International Trade and the Environment

Edited by

Judith M. Dean

International Economist
US International Trade Commission, Washington DC, USA

Routledge
Taylor & Francis Group
LONDON AND NEW YORK

First published 2001 by Dartmouth Publishing Company and Ashgate Publishing

Reissued 2018 by Routledge
2 Park Square, Milton Park, Abingdon, Oxon, OX14 4RN
711 Third Avenue, New York, NY 10017, USA

Routledge is an imprint of the Taylor & Francis Group, an informa business

A Library of Congress record exists under LC control number: 00050268

ISBN 13: 978-1-138-70611-8 (hbk)
ISBN 13: 978-1-138-70607-1 (pbk)
ISBN 13: 978-1-315-20198-6 (ebk)

Contents

PART II TRADE LIBERALIZATION, ENVIRONMENTAL DAMAGE AND DEVELOPING COUNTRIES

Trade Liberalization, Environment and Welfare

Freer Trade and Pollution Havens

PART III TRADE AND TRANSBOUNDARY POLLUTION

Non-cooperative Analyses of Transborder Pollution and Trade Policy

Trade Restrictions and Coordination of Environmental Policy

Transborder Pollution Controls, Trade and Welfare

Acknowledgements

The editor and publishers wish to thank the following for permission to use copyright material.

Academic Press for the essays: Rüdiger Pethig (1976), 'Pollution, Welfare, and Environmental Policy in the Theory of Comparative Advantage', *Journal of Environmental Economics and Management*, **2**, pp. 160–69. Copyright © 1976 Academic Press. Reprinted by permission of the publisher. All rights reserved; Kerry Krutilla (1991), 'Environmental Regulation in an Open Economy', *Journal of Environmental Economics and Management*, **20**, pp. 127–42. Copyright © 1991 Academic Press; Brian R. Copeland (1994), 'International Trade and the Environment: Policy Reform in a Polluted Small Open Economy', *Journal of Environmental Economics and Management*, **26**, pp. 44–65. Copyright © 1994 Academic Press; John H. Mutti and J. David Richardson (1977), 'International Competitive Displacement from Environmental Control: The Quantitative Gains from Methodological Refinement', *Journal of Environmental Economics and Management*, **4**, pp. 135–52. Copyright © 1977 Academic Press; Ramón López (1994), 'The Environment as a Factor of Production: The Effects of Economic Growth and Trade Liberalization', *Journal of Environmental Economics and Management*, **27**, pp. 163–84. Copyright © 1994 Academic Press; John D. Merrifield (1988), 'The Impact of Selected Abatement Strategies on Transnational Pollution, the Terms of Trade, and Factor Rewards: A General Equilibrium Approach', *Journal of Environmental Economics and Management*, **15**, pp. 259–84. Copyright © 1988 Academic Press. Reprinted by permission of the publisher. All rights reserved.

American Economic Association for the essays: Graciela Chinchilnisky (1994), 'North-South Trade and the Global Environment', *American Economic Review*, **84**, pp. 851–74; Brian R. Copeland and M. Scott Taylor (1995), 'Trade and Transboundary Pollution', *American Economic Review*, **85**, pp. 716–37.

Blackwell Publishers for the essays: Horst Siebert (1977), 'Environmental Quality and the Gains from Trade', *Kyklos*, **30**, pp. 657–73; James A. Tobey (1990), 'The Effects of Domestic Environmental Policies on Patterns of World Trade: An Empirical Test', *Kyklos*, **43**, pp. 191–209; Judith M. Dean and Shubhashis Gangopadhyay (1997), 'Export Bans, Environmental Protection, and Unemployment', *Review of Development Economics*, **1**, pp. 324–36. Copyright © 1997 Blackwell Publishers Ltd; H. David Robison (1988), 'Industrial Pollution Abatement: The Impact on Balance of Trade', *Canadian Journal of Economics*, **21**, pp. 187–99. Copyright © 1988 Canadian Economics Association; Rodney D. Ludema and Ian Wooton (1994), 'Cross-Border Externalities and Trade Liberalization: The Strategic Control of Pollution', *Canadian Journal of Economics*, **27**, pp. 950–66. Copyright © 1994 Canadian Economics Association; Carlo Perroni and Randall M. Wigle (1994), 'International Trade and Environmental Quality: How Important are the Linkages?', *Canadian Journal of Economics*, **27**, pp. 551–67. Copyright © 1994 Canadian Economics Association.

Cambridge University Press for the essay: Kym Anderson and Warwick J. McKibbin (2000), 'Reducing Coal Subsidies and Trade Barriers: Their Contribution to Greenhouse Gas Abatement', *Environment and Development Economics*, **5**, pp. 457–81. Copyright © 2000 Cambridge University Press.

Elsevier Science Ltd for the essays: Martin C. McGuire (1982), 'Regulation, Factor Rewards, and International Trade', *Journal of Public Economics*, **17**, pp. 335–54. Copyright © 1982 North Holland; Scott Barrett (1994), 'Strategic Environmental Policy and International Trade', *Journal of Public Economics*, **54**, pp. 325–38. Copyright © 1994 Elsevier Science BV; Michael Hoel (1996), 'Should a Carbon Tax be Differentiated across Sectors?', *Journal of Public Economics*, **59**, pp. 17–32. Copyright © 1996 Elsevier Science BV; James R. Markusen, Edward R. Morey and Nancy Olewiler (1995), 'Competition in Regional Environmental Policies when Plant Locations are Endogenous', *Journal of Public Economics*, **56**, pp. 55–77. Copyright © Elsevier Science BV; James A. Brander and M. Scott Taylor (1998), 'Open Access Renewable Resources: Trade and Trade Policy in a Two-Country Model', *Journal of International Economics*, **44**, pp. 181–209. Copyright © 1998 Elsevier Science BV; Hiro Lee and David Roland-Holst (1997), 'The Environment and Welfare Implications of Trade and Tax Policy', *Journal of Development Economics*, **52**, pp. 65–82. Copyright © 1997 Elsevier Science; James R. Markusen (1975), 'International Externalities and Optimal Tax Structures', *Journal of International Economics,* **5**, pp. 15–29; Scott Barrett (1997), 'The Strategy of Trade Sanctions in International Environmental Agreements', *Resource and Energy Economics*, **19**, pp. 345–61. Copyright © 1997 Elsevier Science BV. With permission from Elsevier Science.

International Association for Energy Economics for the essay: John Whalley and Randall Wigle (1991), 'Cutting CO_2 Emissions: The Effects of Alternative Policy Approaches', *Energy Journal*, **12**, pp. 109–24.

MIT Press Journals for the essay: Brian R. Copeland and M. Scott Taylor (1994) 'North-South Trade and the Environment', *Quarterly Journal of Economics*, **109**, pp. 755–87. Copyright © 1994 The President and Fellows of Harvard College and the Massachusetts Institute of Technology.

Oxford University Press for the essays: Michael Rauscher (1994), 'On Ecological Dumping', *Oxford Economic Papers*, **46**, pp. 822–40. Copyright © 1994 Oxford University Press; Ingo Walter (1973), 'The Pollution Content of American Trade', *Western Economic Journal*, pp. 61–70.

Sage Publications, Inc. for the essay: Nancy Birdsall and David Wheeler (1993) 'Trade Policy and Industrial Pollution in Latin America: Where Are the Pollution Havens?', *Journal of Environment and Development*, **2**, pp. 137–49. Copyright © 1993 Sage Publications, Inc. & Journal of Environment and Development. Reprinted by permission of Sage Publications, Inc.

Every effort has been made to trace all the copyright holders, but if any have been inadvertently overlooked the publishers will be pleased to make the necessary arrangement at the first opportunity.

Personal Acknowledgement

This book was completed while I was an Associate Professor of Economics of SAIS, Johns Hopkins University. I thank my colleagues at SAIS – Jim Riedel, Charlie Pearson, Max Corden, Isaiah Frank, Rob Chase, and Scott Barrett – for their encouragement of my work in trade and environment over many years. Special thanks to Jim, Charlie, and Scott for their suggestions on this volume, and to Lei Liu for her research assistance.

Series Preface

The *International Library of Environmental Economics and Policy* explores the influence of economics on the development of environmental and natural resource policy. In a series of twenty five volumes, the most significant journal essays in key areas of contemporary environmental and resource policy are collected. Scholars who are recognized for their expertise and contribution to the literature in the various research areas serve as volume editors and write an introductory essay that provides the context for the collection.

Volumes in the series reflect the broad strands of economic research including 1) Natural and Environmental Resources, 2) Policy Instruments and Institutions and 3) Methodology. The editors, in their introduction to each volume, provide a state-of-the-art overview of the topic and explain the influence and relevance of the collected papers on the development of policy. This reference series provides access to the economic literature that has made an enduring contribution to contemporary and natural resource policy.

TOM TIETENBERG
WENDY MORRISON
General Editors

Introduction

Overview

The 1990s was a decade of widely publicized debate about the relationship between international trade and the environment. This debate was influential enough to lead to an environmental side agreement to the North American Free Trade Agreement, to a working group in the World Trade Organization on trade and the environment, and to a US presidential mandate that procedures be developed to evaluate the environmental implications of future trade agreements. It also played a key role in the protests against a new WTO round (1999) and against policies of the World Bank and IMF (2000).

Does the presence of environmental damage erode the gains from trade, or imply that trade reduces welfare? Does it give developing countries an unfair advantage in producing pollution-intensive goods? Should trade be restricted in the presence of environmental externalities? Should all countries have the same environmental standards? These questions are not only at the centre of the contemporary debate, but were also at the centre of the debate at least 25 years ago (see Dean, 1992 and Jaffe *et al.*, 1995). The purpose of the present volume is to assemble some of the important theoretical and empirical journal essays which contribute to our understanding of the interface between trade and environment. The collection includes foundational studies from the 1970s and early 1980s, contemporary extensions of early work and contributions on new issues raised in the 1990s. Each of these essays speaks to the issues in the present debate.

Part I of the volume explores the implications of the existence of local environmental damage and environmental regulation on the pattern and gains from trade. Initially the focus is on optimal policy choice in small, perfectly competitive economies. By the 1990s, questions of monopoly power, gradualism and the strategic use of trade and environmental policies were being considered. Part II examines the contemporary debate on trade liberalization and its implications for the environment. These essays focus on trade between industrial and developing countries, since the most heated policy issues have revolved around inter-country differences in standards between these two groups. In Part III policy questions are revisited in the light of the presence of transnational environmental problems. This is a relatively new area of research and many issues are yet to be addressed.

It should be noted that many significant contributions to the trade and environment debate have been published in collected volumes and, therefore, could not be included in this book. Some of the more notable collections include: Anderson and Blackhurst (1992), Low (1992b), Bhagwati and Hudec (1996), Bredahl (1996) and Fredriksson (1999b). This overview cites these where relevant, as well as related journal essays, and some unpublished works.

Two relatively new areas of work are important, though not included in this volume. The first is the political economy of trade and environmental policy. Essays such as Fredriksson (1999a, 1997), Fredriksson and Gaston (1999), Hillman and Ursprung (1992), and Hoekman and Leidy (1992, 1994) explore the interactions between industry, unions and environmental groups in the choice of policy instruments to regulate both trade and the environment. The second area is the development of institutions to address trade and environment issues. Essays such as Eglin (1995) and some of those in Bhagwati and Hudec (Vol. 2, 1996) consider issues such as the revision of the WTO in light of environmental policy.

Environmental Externalities, Comparative Advantage and Optimal Policy Choice

Environmental Abundance and Comparative Advantage

The earliest theoretical studies focus on the implications of environmental damage and environmental policy for the fundamental conclusions of trade theory: the gains from trade, the pattern of trade and the distribution of gains from trade. Most of the analyses assume that countries are small, firms are perfectly competitive and environmental damage is local. Horst Siebert (Chapter 1) asks two questions. First, will countries still gain from trade if unregulated environmental damage exists? Second, will environmental regulations imposed on an open economy raise welfare? Assuming a Ricardian trade model, where environmental damage is generated by production, and defining pollution intensity in terms of emissions per unit of output, Siebert demonstrates that a move from autarky to free trade will always raise the welfare of an importer of pollution-intensive goods. However, trade may raise or lower the welfare of an exporter, since externality costs increase along with production of the exportable. If such an exporter implements an emissions tax, production of the pollution-intensive good will fall and abatement will increase, reducing pollution levels. But the trade volume is also likely to fall, implying a reduction in the gains from trade. Siebert shows that there exists an emissions tax which will raise national welfare, while optimally internalizing the costs of environmental damage.

In Chapter 2 Rüdiger Pethig attempts to clarify whether the existence of environmental damage distorts comparative advantage. He also begins with a Ricardian trade model, where environmental damage is a by-product of production, and shows that, with no regulations on environmental damage, the pattern of trade will still be determined by technological differences in production. Hence, 'pollution-intensity' is not a determinant of the pattern of trade. However, environmental regulations can reduce (increase) a comparative advantage (disadvantage) in the polluting good. If all else is equal, once countries have implemented environmental regulations, differences in those regulations could determine the pattern of trade.

In contrast, Martin McGuire (Chapter 3) focuses on the implications of environmental regulations for the distribution of the gains from trade. He begins with a Heckscher-Ohlin (HO) trade model, in which the production of one of two goods generates pollution. This pollution can be modelled as an input into the production process. In several types of production function this means that environmental regulation amounts to neutral technical 'regress'. Thus, if the sector which pollutes is labour- (capital-) intensive, implementation of environmental regulation will reduce real wages (rents) in the implementing country. If factors are free to move across borders, they will do so in response to these intercountry wage–rent differentials. However, the direction of movement depends on the factor intensity of the polluting good. If, for example, the good were labour-intensive (for example, textiles), environmental regulation would raise real rents in the regulating country, causing foreign investment to flow into the more highly regulated country. This outcome contrasts with the popular idea that foreign investment will move to countries where environmental regulations are lenient.

Optimal Policies, Piecemeal Reform and Strategic Responses

Lack of internalization of environmental damage leads to the underestimation of costs of consumption or production, a potentially distorted pattern of trade and reductions in the gains from trade (or possibly net losses). Standard environmental economics shows the optimal policy response is to internalize environmental damage costs with an appropriate domestic policy, such as emissions taxes or tradeable permits. It is well-known that trade restrictions are not the first-best policy tools to tackle environmental damage, even if they can be designed to reduce output or consumption to socially optimum levels, because they always generate unnecessary additional costly distortions. Yet, in the 1990s, it again became popular to advocate trade restrictions as desirable policy tools to achieve environmental objectives.

Anderson (1992), Snape (1992), and Baumol and Oates (1988) all give detailed analyses of the deadweight losses resulting from a small country attempting to reduce environmental damage with trade restrictions. They also demonstrate the standard finding that a large country's optimal policy is a combination of an optimal tariff (due to its influence over the terms of trade) and an optimal environmental tax. But could trade restrictions be a second-best choice when first-best policies are not available? Kerry Krutilla (Chapter 4) investigates optimal environmental policy when a country is large but cannot use tariffs to influence its terms of trade. He then examines how optimal environmental policy changes when the tariff instrument is available to authorities. If production generates environmental damage, Krutilla shows that the optimal environmental tax is larger (smaller) than the standard Pigouvian tax when the country is a net exporter (net importer), since the tax will also improve (worsen) the terms of trade. The opposite is shown to be the case for a consumption externality. He does, however, verify that the optimal policy combination is a standard Pigouvian environmental tax and a standard optimal tariff.

Two new issues have arisen quite recently. The first comes from the fact that most policy reform is piecemeal, and is done in the presence of multiple distortions. Brian Copeland (Chapter 5) investigates the significance of this 'gradualism' for policy design. He starts with an economy which faces multiple trade and environmental distortions. The country must formulate policies which will reduce these distortions gradually in the direction of an optimum. In some cases, simple rules can be made. Copeland shows that, if all protected industries are also relatively pollution-intensive, then equi-proportionate reductions in all trade barriers or all pollution distortions can improve welfare. However, if export industries are relatively pollution-intensive, then the welfare effect of an equi-proportionate reduction in all tariffs is ambiguous. In general, gradual reform will require coordination of trade and environmental policy in order to ensure welfare improvement. An extension of Copeland's analysis (Beghin, Roland-Holst and Van Der Mensbrugghe, 1997) includes pollution generated by consumption. This is likely to further undermine the case for the use of tariffs as a 'second-best' policy instrument, as tariffs simultaneously tax and subsidize environmental damage.

The second issue comes from the recognition that environmental policy could be used as a strategic tool. Some argue that a country with relatively lenient environmental standards compared to its trading partner is doing this purposely to shift profit to the home firm. Others claim that this country is 'eco-dumping'. The theoretical literature responding to these questions assumes oligopolistic market structures and uses strategic trade theory as an analytical framework.

The strategic trade literature has demonstrated that if a domestic and foreign firm compete as Cournot duopolists in a third market, then the home (foreign) government has an incentive to unilaterally provide a production subsidy to its firm to shift profit toward the home (foreign) country. If the home government is unable to do this, Scott Barrett (Chapter 6) shows that it would have an incentive to use weak environmental standards instead to achieve its profit objective, where weak means that the marginal cost of abatement is less than the marginal damage from pollution. The same incentives would hold for the foreign government. This appears to suggest a potential race to the bottom. However, as Barrett shows, if both countries attempt to shift profit to their own market simultaneously using 'weak' environmental standards, both countries' welfare falls. In addition, if the home industry is an oligopoly, its second-best policy could be either stronger or weaker standards than the environmentally optimal level. Finally, if firms compete in prices, then the incentive to shift profit implies stronger rather than weaker environmental standards. Thus, the incentive to use environmental policy as a strategic tool does not lead conclusively to weaker standards (see also Ulph, 1992; Conrad, 1993).

In Chapter 7 Michael Rauscher examines whether or not it is ever rational for a government to encourage eco-dumping. Following recent economic literature, he defines dumping as selling at a price below marginal cost. If all industries generate the same environmental damage, then eco-dumping would mean weaker environmental standards applied to traded goods compared to non-traded goods. Potential motives might include: improving the terms of trade, shifting profit to the home market, or catering to export lobby pressures. However, Rauscher demonstrates that eco-dumping does not necessarily achieve any of these goals. For example, weaker environmental standards in response to lobbying efforts on the part of the export sector may or may not lead to increased exportable production. Thus, we cannot argue that eco-dumping is the optimal choice of a government which is trying to achieve one of these three objectives.

Environmental Regulations and Loss of Competitiveness

Popular debate in the 1970s and 1990s has also emphasized the potential 'loss of competitiveness' which exporters might face when paying higher environmental control costs (ECC) than competing firms in other countries. In an early contribution, Charles Pearson (Chapter 8) gives five sources of trade changes due to ECC, and examines whether or not each constitutes a case for border adjustments. He eloquently argues that not all such trade changes are distortions and, for those that are, border adjustments appear to be inappropriate responses (at best). In particular, they tend to undermine the achievement of the environmental objective.

Motivated by this concern, empirical work in the 1970s focused on estimating the impact of ECC on industry price and output, and on the trade balance. Ingo Walter (Chapter 9) estimated the pollution content of US exports and imports, using input–output matrices, and found no significant difference between the two. He concluded that ECC are trade neutral at best and marginally damaging to US export industries at worst, although some individual industries might be vulnerable to loss of competitiveness.

Extensions of this approach took two directions: estimation of ECC in a general equilibrium context, including feedback effects through the macro-economy; and estimation of the magnitude of the effects of ECC on the trade balance. John Mutti and David Richardson (Chapter 10) first use a partial equilibrium approach to calculate direct ECC only, and then use elasticities to estimate output effects. They then contrast these results with those found using several other methods: I-O matrices to capture both direct and indirect cost increases due to environmental regulations; incorporation of feedback on industry output through changes in exchange rates, in domestic income, and in demand both at home and abroad due to exchange rate changes. Overall, the comparisons suggest that feedback through other economic variables tends to mitigate the already relatively small direct impact of ECC on industrial output.

Chapter 11 by David Robison updates the Walter's study and finds that the ratio of abatement content of US imports to US exports has risen over time. Robison concludes that US comparative advantage has shifted away from goods which have relatively high abatement costs. He then simulates the impact of a 1 per cent increase in ECC on the trade balance, omitting the general equilibrium effects and assuming full pass-through of ECC to prices, in order to generate upper-bound estimates. Robison argues that marginal changes in abatement costs will affect the US balance of trade, but his figures suggest that the impact would be quite small overall.

In the 1990s, the approach to testing whether or not ECC have any impact on US comparative advantage changed radically, particularly with regard to the explicit introduction of trade models. James Tobey (Chapter 12) employs an HO model to test whether or not ECC have any effect on net exports by sector. For each of five 'pollution-intensive' industry groups, net exports are regressed on endowments of various types of labour, land, capital, natural resources and a measure of the stringency of environmental regulations in each country. He finds no significant impact of stringency of ECC on trade patterns.

This is a significant improvement over earlier approaches, in that a standard trade model is used to specify the explicit relation between ECC and net exports. In addition, econometric testing allows one to examine the statistical significance of any effect ECC might have. However, environmental stringency is difficult to measure. In addition, the sector-specific cross-country regressions may not reveal the effects of environmental regulations on the pattern of specialization across industries within one country. Finally, import restrictions on some of these goods might allow domestic industries to absorb the cost of environmental regulations without impacting trade flows.

Grossman and Krueger (1993) address some of these issues. They explain 1987 US imports from Mexico across industries, using factor shares as explanatory variables. Environmental intensity is proxied by the ratio of US pollution abatement costs (operating costs) to US value-added in that industry. Although the USA does appear to import relatively more (less) labour-(capital-) intensive goods from Mexico, pollution intensity does not affect imports. Since pollution abatement costs as a percent of operating costs are below 2 per cent

(Low, 1992a), many authors conclude that these costs are simply too small to influence trade flows.

Trade Liberalization, Environmental Damage and Developing Countries

Trade Liberalization, Environment and Welfare

Developing countries have been a central part of the trade and environment debate in recent years. The popular assumption has been that developing countries have less stringent environmental standards than industrial countries, and therefore lower relative costs of environmental damage. This has led to concern over three main issues:

1. that liberalizing trade will cause developing countries to increasingly specialize in relatively 'dirty' industries;
2. that 'dirty' industries will shift operations to developing countries (the industrial flight hypothesis);
3. that developing countries may deliberately undervalue the environment in order to attract new investment.

All three phenomena could lead to developing countries becoming 'pollution havens'.

In a separate literature (Grossman and Krueger, 1993; Selden and Song, 1994), it has been argued that income growth has an inverted U relationship with environmental damage. Greater economic activity raises demand for all inputs, and hence increases emissions (the 'scale effect'). But, if people increase their demand for a clean environment as income rises, then higher incomes will be correlated with more stringent environmental regulations. This will encourage firms to shift towards cleaner production processes, reducing emissions (the 'technique effect'). Finally, if income growth shifts preferences towards cleaner goods, then the share of pollution-intensive goods in output will fall, decreasing emissions (the 'composition effect'). At low levels of income, it is argued that the scale effect will outweigh the composition and technique effects, leading to increased environmental damage from income growth. However, at some point, the latter two effects outweigh the former. Thereafter, increased income leads to a net reduction in environmental damage.

This concept has been linked to trade liberalization. If developing countries have a comparative advantage in pollution-intensive goods, then more open trade will have a composition effect which will raise pollution levels. It will also raise the real return to the environmental input, which should result in a technique effect which lowers pollution levels. However, as trade liberalization raises income, it will be accompanied by the three effects of income growth discussed above. For countries at low levels of income, this could imply further increases in pollution levels. Yet, as Bhagwati and Srinivasan (1996) have so eloquently argued, differences in preferences and assimilative capacities are legitimate reasons for environmental standards to differ across countries. As long as environmental damage costs are optimally internalized, more open trade should be beneficial, even if pollution levels rise.

Is it necessarily true that developing countries will have relatively lenient environmental standards compared to industrial countries? If so, will their environmental quality decline with freer trade? Brian Copeland and Scott Taylor (Chapter 13) and Ramón López (Chapter 14) investigate these questions, assuming that environmental damage has been optimally internalized, and hence trade liberalization should be beneficial. Copeland and Taylor develop a multi-good Ricardian trade model, in which Northern countries, with a larger amount of human capital, have higher incomes than Southern. They show that this income pattern is sufficient to generate relatively low environmental standards in the South. More open trade then shifts the composition of output in the South (North) towards (away from) more pollution-intensive goods, while the scale and technique effects of more open trade are assumed to just offset each other. Thus, more open trade must lead to higher pollution levels in the South.

López also evaluates the impact of growth and of trade liberalization on the environment, but models environment as an input in the production process. Depletion of this input may or may not have feedback effects on the stock of productive resources. For the latter case, he argues that the effect of growth on overall pollution levels will be ambiguous. If a clean environment is a luxury good, and if the elasticity of substitution is high between environment and conventional factors of production, then it is more likely that the composition and technique effects of income growth will outweigh the scale effect, and lead to an overall reduction in pollution levels. Under certain assumptions, an inverted U relation can be derived. Trade liberalization is modelled separately as an additional composition effect through changing relative prices. If developing countries have a comparative advantage in agriculture (relative to manufacturing), trade liberalization is likely to reduce production pollution, but to raise consumption pollution. Thus, the impact of trade on pollution levels is ambiguous.

Several other theoretical studies examine this same issue, but focus on property rights over commonly held environmental resources. They begin with the assumption that external costs have not been optimally internalized, thus freer trade may not raise welfare. In Chapter 15 Graciela Chichilnisky argues that, given less well-developed institutions, developing countries are likely to lack well-defined property rights over environmental resources. If the North and South are assumed to be identical except that the environmental resource is held as common property in the South (while held as private property in the North), the South will have an 'apparent' comparative advantage in environmentally-intensive goods. Clearly, this means that overuse of the environment will be aggravated by trade, and welfare in the South will fall.

Brander and Taylor (1997a, 1997b and Chapter 16, this volume) also examine trade in the context of open access renewable resources, but with several differences from Chichilnisky. Growth of the resource is explicitly modelled, and steady state harvesting levels are determined. There is no presumption that developing countries would have a comparative advantage in the resource good, and, therefore, trade could raise both countries' welfare. In Brander and Taylor (1997b) trade occurs between a conservationist country (which has implemented resource management policies to optimize steady-state utility), and a consumer country whose resource is subject to open access. Contrary to popular belief, they show that severe overuse of the resource in the consumer country in autarky will imply a comparative disadvantage in the resource-intensive good in the steady state. Thus, free trade will reduce the overuse in the consumer country, allow its resource stock to rebuild, and raise its welfare. In Chapter 16 Brander and Taylor assume that both countries' environmental policies are lax, and thus allow open access to the renewable resource. In this context, if a country has a comparative advantage in the resource good, and its trade remains diversified, then trade must lower national welfare. Contrary to one's intuition, if the exporter can completely specialize in the resource good, trade will increase the exporter's welfare.

The results of both Chichilnisky, and Brander and Taylor once again raise the issue of optimal policy choice in a second-best world. Chichilnisky demonstrates that a tax on the extraction of the environmental resource could cause further depletion of the resource, as low-income harvesters seek to maintain purchasing power over consumption goods. Brander and Taylor analyse the implications of an import tariff and an export tax. They argue that, starting from free trade, a marginal import tariff will reduce (raise) steady-state stocks of the renewable resource in the importing (exporting) country. This will raise the exporting country's welfare, and could raise the importer's welfare if the terms of trade benefit outweigh the loss from a lower steady-state resource stock. On the other hand, a marginal export tax on the resource good will raise the exporter's welfare and will reduce the importer's welfare.

Judith Dean and Shubhashis Gangopadhyay (Chapter 17) also investigate the case for an export tax as a second-best instrument, when a country has a comparative advantage in a renewable resource and environmental damage costs are not optimally internalized. They consider a three-good (static) HO model in which the resource good is used as an intermediate in the import-competing sector. However, environmental damage from extracting the resource harms the productivity of another exportable sector. The authors investigate whether or not the second-best case for an export tax is strengthened by the possibility that it would not only reduce environmental damage, but encourage expansion of the import-competing sector, where unemployment exists. They find that in the short run, the export tax actually worsens the unemployment problem. In the long run, the opposite occurs. However, if the environmental problem is severe, the case for an export tax is unaffected by the presence of unemployment.

Freer Trade and Pollution Havens

In a recent set of essays, James Markusen, Edward Morey and Nancy Olewiler (1995, Chapter 18, this volume), and Markusen (1997) explore theoretically the impact of environmental regulations on foreign direct investment. These papers incorporate an endogenous market structure, and thus allow trade liberalization and environmental regulation to influence the firm's decisions to maintain a single plant and export or build multiple plants, as well as influence the location of plants. In the essay by Markusen *et al.*(Chapter 18) the authors examine the likelihood of a 'race to the bottom' in environmental regulations, in order to attract foreign investment. They consider a two-stage game where governments of the home and foreign countries choose environmental regulation to maximize consumer surplus net of the disutility of pollution, and the firm then chooses to build plants both at home and abroad, only in one location, or not at all. Complex multiple solutions arise, due to discontinuities when market structure changes. The authors conclude that undercutting of pollution taxes could occur if pollution disutility is low. However, with high enough pollution disutility, governments would increase environmental taxes in order to drive the polluting firm out of their market.

There is still very little statistical work on whether or not industrial flight has occurred due to relatively lenient environmental standards, or whether developing countries have purposely attempted to attract FDI via such standards. The earliest studies (see Walter, 1982; Pearson, 1987) tended to examine trends in FDI from the USA, Europe and Japan, in terms of industry mix and destination. Although they found evidence of a large amount of FDI in pollution-intensive industries, there was little evidence that it had been influenced by differing ECC, or that it flowed faster into developing countries as opposed to industrial countries. The overall conclusion was that there is no evidence that FDI is shifting towards countries with more lenient standards.

Leonard (1988) attempted to improve on the earlier approaches by incorporating theoretical work on the product cycle, industrial location decisions by firms, bargaining processes between multinationals and host countries, and development strategies. Although he finds some evidence that in the 1970s government officials tried to attract FDI with lenient environmental regulations, he argues that these incentives were not substantial enough to offset the other main determinants of location – the level of training of labour, infrastructure and stability. Arik Levinson's 1996 survey of studies of plant-site choice in the USA also supports these conclusions. Results from four conditional logit estimations suggest that interstate differences in environmental regulations do not significantly affect choice of location of plants in the USA. More recently, Eskeland and Harrison (1997) find that abatement costs are not significant determinants of the share of foreign investment in manufacturing industries in Mexico, Côte d'Ivoire, Venezuela, and Morocco. While they do find some evidence of a positive relation between FDI share and air pollution intensity of an industry, they also find a negative relation between FDI share and water pollution and toxic release intensity.

The empirical work of the 1990s concentrated on testing whether or not trade liberalization has shifted the pattern of production in developing countries towards more dirty industries. A study of revealed comparative advantage by Low and Yeats (1992) suggests that there has been such a shift, but that industrial countries remain the largest producers of the more pollution-intensive goods. Lucas, Wheeler and Hettige (1992), using the Industrial Pollution Projection System (IPPS) index of toxic intensity of manufacturing output, find that growth of toxic intensity is lower for poor, rapidly growing open economies compared to those which are closed. Thus openness appears to contribute to cleaner growth in poor countries.

Nancy Birdsall and David Wheeler (Chapter 19) use a similar methodology to Lucas *et al.*, to test whether or not changes in OECD countries' environmental policy caused Latin American countries to specialize in more pollution-intensive products. Regression results on a reduced form equation show that, during the 1970s and 1980s, Latin American countries, at all income levels, had higher growth of toxic intensity of output than in the 1960s. They infer from this support for the idea that increased environmental stringency in OECD countries during this time period led to more pollution-intensive production in Latin America. However, they argue that more openness and faster growth in Latin America actually mitigated this effect.

In Chapter 20 Hiro Lee and David Roland-Holst undertake a computable general equilibrium analysis of trade between Japan and Indonesia. Reminiscent of Walter, the authors calculate the pollution intensity of exports and imports for both countries, using the IPPS index. They find that Indonesia does have a comparative advantage in pollution-intensive goods, and that trade liberalization would indeed increase Indonesia's emission levels of major pollutants. However, they also examine the emissions and welfare implications of various policies, including tariff removal, export taxes, uniform emissions reduction and a uniform effluent tax. They find that a uniform effluent tax, combined with tariff removal, will both lower Indonesia's emissions and raise its overall welfare.

These studies all assess the impact of trade liberalization on emissions via changes in the composition of output only. Thus, new empirical work is attempting to include the implications of scale and technique effects of trade liberalization. Antweiler, Copeland, and Taylor (1998) have developed a theoretical model to decompose the change in emissions (from income growth) into scale, composition effects, and technique effects. This is estimated using cross-country data on SO_2 emissions. Although separate estimates suggest that trade will shift the composition of output towards dirty goods, adding indirect calculations of the scale and technique effects yields an overall beneficial effect of trade liberalization on pollution.

Dean (2000) develops a simultaneous system of equations, based on a two-good HO model with environmental damage modelled as an endogenously supplied input. Estimation of this model, using Chinese data on water pollution, reveals that trade liberalization directly aggravates environmental damage via its influence on the composition of output, but indirectly mitigates it via its effect on income growth (scale and technique effects). Simulations suggest that trade reform had a net beneficial impact on emissions growth.

Trade and Transboundary Pollution

Non-cooperative Analyses of Transborder Pollution and Trade Policy

Although it is clear that unilateral trade restrictions are not first-best policies to address domestic environmental externalities, this result has been questioned in the context of global environmental damage. Is it justifiable for a country to impose unilateral trade restrictions when another country's production or consumption generates damage which spills over borders? If economic activity in all countries generates a global public bad (for example, depletion of the ozone layer or a build-up of greenhouse gases) would trade restrictions be an optimal policy choice?

Theoretical work on the implications of trade for transborder environmental degradation, and vice versa, was largely neglected until the 1990s. One important exception is the 1975 essay by James Markusen (Chapter 21). His study returns to the question of optimal unilateral trade and tax policy for a large country. Domestic and foreign production generate pollution, but the damage from this falls solely on the home country. Clearly, a global optimum would require environmental taxes which internalized these costs into domestic and foreign production. But, in this case, the foreigner does not experience costs from this externality, and hence has no incentive to regulate it. The only influence the home country has on the foreigner is that which it exerts on the terms of trade. Confining his analysis to the home country's unilateral policy choice (already a second-best), Markusen argues for a combination of an effluent tax (here equivalent to a production tax) equal to the marginal social damage from pollution, and an 'optimal' tariff (export tax). However, this optimal tariff (export tax) must be adjusted for its impact on foreign pollution, since pollution abroad spills over onto the home country. Markusen also ranks alternative policy choices when the unilateral first-best combination is not available. In contrast to the case of domestic externalities, he demonstrates that there is no unambiguous second-best unilateral policy choice for a large country facing transborder pollution.

Ludema and Wooton (Chapter 22) investigate the implications of strategic behaviour for Markusen's conclusions regarding unilateral policy. Both governments have an incentive to set tariffs (export taxes) to influence the terms of trade. Ludema and Wooton show that the non-cooperative equilbrium tariffs will exceed the cooperative optimum. In addition, in the non-cooperative case, the foreign government is better off choosing a pollution tax and an export tax – that is, internalizing the externality despite the fact that none of the damage falls on the foreign country. This combination is shown to yield an improvement in the foreigner's terms of trade relative to the case of simultaneous non-cooperative imposition of import tariffs (export taxes).

The authors also investigate whether or not countries might use environmental taxes strategically if they are bound by a free trade agreement, and hence trade taxes are unavailable. In this case, the foreigner again has an incentive to impose a pollution tax, despite the lack of any environmental damage locally, to influence the terms of trade. However, this tax will always be below that which optimally internalizes the environmental damage. If the home country tries to impose a process standard on foreign imports, this competition to influence the terms of trade results in much more restrictive pollution policies and much less trade than would prevail in the global optimum.

Is it more likely that trade liberalization will lead to pollution havens in developing countries, or reductions in welfare, if the pollution is transborder? Brian Copeland and Scott Taylor (Chapter 23) extend their earlier work (Chapter 13) to explore the impact of trade liberalization on global environmental damage and its distribution across regions. They also assess the impact of international trade in permits, tied and untied transfers, and multilateral pollution reduction agreements among a subset of countries. These issues are examined (generally) assuming that countries allocate pollution permits nationally, taking other countries' pollution levels as given. Thus, a global optimum is not reached, and free trade could lead to a welfare loss. The authors argue that with factor price equalization, free trade will actually have no effect on aggregate pollution, but will raise emissions in the developing world and, in response, decrease emissions in the industrial world. Surprisingly, the authors argue that this would lead to increased welfare for the developing world, but decreased welfare for the industrial world, relative to an autarky situation. They also show that pollution reductions by a subset of countries, and transfers tied to pollution reductions could both lead to higher welfare.

Trade Restrictions and Coordination of Environmental Policy

In the presence of transnational externalities, unilateral policies will typically deviate from a global first-best policy, since they do not accurately account for damage falling on all other countries. International coordination of environmental policies is necessary to achieve optimal internalization of the costs of a global public bad. However, the literature on international environmental agreements (IEAs) makes clear the difficulties of designing self-enforcing agreements, and of deterring free-riders. The success of the Montreal Protocol (which includes trade sanctions) and the recently formulated Kyoto Protocol has prompted much debate over two trade policy issues. First, are trade sanctions necessary for the success of an IEA? Second, should trade sanctions be used to deter free-riding?

Michael Hoel (Chapter 24) investigates the necessity of trade taxes to ensure the effectiveness of an IEA. He notes that standard welfare theory calls for optimal carbon taxes to be equal across users, as the environmental damage generated by carbon use is equal regardless of who uses it. But international agreements do not include all countries. Hence, some of the effect of local carbon taxes among signatories is lost, as these regulations encourage the expansion of carbon-intensive tradeable goods production in non-signatory countries. Because of this, Hoel argues, signatories should impose trade taxes or subsidies to influence the terms of trade in such a way as to counteract this 'leakage' problem. He does demonstrate that differentiated carbon taxes could be used to solve the same problem, but argues they would be more difficult to determine than trade taxes. Hoel does, however, acknowledge that his analysis assumes the existence of free-riders and leakage, and that these are not influenced by the specification of the IEA.

In Chapter 25 Scott Barrett examines whether or not the use of trade sanctions could be sufficient to generate full participation in an IEA. In Barrett's framework, transnational pollution is generated by oligopolistic firms which conduct two-way trade in a homogenous good. All countries face the same costs and benefits from pollution, so the only incentive to not participate in the IEA would be to free-ride. Self-enforcing IEAs, with and without trade sanctions, are characterized in terms of equilibrium levels of pollution taxes for both signatories and non-signatories. Barrett then reviews a number of simulation results to compare incentives to free-ride under each type of IEA. Simulation results are ambiguous. If marginal benefits and costs of abatement are very small, the threat of trade sanctions could eliminate all free-riding. However, the welfare of these erstwhile non-signatories could fall vis-à-vis its level under an IEA without sanctions. As multiple equilibria also arise, there is no guarantee that all free-riding will be eliminated through the use of trade sanctions. The issues of necessity and optimality of trade sanctions are not addressed. In addition, as Blackhurst and Subramaniam (1992) point out, in reality, not all non-signatories are free-riders.

Transborder Pollution Controls, Trade and Welfare

Empirical work on transborder externalities and trade is relatively recent and generally involves CGE analyses (Winters, 1992). A relatively early attempt by John Merrifield (Chapter 26) investigates the impact of unilateral environmental taxes when countries are large, pollutants are transborder, and both capital and goods can move across international borders. His model is applied to acid deposition between the USA and Canada. Merrifield shows that the success of unilateral emissions taxes or abatement equipment standards in reducing domestic or global pollution levels may be undermined or reinforced by the secondary effects of movement in capital and changes in the terms of trade.

More recently, Whalley (1991), Whalley and Wigle (Chapter 27) and Piggot, Whalley and Wigle (1992) investigated the trade and welfare implications of various methods of reducing carbon emissions. Quantification should aid in deciphering which regions are likely to have incentives to join in a multilateral agreement. Whalley argues that a global tax, a national production tax or a national consumption tax will all imply major changes in welfare, but also very different distributions of gains and losses. These distributional differences are tied to the differing recipients of the tax revenues under each scheme. For example, if the global tax revenues are rebated on a per capita basis, then developing countries are likely to gain significantly. Both John Whalley and Randall Wigle (Chapter 27) and Piggot, Whalley and Wigle (1992) report large changes in the terms of trade for all regions under the two types of national tax, and large reductions in trade volumes for virtually all regions under the national consumption tax.

In Chapter 28 Carlo Perroni and Randall Wigle use a CGE model to assess the impact of trade on environmental degradation, and the degree to which environmental regulations affect the gains from trade. (Ferrantino and Linkins, 1999, also address the first issue.) Their approach is global, and allows for both local and transnational pollution and sector-specific abatement activities. Differentiated products are traded, but factors are immobile internationally. Simulations are run to assess the implications of full global internalization of externalities in all regions, and unilateral domestic environmental policies in North America under two trading scenarios: free trade or threefold increases in trade barriers. They find environmental damage is significantly reduced by full global internalization of externalities, and these reductions are much larger than those which occur under unilateral policies. Thus, the choice of environmental policy has a significant effect on pollution levels. These results are unaffected by the choice of trade regime. Hence, freer trade appears to have a negligible effect on pollution levels. In contrast, under either environmental regime, welfare gains are significantly increased by a move to free trade. Hence, environmental policy appears to have little effect on the gains from trade.

Complementing the Perroni and Wigle study, a recent analysis by Kym Anderson and Warwick McKibbon (Chapter 29) argues that distortions from existing coal policies have generated excessive carbon emissions. In Western Europe, imports of coal have been restricted, direct subsidies paid to producers, and minimum purchase obligations placed on utilities. In Eastern Europe and the former Soviet Union, coal is underpriced and consumption levels are excessively high. Using a multicountry CGE model, the authors find that removing these distortions would both raise GDP in transition and developing countries, and significantly reduce greenhouse gas emissions globally. Thus, removing trade and domestic policies which distort national markets may go a long way toward achieving mutilateral goals with respect to transfrontier pollution.

Conclusions

Many interesting conclusions and directions for new work emerge from this collection of research. Some brief observations follow. It is clearly critical to design appropriate environmental policies to correct environmental externalities. The absence of such policies can distort the pattern of trade and reduce the gains from trade. Moreover, trade policies are usually ranked well below several domestic environmental policies in terms of effectiveness in correcting damage, and in terms of impact on welfare. The presence of multiple distortions and gradual reform does not appear to alter this conclusion, although it is likely to imply the need to coordinate trade liberalization and environmental regulation.

This conclusion also appears to hold even when damage is transnational, since the unilateral use of trade policies in that context will fail to achieve a globally optimum level of environmental quality. With the presence of strategic incentives or power over the terms of trade, use of such trade restrictions by several countries is likely to yield not only sub-optimal levels of pollution, but also too much restriction of trade. Although countries or firms with strategic interests and market power may have the ability to usurp environmental policy to accomplish other goals (for example, profit-shifting), there is no clear evidence that such a misuse of environmental policy would be effective, nor that a 'race to the bottom' would occur.

There may be, however, an important use of trade restrictions as sanctions in an IEA. They may be needed to ensure the effectiveness of the agreement, since they can potentially correct 'leakage' in the presence of non-signatories. Further work should be done to explore whether or not they are necessary, particularly if the decision to participate in an agreement is endogenous. Trade sanctions may also be sufficient to induce free-riders to participate in an IEA, under certain conditions. However, those conditions appear to be limited. It would be useful to explore whether, and under what conditions, sanctions are the optimal policy choice to achieve this goal.

Empirical work suggests that environmental policies have had virtually no effect on foreign direct investment location choice, although evidence on this is still scarce. Since some theory suggests that more stringent environmental regulations could attract foreign investment, more econometric estimates of location choice between countries would be valuable. However, a large body of evidence does suggest that environmental policies have little impact on trade flows, and that they could have significant beneficial effects on welfare. With respect to tax measures to regulate global pollutants, these welfare effects may vary, depending on the redistribution of revenues. By contrast, trade restrictions (with environmental policies in place) may have very little effect on pollution levels, but significant detrimental effects on welfare. Since much of the empirical work on transnational pollutants is based on CGE simulation, more econometric testing would be illuminating.

Theoretical studies on trade between industrial and developing countries have yielded conflicting results as to whether or not developing countries might find pollution levels rising with freer trade. This outcome appears to be more likely if trade only affects the composition of output. However, this is not necessarily a welfare-reducing result, nor a reason for harmonization of standards. Much of the early empirical work on developing country trade liberalization only tests for its effects on the composition of output. Some of this does suggest that trade liberalization would expand pollution-intensive industries, thereby raising pollution levels in developing countries. More recently, efforts to capture the impact of trade on incentives to abate or to raise environmental standards have yielded some evidence that freer trade may be beneficial for the environment of developing countries. This possibility of an endogenous beneficial relationship deserves further study.

References

Anderson, K. (1992), 'The Standard Welfare Economics of Policies Affecting Trade and the Environment', in K. Anderson and R. Blackhurst (eds), *The Greening of World Trade Issues*, Ann Arbor: University of Michigan Press.

Anderson, K. and Blackhurst, R. (eds) (1992), *The Greening of World Trade Issues*, Ann Arbor: University of Michigan Press.

Antweiler, W., Copeland, B. and Taylor, M.S. (1998), 'Is Free Trade Good for the Environment?', NBER Working Paper No. 6707.

Baumol, W. and Oates, W. (1988), *The Theory of Environmental Policy*, Cambridge: Cambridge University Press.

Beghin, J., Roland-Holst, D. and van der Mensbrugghe, D. (1997), 'Trade and Pollution Linkages: Piecemeal Reform and Optimal Intervention', *Canadian Journal of Economics*, **97**, pp. 442–55.

Bhagwati, J. and Hudec, R. (eds) (1996), *Fair Trade and Harmonization: Prerequisites for Free Trade?*, Vol.1: *Economic Analysis*, Vol. 2: *Legal Analysis*, Cambridge, MA: MIT Press.

Bhagwati, J. and Srinivasan, T.N. (1996), 'Trade and the Environment: Does Environmental Diversity Detract from the Case for Free Trade?', in J. Bhagwati and R. Hudec (eds), *Fair Trade and Harmonization: Prerequisites for Free Trade?* Vol.1: *Economic Analysis*. Cambridge, MA: MIT Press.

Blackhurst, R. and Subramaniam, A. (1992), 'Promoting Multilateral Cooperation on the Environment', in K. Anderson and R. Blackhurst (eds), *The Greening of World Trade Issues*, Ann Arbor: University of Michigan Press.

Brander, J. and Taylor, M.S. (1997a), 'International Trade and Open Access Renewable Resources: the Small Open Economy Case', *Canadian Journal of Economics*, **30**, pp. 526–52.

Brander, J. and Taylor, M.S. (1997b), 'International Trade between Consumer and Conservationist Countries', *Resource and Energy Economics*, **19**, pp. 267–97.

Bredahl, M. (ed.) (1996), *Agriculture, Trade and the Environment*, Boulder, CO: Westview Press.

Conrad, K. (1993), 'Taxes and Subsidies for Pollution-Intensive Industries', *Journal of Environmental Economics and Management*, **25**, pp. 121–35.

Dean, J. (1992), 'Trade and the Environment: A Survey of the Literature', in P. Low (ed.), *International Trade and the Environment*, World Bank Discussion Paper No. 159.

Dean, J. (2000), 'Does Trade Liberalization Harm the Environment? A New Test', CIES Policy Discussion Paper No. 0015, University of Adelaide.

Eglin, R. (1995), 'Trade and Environment in the WTO', *World Economy*, **18**, pp. 769–79.

Eskeland, G. and Harrison, A. (1997), 'Moving to Greener Pastures? Multinationals and the Pollution Haven Hypothesis', World Bank Working Paper No. 1744.

Ferrantino, M. and Linkins, L. (1999), 'The Effect of Global Trade Liberalization on Toxic Emissions in Industry', *Weltwirtschlaftiches Archiv*, **135**, pp. 128–55.

Fredriksson, P. (1997), 'The Political Economy of Pollution Taxes in a Small Open Economy', *Journal of Environmental Economics and Management*, **33**.

Fredricsson, P. (1999a), 'The Political Economy of Trade Liberalization and Environmental Policy', *Southern Economic Journal*, **65**, pp. 513–25.

Fredricsson, P. (ed.) (1999b), *Trade, Global Policy, and the Environment*, World Bank Discussion Paper No. 402.

Fredricsson, P. and Gaston, N. (1999), 'The "Greening" of Trade Unions and the Demand for Ecotaxes', *European Journal of Political Economy*, **15**, pp. 663–86.

Grossman, G. and Krueger, A. (1993), 'Environmental Impacts of NAFTA', in P. Garber (ed.), *The US–Mexico Free Trade Agreement*, Cambridge, MA: MIT Press.

Hillman, A. and Ursprung, H. (1992), 'The Influence of Environmental Concerns on the Political Determination of Trade Policy', in K. Anderson and R. Blackhurst (eds), *The Greening of World Trade Issues*, Ann Arbor: University of Michigan Press.

Hoekman, B. and Leidy, M. (1992), 'Environmental Policy Formation in a Trading Economy: a Public Choice Perspective', in K. Anderson and R. Blackhurst (eds), *The Greening of World Trade Issues*, Ann Arbor: University of Michigan Press.

Hoekman, B. and Leidy, M. (1994), 'Cleaning up While Cleaning Up? Pollution Abatement, Interest Groups, and Contingent Trade Policies', *Public Choice*, **78**, pp. 241–58.

Jaffe, A.B., Peterson, S.R., Portney, P.R. and Stavins, R. (1995), 'Environmental Regulation and the Competitiveness of U.S. Manufacturing', *Journal of Economic Literature*, **33**, pp. 132–63.

Leonard, J. (1988), *Pollution and the Struggle for World Product*, New York: Cambridge University Press.

Levinson, A. (1996), 'Environmental Regulations and Industry Location', in J. Bhagwati and R. Hudec (eds), *Fair Trade and Harmonization: Prerequisites for Free Trade?*, Vol.1: *Economic Analysis*, Cambridge, MA: MIT Press.

Low, P. (1992a), 'Trade Measures and Environmental Quality: The Implications for Mexico's Exports', in P. Low (ed.), *International Trade and the Environment*, World Bank Discussion Paper No. 159.

Low, P. (1992b), *International Trade and the Environment*, World Bank Discussion Paper No. 159.

Low, P. and Yeats, A. (1992), 'Do Dirty Industries Migrate?', in P. Low (ed.), *International Trade and the Environment*, World Bank Discussion Paper No. 159.

Lucas, R.E.B., Wheeler, D. and Hettige, H. (1992), 'Economic Development, Environmental Regulation and the International Migration of Toxic Industrial Pollution: 1960–88', in P. Low (ed.), *International Trade and the Environment*, World Bank Discussion Paper No. 159.

Markusen, J. (1997), 'Costly Pollution Abatement, Competitiveness, and Plant Location Decisions', *Resource and Energy Economics*, **19**, pp. 299–320.

Markusen, J., Morey, E. and Olewiler, N. (1993), 'Environmental Policy when Market Structure and Plant Locations are Endogenous', *Journal of Environmental Economics and Management*, **24**, pp. 69–86.

Pearson, C. (1987), *Multinational Corporations, Environment, and the Third World*, Durham: Duke University Press.

Piggot, J., Whalley, J. and Wigle, R. (1992), 'International Linkages and Carbon Reduction', in K. Anderson and R. Blackhurst (eds), *The Greening of World Trade Issues*, Ann Arbor: University of Michigan Press.

Selden, T.M. and Song, D. (1994), 'Environmental Quality and Development: Is There a Kuznets Curve for Air Pollution Emissions?', *Journal of Environmental Economics and Management*, **27**, pp. 147–62.

Snape, R. (1992), 'The Environment, International Trade, and Competitiveness', in K. Anderson and R. Blackhurst (eds), *The Greening of World Trade Issues*, Ann Arbor: University of Michigan Press.

Ulph, A.(1992), 'The Choice of Environmental Policy Instruments and Strategic International Trade', in R. Pethig (ed.), *Conflicts and Cooperation in Managing Environmental Resources*, Berlin: Springer.

Whalley, J. (1991), 'The Interface between Trade and Environment', *Economic Journal*, **101**, pp. 180–89.

Winters, L. Alan (1992), 'The Trade and Welfare Effects of Greenhouse Gas Abatement: A Survey of Empirical Estimates', in K. Anderson and R. Blackhurst (eds), *The Greening of World Trade Issues*, Ann Arbor: University of Michigan Press.

Part I
Environmental Externalities, Comparative Advantage and Optimal Policy Choice

Environmental Abundance and Comparative Advantage

[1]

KYKLOS, Vol. 30 – 1977 – Fasc. 4, 657–673

ENVIRONMENTAL QUALITY AND THE GAINS FROM TRADE

HORST SIEBERT*

Countries experience welfare gains if they engage in trade. Does this also hold if environmental quality is taken into consideration? And to what extent are the gains from trade altered when effects of trade on environmental quality are not ignored? Assume a two-commodity world with commodity 1 being a pollution-intensively produced commodity. Let the home country have a comparative price advantage in commodity 1 and – after trade has taken place – let the home country specialize in the production of the pollution-intensively produced commodity. As a result of trade then emissions will increase and environmental quality in the home country will decline. Environmental disruption will reduce the overall benefits to society from trade, and *a priori*, it cannot be ruled out that the environmental losses may overcompensate the conventional gains from trade. This problem will be analyzed in *Section II* of this paper with *Section I* presenting the basic assumptions.

Now assume the home country wants to protect itself against a deterioration of its environmental quality by enacting an appropriate environmental policy – for instance, by levying emission taxes. The problem then arises how environmental policy will affect comparative advantage and the gains from trade. This question is studied in *Section III*. In the final section some extensions are indicated and some conclusions are drawn.

* University of Mannheim, Federal Republic of Germany. This study was made possible by a research grant from the 'Deutsche Forschungsgemeinschaft' while the author was Visiting Professor of Economics at New York University and at the University of New Mexico. The author appreciates helpful comments from ROBERT HAWKINS, WILLIAM SCHULTZE and INGO WALTER. Also RALF GRONYCH and RÜDIGER PETHIG have suggested improvements in the manuscript.

HORST SIEBERT

I. ASSUMPTIONS

The frame of reference is a two-sector economy in which production generates pollutants as a joint product. More specifically, the following assumptions are made:

A 1 The home country is small compared to the rest of the world so that after trade takes place the relative price $p = p_1/p_2$ in the home country is determined by the world market.

A 2 The production of commodities $i = 1,2$ generates pollutants as a joint product. For simplifying purposes there is only one type of pollutant. It is assumed that the quantity S_i^p of pollutants emitted rises proportionally or progressively with output, *i.e.*

$$S_i^p = H_i(Q_i) \quad \text{with } H_i' > 0,\ H_i'' \geq 0 \tag{1}$$

A 3 In order to keep the model as simple as possible we assume only one type of resource, R and a production function

$$Q_i = F_i(R_i) \quad \text{with } F_i' > 0,\ F_i'' < 0 \tag{2}$$

A 4 Resources may also be used for pollution abatement purposes. Let S_i^r indicate the quantity of pollutants reduced in Sector i.

$$S_i^r = F_i^r(R_i^r) \quad \text{with } F_i^{r\prime} > 0,\ F_i^{r\prime\prime} < 0 \tag{3}$$

According to equation (3) pollutants are prevented from entering the environment. Additionally it could be assumed that a technology exists that reduces pollutants ambient in the environment (water treatment).

A 5 Net emissions (S) are defined as the difference between emissions generated and emissions reduced

$$S_i = S_i^p - S_i^r \tag{4}$$

Pollutants ambient in the environment S are defined as

$$S = \sum S_i \tag{5}$$

A 6 Pollutants ambient in the environment cause damage to environmental quality U

$$U = G(S) \quad \text{with } G' < 0,\ G'' < 0 \tag{6}$$

A 7 Commodity demand is given by

$$C_i = C_i(p, Y) \quad \text{with } p = p_1/p_2 \tag{7}$$

denoting the relative commodity price.

A 8 In order to close the model, we assume that the government spends the tax income received in form of transfers to households. Consequently, gross national product and personal disposable income are defined as

$$Y = p\,Q_1 + Q_2 \tag{8}$$

Note that Y includes transfers not explicitly shown and that p is consumers price and not producers price. If Y would be defined with respect to producers price, p^*, emission taxes (and transfers) would appear explicitly on the right side of equation (8).

A 9 The resource input can be used for both production and pollution abatement, and is given

$$R_1 + R_2 + R_1^r + R_2^r = \bar{R} \tag{9}$$

A 10 A situation is assumed in which the environment is used as a common property receiving emissions without the polluter being charged *(Section II)*. In *Section III* we assume that the government levies an emission tax z on net emissions S_i, with z being changed parametrically.

A 11 Firms maximize profits and regard commodity prices, factor price (r) and the emission tax as given. The conditions for profit maximizing factor demand are given as

$$r = (p - zH_1') F_1'(R_1') \qquad r = (1 - zH_2') F_2'(R_2) \qquad r = zF_i^{r'}(R_i^r) \tag{10}$$

which yields the usual conditions for $z = 0$.

A 12 If trade takes place, the balance of payments must be in equilibrium

$$pE_1 + E_2 = 0 \tag{11}$$

with

$$E_i = C_i - Q_i \tag{12}$$

II. GAINS FROM TRADE AND ENVIRONMENTAL LOSSES

1. In a situation where no environmental policy is undertaken and $z = 0$, gains from trade exist if trade increases welfare. Assume a social welfare function

$$W = W(C_1, C_2, U) \tag{13}$$

Recalling assumptions (1), (4), (5), (6), (11) and (12), observing that $pdE_1 + E_1dp + dE_2 = 0$ and that $E_1 = 0$ in the autarky situation and finally evaluating commodities at the price p of the trade situation, we have for the change in welfare

$$dW = \left[\frac{\partial W}{\partial C_2}\left(p\frac{dQ_1}{dQ_2} + 1\right) + \frac{\partial W}{\partial U} G'\left(H_1'\frac{dQ_1}{dQ_2} + H_2'\right)\right] dQ_2 \tag{13'}$$

2. Assume $dQ_2 < 0$, so that the country specializes in the production of commodity 1. The first expression in 13′ is positive, if

$$p > -\frac{dQ_2}{dQ_1} = {}^{\circ}p$$

where $^{\circ}p$ is the autarky price of the home country. This is the known condition that country 1 must have a comparative advantage for commodity 1 if it specializes in the production of that commodity after trade takes place.

3. With respect to the second term, two cases have to be distinguished. First, if $(H_1' dQ_1/dQ_2 + H_2') > 0$ or, due to $dR_2 = -dR_1$, $H_1'F_1' < H_2'F_2'$ commodity 2 is the pollution-intensive commodity since $H_i'F_i'$ measures the marginal tendency of pollution of using a resource in Sector *i*. The result is as follows: If a country specializes in the production of the less pollution-intensively produced commodity, the usual gains from trade are increased by an improvement in environmental quality. The country reduces the output of the pollution-intensively produced commodity, the conventional gains from trade are enhanced by an improvement in environmental quality and the country exports pollutants via trade to the rest of the world.

Second, if $H_1'F_1' > H_2'F_2'$, the second term in 13′ is negative. As a result we have the following outcome: If a country specializes in the production of the pollution-intensively produced commodity the welfare gains from trade (in the usual definition) are offset by a deterioration in environmental quality. *A priori* it cannot be ruled out that in the case of a strong preference for environmental quality and of a high marginal damage (in the physical sense) due to high levels of pollutants already in the environment the welfare loss associated with the deterioration in environmental quality may overcompensate the conventional gains from trade.

III. THE TRADE-OFF BETWEEN ENVIRONMENTAL QUALITY AND THE GAINS FROM TRADE

1. In *Section II* it was assumed that no environmental policy is undertaken. Another way of looking at the reduction in the welfare gains from trade due to an environmental deterioration is that the comparative price advantage of a country is not expressed correctly if prices do not include all social costs of production. Assume now that the country undertakes environmental policy. How will that policy affect the gains from trade? Is there a trade-off between the gains from trade and environmental quality? To answer this question we need to discuss how welfare is affected if environmental policy is undertaken when trade is taking place in the initial situation. We

only consider the case in which the country specializes in the production of the pollution intensively produced commodity.

We are interested in the sign of the expression

$$\frac{dW}{dz} = \frac{\partial W}{\partial C_2}\left(\bar{p}\,\frac{dC_1}{dz} + \frac{dC_2}{dz}\right) + \frac{\partial W}{\partial U}\,\frac{dU}{dz} \tag{14}$$

2. In order to analyze how welfare is affected in an open economy if environmental policy is introduced we use the system of equation (1)–(4), (7)–(12) consisting of 19 equations and the 18 variables S_i^p, S_i, S_i^r, Q_i, R_i, R_i^r, Y, C_i, r, E_1 and E_2, with p determined by the world market. The definition of Y states that total demand is equal to income, and the balance of payments equilibrium requires that the excess demand of the economy expressed in terms of commodity 2 is equal to zero, so that in a two-sector-model the definition of E_2 is redundant and can be omitted. Substituting and differentiating with respect to z we have

$$\begin{bmatrix} 1 & 0 & p & 0 & 0 & 0 & 0 \\ 0 & 1 & 0 & -pF_1'C_{2Y}' & -F_2'C_{2Y}' & 0 & 0 \\ 0 & 0 & 1 & F_1'C_{2Y}' & -F_2'C_{1Y}' & 0 & 0 \\ 0 & 0 & 0 & a_1 & 0 & 0 & 1 \\ 0 & 0 & 0 & 0 & a_2 & 0 & 1 \\ 0 & 0 & 0 & 0 & 0 & -zF_1^{r''} & 1 \\ 0 & 0 & 0 & zF_2^{r''} & zF_2^{r''} & zF_2^{r''} & 1 \end{bmatrix} \cdot \begin{bmatrix} dE_2 \\ dC_2 \\ dE_1 \\ dR_1 \\ dR_2 \\ dR_1^r \\ dr \end{bmatrix} = \begin{bmatrix} 0 \\ 0 \\ 0 \\ -H_1'F_1'dz \\ -H_2'F_2'dz \\ F_1^{r'}dz \\ F_2^{r'}dz \end{bmatrix} \tag{15}$$

with

$$C_{2Y}' = 1 - p\,C_{1Y}'$$
$$a_i = zH_i''F_i'^2 - (p_i - zH_i')\,F_i'' > 0$$

Assume commodity 2 is imported and commodity 1 is exported so that $E_2 > 0$ and $E_1 < 0$ when environmental policy is undertaken. Noting that the conditions stated are sufficient conditions so that the results may also occur with other constellations of the parameters, we have the following results:

ENVIRONMENTAL QUALITY AND THE GAINS FROM TRADE

$$\frac{dE_2}{dz}, \frac{d(-E_1)}{dz} < 0: \; H_1'F_1' > H_2'F_2' \tag{16i}$$

$$F_1'C_{2Y}' + F_2'C_{1Y}' > 0 \tag{16ii}$$

$$F_1'C_{2Y}'a_2 > F_2'C_{1Y}'a_1 \tag{16iii}$$

$$\frac{dC_2}{dz} < 0: \; H_1'F_1' > H_2'F_2' \tag{17i}$$

$$C_{2Y}' > 0 \tag{17ii}$$

$$\frac{dR_1}{dz} < 0: \; H_1'F_1' > H_2'F_2' \tag{18}$$

Without any condition additional to those already stated in the assumptions we have from equation (V) in the *appendix* and from the resource constraint

$$\frac{dR_i^r}{dz} > 0 \tag{19}$$

3. With the introduction of environmental policy, resource use in the pollution-intensive sector (and its output) will decline. Environmental policy makes the production of the pollution intensive commodity more costly. Consequently we can expect that the volume of exports will decline. This will be the case if demand conditions are such that the internal demand for commodity 1 rises with the introduction of environmental policy. Observe that income Y will decline with an improvement in environmental quality due to resources used in abatement activities being withdrawn from production (see below). Therefore, internal demand for commodity 1 will rise, if commodity 1 is inferior ($C_{1Y}' < 0$) and if demand for commodity 2 is more income-elastic than for commodity 1 in absolute terms, $|C_{1Y}'| > |C_{2Y}'|$.

Such an exceptional condition is not a necessary one, however. Assume a positive income elasticity of demand for both commodities. Then it may already be sufficient that the demand for commodity 2 is more income elastic than for commodity 1[1]. This ensures that with

1. For a more detailed presentation of the results compare *Beiträge zur angewandten Wirtschaftsforschung*, Institut für Volkswirtschaftslehre und Statistik, Universität Mannheim, Discussion Paper 85/77.

income Y declining, the fall in demand for commodity 1 is smaller than for commodity 2. This relatively income-inelastic demand for the pollution-intensively produced commodity prevents internal demand from falling and makes sure that exports are reduced.

Whereas resource use in Sector 1 decreases, and whereas the resource will be used additionally in the abatement activity of Sector 1, the result on the resource use in Sector 2 is ambiguous if Sector 2 is the less pollution intensive. This is due to the fact that resources used in the pollution abatement of Sector 1 may be withdrawn from Sector 1 only. Also if resources are used in the pollution abatement of Sector 2, they may come from Sector 1[2].

From equation (19) we also know that resources used in the abatement activity of Sector 1 will increase. Further, we have $\sum dR_i^r/dz > 0$ and consequently $\sum dR_i/dz < 0$. These results, however, do not rule out the possibility that resource use increases in Sector 2.

Internal demand for commodity 2 will decline if a positive marginal propensity to spend for commodity 2 prevails. $C'_{2Y} > 0$ does not insure, however, that the quantity of imports will increase.

National income as defined in equation (8) will decline if commodity 1 is the pollution-intensively produced commodity. Observe that it is assumed that taxes are transfered to households, thus having an income effect. It would be more realistic to assume that tax receipts are spent for other purposes such as monitoring environmental quality or administrating environmental programs. Then additional resources would be withdrawn from the private sector and the aforementioned results with respect to resource use will become even more likely.

Environmental quality will increase with the introduction of the emission tax. Using (1)–(6), (9) and solutions III–IV in the *appendix* we have

$$\frac{dU}{dz} = G'\left[H_1'F_1'\frac{dR_1}{dz} + H_2'F_2'\frac{dR_2}{dz} + F_2^{r'}\left(\frac{dR_1}{dz} + \frac{dR_2}{dz}\right)\right] > 0 \qquad (20)$$

4. Pollutants are reduced because of the reallocation of the resource between Sectors 1 and 2 and because the resource is used in

2. Observe, however, that from equations (V) and (VI) in the *appendix*, resource use in Sector 1 is more sensitive to the emission tax than in Sector 2, *i.e.* $|dR_1/dz| > |dR_2/dz|$.

ENVIRONMENTAL QUALITY AND THE GAINS FROM TRADE

Diagram 1

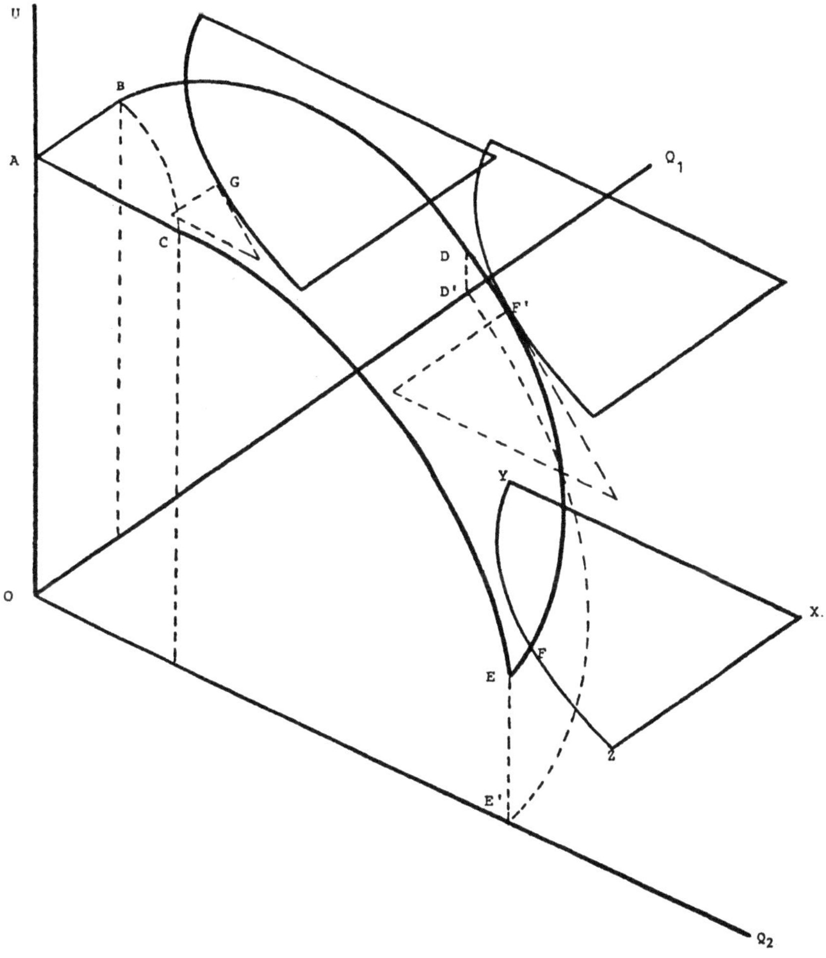

pollution abatement. *Diagram 1* illustrates the results. The concave transformation space can be explained as follows (SIEBERT, 1976). Assume the economy is in a situation of ecological paradise where no production takes place – point *A*. Increasing the production of commodity 1 with $Q_2 = 0$ generates pollutants but up to a certain level all emissions can be reduced by using the resource in pollution-abatement processes – point *B*. Similarly for increasing Q_2 with

$Q_1 = 0$. Curve BC ensures the full employment of resources with no pollutants entering the environment (the assimilative capacity is assumed to be zero). If production of commodity 1 is increased (for $Q_2 = 0$) starting at B, resources are withdrawn from pollution abatement and environmental quality declines for two reasons: (a) increased production with an increasing quantity of pollutants, and (b) withdrawal of resources from pollution abatement. A similar argument holds for increasing the output of commodity 2 with $Q_1 = 0$ starting at point C.

If $R_1^r = 0$, no resources are used for abatement in Sector 1 (D). Similarly point E shows a situation where $R_2^r = 0$. $DD' > EE'$ indicates that commodity 1 is produced relatively more pollution-intensively. Also it is assumed that $H_1'F_1' > H_2'F_2'$ is not offset by a comparative advantage of pollution abatement in Sector 1. Curve DE and its projection to the Q_1–Q_2 plane ($D'D'$) represent the traditional transformation curve with no resource being used in pollution abatement.

In order to keep the diagram simple we do not draw the transformation space of the rest of the world but only its production block (XYZ) which lies horizontally and cuts into the transformation space of the home country at F. Relative price in the home country differs from the world price in the autarky-point F.

Assume a no-trade situation F with both the home country and the rest of the world undertaking no environmental policy and $°p < p$. If trade takes place gains from trade occur as shown by the trade triangle associated with point F'. Environmental quality for the home country, however, has declined. This is the argument presented in *Section II*, above.

Consider now situation F' with the home country levying an emission tax and the rest of the world having no environmental policy. In this case our results indicate that Q_1 will decrease, U will increase and Q_2 may rise or fall. If we define an iso-price-line for varying z, we know that this line will move in such a direction that $dQ_1/dz < 0$ and $dU/dz > 0$. If internal demand for commodity 1 does not fall too much, which we have ruled out, exports of the home country are reduced and, with p given, the quantity of imports falls. Gains from trade are smaller – compare the trade triangle at point G. The gains from trade have been reduced by environmental policy. The improvement in environmental quality is only possible by reducing the gains from trade[3].

5. Substituting the results into equation (14) we have

$$\frac{dW}{dz} = \left(\frac{\partial W}{\partial C_2} + \frac{\partial W}{\partial U}\frac{G'}{z}\right)\frac{dY}{dz} \tag{21}$$

We know that $dY/dz < 0$, *i.e.* the commodity bundle measured in units of commodity 2 decreases due to environmental policy. Consequently we have from equation (21)

$$\frac{dW}{dz} \gtreqless 0 : z\frac{\partial W}{\partial C_2} \lesseqgtr -\frac{\partial W}{\partial U}G' \tag{21'}$$

The term on the right side of equation (21′) indicates prevented marginal environmental damage. The term on the left side denotes the emission tax in value terms, namely the emission tax z in real terms (*i.e.* in quantity units of commodity 2) evaluated with the marginal utility of commodity 2. Welfare will increase if in the initial situation the emission tax in value terms is lower than prevented marginal environmental damage. Welfare will not increase if the emission tax in a given situation is set according to marginal environmental damage prevented. And welfare will fall if in the initial situation the emission tax is set higher than marginal damage prevented.

This result confirms the well-known rule for the setting of the emission tax according to marginal damage prevented in a closed economy for an open economy. It should be pointed out that (21′) is the result of an explanation model and not an optimization model. Using the equations of our open economy as restrictions in an optimization model, it can be shown that the shadow price for emissions must be set according to marginal damage prevented.

3. Due to the small-country assumption the relative price for the rest of the world must be identical in F, F' and G, so that the production print of the rest of the world does not change. Also the production block of the rest of the world is drawn very small. Observe that in the real world the side of the trade triangle cannot be longer than the side of the production block.

Since $zH_1' = p - r/F_1'$ and $zH_2' = 1 - r/F_2'$, (21′) can also be expressed as

$$\frac{dW}{dz} > 0: \frac{\partial W}{\partial C_2} < \frac{\partial W}{\partial C_2}\frac{r}{F_2'} - \frac{\partial W}{\partial U} G' H_2' \qquad (21'')$$

or

$$\frac{\partial W}{\partial C_2} p < \frac{\partial W}{\partial C_2}\frac{r}{F_1'} - \frac{\partial W}{\partial U} G' H_1' \qquad (21''')$$

In (21″) the right side indicates the social costs of producing commodity 2, namely private marginal costs in real terms (r/F_2') evaluated with the marginal social utility of commodity 2 and environmental damage attributable to commodity 2. The right side of equation (21‴) denotes the social costs of producing commodity 1. The left side of both equation denotes the marginal social value of the two commodities[4].

Welfare will increase with environmental policy if in the initial situation (before environmental policy is undertaken) the marginal social costs of producing a commodity (private plus environmental costs) are higher than the value of that commodity.

Since for $z = 0$ the relative price must be equal to private marginal costs of production, environmental costs are not accounted for. Introducing an emission tax will reduce R_1, whereas F_1' will rise and marginal private costs of production will fall[5]. Also pollutants of Sector 1 will be reduced, marginal damage will be reduced due to a lower quantity of emissions and the marginal evaluation of the environment will fall since its quality increases (making the usual assumptions about welfare functions). Consequently, after all adaptions have taken place, commodity price and the social costs of production will be equal [compare equation (10)].

If in (21″) and (21‴) the evaluation of a commodity is higher than its social costs of production before environmental policy is under-

4. In (21‴) p is the relative price of commodity 1, measuring one unit of commodity 1 in quantity units of commodity 2. Multiplying p with $\partial W/\partial C_2$ indicates social value of one unit of commodity 1.

5. It is assumed that the increase in F_1' is not offset by a possible rise in r.

taken, environmental policy cutting back production and reducing emissions will reduce social costs even further. In this case, welfare will decline and environmental policy should not have been undertaken in the first place.

6. As a limiting case we have the possibility that with environmental policy and with an increase in environmental quality the home country loses its comparative advantage by pricing herself out of the world market. Assume the closed country levies an emission tax z^a. Then the autarky price p^a is given by

$$p^a = \frac{r(z^a)}{F_1'(z^a)} + z^a H_1'(z^a)$$

Let z^h denote the emission tax in the open economy. Then we have from $p^a < p$ as a necessary condition for trade to occur (in the direction assumed) that

$$p^a = \frac{r(z^a)}{F_1'(z^a)} + z^a H_1'(z^a) < \bar{p} < \frac{r(z^h)}{F_1'(z^h)} - z^h H_1'(z^h) \qquad (22)$$

If equation (22) holds, the home country will continue to export the pollution-intensively produced commodity, however with a reduced volume. If the left side of (22) does not hold, either the trade equilibrium with environmental policy is identical to the autarky solution with environmental policy, or the direction of trade may be reversed[6].

7. Finally, if a closed country opens up for trade and undertakes environmental policy at the same time, *i.e.* it moves from point F in *Diagram 1* to point G, the change in welfare is indicated by equations (13′) and (14). Whereas equation (14) can be interpreted as the welfare effect of a marginal variation of the emission tax, equation (13′) describes a qualitative variation, that changes the market equilibrium conditions of the closed economy into a balance of payment restraint.

6. Assume the emission tax is set according to marginal damage prevented. Then further inspection of equation (22) allows a comparison on the level of emission taxes in the autarky case and the trade case, if $p^a < p$ is to hold.

IV. EXTENSIONS AND CONCLUSIONS

The following two questions have not been included in the analysis. First, in reality we observe that for a variety of reasons countries tend not to use emission taxes as environmental policy instruments but emission norms and other administrative devices (*e.g.* permits). In this case the question arises whether the country can increase its welfare by introducing a tariff on the non-pollution-intensively produced import substitute. This is an inducement to produce more of the less pollution-intensively produced commodity. The gains from trade may be reduced and environmental quality will rise. Note, however, that in addition to the problems discussed in the theory of an optimal tariff, a tariff will only improve environmental quality by a sectoral change which comes about through a change in relative price from the demand side. Similarly as a product tax on the pollution-intensively produced commodity, a tariff lacks the incentive to reduce pollutants through abatement processes.

Second, if the assumption of the small-country case is given up, opening up a country for trade is accompanied by an improvement in the terms of trade. Also, if environmental policy is undertaken in an initial situation with trade, the terms-of-trade effect will influence the total change in welfare.

In the small-country case we have as conclusions: If a country exports its pollution-intensively produced commodity, its gains from trade are accompanied by a decline in its environmental quality. If environmental policy is undertaken under these circumstances environmental quality will be improved but gains from trade will be reduced. With the introduction of environmental policy, resource-use in the pollution intensive sector (and its output) will decline. Moreover, the quantities exported and imported will fall, and pollution abatement will be increased. There will be an overall welfare gain from environmental policy as long as marginal social costs of producing the commodity (including environmental costs) are higher than the marginal value of the commodity in consumption or as long as the emission tax is lower than marginal environmental damage.

ENVIRONMENTAL QUALITY AND THE GAINS FROM TRADE

APPENDIX[7]

1. The determinant Δ is positive. For the change in the excess demand we have

$$\frac{dE_2}{dz} = \frac{p}{\Delta}\{F_1' C_{2y}' D_1 + F_2' C_{1y}' D_2\} = -\frac{1}{p}\frac{dE_1}{dz} \qquad \text{(I)}$$

with the submatrices

$$D_1 = a_2 (F_1^{r''} + F_2^{r''}) (zH_1' F_1' + r) - z^2 F_1^{r''} F_2^{r''} (H_1' F_1' - H_2' F_2') \qquad \text{(I')}$$

$$D_2 = -a_1 (F_1^{r''} + F_2^{r''}) (zH_2' F_2' + r) - z^2 F_1^{r''} F_2^{r''} (H_1' F_1' - H_2' F_2') \qquad \text{(I'')}$$

2. The change in the home demand for commodity 2 is given by

$$\frac{dC_2}{dz} = \frac{C_{2y}'}{\Delta}\{pF_1' D_1 - F_2' D_2\} \qquad \text{(II)}$$

3. For the change in the resource use we have

$$\frac{dR_1}{dz} = \frac{D_1}{\Delta} \quad \text{and} \quad \frac{dR_2}{dz} = -\frac{D_2}{\Delta} \qquad \text{(III)}$$

4. The change in resource use in the abatement activity is given by

$$\frac{dR_1^r}{dz} = -\frac{F_2^{r''}}{\Delta}\{a_1 (zH_2' F_2' + r) + a_2 (zH_1' F_1' + r)\} \qquad \text{(IV)}$$

5. For the change in income we have from equation (8)

$$\frac{dY}{dz} = \frac{1}{\Delta}\{pF_1 D_1 - F_2' D_2'\} \qquad \text{(V)}$$

REFERENCES

D'ARGE R.C. and KNEESE A.V.: 'Environmental Quality and International Trade', *International Organization*, Vol. 26 (1972), pp. 419–465.

BAUMOL W.J.: *Environmental Protection, International Spillovers and Trade*, Stockholm 1971.

7. For a more detailed presentation of the results compare *Beiträge zur angewandten Wirtschaftsforschung, op. cit.*

GERELLI E.: 'Problèmes Economiques Internationaux de l'Environment: Commerces Internationaux et Pollution Transfrontière', *Schweizerische Zeitschrift für Volkswirtschaftslehre und Statistik*, Vol. 108 (1972), pp. 439–451.

MARKUSEN J. R,: 'International Externalities and Optimal Tax Structures', *Journal of International Economics*, Vol. 5 (1975), pp. 15–29.

PETHIG R.: 'Pollution, Welfare and Environmental Policy in the Theory of Comparative Advantage', *Journal of Environmental Economics And Management*, Vol. 2 (1976), pp. 160–169.

SIEBERT H.: 'Comparative Advantage and Environmental Policy: A Note', *Zeitschrift für Nationalökonomie*, Vol. 34 (1974), pp. 397–400.

SIEBERT H.: 'Environmental Control, Economic Structure and International Trade', in: INGO WALTER (Ed.), *Studies in International Environmental Economics*, 1976, pp. 29–56.

SIEBERT H.: 'Environmental Protection and International Specialization', *Weltwirtschaftliches Archiv*, Vol. 110 (1974), pp. 494–508.

SIEBERT H.: 'Die Grundprobleme des Umweltschutzes. Eine wirtschaftstheoretische Analyse', in: *Soziale Probleme der modernen Industriegesellschaft*, Schriften des Vereins für Socialpolitik, NF, Bd. 92 I und II, Berlin 1977, pp. 141-182.

WALTER I.: *International Economics of Pollution*, New York 1975.

WALTER I.: 'International Trade and Resource Diversion: The Case of Environmental Management', *Weltwirtschaftliches Archiv*, Vol. 110 (1974), pp. 482–493.

WALTER I. (Ed.): *Studies in International Environmental Economics*, New York 1976.

SUMMARY

The paper analyzes the trade-off between environmental quality and the gains from trade. For a world with pollutants as a joint product of output it is shown that gains from trade by exporting a pollution-intensively produced commodity are accompanied by a loss of environmental quality and that improving environmental quality will adversely affect the gains from trade. The paper analyzes with a two sector model which adjustment processes occur, if a country untertakes environmental policy. The results are explained diagrammatically. A condition is specified for a positive change in welfare from environmental policy taking into consideration the reduction in the gains from trade. Finally, the paper suggests that in an open economy emission taxes have to be set according to the same rule as in a closed economy, namely in the optimum the emission tax must equal marginal environmental damage prevented.

ZUSAMMENFASSUNG

Der Artikel diskutiert den Zielkonflikt zwischen Verbesserung der Umweltqualität und den Gewinnen aus Aussenhandel. Für eine Welt mit Emissionen als Kuppelprodukt der Produktion wird gezeigt, dass erstens Gewinne aus Aussenhandel beim Export eines schadstoffintensiv produzierten Gutes von einem Verlust an

ENVIRONMENTAL QUALITY AND THE GAINS FROM TRADE

Umweltqualität begleitet sind und dass zweitens die Verbesserung der Umweltqualität die Gewinne aus Handel tangiert. Der Artikel analysiert mit Hilfe eines Zwei-Sektor-Modells, welche Anpassungsprozesse erfolgen, wenn ein Land Umweltpolitik betreibt. Die Resultate werden graphisch veranschaulicht. Es wird eine Bedingung für eine Wohlfahrtsverbesserung nach Umweltpolitik formuliert, die die Rechnung der Gewinne aus Handel in Betracht zieht. Der Artikel kommt zu dem Resultat, dass in einer offenen Volkswirtschaft die Emissionssteuer nach der gleichen Regel zu setzen ist, die von geschlossenen Volkswirtschaften bekannt ist, nämlich: die Emissionssteuer muss dem verhinderten Grenzschaden entsprechen.

RÉSUMÉ

L'article traite le conflit d'objectifs qui existe entre l'amélioration de la qualité de l'environnement et les avantages de l'échange internationale. On y montre que pour un monde dont les sous-produits sont des déchets nuisants, premièrement, les profits du commerce extérieur à l'exportation d'un bien d'une intense propriété polluante, sont toujours accompagnés d'une perte de la qualité de l'environnement, et deuxièmement l'amélioration de celle-ci est corollaire d'une réduction des avantages de l'échange internationale. L'article analyse au moyen d'un model bisectoriel, les procès d'adaptation qui ont lieu dans un pays pratiquant une politique écologique. On peut observer les résultats selon une courbe graphique. Y est formulée une condition pour le progrès du bien-être en conséquence d'une politique écologique, condition qui tient en considération le compte des advantage de l'échange internationale. L'article en vient au résultat que dans une économie ouverte l'imposition d'une taxe sur les déchets nuisants doit être établie selon la même règle que celle déjà connue des économies sans l'échange internationale, plus précisément: la taxation des sous-produits polluants doit correspondre au domage marginal.

[2]

JOURNAL OF ENVIRONMENTAL ECONOMICS AND MANAGEMENT 2, 160–169 (1976)

Pollution, Welfare, and Environmental Policy in the Theory of Comparative Advantage[1]

RÜDIGER PETHIG

Center for Mathematical Studies in Economics and Management Science, Northwestern University, Evanston, Illinois 60201, and Fakultät für Volkswirtschaftslehre und Statistik, University of Mannheim, 68 Mannheim, Seminargebäude in A5, West Germany

Received February 1, 1975; revised August 25, 1975

Within a simple two-sector general equilibrium model it is shown how some well-known propositions of the neoclassical trade theory can be applied to countries with pollution-generating industries. Results are obtained not only under the assumption that the countries do not enforce any environmental policy but also for the case that one or each country implements an environmental price and standard system. In particular, several versions of the Theorem of Comparative Advantage with respect to environmental scarcity are derived, a theorem on welfare losses from trade, and an emission charge equalization theorem.

I. INTRODUCTION

The important economic impact of the environment and of national environmental policies on international trade have been analyzed recently in [1, 2, 8, 11, 13, 14, 16]. D'Arge and Kneese ([1, p. 434], and similarly [11, 14, 16]) argue that the Theorem of Comparative Advantage applies to trading economies with polluting industries: Countries with relatively large environmental assimilative capacities should specialize in, and export, those commodities which are relatively pollution-intensive in their production.

Such an application of the comparative advantage proposition is suggestive. However, in the literature quoted this proposition and the analytical concept of environmental scarcity are not explicitely rationalized and qualified within a general equilibrium model. The present paper attempts to fill this gap. It will be shown how some positive and normative results of the neoclassical trade theory when properly qualified, modified, and /or reinterpretated can be applied to countries with pollution generating industries and (national) environmental management. In particular, different versions and interpretations of the Theorem of Comparative Advantage with respect to environmental scarcity are derived.

II. THE CLOSED ECONOMY

1. *Assumptions and Definitions*

We consider an economy in which the quantities q_i of the private consumption goods $i = 1, 2$ can be produced by a single resource (labor). Let a_i denote the quantity

[1] I am grateful to Prof. Dr. H. Siebert, W. Gretz, W. Vogt, and two anonymous referees for helpful comments.

of this input used in industry i. Each industry i not only produces the good i, but also a by-product which is of no use to the agents, either in consumption or as a production input. Hence, this by-product must be released into the environment.[2] The environmental service as a receptor for wastes is measured in units of this by-product. We denote by e_i the quantity of the by-product which is produced in industry i and then released into the environment (emission of industry i). Keeping in mind that the environmental service as a waste receptor is measured in units of output, we may interprete e_i as a factor of production [4, 10, 12].

It is assumed that the production technology of industry i consists of many production processes in which the good i and the by-product are generated in (alternative) fixed proportions. These processes will be approximated by a technology in which the ratios of quantities produced are continuously variable. We denote the production technology of industry i by

$$q_i = f_i(a_i, e_i) \quad (i = 1, 2) \tag{1}$$

which satisfies (2a)–(2d): The domain of f_i is

$$D_i \equiv \{(a_i, e_i) | a_i \geq \bar{\bar{k}}_i e_i, \bar{\bar{k}}_i > 0\} \tag{2a}$$

$$\lambda f_i(a_i, e_i) = f_i(\lambda a_i, \lambda e_i) \quad \text{for} \quad \lambda > 0 \tag{2b}$$

$$f_{a_i} > 0; \quad f_{aa_i}, f_{ee_i} < 0 \text{ on } D_i \tag{2c}$$

$$f_{e_i} \gtrless 0 \quad \text{for} \quad (a_i/e_i) \gtrless \bar{k}_i > \bar{\bar{k}}_i \text{ on } D_i. \tag{2d}$$

Assumption (2) implies that, for $(a_i/e_i) > \bar{k}_i$ it is technologically feasible to maintain a given output level of good i by lowering (increasing) the labor input and increasing (lowering) the production of the by-product. If, however, this property would also hold for all $(a_i/e_i) < \bar{k}_i$ one could produce arbitrarily large quantities of the by-product with any given labor endowment. By (2d) such nonconvex production possibilities with respect to the by-product are excluded.

We denote by $k_i \equiv (a_i/e_i)$ the labor intensity in the production of good i. As is known from traditional trade theory, it follows by (2b) that

$$k_i = k_i(f_{e_i}/f_{a_i}) \quad \text{with} \quad dk_i/d(f_{e_i}/f_{a_i}) > 0. \tag{3}$$

To avoid factor reversal difficulties we introduce the familiar strong factor intensity assumption

$$k_2\left(\frac{f_e}{f_a}\right) > k_1\left(\frac{f_e}{f_a}\right) \quad \text{for all} \quad \frac{f_e}{f_a} = \frac{f_{e_1}}{f_{a_1}} = \frac{f_{e_2}}{f_{a_2}} \gtrless 0. \tag{4}$$

This means in the context of the present model that good 1 is relatively environment-intensive and good 2 is relatively labor-intensive.

The labor endowment of the economy is exogenously given and denoted by $\bar{a}$. Let us qualify now in which way the availability of the environment's waste disposal service can also be said to be limited. We ignore the waste being released into the environment by the consumption sector. So the economy's total waste emission is $e \equiv e_1 + e_2$. This emission is transformed into pollutants, whose concentration, denoted by s, depends on e as described by the continuously differentiable "pollution

[2] We do not introduce a third industry "producing" waste abatement services [5, 14] which is economically relevant in particular for the case of increasing returns to scale.

function"

$$s = s(e), \quad \text{where} \quad s(0) = 0,$$

$$ds/de\,|_e \begin{cases} =0, & \text{if} \quad 0 \leq e \leq e^0 \\ >0, & \text{if} \quad e > e^0 \end{cases}, \quad \text{and} \quad d^2s/de^2 \geq 0. \tag{5}$$

According to function (5) the emission has no significant polluting effect unless it exceeds some (low) level e^0. With $e > e^0$, however, pollution rises nondecreasingly as e increases. It will be assumed in addition that at some (high) level $\bar{e} > e^0$ the ecological system "collapses." This collapse is supposed to induce a breakdown of the economy[3] so that for $e > \bar{e}$ there no longer exists what is conventionally called an economic equilibrium.

For the consumers the environmental quality is a pure public consumption good which is determined endogenously by the amount of waste products discharged. It is convenient to define

$$Q = Q(e) \equiv \frac{s(\bar{e}) - s(e)}{s(\bar{e})} \tag{6}$$

to be a normalized index of environmental quality.

The welfare function is $W = W(q_1, q_2, Q)$. For the sake of simplicity it will be specified here by the quasi-concave function

$$W = \min\,(c_1Qq_1, c_2Qq_2) \tag{7}$$

where c_1 and c_2 are positive constants. This special function excludes substitution effects between the goods 1 and 2, i.e., any consumption demand (q_1, q_2) necessarily satisfies

$$q_1 = (c_2/c_1)q_2. \tag{8}$$

Goods 1 and 2 and the labor input are traded on perfectly competitive markets at (nonnegative) prices p_1, p_2, p_A. However, there is no market, and hence no market price, for environmental quality. The environmental service is marketable but need not be marketed. So we assign a price p_E to it which is institutionally restricted to

$$p_E = 0, \tag{9}$$

if the polluters' right principle prevails.

The two industries are profit maximizers. Hence,

$$p_A/p_i = f_{a_i} \quad \text{and} \quad p_E/p_i = f_{e_i} \quad \text{for} \quad i = 1, 2. \tag{10}$$

The consumption sector maximizes welfare, but it does not take into account that ultimately it is their consumption decisions with respect to goods 1 and 2 which determine the level of environmental quality. The total income y of the consumption sector consists of its wages $p_A(a_1 + a_2)$, profits G_i of the two industries and—eventually —transfer payments $p_E(e_1 + e_2)$ from the environmental agency. Thus, by (2b) with

[3] This simple "breakdown" hypothesis is a special case of the more satisfactory approach to treat s as a detrimental external effect in production. Note also that the present model cannot capture the important intertemporal aspects of the concept of environmental assimilative capacity, since the accumulation of pollutants is neglected.

the income

$$y = p_A(a_1 + a_2) + p_B(e_1 + e_2) + G_1 + G_2 = p_1q_1 + p_2q_2 \tag{11}$$

the consumption sector can buy the commodity bundle which is produced.

An equilibrium of the economy is defined by an allocation $(e_1, e_2, a_1, a_2, q_1, q_2)$ and a price system (p_B, p_A, p_1, p_2) such that

$$\begin{aligned} &\text{(a)}\quad p_B \geq 0, \quad p_A, p_1, p_2 > 0 \\ &\text{(b)}\quad e_1 + e_2 \leq \bar{e} \\ &\text{(c)}\quad a_1 + a_2 = \bar{a} \\ &\text{(d)}\quad \text{(8), (10), and (11) are satisfied.} \end{aligned} \tag{12}$$

2. *Equilibrium, Welfare, and Price and Standard Systems*

Before we consider trade some important properties of the closed model are shown.[4] First, we define the transformation function

$$q_1 = q_1(q_2, \epsilon) \tag{13}$$

which is the locus of all efficient production points (q_1, q_2) for a given emission level ϵ $(0 < \epsilon \leq \bar{e})$. A production point (q_1, q_2) is efficient relative to ϵ, if:

(i) It is feasible relative to ϵ, i.e., it satisfies the conditions $q_i = f_i(e_i, a_i)$ for $i = 1, 2$, $a_1 + a_2 \leq \bar{a}$, and $e_1 + e_2 \leq \epsilon$.

(ii) There is no point $(q_1', q_2') \neq (q_1, q_2)$ which is feasible relative to ϵ and $q_i' \geq q_i$, $i = 1, 2$, with $q_i' > q_i$ for some i.

It is easily shown that for alternatively given upper emission bounds ϵ and under assumptions (1), (2), and (4) the transformation function satisfies

LEMMA 1. (a) *If* $\epsilon \geq \bar{a}/\bar{k}_1$, *(13) is given by the affine function*

$$q_1 = \frac{\bar{a}h_1(\bar{k}_1)}{\bar{k}_1} - \frac{\bar{k}_2 h_1(\bar{k}_1)}{\bar{k}_1 h_2(\bar{k}_2)} q_2, \quad \text{where} \quad h_i(k_i) = f_i(k_i, 1).$$

(b) *If* $\epsilon < \bar{a}/\bar{k}_2$, *we have for all* q_2 *in the range of (13)*[5]

(i) $-\dfrac{d^2q_1(q_2, \epsilon)}{dq_2^2} < 0$ (strict concavity),

(ii) $\dfrac{\bar{a}h_1(\bar{k}_1)}{\bar{k}_1} - \dfrac{\bar{k}_2 h_1(\bar{k}_1)}{\bar{k}_1 h_2(\bar{k}_2)} q_2 > q_1(q_2, \epsilon)$.

(c) *If* $\bar{a}/\bar{k}_2 < \epsilon < \bar{a}/\bar{k}_1$, *(13) is continuous and given*

(i) by $q_1 = \dfrac{\hat{a}_1 h_1(\bar{k}_1)}{\bar{k}_1} - \dfrac{\bar{k}_2 h_1(\bar{k}_1)}{\bar{k}_1 h_2(\bar{k}_2)} q_2$

for $q_2 \in [\hat{q}_2(\epsilon), \bar{k}_2/[\bar{a}h_2(\bar{k}_2)]]$ *and*

[4] For a more detailed discussion of the closed model, see [12].

[5] Lemma 1b also holds for $\epsilon = \bar{a}/\bar{k}_2$. In this case, the inequality in Lemma 1b (ii) becomes an equality for $q_2 = \bar{a}h_2(\bar{k}_2)/\bar{k}_2$.

(ii) *by a strictly concave function for* $q_2 \in [0, \hat{q}_2(\epsilon)]$ *where (for* $i = 1, 2$*)* $\hat{q}_i(\epsilon) \equiv f_i(\hat{a}_i, \hat{e}_i)$ *and where the factor allocation* $(\hat{a}_1, \hat{a}_2, \hat{e}_1, \hat{e}_2)$ *is such that,* $\hat{a}_1 + \hat{a}_2 = \bar{a}$, $\hat{e}_1 + \hat{e}_2 = \bar{e}$, *and (for* $i = 1, 2$*)* $\hat{a}_i = \bar{k}_i\hat{e}_i$.

In [12] it is shown that under the assumptions of Section II.1, when no environmental controls are enforced, the closed economy has a unique equilibrium, if and only if the ratio $\bar{a}/\bar{e}$ does not exceed some positive number $\bar{k}_c$. It is also proved in [12] that the closed economy has a unique welfare maximum where the welfare maximal emission value e^* is less than or equal to the economy's equilibrium emission $\tilde{e}$. Hence, environmental controls are always desirable if $e^* < \tilde{e}$. They are even imperative, if $\tilde{e} < (\bar{a}/\bar{k}_c)$, since in this case the economy cannot "survive" without effective environmental protection.

It is widely agreed that the information costs for an environmental protection agency (EPA) to find the optimal value e^* are extremely high. Therefore, we do not require the EPA to have information on e^* but we ask the EPA instead to enforce the less ambitious objective of implementing an "acceptable" emission standard $\epsilon \in]0, \tilde{e}[$ which is to be established by some collective decision procedure [3, 4, 14, 15].

It is clear that such an "acceptable" emission standard should satisfy $\epsilon < (\bar{a}/\bar{k}_c)$. For this case it follows that there is one and only one allocation

$$z^\epsilon = (a_1^\epsilon, a_2^\epsilon, e_1^\epsilon, e_2^\epsilon, q_1^\epsilon, q_2^\epsilon)$$

which is efficient relative to ϵ and simultaneously satisfies (8).[6] Consequently, the "least cost" policy to guarantee the environmental quality $Q(\epsilon)$ requires that the EPA establish an "ϵ-efficient" equilibrium, which is defined by z^ϵ being the equilibrium allocation.

Among the various possible environmental policy instruments we consider only two, which have become known as environmental price and standard systems [15]:

(i) The assumption (9) of Section II.1 is suspended and it is assumed instead that the EPA establishes a market for emission rights, where the total demand for the environmental service e is equated to the EPA's fixed supply ϵ (of emission licences) by a nonnegative market price $w^m \equiv p_E{}^m/p_A$ [7].

(ii) The assumption (9) of Section II.1 is suspended and it is assumed instead that the EPA raises an emission charge (tax)$w^t \equiv p_E{}^t/p_A$ such that the total demand e for the environmental service is reduced to ϵ [4].

These policy instruments are equally efficient in the sense of:

THEOREM 1. *If environmental policies* (i) *or* (ii) *are implemented, for any emission standard* $\epsilon \in]0, \bar{a}/\bar{k}_c[$ *there is a unique* ϵ*-efficient equilibrium with* $w^t = w^m > 0$.

Proof. Denote by $(q_1^\epsilon, q_2^\epsilon)$ the commodity bundle which satisfies (13) and (8) and by $(e_1^\epsilon, e_2^\epsilon, a_1^\epsilon, a_2^\epsilon)$ the factor allocation which is uniquely assigned to this bundle. Since the production $(q_1^\epsilon, q_2^\epsilon)$ is efficient relative to $\epsilon \in]0, \bar{a}/\bar{k}_c[$, it follows that $e_1^\epsilon + e_2^\epsilon = \epsilon$, $a_1^\epsilon + a_2^\epsilon = \bar{a}$ and

$$\frac{f_{a_1}(a_1^\epsilon, e_1^\epsilon)}{f_{e_1}(a_1^\epsilon, e_1^\epsilon)} = \frac{f_{a_2}(a_2^\epsilon, e_2^\epsilon)}{f_{e_2}(a_2^\epsilon, e_2^\epsilon)}$$

[6] This efficiency property is comparable to that established in [4, p. 52n]. See also [15].

Now choose $p_1{}^\epsilon, p_2{}^\epsilon, p_A{}^\epsilon, p_E{}^{t\epsilon} = p_E{}^{m\epsilon} \equiv p_E{}^\epsilon > 0$, such that for $i = 1, 2$

$$\frac{p_A{}^\epsilon}{p_i{}^\epsilon} = f_{a_i}(a_i{}^\epsilon, e_i{}^\epsilon) \quad \text{and} \quad \frac{p_E{}^\epsilon}{p_i{}^\epsilon} = f_{e_i}(a_i{}^\epsilon, e_i{}^\epsilon).$$

Then the vectors $(p_1{}^\epsilon, p_2{}^\epsilon, p_A{}^\epsilon, p_E{}^\epsilon)$ and z^ϵ constitute the unique ϵ-efficient equilibrium of the economy and $p_E{}^{t\epsilon} = p_E{}^{m\epsilon}$ implies $w^{t\epsilon} = w^{m\epsilon}$.

Q.E.D.

According to Theorem 1 the price and standard systems (i) and (ii) are equally efficient environmental policy instruments. The main difference is that for (i) the direct policy variable of the EPA is the emission standard while the equilibrium price for the environmental service is "found" by the market, whereas in policy (ii) the EPA manipulates the charge w^t until the target emission standard is reached. The equivalency in terms of efficiency results from the fact that in both cases the two industries face the same factor price $p_E{}^{m\epsilon}$ or $p_E{}^{t\epsilon}$ and hence by (10) produce at identical marginal factor costs $p_1{}^\epsilon f_{e_1} = p_2{}^\epsilon f_{e_2}$. It should be noted that along a dynamic adjustment path to equilibrium there may well be differences in efficiency for the two systems. The analysis of the comparative dynamics is, however, beyond the scope of this paper.

III. TRADE AND ENVIRONMENT

We can turn now to the two-country case. All variables without an additional superscript refer to country I, while a superscript + indicates that the variables refer to country II. The assumptions made in Section II.1 hold for each country except that the production functions are now specified as

$$q_i = g_i(a_i, e_i) \equiv \lambda_i f_i(a_i, e_i), \tag{14}$$
$$q_i^+ = g_i^+(a_i^+, e_i^+) \equiv \lambda_i^+ f_i(a_i^+, e_i^+), \quad \lambda_i, \lambda_i^+ > 0, \quad i = 1, 2,$$

where the functions f_i are those defined in (1) and (2).

When the goods 1 and 2 can be traded we distinguish between q_i, q_i^+, the quantities produced in each country, and q_i^d, q_i^{d+} the quantities demanded in each country. Thus, the trade model has to determine the allocations

$$z \equiv (a_1, a_2, e_1, e_2, q_1, q_2, q_1{}^d, q_2{}^d), \quad z^+ \equiv (a_1{}^+, a_2{}^+, e_1{}^+, e_2{}^+, q_1{}^+, q_2{}^+, q_1{}^{d+}, q_2{}^{d+})$$

and the prices

$$\pi \equiv (p_E, p_E{}^+, p_A, p_A{}^+, p_1, p_1{}^+, p_2, p_2{}^+).$$

The vector (z, z^+, π) is a trade equilibrium for the countries I and II, if

(a) (12) and (12⁺) is satisfied (where (8) and (8⁺) refer to quantities demanded);
(b) $p_1/p_2 = p_1{}^+/p_2{}^+$;
(c) $q_i{}^d + q_i{}^{d+} = q_i + q_i{}^+$ for $i = 1, 2$.

Let us first state a theorem on the trade pattern between two countries which are not (yet) confronted with severe environmental deterioration (e.g., developing countries):

THEOREM 2. *Under the assumptions (1) to (11), (1⁺) to (11⁺), (14), the conditions* $\bar{e} \geq \bar{a}/\bar{k}_1$, $\bar{e}^+ \geq \bar{a}^+/\bar{k}_1{}^+$, *and when no environmental controls are enforced in either country, it follows (in trade equilibrium):*

(a) *Country I exports and specializes its production on*

$$\left.\begin{array}{l}\textit{good 1}\\ \textit{no good}\\ \textit{good 2}\end{array}\right\}, \quad \textit{if and only if } \frac{\lambda_1}{\lambda_2} \gtreqless \frac{\lambda_1^+}{\lambda_2^+}.$$

(b) *That country which specializes on the production of the environment-intensive good for export may suffer a welfare loss from trade, whereas the other country always gains from trade.*

Proof. (2a) By Lemma 1a both countries have constant rates of transformation. Hence, it is obvious that the case of Theorem 2a is that of the Ricardian theory of trade: Comparative advantages are due to comparative differences in production technologies only.

(2b) Suppose, we have $\bar{e} = \bar{a}/\bar{k}_1$ in the case of Theorem 2a and country I specializes completely in the production of good 1 in the corresponding trade equilibrium. Then by (7), $W = 0$ whatever the equilibrium consumption bundle may be. Since c_2/c_1 is finite, the welfare of country I in its autarkic equilibrium is positive and hence it suffers a welfare loss from trade.

Q.E.D.

If in both countries the "supply" of the environmental service is large relative to the "demand," the analysis leads straight to the Ricardo results, as if labor were the only factor of production. Consequently, Theorem 2a demonstrates that in the model presented here neither the comparative nor the absolute seize of the countries' capacity of environmental services has an impact on the pattern of trade as long as $\bar{e} \geq (\bar{a}/\bar{k}_1)$ and $\bar{e}^+ \geq (\bar{a}^+/\bar{k}_1^+)$. This may be interpreted as a substantial qualification, or even contradiction, of d'Arge and Kneese's conjecture.[7] Theorem 2b demonstrates, however, that the ecological system may have a detrimental welfare impact on one of the economies. This is, in fact, a fundamental challenge for the old liberal free-trade argument which has been rationalized so far by the conventional theorem of gains from trade. For simplicity in the proof of Theorem 2b a rather special case is chosen. More generally, a welfare loss from trade occurs to one of the countries, (i) if it specializes on the environment-intensive good (necessary condition) and (ii) if the welfare loss due to the decreased environmental quality overcompensates the welfare gain from the increased quantities of private consumption goods after trade (sufficient condition).

At some cost of simplification one may classify economies being confronted with severe environmental pollution in the absence of environmental management as industrialized countries, while countries in which the "endowment conditions" of Theorem 2 prevail may be called developing countries. If one of the countries (or both) is industrialized in this sense, we will assume that it already adopted an environmental

[7] Possibly d'Arge and Kneese do not intend to apply their comparative advantage statement to environmental laissez-faire situations, although they do not make this explicit. They only refer to the environmental assimilative capacities, which are defined by them as the countries' "unique attributes in terms of productive resources" [1, p. 434].

price and standard system, and that the emission standard chosen satisfies, respectively,

$$\epsilon \in \,]0, \bar{a}/\bar{k}_c[\tag{15a}$$

$$\epsilon^+ \in \,]0, \bar{a}^+/\bar{k}_c^+[. \tag{15b}$$

THEOREM 3. *Let the assumptions (1) to (8), (10), (11), (1^+) to (11^+) and (14) be given. Furthermore, in country II we have $\bar{e}^+ \geq \bar{a}^+/\bar{k}_1^+$ and no environmental protection, while in country I (15a) holds.*

(a) *Then country I exports and specializes on the production of the labor-intensive good 2, if*

$$(\lambda_1/\lambda_2) \leq (\lambda_1^+/\lambda_2^+).$$

(b) *Let $\{d^n\}$ with $n = 1, 2, \ldots$ be a sequence of vectors $d^n = (q_1^n, q_2^n, \epsilon^n)$ such that ϵ^n converges to zero for $n \to \infty$ and q_1^n, q_2^n satisfy (8) and (13) for $\epsilon = \epsilon^n$, $n = 1, 2, \ldots$. Further, denote by $r \leq 0$ the limit of the increasing sequence $\{\partial q_1(q_2, \epsilon)/\partial q_2 | d^n\}$, which is associated with the sequence $\{d^n\}$. If $(\lambda_1/\lambda_2) > (\lambda_1^+/\lambda_2^+) > (-r)$, then there exists $\hat{\epsilon} \in \,]0, \bar{a}/\bar{k}_c[$ such that country I exports and specializes on the production of the labor-intensive good 2 for all emission standards $\epsilon < \hat{\epsilon}$.*

The proof of Theorem 3 can be omitted, since it is straightforward. The theorem implies that a country's technological comparative advantage for the labor-intensive good can be increased by environmental protection. On the other hand, if one country initially has a technological comparative disadvantage for the labor-intensive good, according to Theorem 3b it can (with a minor technologically determined exception) overcompensate for this disadvantage by choosing a sufficiently restrictive emission standard.

If it is correct that developing countries typically have comparative advantages in the production of the environment-intensive goods, then in trade with industrialized countries they will export and specialize on the production of environment-intensive goods [1, 11, 13]. As indicated above, this is a necessary condition for a welfare loss from trade, unless the developing countries implement environmental controls themselves (thus diminishing or destroying their original comparative advantage).

This leads us to discuss the pattern of trade between two (industrialized) countries both of which have implemented an environmental price and standard system. To compare the "intensity" of these countries' environmental protection policy it is convenient to define:

The environmental control by a price and standard system is said to be more restrictive in country I than in country II.

(α) if $\epsilon/\bar{a} < \epsilon^+/\bar{a}^+$ (criterion of relative emission standards); or alternatively but not equivalently

(β) if $w > w^+$ (criterion of relative emission prices), where w, w^+ denote autarkic equilibrium values.

Applying these concepts we obtain the two following comparative advantage results:

THEOREM 4. *Let the assumptions (1) to (8), (10), (11), (1^+)* to *(8^+), (10^+), (11^+), (14) with $\lambda_i = \lambda_i^+$ for $i = 1, 2$, and (15) be given.*

(a) *Then a country exports and specializes on the production of the environment-intensive good, if* $c_i = c_i^+$ *for* $i = 1, 2$ *and if its environmental control—according to definition* α*—is less restrictive than in the other country.*

(b) *Then a country exports and specializes on the production of the environment-intensive good, if its environmental control—according to definition* β*—is less restrictive than in the other country.*

Theorem 4 is proved as the Heckscher–Ohlin theorem in [9, p. 74]. It rationalizes and qualifies rigorously the d'Arge and Kneese conjecture, if one interpretes the environmental assimilative capacities to be equal to the emission standards ϵ and ϵ^+. Obviously, under the assumptions of Theorem 4, as in the traditional theory, no country can suffer a welfare loss from trade, since by guarantee of the national EPAs the countries' environmental qualities remain unchanged after trade.

In spite of this similarity to the standard theory, the welfare implications of the model presented here are more intricate. Each country's emission standard is a policy instrument, and hence, one country's welfare depends on a decision variable (emission standard) of the other country, so that analytically we are confronted with a typical "oligopoly" problem of interdependent welfare maximization (as long as the number of trading partners is small).

Differences in the restrictiveness of national environmental policies according to either of the two definitions do not generally imply differences in national environmental qualities. Policy divergences not only depend on the restrictiveness definition chosen but also on the difference between diffusion functions (5) and (5+), the qualification of which is an entirely empirical question. Therefore, it is possible (or even likely) that two countries that harmonize their environmental policies in terms of enforcing the same environmental quality do not (or rather, must not) apply equally restrictive environmental controls.

On the other hand, the two countries may well implement equally restrictive environmental controls in trading equilibrium, although they pursue (successfully) different environmental quality objectives. This is specified by

THEOREM 5. *Let the assumptions of Theorem 4 be given and let the restrictiveness of the national price and standard systems be measured by the criterion of the relative emission standards (definition* α*).*

Then the relative emission prices w *and* w^+ *prevailing in the trading equilibrium are the same for both countries, if the environmental controls in one country are not "too" restrictive as compared with those in the other country.*

Theorem 5 is, in both its presuppositions and conclusion, exactly equivalent to the Factor–Price–Equalization theorem and hence need not be proved here. The critical absolute difference $|(\bar{a}/\epsilon) - (\bar{a}^+/\epsilon^+)|$ which is relevant in Theorem 5 may best be analyzed and made precise by the "cone of diversification method" as exposed by Chipman [6, p. 20n.].

REFERENCES

1. R. C. d'Arge and A. V. Kneese, Environmental quality and international trade, *Intern. Organization* **26**, 419–465 (1972).
2. W. J. Baumol, "Environmental Protection, International Spillovers, and Trade," Wicksell Lectures, Stockholm (1971).
3. W. J. Baumol, On taxation and the control of externalities, *Amer. Econ. Rev.* **62**, 307–322 (1972).

4. W. J. Baumol and W. E. Oates, The use of standards and prices for the protection of the environment, *Swedish J. Econ.* **73**, 42–54 (1971).
5. P. Bohm, Pollution, purification and the theory of external effects, *Swedish J. Econ.* **72**, 153–166 (1970).
6. J. S. Chipman, A survey of the theory of international trade: Part 3, The modern theory, *Econometrica* **34**, 18–75 (1966).
7. J. H. Dales, Pollution, property and prices, in "An Essay in Policy-making and Economics," Toronto (1968).
8. GATT, Industrial Pollution Control and Foreign Trade, Submission of the Secretariat of GATT at the UN Conference on Human Environment in Geneva (1971).
9. M. C. Kemp, "The Pure Theory of International Trade and Investment," Prentice-Hall, Englewood Cliffs, N.J. (1969).
10. A. K. Klevorick and G. H. Kramer, Social choice on pollution management: the Genossenschaften, *J. Public Econ.* **2**, 101–146 (1973).
11. A. Majocchi, The impact of environmental measures on international trade, *Rivista Intern. Sci. Econ. Commerciali* **19**, 458–479 (1972).
12. R. Pethig, Umweltverschmutzung, Wohlfahrt und Umweltpolitik in einem Zwei-Sektoren-Gleichgewichtsmodell, *Z. Nationalökonomie* (1975).
13. H. Siebert, Trade and environment, in "The International Devision of Labour. Problems and Perspectives," (H. Giersch, Ed.), Kiel (1974).
14. H. Siebert, Environmental protection and international specialization, *Weltwirtschaftliches Archiv* **110**, 494–508 (1974).
15. T. H. Tietenberg, Controlling pollution by price and standard systems: a general equilibrium analysis, *Swedish J. Econ.* **75**, 193–203 (1973).
16. I. Walter, International trade and resource diversion: the case of environmental management, *Weltwirtschaftliches Archiv* **110**, 482–493 (1974).

[3]

Journal of Public Economics 17 (1982) 335–354. North-Holland Publishing Company

REGULATION, FACTOR REWARDS, AND INTERNATIONAL TRADE

Martin C. McGUIRE*

University of Maryland, College Park, MD 20742, USA

Received February 1980, revised version received July 1981

This paper develops an approach for incorporating regulation into the theory of production, distribution, and trade, using environmental regulation as an example. Four major conclusions emerge in the course of the analysis.

1. Production process regulation is equivalent in its effect on other cooperating factors to *neutral technical regress* (i.e. negative progress).
2. Specific unambiguous income redistribution consequences follow from such regulation. If commodity prices are held constant, the factor used relatively intensively in the *non-regulated* industry will gain *absolutely* in terms of both goods.
3. Unilateral or uncoordinated regulation destroys the link between uniform world commodity prices and identical factor proportions/factors prices across trading countries or regions.
4. If any factor of production is freely mobile across frontiers, the least differential regulation as between countries will entirely drive out the regulated industry from the more to the less regulated economy.

1. Introduction

Policy-makers and policy analysts, as well as the public at large, have recently taken a heightened interest in the real burden and the real incidence of economic regulation. Who actually benefits and who loses from regulatory policies? And are the gains worth the costs? This paper develops an approach for a study of such questions using as an example environmental regulation. The approach developed here applies more generally, however, to any regulation of production processes, and to many service delivery processes.

The stages in the analysis are as follows: first, we characterize regulation as a control over utilization of one factor of production in an N-factor production function; second, we derive a resulting N-1 factor production function, describe its properties, and characterize the profit-maximizing

* This research was sponsored by the Bureau of Business and Economic Research, University of Maryland, under a grant from the Environmental Protection Agency. Support from the National Science Foundation, Grant SES 80–14238, also is gratefully acknowledged. I also thank A.B. Atkinson and a referee for helpful criticisms.

0047-2727/82/0000–0000/$02.75

behavior of competitive firms with and without regulation; third, the general implications of such behavior in a closed two-sector economy are presented; fourth, we apply these conclusions to the standard Heckscher–Ohlin model of international trade, in which factors are not mobile across frontiers; and lastly we allow for international factor mobility.

Four major conclusions will emerge in the course of the analysis.

1. Production process regulation is equivalent in its effect on other cooperating factors to *neutral technical regress* (i.e. negative progress).

2. Specific unambiguous income redistribution consequences follow from such regulation by an extension of the Rybczynski and the Stolper–Samuelson theorems. If commodity prices are held constant the factor used relatively intensively in the *non-regulated* industry will gain *absolutely* in terms of both goods. However, if demand for the regulated product is sufficiently inelastic the factor used intensively in the regulated industry may gain.

3. Unilateral or uncoordinated regulation destroys the link between uniform world commodity prices and identical factor proportions/factor prices across trading countries or regions.

4. If any factor of production is freely mobile across frontiers, the least unilateral or differential regulation as between countries will entirely drive out the regulated industry from the more to the less regulated economy.

2. Regulation and the production function

The most comprehensive simple explanation of a country's economy remains the two-sector model and of its trade with the world, the two country Heckscher–Ohlin model (H–O). Our first task therefore will be to find the minimum change to these models necessary to incorporate environmental or regulated factors in their domain. Once this is accomplished we can describe the autarchic equilibrium and then the trading equilibrium which arises in the absence of all environmental controls. Then we can explore the effects of regulatory control, in turn under autarchy and free trade.

The model to be used is identical to H–O in all respects but one, namely the introduction of a regulated factor of production such as the environment. Thus, we will assume fixed factor supplies of L^{A}, L^{B}, K^{A}, K^{B} in two countries, A and B. (International factor mobility will be allowed later.) Identical linear homogeneous technologies produce two goods, X and Y, in the two countries. Perfect competition and factor mobility within countries entails equal unit-factor rewards across industries. Transportation costs are ignored. Free trade and competition among countries generates common world-wide commodity prices.[1]

[1] All factor and commodity market distortions in the economy are ruled out as are all possible perverse effects identified in Johnson and Mieszkowski (1970), Jones (1971), Magee (1971), and Neary (1978).

We now wish to make the minimum alteration in the H–O setup to accommodate the environmental factor. From one perspective pollution is an unwanted by-product or output from offending industrial processes. From another logically equivalent point of view, however, the environment is a factor of production, which is 'used up' in industrial and agricultural processes. Being a productive factor the environment will be used to the point that its value marginal product equals its price, which in the absence of any regulation is nil. To reduce environmental deterioration the environmental factor must be conserved, either indirectly through post-pollution clean up processes, or directly in the industrial process by substituting other valuable factors such as land, labor, capital, for the environmental factor. From this perspective, the environmental factor can be incorporated in H–O by adding the environment, T, as one factor in *one* industry. We choose X^i as the polluting industry in country i, and Y^i as the non-polluting industry. Accordingly, to represent production we can write

$$X^i = F(L_x^i, K_x^i, T^i), \qquad i = \text{A,B}, \tag{1}$$

$$Y^i = H(L_y^i, K_y^i), \tag{2}$$

where L_j^i denotes i's employment of labor in industry j. T^i, which indicates i's 'useage' or depletion of the environment, is measured in tons (or some physical quantity of effluent output). Whether A's or B's effluent degrades a common global environment (as in the case of atmosphere ozone depletion) or a local environment (rivers, for example) is important for the efficiency properties and normative evaluation of regulation but not for a positive description. This distinction therefore will be considered below. In either country the factor endowments $(L_x^i + L_y^i = L^i)$ and $(K_x^i + K_y^i = K^i)$ are fixed. But there is no constraining physical limit on the amount of effluent which can be discharged. In principle T^i could exceed all bounds. However, we will assume that even in the absence of regulation, pollution reaches a finite equilibrium level because of the technology of the polluting industry.

We will assume therefore, as in the standard H–O case, that technologies in both industries are linear homogeneous, but particularly in the production of good X over some range of values, T, the effluent has positive marginal productivity, over another range T has zero productivity, and over a third range the marginal product of T is negative. Schematically if

$$F_T^i(L_x^i, K_x^i, T^i) \equiv \frac{\partial F(L_x, K_x, T^i)}{\partial T^i}.$$

Then, for some values of L, K, and T, $F_T^i \gtreqless 0$. Naturally, values of L, K, and T for which the marginal product of T is negative will be avoided under normal economic behavior.

In the absence of regulation the polluting industry's technology can be characterized by the two equations

$$X = F(L,K,T), \tag{3}$$

$$F_T(L,K,T) = \beta^0 = 0, \tag{4}$$

the first representing purely a technical relationship and the second a profit-maximizing decision when the price of polluting is zero. Eq. (4) gives an implicit relationship among the variables L, K, T, and the parameter β(0 in this case), which we write explicitly as

$$T = \phi(L,K,\beta^0). \tag{5}$$

By 'folding' eq. (5) into (3) the variable T can be eliminated to derive a mixed profit/production function

$$X = F[L,K,\phi(L,K,\beta^0] = F^0[L,K]. \tag{6}$$

Eq. (6) shows the various combinations of labor and capital which produce designated amounts of X when T is 'automatically' adjusted for each L,K combination to bring $F_T = 0$. Fig. 1 is a pictorial representation of F^0. Everywhere on the surface $F_T = 0$, the marginal product of $T = 0$. The intersection of an L–K–T iso-product shell (not shown) with the surface $F_T = 0$ traces out one L–K isoquant which can be projected back into the L–K plane.

Note that F^0 is first degree homogeneous in L and K as was F in L, K and T.[2] The marginal product of L in F^0 now incorporates an optimal adjustment in T. Accordingly, $\partial F/\partial L \neq \partial F^0/\partial L$. Rather

$$F_L^0 = F_L + F_T \cdot \frac{\mathrm{d}T}{DL},$$

and similarly for the marginal product of capital.

[2] This is seen as follows. The function F^0 is first degree homogeneous provided

$$X = F_L^0 \cdot L + F_K^0 \cdot K$$
$$= \left[F_L + F_T \frac{\mathrm{d}T}{\mathrm{d}L}\right]L + \left[F_K + F^T \frac{\mathrm{d}T}{\mathrm{d}K}\right]K.$$

Since F is first degree homogeneous, the above will hold provided

$$T \cdot F_T = \left[\frac{\mathrm{d}T}{\mathrm{d}L} \cdot L + \frac{\mathrm{d}T}{\mathrm{d}K} \cdot K\right]F_T.$$

This equivalence obtains identically since F_T is homogeneous of degree zero. The terms $\mathrm{d}T/\mathrm{d}K$ come from the implicit relation in (4):

$$\frac{\mathrm{d}T}{\mathrm{d}L} = -F_{TL}\frac{-F_{TL}}{F_{TT}}; \quad \frac{\mathrm{d}T}{\mathrm{d}K} = \frac{-F_{TK}}{F_{TT}}.$$

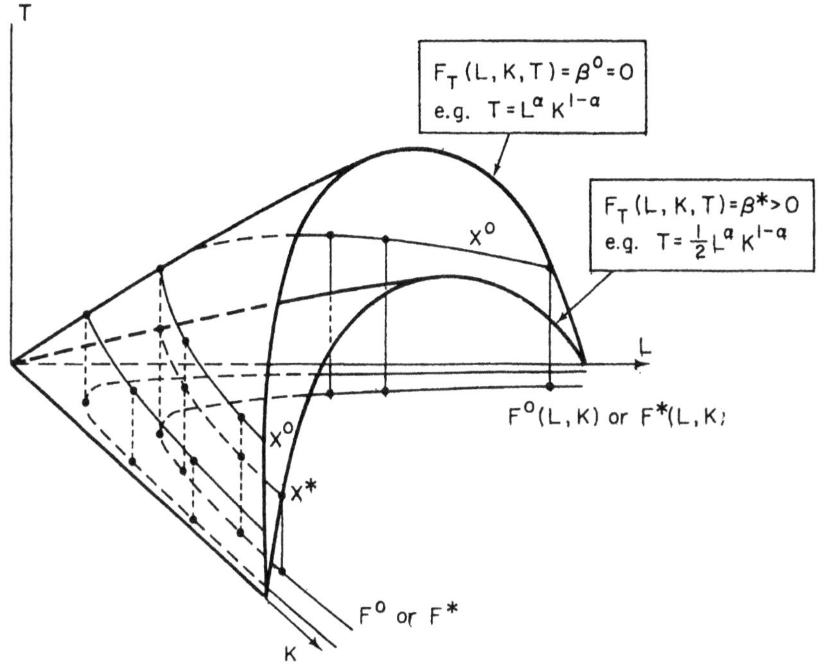

Fig. 1.

Before regulation, the polluting industry's technology in either country is characterized as above. Competition and factor mobility will drive factor allocations to a point such that

$$w = p_X F_L^0 = p_y H_L,$$

where w indicates wage rate and p_X, p_Y commodity prices. Since F^0 is linear homogeneous, factor payments to L and K will exhaust revenues.

Now suppose the government determines to regulate industry X. For the purpose of this analysis we will assume that the marginal social cost of pollution is a known *constant.* If the pollution in question created a pure global public bad, then the marginal social cost of pollution should be the same for all countries. If on the other hand the environmental damage was strictly local, then different countries might properly calculate different marginal social damages. In either case we wish to trace out the consequences of regulation in each country and in the world economic order. First, we will concentrate on a single country. Assume that the government wishes to economize on the environment; efficiency then requires that effluent be restricted up to the point that its value marginal productivity equal its marginal social cost. This restriction might be implemented by imposing the optimal pollution tax on metered effluents from industry X, with the revenues so collected disbursed to consumers. In this case regulation will have both income and substitution effects on the rewards to and productivity of the other factors. Alternatively, the optimal marginal productivity of environmental exploitation might be directly mandated. In this latter case no revenues are collected, the impact of regulation on factor productivities and rewards is limited to a substitution effect. For our analysis we assume regulation takes this latter form, of mandating a minimum allowable marginal productivity of pollution.

When an effective shadow price is placed on effluent output in one country this new cost or mandated conservation will cause industry X to conserve the environment so that its marginal product will have a positive value rather than zero. Whatever post-regulation combinations of K and L are chosen in industry X, a new level of polluting effluent corresponding to $F_T=\beta^*>0$ will be chosen, according to eq. (4), where β^* is a constant with some new higher value than before. That is to say, the imposition of a positive excise tax or an equivalent regulatory policy restricts the choice of other factor inputs to a new family of factor proportion rays, or to a new ruled surface, as in fig. 1. Accordingly, the new 'mixed' profit/production function is

$$X=F[L,K,\phi(L,K,\beta^*)]=F^*(L,K). \tag{7}$$

As before, F^* is linear homogeneous, and $F_L^*=F_L+F_T(\mathrm{d}T/\mathrm{d}L)$. F^* now indicates various combinations of L and K and their designated outputs of X when the environment is optimally exploited/conserved in response to government regulation of $F_T=\beta^*$. Fig. 1 shows the new surface $F_T=\beta^*$ as lying entirely below $F_T=0$.

3. The equivalence between regulation and negative neutral technical progress

Confining our attention to the function F^* and therefore to the representation of production in L–K space (that is the space of non-regulated factors of production), we can see that as the degree of regulation increases from, say, β^0 to β^*, the entire L–K isoquant map will shift outward, so that each L–K combination which produced, say, $X=X^0$ under condition β^0 will now produce some $X<X^0$ under condition β^*. It is not necessary that the new reduced output of X be the same for each of the original L–K combinations. For example, if both (L_1^0,K_1^0) and (L_2^0,K_2^0) produce X^0, the same combinations may yield different outputs under conditions β^*, i.e.

$$F^*(L_1,K_1)<F^0(L_1,K_1)=F^0(L_2,K_2)$$
$$>F^*(L_2,L_2): \qquad F^*(L_1,K_1)\neq F^*(L_2,K_2).$$

However, under certain conditions (which we will explore presently) a change in regulation, say an increase from β^0 to β^*, will shift L–K isoquants out *proportionately*. In this case the effect of regulation is simply to re-number each original isoquant, reducing each by the same proportion. Under these conditions therefore the L–K isoquant map would be geometrically stable, i.e. pictorially identical under different regulatory conditions; isoquants would not twist or wiggle and the relative marginal productivities of non-regulated factors of production as shown by the slopes of the isoquant maps would be invariant under diverse regulatory regimes. In these circumstances the effect of regulation is equivalent to *negative neutral technical progress*. This type of regulation is pictured in fig. 1. The unregulated isoquant X^0 is directly above X^* the regulated isoquant, so they both project the same curve in L–K space.

This type of neutrality will prove to be a 'knife-edge' case for further analysis of the effects of regulation on the autarchic general equilibrium and then on trading equilibrium. Therefore the specific conditions under which regulation is equivalent to neutral technical regress deserve further scrutiny.

4. General conditions under which regulation does not distort other factor productivities

Consider the regulation adjusted production function

$$X = F^* = F[L,K,\phi(L,K,\beta)] = G(L,K,\beta).$$

This adjusted production function has been obtained as a solution to the unconstrained $X = F(L,K,T)$ and the side condition $F_T(L,K,T) = \beta$, where β is a constant. Our concern is to examine the conditions under which $G(L,K,\beta)$ has the multiplicative form

$$G(L,K,\beta) = g(\beta)h(L,K),$$

since in this case a change in β simply would require re-numbering of L–K isoquants. The relative marginal products, therefore, of L and K would be independent of β, and independent of the degree of regulation, i.e. $G_L/G_K = h_L/h_K$. For G to have this multiplicative form requires

$$\frac{\partial\left[\frac{(\partial G/\partial\beta)}{G}\right]}{\partial L} = 0, \tag{8}$$

$$\frac{\partial\left[\frac{(\partial G/\partial\beta)}{G}\right]}{\partial K} = 0. \tag{9}$$

Differentiating (8) gives

$$G_L - \frac{G_{\beta L} \cdot G}{G_\beta} = 0, \tag{10}$$

and a symmetric condition from (9)

$$G_K - \frac{G_{\beta K} \cdot G}{G_\beta} = 0. \tag{11}$$

Application of implicit function theorems and substitution into (10) and (1) gives

$$\frac{F_K}{F_{TK}} + \frac{F \cdot F_{TTK}}{F_{TT}F_{TK}} = \frac{F_L}{F_{TL}} + \frac{F \cdot F_{TTL}}{F_{TT}F_{TL}} = \frac{F_T}{F_{TT}} + \frac{F \cdot F_{TTT}}{(F_{TT})^2} \tag{12}$$

as a condition on the unconstrained production function F, to be satisfied identically. Here F_{ijk} indicates a third cross partial deviative. Eq. (12) will be satisfied identically provided

$$F_K/F_{TK} = F_{KL}/F_{TL} = \gamma F/F_T, \tag{13}$$

where γ is the elasticity of complementarity. That (13) is a sufficient condition for (12) to be satisfied identically is shown as follows. Partial differentiation of (13) gives:

$$\begin{aligned} &\frac{\partial[F_L/F_{LT}]}{\partial T} = \frac{\partial[\gamma F/F_T]}{\partial T}, \\ &\frac{F_{LT}}{F_{LT}} - \frac{F_L \cdot F_{LTT}}{(F_{LT})^2} = \gamma\left(\frac{F_T}{F_T} - \frac{F \cdot F_{TT}}{(F_T)^2}\right), \\ &\frac{F_{TTL}}{F_{TT}} = F_{TL}\left[\frac{1-\gamma}{\gamma}\frac{F_T}{F_{TT} \cdot F} + \frac{1}{F_T}\right] = F_{TL}\sigma. \end{aligned} \tag{14}$$

Similarly

$$\frac{F_{TTK}}{F_{TT}} = F_{TK}\left[\frac{1-\gamma}{\gamma}\frac{F_T}{F_{TT} \cdot F} + \frac{1}{F_T}\right] = F_{TK}\sigma. \tag{15}$$

Since F is homogeneous of degree $+1$, F_{TT} is homogeneous of degree -1:

$$\frac{F_{TTT}}{F_{TT}} = \frac{-1}{T} - \frac{K}{T}\frac{F_{TTK}}{F_{TT}} - \frac{1}{T}\frac{F_{TTL}}{F_{TT}} = \frac{-1}{T} - \frac{K}{T}\sigma F_{TK} - \frac{L}{T}\sigma F_{TL}. \tag{16}$$

However, F_T is homogeneous of degree zero so that

$$\frac{F_{TTT}}{F_{TT}} = \frac{-1}{T} + \sigma F_{TT} = \frac{-1}{T} + F_{TT}\left[\frac{1-\gamma}{\gamma}\frac{F_T}{F_{TT} \cdot F} + \frac{1}{F_T}\right]. \tag{17}$$

Substituting (13), (14), and (17) into (12) gives

$$\frac{\gamma F}{F_T}+F\cdot\sigma=\frac{F_T}{F_{TT}}-\frac{F}{TF_{TT}}+\sigma F,$$

or

$$\frac{\gamma F}{F_T}=\frac{TF_T-F}{TF_{TT}}=\frac{-LF_L-KF_K}{-LF_{LT}-KF_{KT}}.$$

From (13) this last expression is an identity. Note that this is a local condition on the production function F. At different locations on F, the value of γ may be different, provided it is a common value among factors. Eq. (12), therefore, describes a local CES property that partial elasticities of complementarity (and therefore also substitution elasticities) between the regulated factor and each other factor have a common value [See Sato and Koizumi (1973)]. This result will be referred to as the 'neutrality result'.

An alternative direct derivation of this result has been suggested to me by the referee. This derivation utilizes the dual approach as in Atkinson and Stiglitz (1980) or Dixit and Norman (1980). Here the cost minimizing function for X can be written as

$$C=c(r,w,\beta)\cdot X, \tag{18}$$

where c indicates average and marginal costs which are constant under constant returns to scale, r and w factor prices, and β is as defined above. If the unit cost function could be written as

$$c(r,w,\beta)=f(\beta)j(w,r)+\ell(\beta), \tag{19}$$

then the factor demand equations became

$$L=X\cdot f(\beta)\cdot\frac{\partial j}{\partial w},$$

$$K=X\cdot f(\beta)\cdot\frac{\partial j}{\partial r}. \tag{20}$$

Eq. (20) indicates that a cost-minimizing L–K factor input proportions depend only on the unit factor costs w–r, and not on the degree of regulation — which is the neutrality result. Assuming unit costs have the form of eq. (19), the partial elasticities of substitution become

$$\sigma_{KT}=\frac{c\cdot c_{r\beta}}{c_r c_\beta}=\frac{(f\cdot j+\ell)\dfrac{\partial f}{\partial\beta}\cdot\dfrac{\partial j}{\partial r}}{\left(f\cdot\dfrac{\partial j}{\partial r}\right)\left(\dfrac{\partial f}{\partial\beta}\cdot j+\dfrac{\partial\ell}{\partial\beta}\right)}. \tag{21}$$

Since the terms $\partial j/\partial r$ in the numerator and denominator of (21) cancel, $\sigma_{KT}=\sigma_{LT}$, which is the same sufficient condition as eq. (12).

5. Two examples of the equivalence between regulation and negative neutral technical progress

5.1 First example

Consider first a three-factor Cobb–Douglas production function:

$$F=L^{\frac{1}{2}}K^{\frac{1}{3}}T^{\frac{1}{6}}$$

$$F_L/F_T=\tfrac{3}{2}(K/L), \tag{22}$$

$$F_T=F/6T=\beta.$$

Here there is no natural limit on pollution in an unregulated situation; so we must impose one. Suppose therefore that with no regulation $\beta^0=1$. It follows from substitution that

$$F^0=(1/6)^{\frac{1}{5}}\cdot L^{\frac{3}{5}}K^{\frac{2}{5}},$$

$$F_L^0/F_K^0=\tfrac{3}{2}(K/L). \tag{23}$$

The derived, mixed profit/production function is linear homogeneous, and relative marginal productivities of L and K are identical as between F and F^0.

Now assume some regulation changes β to $\beta^*>1$. The result is

$$F^*=\left(\frac{1}{6\beta^*}\right)^{\frac{1}{5}}L^{\frac{3}{5}}K^{\frac{2}{5}}.$$

We observe that F^* is simply a reduced multiple of F^0. The higher the value of β^*, and the more conservation, the greater is the proportional reduction; but that same proportional reduction in output applies to all values of L and K. Similarly, the relative marginal products of the complementary factors L and K are not disturbed at all by regulation

$$\frac{F_L^*}{F_K^*}=\frac{F_L^0}{F_K^0}=\frac{F_L}{F_K}. \tag{24}$$

Therefore if we plot isoquants using L and K as factors, the effect of environmental regulation is simply to re-number those isoquants, reducing each number by the same proportion.

5.2 Second example

A problem with the Cobb–Douglas example is that pollution is not self-limiting in the absence of regulation. According to eqs. (3) and (4) in the production of X there will be some critical family of factor proportions separating production space into two regions, one where using the environment is productive and another where it is counter-productive. Along the crucial factor proportions ray or family of rays the marginal product of polluting is zero. No CES production function could represent such a technology since variable elasticity of substitution is essential to the reversal of factor productivity.

One variable elasticity production function which meets our requirement is

$$F = T^{1-\exp[1-K^{1-\alpha}L^{\alpha}/T]} L^{\alpha\exp[1-K^{1-\alpha}L^{\alpha}/T]} K^{(1-\alpha)\exp[1-K^{1-\alpha}L^{\alpha}/T]}; \qquad 0<\alpha<1. \tag{25}$$

This rather ungainly function is linear homogeneous. Consider first the exponents on T, L, and K, respectively, namely

$$1-e^{1-K^{1-\alpha}L^{\alpha}/T},$$

$$\alpha\, e^{1-K^{1-\alpha}L^{\alpha}/T},$$

$$(1-\alpha)\, e^{1-K^{1-\alpha}L^{\alpha}/T}.$$

These exponents add up to one, yet a proportional increase in all factors leaves each exponent unchanged. Next, consider the surface in T–L–K space defined by

$$K^{1-\alpha}L^{\alpha}/T = 1. \tag{26}$$

This is a ruled surface, a family of proportion rays through the origin. Whenever eq. (26) is satisfied, the exponent on T in (25) is zero. Accordingly, along this ruled surface the marginal product of pollution is zero. (In fig. 1 this is the surface $F_T = 0$.) Now consider other families of factor proportion rays different from (26). For each family of factor proportion rays defined by $K^{1-\alpha}L^{\alpha}/T = a < 1$ the marginal product of pollution has a constant negative value, whereas for $K^{1-\alpha}L^{\alpha}/T = a > 1$ the marginal product of pollution is positive, being a constant for each value of a. Another way of seeing this is to take logs of (25)

$$\log F = (1-e^{1-x})\log T + \alpha\, e^{1-x}\log L + (1-\alpha)\, e^{1-x}\log K,$$

where $x = K^{1-\alpha}L^{\alpha}/T$,

$$\frac{1}{F}\frac{\partial F}{\partial T} = \frac{(1-e^{1-x})}{T} + e^{1-x}\,[\alpha\log L + (1-\alpha)\log K\text{-}\log T]\left(\frac{\partial x}{\partial T}\right),$$

where $\partial x/\partial T < 0$. If $x = 1$, then the first term is zero and $T = K^{1-\alpha}L^{\alpha}$, so that the second term is also zero. If $x > 1$, then the first term is positive and the second term is also (conversely $x < 1$ implies that both are negative).

Before environmental regulation, competition and profit maximization will insure exploitation of the environment until the marginal product of pollution is zero. Setting $\partial F/\partial T = 0$ in (25) and solving for T shows that a competitive profit-maximizing X-industry will choose a value of T corresponding to $K^{1-\alpha}L^{\alpha}$ whatever values of K and L happen to be chosen because they too maximize profits. Substitution of $T = K^{1-\alpha}L^{\alpha}$ into (25) reduces the production function to

$$F(L,K,T^0) = F^0(L,K) = L^{\alpha}K^{1-\alpha}; \qquad T^0 = K^{1-\alpha}L^{\alpha}, \tag{27}$$

The marginal technical rate of substitution becomes

$$\frac{F_L}{F_K} \equiv \frac{F_L^0}{F_K^0} = \frac{\alpha}{1-\alpha} \cdot \frac{K}{L}. \tag{28}$$

By 'folding' the optimal $T = T^0$ into the original production function, one variable T is eliminated. Note again that F^0 is first degree homogeneous in L and K, as was F in L, K, and T; the marginal product of L in F^0 incorporates an optimal adjustment in T. Accordingly, $\partial F/\partial L \neq \partial F^0/\partial L$. Rather,

$$F_L^0 = F_L + F_T \cdot \frac{\partial T^0}{\partial L}. \tag{29}$$

Now to take an example of regulatory control. Suppose pollution is constrained such that the new value of $a = 2$. The production function adjusted for newly constrained environmental exploitation therefore becomes

$$F = T^{1-e^{-1}}L^{\alpha e^{-1}}K^{(1-\alpha)e^{-1}} \qquad \text{(Note that } e^{-1} \simeq 0.36\text{)}. \tag{30}$$

The marginal product of polluting, F_T, is obtained by evaluating $\partial F/\partial T$ at $L^{\alpha}K^{1-\alpha} = aT$:

$$F_T = [a^{e^{1-a}}][1 - e^{1-a}(1 - a\,\mathrm{Ln}(a))] = \beta^*, \tag{31}$$

which makes a an implicit function of $\beta^*; a = \phi(\beta^*)$.

Now with production constrained by

$$T = \tfrac{1}{2}L^{\alpha}K^{1-\alpha} \tag{32}$$

we can substitute for T in the production function to give

$$\begin{aligned}(F^*|a=2) &= (\tfrac{1}{2})^{0.64}(L^{\alpha}K^{1-\alpha})^{0.64}K^{0.36\alpha}K^{0.36(1-\alpha)}\\ &= (\tfrac{1}{2})^{0.64}L^{\alpha}K^{1-\alpha}.\end{aligned} \tag{33}$$

Again the ratio of marginal products is the same as when $a = 1$:

$$\frac{F_L}{F_K} = \frac{F_L^0}{F_K^0} = \frac{F_L^*}{F_K^*} = \frac{\alpha}{1-\alpha}\,\frac{K}{L}.$$

More generally, eliminating T from the production function by use of the marginal productivity constraint yields

$$F^* = (\tfrac{1}{2})^{1-e^{1-\alpha}}[L^{\alpha}K^{1-\alpha}]^{1-e^{1-\alpha}}[L^{\alpha}K^{1-\alpha}]^{e^{1-\alpha}} \tag{34}$$

or

$$F^* = \Psi[\phi(\beta^*)]L^{\alpha}K^{1-\alpha}. \tag{35}$$

As before, the effect of change in $F_T = \beta^*$ is multiplicative on the output from any L–K combination. This example confirms the general result. Environmental regulation which constrains the allowable level of pollution to some given marginal product is equivalent to *negative neutral technological progress*, requiring a simple proportional re-numbering of L–K isoquants. This result is not an accident due to the particular production

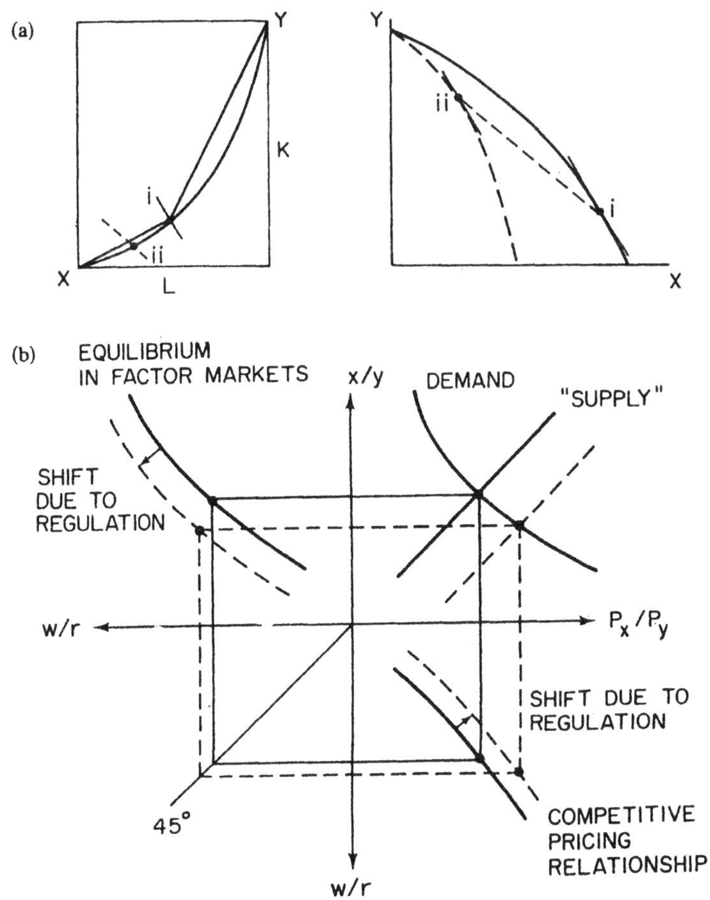

Fig. 2.

functions chosen for illustration. Rather, it is a general feature of all linear homogeneous production functions with equal pairwise elasticities of substitution.

6. Implications of regulation for a closed economy

The general equilibrium effects of factor input regulation are readily examined through the four-quadrant diagram employed by Atkinson and Stiglitz (1980, pp. 171–7). Fig. 2 shows the situation before regulation in unbroken lines. Fig. 2(a) shows the Edgeworth production box and the corresponding transformation curve, fig. 2(b) the four quadrant diagram. Now introduce regulation and re-number the isoquants in the Edgeworth box. Assuming technology in accord with eq. (13), the X-isoquants shift proportionally outward; or, equivalently, each X-isoquant only need be re-numbered, its value reduced by the same proportion as all others. Since the geometry of X- and Y-isoquants in the production box is unaffected by the introduction of a shadow price on T, the contract curve also is unaffected. The effect of regulation is shown in broken lines.

In view of the re-numbering of the X-isoquants there must be an inward shift in the production possibility curve due to regulation [fig. 2(a)]. It follows by Rybcinski's theorem that to maintain the same relative rewards, and the same allocation of factors between X and Y, the relative price of X must increase. Correspondingly, to maintain the same relative commodity prices the return to the factor used intensively in the regulated industry must diminish absolutely in terms of both goods, while the return to the factor used intensively in the unregulated pollution-free industry will increase *absolutely* in terms of both goods.[3] This effect is shown in fig. 2(a) by

[3] To see this, note in each country equilibrium before *and* after regulation requires

$$\frac{P_x}{P_y}=\frac{MP_L^Y}{MP_L^X}=\frac{MP_K^Y}{MP_K^X}=\text{constant.} \tag{1.m}$$

The price ratio P_x/P_y is constant because of the perfectly elastic demand assumption. Now the first-order effect of regulation is to reduce the marginal productivities of L and K in X since less cooperating factor T is available. Therefore both MP_L^Y/MP_L^X and MP_K^Y/MP_K^X are too high. To re-establish the equilibrium conditions given by (1.m), output of X will decline X being relatively labor-intensive. Therefore, MP_K^Y will *increase* since its $(L/K)_y$ ratio will rise. Therefore, MP_K^X must increase above its pre-regulation level to re-establish the equality MP_K^Y/MP_K^X = constant. Similarly, MP_L^Y must fall as Y becomes more labor-intensive, Accordingly, MP_L^X must fall still farther to re-establish the equilibrium MP_L^Y/MP_L^X = constant. It follows that capital benefits absolutely in terms of both goods X and Y, while labor suffers absolutely from the imposition of environmental controls. Evidently, if the demand elasticity for X is highly inelastic the capital/labor ratio in X must increase to compensate for production lost through environmental regulation. In this case regulation may even increase the equilibrium real wage to the factor used intensively in the regulated industry. Contrastingly, if X is relatively capital-intensive, while demand for X is perfectly elastic, labor/capital ratios will fall in both X and Y, real wages will rise, and real rents will fall.

movement from i to ii, two points of identical commodity-price ratios. With constant commodity prices, regulation causes production to shift from i to ii, which changes factor proportions as shown. The assumption of perfect demand elasticity of course implies that the entire 'burden' of regulation will fall not on consumers, but on factors of production. These effects will be attenuated with more of the burden of regulation falling on consumers the closer to zero the price-elasticity of demand for good X. A more general picture of the combined effects of factor income changes together with variable demand conditions is shown in fig. 2(b) by the downward shift in the N.W. quadrant and the rightward shift in the S.E. quadrant. This produces a new 'supply' curve, a higher wage/rent ratio, and a higher relative price of the regulated product. Depending on the relative strength of the effect of regulation on costs and on factor markers, however, wages/rent might decline.

7. The effect of regulation on trade and factor rewards: Immobile factors of production

With the advent of concern over the stress which modern industrial processes place on the environment, many countries have imposed standards or taxes on producers to control their destructive by-products. Very often these controlled products are important in international trade (steel, paper and lumber products, and agriculture come to mind). Characteristically, environmental restrictions may vary widely both in form and effect among different countries. This divergence might be due to differences in perception of a threat to the environment or to differences in the evaluation of such threats. Yet these different producers are linked together by common world commodity prices and world trade. The concern of this section therefore is to analyze the consequences of differential regulation on factor rewards between countries and therefore on comparative advantage, relative specialization, and the location of production between them.

The effect of regulation on trade, production, and factor rewards is unambiguous if the technologies for X^A and X^B are assumed to have the properties of eq. (12). We begin with the supposition that factors are immobile across countries.

Before regulation the standard Heckscher–Ohlin results apply. Identical technologies and free trade lead to identical capital/labor ratios in each industry wherever located, to common commodity prices, and to factor-price equalization; this is shown by points i in fig. 3. Under the H–O assumptions, country B produces the most of good X (the pollution-generating commodity) since B is relatively well-endowed in L, the factor which is used intensively in X (fig. 3).

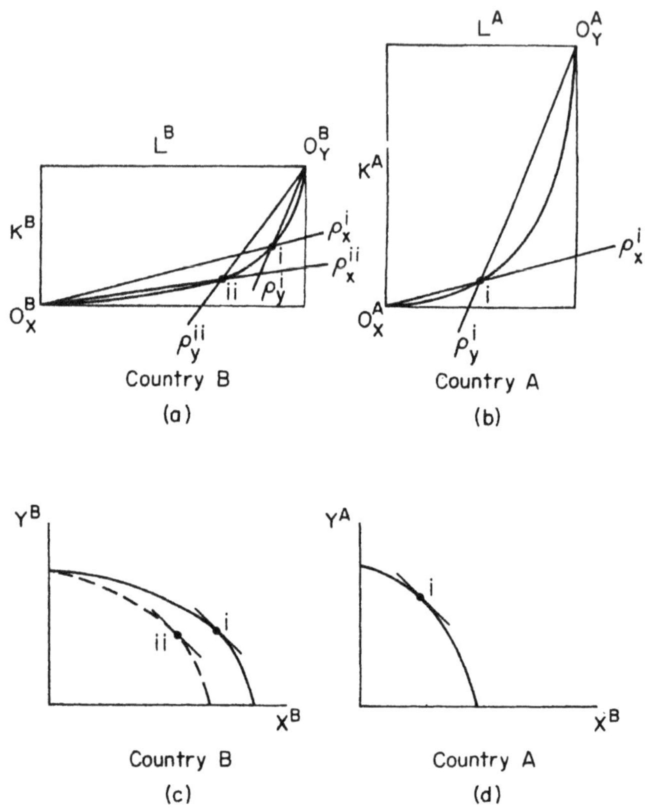

Fig. 3.

7.1. Coordinated environmental control

Suppose first that in both countries *the same* shadow price is levied on T in the production of X. The effect of a proper shadow price on T is to cause the X-producing manufacturers to conserve the environment, raising the value of its marginal product to the optimizing price. Therefore, β in eq. (6) rises. Provided both countries levy *the same tax* on pollution, the qualitative implications of the H–O model are unchanged. A new trade equilibrium will follow from the pollution tax, but the post-tax equilibrium will still feature equal factor proportions and equal factor prices as between countries. The effect of coordinated (equal) regulation on L and K factor incomes now depends on two parameters: the elasticity of demand for good X and the relative capital/labor intensity of X in comparison with Y.

7.2. Uncoordinated or unilateral regulation

Now consider the case of non-uniform, non-coordinated pollution taxes. As a paradigm of this situation suppose only one country (B) imposes a shadow price (or establishes equivalent controls). Then (returning to fig. 3), to maintain world prices requires production at point ii in country B and at point i in country A. At this configuration, however factor proportions and factor prices differ between countries. Moreover, there is no new world commodity price which can equalize factor proportions and therefore equalize factor prices between countries A and B. In other words, non-uniform regulation destroys factor-price equalization. No new interior allocation of factors can simultaneously achieve equal commodity prices and equal factor prices among nations. This is a stark conclusion. For a small country with no influence over world commodity prices regulation of production definitely injures some factor of production and unambiguously benefits others. For a large country its unilateral regulation will raise the world commodity price of the regulated product and elsewhere in the world the factor used intensively in the production of the regulated product will benefit unambiguously.

8. The effect of uncoordinated regulation when factors are mobile

We have just concluded that non-uniform regulation when factors are immobile will cause factor prices to diverge across countries. This difference in factor returns will provide labor and/or capital an incentive to migrate away from low reward areas to high reward areas. If we now relax the factor immobility assumption it is clear that differential regulation will cause labor or capital to move into or out of the regulated country. Multinational companies, for example, may easily transfer capital across borders, where non-uniform regulation provides systematic incentives to re-locate. Note that the direction of migration is not necessarily out of the country imposing regulation. Regulation may attract factors of production. If the factor that is hurt is mobile one should expect migration out of the regulated area. If, however, it is the factor which benefits that is mobile, one should expect migration of that factor into the regulating country. The direction of migration depends on relative factor proportions in the regulated industry. For example, in fig. 3 the effect of regulation is to raise the rent-to-wage ratio in country B, since the regulated industry is assumed to be relatively labor-intensive. Imagine, now, that capital is supplied perfectly elastically to country B; that is, suppose capital flows freely across borders in response to rent/profit differentials. Before regulation, capital just earned its required return (measured in terms of good Y as numeraire). Therefore capital will flow into country B and out of country A until this return is re-established.

To examine the process of factor migration, let us make a corollary 'knife-edge' assumption that world commodity-price ratios are constant. We can call on the Rybczynski theory of a one-to-one correspondence between commodity and factor prices when production is linearly homogeneous. Imagine that when capital flows into country B the manufacture of both goods X and Y continues. To produce at world commodity prices, factor proportions in country B must correspond to ρ_x^{ii} and ρ_y^{ii} in industries X and Y, respectively. To absorb any new capital at these proportions, country B must reduce its output of X and increase its output of Y. The intermediate effect of a capital inflow of ΔK_B^1, into country B is shown as point iii in fig. 4. Evidently, point iii is not a new equilibrium since factor-price ratios between countries A and B are still not equalized. *Capital will continue to flow into B until production of the regulated good reaches zero*, as shown in fig. 5. This requires ΔK_B^2 of new capital. Even at this level, however, factor prices have not been equalized since B specializes in Y at the proportions ρ_y^{ii}. Therefore, still more capital will migrate into B until factor proportions return to ρ_y^{i}. As fig. 5 illustrates, attainment of this new equilibrium requires a capital inflow of ΔK_B^3.

The inflow of capital necessary to equalize factor prices might have come from outside the two-country system. Assuming, however, that A and B constitute the whole world, the capital inflow ΔK_B^3 into B is matched by an equal outflow from A. Again, the Rybczynski theorem insures that proportions ρ_x^{i} and ρ_y^{i} will be maintained, which entails an expansion of X^A and a contraction of Y^A. The conclusion emerges that *the combined effect of unilateral regulation, and factor mobility at a given commodity price ratio is to drive the regulating country out of production of good X entirely.*

Suppose, next, that labor rather than capital was mobile and again that labor is the factor used relatively intensively in the regulated industry. Now, labor will migrate out of B into A; B's Edgeworth production box will close

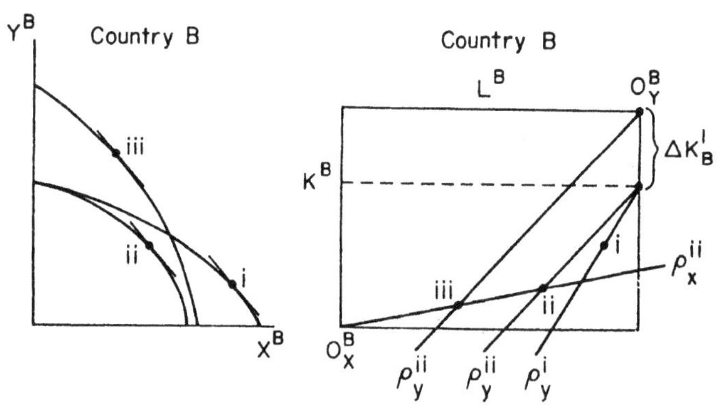

Fig. 4.

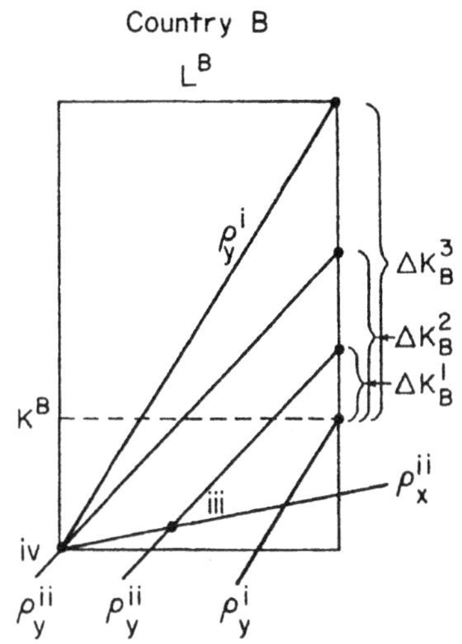

Fig. 5.

up horizontally along the L-axis and A's will expand. Again, a new world equilibrium is reached only when enough labor has migrated out of B to concentrate all B's remaining resources in the production of good Y at factor proportion ρ_y^i. The result emerges that *unilateral regulation, together with factor mobility of any one factor, will drive the regulating country out of producing the regulated good.*

One might think that this result depends on the assumption of fixed commodity prices, but in fact it does not. With less than infinite demand elasticities, unilateral regulation will cause the world price of X to rise and of Y to fall. Production of X will decrease and production of Y will increase. Factor allocations in both countries prior to migration will move along the contract curves toward the origins O_X^A and O_X^B, respectively. But factor proportions and therefore factor prices will diverge between the two countries even after these internal reallocations. Once migration is allowed into the picture, it will proceed until the non-regulating country produces all of good X and the regulating country specializes in the production of Y.

9. Normative and policy conclusions

The normative and/or policy implications of our analysis depend categorically first on whether the factor being regulated creates a local bad (generating disutility only to the consumers in country A or B) or an international public bad, and second, on whether factors of production are mobile or fixed.

If the pollution in question creates a common international global public bad and factors are mobile across national boundaries, then unilateral or uncoordinated regulation is inefficient and ultimately ineffective and useless (subject to all the caveats on realism in the H–O world). When unilateral regulation is undertaken in these circumstances, precisely tailored tax, trade, or commercial policies may compensate for the incentive industry would have to re-locate to control-free havens. The leverage which one country might have on world-wide pollution would then depend on its predominance in the traded goods and on supply and demand elasticities at home and abroad.

If, on the other hand, the environmental damage is local, then factor mobility is desirable from an efficiency standpoint. Differential regulations which reflect differences in local utility loss due to pollution will transfer polluting production processes to regions where the utility cost is low.

References

Atkinson, Anthony B. and Joseph E. Stiglitz, 1980, Lectures on public economics (McGraw-Hill, New York).

Dixit, Avinash K. and Victor Norman, 1980, Theory of international trade, the Cambridge economic handbook (Cambridge University Press).

Johnson, Harry G. and Peter Mieszkowski, 1970, The effect of unionization on the distribution of income: A general equilibrium approach, Quarterly Journal of Economics 84, 539–561.

Jones, Ronald W., 1971, Distortions in factor markets and the general equilibrium model of production, Journal of Political Economy 79, 437–459.

Magee, Stephem P., 1971, Factor market distortions, production distribution, and the pure theory of international trade, Quarterly journal of Economics 85, 623–643.

Neary, J. Peter, 1978, Dynamic stability and the theory of factor market distortions, American Economic Review 68, 671–682.

Sato, R. and T. Koizumi, 1973, On the elasticities of substitution and Complementarity, Oxford Economic Papers 25, 44–56.

Optimal Policies, Piecemeal Reform and Strategic Responses

JOURNAL OF ENVIRONMENTAL ECONOMICS AND MANAGEMENT **20**, 127–142 (1991)

Environmental Regulation in an Open Economy[1]

KERRY KRUTILLA[2]

School of Public and Environmental Affairs, Indiana University, Bloomington, Indiana 47405

Received May 22, 1989; revised September 28, 1989

Environmental regulation by a large trading country affects the world price of traded commodities. A series of second-best environmental taxes are derived which explicitly incorporate trade effects for cases which depend on the type of externality, the regulating country's commodity trade balance, and the presence or absence of trade taxes in the regulated market. A coordinated policy solution using both tax and tariff instruments also is derived. The practical implications for domestic environmental policy-making which emerge from the theoretical results are evaluated. © 1991 Academic Press, Inc.

I. INTRODUCTION

Dating back to Pigou, the traditional policy prescription for environmental regulation has been to levy taxes on polluting activities equal to the marginal social damage—the so called "Pigouvian" tax solution. The implementation of a set of corrective Pigouvian taxes in an economy with externalities can achieve a Pareto-optimal resource allocation if neoclassical assumptions about technology, consumer behavior, and market structure hold [2]. Under these conditions, the second welfare theorem implies that unilateral action by the environmental authorities will lead to a socially efficient resource allocation.

One critique in the literature on the orthodox Pigouvian tax prescription has focused on the underlying market structure assumption. Buchanan [4] showed that a Pigouvian tax could actually reduce social welfare when levied on a monopolized firm, because the tax both reduces environmental damage and further lowers output, which already is suboptimal. If the social cost of the additional output restriction exceeds the corollary environmental cost saving, social welfare will decrease from the Pigouvian taxation policy. Buchanan's study generated further research on the impact of corrective environmental taxes under different market structures [10], and led to the formulation of a second-best environmental policy—a tax which trades off the gain in reduced environmental damage with costs of additional suboptimal output restriction—for the monopoly case [1, 2, 7].[3]

[1] I am indebted to David Good, David Parkhurst, and Tom Snyder, School of Public and Environmental Affairs, Indiana University; Mike Bowes of Resources for the Future; and several anonymous referees for a number of very useful comments. Any remaining errors or oversights in the paper are mine exclusively.

[2] Correspondence should be addressed to Kerry Krutilla, SPEA 325, Indiana University, Bloomington, IN 47405.

[3] The second-best feature of the environmental tax in this case derives from two qualitatively different divergences from the marginal conditions: (1) output is too low; (2) the input mix reflects a socially excessive use of the environment. A single policy instrument, such as a tax on emissions, cannot fully correct both distortions; hence, the tradeoff.

0095-0696/91 $3.00

This paper closely parallels the literature on environmental taxation and market structure but extends the analysis to consider the optimality properties of environmental taxation in an open economy context. It is assumed that the economy, like that of the United States, is large enough to affect world price. In this case, the secondary factor which must be considered in the analysis of environmental tax policy is the impact of the taxation on the economy's terms of trade.

Although the majority of theoretical research in environmental economics is based on a closed economy, the open economy context has received some attention [2, 5, 9, 11]. The existing literature, for the most part, has focused on regulatory impacts *vis-à-vis* comparative advantage, employment, and the balance of trade. Recently, the impact of environmental externalities on the optimality of free trade has been investigated [13]. The possible linkage between environmental policy and the terms of trade has also been discussed in a recent background paper for the Uruguay round of the General Agreement on Tariffs and Trade (GATT) [6].

In contrast to this body of research, the present paper specifically addresses the way in which terms-of-trade ramifications affect the optimality properties of environmental policy. It starts by examining the policy question: at what level should environmental policymakers establish environmental taxes in an open economy when the choice of policy instruments is circumscribed, i.e., the tariff instrument is not available? (If tariffs are present in the regulated market in question, they are taken as exogenous constraints at this stage of the analysis.) Both production and consumption externality cases are evaluated. The paper then goes on to show how the optimal environmental policy changes when the tariff instrument also becomes available to the regulatory authorities. In practice, international law and bilateral treaties will constrain the use and mix of policy instruments. These and other policy issues are addressed in a section of the paper which follows the theoretical developments.

II. THE MODEL

The starting point is formulations which reflect net benefits from the production, consumption, and trade of a homogenous consumption good, Q. Benefits can be represented as the sum of consumer surplus, producer revenues, and tax and tariff revenues. Costs include private production costs plus any environmental costs associated with production or consumption activities. Formulations (1) and (2) below respectively depict net benefits for the case where the environmental cost is associated with a production activity, Bs($\cdot$), and the case where the environmental cost is associated with a consumption activity, Bd($\cdot$),

$$\begin{aligned} \mathrm{Bs} = {} & \int_{\mathrm{Pd}}^{\infty} \mathrm{Qd}(\mathrm{Pd})\, d\mathrm{Pd} + [\mathrm{Ps} + t]\mathrm{Qs}(\mathrm{Ps}) - \mathrm{Cs}(\mathrm{Qs}(\mathrm{Ps})) \\ & - \mathrm{Es}(\mathrm{Qs}(\mathrm{P})) + T[\mathrm{Qs}(\mathrm{Ps}) - \mathrm{Qd}(\mathrm{Pd})] \end{aligned} \tag{1}$$

and

$$\begin{aligned} \mathrm{Bd} = {} & \int_{\mathrm{Pd}}^{\infty} \mathrm{Qd}(\mathrm{Pd})\, d\mathrm{Pd} + t\mathrm{Qd}(\mathrm{Pd}) + \mathrm{PsQs}(\mathrm{Ps}) - \mathrm{Cs}(\mathrm{Qs}(\mathrm{Ps})) \\ & - \mathrm{Ed}(\mathrm{Qd}(\mathrm{Pd})) + T[\mathrm{Qs}(\mathrm{Ps}) - \mathrm{Qd}(\mathrm{Pd})], \end{aligned} \tag{2}$$

where Ps, Pd, and P respectively denote domestic supply price, domestic demand price, and the world price; Qs(Ps) represents domestic supply, $Qs' > 0$; Qd(Pd) represents domestic demand, $Qd' < 0$; Cs(Qs) is total private production costs, $Cs' > 0$, $Cs'' > 0$; Es(Qs) is the total environmental cost associated with production, $Es' > Es'' \geq 0$; and Ed(Qd) is the total environmental cost associated with consumption, $Ed' > 0$, $Ed'' \geq 0$. We also define the tariff, T, which is a specific tax on imports or exports, and the environmental tax, t, which is a specific tax on production in (1) and consumption in (2). The signs indicated for derivatives are sufficient to assure that maxima are attained when (1) and (2) are optimized.

The benefit part of the net benefit formulations include the consumer surplus benefit from consumption, the first term on the right-hand sides, $\int_{Pd}^{\infty} Qd(Pd)\, dPd$; the sum of producer revenue and tax revenue collections, $[Ps + t]Qs(Ps)$ in (1) and $tQd(Pd) + PsQs(Ps)$ in (2); and tariff revenue collections, the final terms on the right-hand side of (1) and (2). Note that (1) and (2) reflect the convention that $T \geq 0$ when the country is a net exporter ($Qs > Qd$), and that $T \leq 0$ when the country is a net importer ($Qs < Qd$), so that the tariff revenue expressions are always nonnegative.[4]

Costs include private production costs, Cs(Qs), and environmental costs, Es(Qs) and Ed(Qd). The cost constructions relate production and environmental costs to the level of output or consumption, and suppress the role of inputs (e.g., the level of abatement, degree of pesticide usage, type of home heat furnace, etc.) in the generation of externalities. This modeling approach sharpens the focus of the analysis on the central point of interest: the connection between environmental regulatory intervention and domestic output or consumption responses, on the one hand, and international trade ramifications on the other. The analytic simplification that externalities are explicitly a function of output or consumption activity levels does not qualitatively affect the conclusions of the analysis.[5]

Environmental costs traditionally have been modeled in the environmental economics literature as a one-period flow process based on static formulations such as (1) and (2) [e.g., 1, 2, 4, 5, 7, 9–11]. The static modeling orientation implicitly rests on the assumption that environmental costs are incurred within one period, or that environmental cost terms reflect a flow of present value for the period in question, without any between-period, intertemporal interactions. An explicitly dynamic formulation would be necessary for other assumptions.[6]

It should also be noted that the environmental costs referred to in (1) and (2) are presumed to be localized in the country initiating the regulation. As such, the

[4]Letting $T \geq 0$ denote an export tax and $T \leq 0$ denote an import tax avoids the need to write out separate and largely redundant formulations for the export and import cases, reducing twofold the amount of mathematics later on.

[5]Focusing the analysis on output and consumption levels means that the environmental policy instruments in question are production and consumption taxes, as noted before. Environmental production and consumption taxes will have the same quantitative impact on output or consumption levels as emissions taxes when emissions are not substitutable with other inputs in the production process, or when reducing output is a lower cost response to an emissions tax than changing the production process. These conditions may hold for relatively low levels of regulation, and/or over the short to medium term when production processes are relatively inflexible.

[6]Current period environmental or trade decisions can affect intertemporal patterns of resource use; e.g., agricultural trade policy can influence the rate of aquifer pumping. These interactions would need to be modeled in a dynamic framework if the object were to determine an optimal intertemporal resource allocation.

net benefit formulations do not model a "transfrontier" pollution process, as analyzed by Segerson [12].

Finally, some terminological clarification is in order. The term "production externality" as used in this paper will denote a spillover generated by a production process—for example, SO_2 emissions associated with power generation—whether or not the impact is on cost or utility functions. Similarly, the term "consumption externality" will refer to a spillover generated by a consumption activity—for example, SO_2 emissions associated with home heat consumption—whether or not the impact is on cost or utility functions. This usage is consistent with the way environmental costs are entered into (1) and (2), and should not be confused with the common externality typology based on cost function and utility effects.

A number of equilibrium conditions underlie the economic model upon which (1) and (2) are based. Since formulation (1) involves the levy of a specific production tax in a market distorted by a preexisting specific tariff, the following equilibrium conditions obtain:

$$\mathrm{Ps} = \frac{\partial \mathrm{Cs}}{\partial \mathrm{Qs}} = P - T - t \quad \text{(Supply-side price equilibrium);} \tag{3}$$

$$\mathrm{Pd} = P - T \quad \text{(Demand-side price equilibrium).} \tag{4}$$

For (2), where a consumption tax is levied, the equilibrium conditions are

$$\mathrm{Ps} = \frac{\partial \mathrm{Cs}}{\partial \mathrm{Qs}} = P - T \quad \text{(Supply-side price equilibrium);} \tag{5}$$

$$\mathrm{Pd} = P - T + t \quad \text{(Demand-side price equilibrim).} \tag{6}$$

A trade equilibrium condition must also be specified to close the model. Excess supply of the regulating country, $Z(\mathrm{Ps}, \mathrm{Pd})$, is

$$Z(\mathrm{Ps}, \mathrm{Pd}) = \mathrm{Qs}(\mathrm{Ps}) - \mathrm{Qd}(\mathrm{Pd}), \tag{7}$$

while world excess demand can be denoted

$$X(P); \quad X' < 0; \quad X(P) > 0, \text{ when Qs} > \text{Qd}; \quad X(P) < 0, \text{ when Qs} < \text{Qd}. \tag{8}$$

Trade equilibrium can then be represented:

$$\mathrm{Qs}(\mathrm{Ps}) - \mathrm{Qd}(\mathrm{Pd}) = X(P). \tag{9}$$

It is assumed initially that the environmental authorities act unilaterally with the policy instrument available, an environmental tax, to maximize (1) and (2), taking preexisting tariffs (if they exist) as exogenous constraints. Subsequently, the exogenous trade policy constraint is relaxed, and a policy coordination scenario maximizing net benefits with respect to both the tax and tariff instruments is explicitly evaluated.

III. NEGATIVE PRODUCTION EXTERNALITY

The policy issue of concern here is the appropriate tax level the environmental authorities should establish in the negative production externality case, assuming that the authorities act unilaterally without coordination with the agencies responsible for commercial trade policy. We want to evaluate how the optimal environmental tax policy under such conditions will compare with the orthodox Pigouvian prescription, which does not consider trade effects. In this case, the optimum tax policy implicitly reflects a constrained optimization because a second policy instrument, the tariff, is held fixed. This gives the optimum environmental tax policy a second-best flavor similar to the environmental taxes derived for the domestic monopoly case previously referred to in [1, 2, 7].

Totally differentiating (1) with respect to the environmental production tax t, and setting the result equal to zero, we have

$$\frac{d\mathrm{Bs}}{dt} = -\mathrm{Qd}\frac{d\mathrm{Pd}}{dt} + \mathrm{Qs}\frac{d\mathrm{Ps}}{dt} + \mathrm{Ps}\frac{\partial \mathrm{Qs}}{\partial \mathrm{Ps}}\frac{d\mathrm{Ps}}{dt} + \mathrm{Qs} + t\frac{\partial \mathrm{Qs}}{\partial \mathrm{Ps}}\frac{d\mathrm{Ps}}{dt} - \frac{\partial \mathrm{Cs}}{\partial \mathrm{Qs}}\frac{\partial \mathrm{Qs}}{\partial \mathrm{Ps}}\frac{d\mathrm{Ps}}{dt}$$
$$- \frac{\partial \mathrm{Es}}{\partial \mathrm{Qs}}\frac{\partial \mathrm{Qs}}{\partial \mathrm{Ps}}\frac{d\mathrm{Ps}}{dt} + T\left(\frac{\partial \mathrm{Qs}}{\partial \mathrm{Ps}}\frac{d\mathrm{Ps}}{dt} - \frac{\partial \mathrm{Qd}}{\partial \mathrm{Pd}}\frac{d\mathrm{Pd}}{dt}\right) = 0. \tag{10}$$

The equilibrium conditions (3) and (4) imply

$$\frac{d\mathrm{Ps}}{dt} = \frac{dP}{dt} - 1 \quad \text{and} \quad \frac{d\mathrm{Pd}}{dt} = \frac{dP}{dt}. \tag{11}$$

Furthermore, totally differentiating the trade equilibrium condition (9) with respect to t implies

$$\frac{\partial \mathrm{Qs}}{\partial \mathrm{Ps}}\frac{d\mathrm{Ps}}{dt} - \frac{\partial \mathrm{Qd}}{\partial \mathrm{Pd}}\frac{d\mathrm{Pd}}{dt} = \frac{\partial X}{\partial P}\frac{dP}{dt}. \tag{12}$$

Making selective substitutions of (11) and (12) into (10), using (3) to eliminate $\partial\mathrm{Cs}/\partial\mathrm{Qs}$, and solving for t yields the optimal environmental production tax,

$$t^* = \frac{\partial \mathrm{Es}}{\partial \mathrm{Qs}} + \alpha(\mathrm{Qs} - \mathrm{Qd}) + \alpha\frac{\partial X}{\partial P}T, \tag{13}$$

where

$$\alpha = -\frac{dP}{dt}\bigg/\left(\frac{\partial \mathrm{Qs}}{\partial \mathrm{Ps}}\frac{d\mathrm{Ps}}{dt}\right).$$

Equation (13) shows that the optimal environmental production tax equals the standard Pigouvian tax $\partial\mathrm{Es}/\partial\mathrm{Qs}$, plus terms which reflect the terms-of-trade impact of taxation, $\alpha(\mathrm{Qs} - \mathrm{Qd})$, and tariff revenue collections, $\alpha(\partial X/\partial P)T$. It is easy to show that α is a nonnegative and equal to[7]

$$-1\bigg/\left(\frac{\partial x}{\partial P} + \frac{\partial \mathrm{Qd}}{\partial \mathrm{Pd}}\right). \tag{14}$$

[7]To determine the sign of α, use (11) to eliminate $d\mathrm{Pd}/dt$ in (12), and rearrange to obtain:

$$1\bigg/\left(\frac{\partial X}{\partial P} + \frac{\partial \mathrm{Qd}}{\partial \mathrm{Pd}}\right) = \frac{dP}{dt}\bigg/\left(\frac{\partial \mathrm{Qs}}{\partial \mathrm{Ps}}\frac{d\mathrm{Ps}}{dt}\right) = -\alpha \le 0,$$

which implies that $\alpha \ge 0$.

α can be interpreted as the absolute value of the reciprocal of the slope of the composite demand for the commodity Q, including both the world component, $\partial X/\partial P$, and the domestic demand component, $\partial \mathrm{Qd}/\partial \mathrm{Pd}$. It indicates the price responsiveness of composite demand. If either demand relationship is infinitely elastic—for example, if $\partial X/\partial P$ or $\partial \mathrm{Qd}/\partial \mathrm{Pd} = -\infty$—then the price effect is nonexistent and α is zero. In this case, the terms-of-trade term in (13) drops out. If in addition to zero price effects, there are no tariffs in the market ($T = 0$), then the third term in (13) also drops out. It is only in this special case that (13) converges to the standard Pigouvian tax.

To interpret (13) when the terms-of-trade effect is operative, maintain the assumption for the moment that tariffs are not present in the market. Under these conditions, Eq. (13) shows that $t^* > \partial \mathrm{Es}/\partial \mathrm{Qs}$ when $\mathrm{Qs} > \mathrm{Qd}$ and $t^* < \partial \mathrm{Es}/\partial \mathrm{Qs}$ when $\mathrm{Qs} < \mathrm{Qd}$. That is, the optimal environmental tax levy is greater than the standard Pigouvian tax if the regulating country is a net exporter, and less than the standard Pigouvian tax if the country is a net importer.

To understand why this is so, it is necessary to consider the impact of the environmental tax on world price and trade volume. When the environmental tax is implemented, domestic production and excess supply decline at the original price level, creating a "supply shock" which raises world price. In the final equilibrium, the regulating country's excess supply will have declined relative to the pre-tax equilibrium.[8]

The excess supply reduction lowers the volume of trade if the country is a net exporter. In conjunction with the higher world price, the export reduction generates a monopolistic surplus gain on the reduced export volume beyond the environmental benefit associated with lower production. The optimal tax policy is thus to raise the tax beyond the Pigouvian level to take advantage of the country's monopolistic price leverage in the world market.

On the other hand, if the regulating country is a net importer, the tax-associated excess supply reduction increases the volume of trade.[9] The increase in the volume and cost of imports represents a welfare loss to the regulating country, which counterbalances the benefit of lower environmental damage. The competing trade and environmental effects lower the optimal environmental tax relative to the standard Pigouvian tax, until the marginal benefits of reduced trade losses equal

[8]The price effect can be found by using (11) and (12) to solve for dP/dt:

$$\frac{dP}{dt} = \frac{\partial \mathrm{Qs}}{\partial \mathrm{Ps}} \Bigg/ \left(\frac{\partial \mathrm{Qs}}{\partial \mathrm{Ps}} - \frac{\partial \mathrm{Qd}}{\partial \mathrm{Pd}} - \frac{\partial X}{\partial P} \right) \geq 0.$$

The trade balance effect can be found by totally differentiating (7) with respect to t, and using (11) and the solution for dP/dt to get

$$\frac{dZ}{dt} = \frac{\partial X}{\partial P} \frac{\partial \mathrm{Qs}}{\partial \mathrm{Ps}} \Bigg/ \left(\frac{\partial \mathrm{Qs}}{\partial \mathrm{Ps}} - \frac{\partial \mathrm{Qd}}{\partial \mathrm{Pd}} - \frac{\partial X}{\partial P} \right) \leq 0.$$

Since $dX/dt = (\partial X/\partial P)(dp/dt)$, clearly $dX/dt = dZ/dt$, i.e. world excess demand must decline to match the regulating country's excess supply reduction.

[9]Since excess supply is negative when the country is a net importer, reducing excess supply further makes it more negative, i.e., increases imports.

the marginal cost of additional environmental damage.[10] To illustrate this situation, we might imagine a large region which produces electricity for domestic consumption by a number of coal-fired power plants and, in addition, imports power from outside the region. The policy question would be at what level regional electricity generation should be taxed to achieve the optimal level of environmental damage reduction. Equation (13) suggests that the tax level will be lower than the Pigouvian level, because the corollary impact of the tax is to increase the price and volume of imported electricity. Depending on the magnitude of the environmental damage and terms-of-trade terms in (13), it would be possible for welfare to go down with a positive tax on regional electricity generation.[11]

Figure 1 graphically illustrates the two tax policy cases. Pd(Qd) and Ps(Qs) denote inverse domestic demand and supply curves. The country is a net exporter at price levels above P Switch (excess supply positive), and a net importer below this price level (excess supply negative). The SMC curve in the figure incorporates the social marginal cost associated with the environmental production externality. For expositional convenience, the graph depicts the special case where $Es'' = 0$.

Consider first the positive excess supply case where the initial equilibrium is at $P^{E0}, Q^{E}s^{0}$. To illustrate the direction that the relevant variables move, imagine that a production of tax of t—the Pigouvian tax level—is imposed. The tax will increase the world price, to P^{E1} for example. Domestic production declines to $Q^{E}s^{1}$. In the post-tax equilibrium, the regulating country will have picked up a net gain of $B + C$ through tax revenue collections—which constitutes monopoly rent association with the world price rise—plus a net gain in environmental cost savings of $E + D$.[12] These gains can be increased by raising the tax beyond the Pigouvian level of t. In the special case where the world excess demand schedule is infinitely elastic at P^{E0}, no monopoly rent would accrue from the environmental tax policy. In this special circumstance, the Pigouvian tax would be the appropriate tax level, generating the usual net social cost savings of $D + E + C$.

For the negative excess supply case, imposing an environmental tax of t moves the system from the initial equilibrium at $P^{I0}, Q^{I}s^{0}$ to a final equilibrium at $P^{I1}, Q^{I}s^{1}$. In this case, the consumer surplus loss associated with the world price rise $(L + M + P + R + S)$ dominates the welfare calculus, so that the net result of the action is a net environment cost savings of only 0 less the net consumer surplus loss of $R + S$.[13] The tax should be lowered until the marginal benefit of

[10] In this case, the environmental tax is conceptually equivalent to the second-best taxes derived in the domestic monopoly case [1, 2, 7], with the terms-of-trade impact of the environmental tax playing the secondary cost role of the suboptimal monopoly output restriction.

[11] In a description of the Sulfur and Nitrogen Emissions Tax Act of 1987 (H.R. 2497)—a bill designed to reduce acid rain through emissions charges—it was recognized that "H.R. 2497... would create incentives to import power produced in Canada" [15, p. 27]. The legislative description added: "power importation would cost domestic companies profits and employment" [15, p. 27]. However, the present paper demonstrates that the principal welfare issue associated with environmental policy-induced power importation from Canada would be the net transfer of U.S. consumer surplus to Canadian citizens through higher import expenditures.

[12] The welfare calculus is as follows: $A + B + C + G + H + I + J$ is collected in tax revenue, while $D + E + F$ is gained as an environmental cost savings. Consumers lose A, while producers lose $J + I + H + G + F$. Summing these gains and losses yields the net gain: $B + C + E + D$.

[13] The welfare calculus in this case: $L + M + N + K$ is gained in tax revenue, and $O + P + Q$ is saved in environmental cost. Counterbalancing these gains is the producer surplus loss of $K + N + Q$ and the consumer surplus loss of $L + M + P + R + S$. Summing these gains and losses we get: $O - (R + S)$.

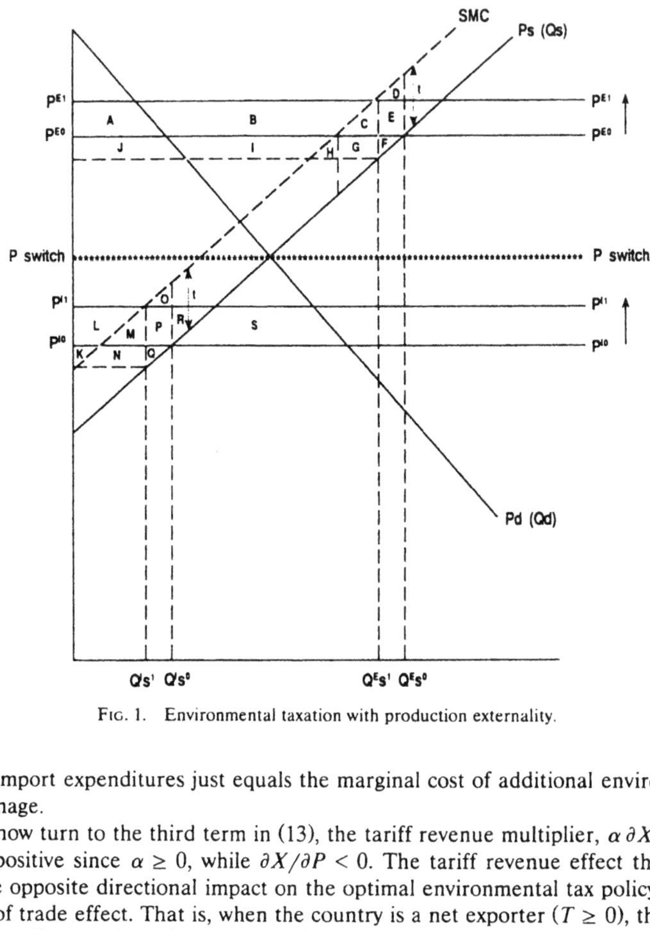

FIG. 1. Environmental taxation with production externality.

lower import expenditures just equals the marginal cost of additional environmental damage.

We now turn to the third term in (13), the tariff revenue multiplier, $\alpha\, \partial X/\partial P$. It is nonpositive since $\alpha \geq 0$, while $\partial X/\partial P < 0$. The tariff revenue effect therefore has the opposite directional impact on the optimal environmental tax policy as the terms of trade effect. That is, when the country is a net exporter ($T \geq 0$), the tariff revenue effect tends to lower the environmental tax. When the country is a net importer ($T \leq 0$), the tariff revenue effect tends to increase the environmental tax.

The intuition behind the tariff revenue effect is easily explained. When the regulating country exports, the environmental tax reduces the volume of trade as described before, and, as a consequence, lower tariff revenue. When the regulating country imports, the environmental tax increases imports and tariff revenue. These ancillary costs (benefits) are reflected in the optimal environmental tax policy by respectively decreasing (increasing) the optimal tax level when the regulating country exports (imports).[14]

[14]Since tariff revenue (TR) is T [Qs(Ps) − Qd(Pd)], we have

$$\frac{d\text{TR}}{dt} = T\frac{\partial X}{\partial P}\frac{dP}{dt}.$$

Thus, $d\text{TR}/dt$ is nonpositive when the country exports ($T \geq 0$), and nonnegative when the country imports ($T \leq 0$).

IV. NEGATIVE CONSUMPTION EXTERNALITY

Now consider the optimal environmental tax when a negative externality is associated with consumption. Totally differentiation (2) and setting the result equal to zero yields

$$\frac{d\text{Bd}}{dt} = -\text{Qd}\frac{d\text{Pd}}{dt} + \text{Qd} + t\frac{\partial\text{Qd}}{\partial\text{Pd}}\frac{d\text{Pd}}{dt} + \frac{d\text{Ps}}{dt}\text{Qs} + \text{Ps}\frac{\partial\text{Qs}}{\partial\text{Ps}}\frac{d\text{Ps}}{dt} - \frac{\partial\text{Cs}}{\partial\text{Qs}}\frac{\partial\text{Qs}}{\partial\text{Ps}}\frac{d\text{Ps}}{dt}$$
$$- \frac{\partial\text{Ed}}{\partial\text{Qd}}\frac{\partial\text{Qd}}{\partial\text{Pd}}\frac{d\text{Pd}}{dt} + T\left(\frac{\partial\text{Qs}}{\partial\text{Ps}}\frac{d\text{Ps}}{dt} - \frac{\partial\text{Qd}}{\partial\text{Pd}}\frac{d\text{Pd}}{dt}\right) = 0. \tag{15}$$

The equilibrium conditions (5) and (6) imply

$$\frac{d\text{Ps}}{dt} = \frac{dP}{dt} \quad \text{and} \quad \frac{d\text{Pd}}{dt} = \frac{dP}{dt} + 1. \tag{16}$$

Making selective use of these relationships and (12), we can solve (15) for t to give

$$t^* = \frac{\partial\text{Ed}}{\partial\text{Qd}} + \gamma(\text{Qs} - \text{Qd}) + \gamma\frac{\partial X}{\partial P}T, \tag{17}$$

where

$$\gamma = -\frac{dP}{dt}\Bigg/\left(\frac{\partial\text{Qd}}{\partial\text{Pd}}\frac{d\text{Pd}}{dt}\right).$$

Equation (17) parallels the structure of the optimal environmental production tax in (13). It is again the Pigouvian tax adjusted by a terms-of-trade effect, $\gamma(\text{Qs} - \text{Qd})$, and tariff revenue effect, $\gamma(\partial X/\partial P)T$. However, γ is nonpositive, so that the trade effects term works in the opposite direction as the positive externality case.[15] Assuming that the terms of trade effect is operative (demand schedules are not infinitely elastic) and that no tariffs exist in the regulated market, we now have the fact that $t^* < \partial\text{Ed}/\partial\text{Qd}$ when Qs > Qd, while $t^* > \partial\text{Ed}/\partial\text{Qd}$ when Qs < Qd. The optimal consumption tax is less than the standard Pigouvian tax if the regulating country is a net exporter, and greater than the standard Pigouvian tax if the country is a net importer.

The terms-of-trade effect works in opposite directions for the environmental consumption and production taxes because the two taxes have the opposite impact on the world price and trade balance. By reducing consumption, the consumption tax increases the regulating country's initial level of excess supply which places a downward pressure on world price. In the final trade equilibrium, the regulating country's excess supply will have increased in the consumption tax case relative to the pre-regulation level.[16]

[15]To determine the sign of γ, (16) can be used to simplify (12) to show that

$$1\Bigg/\left(\frac{\partial X}{\partial P} - \frac{\partial\text{Qs}}{\partial\text{Ps}}\right) = -\frac{dp}{dt}\Bigg/\left(\frac{\partial\text{Qd}}{\partial\text{Pd}}\frac{d\text{Pd}}{dt}\right) = \gamma \le 0.$$

[16]The price and trade balance effects for the consumption tax can be solved analogously to the preceding production tax case.

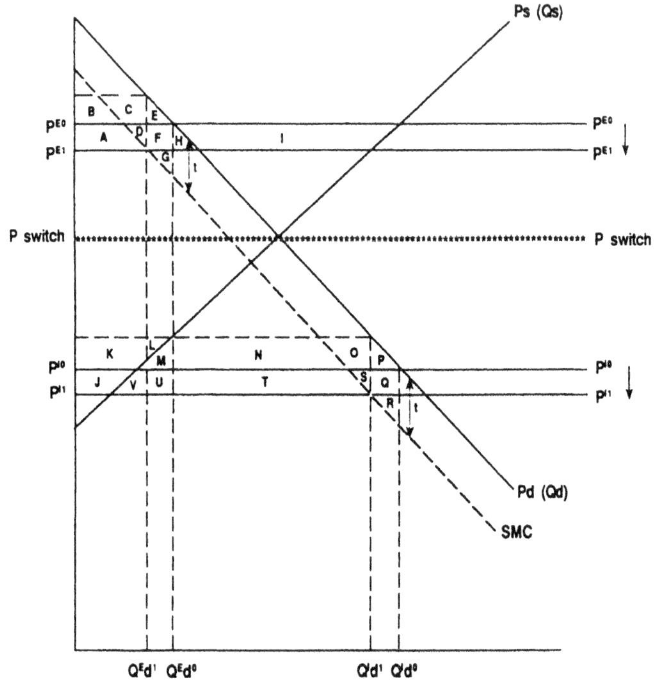

FIG. 2. Environmental taxation with consumption externality.

Given these economic adjustments, the consumption tax effectively increases exports and the volume of trade when the regulating country is a net exporter. The trade expansion and export price drop cause a welfare loss to the regulating country in the form of lost producer surplus—precisely the opposite effect of the monopolistic surplus gain the regulating country achieved in the previous production tax case. The top panel of Fig. 2 illustrates this effect when a tax of t is imposed; the net surplus loss from the action is $H + I$, which is larger than the net environmental cost savings of G. Under these circumstances, the optimal environmental tax should be lower than the Pigouvian level, to provide the optimal trade-off between the cost of trade surplus losses and the benefit of environmental cost reduction associated with lower consumption.[17]

[17]The welfare calculus: $B + C + D + A$ is gained in tax revenue, and $E + F + G$ in environmental cost savings. $B + C + E$ is lost is consumer surplus, and $A + D + F + H + I$ in producer surplus. The net impact: the net environmental cost savings G, less the net export surplus loss $H + I$. These welfare calculations based on Fig. 2 are premised on the special case that $Ed'' = 0$. There are other functional form possibilities. One interesting case is where a positive national security externality attaches to the domestic production of the commodity. The national security benefit would lower the valuation of the negative externality over the domestic consumption range, and result in a sharp increase in the valuation of the negative externality when the commodity becomes traded. The graphical representation in Fig. 2 abstracts from this type of complication.

TABLE I

Welfare Impact of Environmental Taxes and Subsidies Through Terms-of-Trade (TOT) and Tariff Revenue (TR) Channels

	Exporter		Importer	
	TOT	TR	TOT	TR
	Negative externality—Taxes			
Production	+	−	−	+
Consumption	−	+	+	−
	Positive externality—Subsidies			
Production	−	+	+	−
Consumption	+	−	−	+

When the regulating country imports, the excess supply increase reduces imports and the volume of trade. The decrease in the cost and volume of imports represents a welfare gain to the regulating country beyond the environmental damage reduction from lower consumption. The environmental tax can be raised above the Pigouvian level until the marginal benefit of the trade surplus gain just equals the marginal cost of suboptimal consumption and environmental damage. The bottom panel of Fig. 2 illustrates this situation. In the post-tax equilibrium at $P^{11}, Q^{1}d^{1}$, there is a net welfare gain of $S + T + U + V$ from import cost savings, and a net gain of $Q + R$ in environmental cost savings.[18] The optimal environmental tax reflects the additional gain in import cost savings with a higher rate than the Pigouvian tax level of t.

The impact of tariff revenue collections also affects the consumption tax in the opposite direction of the production tax. For the positive excess supply case, the post-tax excess supply shift increases trade and tariff revenue. Equation (17) thus shows that the tariff effect is non-negative under these circumstances, i.e., $T \geq 0$, and $\gamma\, \partial X/\partial P \geq 0$. When excess supply is negative (the country imports), the consumption tax-induced excess supply increase reduces imports, the volume of trade, and, consequently, tariff revenue. As a result, the tariff revenue effect is nonpositive. These effect works against the terms-of-trade effect, moving the optimal tax back in the direction of the Pigouvian tax.

It should be noted that the results derived in this and the previous section can easily be extended to parallel positive production and consumption externality cases. Positive externalities require subsidies, and domestic subsidies have the opposite impact on the world price, trade volume, and tariff revenue collections as taxes. Table I summarizes the directional impacts of the terms-of-trade and tariff revenue effects on Pigouvian taxes for the negative externality cases, and also the directional impact for environmental subsidies.[19] Pluses in the table indicate that

[18] We have a tax revenue gain of $K + L + M + N + O + S + T + U + V + J$ and an environmental cost savings of $P + Q + R$. Consumer and producer surplus losses are respectively $K + L + M + N + O + P$ and J. Summing these we have a net gain of $Q + R + S + T + U + V$.

[19] Since subsidies and taxes move trade effects in opposite directions, it follows that a production subsidy (tax) will have an identical impact on trade to a consumption tax (subsidy). Either a production subsidy or a consumption tax will increase excess supply and lower world price, and either a production tax or consumption subsidy will reduce excess supply and raise world price. (A detailed derivation of the subsidy results is available from the author upon request.)

the factor in question—either the terms of trade channel or tariff revenue channel—increases the environmental tax or subsidy relative to the Pigouvian level, while negative signs indicate that the factors tends to lower the tax or subsidy relative to the Pigouvian level.

Consider, for example, a positive externality associated with consumption where the country is a net importer, and assume tariffs are not present, so that only the terms-of-trade channel is operative. The commodity in question could be a medical vaccine, the consumption of which the government wishes to subsidize because of the positive externality associated with reduced communicable disease in the general population. Table I shows that the consumption subsidy should be lower than the Pigouvian level when the country imports (sign negative). The consumption subsidy, by increasing domestic demand, will increase the world price and the volume and cost of imports. The consumer surplus loss from the deteriorated terms-of-trade could exceed the social gain from the subsidy, in which case, a do-nothing policy would be socially preferable to a subsidy policy.

On the other hand, if the country is a net exporter of the medical vaccine, the consumption subsidy should be higher than the Pigouvian level (sign positive in Table I). The increase in domestic demand again raises the world price, but the effect now is to increase export earnings. The consumption subsidy can be increased above the Pigouvian level to capitalize on the additional welfare gain associated with the increased export surplus.

V. POLICY COORDINATION

In the preceding sections, commodity tariffs have been taken as exogenous constraints. Equations (13) and (17), in fact, can be viewed as formulae which generate a range of optimal environmental taxes, t^*, for parametric variation of the exogenous tariff parameter, T. Two solution pairs have been considered, $(t^*, 0)$ and (t^*, T), where T in the latter case was arbitrary. Another interesting pair is $(0, T^*)$, where T^* is the tariff level which makes environmental regulation unnecessary. Using (13) as an example, we can find T^* by setting t^* equal to 0 and solving to get

$$T^* = -\left(\frac{\partial \text{Es}}{\partial \text{Qs}} + \alpha(\text{Qs} - \text{Qd})\right) \bigg/ \left(\alpha \frac{\partial X}{\partial P}\right) \tag{18}$$

or

$$T^* = -\frac{P}{\eta} - \frac{\partial \text{Es}}{\partial \text{Qs}} \bigg/ \left(\alpha \frac{\partial X}{\partial P}\right), \tag{19}$$

where $\eta = (\partial X/\partial P)(P/X)$ is the elasticity of world excess demand.[20] Equation (19) accomplishes the same objective as the environmental production tax, but with

[20] Note that η will be negative (positive) as the country export (imports). This is true because $\partial X/\partial P < 0$, whereas $X = \text{Qs} - \text{Qd}$ is positive (negative) as the country exports (imports). Note also that because of the convention that $T \leq 0$ when the country imports, (19) must be multiplied by -1 to get a positive expression for the import tariff. This holds also for the optimal tariff derived subsequently in (23).

a different instrument—a tariff. It denotes the standard optimal tariff of international trade theory (the first term in (19)), adjusted for environmental damage (the second term).

This example highlights the fact that the same regulatory objective can be accomplished with a tariff, a production tax, or some combination. The relevant question then, is: Of the infinite number of pairs (t^*, T) which solve (13), which yields the highest level of net benefits? To find out, a coordinated environmental–trade policy must be formulated. Using the production externality case as an example, a coordinated policy solution can be generated by maximizing Bs($\cdot$) in (1) with respect to both t and T. Letting t^{c*} and T^{c*} denote the optimal values of the tax and tariff respectively when they are derived simultaneously, we have (after some manipulation) the first-order conditions[21]

$$\frac{\partial \mathrm{Bs}}{\partial t} = (\mathrm{Qs} - \mathrm{Qd})\frac{\partial P}{\partial t} + \left(t - \frac{\partial \mathrm{Es}}{\partial \mathrm{Qs}}\right)\frac{\partial \mathrm{Qs}}{\partial \mathrm{Ps}}\frac{\partial \mathrm{Ps}}{\partial t} + T\frac{\partial X}{\partial P}\frac{\partial P}{\partial t} = 0, \qquad (20)$$

$$\frac{\partial \mathrm{Bs}}{\partial T} = (\mathrm{Qs} - \mathrm{Qd})\frac{\partial P}{\partial T} + \left(t - \frac{\partial \mathrm{Es}}{\partial \mathrm{Qs}}\right)\frac{\partial \mathrm{Qs}}{\partial \mathrm{Ps}}\frac{\partial \mathrm{Ps}}{\partial T} + T\frac{\partial X}{\partial P}\frac{\partial P}{\partial T} = 0. \qquad (21)$$

Letting $t^{c*} = \partial \mathrm{Es}/\partial \mathrm{Qs}$ in (20) and (21), the same equation results,

$$(\mathrm{Qs} - \mathrm{QD}) + T\frac{\partial X}{\partial P} = 0, \qquad (22)$$

which implies

$$T^{c*} = -\frac{P}{\eta}. \qquad (23)$$

Equation (23) is the optimal tariff of international trade theory. In short, the optimal policy is a combination of the standard Pigouvian tax and the standard optimal tariff. This combination represents the "first-best" solution to the problem of environmental cost and the terms of trade. The first-best solution will not be attained by maximization of the net benefit formulation with respect to only one of the two relevant policy instruments, unless the other instrument is fortuitously at the level t^{c*} or T^{c*}.[22]

VI. POLICY ISSUES

Although a coordinated strategy employing both environmental and trade policies is theoretically optimal in the open economy context, political constraints limit the feasibility of joint policy action. A primary objective of trade policy is to protect special interests, rather than improve and/or maintain the terms of trade [3], and environmental policy-making is not necessarily consistent with this objective. Activist trade policy also is increasingly constrained by international negotiations

[21] This derivation makes use of (3), (4), and (9), and the fact that $\mathrm{Ps} = \partial \mathrm{Cs}/\partial \mathrm{Qs}$. The complete derivation is available from the author upon request.

[22] The results of this section can be extended symmetrically to the consumption externality case.

and treaty agreements such as the GATT trade liberalization process and the recent bilateral free trade agreement between the United States and Canada. These international protocols limit the flexibility of tariff-setting as an activist policy instrument. As a consequence, it is reasonable to presume that environmental policy-making will continue to rely exclusively on non-tariff instruments, as it has in the past.

Given these realities, it is worth inquiring if the theoretical results of Sections III and IV suggest any practical insights for environmental policy-making in view of the actual protective tariff structure that exists in the United States.[23] Since environmental policy-making is generally conducted with less than complete information, we also want to determine whether the theoretical results yield any insights about informational requirements associated with environmental policy-making; for example, cases where the premium on good information is high, or the costs of wrong information are low.

Consider first a commodity for which the United States is a net exporter. Since export taxes are not levied in the United States, only the terms-of-trade channel is of concern. When the commodity is exported and the externality at issue is a production externality, both the terms of trade and environmental effects of the regulation are positive and move in the same direction (see Table I). Thus, even if some uncertainty exists about the magnitude of the environmental damage term and the calculation of the optimal tax policy, the environmental authority can take an incremental regulatory step (from a no-regulation baseline) and be confident that social welfare will improve.

However, when the commodity is exported but the externality at issue is a consumption externality, the terms-of-trade effect of environmental regulation is negative, tending to offset the environmental gain. As a consequence, there is no way to know a priori, for example, whether the health benefit associated with a consumption tax on cigarettes (to reflect the social cost of smoking) would exceed the associated cost of export price declines and lost export earnings. This situation demands better information than the preceding case for the environmental policy maker to ascertain the impact of the proposed regulation.

Turning to the policy permutations when the regulated commodity is imported, the complication of import taxes arises. The previous results indicate that the terms-of-trade and tariff revenue effects move in opposite directions. Equations (13) and (17) imply that the terms-of-trade channel will dominate the tariff revenue effect if existing tariffs are less than the optimal tariff level; conversely, the tariff revenue effect will dominate if existing tariffs are above the optimal tariff level. To determine how existing import tariffs in the United States compare to "optimal" tariff levels for specific commodities it is necessary to consider commodity import supply (negative excess demand) elasticities.[24] Unfortunately, empirical information in import supply elasticities is scarce and of uncertain reliability, and it is therefore difficult to state conclusively whether the existing level of tariff protec-

[23]Export taxes are illegal in the United States, but import taxes are common, and generally escalate with the degree of manufacturing. Imported raw materials and primary processed products do not have tariffs or have only very low tariffs, while more highly processed products and consumption goods have ad valorem tariffs which may be 20% or higher [16].

[24]In ad valorem terms, the optimal import tariff is $T/P = 1/\eta$. This formula shows that when η is less than 1, the optimal ad valorem import tariff will exceed 100%; if η is greater than 1, the optimal ad valorem tariff will be less than 100%.

tion in the United States is below or above optimal levels.[25] As a result, it is difficult to make a presumptive statement about the impact of environmental regulation for commodities which are imported.[26]

As a final issue, it should be noted that, as trade barriers have been lowered and/or negotiated away, attention of the international community has increasingly focused on other trade-distorting policies. For example, a study of the trade ramifications of environmental policies in the agricultural sector is now taking place as a part of a background review for the current GATT round. According to the background report, "Clear guidelines need to be established in the GATT that will distinguish legitimate sets of policies to reduce socially recognized environmental costs of private production decisions from those that primarily reduce commodity supply" [6, p. 19].[27] The growing awareness of the interconnection between environmental intervention and terms-of-trade ramifications may create new political constraints on the conduct of domestic environmental policy.

VII. CONCLUSION

Environmental regulation in the open economy context appears to be a more complicated process than the traditional analysis suggests. In particular, whether a commodity is exported or imported and the level of tariff protection are critical variables in determining the welfare effect of an environmental tax. The analysis shows that the structure of environmental taxes should be modified to reflect the existence of trade, unless terms-of-trade effects are explicitly addressed through the trade policy channel. Since political constraints limit the feasibility of activist trade policy, however, the trade ramifications of environmental intervention most likely will fall within the domain of environmental policy-making itself. Such a requirement goes beyond the traditional purview of domestic environmental policy-making, and, in conjunction with growing international interest in policy-

[25] Although there are many empirical studies in the economics literature on import and export demand elasticities, there is very little work on the supply side. Magee has estimated an aggregate import supply elasticity to the United States of 8.5, but has "some reservations" about the estimate [8, p. 204]. The optimal tariff calculated from this elasticity would be about 12%. Tarr [14] reports an estimated elasticity for U.S. auto import supply of 5 for use in an FTC-developed general equilibrium model, yielding an optimal tariff of 20% for automobiles. Boyd and Krutilla [3] use an elasticity of Canadian lumber import supply which is varied in sensitivity analysis between .89 and 1.35, yielding optimal tariffs for lumber in the range of 112% to 74%.

[26] The impact of environmental regulation can probably be differentiated between raw material and semimanufactured products which receive relatively low levels of tariff protection, and final consumption goods which are more highly protected. In the former case, the terms-of-trade effect likely dominates. (The net benefit formulation can be construed to represent the production, consumption, and trade of a raw material or semimanufactured product by letting Qd(Pd) in (1) and (2) denote an input demand.) For final consumption goods, the relative dominance of trade and revenue effects is less clear. However, successive GATT rounds have continued to lower protection on final goods [16], and as the GATT process of multilateral trade liberalization continues, the terms-of-trade channel should eventually also come to dominate for consumption goods.

[27] A related issue: under current international law, a countervailing duty can be applied against the imported product from a foreign industry which is subsidized and injures a domestic industry. The statute makes no distinction as to whether or not the subsidy is conceptually justified by theoretical welfare economics.

associated trade ramifications, augers a more complicated policy landscape for the definition and conduct of future environmental policy.

REFERENCES

1. A. J. Barnett, The Pigouvian tax rule under monopoly, *Amer. Econom. Rev.* **70**, 1037–1041 (1980).
2. W. J. Baumol and W. E. Oates, "The Theory of Environmental Policy," 2nd ed., Cambridge Univ. Press, New York (1988).
3. R. G. Boyd and K. Krutilla, The politics and consequences of protectionism: A case study in the North American lumber market, *J. Pol. Mod.* **10**, 601–609 (1988).
4. J. M. Buchanan, External diseconomies, corrective taxes, and market structure, *Amer. Econom. Rev.* **59**, 174–177 (1969).
5. R. C. d'Arge and A. V. Kneese, Environmental quality and international trade, *Int. Organ.* **26**, 419–465 (1972).
6. International Agricultural Trade Research Consortium, "Bringing Agriculture into the GATT: Designing Acceptable Agricultural Policies," Cornell University, New York (1988).
7. D. R. Lee, Efficiency of pollution taxation and market structure, *J. Environ. Econom. Management* **2**, 69–72 (1975).
8. S. P. Magee, Prices, incomes, and foreign trade, *in* "International Trade and Finance" (P. Kenen, Ed.), Camridge, Univ. Press, New York (1975).
9. M. McGuire, Environmental regulation, factor mobility, and international trade, *in* "The Economics of Managing Chlorofluorocarbons" (J. C. Cumberland, J. R. Hibbs, and I. Hoch, Eds.), Resources for the Future, Washington, DC (1982).
10. E. Oates and D. L. Strassmann, Effluent fees and market structure, *J. Public Econom.* **24**, 29–46 (1984).
11. R. Pethig, Pollution, welfare, and environmental policy in the theory of comparative advantage, *J. Environ. Econom. Management* **2**, 160–169 (1976).
12. K. Segerson, Unilateral transfrontier pollution: The role of economic interdependence, *Land Econom.* **61**, 83–87 (1985).
13. E. Segarra and M. Dicks, "Agricultural Production Externalities: The Welfare Implications of Agricultural Trade," Texas Tech University College of Agricultural Sciences Publication No. T-27, April (1988).
14. D. Tarr, World Bank, Personal communication (August 1989).
15. U.S. Government Printing Office, Description of H.R. 2497 (Sulfur and Nitrogen Emissions Tax Act of 1987), Prepared by the staff of the Joint Committee on Taxation (August 1987).
16. B. V. Yarbrough and R. M. Yarbrough, "The World Economy Trade and Finance," Dryden, New York (1988).

[5]

JOURNAL OF ENVIRONMENTAL ECONOMICS AND MANAGEMENT 26, 44–65 (1994)

International Trade and the Environment: Policy Reform in a Polluted Small Open Economy

BRIAN R. COPELAND*

University of British Columbia

Received May 15, 1991; revised November 14, 1991

This paper investigates sufficient conditions for welfare-improving policy reforms in a small open economy facing many trade and pollution distortions. We investigate and compare reform in tax regimes, quota regimes, and mixed regimes, where some pollutants are regulated with taxes and others with quotas. It is also shown that the welfare benefits of reforming pollution policy are greater in an economy with international factor mobility than in an economy not subject to such mobility. © 1994 Academic Press, Inc.

1. INTRODUCTION

As the world economy has become more integrated, the relation between international trade and the environment has emerged as an important policy issue. Since the imposition of taxes or regulations to control pollution typically increases production costs, those in affected industries often raise concerns about how such policies will hinder their ability to compete with foreign firms. Similar issues arise when liberalization of trade policy is considered, since a trade barrier can provide shelter from foreign competition for a firm which is subject to environmental regulations.

There are many examples of practical policy matters where such linkage has become an issue. In the context of trilateral free trade negotiations between Canada, Mexico, and the United States, many have argued that an agreement on environmental policy should be linked to a trade agreement since otherwise relatively lax environmental standards could be used as a substitute for trade policy. In the EEC, where trade barriers have already been reduced substantially, concerns have been raised that some countries have used environmental regulations as a non-tariff barrier to trade.[1] Because this issue is likely to increase in importance as public pressure for protection of the environment grows in an era when the world economy is becoming more integrated, it is important that we develop an understanding of the way in which reforms of trade policy and environmental policy interact in standard economic models.

The linkage between international trade and the environment has been the subject of an interesting literature.[2] In particular, several authors have considered optimal trade and environmental policies in an open economy which can influence its terms of trade. As is well known from the literature on distortions

*This work was supported in part by a grant from the Social Sciences and Humanities Research Council of Canada. The paper has also benefited from the helpful suggestions of two anonymous referees.

[1]The September 8, 1990, issue of the *Economist* discusses the European case, as well as other examples on p. 24 of its survey on the environment.

[2]See [2, 12, 14, 16, 17, 19, 20], and others.

0095-0696/94 $6.00

(e.g., Bhagwati [3]), the first-best policy requires two instruments: a trade tax tc improve the terms of trade and pollution tax to offset the externality. Much of the interest has centered on second-best policies for the case where only one instrument is available. If trade policy is the only instrument, Baumol and Oates [2] and Markusen [14] show that in the presence of pollution, the optimal tariff may be higher or lower than that which would maximize rent extraction from foreigners, since the policymaker must also consider the effect of the tariff on pollution levels. Similarly, if tariff levels are exogenous, Markusen [14] and Krutilla [12] show that optimal second-best pollution taxes will be either higher or lower than those which would fully internalize the externality, since terms of trade effects must be considered.

In this paper, I investigate the welfare effects of reforms of trade and environmental policy in a distorted small open economy. This work differs from the above literature in several ways. First, while Markusen and Krutilla characterize *optimal* policies with one pollution distortion and one trade distortion, I instead focus on small changes in policy which move an economy with many pollution and trade distortions in the direction of the optimum. In addition, while Markusen and Krutilla consider only tax instruments, I compare regimes where taxes have been used to control pollution with regimes where quotas are used instead (I also allow for mixed regimes) and find that the results can be quite different across regimes. Finally, I extend the analysis to allow for international factor mobility.[3]

While the motivation for extending the analysis to consider quotas and international factor mobility is likely self-evident, the decision to consider gradual policy reforms in a multi-distortion world perhaps needs some elaboration. An important advantage of the gradual approach to policy reform is that the sufficient conditions for a small welfare-improving policy change make use of elasticities in the region of the initial distorted equilibrium, while formulas for the optimal tax policies found in Markusen [14] and Krutilla [12] require information on elasticities in the region of the optimum (which typically is not available). Hence, this approach is potentially useful for practical policy matters. In addition, governments may be more receptive to proposals for small reforms than for large ones. As a result, the gradual approach has been very influential in the public finance and trade policy literature.[4]

The emphasis on multiple distortions is also motivated by policy relevance. Most practical policy issues concern situations with many goods and pollutants. However, as is well known, the results for the case of one distortion do not hold in the case of many distortions.[5] Models with many trade distortions have received a great deal of attention in the international trade literature, perhaps in part because trade policy reforms frequently occur through the GATT process or in the

[3]Another difference between this paper and those of Markusen and Krutilla is that I focus on a small open economy, rather than a large one which can influence its terms of trade. In a model which is already complicated by the presence of many distortions, the small open economy case allows one to focus clearly on the linkage between trade and pollution distortions. While this is a simplification, it is probably the relevant case to consider for most countries in the world. The multi-country case with market power and transboundary pollution will be considered in a follow-up paper.

[4]There is a large literature on gradual trade policy reform. Dixit [8] and Vousden [21] provide excellent surveys. There is also a large public finance literature on the reform of distorted economies. See Dixit [7] and Auerbach [1].

[5]See, for example, [2, 8].

context of setting up free trade areas, in which case coordinated changes in large numbers of trade policy instruments occur. Reforms of pollution policy, on the other hand, typically occur on a piecemeal basis, and for this reason, it may seem natural to focus on one-distortion models. However, this, if anything, strengthens the case for looking at models with many distortions, since it forces the policy-maker to design policies that take into account any important undesirable spillover effects arising from an inability to deal simultaneously with all distortions.

The plan of the paper is as follows. The basic model is set up in Section 2. In Section 3, I give conditions for a tariff change to increase welfare in the presence of pollution distortions and conditions for a reform of pollution taxes to increase welfare in the presence of trade distortions. In either case, attempts to deal with one distortion can have spillover effects which may exacerbate other distortions, and hence policy reform is complex in general. In some cases, simple rules for reform can result in welfare improvements. For example, if industries which are subject to trade protection tend to be heavy polluters (i.e., if they are what I call *pollution damage intensive*), then an equiproportionate reduction in either trade barriers or pollution distortions can improve welfare. More generally, however, such simple rules of thumb need not improve welfare, and hence the analysis lends support to the view that reforms in trade and pollution policy should be coordinated. The work in this section is an application and extension of the general models of policy reform in open economies (e.g., Dixit [8]) to the specific problem of pollution and trade distortions.

Quota regimes are investigated in Section 4. If one searches for the optimal policy, as in the case of Markusen and Krutilla, then tax and quota regimes are equivalent. However, if one considers small reforms of policy, as in the present paper, the two regimes are no longer equivalent, since an economy constrained by quotas on pollution or trade responds to policy changes differently than an economy in which only tax instruments have been imposed. The main result is that in some cases, policy reform can be easier in quota regimes than in tax regimes. For example, if all pollutants are constrained by binding quotas, then small reforms of trade policy in the direction of first-best tariff levels can improve welfare. Corden and Falvey [5] and Falvey [10] have previously considered reform of an economy in which both taxes and quotas are used to restrict trade, but where there is no pollution. This section extends their work to allow for pollution distortions.

Finally, in Section 5, the model is extended to allow for free international factor mobility.[6] Concerns are sometimes raised over the possible adverse welfare effects of capital flight induced by more stringent pollution policy. Markusen *et al.* [15] show that in the presence of imperfect competition, the international pattern of production may be very sensitive to pollution policy. In the presence of perfect competition, I show that the benefits of a given increase in pollution taxes toward the first-best level are larger in an economy with mobile factors than in a similar economy without such factor mobility. In this sense, one can argue that increased "globalization" of the world economy provides incentives for reforming pollution policy even stronger than those which existed before.

[6] In Markusen [14] and Krutilla [12] all factors of production are assumed to be internationally immobile.

The final section discusses the practical policy relevance of the results and considers directions for future work in this area.

2. THE MODEL

I consider a standard model of a perfectly competitive small open economy[7] and modify it to allow for pollution. The economy is endowed with a vector, v, of M primary factors of production, which are supplied inelastically. Agents in the economy may produce or consume $N_g + 1$ goods and N_p types of pollutants. The output of good 0 (the numeraire) is denoted by y_0, and its domestic consumption by c_0. The output and consumption of goods $1, \ldots, N_g$ are denoted by the vectors y and c, respectively.

Pollution is modeled as a by-product of goods production, and the level of its output is denoted by the vector z. I assume that pollution adversely affects the utility of consumers, but that it does not generate external effects on production functions. That is, an increase in the level of pollution produced by one firm does not affect the cost function of any other firm, but does affect the utility function of consumers.[8] The set of feasible pollution and output combinations (y_0, y, z) is given by the technology set $T(v)$, which I assume is strictly convex.

Because of the small country assumption, world prices are treated as fixed. No tariff is levied on the numeraire (good 0), and hence its domestic and world price are both set equal to one. The vector of world prices for goods $1, \ldots, N_g$ is denoted by p; the corresponding vector of domestic goods prices is denoted by q. If a vector of trade taxes or subsidies t is imposed, then $q = p + t$. Firms may also face a vector of pollution taxes s.

I assume a representative consumer, with a utility function $U(c_0, c, z)$, where consumption of goods is a choice variable for the consumer, but where pollution takes the form of a public bad, and hence the level of its consumption is beyond the control of the consumer. Equivalently, the consumer's preferences may be represented with an expenditure function $E(1, q, z, u)$,[9] which is concave in q, non-decreasing in q, and increasing in u and z.[10] This is the minimum cost of attaining utility level u given goods prices q and the current pollution level z. Note that by Shepherd's Lemma, the consumer's compensated demand vector for good 0 is given by E_0 and for goods $1, \ldots, N_g$ by $E_q \equiv \partial E / \partial q$. Similarly, E_z is the vector of marginal willingness to pay for reductions in pollution. Thus, E_z represents the marginal damage caused by pollution.

As is the convention in the recent international trade literature, it is convenient to work with the aggregate revenue function for the economy. This is also known as the GNP function, and it has the properties of a restricted profit function. Given q and s, firms maximize their individual profits, and in doing so, they

[7] Dixit and Norman [9] and Woodland [22] provide expositions of the standard model.

[8] Markusen [14] also restricted his analysis to pollution of this type. This simplification allows a clear exposition of some important relationships between trade policy and pollution policy. A more general analysis, incorporating both production and consumption externalities and allowing for multiple countries, will be carried out in subsequent research.

[9] The numeral "1" here refers to the price of the numeraire.

[10] It is increasing in z since an increase in the level of any pollutant is assumed to harm the consumer; hence, the minimum cost of attaining a given utility level increases with z.

collectively maximize GNP at domestic prices (less pollution tax costs). Denoting the economy's revenue function by G, the private sector of the economy thus acts as if it solves the problem

$$G(1, q, s, v) = \max_{\{y, z\}} \{ y_0 + q'y - s'z \text{ s.t. } (y_0, y, z) \in T(v) \},$$

where a prime (′) denotes transpose. By the envelope theorem, the output vector for goods $1, \ldots, N_g$ is $y = G_q$ and the vector of pollutants is $z = -G_s$. The function G is convex in (q, s) and concave in v.[11]

Any revenue collected by the government is assumed to be rebated in lump-sum form to the consumer. Hence, given a vector of trade taxes and subsidies t and a vector of pollution taxes s, the equilibrium of the economy is given by

$$E(1, q, z, u) = G(1, q, s, v) + s'z + t'M, \tag{1}$$

$$M = E_q(1, q, z, u) - G_q(1, q, s, v), \tag{2}$$

$$z = -G_s, \tag{3}$$

where M is the vector of net imports of goods $1, \ldots, N_g$ (negative components of M correspond to exports). Equation (1) requires that consumer expenditure be equal to the net value of output plus tax and tariff revenue, Eq. (2) defines compensated net imports as the difference between compensated demand (E_q) and goods output (G_q), and Eq. (3) uses the envelope theorem (as noted above) to recover pollution levels from the economy's revenue function.

3. WELFARE EFFECTS OF SMALL CHANGES IN POLLUTION TAXES AND TRADE TAXES

In this section, I consider a distorted economy in which both trade taxes and pollution taxes initially may be set sub-optimally and investigate conditions under which small changes in these instruments can improve welfare. A general expression for the welfare effects of trade and pollution tax changes is found in Subsection 3.1. This is used to derive conditions for policy reform in subsequent subsections. To place the work in context and to motivate what follows, some known results are reviewed briefly in Subsection 3.2. The next two subsections then consider conditions under which pollution policy and trade policy can be reformed independently.

3.1. The General Case

To find an expression for the effects of policy changes on welfare, note that the utility of the consumer is determined by Eq. (1). Totally differentiating (1), using (2) and (3), and noting that $dq = dt$, since the world prices are assumed to be fixed, we obtain

$$E_u\, du = -(E_z - s)'\, dz + t'\, dM. \tag{4}$$

[11]See [22] for further discussion of these and other properties of the GNP function.

Note that $E_u > 0$ is the inverse of the marginal utility of income, and hence $E_u\, du$ is a measure of the change in welfare. This has two components, reflecting the two types of distortions (due to trade barriers and suboptimal pollution taxes).

The vector $E_z - s$ measures the pollution distortions as the difference between the marginal damage caused by pollutants, E_z, and the taxes charged to firms which emit these pollutants. Hence, the first term in (4), $-(E_z - s)' dz$, measures the effect of a policy change on the pollution distortion: if pollution taxes are initially too low, we have $E_z > s$, and hence reductions in pollution ($dz < 0$) improve welfare. The second term, $t'\,dM$, measures the effect on the trade distortion. For example, if the only trade distortions are due to import tariffs, then imports are initially too low on average, and hence a policy which increases imports on average ($t'\,dM \geq 0$) has a first-order positive effect on welfare.

Although Eq. (4) is instructive, it expresses welfare changes as a function of the targets (pollution and imports), rather than the policy instruments (pollution taxes and trade taxes). To remedy this, totally differentiate (3) to obtain the policy-induced change in pollution,

$$dz = -(G_{sq}\, dt + G_{ss}\, ds), \tag{5}$$

and differentiate (2) to obtain the change in net imports,

$$dM = (E_{qq} - G_{qq})\, dt + E_{qz}\, dz + E_{qu}\, du - G_{qs}\, ds. \tag{6}$$

Substituting (5) and (6) into (4) and defining $m \equiv E_{qu}/E_u$ (this is the vector of marginal propensities to consume) and $H_{qq} \equiv G_{qq} - E_{qq}$, which is a positive semidefinite matrix of pure substitution effects, we obtain our fundamental equation which measures the welfare effects of small policy changes,

$$E_u\, du(1 - t'm) = [\delta_z G_{sq} - t'H_{qq}]\, dt + [\delta_z G_{ss} - t'G_{qs}]\, ds, \tag{7}$$

where $\delta_z \equiv E'_z - t'E_{qz} - s'$, and stability implies that the tariff multiplier $1 - t'm > 0$.[12]

The term denoted by δ_z is the gap between the relevant measure of marginal external damage to consumers from pollution ($E'_z - t'E_{qz}$) and the pollution tax vector. In the presence of trade taxes, an increase in pollution has two effects on consumers: the direct effect of the pollution (E'_z) and the indirect effect on the trade distortion ($-t'E_{qz}$). If the compensated demand for goods which are protected by import tariffs falls in response to an increase in pollution, then the trade distortion is exacerbated by the pollution. For example, if hiking boots are protected by a tariff, the country's imports of hiking boots are too low, thus yielding a tariff-induced consumption distortion. If an increase in pollution destroys wilderness areas and discourages hiking, then imports of hiking boots will fall even further below their optimal level, thus worsening the effects of the tariff distortion.

Hence, we see from (7) that an increase in tariff rates ($dt > 0$) has two effects: there is a direct effect on the trade distortion, measured by $-t'H_{qq}\, dt$, and an

[12] See Neary and Ruane [18] for discussion of the tariff multiplier and its relation to the stability condition.

indirect effect on the pollution level, the welfare cost of which is measured by $\delta_z G_{sq}\, dt$. Conversely, an increase in pollution taxes ($ds > 0$) has a direct effect on pollution and an indirect effect on the trade distortion. In the following subsections, we will analyze the interactions between these various effects, beginning with some familiar special cases.

3.2. A Brief Review of Some Special Cases

In the presence of many distortions, an arbitrary reduction in any given distortion may raise or lower welfare because of well-known problems of the second best. For example, if there are no trade distortions, if all pollution is initially unregulated, and if a particular pollutant is selected as a target of regulation, it may be welfare improving to *subsidize* rather than tax that pollutant.[13] Similarly, if there is no pollution, then although free trade is optimal in our model, the reduction of an arbitrary tariff may worsen welfare.[14] Policy analysis is thus complex. However, a general rule which has emerged from the literature on gradual reform in the presence of many distortions is that uniform proportional reductions in *all* distortions will improve (or at least not reduce) welfare.[15] To illustrate, consider some special cases.

Let us first suppose that there is no pollution; that is, suppose $z \equiv 0$ (hence also $s \equiv 0$). Then as is well known (see Lloyd [13], Dixit [7], Hatta [11], Diewert *et al.* [6], and others), a uniform reduction in all tariffs will not worsen welfare (and will typically improve it): in (7) let $dt = -t\, d\lambda$, where λ is a scalar and where $d\lambda > 0$. Then

$$E_u\, du(1 - t'm) = t'H_{qq} t\, d\lambda \geq 0,$$

since H_{qq} is positive semidefinite.

Next suppose now that there are pollution distortions, but that all tariffs are zero. Then (7) reduces to

$$E_u\, du = (E_z - s)'G_{ss}\, ds. \tag{8}$$

If there is only one pollutant, then if the pollution tax is below marginal damage ($E_z > s$), it should be increased; and if the tax is above marginal damage ($E_z < s$), it should be decreased. This result no longer holds if there are many pollutants;

[13] See Baumol and Oates [2]. As an example of how this could arise in the present model, suppose that there are only two pollutants and that they are initially unregulated (i.e., $s_1 = s_2 = 0$). If a tax is imposed on pollutant 1 only, then from (7) we have $E_u(du/ds_1) = -E_{z_1}(\partial z_1/\partial s_1) - E_{z_2}(\partial z_2/\partial s_1)$. The tax will reduce the output of pollutant 1, which is beneficial; however, it may also induce substitution toward pollutant 2, which may be much more damaging than pollutant 1. That is, if $\partial z_2/\partial s_1 > 0$, then there exist preferences with $E_{z_2} > E_{z_1}$, for which $du/ds_1 < 0$. In this case, if the policy maker is constrained to intervening only with respect to type 1 pollution, the optimal policy is to subsidize type 1 pollution. (Note that the response $\partial z_2/\partial s_1 > 0$ will be obtained in a wide range of non-perverse models. For example, consider a Heckscher–Ohlin model with two goods and two factors. Suppose good 1 generates type 1 pollution and good 2 generates type 2 pollution, with each type of pollution being directly proportional to output. Then taxing type 1 pollution will cause sector 1 to contract and sector 2 to expand, and thus type 2 pollution will increase.)

[14] Dixit [8] provides a good discussion of these issues.

[15] See Dixit [8].

however, in that case, equiproportionate reductions in all pollution distortions can improve welfare. To see this, let $ds = (E_z - s)\,d\lambda$, where λ is a scalar and $d\lambda > 0$. That is, for each pollutant, the increase in pollution taxes should be proportional to the difference between marginal damage and the initial pollution tax. Then (8) becomes

$$E_u\,du = (E_z - s)'G_{ss}(E_z - s)\,d\lambda \geq 0,$$

since G_{ss} is positive semidefinite.

Finally, suppose now that there are both pollution and trade distortions. Then if pollution and trade policy can be reformed simultaneously, a sufficient condition for policy reform can be obtained easily: all distortions should be reduced equiproportionately. To see this, let $dt = -t\,d\lambda$ and $ds = \delta_z'\,d\lambda$, with $d\lambda > 0$. Then (7) yields

$$E_u\,du(1 - t'm) = (-t', \delta_z)\begin{bmatrix} G_{qq} & G_{qs} \\ G_{sq} & G_{ss} \end{bmatrix}(-t, \delta_z')\,d\lambda - t'E_{qq}t\,d\lambda \geq 0,$$

since G is convex in (q, s) and E_{qq} is negative semi-definite.

The three examples considered in this section illustrate the point that if all distortions can be adjusted simultaneously, then small coordinated movements toward the first best can improve welfare. However, in practice, such coordination does not often occur. The next subsections consider sufficient conditions for policy reform when each type of policy is set independently.

3.3 Tariff Reform Without Pollution Reform

In practice, trade policy and environmental policy are typically conducted independently. As indicated in the previous section, this is less than ideal, since changes in one type of distortion can exacerbate other types of distortions. However, if the policymaker is aware of the potential spillover effects, then it is possible to design piecemeal rules for reform which will lead to welfare improvement. This section considers the effects of tariff reform, while leaving pollution policy in place; the following section considers pollution reform while leaving tariffs in place. I show that under some conditions, the simple rules of thumb of Section 3.3 continue to be valid. In general, however, the direction of reform may have to be modified to take into account the inevitable spillover effects that occur as a result of the constraint on the policymaker.

If the pollution tax vector is unchanged, we have $ds = 0$, and hence (7) becomes

$$E_u\,du(1 - t'm) = \left[\delta_z G_{sq} - t'H_{qq}\right] dt. \tag{9}$$

Let us first consider the effects of a uniform reduction in tariff levels; i.e., let $dt = -t\,d\lambda$, with $d\lambda > 0$. As shown in Section 3.2, this will reduce the tariff distortion, but the effect on the pollution distortion is ambiguous. If the shift in production induced by the tariff change stimulates pollution-intensive industries, then the increased damage from pollution must be weighed against the benefits of tariff reduction. On the other hand, if pollution-intensive industries decline in response to the tariff changes, then the reduced damage from pollution can reinforce the benefits of tariff reduction.

In order to obtain some unambiguous results, it is useful to have the following definitions which make precise the notion that some industries tend to be relatively more pollution intensive than others.

DEFINITION 1. Industry k is *intensive in pollutant* i if $\partial z_i/\partial q_k > 0$.

An increase in the price of good k will increase the output of good k by drawing resources away from the rest of the economy toward producers of good k. If, at the margin, the expanding part of the economy tends to produce more of pollutant i than the contracting part, then we have $\partial z_i/\partial q_k > 0$, and we say that industry k is intensive in that pollutant.[16]

With many pollutants, an industry may be intensive in some types of pollutants, but not others. It is useful to be able to sum up the net harmful effects of the changes in levels of a given group of pollutants generated by a price-induced expansion of industry k. One way of doing this is to weight the changes in different pollution levels with the pollution distortion terms which are given by the vector δ_z. This is done in the following:

DEFINITION 2. Let S be a set of pollutant types. Then industry k is *damage intensive with respect to pollutants of type* S if $\Sigma_{i \in S}\delta_{z_i}(\partial z_i/\partial q_k) > 0$.

DEFINITION 3. Industry k is *pollution damage intensive* if it is damage intensive with respect to the set of all pollutants.

Hence, to determine pollution damage intensivity, positive weight is put on increases in pollutants for which the marginal damage to consumers is in excess of the corresponding pollution tax.

We can now give a condition under which an equiproportionate reduction of tariffs can improve welfare in the presence of pollution distortions.

PROPOSITION 1. *Assume stability* (*i.e.*, $1 - t'm > 0$). *Suppose that the only trade barriers are import tariffs and/or export subsidies. Suppose also that all industries which are subject to trade protection are pollution damage intensive. Then a small equiproportionate reduction in trade taxes and subsidies will not reduce welfare.*

Proof. Let $dt = -t\,d\lambda$ with $d\lambda > 0$ in (9). By our restrictions on policy instruments, $t \geq 0$. This, combined with the pollution damage intensivity assumption, implies that $-\delta_z G_{sq} t \geq 0$. Recalling also that H_{qq} is positive semidefinite, we have our result. □

The intuition for this result is as follows. Import taxes and export subsidies are policies which stimulate domestic output of the protected sector at the expense of the rest of the economy. A reduction in trade barriers will thus cause the protected sector to contract. This will lessen the trade distortions, but will have a spillover effect on pollution. If the protected sector is pollution damage intensive, a contraction of this sector will reduce the pollution distortion, thereby yielding an additional boost to social welfare. Hence, the trade policy reform has a positive

[16]An alternative characterization of the above definition can be obtained by noting that $\partial z_i/\partial q_k = -G_{s_i q_k} = -G_{q_k s_i} = -\partial y_k/\partial s_i$. Hence, we have the result that industry k is intensive in pollutant i if and only if an increase in the pollution tax on pollutant i leads to a reduction in the output of good k.

spillover effect on pollution in this case.[17] Although Proposition 1 requires that all goods subject to protection be pollution damage intensive, more generally one can say if tariffs and export subsidies are the only type of protection, and if goods which have relatively high protection tend on average to also be relatively pollution damage intensive, then a uniform reduction in trade barriers will tend to increase welfare.

Proposition 1 deals with a case where the spillover effect of tariff reduction on the pollution distortion reinforces the gains from tariff reductions. If, instead, the protected sector is not pollution damage intensive, then a uniform tariff reduction may stimulate the output of industries which produce pollutants that are not subject to appropriate taxes, and the net effect on welfare will be ambiguous. To obtain a rule which will be sufficient for a welfare improvement, let us deviate from the notion of uniform tariff reductions and instead consider a uniform movement toward a second-best tariff vector.

PROPOSITION 2. *Assume stability (i.e., $1 - t'm > 0$) and that H_{qq} is of full rank. Define*

$$\tau(t)' = \delta_z G_{sq}(H_{qq})^{-1}.$$

Then an equiproportionate movement of tariffs toward the vector $\tau(t)$ will not reduce welfare.

Proof. Note that we can write (9) as

$$E_u\, du(1 - t'm) = -[t - \tau(t)]' H_{qq}\, dt.$$

Let $dt = -[t - \tau(t)]\, d\lambda$, with $d\lambda > 0$. Then

$$E_u\, du(1 - t'm) = [t - \tau(t)]' H_{qq} [t - \tau(t)]\, d\lambda \geq 0,$$

since H_{qq} is positive semidefinite. □

Note that the second-best optimal tariff vector satisfies $t^* = \tau(t^*)$. Thus, the function $\tau(t)$ indicates the direction in which tariffs should be adjusted in order to move closer to the second-best optimum. If $t_i > \tau_i(t)$, then t_i should be reduced; if $t_i < \tau_i(t)$, it should be increased. However, note that the desirable direction of movement for tariffs is heavily dependent on the size of the pollution distortion. In particular, Proposition 2 does not indicate a movement toward free trade unless either (1) $\delta_z = 0$, in which case there is no pollution distortion, or (2) $G_{sq} = 0$, in which case output changes do not affect pollution.

To interpret Proposition 2 further, it is useful to consider a special case where there are many pollutants, but only two goods. Suppose good 0, the numeraire, is exported, and that there is an import tariff, t, on good 1. Then $H_{qq} > 0$ is a scalar,

[17]The form of protection stipulated in Proposition 1 is probably the most relevant case to consider. However, one can restate the proposition for other forms of protection. If, instead, export taxes were the only forms of protection, then a reduction in trade taxes would simulate output of goods subject to these taxes, and hence the pollution spillover effect would be beneficial only if goods subject to export taxes were not pollution damage intensive.

and

$$\tau(t) = -\frac{\Sigma_i \delta_{z_i}(\partial z_i/\partial q)}{H_{qq}}.$$

Hence, τ is negative if the import-competing industry is pollution damage intensive, zero either if output does not affect pollution or if pollution taxes just offset the pollution distortion, and positive otherwise. This implies that the tariff should continue to be reduced past the point where it takes on the free trade level of zero (hence an import subsidy is called for) if the import-competing industry is pollution damage intensive, since the effect of an import subsidy is to force domestic output below the free trade level and thus indirectly reduce pollution. On the other hand, if the import-competing sector is not pollution damage intensive, then the second-best optimal tariff is positive. In this case, aggregate damage from pollution can be reduced by encouraging output in the import-competing sector at a level above that which would be attained in free trade either because this sector does not pollute much or because pollution is well regulated in this sector relative to the export sector. To sum up, note that in either case, trade policy can be used to correct partially for inefficient pollution policy, a result which generalizes that obtained in the one-pollutant case in Markusen [14].

3.4. Pollution Reform without Tariff Reform

We now consider reform of pollution policy in the presence of exogenous trade distortions. Holding tariffs constant, (7) becomes

$$E_u\, du(1 - t'm) = \left[\delta_z G_{ss} - t'G_{qs}\right] ds. \tag{10}$$

In this case, uniform reductions in the pollution distortion (δ_z) need not improve welfare, despite the fact that our definition of the pollution distortion ($\delta_z = E_z' - t'E_{qz} - s'$) already takes into account the effect of the tariff distortion on the cost of pollution to consumers. This is because a reduction in pollution will indirectly affect the tariff distortion through a production effect (measured by $-t'G_{qs}$), as well as through the demand effect already included in δ_z.

However, we can obtain a sufficient condition for an uniform reduction in pollution distortions to improve welfare.

PROPOSITION 3. *Assume stability (i.e.,* $1 - t'm > 0$*). Suppose that the only trade barriers are import tariffs and/or export subsidies. Suppose also that all industries which are subject to trade protection are pollution damage intensive. Then a small reduction in pollution taxes proportional to the pollution distortion vector* δ_z *will not reduce welfare.*

Proof. In (10), let $ds = \delta_z\, d\lambda$, with $d\lambda > 0$. The proof is then similar to that of Proposition 1. □

A weaker sufficient condition for a uniform pollution reform to improve welfare is that $-t'G_{qs}\delta_z \geq 0$, which requires that on average, industries subject to relatively high protection should be relatively pollution damage intensive.[18] The intuition is as follows. A reform of pollution policy will typically raise pollution taxes. This is a relative price change, and in response, some industries will contract while others will expand. Since the pollution-damage-intensive industries will be hardest hit by the pollution reform, they will be the most likely to contract. This is desirable from the perspective of pollution policy, but will have a spillover effect on the trade distortion. Whether the spillover effect is positive or negative depends on whether trade policy results in too much or too little output in the affected sector. If industries which are pollution damage intensive are also subject to protection from imports, then the initial output of these industries is too high from the perspective of the trade distortion, and hence the spillover effect is positive: the pollution reform helps by partially correcting the trade distortion.

An alternative sufficient condition for pollution reform can be developed which allows for the possibility that a uniform reform of pollution distortions could have a negative spillover effect on the trade distortion. In this case, the direction of reform must be adjusted to take into account the trade distortion.

PROPOSITION 4. *Assume stability (i.e., $1 - t'm > 0$) and that G_{ss} is of full rank. Define*

$$\sigma(s)' = E_z' - t'E_{qz} - t'G_{qs}(G_{ss})^{-1}. \tag{11}$$

Then an equiproportionate movement of pollution taxes toward the vector $\sigma(s)$ will not reduce welfare.

Proof. Letting $ds = [\sigma(s) - s]\,d\lambda$, with $d\lambda > 0$, we can write (10) as

$$E_u\,du(1 - t'm) = [\sigma(s) - s]'G_{ss}[\sigma(s) - s]\,d\lambda \geq 0,$$

since G_{ss} is positive semi-definite. □

To interpret the direction of the reform, note that since $dz = G_{ss}\,ds$, we can, with a slight abuse of notation, write (11) as

$$\sigma(s)' = E_z' - t'(\partial M/\partial z),$$

where M is the compensated net import vector, and the change in z is to be interpreted as that induced by the pollution tax changes. If there were no tariffs, then $\sigma = E_z$, and the difference between direct marginal damage and pollution taxes indicates the desired direction of reform. In the presence of tariffs, this direction must be adjusted to compensate for the spillover effect on the tariff distortion. From Eq. (4), the change in tariff revenue is a measure of the welfare effects of any induced changes in imports. Hence, in the above, the direction of reform is adjusted by the term $t'(\partial M/\partial z)$, which measures the effects of increases

[18]These conditions are based on reductions in δ_z, which takes into account the consumption effects of the tariff distortion. An alternative approach is to ask under what conditions uniform reductions in $E_z - s$ will improve welfare. The attractiveness of this approach is that the pollution taxes are adjusted toward the direct marginal damage. In this case, a sufficient condition for a welfare improvement is that $t'(\partial M/\partial s)(E_z - s) > 0$, where M is the compensated net import vector. Note that if $t'(\partial M/\partial s_i) > 0$, then an increase in the tax on pollutant i results in an increase in tariff revenue, which mitigates the trade distortion (imports are simulated). Hence, if pollution taxes are initially below marginal damage, a sufficient condition for welfare to improve if they are increased in proportion to $E_z - s$ is that tariff revenue also increases.

in the levels of pollutants on aggregate tariff revenue. If a reduction in the level of pollutant i tends to reduce tariff revenue, then $t'(\partial M/\partial z_i) > 0$, and hence $\sigma_i < E_{z_i}$. On the other hand, if a reduction in pollutant j stimulates tariff revenue, we have $\sigma_j > E_{z_j}$. Thus the direction of pollution tax reform is adjusted to lessen any adverse effects on the level of imports in the protected sector and to reinforce any positive effects.

4. REFORM OF QUANTITATIVE RESTRICTIONS ON TRADE AND POLLUTION

4.1. *The Model*

Governments frequently use quantitative restrictions to regulate trade and pollution. Since a quota-constrained economy will respond quite differently to exogenous changes than will an economy subject to taxes and subsidies, it is important to extend our analysis to quota regimes. Corden and Falvey [5] and Falvey [10] have previously investigated the reform of economies subject to both tariffs and import quotas; this section extends their analysis to consider economies that have pollution distortions as well as trade distortions.

There are a number of possible types of regimes: both pollution and trade could be regulated only with quotas, or various combinations of taxes and quotas could be used. I begin by setting up a framework which can be used to analyze mixed regimes where some pollutants are controlled by quotas, while others are subject to taxes (which may be zero). Trade may also be regulated by taxes or quotas. This framework will then be used to study some special cases which highlight the differences between taxes and quotas.

Relabel pollutants so that z^R is the vector of pollutants regulated by quotas, and z^T is the vector of pollutants regulated by taxes s^T. I assume that pollution permits are marketable; the government prints a fixed supply z^R of permits, and the market determines a price s^R for the permits. Moreover, I assume that the pollution quotas represent a binding constraint on the private sector.

It is useful to redefine the GNP function as follows to reflect the pollution quota constraint. Profit-maximizing behavior by individual firms will result in the private sector maximizing GNP subject to the quota constraint on pollutants:

$$G(1, q, z^R, s^T, v) = \max_{\{y, z^T\}} \left\{ y_0 + q'y - s^{T\prime}z^T \text{ s.t. } (y_0, y, z^R, z^T) \in T(v) \right\}.$$

Note that s^R can be obtained as $s^R = \partial G/\partial z^R$. Equilibrium is then given by

$$E(1, q, z^R, z^T, u) = G(1, q, z^R, s^T, v) + s^{T\prime}z^T + t'M, \quad (12)$$

$$M = E_q - G_q, \quad (13)$$

$$z^T = -G_T, \quad (14)$$

$$t = q - p, \quad (15)$$

where G_T denotes differentiation with respect to s^T, etc. Equations (12)–(14) have the same meaning as in Section 2, with the exception of the interpretation of the vector t. If good i is subject to a trade tax, then t_i is the exogenous tax, net imports M_i are determined endogenously by (13), and the domestic price q_i is given by the world price plus the tax as in (15). On the other hand, if good j is subject to a binding import quota M_j, then M_j is exogenous, the domestic price q_j is determined endogenously by (13), and the endogenous wedge t_j between the domestic and world price is given by (15). Note that if there is neither a tax nor a quota on trade in good j, then $t_j = 0$.

4.2. *Preliminary Results*

In this subsection, I investigate some special cases which highlight the difference between reform in economies regulated by taxes and those subject to quotas.

First, let us suppose that the government uses *only* quantitative instruments for both trade and pollution regulation, and moreover suppose that all *all* pollution is subject to binding quotas. Imports may or may not be restricted. In this case, totally differentiating (12) yields

$$E_u\, du = -\left[E_{\mathrm{R}} - s^{\mathrm{R}}\right]' dz^{\mathrm{R}} + t'\, dM, \tag{16}$$

which is the same as (4), except that in this case our control variables are z and those components of M for which $q_i \neq p_i$, whereas in (4), z and M could be controlled only indirectly by taxes. This is a crucial difference, since (16) implies that any small reduction in any distortion will improve welfare.

PROPOSITION 5. *Suppose that the government uses* only *quantitative instruments for both international trade and pollution regulation, and moreover suppose that all* all *pollution is subject to binding quotas. Then a small reduction in any distortion brought about by adjusting a binding quota will improve welfare.*

Proof. The proof follows directly from (16). □

Thus, the government can increase welfare by relaxing any binding quota on trade, or by reducing the supply of permits for any pollutant for which the marginal external damage is in excess of the pollution permit price. This is a simple generalization of a result due to Corden and Falvey [5], who showed that in an economy subject to quantitative restrictions on international trade, a small relaxation of any binding quota on trade will improve welfare.

Piecemeal reform is feasible in a fully quota-constrained economy because the quotas prevent spillovers of distortions. In a tax regime, a tax change designed to reduce one type of pollutant can have the undesirable side effect of increasing the output of another type of pollutant, or of reducing imports further below their first-best level, but in a quota regime, these side effects are prevented from occurring because of the quotas.

A slightly different result can be obtained if tariffs, instead of quotas, are used to restrict trade. Suppose now that all pollution is regulated with binding quotas (which need not be optimal), while all trade is regulated with trade taxes. Then since changes in trade policy will be prevented by pollution quotas from having spillover effects on the pollution distortions, we have the following.

PROPOSITION 6. *Suppose that all pollutants are controlled with binding quotas, and that all trade barriers take the form of trade taxes. Assume stability* ($1 - t'm > 0$). *Then an equiproportionate reduction of trade taxes will not reduce welfare.*

Proof. Let $dt = -t\,d\lambda$, where λ is a scalar with $d\lambda > 0$. The change in imports induced by the tariff change is $dM = -H_{qq}\,dq + E_{qu}\,du$. Hence, $E_u\,du(1 - t'm) = -t'H_{qq}t\,d\lambda \geq 0$, since H_{qq} is positive semidefinite. □

Thus, trade policy can be reformed independently of pollution policy, provided that all pollutants are covered by quotas. However, whereas in a fully quota-constrained economy, reducing any distortion would improve welfare, this is no longer true in the mixed regime of Proposition 6. Reducing an arbitrary tariff may lower welfare, because of spillover effects to other trade distortions. Hence, a coordinated reform of trade distortions is necessary to ensure welfare improvement; a uniform reduction of tariffs is sufficient to accomplish this.

4.3. Mixed Regimes

The preceding two results illustrate that, in principle, policy reform is easier in a quota regime than in a tax regime. Note, however, that in both cases, we require that *all* pollutants be constrained by quotas. In practice, many pollutants are likely to be unregulated, in which case the above argument fails, since a reduction in the level of a regulated pollutant can stimulate the output of an unregulated pollutant. Hence, in this section, I turn to the study of mixed regimes. To avoid producing a lengthy catalogue of all the possible cases, I will focus on regimes where only tariffs are used as instruments of trade policy, but where both taxes and quotas are used for pollution policy. A similar analysis could be carried out for mixed trade policy regimes.

An equation which links welfare changes to policy changes [i.e., the analogue to Eq. (7)] can be obtained by totally differentiating (12)–(14) to obtain

$$E_u\,du(1 - t'm) = -\left[\delta_{\mathrm{R}} - \delta_{\mathrm{T}}G_{\mathrm{TR}} + t'G_{q\mathrm{R}}\right]dz^{\mathrm{R}} + \left[\delta_{\mathrm{T}}G_{\mathrm{TT}} - tG_{q\mathrm{T}}\right]ds^{\mathrm{T}} + \left[\delta_{\mathrm{T}}G_{\mathrm{T}q} - t'H_{qq}\right]dt, \qquad (17)$$

where $\delta_{\mathrm{R}} \equiv E'_{\mathrm{R}} - t'E_{q\mathrm{R}} - s^{\mathrm{R}'}$ and $\delta_{\mathrm{T}} \equiv E'_{\mathrm{T}} - t'E_{q\mathrm{T}} - s^{\mathrm{T}'}$. Note that δ_{R} and δ_{T} have the same interpretation as in Section 3; they are measures of the gap between the marginal external damage to consumers due to an increase in pollution and the price the firm pays for producing an extra unit of pollution.

For clarity, let us initially suppose that there is no trade distortion and hence focus on the pollution distortions. In this case, (17) becomes

$$E_u\,du = -\left[\left(E'_{\mathrm{R}} - s^{\mathrm{R}'}\right) - \left(E'_{\mathrm{T}} - s^{\mathrm{T}}\right)G_{\mathrm{TR}}\right]dz^{\mathrm{R}} + \left[\left(E'_{\mathrm{T}} - s^{\mathrm{T}}\right)G_{\mathrm{TT}}\right]ds^{\mathrm{T}}. \qquad (18)$$

Note that in the present framework, pollutants have been divided into two groups: those controlled by quotas and those either unregulated or subject to taxes. If instead we had a pure tax regime, we could also divide pollutants into two groups (say, group A and group B) and consider reforming taxes in only one group. In this case there would be two spillover effects to consider: within and across groups. Reducing a tax on a pollutant in group A will affect the level of other pollutants in group A, as well as the level of pollutants in group B.

In contrast, in our mixed tax and quota regimes, some of these spillover effects are contained by quotas. As a first indication of this, note from (18) that reforms in the tax sector (i.e., changes in s^{T} with $dz^{\mathrm{R}} = 0$) must take into account intra-group spillovers (induced changes in levels of other pollutants covered by taxes), but not inter-group spillovers, since the pollution quotas prevent spillovers into the quota sector. Thus, reform of the tax sector can be carried out independently of the quota sector. Hence, we have:

PROPOSITION 7. *Suppose there are no trade distortions and that some pollutants are controlled with binding quotas, while others are controlled with taxes (which may be zero). Then an equiproportionate movement of all pollution taxes toward direct marginal damage will not reduce welfare.*

Proof. In (18), let $dz^{\mathrm{R}} = 0$, and let $ds^{\mathrm{T}} = (E'_{\mathrm{T}} - s^{\mathrm{T}})\,d\lambda$, with $d\lambda$ a positive scalar. □

On the other hand, note from (18) that reforms of the quota sector cannot be carried out without reference to the effect on the taxed (or possibly unregulated) sector. The coefficient of dz^{R} has two terms: the first is the direct effect of a quota reform on the pollution damage in the quota sector, while the second term captures the effects of reform of a pollution quota on pollution levels in the taxed sector. Thus, firms might respond to a tightening up of pollution quotas by increasing their output of a pollutant regulated with a tax. As noted above, a similar spillover effect occurs in a pure tax regime; the mixed regime differs in that the spillovers are confined to those pollutants regulated by taxes. Hence, using (18), we have:

PROPOSITION 8. *Suppose that there are no trade distortions, and that some pollutants are controlled with binding quotas, while others are controlled with taxes (which may be zero). Then if*

$$E_{\mathrm{R}_i} + \left(E_{\mathrm{T}} - s^{\mathrm{T}}\right)\left(\partial z^{\mathrm{T}}/\partial z_i^{\mathrm{R}}\right) - s_i^{\mathrm{R}} > 0, \tag{19}$$

tightening up the quota on pollutant i will increase welfare.

In this case, intra-group spillovers do not occur, but inter-group spillovers do. Condition (19) compares the existing price of a pollution permit with the marginal damage to the economy of an increase in the level of pollutant i. This has two components: the damage directly caused by pollutant i and the effects of induced changes in the levels of pollutants in the taxed sector, weighted by the distortions in that sector. The presence of quotas allows us to disregard other pollutants constrained by quotas.

Let us now return to the more general case, where there are tariff distortions as well as pollution distortions. The results have much the same character as those outlined above: spillover effects of reform must be taken into account, but the presence of quotas narrows the range of possible spillover effects and thus to some extent reduces the complexity of the reform problem. First, consider the reform of pollution taxes.

PROPOSITION 9. *Assume stability (i.e., $1 - t'm > 0$). Suppose (i) that some pollutants are controlled with binding quotas, while others are controlled with taxes (which may be zero); (ii) the only trade barriers are import tariffs and/or export subsidies; and (iii) all industries which are subject to trade protection are damage* *intensive with respect to pollutants covered by taxes. Then a small reduction in pollution taxes proportional to the pollution distortion vector* δ_T *will not reduce welfare.*

Proof. In (17), set $dz^R = 0$, $dt = 0$, and $ds^T = \delta_T\, d\lambda$, where λ is a scalar and $d\lambda > 0$. □

This result is similar to Proposition 3, which applies when taxes are the only instrument of pollution control. However, in that case, a reform of all pollution distortions was required, and one had to check for pollution damage intensity with respect to all pollutants. When quotas are present, one can reform the tax sector independently of the quota sector: taxes can be adjusted without also adjusting quotas, and pollution damage intensity must be checked only with respect to those pollutants subject to taxes. The intuition is essentially the same as above. The reform of pollution taxes induces two types of spillover effects: intra-group spillover effects on pollution (all pollutants subject to taxes or which are unregulated are potentially affected) and spillover effects onto the trade distortion. However, because of the pollution quotas, there are no inter-group spillover effects on pollution, and hence the tax sector can be reformed independently of the quota sector.[19]

Let us now turn to quota reform [i.e., set $ds^T = dt = 0$ in (17)]. In this case, if we assume stability, a sufficient condition for tightening up the quota on pollutant i to increase welfare is

$$\delta_{R_i} + t'G_{qR_i} - \delta_T G_{TR_i} > 0, \tag{20}$$

which can also be written as

$$\partial E/\partial z_i^R - t'(\partial M/\partial z_i^R) + \delta_T(\partial z^T/\partial z_i^R) > s_i^R, \tag{21}$$

where M is the compensated net import demand vector. As in the case of pollution taxes, a reform of pollution policy has an effect on the trade distortion, which is captured in (21) by the effect of the pollution reform on net trade tax revenue. In addition, there is an inter-group spillover effect on pollution, captured by the term $\delta_T(\partial z^T/\partial z_i^R)$, which measures the effect of a change in pollution quotas on the damage caused by induced changes in the levels of those pollutants controlled by taxes. However, there is no intra-group spillover effect, since the levels of other pollutants in the quota sector are constrained by the quotas.

Finally, let us consider the reform of trade policy in the presence of pollution quotas. The following result illustrates the difference between the pure tax regime and the mixed regime.

PROPOSITION 10. *Assume stability (i.e.,* $1 - t'm > 0$*). Suppose (i) that some pollutants are controlled with binding quotas, while others are controlled with taxes (which may be zero); (ii) the only trade barriers are import tariffs and/or export subsidies; and (iii) all industries which are subject to trade protection are damage*

[19]One can also derive an analogue to Proposition 4; however, this is straightforward and left to the reader.

intensive with respect to pollutants covered by taxes. Then a small equiproportionate reduction in trade taxes and subsidies will not reduce welfare.

Proof. In (17), set $ds^{\mathrm{T}} = dz^{\mathrm{R}} = 0$ and $dt = -t\,d\lambda$, where λ is a scalar and $d\lambda > 0$. □

This is the same result as that obtained in Proposition 1 for the pure tax regime, except that pollution damage intensity with respect to those pollutants controlled by quotas is not relevant. Uniform tariff reductions do not necessarily improve welfare since they can affect pollution levels. However, those pollutants regulated with binding quotas will be unaffected by tariff reductions, and hence the policy-maker need be concerned only with the response of those pollutants regulated by taxes. Thus, the presence of pollution quotas simplifies the tariff reform problem by reducing the dimension of the spillover problem. Note that if *all* pollutants were governed by binding pollution quotas, then from Proposition 5, uniform tariff reductions would improve welfare: the pollution distortions could be ignored in small tariff reforms.

5. POLLUTION REFORM IN THE PRESENCE OF INTERNATIONAL FACTOR MOBILITY

One of the concerns sometimes raised about pollution regulation in an open economy is that increases in pollution control may discourage foreign investment and that this may have a negative effect on welfare. I investigate this issue briefly in this section by considering changes in pollution taxes in an economy where a subset of the primary factors of production is freely mobile internationally. To focus on the factor mobility issue, I assume that the only distortions in the economy arise from pollution: there are no trade taxes or taxes on factor mobility.

The vector of primary factors is now written as (v, k), where the factors v are not mobile internationally, while the factors k are freely mobile internationally. Let k^0 be the endowment of these factors owned by agents in the home country, and let k be the vector of these types of factors employed in the home country. Then $(k - k^0)$ is the vector of net foreign investment in the home country: positive components correspond to foreign investment in the home country, and negative components correspond to domestically owned factors which are invested in other countries. The vector of rates of return on mobile factors, r, is assumed to be fixed in international markets.

The equilibrium condition for the country is given by

$$E(1, p, z, u) = G(1, p, s, v, k) - r'(k - k^0) + s'z, \tag{22}$$

$$r = G_k(p, s, v, k), \tag{23}$$

$$z = -G_s(p, s, v, k), \tag{24}$$

where $r(k - k^0)$ is net repatriation of factor earnings to foreigners. Let us now consider the effects of a change in the level of pollution taxes. Totally differentiating (22) yields

$$E_u\,du = (s - E_z)'\,dz. \tag{25}$$

That is, changes in pollution policy affect welfare only through their effect on pollution, since that is the only distortion that the economy faces.

From (24), we have

$$dz = -[G_{ss}\,ds + G_{sk}\,dk], \tag{26}$$

and using (23), we have, if G_{kk} is invertible,

$$dk = -(G_{kk})^{-1}G_{ks}\,ds. \tag{27}$$

Substituting (26) and (27) into (25) yields

$$E_u\,du = (E_z - s)'G_{ss}\,ds - (E_z - s)'G_{sk}(G_{kk})^{-1}G_{ks}\,ds. \tag{28}$$

Hence, if we let $ds = (E_z - s)\,d\lambda$, we have $du/d\lambda \geq 0$, since G_{ss} is positive semidefinite and G_{kk} is negative semidefinite (G is concave in k). Thus, equiproportionate reductions in the gap between pollution taxes and the marginal external damage caused by pollution are a sufficient condition for a non-welfare-reducing policy reform in the presence of international factor mobility. Moreover, note that the first term in (28) corresponds to the welfare improvement before factors move, while the second term measures the welfare effect due to the induced factor mobility, which may involve an exodus of foreign capital. Since both of these terms are non-negative for an equiproportionate reform, we have the following result:[20]

PROPOSITION 11. *Assume that G_{kk} is non-singular and compare two equilibria which have identical initial allocations of the factors k and v. Then the gains from a small equiproportionate reform of pollution policy are at least as large when the vector of factors k are freely mobile internationally as when such factor mobility is prohibited.*

That is, if pollution taxes are initially too low, the welfare gains from a small increase in pollution taxes will typically be larger when factors are freely mobile internationally than when factors cannot move. This is because the supply response of the economy is more elastic when factors are mobile. Hence, a given change in taxes will result in a larger drop in pollution (and thus yield more benefits) when factors are mobile. Of course, the reverse is also true: a small reduction in pollution taxes which exacerbates the pollution distortion will have a larger negative effect on the economy when factors are mobile than when they are not. In this sense, one can argue that globalization of the world economy tends to amplify

[20] Neary and Ruane [18] have obtained a similar result in analyzing the effects of increases in tariff distortions in the presence of factor mobility. They show that small increases in tariffs are more damaging in the presence of freely mobile foreign capital than in the absence of such mobility.

the mistakes of government policy: the negative consequences of neglecting pollution policy are likely to be larger as capital mobility increases.[21]

6. CONCLUSIONS AND IMPLICATIONS FOR PUBLIC POLICY

This paper examines an economy which has many distortions. As is well known from the second-best literature, policy reform in such economies is complex: the simple rules which emerge from one-distortion models are not helpful. There is a danger that second-best analysis can appear nihilistic; that is not the intention of this paper. Rather, the central theme is that if pollution and trade distortions are both important, then linkages between them cannot be ignored, and policy analysts must confront the spillover effects that will result from piecemeal reform.

Ideally, reforms of trade policy and pollution policy should be coordinated. In the economy examined in this paper, an equiproportionate reform of all distortions will typically improve welfare. If this is not feasible, then the critical issue is the magnitude and direction of the spillover effects. This paper identifies two features which may be useful in assessing spillover effects: the mix between taxes and quotas as instruments of regulation and the notion of pollution damage intensity.

Quotas tend to inhibit spillover effects. In the absence of quotas, a policy which succeeds in reducing the level of one pollutant can backfire if it stimulates the production of some other pollutant. If a quota is place, then this feedback effect need not occur, and hence the policymaker can be more confident that the policy reform will not have an unintended side effect. The paper explores a number of cases where the presence of quotas can be exploited to engage in piecemeal reform.

When spillovers are not contained by quotas, the concept of pollution damage intensity can provide some guidance. Typically trade policy reforms will lead to a contraction of output in protected sectors and an expansion of output in the rest of the economy. The issue for the policymaker is whether or not this change in the pattern of production will exacerbate pollution distortions. As shown in Propositions 1 and 10, if the protected sectors are pollution damage intensive with respect to those pollutants not constrained by quotas, then the spillover effect will

[21] Instead of assuming that some factors are freely mobile, one can also consider the effects of exogenous increases in foreign investment. That is, suppose that the level of foreign-owned factors in the economy, k^*, is exogenous and that r is determined endogenously in the home economy, given the domestic and foreign supply of factors. Then one can show

$$E_u\, du = (E_z - s)' G_{sk}\, dk^* - k^{*\prime} G_{kk}\, dk^*.$$

The first term is the effect of increased foreign investment on the pollution distortion, and the second term is the factoral terms of trade effect. Both terms are ambiguous in sign in general. However, for equiproportionate increases in foreign investment (i.e., $dk^* = k^*\, d\lambda$), the factoral terms of trade can never worsen, so the second term is non-negative. However, the first term will be negative if pollution taxes are too low and if the foreign-owned factors are used relatively intensively by pollution-intensive industries. In a two-good (y_1 and y_2), two-factor (capital and labor) Heckscher–Ohlin model, with one pollutant whose level is given by $z = Z(y_1, y_2)$, if the capital intensive industry is also relatively pollution intensive, a small amount of foreign investment, starting from point $k^* = 0$, will reduce welfare if the pollution tax is too low. The argument is the same as that used to demonstrate that foreign investment can be immiserizing in the presence of tariff distortions (Brecher and Diaz-Alejandro [4]).

reinforce the benefits of reducing the trade distortions. That is, a trade policy which protects industries which are also very pollution damage intensive is a particularly bad policy, and one can feel fairly confident that a reform of such a policy will not backfire. On the other hand, if the unprotected sector of the economy is pollution damage intensive, then trade policy reform will stimulate pollution and the case for liberalizing trade is considerably weaker, unless pollution policy can also be reformed.

Another implication of the paper is that the globalization of international capital markets makes the case for control of pollution externalities more compelling. Although increased international factor mobility does increase the output effects of a change in pollution policy, it also magnifies the external damage arising from pollution taxes which are too low. Thus, although the relation between trade and pollution policy is complex, the cost of doing nothing will likely increase as markets become more integrated.

This paper has focused on a small open economy. An important issue which is not addressed here is the role of international spillovers. In a multi-country world, reform of pollution or trade policy in one country can affect pollution and trade distortions in another country. This raises many issues regarding the extent to which treaties on trade policy should be linked to treaties on environmental policy. The analysis of such issues should be a fruitful area for future research.

APPENDIX: LIST OF SYMBOLS

v Vector of primary factors of production
M Number of primary factors
N_g Goods are indexed $0, \ldots, N_g$
N_p Pollutants are indexed $1, \ldots, N_p$
c Consumption vector for goods $1, \ldots, N_g$
y Output vector for goods $1, \ldots, N_g$
c_0 Consumption of the numeraire good
y_0 Output of the numeraire good
z Vector of pollutants
T Set of feasible output and pollution vectors (i.e., the technology set)
p World price vector for goods $1, \ldots, N_g$
q Domestic price vector for goods $1, \ldots, N_g$
t Either the vector of trade taxes or subsidies or, if trade quotas are imposed, the endogenous gap between domestic and world prices; in either case, it is equal to $q - p$
s Vector of pollution taxes
u Utility
E Expenditure function
G GNP function
M Net import vector
m Vector of marginal propensities to consume
H_{qq} $G_{qq} - E_{qq}$
δ_z Pollution distortion vector
λ A scale factor

τ A vector of local second-best tariff targets
σ A vector of local second-best pollution tax targets
z^{R} Vector of pollutants controlled by binding quotas
s^{R} Price of pollution permits for pollutants z^{R}
z^{T} Vector of pollutants controlled by taxes
s^{T} Vector of pollution taxes for pollutants z^{T}
δ_{R} Pollution distortion vector for pollutants controlled by quotas
δ_{T} Pollution distortion vector for pollutants controlled by taxes
k Vector of internationally mobile factors currently employed in home country
k^0 Home's endowment of factors which are internationally mobile
r Vector of rates of return on internationally mobile factors

REFERENCES

1. A. J. Auerbach, The theory of excess burden and optimal taxation, *in* "Handbook of Public Economics" (A. J. Auerbach and M. Feldstein, Eds.), Vol. 1, North-Holland, Amsterdam (1985).
2. W. J. Baumol and and W. E. Oates, "The Theory of Environmental Policy," Cambridge Univ. Press, Cambridge (1988).
3. J. Bhagwati, The generalized theory of distortions and welfare, *in* "Trade, Balance of Payments, and Growth" (J. N. Bhagwati *et al.*, Eds.) North-Holland, Amsterdam (1971).
4. R. A. Brecher and C. Diaz-Alejandro, Tariffs, foreign capital and immiserizing growth, *J. Internat. Econom.* **7**, 317–322 (1977).
5. W. M. Corden and R. E. Falvey, Quotas and the second best, *Econom. Lett.* **18**, 67–70 (1985).
6. W. E. Diewert, A. H. Turunen-Red, and A. D. Woodland, Productivity- and Pareto-improving changes in taxes and tariffs, *Rev. Econom. Stud.* **56**, 199–216 (1989).
7. A. K. Dixit, Welfare effects of tax and price changes, *J. Public Econom.* **4**, 103–123 (1975).
8. A. K. Dixit, Tax policy in open economies, *in* "Handbook of Public Economics" (A. J. Auerbach and M. Feldstein, Eds.), Vol. 1, North-Holland, Amsterdam (1985).
9. A. K. Dixit and V. Norman, "Theory of International Trade," Cambridge Univ. Press, Cambridge (1980).
10. R. E. Falvey, Tariffs, quotas, and piecemeal policy reform, *J. Internat. Econom.* **25**, 177–183 (1988).
11. T. Hatta, A recommendation for a better tariff structure, *Econometrica* **45**, 1859–1869 (1977).
12. K. Krutilla, Environmental regulation in an open economy, *J. Environ. Econom. Management* **20**, 127–142 (1991).
13. P. J. Lloyd, A more general theory of price distortions in open economies, *J. Internat. Econom.* **4**, 365–386 (1974).
14. J. R. Markusen, International externalities and optimal tax structures, *J. Internat. Econom.* **5**, 15–29 (1975).
15. J. R. Markusen, E. Morey, and N. Olewiler, Optimal pollution taxes when market structure and plant location are endogenous, *J. Environ. Econom. Management* **24**, 69–86 (1993).
16. M. McGuire, Regulation, factor rewards, and international trade, *J. Public Econom.* **17**, 335–354 (1982).
17. J. D. Merrifield, The impact of selected abatement strategies on transnational pollution, the terms of trade, and factor rewards: A general equilibrium approach, *J. Environ. Econom. Management* **15**, 259–284 (1988).
18. P. Neary and F. Ruane, International capital mobility, shadow prices, and the cost of protection, *Internat. Econom. Rev.* **29**, 571–585 (1988).
19. R. Pethig, Pollution, welfare, and environmental policy in the theory of comparative advantage, *J. Environ. Econom. Management* **2**, 160–169 (1976).
20. H. Siebert, J. Eichberger, R. Gronych, and R. Pethig, "Trade and Environment: A Theoretical Enquiry," Elsevier, Amsterdam (1980).
21. N. Vousden, "The Economics of Trade Protection," Cambridge Univ. Press, Cambridge (1990).
22. A. D. Woodland, "International Trade and Resource Allocation," North-Holland, Amsterdam (1982).

[6]

Journal of Public Economics 54 (1994) 325–338. North-Holland

Strategic environmental policy and international trade

Scott Barrett*

Faculty of Economics, London Business School, Sussex Place, Regent's Park, London NW1 4SA, UK and Centre for Social and Economic Research on the Global Environment, University College London, Gower Street, London WC1E 6BT, UK

Received April 1992, final version received September 1992

This paper demonstrates that governments may have incentives to impose weak environmental standards on industries that compete for business in imperfectly competitive international markets, where 'weak' means that the marginal cost of abatement is less than the marginal damage from pollution. However, such an intervention is not as efficient as an export or R&D subsidy in improving competitiveness, and depending on the form of competition and market structure, it may instead be optimal for governments to impose strong environmental standards, where 'strong' means that the marginal cost of abatement exceeds the marginal environmental damage.

> The existence of less strict environmental standards in a lower income country ... is not a sufficient basis for claiming that the environmental standards are 'too low' or that the country is manipulating its environmental standards in order to improve the competitiveness of its producers. To substantiate such a claim, it would be necessary at the very least to demonstrate that the standards are even lower than would be expected on the basis of such factors as the level of per capita income and the characteristics of the physical environment.
>
> Clearly, that would be very difficult to do. Moreover, the charge might also be aimed at highly developed countries in which stringent environmental standards may have been adopted in some areas but where, because of competitiveness considerations, governments have shied away from high standards in others. [GATT (1992, p. 29)].

1. Introduction

Concern is growing that environmental policy may not only interfere with free trade, but in some instances may be purposefully designed to confer competitive advantage upon the home country industry at the expense of

Correspondence to: Scott Barrett, Associate Professor, Faculty of Economics, London Business School, Sussex Place, Regent's Park, London NW1 4SA, UK.

*I am grateful to Paul Geroski, Michael Hoel, David Pearce, Candice Stevens and two anonymous reviewers for commenting on an earlier version of this paper.

SSDI 0047-2727(93)01382-K

competitive disadvantage abroad.[1] As an example, a recent article appearing in the European edition of the *Wall Street Journal* (8 July 1991), reports that U.S. environmental policy, as devised by the Environmental Protection Agency, has in some instances been modified to accommodate concerns expressed by the White House Council on Competitiveness. Such interventions are potentially worrying, not only because they may worsen environmental quality, but also because they cannot be challenged under the GATT,[2] and hence may inspire offended countries to retaliate by changing their standards or by imposing countervailing duties on imports.[3]

Are the incentives to distort environmental standards for reasons of competitiveness quantitatively important? They may be in some cases,[4] but recent empirical work is ambivalent on the related question of whether sectoral trade flows are affected by environmental standards. Low and Yeats (1992) find that environmentally 'dirty' industries have migrated over the last two decades towards lower income countries where environmental standards are weaker. Lucas et al. (1992) find that stricter regulation of pollution-intensive production in the OECD countries 'has led to significant locational displacement, with consequent acceleration of industrial pollution intensity in developing countries'. However, Grossman and Krueger (1992) find that the sectoral pattern of trade between the United States and Mexico has not been influenced by pollution abatement costs in U.S. industry. Several earlier studies support the view that the link between trade flows and environmental standards is weak, or non-existent [Dean (1992)].

Recent theoretical papers consider related questions of strategy.[5] Ulph (1992), using a three-stage model in which governments choose environmental policies (to meet a fixed environmental target) in the first stage and firms choose capital stocks and output levels in the second and third stages, shows that if governments behave strategically, they will want to impose quantity

[1]For discussions of this issue, see Grimmett (1991), Reistein (1991), Whalley (1991), Anderson and Blackhurst (1992), GATT (1992), Low (1992), Pearce (1992) and *The Economist* (30 May 1992).

[2]In the words of the GATT (1992, p. 23): 'Generally speaking, a country can do anything to imports or exports that it does to its own products, and it can do anything it considers necessary to its own production processes'.

[3]It is this last possibility that worries the GATT most. Using uncharacteristically strong language, the GATT (1992, p. 30) argues: 'To allow each contracting party unilaterally to impose special duties against whatever it objects to among domestic policies of other contracting parties would risk an eventual descent into chaotic trade conditions similar to those that plagued the 1930s'.

[4]Grossman and Krueger (1992, p. 22) cite a survey by the U.S. General Accounting Office, 'suggesting that a few American furniture manufacturers may have moved their operations to Mexico in response to the State of California's tightening of air pollution control standards for paint coatings and solvents'.

[5]The literature on trade and the environment is large, and growing. For recent surveys, see Cropper and Oates (1992) and Dean (1992).

standards rather than pollution taxes [see also Rauscher (1991)]. The reason, roughly, is that quantity standards allow firms to commit to producing lower output levels, and hence to earn higher profits.[6] Markusen et al. (1992) also employ a stage game to consider whether governments might want to distort their environmental policies in order to influence the location decision of a single polluting firm. They show that governments may compete by weakening environmental policy in order to attract investment, or by strengthening policy in order to induce the firm to locate elsewhere. Finally, Copeland (1990a), again employing a stage game, shows that countries may wish to 'overinvest' or 'underinvest' in activities that affect the costs and benefits of exploiting a shared resource (a fishery). For example, if enhancement of fish stocks by one country lowers harvesting costs more for its fishermen than its rivals' fishermen, then the effect of the investment may be to decrease harvesting effort by rivals, to the benefit of the home country. In a related paper, Copeland (1990b) shows that a similar result can be obtained for transboundary pollution when governments choose R&D in pollution control as well as pollution levels.[7]

This paper considers the strategic role of environmental policy from a different perspective. Unlike Ulph (1992), this paper is not concerned with the choice of policy instrument, and solves endogenously for the environmental target. Unlike Markusen et al. (1992), this paper is not concerned with the location decisions of firms, but with the competitiveness of existing industries (as determined by their ability to commit to output and price levels). Unlike Copeland (1990a, b), in this paper the interdependence that exists between countries is transmitted not through a shared resource (here, environmental damage is strictly local), but through competition in international markets. Unlike all of the above papers, this one also considers alternative market structures and alternative forms of industry competition.

The basic model employed is a stage game involving two governments and their respective industries, which sell all their output in a third market. Governments move first by choosing environmental standards for their own firms. Firms take these standards as given and compete by choosing either output levels or prices. It is assumed that environmental damage is local, and that the governments of consumer countries have no means of influencing

[6]Copeland (1992) provides a richer model of the strategic implications of taxes versus standards under various forms of imperfect competition, but does not consider the international dimension. Markusen et al. (1991) analyze the effect of taxes on the location decisions of firms under imperfect competition.

[7]Oates and Schwab (1988) also find that it may be optimal for governments to set 'weak' or 'strong' standards, but not for strategic reasons. Employing public choice theory, they show that government officials may want to impose weak environmental standards in order to attract capital investment. Assuming a median-voter rule and a heterogeneous population, environmental standards could be either weak or strong, depending on whether the majority of the population preferred to tax or subsidize capital.

environmental standards in producer countries. This last assumption is entirely consistent with the GATT [see Pearce (1992)].

The paper shows that if the domestic industry is a monopoly, the foreign industry is imperfectly competitive, and industrial competition is Cournot, then the domestic government has an incentive to set a weak environmental standard, where 'weak' means that the marginal cost of abatement is less than the marginal damage from pollution. However, this conclusion hinges on the inability of the domestic firm to act like a Stackelberg leader, and on the inability of the domestic government to employ industrial policy for the same strategic purpose. What is more, if the domestic industry is an oligopoly, then the incentive to impose weak environmental standards is diminished, and it may even become attractive to impose strong environmental standards, where 'strong' means that marginal abatement costs exceed the associated marginal environmental damage. If firms compete in prices rather than quantities, then strategic considerations will favor strong standards, whatever the structure of the domestic industry. The conclusion that strategy may demand either weak or strong environmental standards is reminiscent of the results obtained by Copeland (1990a, b) and Markusen et al. (1992), but arises for quite different reasons.

These theoretical findings are as ambivalent as those appearing in the empirical literature. Taken together, they suggest that the incentives for governments to behave strategically in devising environmental policy are limited. Competitiveness may be more effectively enhanced by improving the efficiency of *non*-strategic environmental policy, which is exactly what economists have long argued [Cropper and Oates (1992)].

2. Unilateral strategic environmental policy

Denote the domestic firm's output by q^1 and the foreign firm's output by q^2, and let $C^i(q^i)$ be firm i's production cost function. Denoting derivatives by subscripts, assume $C^i_q > 0$. Total revenues are $R^i(q^1, q^2)$. Assuming that the two outputs are substitutes, $R^i_j < 0$. Abatement costs depend on the level of output and the emission standard, which is set by government. Denote the domestic emission standard by e^1 and the foreign standard by e^2. The abatement cost function for firm i is $A^i(q^i, e^i)$, with $A^i_q \geqq 0$, $A^i_e \leqq 0$, and $A^i_{qe} \leqq 0$. If the emission standards are binding, then all of these inequalities are likely to hold strictly. Assume that this is the case. Each firm chooses its output taking as given both the rival's output and the emission standard set by government. Formally, letting π^i denote firm i's profits, the following optimization problem is solved:

$$\max_{q^i} \pi^i = R^i(q^1, q^2) - C^i(q^i) - A^i(q^i, e^i). \tag{1}$$

The Nash equilibrium quantities, given emission standards e^i, are determined by

$$\pi_i^i = R_i^i - C_q^i - A_q^i = 0. \tag{2}$$

Second-order conditions for a maximum are

$$\pi_{ii}^i = R_{ii}^i - C_{qq}^i - A_{qq}^i < 0. \tag{3}$$

Also assume

$$R_{ij}^i < 0. \tag{4}$$

and

$$\pi_{11}^1 \pi_{22}^2 - \pi_{12}^1 \pi_{21}^2 > 0. \tag{5}$$

Conditions (4) ensure that the reaction functions are downward sloping. Condition (5) ensures stability.

The domestic and foreign governments choose their emission standards e^i so as to maximize their respective net benefits, NB^1 and NB^2. Recalling that firm i's output is not consumed within country i, the maximization problem may be stated formally as

$$\max_{e^i} NB^i = \pi^i(q^1, q^2, e^i) - D^i(e^i), \tag{6}$$

where $D^i(e^i)$ is the (purely local) environmental damage suffered by country i; $D_e^i \geqq 0$. If the emission standards are binding, it is likely that these inequalities will hold strictly. Assume that this is the case. The first-order conditions are

$$NB_e^i = -A_e^i - D_e^i = 0, \tag{7}$$

and the corresponding second-order conditions are

$$NB_{ee}^i = -A_{ee}^i - D_{ee}^i < 0. \tag{8}$$

Stability requires

$$NB_{ii}^i NB_{ee}^i - NB_{ie}^i NB_{ei}^i > 0 \tag{9}$$

$$NB_{ii}^i NB_{je}^j NB_{ej}^j + NB_{ij}^i NB_{ji}^j NB_{ee}^j - NB_{ii}^i NB_{jj}^j NB_{ee}^j > 0. \tag{10}$$

Eq. (7) can be rewritten as $\tilde{e}^i = \phi^i(q^i)$. Define these schedules as the *environmentally optimal emission standards* (EOSs). These standards obey the usual optimality rule in environmental economics: pollution is reduced to the level where the marginal damage caused by the pollution (D_e^i) just equals the marginal cost of abatement ($-A_e^i$). These schedules may vary depending on environmental assimilative capacities, incomes, preferences, and abatement costs.

The domestic firm can earn higher profits if it can commit to producing a higher level of output compared with the Nash equilibrium. While the firm cannot make such a commitment credible, its government may do so on its behalf by departing from the EOS. Suppose, then, that the domestic government solves (6) subject to (2) and eq. (7) for country 2. Then we have the first-order condition

$$\pi_1^1 dq^1/de^1 + \pi_2^1 (dq^2/dq^1)(dq^1/de^1) + NB_e^1 = 0. \tag{11}$$

Upon substitution, (11) can be written as $\bar{e}^1 = \xi^1(q^1)$. Define $\bar{e}^1$ as country 1's *strategically optimal emission standard* (SOS). We know that the domestic firm will set $\pi_1^1 = 0$. However, the second term in (11) may be positive, in which case the dometic government would want to choose an emission standard (for given q^1) at which the marginal damage of pollution exceeds the marginal cost of abatement. Proposition 1 establishes that this is indeed the case.

Proposition 1. The SOS is weaker than the EOS ($\bar{e}^1 > \tilde{e}^1$ for q^1 given).

Proof. By assumption, $R_2^1 < 0$; hence $\pi_2^1 < 0$. To sign dq^2/dq^1, totally differentiate (2) for firm 2 and (7) for country 2:

$$NB_{ee}^2 de^2 = -NB_{e2}^2 dq^2, \tag{12}$$

$$NB_{21}^2 dq^1 + NB_{22}^2 dq^2 + NB_{2e}^2 de^2 = 0. \tag{13}$$

Combining (12) and (13) and rearranging yields

$$dq^2/dq^1 = (-NB_{21}^2 NB_{ee}^2)/(NB_{22}^2 NB_{ee}^2 - NB_{2e}^2 NB_{e2}^2). \tag{14}$$

By (9), the denominator of (14) is positive. By (4), $NB_{21}^2 < 0$, and by (8), $NB_{ee}^2 < 0$. Hence, the numerator of (14) is negative, and $dq^2/dq^1 < 0$.

It remains to sign dq^1/de^1. Totally differentiating (2) yields

$$NB_{11}^1 dq^1 + NB_{12}^1 dq^2 + NB_{1e}^1 de^1 = 0. \tag{15}$$

Rearranging (15) and substituting (14) yields

$$dq^1/de^1 = [NB_{1e}^1 (NB_{22}^2 NB_{ee}^2 - NB_{2e}^2 NB_{e2}^2)]/(NB_{11}^1 NB_{2e}^2 NB_{e2}^2 + NB_{21}^2 NB_{ee}^2 NB_{12}^1 - NB_{11}^1 NB_{22}^2 NB_{ee}^2). \tag{16}$$

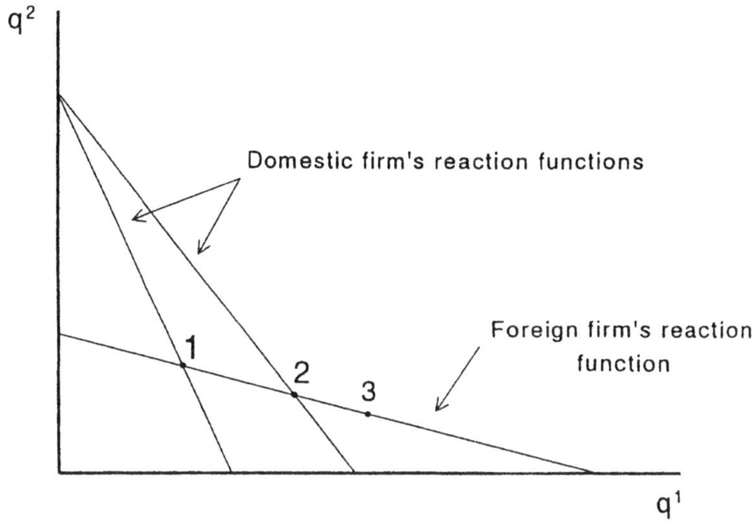

Fig. 1. Strategic environmental policy.

$NB^1_{1e} > 0$ if the standard is binding. The term in brackets in the numerator of (16) is positive by (9), and the denominator is positive by (10). Hence $dq^1/de^1 > 0$. Since $\pi^1_2 < 0$ and $dq^2/dq^1 < 0$, eq. (11) implies $NB^1_e < 0$, or $-A^1_e < D^1_e$. □

The reason for this result is as follows. If the domestic government increases the domestic standard above $\tilde{e}^1$, then the domestic firm will increase its output, and the foreign firm will decrease its output. Profits will be shifted away from the foreign firm to the domestic firm. This shift in profits compensates the domestic government at the margin for higher environmental damages.[8]

The result is illustrated in fig. 1.[9] The action by the domestic government shifts the domestic firm's reaction function to the right, moving the equilibrium from point 1 to point 2. This result is similar to Spencer and Brander's (1983) analysis of R&D subsidies and Brander and Spencer's

[8]If the foreign industry is perfectly competitive, then the domestic firm faces a downward-sloping demand curve that reflects both third-country demand and the response of foreign firms to price changes, and it is optimal for the domestic government to impose the EOS. Similarly, if the domestic industry faces a horizontal demand curve, the domestic government has no incentive to behave strategically. While this last observation is invariant to the structure of the domestic industry, the former is not; see section 4.

[9]The figure assumes that domestic and foreign output are homogeneous products with linear demand; marginal production costs are constant; the first partial derivatives of $A^i(q^i, e^i)$ are linear; and marginal damages are linear in emission levels.

(1985) analysis of export subsidies. However, in contrast to these analyses of industrial policy, strategic environmental policy does not make the domestic firm a de facto Stackelberg leader – that is, if the domestic firm were a Stackelberg leader, it would produce an even greater level of output than is optimal under the SOS.

Proposition 2. The SOS does not make the domestic firm a de facto Stackelberg leader. If the domestic firm is a Stackelberg leader, then the domestic government does not have an incentive to behave strategically. Domestic net benefits are higher when the domestic firm is a Stackelberg leader and the domestic government chooses the EOS than when the domestic firm plays Cournot and the domestic government chooses the SOS.

Proof. If the domestic firm is a Stackelberg leader, the foreign firm a follower, and neither government behaves strategically, then the equilibrium is defined by

$$\pi_1^1 + \pi_2^1 \mathrm{d}q^2/\mathrm{d}q^1 = 0, \quad \text{with } NB_e^1 = 0, \tag{17}$$

plus eqs. (2) and (7) for $i=2$. If the domestic government imposes the SOS, the foreign government imposes the EOS, and both firms compete Cournot, then the equilibrium is defined by

$$\pi_2^1 \mathrm{d}q^2/\mathrm{d}q^1 + NB_e^1 \mathrm{d}e^1/\mathrm{d}q^1 = 0, \quad \text{with } \pi_1^1 = 0, \tag{18}$$

plus eqs. (2) and (7) for $i=2$. The first part of the proposition is proved by noting that (17) and (18) are different.

To prove the second part of the proposition, notice that if the domestic firm were a Stackelberg leader, and the domestic government behaved strategically, the equilibrium would be defined by

$$(\pi_1^1 + \pi_2^1 \mathrm{d}q^2/\mathrm{d}q^1)\mathrm{d}q^1/\mathrm{d}e^1 + NB_e^1 = 0, \quad \text{with } \pi_1^1 + \pi_2^1 \mathrm{d}q^2/\mathrm{d}q^1 = 0, \tag{19}$$

plus eqs. (2) and (7) for $i=2$. Eq. (19) implies $NB_e^1 = 0$, which defines the EOS.

To prove the final point of the proposition, suppose the domestic government could choose both q^1 and e^1. Then the equilibrium would be defined by

$$\pi_1^1 + \pi_2^1 \mathrm{d}q^2/\mathrm{d}q^1, \quad \text{with } NB_e^1 = 0, \tag{20}$$

plus eqs. (2) and (7) for $i=2$. But (20) is identical to (17), which is different from (18). □

In the Spencer and Brander (1983) and Brander and Spencer (1985) models, the optimal export and R&D subsidies move the industry equilibrium to the Stackelberg point: 'The government does for the domestic firm what the firm cannot do for itself' [Spencer and Brander (1983, p. 714)]. Strategic environmental policy moves the industry equilibrium *closer* to the Stackelberg point, but it is not optimal for the domestic government to reach that point. In fig. 1, point 2 is the equilibrium where the domestic government imposes the SOS, while point 3 is the equilibrium where the domestic firm is the Stackelberg leader and its government imposes the EOS. The reason for this result is that weaker environmental standards offer an 'implicit subsidy', but one that is costly; society suffers because the subsidy worsens domestic pollution. Export and R&D subsidies are not costly to society; they simply transfer resources from the domestic government to domestic industry. Indeed, it can be shown that if the domestic government could subsidize production or exports directly, it would have no incentive to depart from the EOS.[10]

3. Bilateral strategic environmental policy

If the domestic firm's government has an incentive to behave strategically, so would the foreign firm's. Suppose, then, that each government chooses its environmental standard, taking as given the foreign government's environmental standard, but recognizing how this choice will affect the industry equilibrium. Then we have

Proposition 3. The Nash environmental policy equilibrium involves both exporting countries choosing SOSs that are weaker than their respective EOSs.

Proof. The Nash environmental policy equilibrium is defined by (2), (11), which defines the domestic government's SOS, and

$$\pi^2_1(\mathrm{d}q^1/\mathrm{d}q^2)/(\mathrm{d}q^2/\mathrm{d}e^2)+NB^2_e=0, \tag{21}$$

which defines the foreign government's SOS. Totally differentiating (2), setting $\mathrm{d}e^2=0$ and substituting yields

$$\mathrm{d}q^2/\mathrm{d}q^1=-\pi^2_{21}/\pi^2_{22} \quad \text{and} \quad \mathrm{d}q^1/\mathrm{d}e^1=(\pi^2_{22}\pi^1_{1e})/(\pi^1_{12}\pi^2_{21}-\pi^1_{11}\pi^2_{22}). \tag{22}$$

Substituting (22) into (11) and repeating the process for the foreign country yields

[10]If the domestic government could choose both e^1 and a domestic export/production subsidy s^1, the optimal values must satisfy $(\pi^1_1-s+\pi^1_2\mathrm{d}q^2/\mathrm{d}q^1)\mathrm{d}q^1/\mathrm{d}s^1=0$ and $(\pi^1_1-s+\pi^1_2\mathrm{d}q^2/\mathrm{d}q^1)\mathrm{d}q^1/\mathrm{d}e^1+NB^1_e=0$. It is easy to show that $\mathrm{d}q^1/\mathrm{d}s^1>0$. Hence, the term in parentheses must equal zero. That means NB^1_e must equal zero, which defines the EOS.

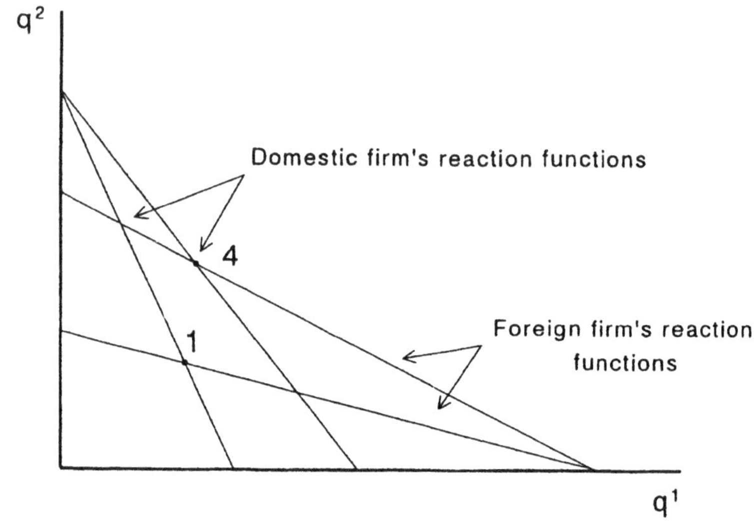

Fig. 2. Nash environmental policy equilibria.

$$NB^i_e = (NB^i_j NB^j_{ji} NB^i_{ie})/(NB^i_{ij} NB^i_{ji} - NB^i_{ii} NB^j_{jj}). \tag{23}$$

Hence, the Nash environmental policy equilibrium is the solution to (23) and (2). It is easy to verify that our assumptions imply $NB^i_e < 0$. Hence, eqs. (8) imply that in equilibrium the e^i are greater than their EOS levels (for q^i given). □

The consequence of bilateral strategic environmental policy is shown in fig. 2. Point 1 is the Nash industry equilibrium, assuming governments impose their EOSs. If both governments impose their SOSs, the reaction curves tilt outwards, and a new equilibrium is reached at point 4. At this new equilibrium, both countries earn lower net benefits compared with point 1, but neither has an incentive to impose its EOS unilaterally.

4. Strategic environmental policy for oligopolistic industries

Would these results hold for a domestic oligopoly? It seems that they might not. If the foreign industry were perfectly competitive, and the domestic industry oligopolistic, domestic profits could be increased if domestic output were lowered. Hence, the domestic government would have an incentive to impose strong environmental standards unilaterally. When there is imperfectly competitive foreign competition, this incentive must be balanced against the incentive to impose weak environmental standards in order to shift profits away from foreign rivals.

To formalize these points, suppose the domestic industry consists of n producers, the kth of which has profit function

$$\pi^k = R^k(\mathbf{q}, q^2) - C^k(q^k) - A^k(q^k, e^k),$$

where $\mathbf{q}$ is a vector of n output levels, q^k is k's output and e^k is k's emission standard. For simplicity, it can be assumed that the foreign producer's industry is a monopoly, and produces output q^2 as before. If the foreign industry were oligopolistic, the results would not change substantively; all that matters is that the foreign rival industry respond to changes in the output of the domestic industry.[11]

The domestic government has net benefit function

$$NB^1 = \sum_{k=1}^{n} \pi^k - D^1(\mathbf{e}),$$

where $\mathbf{e}$ is a vector of domestic emission levels. The EOS for firm k is given by

$$\frac{-\partial A^k}{\partial e^k} - \frac{\partial D^1}{\partial e^k} = 0.$$

The SOS must satisfy

$$\frac{-\partial A^k}{\partial e^k} - \frac{\partial D^1}{\partial e^k} + \sum_{l=1}^{n} \frac{\partial \pi^l}{\partial q^2} \cdot \frac{\mathrm{d}q^2}{\mathrm{d}q^k} \cdot \frac{\mathrm{d}q^k}{\mathrm{d}e^k} + \sum_{l=1}^{n} \frac{\partial \pi^l}{\partial q^k} \cdot \frac{\mathrm{d}q^k}{\mathrm{d}e^k} = 0. \tag{24}$$

The second term in (24) indicates the contribution to net benefits of the shift in profits from the foreign to the domestic industry. If reaction functions are downward sloping and all goods are substitutes, this term will be positive. What is substantially different about eq. (24) is the last term, which captures the effect of changes in k's emission standard on the profitability of the other domestic firms. If one domestic firm's output is a substitute for another's, this term will be negative. Hence, eq. (24) implies:

Proposition 4. Where the domestic industry is oligopolistic, the SOSs may be either weaker or stronger than the EOSs.

[11] If the foreign industry is perfectly competitive and the domestic industry faces a downward-sloping demand curve, the SOS will be stronger than the EOS. Under these conditions, profits cannot be shifted away from the foreign industry, but strong standards limit domestic production and hence increase domestic industry profits.

Proposition 4 holds for both unilateral policies and the Nash environmental policy equilibrium.

5. Strategic environmental policy under price competition

It is well known that if firms compete in prices rather than quantities, the strategically optimal policy can be reversed [Bulow et al. (1985)]. In the case of strategic trade policy, if an export subsidy is optimal under quantity competition, an export tax is optimal under price competition [Eaton and Gossman (1986)]. A similar qualitative conclusion emerges from the analysis of strategic environmental standards.

Let the prices chosen by the domestic and foreign firms be denoted by p^1 and p^2, respectively. At these prices, firm i sells $S^i(p^1,p^2)$. i's profit function can be written

$$\pi^i = p^i S^i(p^1,p^2) - C^i(S^i(p^1,p^2)) - A^i(S^i(p^1,p^2),e^i).$$

The EOS is unchanged from before; the domestic country's EOS satisfies eq. (7) under Bertrand competition. However, the rule for choosing the SOS now becomes (denoting $\partial\pi^1/\partial p^1$ by π^1_1, etc.)

$$\pi^1_1 \mathrm{d}p^1/\mathrm{d}e^1 + \pi^1_2(\mathrm{d}p^2/\mathrm{d}p^1)(\mathrm{d}p^1/\mathrm{d}e^1) + NB^1_e = 0.$$

The domestic firm chooses price p^1 such that $\pi^1_1=0$. If the two goods are substitutes, $\pi^1_2>0$. Assuming that the reaction functions are upward sloping (i.e. $\pi^1_{12}>0$), $\mathrm{d}p^2/\mathrm{d}p^1>0$ if the stability conditions for Bertrand competition are satisfied. These conditions also imply $\mathrm{d}p^1/\mathrm{d}e^1<0$ if the emission standard is binding. Hence, we have $NB^1_e>0$, or

Proposition 5. Under Bertrand competition, the unilateral SOS is stronger than the EOS.

Setting a strong emission standard raises marginal costs, thus making it credible for the domestic firm to increase price. Unlike the Cournot case, the foreign firm welcomes this unilateral policy; its profits *rise* as a consequence.

Proposition 2 can be shown to hold for Bertrand competition as well as Cournot competition. However, in contrast to quantity competition, the leader under Bertrand competition may suffer a reduction in profits.[12]

Using the same procedure as in the proof to Proposition 3, it is easy to show that if both countries behave strategically, the Nash equilibrium satisfies

[12]See Tirole (1988, pp. 330–331).

$$NB_e^i = \frac{-NB_j^i NB_{ji}^j NB_{ie}^i}{(NB_{ii}^i NB_{jj}^j - NB_{ij}^i NB_{ji}^j)}. \tag{25}$$

If the two goods are substitutes, $NB_i^i > 0$. If the reaction curves are upward sloping, $NB_{ij}^i > 0$. Under our assumptions, $NB_{ie}^i < 0$. The denominators of (25) are positive if the stability conditions are satisfied. Hence, $NB_e^i > 0$.

Proposition 6. Under Bertrand competition, the Nash environmental policy equilibrium involves both countries choosing SOSs that are stronger than their respective EOSs.

Finally, note that if the domestic industry is oligopolistic, all the results presented in this section are reinforced. A strong SOS induces domestic firms, as well as foreign rivals, to raise price, thereby increasing domestic industry profits.

6. Conclusions and policy implications

This paper has shown that if the domestic industry consists of one firm, the foreign industry is imperfectly competitive, and competition in international markets is Cournot, then the domestic government has an incentive to impose a weak environmental standard, where 'weak' means that the marginal damage from pollution exceeds the marginal cost of abatement. While this result confirms fears that governments may want to weaken standards to improve competitiveness, the paper shows that environmental policy is inferior to industrial policy as an instrument for improving competitiveness. A production subsidy, for example, would effectively make the domestic firm a Stackelberg leader at no cost to the domestic economy. Hence, governments would only want to interfere in environmental policy if other, more efficient policy interventions could not be made. Furthermore, the conclusion that weak standards improve competitiveness is not robust. If the domestic industry consists of more than one firm, the incentive to weaken standards is reduced, and may even be reversed. If firms compete in prices (Bertrand) rather than quantities (Cournot), countries have an incentive to impose strong standards, where 'strong' means that the marginal damage from pollution is less than the marginal cost of abatement, whether the domestic industry is a monopoly or oligopoly. Taken together, the results suggest that incentives to distort environmental standards will typically not be significant and may be of the opposite direction than is usually assumed.

References

Anderson, K. and R. Blackhurst, eds., The greening of world trade issues (Harvester Wheatsheaf, London).

Brander, J.A. and B.J. Spencer, 1985, Export subsidies and international market share rivalry, Journal of International Economics 18, 83–100.
Bulow, J.I., J.D. Geanakoplos and P.D. Klemperer, 1985, Multimarket oligopoly: Strategic substitutes and complements, Journal of Political Economy 93, 488–511.
Copeland, B.R., 1990a, Strategic enhancement and destruction of fisheries and the environment in the presence of international externalities, Journal of Environmental Economics and Management 19, 212–226.
Copeland, B.R., 1990b, Endogenous spillovers, R&D, and transboundary pollution, Mimeo. (Department of Economics, University of British Columbia).
Copeland, B.R., 1992, Taxes versus standards to control pollution in imperfectly competitive markets, Mimeo. (Department of Economics, University of British Columbia).
Cropper, M.L. and W.E. Oates, 1992, Environmental economics: A survey, Journal of Economic Literature 30, 675–740.
Dean, J.M., 1992, Trade and the environment: A survey of the literature, in: P. Low, ed., International trade and the environment (The World Bank, Washington, DC) 15–28.
Eaton, J. and G.M. Grossman, 1986, Optimal trade and industrial policy under oligopoly, Quarterly Journal of Economics 101, 383–406.
GATT Secretariat, 1992, International trade 90–91 (GATT, Geneva).
Grimmett, J.J., 1991, Environmental regulation and the GATT, Report for congress, Congressional Research Service.
Grossman, G.M. and A.B. Krueger, 1992, Environmental impacts of a North American Free Trade Agreement, Centre for Economic Policy Research Discussion Paper 644.
Low, P., 1992, International trade and the environment, Discussion Paper 159 (The World Bank, Washington, DC).
Low, P. and A. Yeats, 1992, Do 'dirty' industries migrate?, in: P. Low, ed., International trade and the environment (The World Bank, Washington, DC) 89–103.
Lucas, R.E.B., D. Wheeler and H. Hettige, 1992, Economic development, environmental regulation and the international migration of toxic industrial pollution: 1960–1988, in: P. Low, ed., International trade and the environment (The World Bank, Washington, DC) 67–86.
Markusen, J.R., E.R. Morey and N. Olewiler, 1991, Environmental policy when market structure and plant locations are endogenous, National Bureau of Economic Research Working Paper 3671.
Markusen, J.R., E.R. Morey and N. Olewiler, 1992, Noncooperative equilibria in regional environmental policies when plant locations are endogenous, National Bureau of Economic Research Working Paper 4051.
Oates, W.E. and R.M. Schwab, 1988, Economic competition among jurisdictions: Efficiency enhancing or distortion inducing? Journal of Public Economics 35, 333–354.
Pearce, D., 1992, Should GATT be reformed for environmental reasons?, CSERGE Discussion Paper GEC 92-06 (University of East Anglia and University College London).
Rauscher, M., 1991, Foreign trade and the environment, in: H. Siebert, ed., Environmental scarcity: The international dimension (J.C.B. Mohr, Tübingen).
Reinstein, R.A., 1991, Trade and environment, Mimeo. (U.S. State Department).
Spencer, B.J. and J.A. Brander, 1983, International R&D rivalry and industrial strategy, Review of Economic Studies 50, 707–722.
Tirole, J., 1988, The theory of industrial organization (MIT Press, Cambridge, MA).
Ulph, A., 1992, The choice of environmental policy instruments and strategic international trade, in: R. Pethig, ed., Conflicts and cooperation in managing environmental resources (Springer-Verlag, Berlin).
Whalley, J., 1991, The interface between environmental and trade policies, Economic Journal 101, 100–189.

[7]

Oxford Economic Papers 46 (1994), 822–840

ON ECOLOGICAL DUMPING

By MICHAEL RAUSCHER

Institut für Weltwirtschaft, Universität Kiel, D—24100 Kiel, Germany
Centre for Economic Policy Research

1. Introduction

ENVIRONMENTAL legislation provides a means to the government to influence the competitiveness of an economy or of some of its sectors. According to the standard theorems of international-trade theory, a restrictive policy towards the users of environmental resources will distract internationally mobile factors of production and, inside the economy, cause factor movements from the pollution-intensive sectors of the economy to the cleaner sectors. The comparative advantage of the former is diminished by such a policy. Thus, environmental legislation affects the international division of labour and can be used to achieve trade-policy objectives. This is particularly appealing if the traditional instruments of trade policy, tariffs and quotas, are not available, for instance if the country has signed treaties that prohibit restrictions on imports from other countries. Examples are the EC treaties and the GATT. Thus, the politician may be tempted to use the tools of environmental policies to achieve objectives other than the internalisation of the social costs of pollution. The objectives may be terms-of-trade improvements, strategic trade-policy considerations, or the protection of infant or ailing industries or sectors which are supported by powerful lobbies.

The protection of particular sectors or subgroups of a society by means of environmental policies may result in an environmental legislation which is too lax in some sense. Producers obtain hidden subsidies in terms of low pollution abatement requirements and they can dump their products in international markets at prices that do not reflect the true cost of production. This is considered to be a practice of unfair trade. Thus, the term 'ecological dumping' is often used in the public discussion to paraphrase the phenomenon. This catchphrase will be taken up for the following investigation. It should be kept in mind, however, that, in contrast to normal dumping, ecological dumping is an activity performed by the government and not by an individual firm. Moreover, it does not in the first place affect the price of a tradable commodity but that of a factor of products which is internationally immobile: nature's capability to provide environmental resources.

This paper is an attempt to cast some more light on the issue of ecological dumping. In a first step, a sensible definition of the subject is sought. What is ecological dumping and how can it be measured? We shall then try to identify economic motives underlying a government's decision to engage in ecological dumping. It will be assumed that the government follows a rational strategy, i.e. it maximises national welfare or another objective function. Firstly, the terms-of-trade argument will be addressed. It will be seen that the terms of trade of a country are not in general improved by lax environmental policies. Thus, two alternative approaches to explaining ecological dumping are presented. One of is them strategic trade policy: lax environmental standards may be used to improve the market position of a domestic oligopolist and to shift profits from abroad to the domestic economy. The other approach is to model the impact of domestic exporters' lobbies on the political decision-making process. Some final remarks conclude the paper.

Finally, it may be useful to say what is missing in this paper. The theoretical framework of the analysis is an international-trade model in which the production of traded commodities harms the environment. Of course, there are also environmental problems connected with the consumption of these goods and they may have strong implications on international trade (as the Danish bottle case in the EC has vividly demonstrated). Nonetheless, since the term 'ecological dumping' has been used to characterise the regulation of production activities, consumption externalities are of minor interest here. Another omission is the neglect of transfrontier pollution. It has been shown by Merrifield (1988) and Rauscher (1991), that the combination of transfrontier pollution spill-overs and international trade create interesting phenomena in the standard model of international trade. But it would be trivial to identify transfrontier externalities as an explanation of too-lax environmental regulation and the term 'ecological dumping' has not been used in this sense. Therefore, I shall deal with purely national environmental problems. The final restriction of the model is the absence of trade interventions. Many countries have signed international agreements that prohibit the use of these instruments. Therefore, environmental regulation may serve as a second-best alternative to tariffs and quotas in a world of free trade.

2. Three definitions of ecological dumping

Environmental dumping characterises a situation in which a government uses lax environmental standards to support domestic firms in international markets. Low emission taxes and pollution-abatement requirements enable these firms to dump their goods into foreign markets at relatively low prices. This is viewed as being unfair and should be prevented. It is, however, far from clear what is meant by too-lax environmental standards.

In the public opinion, the term 'ecological dumping' characterises a situation in which the environmental standards in one country are lower than those in other countries. By undercutting the environmental standards of other countries, a government reduces the production costs of domestic firms. They can produce at lower costs than their foreign competitors and this is often considered to be unfair. As a consequence, a desirable world of fair trade would be characterised by perfect harmonisation of environmental policies: all countries should use the same environmental standards.

There are two objections against applying this concept to international differences in environmental regulations. First, if one believes in factor price equalisation, the implicit prices of environmental resources should be the same in all countries if there is trade. Differences in emission taxes across countries would not occur. To detect eco-dumping activities, one would have to employ the autarky prices. The second critique is more important. To a trade theorist, it does not make much sense to postulate that all countries should use the same level of environmental regulation. International differences in the endowments with environmental resources do exist, be it because of differences in physical characteristics of the countries, be it due to differences in the tastes of the people. Removing these differences by means of harmonisation is equivalent to removing a part of the basis of gains from trade. See Hansson (1990) for instance. Thus, ecological dumping by employing lower environmental standards than the rest of the world can be a good thing and there is no need to rack one's brains about it as a problem.

Nonetheless, I think that ecological dumping is a problem. With another definition of the subject, this becomes obvious at once. The definition is related to the modern view of dumping in commodity markets which defines the subject of its analysis as pricing at less than marginal cost.[1] See Davies and McGuinness (1982) and Ethier (1982). Correspondingly, ecological dumping can be defined as a policy which prices environmentally harmful activities at less than the marginal cost of environmental degradation, i.e. a policy which does not internalise all environmental externalities. Therefore, firms can dump their output into international markets at prices which do not meet the marginal social cost of production.[2]

The problem with this definition is that there are many reasons for too low a level of environmental regulation and it may be hard to distinguish between ecological dumping and other kinds of under-regulation. For instance, it is often argued that producers' lobbies are more influential in the political decision making process than the consumers of environmental quality. If this is true, the under-internalisation of external effects would be possible even in closed economies and this can hardly be called ecological dumping. A way out of this dilemma is to compare different sectors of the economy. One may argue that trade-related measures of environmental policy are targeted primarily at the producers of traded goods, who face competition in international markets, but not at the producers of non-traded goods, that are not subject to international

[1] For the traditional view of dumping as price discrimination between foreign and domestic markets, see Viner (1923).

[2] There may be additional components of the social costs of using environmental resources that are neglected by this definition. The full social cost would also include the effects of environmental regulation on the terms of trade or on other variables that affect welfare. Nonetheless, it appears to be sensible to restrict the definition of ecological dumping to pure production costs, i.e. the private costs of production plus the environmental damage. The same concept has been used by Davies and McGuinness (1982) for their definition of dumping in goods markets. One of the scenarios they consider is that of a monopolist who uses a dumping strategy to deter the entry of a competitor. The definition of dumping as pricing at less than marginal production cost neglects the fact that the entry of a competitor is costly to the incumbent and may be viewed as a part of her cost function.

competition. One could, therefore, take the non-traded-goods sector as a point of reference and define ecological dumping as a scenario in which environmental standards are tighter in the non-tradables than in the tradables sector. A prerequisite for this to be possible is that the government has the power to use sector-specific instruments of environmental policy. Anecdotal evidence tells us that this is indeed the case. There are even plant-specific differences in pollution abatement requirements, as is vividly testified by the electricity generation sectors in various countries. In practical applications, however, it may turn out to be difficult to compare the tightness of environmental standards across different sectors. Matters are simple if both sectors discharge the same pollutant and cause the same environmental damage at the margin. This will be assumed in the theoretical parts of this paper and the emission tax rate is an appropriate measure of the tightness of environmental standards. In the more general case of different pollutants and different marginal damages, one should compare the degrees of internalisation of social costs across different sectors of the economy.

Given that the public-opinion view does not provide a sensible definition of ecological dumping, there remain two approaches to the subject of investigation. The major difference between the two definitions of ecological dumping is their point of reference. In the first case, it is the full internalisation of the social costs of production. In the second case, it is the policy applied to the non-tradables sector (which does not necessarily internalise the external effects of production).

3. The model

Since one of the definitions of ecological dumping uses the non-traded goods sector as a point of reference, a three-goods model of the economy is needed. There are imported goods, exported goods, and non-tradables and they are produced with two factors. In order to reduce complexity, I assume that only two goods are produced domestically. Sector 1 of the economy produces non-tradable goods and sector 2 produces the export good. Commodity 3 is produced only in the foreign country.[3] The two factors of production are capital and an environmental resource, which will also be referred to as 'emission'. Let K^i be the capital stock and E^i be the quantity of the environmental resource employed in the ith sector. The output of this sector, Q^i, then is

$$Q^i = F^i(K^i, E^i), \qquad i = 1, 2 \tag{1}$$

The production functions are assumed to be well-behaved. They are concave and exhibit constant returns to scale. Marginal productivities are positive and declining and the cross derivatives F^i_{KE} are positive. This implies that capital and emissions are imperfect substitutes or, more technically speaking, that their elasticity of substitution is finite and has the normal sign.[4]

[3] A similar model with traded and non-traded goods has been analysed by Jones (1974). In his model, however, the exported good is not consumed in the home country.

[4] Algebraically, the condition $f^i_{KE} > 0$ follows from constant returns to scale and the concavity of the production function.

Let P^2 and P^3 be the prices of commodities 2 and 3 in terms of the non-traded good which serves as the numéraire. $P = P^2/P^3$ denotes the country's terms of trade, i.e. the price of the export good in terms of the import good. Moreover, let C^i denote the domestic consumption and let $m(P)$ be the foreign country's excess demand function for commodity 2. An equilibrium requires that the excess supply of the home country equals the excess demand of the foreign country

$$Q^2 - C^2 = m(P) \tag{2}$$

Moreover, if international trade is balanced, we have

$$P^2(C^2 - Q^2) + P^3C^3 = 0 \tag{3a}$$

or, together with (2)

$$C^3 = Pm(P) \tag{3b}$$

The demand for commodities 1, 2, and 3 and the optimal environmental policy can be derived from the national welfare function $W(.,.,.,.)$ which has as its arguments the consumption of the three goods and environmental quality, A. For the sake of simplicity, I assume that the welfare function is additively separable in its arguments.[5] Therefore

$$W(C^1, C^2, C^3, A) = U^1(C^1) + U^2(C^2) + U^3(C^3) + V(A) \tag{4}$$

with positive but decreasing partial derivatives.[6]

There is a fixed capital stock, K, which can be moved without costs between sectors 1 and 2

$$K = K^1 + K^2 \tag{5}$$

For reasons of comparability, let us assume that all sectors discharge the same pollutant. Then, the environmental quality may be defined as

$$A = -E^1 - E^2 \tag{6}$$

Inserting eqs (1), (2), (3b), (5), and (6) into the welfare function yields

$$W = U^1[F^1(K^1, E^1)] + U^2[F^2(K - K^1, -A - E^1) - m(P)] + U^3[Pm(P)] + V[A] \tag{7}$$

This welfare function is to be maximised by the government, which chooses the optimal state of the environment, A. The firms decide on the allocation of capital to the producing sectors of the economy. The emission levels E^1 and E^2 can be chosen either by the producers or by the government. In one case, the government chooses just the level of environmental policy and then leaves

[5] Even with this restrictive assumption, there will be a large variety of feasible results and a more general welfare function would not add much to the analysis in this respect.

[6] This type of welfare function is known from models with endogenous factor supply. See Kemp and Jones (1962).

it to the producers to allocate the emissions. This can be done by choosing appropriate emission taxes or by using a tradable permits scheme. On the other hand, the government itself may wish to determine the emissions of the two producing sectors.

If the country is small, P is given and the excess demand of the rest of the world is perfectly elastic. The optimal level of environmental quality, A, is determined by

$$U_C^2 F_E^2 = V' \tag{8}$$

where primes and subscripts denote (partial) derivatives of functions. Under the assumption of perfect competition, factors are remunerated according to their marginal productivity. If the government left the allocation decision to the producers, the equilibrium price of environmental resources (equalling the Pigouvian tax rate), T, would be

$$P^2 V'/U_C^2 = P^2 F_E^2 = F_E^1 = T \tag{9}$$

If the government itself decides on the allocation issue, it maximises (7) also with respect to E^1, which implies

$$U_C^1 F_E^1 = U_C^2 F_E^2 \tag{10}$$

Noting that utility maximisation of the households implies $U_C^1 = U_C^2/P^2 = U_C^3/P^3$, it follows from (10) that $F_E^1 = P^2 F_E^2$.

This implies that the results of economy-wide and sector-specific environmental regulation are the same. The same tax rate will be applied to all sectors. Thus, it does not pay to discriminate against one sector and favour another if the country under consideration is small. Moreover, the emission tax rate covers the marginal social cost of environmental degradation. Thus, there is no ecological dumping, independently of the definition applied.

4. The terms-of-trade argument

Matters may be different if the country under consideration is large. It has an impact on its terms of trade and this affects its welfare. The effect is

$$\mathrm{d}W = [-U_C^2 m' + U_C^3(m + Pm')]\,\mathrm{d}P$$

Noting that due to utility maximisation of the households $U_C^2 = PU_C^3$, this can be rewritten

$$\mathrm{d}W = U_C^3 m\,\mathrm{d}P \tag{11}$$

As an exporter of good 2, the country will benefit from an increase in the relative price of this good compared to the imported good. On can now determine the impact of the supply of the environmental factor of production on the terms of trade.

In a first step, we shall deal with a scenario in which the government determines merely the level of environmental quality and then imposes a tradable-permits scheme or levies an emission tax, which the firms use to decide on the allocation of the environmental factor of production to the two producing sectors of the economy. For the standard model without non-tradable goods, the optimal environmental policy has been investigated by Markusen (1975) and Rauscher (1991). A country should use its public policy to increase the relative price of the factor with which it is relatively well-endowed to improve its terms of trade. The reduction of the availability of this factor tends to increase its price and the relative price of the commodity that uses this factor intensively in its production. Since this good is the export good, the terms of trade are improved by such a policy. Applying this to a model with environmental resources yields the result that a country well-endowed with environmental resources should employ a particularly restrictive policy towards users of environmental policy. In contrast, countries not so well endowed with environmental resources should reduce their emission tax rates in order to improve their terms of trade.

Matters are different in a case of complete specialisation, i.e. if there is no domestic consumption of the imported good. Under normal parameter constellations, it is optimal to reduce the supply of the export good in order to raise its price. This can be done by reducing the supply of the environmental factor of production—regardless of whether the country is well-endowed with resources or not. In the model considered here, there is an additional complication since there is the non-traded goods sector which itself uses environmental resources. The impact of a change in the environmental policy A on the terms of trade, P, is determined by

$$U_C^2 - P^2 U_C^1 = 0 \tag{12a}$$

$$U_C^2 - P U_C^3 = 0 \tag{12b}$$

$$F_K^1 - P^2 F_K^2 = 0 \tag{12c}$$

$$F_E^1 - P^2 F_E^2 = 0 \tag{12d}$$

Eqs (12a, b) are derived from utility maximisation by consumers whereas (12c, d) follows from profit-maximising behaviour of firms. Eliminating P^2 yields

$$U_C^2 - P U_C^3 = 0 \tag{13a}$$

$$U_C^1 F_K^1 - U_C^2 F_K^2 = 0 \tag{13b}$$

$$U_C^1 F_E^1 - U_C^2 F_E^2 = 0 \tag{13c}$$

Total differentiation with respect to P, K^1, E^1, and A gives the desired result. Some basic but cumbersome algebraic exercises show that the sign of dP/dA

is ambiguous: there are nine positive and two negative terms.[7] This is due to the fact that both sectors compete for the environmental factor of production. A reduction of the availability of these resources reduces the marginal productivity of capital in both sectors since $F^i_{KE} > 0$. If this reduction is larger in the non-tradables than in the tradables sector, capital will be moved from the non-tradables to the tradables sector of the economy. Thus, the output of traded goods may actually rise if the reduction of emissions is dominated by an increase in the capital stock. As a consequence, the terms of trade may be reduced. Under certain circumstances, it may be advisable to relax environmental regulations to improve the terms of trade. It is not optimal to fully internalise the domestic costs of environmental disruption and this may be called ecological dumping. If, however, the direct effects of environmental policy changes dominate the indirect general-equilibrium effects, it is advisible to use more-restrictive policies.

The type of environmental policy considered here uses one instrument to cope with two distortions. There are the social costs of environmental degradation and the potential to improve the terms of trade. In this case, two policy instruments are better than one. Of course, the optimal combination of policy measures would be an emission tax plus a tariff. However, if tariffs are not available as an instrument of economic policy, the government may wish to enlarge its set of policy measures by imposing sector-specific environmenta' policies. The question to be considered here is whether such a policy tends to discriminate against the sectors producing non-traded goods. For this purpose it is convenient to rewrite the objective function by substituting for A

$$W = U^1[F^1(K^1, E^1)] + U^2[F^2(K - K^1, E^2) - m(P)] + U^3[Pm(P)] + V[-E^1 - E^2] \tag{7'}$$

The allocation of capital and the terms of trade are determined by

$$U_C^2 - PU_C^3 = 0 \tag{13a}$$

and

$$U_C^1 F_K^1 - U_C^2 F_K^2 = 0 \tag{13b}$$

Using (13a, b), one can derive the welfare effects of changes in sector-specific environmental policies. Optimal policies are characterised by

$$\frac{dW}{dE^1} = U_C^1 F_E^1 - V' + U_C^3 m \frac{dP}{dE^1} = 0 \tag{14a}$$

[7] An additional ambiguity arises when the determinant of the matrix of the partial derivatives of (13a, b, c) with respect to P, E^1, and E^2 has the 'wrong' sign. An explanation of this will be given below.

and

$$\frac{\mathrm{d}W}{\mathrm{d}E^2} = U_C^2 F_E^2 - V' + U_C^3 m \frac{\mathrm{d}P}{\mathrm{d}E^2} = 0 \tag{14b}$$

Noting that in a competitive economy the marginal productivities of emissions equal the emission tax rates, i.e. $T^1 = F_E^1$ and $T^2 = P^2 F_E^2$ where $P^2 = U_C^1 / U_C^2 F_E^2$, one can easily determine a condition for ecological dumping defined in the sense of discrimination of non-traded goods production. Ecological dumping according to this definition is when the emission tax rate in the export sector is lower than that in the non-traded goods sector or, equivalently

$$T^2 < T^1 \quad \text{iff} \quad \frac{\mathrm{d}P}{\mathrm{d}E^1} < \frac{\mathrm{d}P}{\mathrm{d}E^2} \tag{15}$$

Ecological dumping is optimal if the terms-of-trade effect of additional emissions in the non-tradables sector is smaller than the corresponding effect in the sector producing traded commodities. If this condition holds, the improvement in the terms of trade by an additional unit of emissions in the tradables sector exceeds the improvement achieved by increasing emissions in the non-tradables sector. Therefore, it is optimal to apply lower environmental standards to the exporting industries.

The terms-of-trade effects of sector-specific environmental policies can be determined by total differentiation of the private sector's optimality conditions (13a, b). This yields

$$\begin{pmatrix} -m'U_{CC}^2 - U_C^3 - P(m + Pm')U_{CC}^3 & -U_{CC}^2 F_K^2 \\ m'U_{CC}^2 F_K^2 & U_C^1 F_{KK}^1 + U_{CC}^1 (F_K^1)^2 + U_C^2 F_{KK}^2 + U_{CC}^2 (F_K^2)^2 \end{pmatrix}$$

$$\times \begin{pmatrix} \mathrm{d}P \\ \mathrm{d}K^1 \end{pmatrix} = \begin{pmatrix} 0 & -U_{CC}^2 F_E^2 \\ -U_C^1 F_{KE}^1 - U_{CC}^1 F_K^1 F_E^1 & U_C^2 F_{KE}^2 + U_{CC}^2 F_K^2 F_E^2 \end{pmatrix} \begin{pmatrix} \mathrm{d}E^1 \\ \mathrm{d}E^2 \end{pmatrix} \tag{16}$$

The sign of the determinant, D, of the matrix on the left-hand side is ambiguous. This is due to the terms occurring in its first-row first-column element. If the foreign country's import demand is inelastic, then m' is close to zero, implying that this element may be positive. In this case, the determinant is negative. But the opposite scenario is also feasible. In order to give an economic interpretation, imagine a situation in which the supply of good 3 is increased exogenously, e.g. by some manna from heaven. The intuition is that this should improve the terms of trade, since the scarcity of the import good is reduced and its gets cheaper. It can be shown that this happens only if the determinant is positive.[8] If the determinant is negative, general-equilibrium interdependencies produce the counter-intuitive result of declining terms of trade. In what follows, I will assume that the intuition is correct and that the determinant has a positive sign.

[8] Let M be the quality of manna falling from heaven. Then

$$\mathrm{d}P/\mathrm{d}M = D^{-1} P U_{CC}^3 (U_C^1 F_{KK}^1 + U_{CC}^1 (F_K^1)^2 + U_C^2 F_{KK}^2 + U_{CC}^2 (F_K^2)^2)$$

It follows that sign $(\mathrm{d}P/\mathrm{d}M)$ = sign (D).

The terms-of-trade effects of sector-specific environmental policies can be determined by applying Cramer's rule to eq. (16). This yields

$$\frac{\mathrm{d}P}{\mathrm{d}E^1} = -D^{-1}U^2_{CC}F^2_K[U^1_C F^1_{KE} + U^1_{CC}F^1_K F^1_E] \tag{17a}$$

$$\frac{\mathrm{d}P}{\mathrm{d}E^2} = D^{-1}[U^2_{CC}F^2_K U^2_C F^2_{KE} - U^2_{CC}F^2_E(U^1_C F^1_{KK} + U^1_{CC}(F^1_K)^2 + U^2_C F^2_{KK})] \tag{17b}$$

The terms-of-trade effect of an increase in emissions is negative in the traded commodities sector and ambiguous in the non-tradables sector. This can be explained as follows. An increase in the availability of environmental resources in sector 2 increases the supply of exportable goods and, under normal circumstances, their price will decline. For sector 1, which produces the non-traded good, there are two opposing effects. On the one hand, an increase in emissions raises the marginal productivity of capital since $F^1_{KE} > 0$. If commodity prices are given, capital is moved from sector 2 to sector 1. This reduces the supply of the export good and tends to improve the terms of trade. On the other hand, the increase in the availability of the environmental factor of production in the non-tradables sector increases the supply of this good. Its price relative to that of the other good which is produced at home is reduced. For given productivities, capital tends to move from sector 1 to sector 2, this raises the supply of the exported good and leads to a deterioration of the terms of trade.

Given the terms-of-trade effects of sector-specific environmental policies, the policy implications can easily be derived. Since under normal circumstances the terms-of-trade effect of additional emissions in the export sector is negative, one should attempt to reduce these emissions below those of the reference scenario in which the terms-of-trade effects are not taken into account. The policy implication for the non-tradables sector is ambiguous. If capital and emissions are good substitutes in these sectors (if F^1_{KE} is large), then there is a positive terms-of-trade effect, and the environmental policy measures applied to the non-tradables sector should be relaxed. In this scenario the policy implications is the opposite of ecological dumping: discriminating against the sector which produces traded goods. It should be noted, however, that a number of different scenarios are imaginable some of which can indeed result in discrimination against the non-tradables sector. But such an outcome is not particularly likely.

We can summarise that there is a tendency towards stricter environmental legislation, either in the export sector or for the economy as a whole, if policy makers wish to improve the terms of trade. Due to general-equilibrium considerations, however, the opposite policy recommendation is also possible for some parameter combinations. It should be noted that the tendency towards better protection of the environment is an artifact of the assumptions used in this model. The crucial assumption is the absence of an import-competing industry. If such a sector existed, the policy recommendation would mainly depend upon whether the economy is well-endowed with environmental resources or not.

5. Strategic trade policy

In the previous sections, it has been assumed that perfect competition prevails on factors and goods markets. Over the last decade, numerous models have been developed which differ from the standard Heckscher–Ohlin–Samuelson framework in this respect and allow the derivation of interesting policy implications. One of them is the strategic trade policy framework which shows that, under certain circumstances, it may be advisable to subsidise domestic firms in order to increase their market power in international markets.

The basic model is that of Brander and Spencer (1985). They show that the government can turn a firm playing Nash–Cournot into a Stackelberg leader by subsidising its production. Rents are shifted to the home country and this is welfare-improving. Direct subsidies, however, can easily be detected by foreign competitors. Therefore, it may be better to use indirect methods of subsidisation. One possibility is to subsidise domestic research and development. See Spencer and Brander (1983). Another alternative is to impose relatively modest pollution abatement requirements on the firms competing in international oligopoly markets. There have been some recent attempts to analyse this possibility in theoretical models. See Barrett (1992), Ulph (1992), and Conrad (1993). I will refer mainly to Barrett's paper and try to apply his results to the general-equilibrium framework used above.

Barrett (1992) uses the standard model of stategic trade policy extended by the introduction of costly pollution abatement. There are two firms, one domestic and one foreign. They sell their production in a third country. Each firm takes as given the quantity supplied by the other firm and the environmental policy of its home government. In this situation, the market solution is the Nash equilibrium which is represented by point N in Fig. 1. Q and q denote the quantities supplied by the domestic and the foreign firm, respectively, and R and r are their reaction curves. Let B and b be the iso-profit curves of the two firms. If a direct subsidy is given to the domestic firm, it increases its output and its curve is shifted to the right. The equilibrium moves along the foreign country's reaction curve. This is beneficial to the home country as long as the net profits (profits minus subsidies) of the domestic are industry raised. The optimum is given by point S, where the foreign firm's reaction curve touches the best-possible domestic iso-profit curve. This is the Stackelberg solution.

Matters are slightly different if the subsidy is given indirectly by relaxing environmental standards. This kind of subsidy is not merely a purely redistributive policy instrument but its application incurs some real cost. The environmental quality deteriorates and this has to be taken into account by the government. The emission tax rate should be chosen such that the marginal

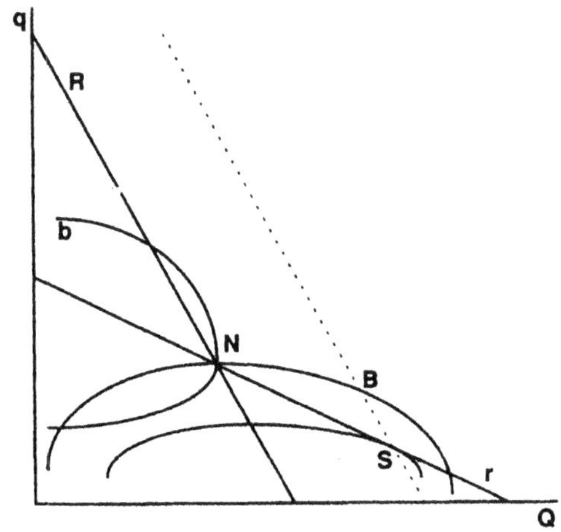

FIG. 1. Strategic environmental policy

social cost due to environmental degradation and the marginal benefit from the increase in the market position of the domestic firm are equated. The optimal solution is to be found somewhere between the Nash and the Stackelberg points N and S.

Applying these results to the eco-dumping problem yields the following propositions. It can be optimal to favour the export industries if the supply side of the international market is oligopolistic. This implies that the non-tradables sector is discrimated against. Moreover, the environmental standards are lower than those that internalise the pure social cost of pollution. Therefore, ecological dumping according to both our definitions may be explained by strategic trade policy considerations. Finally, there may be an international competition in environmental regulations which leads to undesirably low levels of environmental quality in many countries.

Matters can be rather different if the general-equilibrium effects are taken into account. As can be seen in Fig. 1, the objective of strategic trade policy is to raise the production of the domestic export industry for any given quantity supplied by the foreign competitor. In a partial equilibrium, this is achieved by increasing the supply of the environmental factor of production for this sector. In a general equilibrium, the change in the allocation of capital must also be taken into account. We will look at a situation in which the government chooses sector-specific environmental measures. Let us, for the rest of this part of the paper, use the assumption often employed in the strategic trade literature that the good is not sold on the domestic market, i.e.

$$m(P) = F^2(K^2, E^2) \tag{18}$$

Let $m(P)$ now be the inverse demand function faced by the domestic oligopolist for a given level of production of its foreign competitor. If this firm acts as a price taker on domestic factor markets, its profits are passed over to the factor owners. The factors are remunerated at more than marginal cost. This implies

$$F_K^1 = (1+e)P^2F_K^2 \tag{19}$$

where $e = m/(m'P)$, $-1 < e < 0$, is the elasticity of the residual demand function which will be assumed to be constant. Noting that $P^2 = P^3P$ and $P^3U_C^1 = U_C^3$, we obtain

$$U_C^1F_K^1 - (1+e)U_C^3PF_K^2 = 0 \tag{19'}$$

Comparative static results can be derived by totally differentiating eqs (18) and (19′)

$$\begin{pmatrix} m' & F_K^2 \\ -F_K^2(1+e)[U_C^3 + U_{CC}^3P(m+Pm')] & U_{CC}^1(F_K^1)^2 + U_C^1F_{KK}^1 + U_C^3PF_{KK}^2(1+e) \end{pmatrix}$$

$$\times \begin{pmatrix} \mathrm{d}P \\ \mathrm{d}K^1 \end{pmatrix} = \begin{pmatrix} 0 & F_E^2 \\ -U_{CC}^1F_K^1F_E^1 - U_C^1F_{KE}^1 & U_C^3PF_{KE}^2(1+e) \end{pmatrix}\begin{pmatrix} \mathrm{d}E^1 \\ \mathrm{d}E^2 \end{pmatrix} \tag{20}$$

It can be shown that the determinant of the matrix on the left-hand side, D, is positive since the world market demand for 2 is elastic. The impact of changes in environmental policy on the allocation of capital turns out to be

$$\frac{\mathrm{d}K^1}{\mathrm{d}E^1} = D^{-1}m'(-U_{CC}^1F_K^1F_E^1 - U_C^1F_{KE}^1) \tag{21a}$$

$$\frac{\mathrm{d}K^1}{\mathrm{d}E^2} = D^{-1}(1+e)(m'U_C^3PF_{KE}^2 + F_E^2F_K^2[U_C^3 + U_{CC}^3P(m+Pm')]) \tag{21b}$$

In both cases, the effects of environmental policy changes are ambiguous. An increase in emissions in a sector makes capital more productive at the margin since F_{KE}^1 and F_{KE}^2 are positive. Thus, a policy which increases emissions in a sector attracts capital. On the other hand, a good produced in a more pollution-intensive process becomes cheaper and the marginal value product of capital tends to be reduced. This induces a capital movement into the opposite direction. In the case of a change in E^2, however, this capital removal due to price changes is always dominated by the direct output expansion effect of the increase in emissions.[9] Thus, in order to increase the output of the export history, it is advisable to relax the sector-specific environmental policy. But it may be optimal to relax the policy for the other sector even more if this induces a very massive capital flow to the export sector. Although this is not particularly likely, it may be optimal to use an environmental policy which is the opposite of ecological dumping.

Matters become more complicated algebraically, if an economy-wide policy is sought which increases the output of the export industry. An additional equation for the cross-sector equalisation of emission taxes has to be introduced

[9] This can be verified by computing $\mathrm{d}Q^2/\mathrm{d}E^2 = F_E^2 - F_K^2(\mathrm{d}K^1/\mathrm{d}E^2)$.

and the effect of a change in environmental policy on the allocation of emissions to the two sectors has to be considered too. The result is ambiguous: at least one of the sectors will raise its output if pollution abatement requirements are reduced. It may, however, happen that factors move to the non-tradables sector of the economy. In this case, the output of the export industry may be reduced by ecological dumping.

Summarising the results of this part of the paper, we can conclude that strategic behaviour in international trade does not necessarily lead to eco-dumping, independently of the definition applied. As an additional caveat, one should note that, as Eaton and Grossman (1986) have shown, the policy implications are turned into the opposite direction when the oligopolists play Bertrand instead of Cournot.

6. Towards a public-choice explanation of environmental policies in open economies

In the previous sections environmental policies have been investigated which maximise an index of national well-being. It is a commonplace thing, however, that real-world political decision makers do not use this kind of welfare criterion. Instead, they try to follow their own objectives. In what follows, I shall consider two models in which these objectives are taken into account. The first one looks at some of the intrinsic driving forces of a public bureaucracy, the second approach considers the impact of the power of sector-specific interest groups on governmental decisions. In order to make matters simpler and to separate the effects from the terms-of-trade effects, we shall consider a small economy for which the world market prices are given.

According to Niskanen (1977) and others, one major characteristic of a governmental bureaucracy is the desire to maximise the budget it has to administer. Taking this into account, the objective function has to be rewritten. Assume that the policy maker maximises a weighted average of measure of national welfare and the benefits from tax revenues. Let the benefits from tax revenues be measured by an increasing and strictly concave fuction $G(.)$. The new objective function turns out to be

$$W^G = W + G(T^1E^1 + T^2E^2) \qquad (22)$$

where W is given by eqs (7) or (7′).

If $T^1 = T^2$, both sectors face identical environmental regulations. In order to detect ecological dumping, one should compare the solution of the maximisation of W^G with a policy that maximises national welfare. There are two effects of a change in the emission tax rate on the tax revenue. First, for given emissions, the revenue will increase by $(E^1 + E^2)$ times the change in the tax rate. But with an increasing tax rate, emissions should be reduced which implies that, for given levels of the tax rate, the revenue is reduced. Either of these effects may dominate or there may be a bell-shaped Laffer curve. Depending on whether the revenue function is an increasing or decreasing function in the social optimum, the policy maker may wish to raise or reduce the tax rate. Of course, similar arguments apply to a situation in which the government chooses sector-specific environmental policies and it is not clear which sector is discriminated against in an optimum.

A more promising approach to indentifying motives of ecological dumping is the consideration of sector-specific interest groups. In a representative democracy, the voter does not decide directly upon all the relevant issues but merely elects a government to represent her will. The government has some discretion in interpreting the will of the electorate. Due to this discretion, interest groups have a chance to influence the government's decisions by lobbying, which may range from spending resources on public relations and financial support of campaigns to bribing and blackmailing. There are good arguments in favour of the hypothesis that the traded-goods industries (cars, chemicals, pharmaceuticals, etc.) have a stronger impact on the government than the producers of non-traded goods (mainly services). If this is true, then the policy maker's objective function is changed by the impact of lobbying.

In what follows, it will be assumed that the lobbyists are concerned about the output of the export industry. This is a sensible approach if there are structural problems with a threat of unemployment and declining profits or if there are sector-specific factors that experience income increases when the output of the sector is increased. If the lobby's impact on political decisions is sufficiently large, the government will maximise an objective function which is a weighted average of the national welfare function and the utility function of the lobbyists. Thus, we have

$$W^L = W + L(Q^2) \tag{23}$$

where $L(.)$ is increasing and strictly concave and W is defined by eq. (7′).

To get an idea of what the major impacts are, the impact of a change in environmental policies on the government's objective function can be determined. In a first step, it is necessary to consider the impacts of the environmental policy on the allocation of the factors of production. This can be done by total differentiation of the first-order optimality conditions of the households and firms

$$U_C^1 F_K^1 - U_C^2 F_K^2 = 0 \tag{13b}$$

$$U_C^1 F_E^1 - U_C^2 F_E^2 = 0 \tag{13c}$$

Total differentiation with respect to K^1, E^1 and A shows that the impact of a change in environmental policy, A, on the allocation of factors is ambiguous. In the case of capital this may have been expected. But the same is true for emissions: although the overall level of emissions is increased by a relaxation of environmental policy, emissions in one of the two sectors may be reduced. The impact on production is also ambiguous. Ecological dumping may result either in an increase or a reduction of the export industry's output.

Matters are a bit simpler if we consider sector-specific environmental policies. Equation (13c) is no longer relevant and total differentiation of (13b) yields

$$\frac{\mathrm{d}K^1}{\mathrm{d}E^1} = \frac{-U_C^1 F_{KE}^1 - U_{CC}^1 F_K^1 F_E^1}{U_C^1 F_{KK}^1 + U_{CC}^1 (F_K^1)^2 + U_C^2 F_{KK}^2 + U_{CC}^2 (F_K^2)^2} \tag{24a}$$

$$\frac{\mathrm{d}K^1}{\mathrm{d}E^2} = \frac{U_C^2 F_{KE}^2 + U_{CC}^2 F_K^2 F_E^2}{U_C^1 F_{KK}^1 + U_{CC}^1 (F_K^1)^2 + U_C^2 F_{KK}^2 + U_{CC}^2 (F_K^2)^2} \tag{24b}$$

An increase in emissions in sector 1 moves capital into this sector if F_{KE}^1 is large, i.e. if there is a substantial increase in capital productivity, or if $-U_{CC}^1$ is small. The latter condition means that the price elasticity of demand is large and this implies that an increase in supply results only in a small price reduction. Thus the increase in E^1 has only a small effect on the marginal value product of capital for a given level of the physical productivity. The same arguments apply for the other sector of the economy.

Now consider the welfare effects of a change in environmental policy

$$\mathrm{d}W^L/\mathrm{d}E^1 = \mathrm{d}W/\mathrm{d}E^1 - L'F_K^2(\mathrm{d}K^1/\mathrm{d}E^1) \tag{25a}$$

$$\mathrm{d}W^L/\mathrm{d}E^2 = \mathrm{d}W/\mathrm{d}E^2 + L'(F_E^2 - F_K^2(\mathrm{d}K^1/\mathrm{d}E^2) \tag{25b}$$

Starting from a situation of a social optimum in which $\mathrm{d}W/\mathrm{d}E^1 = \mathrm{d}W/\mathrm{d}E^2 = 0$, ecological dumping by discriminating against the non-traded goods sector is beneficial to the government if

$$(F_E^2 - F_K^2\,\mathrm{d}K^1/\mathrm{d}E^2) > -F_K^2(\mathrm{d}K^1/\mathrm{d}E^1) \tag{26}$$

Inserting eqs (24a, b) yields

$$\frac{F_E^2(U_C^1 F_{KK}^1 + U_{CC}^1 (F_K^1)^2 + U_C F_{KK}^2) - F_K^2(U_C^1 F_{KE}^1 + U_C^2 F_{KE}^2 + U_{CC}^1 F_K^1 F_E^1)}{U_C^1 F_{KK}^1 + U_{CC}^1 (F_K^1)^2 + U_C^2 F_{KK}^2 + U_{CC}^2 (F_K^2)^2} > 0 \tag{27}$$

The last term in the numerator in eq. (27) may exhibit the 'wrong' sign. Thus it is possible that the export industry is supported best by applying more restrictive environmental policies there than in the non-tradables industry. This is just the opposite of ecological dumping defined as the preferential treatment of the export industry in terms of low emission tax rates. However, this result requires a very particular parameter constellation and in the normal case it is advisable to apply lower levels of environmental regulation in the export industry than in the non-traded goods sector.[10]

Summarising the results of the models presented in this section, one arrives

[10] It follows from eq. (24b) that an increase in emissions in the export industry will always raise its output. At least in this model framework, a situation in which exporters benefit from more rigid environmental policies in their own sector is not possible. This may, however, change if more complicated versions of the model are considered, e.g. if the country is large and if more general utility functions are introduced.

at the conclusion that it is by no means clear that it is in the interest of the exporters' lobby or the government itself to have eco-dumping as an environmental policy.

7. Summary and conclusion

The preceding investigation has been an attempt to give more economic content to the catchword of ecological dumping, which has frequently been (mis)used in the recent public discussion on environmental policies in open economies. In a first step a definition of ecological dumping has been sought. Three definitions have been proposed and one of them, which is based on an international comparison of environmental policies, has been rejected. Of the remaining two, one uses the optimal internalisation of social costs as its point of reference, the other one is based on the comparison of regulations applied to sectors producing traded and non-traded commodities. We have then tried to find the economic motives of ecological dumping. Under which circumstances is it optimal to employ a policy which may be termed 'ecological dumping' according to one of the two criteria? It has been seen that neither terms-of-trade considerations nor maximisation of the revenues from emission taxation explain ecological dumping. Depending on parameters of the demand and supply side, these objectives may be achieved sometimes by ecological dumping and sometimes by its converse. Strategic trade policy and lobbying activities of the exporters are more successful in explaining ecological dumping. However, there are still a number of ambiguities and the general equilibrium reprecussions of changes in environmental policy may turn the results around. Lobbyists would sometimes be surprised if they knew that relaxing environmental standards can make the exporters worse off.

Applied to the real world, the interest group approach is the most promising among different candidates for an explanation of ecological dumping. If an explanation of economic policy decisions is sought, it is not important what is optimal but what is thought to be optimal. It is a truism (but not always the truth) that a producer will benefit from relaxed pollution abatement requirements applied to the production processes she uses. But this conjecture, wrong as it may be, provides incentives to lobby for lower emission tax rates. If the exporters' lobbies are more influential than other lobbies, then this may explain ecological dumping. The model presented here has used a shortcut to translate the interest of lobbyists into political decisions. A complicated process has been modelled by simply adding some terms to the government's objective function. It is desirable to model this process more explicitly. A promising approach originates in Hillman and Ursprung (1992) who model the impact of interest groups with motives related to emissions, pollution, and the environment on international trade. If a similar analysis could be undertaken for the opposite problem of how trade-related interests affect environmental policies, this would be another major step towards an understanding of the driving forces of ecological dumping.

Another problem which has been neglected in the preceding analysis is that of retaliation. What happens if the other country also uses environmental policy measures to improve its terms of trade or to support its export industries? Will there be prisoners' dilemma situations in which both countries undercut each other's environmental taxes in order to keep their traded-goods industries competitive? This may lead to undesirably low levels of environmental regulation everywhere and to disastrous consequences for environmental quality. The question arises under which circumstances this result of an international environmental-policy game is feasible and what kind of institutions are necessary to cope with this prisoners' dilemma. Future research into the problem area is desirable.

ACKNOWLEDGEMENTS

Earlier versions of the paper have been presented in seminars at the Kiel Institute of World Economics, the Universities of Munich and Konstanz, and during the 1992 European Research Workshop in International Trade held at the Universidade Nova of Lisbon and I am indebted to the participants for helpful comments and suggestions. Moreover, I have benefited considerably from discussing problems of environmental policies in open economics with Kym Anderson, Richard Blackhurst, Scott Barrett, Carlo Carraro, and Henry Tulkens. Last but not least, I received useful comments by one of the editors and a referee. The responsibility for remaining deficiencies of this paper is solely mine.

REFERENCES

Barrett, S. (1992). *Strategic Environmental Policy and International Trade*, CSERGE working paper GEC 92-19, Norwich.

Brander, J. A. and Spencer, B. (1985). 'Export Subsidies and International Market Share Rivalry', *Journal of International Economics*, **18**, 83–100.

Conrad, K. (1993). 'Taxes and Subsidies for Pollution-Intensive Industries', *Journal of Environmental Economics and Management*, **25**, 121–35.

Davies, S. W. and McGuinness, A. J. (1982). 'Dumping at Less than Marginal Cost', *Journal of International Economics*, **12**, 169–82.

Eaton, J. and Grossman, G. M. (1986). 'Optimal Trade and Industrial Policy under Oligopoly', *Quarterly Journal of Economics*, **102**, 383–406.

Ethier, W. J. (1982). 'Dumping', *Journal of Political Economy*, **90**, 487–506.

Hansson, G. (1990). *Harmonization and International Trade*, London.

Hillman, A. L. and Ursprung, H. W. (1992). 'The Influence of Environmental Concerns on the Political Determination of International Trade Policy', in K. Anderson and R. Blackhurst (eds), *The Greening of World Trade Issues*, Harvester-Wheatsheaf.

Jones, R. W. (1974) 'Trade with Non-traded Goods: The Anatomy of Interconnected Markets', *Economica*, **41**, 121–38.

Kemp, M. C. and Jones, R. W. (1962). 'Variable Labor Supply and the Theory of International Trade', Journal of Political Economy, **70**, 30–6.

Markusen, J. R. (1975). 'International Externalities and Optimal Tax Structures', Journal of International Economics, **5**, 15–29.

Merrifield, J. D. (1988). 'The Impact of Abatement Strategies in Transnational Pollution, the Terms of Trade, and Factor Rewards: A General Equilibrium Approach', *Journal of Environmental Economics and Management*, **15**, 259–84.

Niskanen, W. (1977). *Bureaucracy and Representative Government*, Chicago.

Rauscher, M. (1991). 'Foreign Trade and the Environment', in H. Siebert (ed.), *Economics and the Environment: The International Dimension*, Mohr, Tübingen.

SPENCER, B. and BRANDER, J. A. (1983). 'International R & D Rivalry and Industrial Strategy', *Review of Economic Studies*, **50**, 707–22.

ULPH, A. (1992). 'The Choice of Environmental Policy Instruments and Strategic International Trade', in R. Pethig (ed.), *Conflicts and Cooperation in Managing Environmental Resources*, Springer, Berlin.

VINER, J. (1923). *Dumping: A Problem in International Trade*, University of Chicago Press, Chicago.

Environmental Regulations and Loss of Competitiveness

[8]

ENVIRONMENTAL CONTROL COSTS AND BORDER ADJUSTMENTS

CHARLES PEARSON*

ABSTRACT

Border adjustments (export rebates, import taxes) to offset international differences in environmental control costs are analyzed. The paper first notes conflicting national and international policy developments concerning border adjustments. After examining the international economic consequences of environmental control costs, the paper argues that border adjustments would subvert environmental objectives, distort international trade, probably violate GATT obligations, and present extraordinary administrative problems. Reliance on alternative policies, including exchange rate adjustments and compliance with OECD principles, is preferable.

Introduction

THERE are now several good general expositions of possible international economic consequences of environmental control (EC) measures and two quantitative studies of the international macro economic implications.[1] Since the publication of these studies, however, two potentially conflicting policy initiatives have developed which give focus to the discussion and oblige us to examine these matters once again. One policy initiative is at the international level — the May 1972 agreement within the OECD establishing guiding principles for international economic policy response to EC measures — and the other is buried within domestic legislation — Section 6 of the 1972 Federal Water Pollution Control Act Amendments.[2]

The potential conflict is over the use of border adjustments to offset differences in EC costs. The OECD agreement renounces the use of border adjustments (import charges, export rebates) to equalize EC costs. In contrast, Section 6 of the 1972 Federal Water Pollution Control legislation requires the Department of Commerce to initiate a study of U.S. and foreign EC cost differences and the possibilities for equalizing any difference at the U.S. border. The purpose of this paper, then, is to examine in some depth the issue of using border adjustments to neutralize EC induced changes in international trade.[3]

The discussion is divided into four parts. Section I presents a brief review of the international economic implications of government intervention to correct environmental externalities, and notes national and international policy developments in this area. Section II analyzes these applications, and concludes that the issue of major concern is change in the competitive position of individual industries. Furthermore, the sources of EC induced trade changes

*Associate Professor of International Economics, School of Advanced International Studies, The Johns Hopkins University. Research for this paper was supported in part by the SAIS International Environment for Multinational Business Program. I wish to thank Isaiah Frank, Bart Fisher and Wendy Takacs for helpful comments.

[1]S. Magee & W. Ford, "Environmental Pollution, the Terms of Trade & Balance of Payments of the U.S.," *Kyklos*, Vol. XXV, 1972 Fasc. 1; C. Pearson & W. Takacs, "International Economic Implications of Environmental Controls" in Commission on International Trade & Investment Policy, *Papers Vol. I*, Washington, D.C.: GPO, 1971; C. Russell & H. Landsberg, "International Environmental Problems — A Taxonomy," *Science 173 (3994)* July 23, 1971; I. Walter, "Environmental Control & Patterns of International Trade & Investment," *Banca Nazionale del Lavoro Quarterly Review*, Vol. XXV No. 100, March 1972; R. d'Arge, "International Trade, Domestic Income, and Environmental Controls: Some Empirical Results," Appendix F of Kneese, Rolfe, Harned (eds.), *Managing the Environment*, New York: Praeger, 1971; and R. d'Arge & A. Kneese, "Environmental Quality & International Trade," *International Organization*, Vol. 26 No. 2, Spring 1972.

[2]"Guiding Principles Concerning Internation Economic Aspects of Environmental Policies" adopted at the May 1972 Ministerial Meeting of the OECD, and P.L. 92-500 "Federal Water Pollution Control Act Amendments of 1972," October 1972.

[3]As noted below, the focus of this paper is on environmental control costs in production rather than consumption activities.

are identified, and the desirability of initiating compensatory policies is examined. Section III evaluates border adjustments in light of U.S.-GATT obligations. Section IV summarizes the case for and against border adjustments.

I. *Government Intervention and Policy Developments*

External diseconomies associated with the use of common property resources are at the center of the economic interpretation of environmental deterioration. The allocative inefficiencies associated with environmental common property resources provide the rationale for government intervention to improve social welfare.[4] In contemplating intervention, three conclusions emerge that have direct bearing on the international economic implications of EC measures.

First, there are strong economic efficiency arguments supporting modes of government intervention which force polluters to internalize the external costs of their activities. Both effluent and emissions charges systems, and government established standards on private waste discharges have this effect, although there has been considerable debate as to which approach is more efficient in reaching pollution abatement objectives. In contrast government assistance to industry in absorbing pollution abatement costs, through direct grants, tax breaks or interest subsidies, does not force the internalization of external costs and bring about the desired readjustment of relative prices. Second, environmental quality goals should be established according to the principle that marginal pollution abatement costs equal marginal benefits from abatement. Third, efficiency in the allocation of environmental resources will be improved if the location of economic activity responds to spatial differences in the availability and implicit prices of these resources. One expects and welcomes spatial reallocation of production as relatively "dirty" industries locate in areas where assimilative capacity is large, and clean industries locate in areas of low assimilative capacity and high demand for environmental quality.

The international economic dimension of these conclusions is clear. International agreement on the principle that private sector EC costs should not be absorbed by governments serves domestic allocative efficiency objectives, and also minimizes changes in trade arising from differences among countries in allocating EC costs between the public and private sector. With respect to the establishment of environmental quality goals, it is unlikely that cost and benefit functions will be identical internationally. Differences will arise from such factors as dissimilar technology, composition of output, age structure of plants, and assimilative capacity of environmental resources. Additionally the valuation of environmental quality is a function of income levels, tastes and so forth. Accordingly, as states select environmental goals which maximize their welfare, one does not expect uniformity of environmental standards internationally. Attempts to impose uniform standards internationally would deny legitimate differences. Finally, the expected spatial reallocation of economic activity, consequent to incorporation of environmental control costs in product prices is merely an extension of traditional comparative advantage theory. Trade, based in part on relative endowments of environmental resources, and in part on international differences in preferences for environmental quality, serves its traditional function of improving global productivity.

Moving to forestall new trade distortions arising from the implementation of EC measures, the OECD in 1972 adopted "Guiding Principles" for the treatment of EC costs.[5] Chief among these was the "Polluter-Pays Principle" which places the pollution abatement cost burden in the private rather than the public sector.[6] This is

[4]With no restrictions on waste disposal, implicit "rights" to CPR's are awarded to polluters. Note that the case for government intervention is strongest when private transactions costs among polluters and victims are greatest.

[5]The Principles follow closely the recommendations of the Williams Commission. See Commission on International Trade and Investment Policy, *United State International Economic Policy in an Interdependent World*, Washington: GPO, 1971.

[6]The term is somewhat unfortunate. First it confuses the issue of government vs. private

consistent with the objective of incorporating social costs, including environmental control costs, in product prices. With regard to international harmonization of environmental standards, the Guiding Principles are ambivalent. Harmonization is urged where possible, but the OECD acknowledged that differences in assimilative capacity, priorities and levels of industrialization justify different policies and standards. Finally, the member countries agreed not to use border adjustments to offset cost differences arising from different environmental policies.

Despite the OECD condemnation, border adjustments for differential EC costs continue to exert an appeal, and re-emerge in Section 6 of the 1972 Federal Water Pollution Control legislation. Specifically, the Department of Commerce is required to report on international EC cost differences by commodity, and to study alternative means by which cost differences could be equalized as, for example, by the use of border adjustments involving special import duties and perhaps export rebates. Indeed, the legislation expresses the intent that other countries undertake EC programs with goals at least as stringent as those of the U.S., and requests study of the impact border adjustments could have on encouraging others to increase their environmental controls.[7]

II. *International Economic Implications of EC Measures*[8]

To keep the presentation within the bounds of Section 6, and specifically the use of border adjustments, we do not investigate the international economic consequences of trans-national pollution, or the movement of pollutants, originating within the territory of one country and degrading the environment of another, or international common property resources such as the oceans. Nor do we address trade problems associated with the control of pollution from consumption activities.[9] The concern here is with EC measures that increase production costs.

Terms of Trade Effect

As Magee and Ford have shown, the terms of trade will improve if EC measures are initiated in the export sector, deteriorate if initiated in the import competing sector and foreign supply is not infinitely elastic, and remain unchanged if the import competing and foreign elasticities of supply are infinite. If costs increase in both import competing and export sectors, the terms of trade effect is indeterminate without knowledge of the relevant elasticities and cost increases.[10] While little can be said *a priori* about the terms of trade impact of EC controls, there is no justification for using a system of special import duties and export rebates to equalize EC costs internationally for the purpose of restoring a potential adverse change in the terms of trade, nor does this appear to be the purpose of Section 6.

Balance of Trade Effect

Assuming infinite supply elasticities, the immediate effect of EC related production

sector financing with another issue discussed in the literature — whether abatement cost should fall on the polluter or the victim. Further, the term is misleading in popular usage. The producer, if a polluter, need not pay but is free under the principle to pass forward abatement costs to the consumer. Finally, the principle does not oblige payment of compensation for residual damages.

[7]Section 6 and Title I, Section 101c.

[8]In addition to references cited earlier, see also GATT Studies in International Trade, "International Pollution Control and International Trade," Geneva: GATT, July 1971 and A. Scott, "The Economics of International Transmission of Pollution" in *Problems of Environmental Economics*, Paris: OECD, 1972.

[9]The trade consequences of product pollution control such as auto emission standards are similar to the non-tariff trade barrier issues thrown up by health and safety standards.

[10]Price elasticity of demand for imports and exportables, foreign price elasticity of demand for our exports, supply elasticities for exports and imports, and cross price elasticity of demand for import competing goods. Note EC cost increases are magnified in decreasing cost industries and dampened in increasing cost industries if output level is affected.

These conclusions are based on several limiting assumptions including constant real income and no EC induced exchange rate changes.

cost increases on the trade balance will be negative if the sum of the import and export demand elasticities are greater than one (Marshall-Lerner conditions). This effect will be modified or reversed, however, as domestic and foreign income effects associated with the trade balance change work through the system.[11] In any event, the trade balance effect should be considered a *macro* economic consequence. Even if the overall impact is zero, individual industries may well find their international competitive position affected.

If the trade balance is left in an unsatisfactory position as a result of EC measures, the appropriate policy response would employ macro-economic policy instruments, and especially an exchange rate adjustment sufficient to restore equilibrium. An exchange rate change is superior to attempting protection of EC impacted industries through special import duties and export rebates. If necessary, the exchange rate charge would automatically offer greater incentive to relatively "clean" export and import competing industries, and disincentive to high abatement cost industries. The structure of trade goods production would shift in an environmentally desirable direction. In contrast, border adjustments would frustrate environmentally desirable changes in the composition of export and import competing production in addition to violating international obligations and inviting retaliation as described below. The increased exchange rate flexibility in recent months essentially removes the trade balance effect as a justification for border adjustments.

EC Induced Changes in Comparative Advantage[12]

Although macro consequences of EC measures may be small or better dealt with through macro instruments, individual industries may find export markets eroded, or increasingly keen import competition. Before concluding that any compensatory policy such as border adjustments are called for we must examine the sources of trade changes in the light of the three conclusions developed in Section I.

EC induced trade changes can arise from the following:

(1) different standards imposed internationally
(2) identical standards, but costs of meeting standards differ due to differences in assimilative capacity, age structure of plant, abatement technology and so forth
(3) standards and costs identical, but timing differs
(4) standards, costs, and timing identical, but allocation of costs between private and public sectors differs
(5) all of the above identical, but willingness or ability of firms to pass on cost increases in product prices differs.

With regard to the first source, different standards, it was argued earlier that as environmental supply and demand conditions vary internationally, so too will environmental quality standards. To show that a trade shift resulting from different standards is a *distortion* to international trade it would be necessary to demonstrate that the foreign standard was not a legitimate reflection of that country's supply and demand for environmental quality, but was a covert attempt to subsidize its exports on world markets and its import competing sector at home. Even if such were the case a policy response of border adjustments by the higher standard country need not be warranted. The foreign standard set below optimal level implies a welfare transfer from the foreign residents who (perhaps unwittingly) accept a degraded environment, to the country importing products at less than full social cost. The traditional objections to accepting subsidized imports — potential for ultimate monopoly exploitation and trade balance impact — do not seem compelling. Nor does an argument for using border adjustments to reduce resource reallocation costs (transition costs) appear persuasive. Existing and proposed trade adjustment assistance programs will ease transition costs. Furthermore, EC mea-

[11] For tentative quantitative conclusions in the income and trade balance effect see d'Arge, and d'Arge & Kneese, *op. cit.*

[12] The distinction between changes in overall competitive position and comparative advantage is made by Ingo Walter, *op. cit.*

sures are implemented over substantial time periods which minimizes transition costs.

Concerning the second source of trade change, differential costs of meeting identical standards, there is no economic rationale for offsetting at the border cost differences reflecting environmental comparative advantage. Carried to its extreme, offsetting cost differences based on comparative advantage eliminates the basis for and gains from international trade. With regard to timing differences, however, and where ultimate similarity of standards can be contemplated, mutual consultation and harmonization can contribute to reducing unnecessary disruptions in the pattern of international trade.

Trade shifts due to differences in cost allocation between the public and private sector are in fact distortions to international trade. As argued in Section I, government assumption of private pollution abatement cost burden prevents the internalization of externalities. Product prices continue their failure to reflect social costs, and productive resources continue to be misallocated. It was to prevent this misallocation and minimize distortions to international trade that moved the OECD to adopt the Polluter Pays Principle. Even if this principle is not honored by others, however, the case for border adjustments by a country adhering to the principle is ambiguous. The cost of employing border adjustments would be to block domestically desirable changes in the structure of production, and to forego subsidized imports. Set against this would be protection of domestic producers from "unfair" competition, and the possibility of inducing foreign competitors to move toward a more efficient cost allocation regime.

Finally, trade shifts arising from differential ability to shift EC costs forward cannot justify compensatory policies such as border adjustments. *A priori,* there is no reason to believe that, internationally, firms will systematically react differently to EC costs.

The conclusions that emerge from considering EC induced changes in the competitive position of individual industries are as follows. First, not all trade changes consequent to EC measures should be viewed as trade distortions. Indeed the current pattern of trade is distorted to the extent that environmental resource costs are not incorporated in market prices. EC measures will necessarily and desirably lead to shifts in trade.[13] Second, trade changes resulting from either foreign government financing of private abatement costs or foreign standards that do not accurately reflect their environmental priorities should be viewed as trade distortions. The case for a compensatory border adjustment scheme, however, is weak. Third, efficiency and equity objective will be served if transition costs are minimized, regardless of the reason for reallocating resources.

III. *Section 6 and the GATT*[14]

While a full legal treatment of the relation between Section 6 issues and GATT obligations is beyond the scope of this paper, we do attempt to illustrate how EC policy meshes with the system of commercial policy regulations embodied in GATT. The issues are considered sequentially, first examining EC policies themselves, and then moving to the more complicated question of border adjustments.

A. Would government subsidies to industry for offsetting private pollution abatement costs represent subsidized production in violation of GATT obligations, and could importing countries consider countervailing duties? Article XVI, dealing with subsidies, distinguishes between production subsidies and export subsidies. If the government subsidization of private pollution abatement costs was applied equally to products destined for export and for domestic consumption, there does not seem to be any GATT violation, nor could the importing country avail itself of countervail-

[13] For elaboration of the proposition that government intervention designed to correct market failure resulting from externalities should not be viewed as distorting trade, and that compensatory trade policy to neutralize the effects of government intervention is undesirable, see W. Schwartz & E. Harper, "The Regulation of Subsidies Affecting International Trade," *Michigan Law Review* Vol. 70(5), April 1972.

[14] See in particular F. Kirgis, "Effective Pollution Control in Industrial Countries," *Michigan Law Review*, Vol. 70(5), April 1972, for a thoughtful analysis.

ing duties under Article VI. While such subsidization would violate the OECD principles, the GATT obligations would remain intact.[15]

B. Would a system of government *export* rebates to compensate U.S. producers for additional costs incurred through EC policies be permitted under GATT? The answer depends in part on the mechanism through which the additional EC costs were incurred. The case for export rebates would be weakest if the costs were incurred by firms in the process of meeting regulations and standards established by the government. This is the usual form of U.S.-EC policy, and nowhere in the GATT is there justification for rebating at the border costs incurred in meeting domestic regulations.

A more complicated question arises, however, if the form which the EC measure takes is a production tax designed to bring social and private costs into alignment. A production tax will be shifted partially or fully into product prices and it can be argued that the general GATT principle, permitting rebate of indirect taxes on the grounds that they are shifted forward into product prices, would be applicable. This argument then would treat environmentally motivated production taxes as indirect taxes which could be rebated (although this would undermine the purpose of the tax to limit pollution). The still unresolved question of *tax occult,* or the pyramiding of taxes up through the production structure, would however be raised.

Two other EC tax schemes are possible. Instead of taxing output to control pollution, inputs into production could be taxed for environmental purposes (as for example, a tax based on the sulphur content of fuels used in production). This again raises the *tax occult* issue. The final type of tax, which finds favor among many economists on the grounds of efficiency, is to tax emissions or effluents. Such a tax is neither a production tax nor a tax on intermediate inputs. An emission or effluent tax would most likely increase prices, and border rebates could be supported on the traditional grounds which distinguish between direct and indirect taxes. A contrary argument could be made persuasively that the effluent tax was not a tax, but the pricing of an input into production (environmental services) which previously had been supplied at less than cost. From that perspective, the effluent tax would be viewed as simply another payment to a factor of production. As prices paid to primary or intermediate inputs cannot be rebated, there would be no grounds for rebate of the emissions tax. Indeed, this last argument can be applied against rebates in the case of production taxes, although it is not an equally strong ground.[16]

C. Would a system of *import* duties, designed to offset the competitive disadvantage faced by domestic import competing producers be justified under GATT? Some of the issues raised by import duties are similar to those arising from export rebates. If the domestic EC costs were occasioned by government regulation and standards there does not appear to be a valid case for EC related import charges.[17] If, however, the EC measure is of the production tax form it could again be argued that the effect is similar to an indirect tax, raising product prices, and imports could be subject to an equivalent duty. This would, of course, again run counter to domestic environmental policy as it would help preserve the polluting industry. If the EC measures were of the effluent tax type, a case for and a case against duties could be made along the lines discussed earlier, but two potentially serious objections arise.

The first concerns equity for domestic producers. The purpose of an effluent tax

[15]The GATT does provide for a consultation process with a view toward limiting the subsidy if the latter operates directly or indirectly to encourage exports.

[16]An additional case might involve consumption pollution — or pollution by a product during the process of consumption — which is attacked by a production tax, perhaps for administrative convenience. In this (rare) situation the case for rebating the tax is stronger, for the external diseconomy occurs at the consumption location rather than the location of production.

[17]Unless the question is raised within the context of Article XIX, the escape clause provisions. Protection under the escape clause would presumably be limited to a very few highly sensitive items and could not be used as the basis for a widespread system of EC related duties on imports. See Kirgis, *op. cit.,* p. 903.

is efficiency in pollution abatement; effluent taxes are claimed to be more efficient than standards for they automatically distinguish between firms which face high abatement costs and firms which face relatively low abatement costs.[18]

So long as firms differ with respect to abatement costs, it is more efficient to respect these differences and this is done automatically using effluent taxes. An equity problem would arise, however, if firms which chose low abatement and high tax payments were given protection by import duties equal to their tax payments, while high abatement, low tax payment firms were granted lower protection according to their lower tax payment. In practice, a compensatory import charge would protect products, and there would be no method for distinguishing between firms according to their abatement vs tax payment behavior.

The second special problem relating to import charges and the GATT involves Article I and the Most-Favored-Nation principle.[19] If import charges to offset domestic EC costs were to be introduced, it seems reasonable that they would be related to the *differential* between domestic and foreign EC costs. They would lose their justification if foreign EC costs equalled domestic EC costs. The difficulty arises because each foreign competitor will have its own EC costs, and to equalize these foreign costs with domestic costs would require a separate duty computed by commodity and by individual competitor country. Beyond the enormous practical difficulty of establishing a duty rate for each commodity and each country, such a system would be directly counter to the non-discriminatory principle embodied in MFN and would be open to serious challenge from abroad. The alternative, to apply duties on the basis of some average of foreign EC costs, would penalize foreign competitors who have undertaken substantial environmental quality program and would be a disincentive for countries to move beyond the limits set by the average duty.[20]

In short, GATT would appear to preclude protection to offset certain types of EC costs such as government regulations and standards, and while perhaps permitting protection for other types of EC costs such as effluent taxes, would raise domestic equity problems and invite discriminatory trade practices.

IV. *Evaluation of Border Adjustments and Conclusions*

Economic and Environmental Considerations

Section II distinguishes between the macro and micro international economic implications of EC measures. It concluded that neither the terms of trade nor trade balance were the major concerns of Section 6, and that the use of border adjustments would be economically and environmentally inferior to macro-economic policy instruments in restoring any overall loss in international competitiveness. With regard to the impact of EC measures on the competitive position of individual industries, it was pointed out that not all shifts in the pattern of international trade consequent to EC measures are trade distortions warranting border adjustments or other compensatory policies. The case for border adjustments is strongest when trade shifts result from foreign government subsidization of foreign private EC costs, and when foreign environmental standards do not conform to environmental resource supply and demand, but are covertly set to gain a trade advantage. The latter is almost impossible to document. In any event border adjustments

[18]High abatement cost firms will undertake less abatement and pay higher taxes while low abatement cost firms will undertake more abatement and reduce their tax burden.

[19]The Most-Favored-Nation principle (MFN) remains the basic foundation of international commerce. It means that tariff advantages extended to one country are automatically extended to all others with whom you have negotiated MFN treatment. Thus, all exporting countries face identical non-discriminatory tariff rates in the import market.

[20]This particular problem could be avoided if all countries treated EC costs as they do indirect taxes — i.e., all countries rebate EC costs fully on exports and applied the full equivalent of EC costs on imports. Such a system would, however, violate the OECD obligation, be extremely questionable under GATT, and frustrate the potential for improving environmental resource allocation.

would not be consonant with allocative efficiency, but could only be justified on equity grounds — placing domestic producers on an equal footing with foreign competitors.

OECD and GATT Obligations

Border adjustments would violate OECD commitments provided that foreign competitors are abiding by two operative principles, the Polluter Pays Principle, and the establishment of standards which reflect environmental supply and demand conditions. Should these principles not be honored by others, the U.S. renouncement of the use of border adjustments loses considerable strength. For Section 6 purposes, then, the United States should monitor closely competitors' adherance to the OECD Guiding Principles.

Within GATT, border adjustments present a curious anomaly. The legitimacy of using export rebates would depend on the choice of government instruments used to force the internalization of EC costs — regulations and standards would not qualify, effluent taxes might qualify given a very strained argument, and production taxes would be most likely to qualify for rebate. The same holds true for import duties to equalize EC costs, but if these duties are calculated on a by-country basis the import charge would run afoul of the MFN doctrine. In a broader context, if GATT is seen as an instrument for improving global resource allocation by permitting comparative advantage to work, border adjustments would be undesirable when EC trade shifts are a result of legitimate differences in international environmental conditions, and most reasonable when the shifts result from foreign government subsidies and covert attempts to improve competitive conditions by setting unreasonably low standards.

Practical Aspects

Assuming the export rebate/import charge system is designed to neutralize cost differences arising from foreign government subsidization or artificially low standards, the informational and administrative requirements would be enormous. For each major competitor and for the United States it would be necessary to determine, by industry and perhaps product, the EC policies in effect and their impact on costs, channels for and cost saving equivalent of government assistance, and the extent to which EC standards accurately reflect environmental supply and demand conditions. Additional problems would remain. Information must be current, and duty and rebate levels adjusted frequently as EC policies evolve. With respect to export rebate rates, a problem arises in choosing appropriate foreign costs. If average foreign costs are chosen, environmentally progressive foreign competitors are penalized and others rewarded. Conversely, if export rebates are based on EC costs in the country of destination, the problem of equalizing competitive position in exporting to third country markets remains. Further, would we be consistent and *subsidize* imports and *tax* exports if foreign EC costs exceed U.S. costs, as is likely in certain product lines? Would domestic producers relax efforts to minimize abatement costs if they expected to receive rebates and protection?

International Reaction

The international response to unilateral imposition of border adjustments would depend, *inter alia,* upon the degree to which they were deemed consistent with our OECD and GATT obligations, and the size of the EC related rebates and changes. Clearly any system of rebates and import duties would be wide open to challenge, and the potential for friction among trading partners is large. Furthermore, such an action by the United States would invite other countries to take similar measures, and an intricate web of highly questionable rebates and duties would be superimposed on trade relations. The opportunity for protectionism would be substantial.[21]

[21]An attempt by one country to equalize one element of production costs (EC costs) would encourage other equalization schemes in other areas — for example, industrial health and safety regulations.

A major concern of Section 6 is the impact border adjustments might have on encouraging foreign competitors to implement EC measures.[22] If rebates and import charges were based on average foreign EC costs (which is administratively easier) a perverse incentive would be given. Countries with low EC costs would be discouraged from tightening EC policy while facing the same EC duty in the U.S. market. Countries with EC costs above the average EC duty rate would improve their competitive position by lowering EC standards. Similar conclusions obtain if U.S. export rebates were based on average foreign EC costs. Import charges and export rebates based on EC costs in individual countries of origin or destination would be better from the incentive standpoint, but at most would remove a disincentive to upgrading foreign EC standards, and would not provide a positive incentive.

In summary, the case for border adjustments has a patina of respectability on the grounds of "fair competition" for domestic producers, but on closer inspection the argument is quite dubious. Reliance should be placed on measures to improve the domestic mobility of resources and to insure reasonable compliance internationally with the OECD principles.

[22]As noted earlier, the Water Pollution Control Act also endorses the objective that foreign EC standards be brought up at least to U.S. levels. See Title I.

BIBLIOGRAPHY

R. d'Arge, "International Trade, Domestic Income, and Environmental Controls: Some Empirical Results," Appendix F of Kneese, Rolfe, Harned (eds.), *Managing the Environment,* New York: Praeger, 1971.

R. d'Arge and A. Kneese, "Environmental Quality & International Trade," *International Organization,* Spring 1972.

GATT, "Industrial Pollution Control & International Trade," Studies in International Trade, July 1971.

F. Kirgis, "Effective Pollution Control in Industrial Countries," *Michigan Law Review,* April 1972.

S. Magee and W. Ford, "Environmental Pollution, the Terms of Trade & Balance of Payments of the U.S.," *Kyklos,* 1972 Fasc. 1.

C. Pearson and W. Takacs, "International Economic Implications of Environmental Controls" in Commission on International Trade & Investment Policy, *Papers Vol. I,* Washington, D.C.: GPO, 1971.

C. Russell and H. Landsberg, "International Environmental Problems — A Taxonomy," *Science,* July 25, 1971.

W. Schwartz and E. Harper, "The Regulation of Subsidies Affecting International Trade," *Michigan Law Review,* April 1972.

A. Scott, "The Economics of International Transmission of Pollution," in *Problems of Environmental Economics,* Paris: OECD, 1972.

I. Walter, "Environmental Control & Patterns of International Trade & Investment," *Banca Nazionale del Lavoro Quarterly Review,* March 1972.

[9]

THE POLLUTION CONTENT OF AMERICAN TRADE

INGO WALTER*
New York University

The emergence in recent years of the human environment as a matter of serious economic, social and political concern has stimulated some potentially useful, albeit preliminary, research on the international economics of pollution. For example, the capacity of the environment to assimilate pollutants represents a determinant of supply conditions and is therefore a factor affecting comparative advantage.[1] There is also reason to believe that national political collectivities will differ at least to some degree in their assessments of what is an "acceptable" environment, viewed as a question of social preference.[2] Both will have a bearing on the determination of national environmental-control (EC) standards, and on the economic cost of meeting those standards. As these costs are passed forward to purchasers or backward to productive factors and taxpayers, and as productive resources are increasingly devoted to maintenance and restoration of environmental balance, patterns of international trade and investment will inevitably shift.[3]

Very little evidence is available as yet on international differences in environmental assimilative capacities, social preferences and techniques of implementing whatever EC standards are set—e.g., Pigovian taxation based on the volume of pollutive discharge *versus* enforcement of standards on a "polluter pays" basis *versus* government subsidization of EC equipment and technology.[4] Recent studies [1] [2] [12] [13] have made some progress in evaluating whether EC costs related to production processes or to traded products themselves are *in fact* important enough to cause significant international competitive shifts and their derivative economic effects.

The purpose of this paper is to determine at least in a preliminary way whether EC charges actually incurred by industry form an essentially "trade-neutral" pattern, or whether they are fundamentally export-biased

*The author is indebted to Falih Alsaaty for statistical assistance and to Robert G. Hawkins for helpful comments on an earlier draft. The research was made possible by a grant from the Ford Foundation.

1. See, for example, the discussion contained in [6] [8] and [28].

2. See [26] for an evaluation of these differences in terms of their impact on corporate decision-making.

3. Environmental control may affect the volume, composition, balance, direction and terms of international trade, industrial location, transport costs, and a variety of related variables, including national policy responses. For a detailed discussion see [27], [28], and [15]. With respect to the developing countries, see [19] and [23]. As related to conventional trade theory and transboundary pollution, see [11].

4. For some research priorities, see [5].

or import-biased. If U.S. exports are inherently more pollution-intensive than imports, then *whatever* pattern of environmental policies eventually emerges among the major trading nations will impact disproportionately on U.S. performance in the international market.[5]

Measuring EC Loadings. One way to approach this problem is to determine—for a given tradeable product or product-group—what proportion of its final value, at market prices, is attributable to internalization of environmental externalities arising in the production *process* or in rendering the product *itself* environmentally acceptable—either in its normal use or as a residual at the end of its useful life. This can be done by estimating what the value of that product *would be* if it and its production process fully conformed to accepted environmental norms without absorbing any economic resources to achieve this conformity. The hypothetical value of a given internationally-traded product (P_H) can then be compared with its actual market price (P_A) in order to determine its "direct EC loading" (*DECL*):

$$DECL = (P_A - P_H)/P_A \tag{1}$$

Since each of the raw-material and intermediate inputs into the traded product is also subject to an environmental charge, the "overall EC loading" (*OECL*) of a given tradeable product is its own *DECL* plus that of each input weighted by the contribution of the input to final export or import value. If we let j represent the traded product, i a given input, and a_{ij} the contribution of i to the unit trade-value of j, then:

$$OECL_j = [(P_A - P_H)_j + \sum_{i=1}^{n} a_{ij}(P_A - P_H)_i]/P_{A_j} \tag{2}$$

While it is impossible to generate observable values for P_H, direct and indirect costs attributable to environmental management can be estimated. These are assumed to approximate $(P_A - P_H)_j$ for tradeable products and $(P_A - P_H)_i$ for inputs,[6] and estimates for the overall environmental-control loadings can be developed using Equation (2).

The Data. For purposes of this paper, environmental-control costs are broken down into (a) current research and development expenditures, (b) depreciation charges on in-place pollution-control equipment, (c) the capital cost of in-place pollution-control equipment, and (d) current operating

5. The point is to examine the product-profile of U.S. exports and imports and to compare it with a pollution-profile covering the same spectrum of tradeable goods and services.

6. We assume constant costs; the price-response to EC costs will clearly differ for increasing- and decreasing-cost industries. See [5].

costs associated with environmental management.[7] The cost estimates for this study were obtained directly for R&D and inferentially for operating-cost requirements. The capital-cost and depreciation components were derived from estimates of the in-place stock of EC equipment. Since no data for the latter yet exist, the estimates were developed from current increments in that stock, and as such represent a composite of past, present and anticipated future requirements for pollution-control hardware. Although there is considerable margin for error in such estimates, their ordinal ranking by industry may be relatively close to the mark.[8]

The sum of the above charges for each of 18 manufacturing industries, and for aggregate mining, transportation, utilities, commercial services, communications and agriculture was divided in each case by gross sales or billings in 1971 to obtain for each sector estimated EC costs per dollar of sales. The results are presented in Table 1.

It is important to remember that the values presented incorporate three factors: (a) internalization of environmental externalities attributable to the production process; (b) expenditure required to render products environmentally acceptable; and (c) costs attributable to the production of EC-hardware and technology—which are responsible for the high EC-loading indicated for the instruments sector, for example. Separation of the latter EC cost element is impossible. Hence, while high EC charges per dollar of sales generally bear a negative international competitive connotation, this is not uniformly true.

In order to disaggregate the industry-based estimates of environmental costs into product-based *DECL* estimates useful for application in an international trade context, 83 goods and services categories contained in the U.S. input-output table [24] were employed.[9] The relevant values shown in the first column of Table 2, together with 1966 U.S. input-

7. Information on what it costs individual firms and industries to meet existing or anticipated environmental standards is generally notoriously poor in quality, in part because of problems encountered in separating EC charges from other kinds of production costs. R & D costs were taken from [17]. Estimates of in-place EC hardware were derived by multiplying the proportion of EC in total 1971 investment by total industry capital stock in that year according to data contained in [18], [7] and [25], under the assumption that the proportion of EC investment in total investment is indicative of what the proportion of EC-related capital stock should be, by industry. The depreciation cost was derived by applying the industry capital consumption rate [7] to the corresponding estimate of in-place EC hardware. The capital cost was derived by applying the net pre-tax industry rate of return [7] to the in-place EC hardware estimate. Operating cost estimates from [14] applied in proportion to the estimate of in-place EC capital stock.

8. For industries producing more than one I/O category of products or services, a judgment based on the engineering nature of the output was made whether it is at, above, or below average for the industry relative to its value-added. In the latter two cases, the estimates were accordingly adjusted upward or downward on that basis.

9. A concordance was developed between the various I/O product groups and the Standard International Trade Classification product groups described in [22]. Trade data from [21].

Table 1 – Estimated Environmental Control Costs Per Dollar of Gross Industry Sales, 1971

Industry	*EC Cost: Cents Per Dollar of Sales*
Iron & steel	1.47
Nonferrous metals	1.76
Electrical machinery	0.49
Machinery	1.03
Autos, trucks & parts	1.19
Aerospace	0.57
Other transportation equipment	0.72
Fabricated metals	0.52
Instruments	3.37
Stone, clay & glass	1.75
Other durables	0.60
Chemicals	2.19
Paper	1.63
Rubber	0.63
Petroleum	3.73
Food & beverages	0.36
Textiles	0.38
Other nondurables	0.10
Mining	0.82
Railroads	0.46
Airlines	0.27
Other transportation	0.63
Communications	0.08
Electric utilities	7.00
Gas utilities	0.12
Commercial	0.32
Agriculture & fisheries	0.11
Total durables	1.18
Total nondurables	1.15
All business	1.16

Data: [7] [14] [17] [18] [25]. Computations are explained in footnote 7.

Table 2

Pollution Content of American Exports and Imports: Estimated Direct (DECL) and Overall (OECL) Environmental-Control Loadings Entering U.S. International Trade Flows, 1968-70

	(1)	(2)	(3)	(4)	(5)	(6)
I/O Product or Service Group	DECL[a]	OECL[a]	Export/Import Ratio U.S.-Rest of World	OECL Exports[b]	OECL Imports[b]	Relative Impact Index[c]
1. Livestock & products	1.28	1.98	0.61	$ 10.06	$ 16.49	1.10
2. Other agricultural products	1.92	2.46	1.84	117.93	64.12	4.52
3. Forestry and fishery products	0.64	1.05	0.11	0.83	7.40	0.12
5. Iron & ferroalloy ores mining	0.82	1.16	0.15	0.77	5.14	0.18
6. Nonferrous metal ores mining	0.82	1.29	0.36	2.41	6.66	0.47
7. Coal mining	1.76	2.21	42.02	16.22	0.39	92.86
8. Crude petroleum & natural gas	0.41	0.64	0.08	0.86	10.54	0.05
9. Stone & clay mining and quarrying	0.41	0.95	0.73	1.62	2.23	0.69
10. Chemical & fertilizer mining	0.82	1.31	2.42	1.51	0.81	3.17
13. Ordnance & accessories	0.53	2.36	12.72	15.81	1.24	30.02
14. Food and kindred products	0.36	1.01	0.28	5.47	19.33	0.29
15. Tobacco manufactures	0.18	0.51	4.93	3.50	0.71	2.51
16. Broad & narrow fabrics, yarn, thread	0.38	1.02	0.47	3.87	8.19	0.48
17. Misc. textile goods and floor covering	0.38	1.10	0.93	1.06	1.15	1.02
18. Apparel	0.19	0.50	0.20	1.08	5.38	0.10
19. Misc. fabricated textile products	0.19	0.55	0.70	0.49	0.70	0.38
20. Lumber & wood prods. except containers	0.10	0.45	0.60	2.80	4.68	0.27
21. Wooden containers	0.05	0.56	0.66	0.01	0.02	0.30
22-23. Furniture & fixtures	0.05	0.59	0.29	0.57	1.97	0.17
24. Paper & allied prods. exc. containers	1.63	2.33	0.60	21.35	35.48	1.40
25. Paperboard containers & boxes	1.63	2.50	9.42	0.73	0.08	23.56
26. Printing & publishing	0.08	0.56	2.32	1.73	0.75	3.25
27. Chemicals & selected chemical prods.	2.19	3.25	2.01	55.71	27.71	6.53
28. Plastics & synthetic materials	2.19	3.34	4.40	23.17	5.26	14.71
29. Drugs, cleaning, toilet preparations	1.10	1.78	3.34	9.44	2.83	5.94
30. Paints & allied products	3.29	4.27	1.60	5.44	3.34	6.84
31. Petroleum refining & related products	3.73	4.58	0.39	20.55	53.04	1.77
32. Rubber & misc. plastic prods.	0.63	1.38	0.82	5.00	6.12	1.13
33. Leather tanning & industrial leather	0.95	1.38	0.21	1.04	4.89	0.29
34. Footwear & other leather products	0.32	0.57	0.02	0.05	2.86	0.10

Table 2 (continued)

I/O Product or Service Group	(1) DECL[a]	(2) OECL[a]	(3) Export/Import Ratio U.S.-Rest of World	(4) OECL Exports[b]	(5) OECL Imports[b]	(6) Relative Impact Index[c]
35. Glass & glass products	0.86	1.55	0.93	$ 2.57	$ 2.80	1.44
36. Stone & clay products	1.72	2.40	0.35	6.57	18.68	0.84
37. Primary iron & steel	1.47	2.16	0.44	20.55	42.41	0.94
38. Primary nonferrous metals	1.76	3.09	0.49	25.67	52.78	1.50
39. Metal containers	0.53	1.35	2.29	0.44	0.20	3.09
40. Heating, plumbing, structural metal	0.53	1.28	5.06	1.71	0.34	6.47
41. Stamping, screw machine products	0.53	1.21	0.42	0.79	1.87	0.51
42. Other fabr. metal products	0.53	1.23	0.28	0.74	2.67	0.34
43. Engines and turbines	1.03	1.66	2.01	21.16	10.57	3.33
44. Farm machinery & equipment	1.03	1.66	2.48	10.48	4.23	4.11
45. Construction, mining, oil field equipt.	1.03	1.94	14.83	12.45	0.84	28.77
46. Metals handling mach. & equipt.	1.03	1.75	6.48	1.94	0.30	11.35
47. Metalworking mach. & equipt.	1.03	1.53	1.95	5.47	2.81	2.98
48. Special industrial mach. & equipt.	1.03	1.61	0.94	5.88	6.24	1.52
49. General industrial mach. & equipt.	1.03	1.63	4.32	43.63	10.11	7.04
50. Machine shop products	1.03	1.58	1.28	5.81	4.55	2.02
51. Office computing & acct. machines	0.49	0.89	2.95	9.92	3.36	2.63
52. Service industry machines	1.03	1.63	1.88	2.05	1.09	3.06
53. Electric industrial equipt.	0.49	1.07	2.79	6.12	2.20	2.98
54. Household appliances	0.49	1.22	1.09	1.51	1.38	1.33
55. Electric lighting & wiring equipt.	0.49	1.14	0.65	1.15	1.75	0.75
56. Radio, TV, commun. equipt.	0.49	0.84	0.64	5.07	7.97	0.54
57. Electronic components & access.	0.49	1.04	2.33	4.33	1.85	2.42
58. Misc. elect. mach. & supplies	0.49	1.11	2.42	9.60	3.96	2.69
59. Motor vehicles & equipt.	1.19	2.04	0.75	75.78	97.03	1.53
60. Aircraft & parts	0.57	1.06	8.66	26.02	3.01	9.18
61. Other transportation equipment	0.72	1.31	2.41	3.47	1.44	3.15
62. Scientific & controlling instr.	3.37	4.03	5.66	22.07	3.90	22.82
63. Optical, opthalmic, photographic equipt.	3.37	3.96	0.98	8.80	9.03	3.86
64. Misc. manufacturing	1.17	1.67	0.53	16.36	30.66	0.89
65. Transportation & warehousing	0.53	0.85	0.80	25.90	29.20	0.75
70. Finance & insurance	0.16	0.38	0.13	0.08	0.61	0.05
77. Medical, educational, nonprofit	0.01	0.29	0.42	6.42	15.30	0.12
RR. Misc. services[d]	0.69	1.16	4.97	29.29	5.90	5.76
Total			0.99	$751.40	$608.50	

Data: [7] [14] [17] [18] [23] [25]. For computations, see footnotes 7, 8, and 9.

[a] Cents per dollar of final sales.

[b] Millions of dollars.

[c] Export/Import ratio multiplied by OECL value.

[d] Includes I/O Nos. 4, 11, 12, 66, 67, 68, 69, 71. 72. 73, 75, 76.

output (I/O) coefficients, were used to derive the *OECL* values presented in the second column of that table.

EC Loadings and U.S. Trade. Use of the foregoing estimates of overall environmental-control loadings by product groups yields a pollution-loading profile of U.S. trade. On the export side, the *OECL* values in Table 2 are simply multiplied by the value of sales abroad for each product or service group. The product mix within each group for exports is assumed identical to the product mix for total sales, and average prices charged on exports are assumed to be the same as on domestic sales. The result is Column 4 of Table 2, indicating that the average annual *OECL* of U.S. exports during the 1968-70 period was about $751 million, or 1.75 percent of total exports.

Since there is no way of knowing the *OECL* values of foreign suppliers, we assume them to be the same as for domestic import-competing suppliers and estimate what the overall EC loading of U.S. imports would have been if the imported goods had been produced at home. We again assume that the product-mix of imports within each group is identical to the mix of total sales of the import-competing industry, and that imported and import-competing product prices are the same. The results, given in Column 5 of Table 2, indicate that in 1968-70 the U.S. average annual *OECL* on imports was about $609 million, or 1.52 percent of total imports.

Over the entire range of traded goods and services, it appears that 1.75 percent of the value of U.S. exports consisted of pollution-related costs, which is about 15 percent higher than the 1.52 percent estimated for U.S. imports. This difference does not appear very significant and suggests that EC measures bearing on the respective suppliers of U.S. exports and imports will be trade-neutral, or at worst only marginally biased against the U.S. In short, the product-profile of American exports does not seem to be systematically more or less pollution-intensive than the product-profile of American imports.[10]

This does not mean, however, that U.S. trade in individual industries may not be vulnerable to increased environmental costs in terms of their international competitiveness. This vulnerability of a given industry will be larger (a) the more competitive its products are in the international marketplace, and (b) the higher its overall environmental-control loading.[11]

A proxy for international competitiveness is the export/import ratio given in Column 3 of Table 2. When this is multiplied by the *OECL* values

10. For another view, and reconciliation with the findings of the present paper, see [9].

11. For some case studies, see [2].

given in Column 2, the "relative impact index" given in Column 6 of Table 2 results. These values show that, all else equal, the U.S. international competitive position may be affected in industries such as ordnance and accessories, construction and mining equipment, and plastics, relative to industries such as apparel, fishery and forest products, and footwear, which are already characterized by a substantial competitive disadvantage or where EC costs are not very important.[12]

It follows that American trade with individual foreign countries may be affected differently in terms of trade-neutrality of EC regulations. For example, the average annual pollution-control loading of U.S. exports to Canada during the 1968-70 period was $157 million, compared with $174 million for imports—representing *OECL* percentage values of 1.75 for exports and 1.70 for imports. During the same period, the pollution loading of American exports to Japan was $68 million compared with $88 million for imports, but with percentage *OECL* values of 1.70 for exports and 1.50 for imports. Relative to imports from Japan, therefore, U.S. exports to Japan appear to be relatively pollution-intensive, which is much less true of U.S.-Canada trade.

Some Concluding Comments. It is clear that U.S. trade will be affected if the world's nations adopt different environmental standards and/or ways of implementing such standards. Application of disaggregated price elasticities of U.S. imports and exports to the *OECL* values presented in Table 2 would, for example, indicate the possible trade-impact under the extreme assumption that no other country applied EC-measures of any kind. At the other extreme is the assumption that all countries apply and enforce identical EC norms, which will affect trade flows of individual countries differently depending on their relative pollution intensity.

The findings presented here appear to indicate that for the U.S. such a bias might be adverse, but only marginally so. The impact on the direction of trade and on the international competitiveness of individual economic sectors could nevertheless be substantial. Unfortunately, in view of the quality of the data and overriding uncertainties with regard to future costs of environmental management, a discussion of this type can only be regarded as preliminary.

12. The special case of scientific and controlling instruments, where the direction of impact would tend to be the opposite, has already been explained.

REFERENCES

1. J. Brashares, "Cost Estimates for Environment Improvement Programs," in *Managing the Environment: International Cooperation for Pollution Control*, eds., A. V. Kneese *et al.*, New York 1971.

2. Council on Environmental Quality, Department of Commerce, and Environmental Protection Agency, *The Economic Impact of Pollution Control*, Washington 1972.

3. R. C. D'Arge, "International Trade and Domestic Environmental Control: Some Empirical Estimates," in *Managing the Environment: International Cooperation for Pollution Control*, eds., A. V. Kneese *et al.*, New York 1971.

4. ———, "Trade, Environmental Controls, and the Developing Economies," in *Problems of Environmental Economics*, OECD, Paris 1972.

5. ———, G. C. Hufbauer and I. Walter, "International Economic and Environmental Aspects of a National Materials Policy," Environmental Studies Board, National Academy of Sciences, Washington (mimeo.) 1973.

6. ——— and A. V. Kneese, "Environmental Quality and International Trade," *International Organization*, Spring 1972, *26*, 419-65.

7. Federal Trade Commission, *Quarterly Financial Reports*, No. II, Washington 1972.

8. General Agreement on Tariffs and Trade, *Industrial Pollution and International Trade*, Geneva 1971.

9. F. Huynh, "The Relative Pollution Intensity of U.S. Trade," Department of Economics, Michigan State Univ. (unpublished), 1973.

10. B. P. Klotz, "The Trade Effects of Unilateral Pollution Standards," in *Problems of Environmental Economics*, OECD, Paris 1972.

11. A. Y. C. Koo, "Environmental Repercussions and Trade Theory," Michigan State Univ., Econometric Workshop Paper No. 7102, Oct. 1971.

12. W. Leontief, "Environmental Repercussions and Economic Structure: An Input-Output Approach," *Rev. Econ. Stat.*, Aug. 1970, *52*, 374-81.

13. ——— and W. F. Ford, "Air Pollution and Economic Structure: Empirical Results of Input-Output Computations," Harvard Univ. (unpublished), 1972.

14. L. Lund, *Industry Expenditures for Water Pollution Control*, National Industrial Conference Board, New York 1972.

15. S. P. Magee and W. F. Ford, "Environmental Pollution, the Terms of Trade and the Balance of Payments of the United States," *Kyklos*, Fasc. 1, 1972, *25*, 101-18.

16. A. Majocchi, "The Impact of Environmental Measures on Trade: Some Policy Issues," in *Problems of Environmental Economics*, OECD, Paris 1972.

17. McGraw-Hill Economics, *5th Annual McGraw-Hill Survey of Pollution Control Expenditures*, New York, May 12, 1972.

18. ———, *25th Annual McGraw-Hill Survey of Business Plans for New Plant and Equipment*, New York, April 28, 1972.

19. M. Ozorio de Almeida *et al.*, "Environment and Development: The Founex Report," *International Conciliation*, Jan. 1972, *586*, 7-83.

20. C. Pearson and W. Takacs, "International Economic Implications of Environmental Control and Pollution Abatement Programs," in *United States International Economic Policy in an Interdependent World*, Report of the Williams Commission, Washington, July 1971.

21. United Nations, Statistical Office, *Commodity Trade Statistics*, Stat. Papers Ser. D, New York 1969-71.

22. ———, *Standard International Trade Classification*, Rev., Stat. Papers Ser. M, No. 34, New York 1961.

23. United Nations Conference on Trade and Development, *The Implications of Environmental Measures for International Trade and Development*, Document TD/130, Santiago 1972.

24. U.S. Department of Commerce, *Input-Output Transactions: 1966*, Document BEA-SP 72-019, Washington, Feb. 1972.

25. ———, *Survey of Current Business*, Washington, June 1972.

26. I. Walter, *Environmental Control and Consumer Protection: Emerging Forces in Multinational Corporate Operations*, Center for Multinational Studies Occasional Paper No. 2, Washington 1972.

27. ———, "Environmental Control and the Patterns of International Trade and Investment: An Emerging Policy Issue," *Banca Naz. Lavoro Quart. Rev.*, March 1972, *100*, 82-106.

28. ———, "Environmental Management and the International Economic Order," Ford Foundation-Brookings Institution Project on the Future of the International Economic Order, Washington (unpublished), 1972.

[10]

JOURNAL OF ENVIRONMENTAL ECONOMICS AND MANAGEMENT 4, 135–152 (1977)

International Competitive Displacement from Environmental Control

The Quantitative Gains from Methodological Refinement[1]

JOHN H. MUTTI

Department of Economics, University of Wyoming, Laramie, Wyoming 82070

AND

J. DAVID RICHARDSON

Department of Economics, University of Wisconsin–Madison, Madison, Wisconsin 83706

Received November 2, 1976; revised January 11, 1977

This paper demonstrates empirically the gain from adopting more general equilibrium approaches in projecting the effects on domestic output and international trade of environmental controls. The suggested models include a partial equilibrium case where all industries are treated independently, an intermediate case incorporating effects in supplying industries, and general equilibrium formulations based on alternative macroeconomic conditions. U. S. data is used to evaluate these models. Under both pollutor pays and subsidy financing schemes, moving from the simplest case to the intermediate model results in quite different industry projections. Including macroeconomic factors appears particularly important in the classical setting.

This paper evaluates the relative merits and predictions of several simple and sophisticated methodologies for estimating the industry-by-industry displacement caused by deterioration in the U. S. international competitive position, deterioration induced specifically by unilateral environmental control. Its genesis lies partially in the response to an earlier empirical general-equilibrium approach to the same problem [12]. What, it was asked, does a carefully specified general-equilibrium approach tell us that a casually specified partial-equilibrium approach (or even simple intuition) does not? Was it really worth the effort? In general, our results below support the answers "a lot" and "yes." Methodological refinements of the sort we illustrate turn out usually to have sizable quantitative effects on both the extent of industrial displacement from environmental control, and on its incidence from industry to industry. We believe that this conclusion would also characterize alternative approaches to estimating the impacts of a wide range of shocks to domestic costs, besides environmental control.

[1] The authors gratefully acknowledge the helpful comments of Ingo Walter and an anonymous referee, the research assistance of Robert A. Feldman and Peter Yashua and the financial support of the Ford Foundation in its grant to the Universities of Wisconsin and Wyoming to support research in International Economic Order.

ISSN 0095-0696

I. INTRODUCTION

Unilateral environmental control by the United States confronts every U. S. tradeables industry with a loss of business. If financed according to the "polluter pays" principle, then every industry's costs are raised directly by the expense of its environmental clean-up. If financed with subsidies which are raised by explicit or implicit taxation (e.g., higher rates of inflation), then every industry's costs are raised indirectly by higher taxes. Either way, U. S. industries lose international competitiveness, and the time path describing present and future output is displaced negatively from what it otherwise would have been. Any resulting unemployment or excess capacity because of immobile productive factors and inflexible prices, whether transitory or permanent, is properly reckoned as a social cost of environmental control [1, 11].

Attempts to measure these displacements quantitatively are familiar: Magee and Ford [10], d'Arge [6], d'Arge and Kneese [7], Walter [20], Council on Environmental Quality [5], U. S. Department of Commerce [16], and Mutti and Richardson [12], among others. Each attempt has differed from the others in approach and methodology. Some have focused on aggregate economy-wide data, others on particular industries in isolation, and still others on interindustry linkages. Some have controlled for the effect of environmental control on macroeconomic well-being and the international terms of trade, others have not. Some have allowed the cost of environmental control to pass through fully to the U. S. price level, others have allowed a portion to be absorbed by lower wages, profits, and other factor prices. Efforts to evaluate the diverse empirical conclusions founder for the same reasons that the studies differ. One cannot compare the incomparable. And as a result, one cannot suggest very forcefully the direction in which methodological refinement should go.

However, in a given study, it is possible to proceed sequentially, beginning with the simplest "models" that are usually employed for these purposes, and advancing to more complicated ones that incorporate many of the sophisticated features found in less casual work. Quantitative comparisons across levels of sophistication *are* then possible. One can infer just how much difference it makes to allow for complications, and therefore whether allowing for them is "worth it" in calculations of the economic cost of unilateral environmental control.

Assessments of industrial dislocation from *unilateral* environmental control may be a fool's errand, of course. One can argue that it is precisely these potential dislocation costs that make government-mandated environmental control either multilateral or nonexistent. Yet such an argument seems both extreme and irrelevant to the work below. The argument is extreme because unilateral environmental control is observed in reality, especially among the most developed countries. And when it has been multilateral, countries have often differed significantly in their phasing of controls, and in their administration and financing of them.[2] Furthermore, "multilateral" has almost never spanned the large group of less developed countries who are major polluters themselves. Ultimately, the argument seems irrelevant to the purpose of this paper. The proportional dif-

[2] For a good summary of European environmental control programs, which suggests support along these lines for a less extreme perspective, see Barde [2]. Significant intercountry differences in environmental control programs are also documented in Walter [18].

ferences in quantitative results across alternative approaches and methodologies are probably only slightly affected by focusing on the effects of multilateral, rather than unilateral, environmental control.[3]

Several features are common across all of the methodological approaches summarized below. First, our interest is always in the disaggregated output shocks that unilateral environmental control imposes on U. S. industries through loss of international competitiveness, both in their importance as a percentage of output and in their evenness from industry to industry. Second, the level of industrial detail is uniform across approaches. Attention is fixed on the 81 industries distinguished in the most familiar (1967) U. S. input–output table. Third, the time horizon is uniformly a five-to-ten-year "medium run." The medium run is defined as being long enough for current employment-output decisions to be adjusted fully to the altered pattern of wages, profits, and prices, yet short enough that the impacts of environmental control on new capital spending, technological best-practice methods, and lifetime labor-force participation rates are still dominated by current employment-output decisions.[4] Finally, each approach is carried out under pure versions of the two most familiar methods of financing environmental control: the "polluter pays" principle and subsidization out of general tax revenues.[5]

What differs is the methodological approach to the central question. Schema 1 illustrates verbally the four approaches that we compare in this paper. These four were selected because they, or compromises among them, appear to encompass the methodology of much previous work on this subject.[6]

Each of the four approaches is outlined in greater detail in Section II of the paper. In Section III, each is applied to estimate U. S. industrial displacement from the international competitive effects of environmental control. The methodologies are compared by evaluating how well displacements calculated by the

[3] One *would* expect the quantitative dislocations from multilateral environmental control to be ***absolutely*** smaller than those from unilateral environmental control, of course.

[4] Maintaining this time horizon makes defensible several operational assumptions in the empirical analysis below, e.g., that long-run price elasticities of demand and supply can be appealed to, yet that constancy of both input–output coefficients and the industrial mix of final demand for capital goods are not too unrealistic to be invoked.

[5] Neither method of financing is relevant to environmental control programs actually adopted from nation to nation. The "polluter pays" method comes closest, having been agreed to as a guiding principle by the 24 member nations of the Organization for Economic Co-operation and Development. Yet elements of subsidy methods are still prominent under "polluter pays" as documented extensively in Walter [18]. Industries that are particularly burdened by environmental control often qualify for subsidies under policies to alleviate "structural dislocation" or aimed at easing the adjustment problem facing "sick-man" sectors. Such subsidies are often directed specifically toward older plants within an industry. Other subsidies are aimed at newer plants, under government programs to stimulate investment and promote modernization. These subsidies will often help to finance the capital outlays (fixed costs) associated with environmental control. Thus in practice, the financing of environmental control is almost always a combination of "polluter pays" and subsidization out of general tax revenue. Most of our findings below hold under both pure forms of financing, and probably also hold therefore for realistic compromises between the two extremes. A few findings differ for the two pure extremes. For these it is necessary to know a nation's exact combination of financing methods in order to draw conclusions about ideal methodological approaches.

[6] Mutti and Richardson [12], for example, calculated industrial dislocation from unilateral environmental control with the intermediate methodology and with the classical methodology.

SCHEMA 1

Alternative Methodological Approaches to Industrial Displacement Due to the Effects of Environmental Control on International Competitiveness

Partial Equilibrium Approach

Demand-Oriented Industry-by-Industry Approaches (Partial Equilibrium)

No inter-industry linkage
No inter-industry substitutability of demand
No secondary multiplier effects of reduced outputs on aggregate real economic activity
No exchange-rate consequences
Full pass-through of environmental control costs into prices

Intermediate Approach

Demand-Oriented Comprehensive Approaches

Inter-industry linkage considered
Otherwise same as above

General Equilibrium Approaches

Demand-Oriented "Macro-Orthodox" Approaches (General Equilibrium)

Inter-industry linkage considered
Inter-industry substitutability of demand considered
Secondary multiplier effects of reduced output on aggregate real economic activity considered

Exchange-rate consequences considered
Full pass-through of environmental control costs into prices

Supply-Demand Oriented "Classical" Approaches (General Equilibrium)

Inter-industry linkage considered
Inter-industry substitutability of demand considered
Flexible factor returns and prices, or compensating policy, leave aggregate real economic activity unaffected
No exchange-rate consequences considered
Partial pass-through of environmental control costs into prices, partial absorbtion into factor rents

less demanding approaches predict displacements calculated by the more complex approaches. In general, the answer is "not well" in a regression context. By contrast, rank correlations of percentage displacements (most displaced industry to least displaced industry) from approach to approach are high. Worth emphasis is the finding that the predictions of the "macro-orthodox" approach for the size and cross-industry pattern of displacements differ notably from those of the "classical" approach, especially under subsidy-tax financing. This suggests the crucial methodological importance of assumptions regarding macroeconomic feedback, exchange rates, supply, producer pricing behavior, and the incidence of environmental control taxes.[7]

II. ALTERNATIVE METHODOLOGICAL APPROACHES

In this section of the paper we explain in greater detail the alternative models portrayed in Schema 1. We begin with the most simplistic, partial-equilibrium models. Because all of the percentage increase in direct costs entailed in meeting environmental control is assumed to be passed on to the purchaser under "polluter pays" financing, domestic supply curves must be infinitely price elastic To determine the percentage effect on domestic output, dQ_1/Q_1, we multiply these cost changes, EC, by the own price elasticity of demand facing domestic producers, η

$$dQ_1/Q_1 = \eta \cdot \mathrm{EC}, \qquad \text{(A)}$$

where η is an 81×81 diagonal matrix and EC and dQ_1/Q_1 are 81×1 vectors.

[7] Finally, and not surprisingly, for the most sophisticated methodologies, the industrial incidence of environmental control under "polluter pays" financing is almost totally unrelated to that under subsidy-tax schemes. Financing in fact seems to be the chief determinant of the distribution (incidence) of environmental control costs from industry to industry.

Because the price elasticity of demand facing domestic producers is a weighted average of home and foreign demands, two separate elasticities must be known.[8] But price is predetermined and constant for all levels of output, allowing us to suppress the supply side of the market.

Alternatively, if the costs of meeting environmental controls are subsidized by the government, then we must calculate the total subsidy payment necessary and determine the appropriate tax and corresponding tax rate to raise it. We approximate the total subsidy payment required by multiplying the percentage cost vector (EC) by the vector of current output. We approximate the appropriate tax by considering a proportional "income" tax. For purposes of computation, we assume that the same tax rate is levied on value added in each industry. Clearly our example only approximates reality, since the effective U. S. personal and corporate income tax rates are not equal or necessarily proportional, and the value added figure does not correspond directly to taxable income. Also, we ignore how the collection of existing taxes would be changed with this new shock to the system. We emphasize this alternative only to illustrate the markedly different implication of a subsidy-tax versus "polluter pays" policy, and not to give precise numerical projections for a specific subsidy-tax system.

Since the simple approaches assume implicitly that the money supply is increased sufficiently to maintain the money income of capital and labor,[9] the effect of the environmental-control tax, VAT, on domestic output can be calculated in a manner analogous to that above

$$dQ_1^*/Q_1^* = \eta \cdot \text{VAT}. \qquad (\text{A}^*)$$

The intermediate model proposed in Schema 1 merely requires that we allow for the cost increase of inputs as well as direct cost increases from meeting control standards in the given industry. The model still is demand oriented, and an appropriate tool to use is input–output analysis.[10] One drawback of the available U. S. coefficients is that they reflect inputs demanded from both domestic and foreign producers. If foreign prices remain constant upon unilateral environmental control, we want to allow only for the increased cost from domestic price increases. To do so, we calculated a new set of fixed, input–output coefficients, a_{ij}^D, where each row entry was multiplied by the domestic share of total intermediate sales.[11] Such a procedure implies that the import share of the market is fairly stable, which may not be too inappropriate if the tax changes we con-

[8] Sources of the required data to implement this and the subsequent sophisticated approaches are discussed in the Appendix.

[9] It is doubtful that such a policy is neutral toward interest rates. Yet another step toward sophistication, not considered in this paper, is to allow for the influence of any interest-rate changes on industry output, which we should expect to be larger in more capital- or inventory-intensive industries.

[10] Shortcomings of input–output analysis are that available tables generally reflect current input flows only, which may mean our estimates for capital intensive industries are understated. Even when capital flow tables are available as well, the coefficients refer to technical relationships for some past period, which may be quite different from new pollution abatement technologies. Consequently the relevant time horizon for prediction falls in the five-to-ten year range mentioned above.

[11] The domestic share of total intermediate sales is calculated as the quotient of (intermediate outputs, total *less* transfers out *less* transferred imports) and (intermediate outputs, total *less* transfers out).

sider are small. It also implies that average propensities to import a given intermediate input are the same from industry to industry. Using this pure "domestic base" table, A^D, the change in output from environmental control now becomes

$$dQ_2/Q_2 = \eta \cdot [I - A^{D'}]^{-1} \cdot \text{EC} \tag{B}$$

under "polluter pays" financing. The corresponding solution for the subsidy-tax alternative is

$$dQ_2^*/Q_2^* = \eta \cdot [I - A^{D'}]^{-1} \cdot \text{VAT}. \tag{B*}$$

The "macro-orthodox" general equilibrium approach is similar to the simpler models presented because it, too, is demand oriented. However, if the economy is not at full employment, so that the assumption of infinitely elastic domestic supply is appropriate, and if there is no automatic tendency toward full employment (through policy or otherwise), then we must pay attention to the macroeconomic determination of income. Additionally, if domestic prices are invariant to the scale of economic activity, then balance of trade disequilibria must be eliminated through exchange rate changes. To capture both factors, we add an income determination equation and a balance of trade constraint to the model. By making these two variables endogenous, we alter several of the relationships explained earlier. For instance, domestic prices will no longer depend parametrically on environmental costs or taxes alone, but also on the dollar price of imported inputs, which will vary with the exchange rate. The appropriate price-determination equation under "polluter pays" financing is

$$dP/P = [I - A^{D'}]^{-1} \cdot \text{EC} + [I - A^{D'}]^{-1} \cdot A^{M'} \cdot i \cdot (dE/E), \tag{C1}$$

where A^M is the matrix of imported input coefficients, E is the dollar price of foreign currency, and i is a unit vector.

Demand facing domestic producers must now be broken into home and foreign market components. We allow for the role of variations in aggregate income on domestic demand, and for the relative price effect of exchange rate changes on both domestic demand and exports. The appropriate change in output due to environmental control is [12]

$$\frac{dQ_3}{Q_3} = \theta_F \eta_X \left(\frac{dP}{P} - \frac{dE}{E} \right)$$
$$+ \theta_H \left(\eta_H \frac{dP}{P} + \eta_H{}^{\text{CP}} i \frac{dE}{E} + \eta_H{}^{\text{RP}} \frac{dP_r}{P_r} + \eta_H{}^{Y} i \frac{dY}{Y} \right), \tag{C}$$

where θ_F and θ_H are the share of total domestic output going to foreign and home markets, respectively, η_X and η_H are the own-price elasticities of demand facing domestic producers in the two markets, $\eta_H{}^{\text{CP}}$ is the cross-price elasticity of home demand with respect to import prices, $\eta_H{}^{\text{RP}}$ is the cross-price elasticity of

[12] We assume foreign prices are constant (infinitely price-elastic import supply), and ignore any changes in foreign income. Also, we do not specify the foreign demand equation in as great detail as the domestic demand equation. In particular we constrain the foreign own and cross-price elasticities to be equal in absolute value, ruling out any price substitution with all other goods.

home demand with respect to the prices of all other goods, and $\eta_H{}^Y$ is the income elasticity of home demand. (All elasticity and market share expressions are diagonal matrices.)

The change in aggregate money income is based on a weighted average of the change in value added for all domestic industries

$$dY/Y = i'\theta_Y[(dP/P) + (dQ/Q)], \tag{C2}$$

where θ_Y is the diagonal matrix of industry shares of total income. Because we treat value added as a constant percentage of the value of output, the percentage change in each industry's valued-added is equal to the percentage change in its total output $[(dP/P) + (dQ/Q)]$. The residual price index which appears in the demand equation for home goods is calculated as

$$dP_r/P_r = \psi(dP/P), \tag{C3}$$

where the matrix ψ represents a set of weights based on each industry's value-added share in income, excluding the industry under consideration.

Treating foreign currency prices as constant and assuming initially balanced trade, we rule out international capital flows and specify the constraint that trade always be balanced to determine the equilibrium change in exchange rates

$$i'\theta_M\left(i\frac{dE}{E} + \frac{dM}{M}\right) = i'\theta_X\left(\frac{dP}{P} + \frac{dX}{X}\right) \tag{C4}$$

where θ_M and θ_X reflect the share of total imports (M) and exports (X), respectively, accounted for by each industry. The import demand equation will be a function of income, the exchange rate, competing domestic goods' prices and all other prices, variables cited in Eq. (C).

The subsidy-tax variant of the "macro-orthodox" approach is derived simply by changing the initial price determination equation

$$dP^*/P^* = [I - A^{D'}]^{-1}\cdot \text{VAT} + [I - A^{D'}]^{-1}\cdot A^{M'}\cdot i\cdot (dE/E). \tag{C*1}$$

We now turn to the "classical" general-equilibrium approach. The main feature of this case is that we do *not* assume that the economy operates so far below full employment that output prices will be constant. Rather we try to capture the necessary increase in price which occurs when industry output expands, drawing in primary resources which are progressively less suited to the industry, which utilizes them with a given amount of industry-specific resources. Determining which resources are industry-specific is an empirical issue, and we treat our intermediate run elasticities as relevant for the five-to-ten-year period mentioned earlier. Clearly if we could accurately project investment decisions and input–output coefficients for a longer period of time, the relevant supply elasticities would be larger, as more resources are able to adjust.

Because the supply of industry-specific resources tends to be fixed, at least in our intermediate run, not all of the environmental costs or taxes will be passed on to purchasers. Rather, some will be absorbed by the producer in the form of reduced rents for the industry-specific resources. Analytically we no longer regard price as predetermined and we must introduce a supply equation explicitly into the model. Price and output are then solved for simultaneously, and we report the output solutions below for "polluter pays" and subsidy-tax financing

$$\frac{dQ_4}{Q_4} = \eta \cdot \frac{\epsilon}{\epsilon - \eta} \cdot \left[I - \frac{\epsilon}{\epsilon - \eta} A^{D'} - \frac{\vartheta_H \eta_H^{RP}}{\epsilon - \eta} \psi \right]^{-1} \cdot \mathrm{EC}, \qquad \text{(D)}$$

$$\frac{dQ_4^*}{Q_4^*} = \eta \cdot \frac{\epsilon}{\epsilon - \eta} \cdot \left[I - \frac{\epsilon}{\epsilon - \eta} A^{D'} - \frac{\theta_H \eta_H^{RP}}{\epsilon - \eta} \psi \right]^{-1} \cdot \mathrm{VAT}, \qquad \text{(D*)}$$

where ϵ denotes the domestic supply elasticity and $\epsilon/\epsilon - \eta$ is an 81×81 diagonal matrix.[13]

Changes in aggregate income are not incorporated into this extreme "classical" approach because involuntary unemployment is assumed to be zero. In a longer-run perspective than that taken here, there might nevertheless be effects of environmental control on aggregate income through alterations in capacity-enhancing investment, and in labor-force participation rates (labor-leisure choices). But these will be relatively small in the medium run.

Exchange-rate changes are also ignored in the "classical" approach. This is because the natural general-equilibrium macroeconomic correspondent to "classical" assumptions about wage-price flexibility and exogenous (or more strongly, constant) aggregate real economic activity is the "monetary approach" to the balance of payments and exchange rates. In the monetary approach, with flexible prices and exogenous aggregate real economic activity, the foreign-exchange-market value of domestic currency (exchange rate) varies inversely with aggregate monetary growth, and with nothing else. There seems little reason to construct any link between environmental control and monetary growth, and therefore there seems little reason to suggest any impact of environmental control on the exchange rate, even though it tends to make the trade balance deteriorate. The deteriorated trade balance is offset in the short and medium runs by a capital inflow, caused by the reduction in the stock supply of *real* cash balances brought about by higher domestic prices, and its consequent tendency to push domestic interest rates and other rates of return up and attract foreign investors.

III. ALTERNATIVE METHODOLOGIES COMPARED EMPIRICALLY

Each of the four different approaches from Sections I and II was applied to U. S. data, summarized in the Appendix, first under a "polluter pays" financing scheme, then under a subsidy-tax financing scheme. Table I records a representative sample of the projected physical output displacements (from what output otherwise would have been) for the two general equilibrium approaches.[14]

[13] In the classical general-equilibrium calculations of the next section, η_H^{RP} was set equal to zero because of computational difficulties (it was not in the "macro-orthodox" approach). We believe that the quantitative effects of this omission are small. On the details of the derivation of (D) and (D*), see Mutti and Richardson [12, pp. 65, 98].

[14] A full tabulation of results for each of the 81 two-digit input–output industries under the two general-equilibrium approaches is available from the authors on request. At first blush, these results may seem small in absolute magnitude. However, projected displacements of 1 to 5% of industry output can be highly significant, especially if they are concentrated on

TABLE I

Percentage Decreases in Industrial Output from Environmental Control's Effect on International Competitiveness: Alternative General-Equilibrium Predictions for a Sample of Industries

Industry Input-Output Number and Title	Polluter-Pays		Subsidy-and-Tax	
	Macro-orthodox	Classical	Macro-orthodox	Classical
AGRICULTURE, FORESTRY, AND FISHERIES				
1. Livestock and livestock products	2.98	0.51	1.12	0.23
2. Other agricultural products	2.62	0.58	1.01	0.29
MINING				
5. Iron and ferroalloy ores	1.52	0.25	0.97	0.21
7. Coal mining	2.30	0.37	1.03	0.21
MANUFACTURING				
14. Food and kindred products	1.88	0.81	1.08	0.79
18. Apparel	1.14	0.81	1.13	1.14
24. Paper and allied products, except containers	2.81	1.68	1.11	0.81
27. Chemicals and selected chemical products	3.75	3.25	1.03	1.09
28. Plastics and synthetic materials	4.21	3.77	1.07	1.25
31. Petroleum refining and related industries	4.64	2.38	1.06	0.46
37. Primary iron and steel manufacturing	2.73	2.39	1.06	1.21
38. Primary nonferrous metal manufacturing	3.77	1.93	1.12	0.68
49. General industrial machinery and equipment	1.98	1.77	1.05	1.24
59. Motor vehicles and equipment	2.66	2.62	1.03	1.37
SERVICES, GOV., DUMMY, AND SPECIAL INDUSTRIES				
68. Electric, gas, water and sanitary services	5.27	5.18	1.14	1.33
69. Wholesale and retail trade	0.60	0.64	1.15	1.48

The results indicate consistent negative impacts of environmental control on industry output, through loss of international competitiveness.[15] But the results also indicate considerable diversity of the impacts from industry to industry.

The principal purpose of this paper is to compare displacements from approach to approach. If it were true that they varied very little between the simple partial-equilibrium approach and the computationally complicated general-equilibrium approaches, then there would be little merit in adopting the latter. They would not be worth the effort. Furthermore, if there were significant variation between the partial- and general-equilibrium approaches, yet most of it were accounted for by the intermediate consideration of interindustry linkages (Schema 1), then there would be little merit in going beyond the intermediate approach.

To form judgments on these matters, both regression and rank-correlation methods were adopted. The vector of predicted percentage displacements from a more refined approach was regressed in linear fashion on the same vector from a less refined approach. The significance of the regression as a whole indicated

slow-growing or contracting industries in nondiversified regional economies. Then adjustment problems and political repurcussions can be severe. Such problems are compounded by the tendency of displacements to occur in older plants with higher labor–output ratios. In any event, the absolute magnitude of the displacements is not the focus of this paper. It is concerned with how these projected displacements *change* as a progressively wider set of economic influences and interactions is introduced.

15 An underlying assumption in the calculations is that the resources freed from all 81 input–output industries combine implicitly to produce the environmental control services whose "cost" was initially levied on each industry as an exogenous shock. Environmental control is thus a missing 82nd industry whose output must be counted when calculating aggregate real economic activity, assumed constant under the "classical" approach.

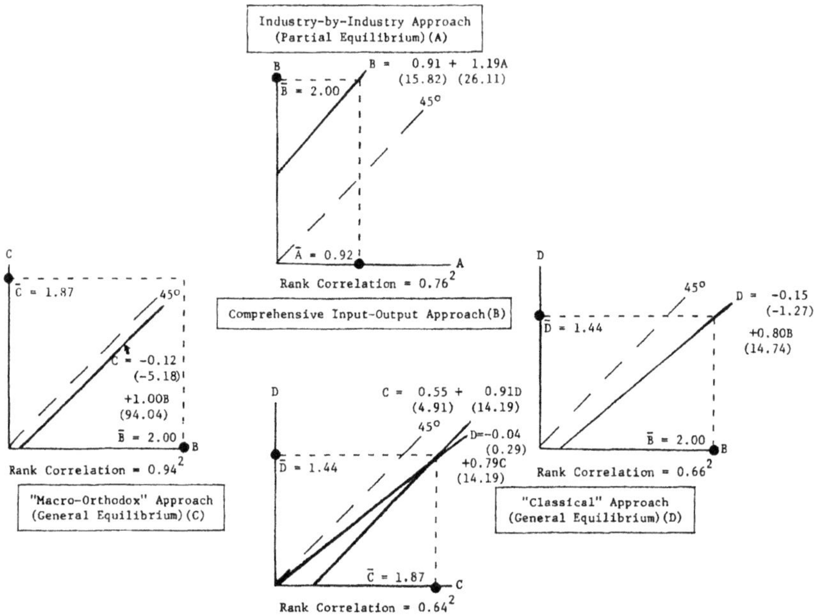

FIG. 1. "Polluter pays" financing: Comparability of industrial displacement shocks (percentages) under alternative methodological approaches.[1]

[1] Significance of regressions indicated by t-value of slope coefficient (in parentheses below coefficient), equivalent to an F-statistic calculated on the hypothesis that the entire regression explains nothing.

[2] Kendall rank correlation coefficient, significant at 1% level.

the degree to which results from simpler approaches were good predictors of results from complicated approaches. The estimated slopes and intercepts also have important interpretations that are elaborated below. As one final check of the gains to methodological refinement, elements of the displacement vectors were ranked by size, and rank correlations performed between different vectors.[16]

The results of these procedures are summarized in Fig. 1 for "polluter pays" financing, and in Fig. 2 for subsidy-tax financing. In each diagram, the important conclusions derive from the relation of the estimated regression line to the 45° line. Two methodologies that generated exactly the same estimates of industrial displacement from environmental control would yield a regression line that was coincident with the 45° line. Two methodologies that generated proportionally different displacements (e.g., percentage displacements twice as big in

[16] The regression and rank-correlation methods alleviated our uneasiness about the reliability of our data. As the Appendix reveals, demand and supply elasticities were estimated under sensible but highly restrictive assumptions (Mutti and Richardson [12, pp. 97–98, fnts. 3, 7, 9, 14]). This was true also of the basic industry-by-industry environmental costs taken from Walter [20]. See his caveats on pp. 62–63. Thus our estimated displacements under any methodological approach are subject to a wide margin of error. However, errors due to data reliability are likely to be qualitatively similar from approach to approach. Since our aim is to compare approaches to each other, we have some confidence in the reliability of our relative findings, despite any unreliability of the underlying data.

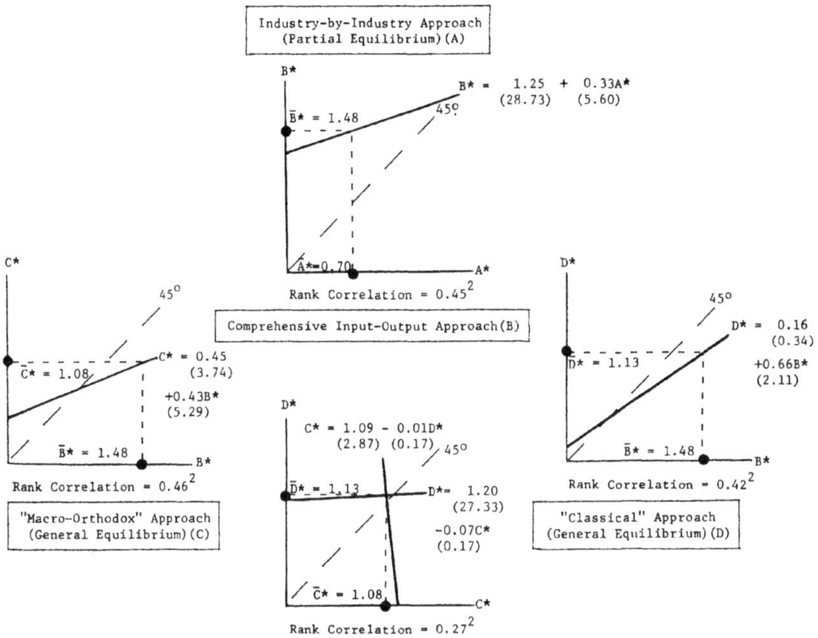

FIG. 2. "Subsidy-and-tax" financing: Comparability of industrial displacement shocks (percentage) under alternative methodological approaches.[1]

[1] Significance of regressions indicated by *t*-value of slope coefficient (in parentheses below coefficient), equivalent to an *F*-statistic calculated on the hypothesis that the entire regression explains nothing.

[2] Kendall rank correlation coefficients significant at 1% level.

one case as in another) would yield a regression line through the origin with a different slope than 45°. A flat regression line with a positive intercept indicates that the "vertical" sophisticated methodology predicted more comparably sized displacements from industry to industry than did the "horizontal" simpler methodology: Industries with below-average displacement according to the simple methodology tended to be displaced more severely than initially indicated, once methodological refinements were made, while those with above-average displacement according to the simple methodology tended to be displaced less severely. Similarly, a steep regression line with a negative intercept indicates that simpler methodologies understated the displacement dispersion from industry to industry. In such a case, methodological refinements suggested that displacements were more divergent (less "equitable"?) from industry to industry than was indicated by the less complicated approach.[17]

[17] The slope of the regression line is in fact a cross-sectional elasticity of one set of displacements with respect to the other, given that A, B, C, and D are all measured as percentage displacements. A slope of 1.19 in the top diagram of Fig. 1, for example, indicates that if some industry appeared to suffer twice as badly (in percentage terms) under a partial-equilibrium approach as some other industry did, then once interindustry linkages are taken account of, the first industry would fare 2.38 times worse than the second.

Several broad results stand out from Figs. 1 and 2 together.

(1) Regardless of financing method, partial-equilibrium methods understate industrial displacements from the international competitive effects of environmental control by half on average, compared to what they are when interindustry linkages are taken into account [$\bar{A}$, $\bar{A}^*$ = roughly (0.5)($\bar{B}$, $\bar{B}^*$)]. In other words, in an intermediate level approach, on an average only half of an industry's displacement of output is due to its own cost of environmental clean-up. The other half is due to higher input costs caused by environmental control in intermediate supplier industries. Price rises in intermediate supplier industries translate into cost increases to user industries. The existence of this cascading or multiplier effect is not surprising, but its large magnitude (two) is.

(2) Interindustry linkage makes the distribution of environmental-control displacement across industries dramatically more equal under subsidy-tax financing, and somewhat more unequal under the "polluter pays" principle. Industries that find themselves especially severely impacted by a polluter pays environmental control system turn out also to be disproportionately dependent on other severely impacted industries for intermediate inputs. The opposite is true for severely impacted industries under subsidy-tax systems. Their structure of input–output dependence cushions the impact of environmental control on their output.

Both conclusions (1) and (2) suggest the crucial quantitative importance of taking at least the first simple step beyond partial-equilibrium modeling of these matters. Single-industry studies of displacement from environmental control programs (e.g., Council on Environmental Quality [5], U. S. Department of Commerce [16]) are likely to be seriously misleading if they focus narrowly on environmental-control costs in the particular industry alone, ignoring those in supplier industries.

(3) Taking the next methodological step and adding general-equilibrium refinements has little impact on estimated dislocation if the refinements tend toward "macro-orthodoxy," and if environmental control is financed according to the "polluter pays" principle. "Macro-orthodox" general-equilibrium refinements reduce predicted percentage displacements by only 5% on average ($\bar{C}$ = approximately 95% of $\bar{B}$), and do virtually nothing to the interindustry incidence of displacement.

(4) But taking the next methodological step has significant impacts in all other cases, "macro-orthodoxy" under subsidy-tax schemes, and both "classical" approaches. For these three cases, general-equilibrium refinements reduce predicted percentage displacements by almost 30% and even out the interindustry incidence of displacement markedly. Industry displacements "regress toward the mean" displacements by as much as 57% (of the predicted intermediate-level-approach figure), and by at least 20%.[18] It would appear on an average that industries which *seem* casually to be heavily impacted by environmental control are also industries which enjoy all or some of the following features that reduce displacement in a general-equilibrium setting (i) inelastic supply conditions and high rents; (ii) inelastic foreign demands (so that the exchange-rate depreciation brought about by *average* aggregate loss of international competitiveness may *more* than compensate them for the slight loss in international com-

[18] 57 = 100 (1.00 − 0.43) from Fig. 2. 20 = 100 (1.00 − 0.80) from Fig. 1.

petitiveness that environmental control imposes on them in particular); (iii) low scale elasticities of domestic demand; and (iv) more pronounced than average demand-substitution relationships with industries whose prices rise more than its own.

Conclusion (4) suggests that the prediction error introduced by ignoring general-equilibrium complexities is not quantitatively trivial. It reinforces quantitatively a familiar qualitative conclusion from general-equilibrium analysis. Partial-equilibrium or comprehensive "fixed-coefficient" approaches to the effects of most exogenous shocks tend generally to overstate their consequences. The conclusion has an important political-polemical corollary: Industries pleading for relief from severe dislocation might well choose a partial-equilibrium input–output approach to bolster their case; but governments should be wary of such analyses, because the general-equilibrium offsets can in many cases be significantly large.

(5) Methodological refinements appear to have a larger payoff in predicting displacement under subsidy-tax systems than under "polluter pays" financing. This can be seen graphically by comparing Fig. 1 to Fig. 2, and numerically by cumulating the methodological refinement and calculating how precisely the simple partial-equilibrium displacements forecast the complicated general-equilibrium displacements. (How well does A, A^* forecast C, C^* or D, D^*?).[19] The cumulative effect of the methodological refinements that we consider raises casually calculated percentage displacements by from 50 to 100%, regardless of financing scheme. But with subsidy-tax arrangements, these methodological refinements also have a profound leveling effect on the dispersion of dislocation from industry to industry. The refinements reduce substantially the unevenness with which different industries bear the cost of environmental control.

(6) Granted the quantitative importance of general-equilibrium refinements in calculating industrial dislocation from environmental control, it is nevertheless unclear what *sort* of general-equilibrium refinements to add. There is moderate similarity between the predictions of the "macro-orthodox" and "classical" models under "polluter pays" financing, but no similarity at all between the predictions under subsidy-tax schemes. Neither pattern has any explanatory power at all in forecasting the other. Even where there is moderate similarity, the two regressions (of C on D and D on C) conflict as to whether industries

[19] The cumulative effect of moving directly from a partial-equilibrium approach to a general-equilibrium approach can be illustrated by the following regressions, although the properties of ordinary-least-squares regression guarantees that they are implied by substitution of the top regression in each figure into the middle two.

Fig. 1, "Polluter Pays":

$$C = \underset{(13.18)}{0.78} + \underset{(25.30)}{1.19A},$$
$$D = \underset{(5.88)}{0.56} + \underset{(12.84)}{0.96A},$$

Fig. 2, Subsidy Tax:

$$C^* = \underset{(23.86)}{0.97} + \underset{(2.80)}{0.15A^*}$$
$$D^* = \underset{(6.54)}{0.94} + \underset{(1.41)}{0.27A^*}.$$

are displaced more unevenly under "macro-orthodox" assumptions or under "classical" assumptions. Conflicts and lack of similarity in the predictions of alternative general-equilibrium methodologies are not surprising, and are by nature insoluble, since they arise from different opinions over which alternative set of assumptions are most descriptive in a real-world setting. But our results highlight quantitatively the importance of alternative assumptions, and suggest caution in any attempt to find a methodological approach that is uniformly "best" under all circumstances.

(7) Rank correlation coefficients that compare alternative methodological approaches are fairly large, positive, and statistically significant. (See Figs. 1 and 2, below each diagram.) Thus alternative methodologies do not tend to affect the *identity* of the industries who suffer above-or-below-average displacement from the international competitive effects of environmental control. But as we have seen in conclusions (1) through (6), alternative methodologies do have important effects on the absolute size of these percentage displacements and on their relative size from industry to industry.[20]

IV. CONCLUSIONS

Evaluating the international competitive impacts of unilateral environmental control is an important exercise. The paths of domestic industrial outputs over a medium-term time period are displaced by such impacts from what they otherwise would have been. Yet little agreement exists in the literature on an empirical strategy for evaluating these displacements. There appears to be widespread recourse to partial-equilibrium methods, and frequent skepticism that more complex general-equilibrium approaches can produce anything additional that would justify the extra demands that they make on researchers. This paper undercuts such skepticism by quantifying the differences that general-equilibrium approaches do make. In most cases they are not trivial, and in some, they are substantial.[21]

We believe that our findings are not specific to the particular problem that we have examined. Given the structure of the alternative models, our conclu-

[20] The extent and pattern of industrial displacement from lost international competitiveness differs dramatically, depending on the way in which environmental control is financed. While this conclusion is not demonstrable in Figs. 1 and 2, it can be shown by examining the similarity between the "polluter-pays" displacement vector and the subsidy-tax displacement vector for any given methodological approach, using the same regression approach. In the "macro-orthodox" general-equilibrium approach, industrial dislocation under "polluter pay" financing bears absolutely no resemblance to that under subsidy-tax financing. In the classical approach, the resemblance is slight at best. These findings reinforce the well-known importance of financing schemes in determining the industrial incidence of environmental control, those industries which bear the most severe impacts under one scheme do not under the other; those industries which escape displacement under one scheme do not under the other. In fact, under "macro-orthodox" assumptions, if one ranks the industries by the size of their percentage dislocation under each scheme, the two rankings are negatively (and significantly) correlated. Under classical assumptions, the rank correlation is positive but very slight.

[21] Whalley [19] draws virtually the same conclusion in his comparison of alternative methodologies for estimating the effects of the British capital income tax on capital usage. His concern with linearization approximations is not mirrored here. Thus the only reason that our calculations differ from methodology to methodology is the progressive removal of ceteris paribus assumptions.

sions should hold for any shock to the domestic cost of primary factors, shocks that undermine international competitiveness and displace domestic producers. Thus there would seem to be substantial practical merit in adopting general-equilibrium approaches to the interindustry effects of generalized wage-push inflation, occupational safety and health standards, domestic tax incentives like Domestic International Sales Corporations (DISC's), and other similar shocks. We also suspect practical payoffs of a similar quantitative magnitude from adopting general-equilibrium approaches to calculating the domestic impacts of exogeneous foreign price shocks (e.g., changes in tariffs, energy prices, etc.).[22]

APPENDIX: DATA SOURCES

Data sources and construction methods are described generally below. Additional information is available from the authors on request, including a table recording the 81 calculated values of the elasticities of domestic demand with respect to own-price, cross-prices, and scale, and also recording the 81 calculated supply elasticities.

In general, each step toward sophistication in our estimation of the industrial dislocation brought about by unilateral environmental control required additional data. Indeed, these extra data demands are the chief practical cost of general-equilibrium methods that must be offset against the gains from such. To be specific:

Partial-Equilibrium Approaches; Equations (A) and (A*). Required data: η, EC, VAT. η = weighted average of elasticities of foreign export and domestic demand facing domestic producers. Source for elasticity of foreign (export) demand: aggregation of Buckler-Almon [4] estimates. Source for elasticity of domestic demand: aggregation and transformation of Buckler-Almon [4] estimates of import demand elasticities. See Mutti and Richardson [12, pp. 62–65] for details. Source for weights: U. S. Department of Commerce [16]. EC = direct environmental control costs as a percentage of the value of production in each industry. Source: Walter [20], as adjusted by Mutti and Richardson [12, pp. 92–96]. VAT = taxes levied on each industry to support environmental control under a subsidy-tax financing scheme. Source: solution of

$$(\mathrm{VAT})_i = \frac{(T)\cdot(VA)_i}{(\mathrm{PQ})_i} \qquad \text{for all 81 } i;$$

$$\sum_{i=1}^{81} (\mathrm{VAT})_i \cdot (\mathrm{PQ})_i = \sum_{i=1}^{81} (\mathrm{EC})_i \cdot (\mathrm{PQ})_i;$$

for 81 $(\mathrm{VAT})_i$'s and one T, where

i subscripts denote the value of a variable appropriate to industry i;

T = the uniform tax rate on value-added ("incomes" of primary factor owners) in each industry;

VA = value added in each industry.

[22] As examples of general-equilibrium approaches to these international shocks, see Taylor and Black [14], Boadway and Treddenick [3], and ongoing work at the Universities of Wisconsin and Wyoming.

VAT was expressed as a proportion of production (PQ) to make it comparable to EC. Operationally, tax rates were set so that the same environmental control costs were covered as under "polluter pays" financing, but so that every industry paid the same tax rate on value-added. Taxes were levied according to the origin principle to make them more comparable to U. S. direct income taxes. For additional computation detail, and the exact value of the calculated vector VAT, see Mutti and Richardson [12, pp. 66–69, 71–80, 98–99].

Intermediate Approaches; Equations (B) and (B*). Additional required data, A^D. A^D = a matrix of input–output requirements for domestic goods only. Source: U. S. Department of Commerce [16], adjusted to "domestic-base" table as indicated in the text of this paper.

General-Equilibrium "Macro-Orthodox" Approach; Equations (C) and (C*). Additional required data, A^M, η_X, η_H, $\eta_H{}^{CP}$, $\eta_H{}^Y$, $\eta_H{}^{RP}$. A^M = a matrix of input–output requirements for imported goods only, equal to A-A^D, where A is the standard input–output table, and A^D is as above. Source: U. S. Department of Commerce [16]. η_X, η_H = the own-price elasticities of foreign and domestic demand, respectively, facing domestic producers. Source: already calculated as the two components whose average yields η above. See Mutti and Richardson [12, pp. 62–65]. $\eta_H{}^{CP}$ = the cross-price elasticity of domestic demand facing domestic producers, with respect to import prices. Source: Solution of

$$\theta_H \eta_H{}^{CP} + \bar{\theta}_M \bar{\eta}_M = -\theta_M ;$$

an adding-up property implied by Buckler and Almon's [4] use of total domestic spending (say, A) on an industry's domestic output and its imports ($A = PH + EP_fM$, where H = domestic demand facing domestic producers) as the scale variable in their import demand equations, and where

$$\theta_H = PH/A ;$$

$$\theta_M = EP_fM/A ;$$

η_M = the own-price elasticity of import demand.

The key to solving the equation is to observe that Buckler and Almon [4] regress the *value* of imports on EP_f/P, thereby implying that their estimated own-price elasticity of import demand (η_M) is equal to the coefficient on EP_f/P *less one*. The estimated cross-price elasticity of import demand ($\eta_M{}^{CP}$) is equal to the negative of the coefficient itself, and therefore, $\eta_M = -\eta_M{}^{CP} - 1$ can be substituted into the equation above to yield

$$\theta_H \eta_H{}^{CP} + \theta_M(-\eta_M{}^{CP} - 1) = -\theta_M ;$$

implying

$$\eta_H{}^{CP} = (\theta_M/\theta_H)\eta_M{}^{CP}.$$

Data on $\eta_M{}^{CP}$ is drawn directly from Buckler and Almon [4]. $\eta_H{}^Y$ = the income elasticity of domestic demand facing domestic producers. Source: the assumption that total domestic spending on an industry's domestic output and imports (A) is unit income elastic, so that $\eta_H{}^Y = \eta_H{}^A \cdot \eta_A{}^Y = \eta_H{}^A$, and solution of the equation

$$\eta_H{}^A = (1/\theta_H) - (\theta_M/\theta_H)\eta_M{}^A ;$$

which is implied by the fact that $A = PH + EP_fM$. Data on $\eta_M{}^A$ were computed from Buckler-Almon [4], who provide estimates of $(\eta_M{}^A)\cdot(\theta_M)$. $\eta_H{}^{RP}$ = the cross-price elasticity of domestic demand facing domestic producers, with respect to all other goods. Source: the assumption that Buckler and Almon's [4] estimates are not significantly biased by their omission of all other prices, coupled with the assumption that money illusion is absent in reality at this level of aggregation, implying that

$$\eta_H{}^{RP} = \eta_H - \eta_H{}^{CP} - \eta_H{}^Y.$$

General-Equilibrium "Classical" Approach; Equations (D) and (D*). Additional required data, ϵ. ϵ = the domestic price elasticity of supply, or less rigidly, a measure of the incidence of a demand shock, i.e., how it is split between price changes and rent changes. Source: directly estimated supply elasticities from Tweeten [15]; implied supply elasticities from inverted price-determination equations (Perry [13], Eckstein and Wyss [8], Goldstein [9]); casual empiricism and guesstimates for some agriculture and much mining and services. See Mutti and Richardson [12, pp. 65–66] for additional detail.

REFERENCES

1. R. E. Baldwin and J. H. Mutti, Policy problems in the adjustment process, in "Prospects for Partnership: Industrialization and Trade Policies in the 1970's" (Helen Hughes *et al.*, Eds.), Johns Hopkins Press, Baltimore (1973).
2. J. P. Barde, National and international policy alternatives for environmental control and their economic implications, in "Studies in International Environmental Economics" (I. Walter, Ed.), Wiley, New York (1976).
3. R. Boadway and J. Treddenick, "Computing the Effects of Tariffs in a Multi-Sector General-Equilibrium Model With Interindustry Flows: An Application to Canada," Queen's University Institute for Economic Research, Discussion Paper No. 176, Kingston, Ontario (1975).
4. M. Buckler and C. Almon, Imports and exports in an input-output model, in "1972 Proceedings of the Business and Economics Statistics Section of the American Statistical Association," American Statistical Association, 175-84, Washington (1972), appearing also as Chapter 6 of Clopper Almon, Jr., Margaret B. Buckler, Lawrence M. Horwitz, and Thomas C. Reimbold, "1985: Interindustry Forecasts of the American Economy," Lexington, Massachusetts: D. C. Heath (1974).
5. Council on Environmental Quality, U. S. Department of Commerce, and Environmental Protection Agency, "The Economic Impact of Pollution Control: A Summary of Recent Studies," U. S. Government Printing Office, Washington, D. C. (1972).
6. R. C. d'Arge, "International Trade, Domestic Income, and Environmental Controls: Some Empirical Estimates," in "Managing the Environment: International Economic Cooperation for Pollution Control" (Allen V. Kneese, Sidney E. Rolfe, and Joseph W. Harned, Eds.), Praeger, New York (1971).
7. R. C. d'Arge and A. V. Kneese, "Environmental Quality and International Trade," *International Organization*, Spring 1972. Reprinted in David A. Kay and Eugene B. Skolnikoff, "World Eco-Crisis: International Organization in Response," pp. 255–301, Univ. of Wisconsin Press, Madison.
8. O. Eckstein and D. Wyss, Industry price equations, in "The Econometrics of Price Determination Conference" (Eckstein, Ed.), Board of Governors of the Federal Reserve System, Washington (1972).
9. M. Goldstein, "Anti-Inflationary Demand Management in the United States: A Selective Industry Approach," *International Monetary Fund Staff Papers*, pp. 344–394 (July 19, 1972).

10. S. P. Magee and W. F. Ford, Environmental pollution, the terms of trade and balance of payments of the United States, *Kyklos* **25**, 101–118 (1972).
11. J. H. Mutti, "Foreign Trade, Employment, and Welfare," unpublished doctoral dissertation, University of Wisconsin, Madison (1974).
12. J. H. Mutti and J. D. Richardson, Industrial displacement through environmental controls: The international competitive aspects, in "Studies in International Environmental Economics" (I. Walter, Ed.), Wiley, New York (1976).
13. G. L. Perry, Capacity in Manufacturing, *Brookings Papers on Economic Activity* 3, 701–742 (1973).
14. L. Taylor and S. L. Black, Practical general equilibrium estimation of resource pulls under trade liberalization, *J. Inter. Econ.* **4**, 37–58 (1974).
15. L. Tweeten, "Foundations of Farm Policy," Univ. of Nebraska Press, Lincoln (1970).
16. United States Department of Commerce, The Input-Output Structure of the U. S. Economy: 1967, *Survey of Current Business* **54**, 24–56 (1974).
17. I. Walter (Ed.), "Studies in International Environmental Economics," Wiley, New York (1976).
18. I. Walter, "Implications of Environmental Policies for the Trade Prospects of Developing Countries: Analysis based on an UNCTAD Questionnaire," New York University Faculty of Business Administration Working Paper Series, No. 76-33 (1976).
19. J. Whalley, How reliable is partial equilibrium analysis, *Rev. Econ. Statist.* **57**, 299–310 (1975).
20. I. Walter, The pollution content of American Trade, *Western Economic Journal*, **11**, 61–70 (1973).

[11]

Industrial pollution abatement: the impact on balance of trade

H. DAVID ROBISON Louisiana Tech University

Abstract. This paper uses an ex-post partial-equilibrium framework to measure the impact of marginal changes in industrial pollution abatement costs on the U.S. balance of trade in general, and balance of trade with Canada in particular. The impacts are found to be negative for most industries, growing with trade volume, and small relative to domestic consumption. In addition, some evidence is found that pollution control programs have changed the U.S. comparative advantage such that more high-abatement-cost goods are imported and more low-abatement-cost goods are exported.

La réduction de la pollution industrielle: l'impact sur la balance commerciale. Ce mémoire utilise un cadre d'analyse d'équilibre partiel ex-post pour calibrer l'impact de changements à la marge dans les coûts de la réduction de la pollution industrielle sur la balance commerciale des Etats-Unis et en particulier sur la balance commerciale avec le Canada. Il appert que les impacts sont négatifs pour la plupart des industries, qu'ils croissent avec la taille des flux commerciaux, et qu'ils sont petits relativement à la consommation domestique. De plus, il semble que les programmes de lutte à la pollution ont transformé l'avantage comparatif des Etats-Unis de telle manière qu'on importe davantage de biens pour lesquels les coûts de réduction de la pollution sont élevés et qu'on exporte davantage de biens pour lesquels ces coûts sont bas.

Although economists agree that, by raising the prices of domestically produced products, pollution abatement expenditures alter a country's comparative advantage and trading pattern, no formal measurement of the impact has been made. This paper attempts to measure on an ex post basis the impact of marginal changes in industrial pollution abatement on U.S. balance of trade in general, and balance of trade with Canada as a special case. More specifically, Baumol and Oates's (1975) theoretical work on the trade impacts of industrial

I would like to thank Wallace Oates, Clopper Almon, Matt Hyle, Ralph Monaco, Margaret McCarthy, and Don Meyer for their helpful comments on earlier drafts. I would also like to thank Douglas Nyhus and Lorraine Sullivan of the INFORUM staff for their assistance with some of the data work.

Canadian Journal of Economics Revue canadienne d'Economique XXI, No. 1
February février 1988. Printed in Canada Imprimé au Canada

0008-4085 / 88 / 187-199 $1.50

pollution abatement is extended from a two final-good model to a seventy-eight sector model with all interindustry effects considered. Using this extended model, measurements of the trade impacts of marginal increases in abatement expenditures are made for each sector. These measurements are an upper bound to potential impacts on the balance of trade because all mitigating variables such as improved terms of trade, offsetting governmental policies, and adjustments in exchange rates are ignored. The results for 1977 range from \$−0.1 through \$−80.9 to \$−566.6 million for transportation services, electric utilities, and ferrous metals, respectively.

In addition, this paper uses Walter's (1973) concept of the abatement content of trade to test the proposition, discussed by Baumol and Oates among others,[1] that undertaking pollution abatement will reduce the abating country's comparative advantage in producing high-abatement-cost goods and improve the comparative advantage in low-abatement-cost goods. Results indicate that the abatement content of imports has grown more rapidly than that of exports, thus supporting this proposition.

Baumol and Oates define and discuss the conditions by which increased industrial abatement costs can improve or hurt a country's balance of trade in a two-country, two-good world.[2] No intermediate product flows are considered in the Baumol-Oates world, which would be sufficient if most abatement costs were incurred in producing final goods. However, most industrial pollution abatement (IPA) costs occur at basic levels of production, requiring the incorporation of interindustry effects, as is done in this study.

Measuring the price changes caused by IPA is a straightforward application of input-output analysis as discussed in Leontieff (1970) and performed in Walter (1973), Pasurka (1984), and Robison (1985). The Robison method for measuring the price change is used in the current study.

A general-equilibrium framework, including an input-output table, would seem the appropriate approach for this type of study. D'Arge (1971), Mutti and Richardson (1977), Evans (1973), and two commercial economic consulting firms[3] provide 'general equilibrium' based forecasting studies designed to examine the impact of IPA on the macro economy and trade. There are, however, at least two problems with each of these studies. First, because the studies use ex-ante forecasting, they must assume or estimate abatement costs. Second, assumptions are made as to how the abatement costs are allocated between return to capital, labour, etc. in order to run the forecasting routines.[4]

1 See D'Arge (1971), Mutti and Richardson (1977), and Magee and Ford (1972) for additional discussions.

2 A less general approach to this issue can be found in Magee and Ford (1972).

3 These forecasts are discussed in Portney (1981).

4 A third problem, argued by Dorfman (1973) in response to Evans (1973) but not treated in the current study, is that there will never be a true general-equilibrium model until pollution emitted by all sources is included in the production functions of all industries. Given this point, a partial equilibrium framework is the only alternative.

By choosing an ex post partial-equilibrium approach, these problems are avoided.

MODEL FRAMEWORK

The Baumol and Oates work derives the balance of trade conditions for a two-good two-country world. In doing so, one good has pollution associated with its production, while the other does not. In this simple world only direct abatement costs affect prices and trade. Here more general conditions are derived for the seventy-eight industries of the INFORUM interindustry macro model.

The balance of trade is obtained by

$$\mathrm{BT} = \sum_{i=1}^{78} (P_i \mathrm{EX}_i - P_i \mathrm{IM}_i), \tag{1}$$

where

BT = balance of trade

P_i = US domestic price of good i

EX_i = US exports for sector i

IM_i = US imports for sector i

$i = 1, 2, 3, \ldots, 78.$

If environmental regulations affect the price of products produced by industry j, the change in the balance of trade is found by

$$\partial \mathrm{BT}/\partial P_j = \sum_{i=1}^{78} [(\partial P_i/\partial P_j)\, \mathrm{EX}_i + P_i\, (\partial \mathrm{EX}_i/\partial P_j) - (\partial P_i/\partial P_j)\, \mathrm{IM}_i - P_i\, (\partial \mathrm{IM}_i/\partial P_j)]. \tag{2}$$

Note:

$$(\partial \mathrm{EX}_i/\partial P_j) = (\partial \mathrm{EX}_i/\partial P_i)\, (\partial P_i/\partial P_j), \tag{3}$$

and

$$(\partial \mathrm{IM}_i/\partial P_j) = (\partial \mathrm{IM}_i/\partial P_i)\, (\partial P_i/\partial P_j), \tag{4}$$

substituting (3) and (4) into (2) and rewriting:

$$\partial \mathrm{BT}/\partial P_j = \sum_{i=1}^{78} [(1 + \eta_i E)\, \mathrm{EX}_i (\%\, \Delta\, P_i/\%\, \Delta\, P_j)\, (P_i/P_j) - (1 + \eta_i I)\, \mathrm{IM}_i\, (\%\, \Delta\, P_i/\%\, \Delta\, P_j)\, (P_i/P_j)], \tag{5}$$

where

$\eta_i E$ = export own price elasticity for industry i

$\eta_i I$ = import own price elasticity for industry i.

In equation (5) the ratios of the percentage change in price of good i to the percentage change in price of good j are the terms through which the interindustry impacts are felt. These terms are the j, ith coefficient in the total requirements matrix.[5] Thus, exports of industry i are indirectly affected by a change in the price of good j.

The abatement induced price increase for industry j can increase or decrease export revenues depending on the export price elasticities, export volume, the coefficients of the jth row of the total requirements matrix, and industry prices. The impact of a change in the price of industry j on the export revenues of each industry i is found by multiplying exports of i times the j, ith element of the total requirements matrix times the price ratio times one plus $\eta_i E$. Revenues will rise, remain constant, or fall if $\eta_i E$ is greater than, equal to, or less that -1, respectively.

The dollar value of imports will rise for two reasons. First, with a higher domestic price more goods will be imported. Second, higher domestic prices will permit foreign producers to charge higher prices for the larger quantity they are shipping to the United States. Obviously, the lower the import price elasticity is, the smaller the impact on the balance of trade.

In order for an abatement cost induced change in the price of industry j to have a positive net effect on the balance of trade, the export impact must be positive and greater than the import impact. While not the case in the current study, this condition might occur if the import and export price elasticities for all sectors were small in absolute value. It might also occur if the United States exports several times more of product j than it imports (a strong net exporter), with low export and import price elasticities.

The assumption of full-cost pass-through into prices is reasonable in the long run. Alternate assumptions and their implications are discussed in detail in Lake, Hanneman, and Oster (1979), but a summary is warranted. Greater than full-cost pass-through is possible in oligopolistic industries. This non-competitive behaviour has the effect of encouraging more foreign firms to compete for domestic markets than would simple cost pass-through. Conversely, foreign firms would be discouraged from competing in U.S. markets by price increases smaller than cost increases, as might occur in highly competitive

5 This simple result comes from the input-output price determination equation: $p = pA + v$, where: p = vector of 78 sector prices; v = vector of 78 sector value added; A = 78 by 78 input-output coefficient matrix. Solving this equation for prices: $p = (I - A)^{-1}v$. A change in industrial pollution abatement for a sector changes the value added for that sector and prices of all sectors according to the coefficients of the total requirements matrix, $(I - A)^{-1}$.

industries. Use of the full-cost pass-through assumption helps ensure that the estimates are, in fact, upper bounds.

Most studies using input-output to measure price changes caused by environmental regulations simply multiply the abatement cost vector by the standard total requirements matrix (see, e.g., Pasurka, 1984; Mutti and Richardson, 1977; Walter, 1973). This approach misses a small portion of abatement costs, those implicit in capital goods used in the production process. To account for these additional costs, a 'capital-included' total requirements matrix is formed following the method described in Robison (1985). The general procedure is to add to the standard coefficient 'A' matrix a capital flows coefficient, or 'B' matrix that has been scaled so that the columns sum to the depreciation to output ratio of that industry. Given this modified A matrix, called A^*, the capital-included total requirements matrix is formed $(I - A^*)^{-1}$. Each j, i element of the total requirements shows the percentage price increase for industry i caused by a one percent increase in the price of input j.

DATA

All economic data and the estimated import and export price elasticities are provided by the INFORUM project.[6] A discussion of the general form of the merchandise import and export equations can be found in Almon, et al. (1974), while modifications, recent estimation results, and the non-merchandise equations are described in the INFORUM staff paper (1986).[7]

Abatement costs for each firm are defined as including only the costs of abating pollution generated by the firm, not the cost of abatement equipment built into the goods the firm produces. For example, the costs of abatement equipment built in U.S. automobiles are classified as being incurred by the auto's purchaser, not the producer.

The abatement data for the manufacturing sectors are taken from *Pollution Abatement Costs and Expenditures* for 1973, 1977, and 1983 (1976, 1979, 1984). No annual operating cost data are available for the non-manufacturing sectors. Capital expenditures on abatement equipment are, however, available for non-manufacturing in *The Survey of Current Business* (1984, 1978, 1980). Operating costs are approximated by assuming that the ratio of capital expenditures for abatement equipment to annual operating costs is the same for non-manufacturing as for manufacturing.[8]

6 INFORUM is the Interindustry Forecasting Project of The University of Maryland.

7 The general forms of the merchandise trade equations are $M_t = (a + bD_t)P_t^{\eta}$ and $E_t = (a + bF_t)P_t^{\eta}$ where: M_t = imports in domestic-port prices; D_t = domestic demand for the product; P_t = the effective ratio of the foreign price to the domestic price; η = the price elasticity; E_t = exports; F_t = foreign demand index. The non-merchandise equations are too sector specific to present a general form. See Almon (1974) and INFORUM staff (1986) for details.

8 More detailed information about the data is available from the author upon request.

TABLE 1

Average abatement content of U.S. trade (1.00 Means 1 cent per dollar)

	1973	1977	1982
Total U.S. imports	0.428	0.628	0.993
Total U.S. exports	0.372	0.538	0.715
Total U.S. output	0.499	0.692	0.927
Ratio of import content to export content	1.151	1.167	1.389
U.S. imports from Canada[a]	0.652	0.971	1.512
U.S. exports to Canada[a]	0.586	0.893	1.319
Ratio of import content to export content	1.113	1.087	1.146

a U.S.-Canada trade data is available only for the merchandise sectors. For this reason, the results are not directly comparable to the total trade figures.

RESULTS

The two major findings of this study are much as expected. First, there is some evidence that U.S. pollution control programs have changed the U.S. comparative advantage such that more high-abatement-cost goods will be imported and more low-abatement-cost goods exported. Second, the impact on the U.S. balance of trade of marginal changes in IPA is negative for most industries, growing with trade volume, and small relative to domestic consumption.

Table 1 presents the average abatement content of U.S. total and U.S.-Canadian trade for the years 1973, 1977, and 1982 as well as the average abatement content of U.S. output.[9] No detailed abatement data are available for countries (including Canada) for which similar input output tables are available. Hence, what is reported as abatement content of imports is, in fact, the abatement content of the goods had they been produced in the United States. Because of this data restriction, a rise in the abatement content of imports relative to exports indicates that the United States is importing goods with high U.S. abatement costs.

While the level of abatement costs implicit in both imports and exports rose rapidly over the period, they rose relatively more quickly for total imports than total exports. Relative shifts can be seen by looking at the ratio of import to export abatement content, which rose from 1.17 to 1.39 between 1977 and 1982. The rise in the abatement content ratio clearly indicates a shift towards importing goods with high U.S. abatement costs. Further evidence of a shift in comparative advantage is found in comparing the abatement content of U.S. exports, imports, and output. Over the 1973 to 1982 period the abatement costs implicit in U.S. exports and output grew proportionately. The abatement content of imports grew more quickly, rising above that of output in 1982.

9 A 1972 input-output table is used for the 1973 computations. The 1977 input-output table is also used for the 1982 computations, given that no 1982 table is available.

Thus, in 1982, the average dollar's worth of imports had more abatement costs implicit in it than the average dollar's worth of U.S. output. Stated another way, if the United States had produced the goods it imported, the average abatement content of U.S. output would have been higher.

Table 1 shows virtually no change in the abatement content ratio for U.S.-Canadian trade, thus implying no major shift in trading pattern. Given Canada's adoption of environmental quality regulations, this result is not surprising. In total trade, rising U.S. abatement costs increased the price differential for some products relative to countries with little or no environmental regulation and induced a change in the trading pattern. Canada, by adopting environmental regulations, prevented the price differential and corresponding shift in trading pattern from occurring. The Canadian results also suggest that the trading pattern shift is stronger for all other countries than in indicated in table 1. No shift is apparent for trade with Canada, which accounts for approximately 15 per cent of all U.S. trade. Thus, to get the total trade shift of table 1, the change in trading patterns with all other countries must be greater than the average indicated.

Table 2 presents the results of equation (5) for selected sectors under the assumption that additional abatement costs raised the sectoral price by 1 per cent. Thus, the value of −245.1 for the agricultural products sector indicates that, if additional abatement costs raised the price of agricultural products holding everything else constant, the U.S. balance of trade would have been reduced by at most $245.1 million. Of the $245.1 million impact, $95.8 million is attributed to reduced agricultural exports and increased agricultural imports, while the remainder is the result of indirect effects of agricultural prices on other sectoral prices.

As can be seen in table 2, the direct impacts are large relative to indirect impacts in most manufacturing sectors such as food and tobacco, ferrous metals, and motor vehicles. The indirect effects are relatively large for service sectors such as gas utilities, retail trade, and business services. The importance of the indirect effects is best exemplified by electrical utilities (sector 56), which has large abatement costs but a small trade volume. A 1 per cent increase in the price of electrical utilities would have only a $−1.5 million direct impact on the balance of trade, yet an $−80.9 million total impact.

Table 2 and appendix tables A1 and A2 strongly support most economists' intuitive position that higher abatement costs will reduce the U.S. balance of trade. The only sectors with positive impacts on the trade balance are coal mining (1973 and 1982 for all trade, and all years for trade with Canada), transportation services (1973 for all trade), and special industry machinery (1973 and 1982 for trade with Canada). All three sectors have low export and import elasticities, and the United States is a strong exporter of coal and transportation services. In trade with Canada, the United States is a strong net exporter of special industry machinery, whereas in total trade the United States is a net importer.

TABLE 2

Impacts on U.S. balance of trade for 1 per cent price increases (in millions of 1977 dollars)

	Total U.S.		U.S.-Canadian		
	Direct impact	Total impact	Direct impact	Total impact	Total U.S. domestic consumption
1 Agriculture	−95.8	−245.1	−52.3	−71.9	133,273.
2 Iron ore mining	−12.8	−41.0	−7.4	−12.7	3,567.
4 Coal mining	22.1	−6.3	8.1	2.1	16,701.
6 Crude petroleum	−316.4	−434.5	−16.7	−36.0	64,920.
9 Food and tobacco	−249.4	−285.8	−17.3	−28.2	210,733.
13 Paper	−111.0	−180.0	−75.4	−86.0	52,294.
15 Agricultural fertilizers	−5.6	−25.2	−8.3	−13.7	10,523.
16 Other chemicals	−132.5	−314.6	−26.9	−63.3	99,808.
17 Petroleum refining	−82.0	−201.5	−5.2	−32.3	104,290.
20 Plastic products	−24.3	−78.6	−6.1	−16.2	24,206.
24 Stone, clay & glass	−46.5	−83.1	−5.6	−12.9	35,462.
25 Ferrous metals	−376.4	−566.5	−54.5	−106.7	71,719.
26 Copper	−28.2	−64.4	−4.9	−14.0	9,300.
27 Other nonferrous metals	−76.0	−172.5	−26.8	−47.4	35,033.
28 Metal products	−91.4	−219.8	−22.1	−54.8	86,228.
29 Engines & turbines	−13.3	−28.9	−9.1	−13.4	9,454.
32 Metalworking machinery	−15.3	−42.3	−1.6	−7.4	13,734.
33 Special industry machinery	4.9	−4.5	2.9	1.1	7,547.
35 Computers	−29.5	−34.4	−6.6	−7.5	10,424.
40 Household appliances	−20.1	−22.7	−1.2	−1.8	10,728.
42 TV, radio & phonographs	−50.9	−52.5	−4.0	−4.6	9,492.
43 Motor vehicles	−285.5	−330.2	−119.2	−126.5	128,208.
54 Transportation services	3.3	−0.1	*a*	−0.5	2,025.
55 Communication services	−7.5	−50.4	*a*	−7.9	60,105.
56 Electrical utilities	−1.5	−80.9	*a*	−17.2	63,568.
57 Gas utilities	−3.0	−62.0	*a*	−13.4	46,708.
60 Retail trade	−0.4	−11.2	*a*	−2.0	194,613.
61 Eating & drinking places	0.0	−33.4	*a*	−6.5	87,819.
62 Finance & insurance	−9.0	−57.0	*a*	−9.5	127,952.
66 Business services	−17.7	−210.9	*a*	−37.1	161,049.

a No direct effects can be measured, owing to data limitations.

Relative to domestic consumption of the respective sector, the impacts on the balance of trade are quite small, with a range of 0.006 per cent (retail trade) to 0.8 per cent (ferrous metals). When measured as a percentage of total U.S. trade (exports plus imports) of individual sectors, the impacts range from −0.12 per cent (special industry machinery) to −7.08 per cent (copper) for the

TABLE 3

Total impact of industrial pollution abatement on trade (in millions of 1977 dollars)

	1973	1977	1982
Total trade			
U.S. export impact	−133.5	−258.8	−426.3
U.S. import impact	−1,247.9	−2,133.5	−3,978.9
Total trade impact	−1,381.4	−2,392.3	−4,405.3
Total U.S. trade volume	256,405.0	354,895.0	453,825.0
U.S.-Canadian trade			
Export impact	−33.7	−63.2	−64.0
Import impact	−303.7	−480.8	−786.0
Total trade impact	−337.4	−544.0	−850.0
U.S.-Canadian trade volume	48,467.0	53,413.0	51,733.0

merchandise sectors, with an average of −2.69 per cent. For trade with Canada, the impacts range from 0.2 (coal mining) to −8.9 (petroleum refining) per cent, with an average of −2.53 per cent.

Table 2 also provides a measure of a side benefit derived from the U.S. governmental policy of paying a large portion of farmers' abatement costs. If this program held agricultural prices down by 1 per cent, the 1977 U.S. balance of trade was improved by $245.1 million.

Little can be said about the growth in the effects shown in tables A1 and A2. Although additional abatement costs will have an impact on trade patterns, other influences such as macro-economic policies and influences of changing exchange rates make it impossible to determine exactly what portion of the shifts can be attributed to increased abatement costs.

Table 3 presents estimates of the total impact of IPA on the balance of trade under the assumption that the INFORUM import and export price elasticities hold for the full price change. In addition, all general equilibrium mitigating effects that might occur through changes in income or exchange rates are ignored. Therefore, these estimates should be the maximum potential effects. Given these caveats, the net reduction in the balance of trade for 1977 is $2,392.3 million for all trade and $544 million for trade with Canada. These figures are 0.67 and 1.02 per cent of the respective trade volumes.

The total impacts found in this study are above those forecasted in Evans (1973) and the Chase Econometrics (1981) studies but below those in the Data Resources Study (1981). The most striking difference between the current study and previous work is the growth in the size of IPA's impact over time. This study finds the impact grew by 218.9 per cent in constant dollars between 1973 and 1982, compared with a high of 28 per cent (the Data Resources study) among the other studies. The tremendous difference may in part be due to general equilibrium effects in the forecasting studies, but it is likely that these studies mis-estimated both the size of IPA costs and the length of the adjustment period.

CONCLUDING REMARKS

By providing a framework for examining the impact industrial pollution abatement has on the U.S. balance of trade, this paper has moved one step towards a more accurate assessment of U.S. environmental policy. General conditions for positive and negative impacts are derived in an interindustry framework under the assumption of full cost pass-through. This framework establishes an upper bound for the impact by explicitly ignoring all offsetting general-equilibrium effects such as changes in exchange rates. The statistical results indicate that marginal changes in IPA will reduce the U.S. balance of trade for all but a few industries. In addition, empirical support is found for the proposition that IPA is inducing changes in the U.S. comparative advantage such that the abatement content of imported goods is rising relative to that of exported goods.

The implications of this work for U.S. policy makers are fairly obvious. First, marginal changes in abatement costs, such as those resulting from the recent acid-rain talks with Canada, will result in a reduction in the U.S. balance of trade. Second, the inefficiency of the current regulatory system contributes substantially to the impact on the balance of trade. A 1982 Government Accounting Office report (1982) suggests that, if a more efficient regulatory scheme were used, air pollution abatement costs could be reduced 40 to 90 per cent, which would in turn improve the U.S. balance of trade. Finally, the adoption of similar environmental regulations by other countries will reduce the impact on the trade balance, although high-abatement-cost industries are likely to move to countries that do not adopt an environmental policy.

REFERENCES

Almon, Clopper Jr, Margaret Buckler, Lawrence Horwitz, and Thomas Reimbold (1974) *1985: Interindustry Forecasts of the American Economy* (Lexington, MA: Lexington Books)

Baumol, William J. and Wallace E. Oates (1975) *The Theory of Environmental Policy* (New Jersey: Prentice-Hall Inc.)

D'Arge, Ralph C. (1971) 'International Trade, Domestic Income, and Environmental Controls: Some Empirical Estimates.' In *Managing the Environment* edited by Allen V. Kneese, Sidney E. Rolfe, and Joseph W. Harned (New York: Praeger Publishers)

Dorfman, Robert (1973) Discussion of presented papers. *American Economic Review* 63, 253–6

Evans, Michael K. (1973) 'A forecasting model applied to pollution control costs.' *American Economic Review* 63, 244–52

INFORUM Staff (1986) 'The INFORUM models: a closer look.' INFORUM Research Report No. 75

Lake, Elizabeth E., William M. Hanneman, and Sharon M. Oster (1979) *Who Pays for Clean Water? The Distribution of Water Pollution Control Costs* (Boulder, CO: Westview Press)

Leontief, Wassily (1970) 'Environmental repercussions and the economic structure: an input-output approach.' *The Review of Economics and Statistics* 52, 262–71

Magee, Stephen P. and William F. Ford (1972) 'Environmental pollution, the terms of trade and the balance of payments.' *Kyklos* 25, 101–18

Mutti, John H. and David J. Richardson (1977) 'International competitive displacement from environmental control: the quantitative gains from methodological refinement.' *Journal of Environmental Economics and Management* 4, 135–52

Pasurka, Carl A. (1984) 'The short-run impact of environmental protection costs on U.S. product prices.' *Journal of Environmental Economics and Management* 11, 380–90

Portney, Paul R. (1981) 'The macro-economic impacts of federal environmental regulation.' In Henry M. Peskin, Paul R. Portney, and Allen V. Kneese, eds, *Environmental Regulation and the U.S. Economy* (Baltimore: Johns Hopkins University Press)

Robison, H. David (1985) 'Who pays for industrial pollution abatement?' *Review of Economics and Statistics* 67, 702–6

Russo, William J. and Gary L. Rutledge (1984) 'Plant and equipment expenditures by business for pollution abatement, 1983 and planned 1984.' *Survey of Current Business* 64, 31–4

Rutledge, Gary L., F.J. Dreiling, and B.C. Dunlap (1978) 'Capital Expenditures by Business for Pollution Abatement 1973–7 and Planned 1978.' *Survey of Current Business* 58, 33–8

Rutledge, Gary L. and Betsy O'Connor (1980) 'Capital expenditures by business for pollution abatement, 1977, 1978, and planned 1979.' *Survey of Current Business* 60, 19–22

U.S. Bureau of the Census (1976) *Pollution Abatement Costs and Expenditures 1973* (Washington, D.C.: U.S. Government Printing Office)

U.S. Bureau of the Census (1979) *Pollution Abatement Costs and Expenditures 1977* (Washington, D.C.: U.S. Government Printing Office)

U.S. Bureau of the Census (1984) *Pollution Abatement Costs and Expenditures 1982* (Washington, D.C.: U.S. Government Printing Office)

U.S. General Accounting Office (1982) *A Market Approach to Air Pollution Control Could Reduce Compliance Costs Without Jeopardizing Clean Air Goals* (Washington, D.C.: U.S. Government Printing Office)

Walter, Ingo (1973) 'The pollution content of American trade.' *Western Economic Journal* 11, 61–70

APPENDIX

TABLE A1

Impacts on U.S. balance of trade for 1 per cent price increases (in millions of 1977 dollars)

	1973	1977	1982
1 Agriculture	−258.3	−245.1	−295.0
2 Iron ore mining	−27.4	−41.0	−41.5
4 Coal mining	4.6	−6.3	5.8
6 Crude petroleum	−225.0	−434.5	−469.7
9 Food and tobacco	−249.4	−285.8	−319.7
13 Paper	−151.6	−180.0	−221.8
15 Agricultural fertilizers	−8.4	−25.2	−25.7
16 Other chemicals	−210.5	−314.6	−445.7
17 Petroleum refining	−149.3	−201.5	−335.3
20 Plastic products	−43.5	−78.6	−111.3
24 Stone, clay & glass	−74.1	−83.1	−108.7
25 Ferrous metals	−429.2	−566.5	−651.1
26 Copper	−65.9	−64.4	−78.0
27 Other nonferrous metals	−127.1	−172.5	−251.1
28 Metal products	−167.7	−219.8	−284.3
29 Engines & turbines	−22.0	−28.9	−46.3
32 Metalworking machinery	−33.0	−42.3	−71.8
33 Special industry machinery	−6.9	−4.5	−32.3
35 Computers	−29.4	−34.4	−97.2
40 Household appliances	−17.7	−22.7	−27.0
42 TV, radio & phonographs	−47.0	−52.5	−70.1
43 Motor vehicles	−269.0	−330.2	−438.9
54 Transportation services	0.7	−0.1	−1.8
55 Communication services	−47.7	−50.4	−65.1
56 Electrical utilities	−43.1	−80.9	−126.9
57 Gas utilities	−25.9	−62.0	−108.6
60 Retail trade	−10.0	−11.2	−13.0
61 Eating & drinking places	−29.4	−33.4	−50.1
62 Finance & insurance	−60.8	−57.0	−72.7
66 Business services	−173.2	−210.9	−284.7

TABLE A2

Impacts on U.S. balance of trade with Canada for 1 per cent price increases (in millions of 1977 dollars)

	1973	1977	1982
1 Agriculture	−76.6	−71.9	−82.3
2 Iron ore mining	−8.4	−12.7	−11.9
4 Coal mining	3.1	2.1	0.8
6 Crude petroleum	−49.1	−36.0	−58.1
9 Food and tobacco	−26.8	−28.2	−31.1
13 Paper	−78.2	−86.0	−90.7
15 Agricultural fertilizers	−7.1	−13.7	−13.0
16 Other chemicals	−47.2	−63.3	−86.3
17 Petroleum refining	−23.5	−32.3	−56.0
20 Plastic products	−11.6	−16.2	−18.1
24 Stone, clay & glass	−12.8	−12.9	−13.4
25 Ferrous metals	−78.7	−106.7	−104.4
26 Copper	−19.8	−14.0	−13.6
27 Other nonferrous metals	−45.5	−47.4	−50.0
28 Metal products	−45.1	−54.8	−60.8
29 Engines & turbines	−11.1	−13.4	−10.6
32 Metalworking machinery	−7.0	−7.4	−8.9
33 Special industry machinery	1.2	1.1	−0.4
35 Computers	−6.5	−7.5	−7.6
40 Household appliances	−1.7	−1.8	−2.1
42 TV, radio & phonographs	−4.3	−4.6	−5.6
43 Motor vehicles	−96.3	−126.5	−136.1
54 Transportation services[a]	−0.3	−0.5	−0.7
55 Communication services[a]	−9.2	−7.9	−8.2
56 Electrical utilities[a]	−10.2	−17.2	−22.6
57 Gas utilities[a]	−5.3	−13.4	−20.5
60 Retail trade[a]	−2.3	−2.0	−2.1
61 Eating & drinking places[a]	−6.8	−6.5	−7.8
62 Finance & insurance[a]	−11.9	−9.5	−10.1
66 Business services[a]	−35.9	−37.1	−42.8

a Includes only the indirect impacts on merchandise sectors due to data limitations.

[12]

KYKLOS, Vol. 43, Fasc. 2, 191–209

The Effects of Domestic Environmental Policies on Patterns of World Trade: An Empirical Test

JAMES A. TOBEY *

I. INTRODUCTION

In theory, environmental control costs encourage reduced specialization in the production of polluting outputs in countries with stringent environmental regulations [PETHIG, 1976; SIEBERT, 1977; MCGUIRE, 1982]. In contrast, countries that fail to undertake an environmental protection program presumably increase their comparative advantage in the production of items that damage the environment. This relationship between trade and environmental policy receives considerable attention whenever countries are in the process of passing new pollution control measures. Groups who oppose existing measures, or the implementation of stiffer measures, argue that they reduce the ability of polluting industries to compete internationally [1]. With foreign trade an increasingly important sector in many of the world's economies, the arguments of such groups are now frequently weighted very heavily.

The premise that trade suffers from the imposition of environmental policy has a strong element of a priori plausibility but, surprisingly, has little empirical support. Several macroeconometric models [D'ARGE, 1974; ROBISON, 1986; OECD, 1985] have predicted that

* Affiliated with the United States Department of Agriculture, Economic Research Service, Research and Technology Division. This paper does not necessarily represent the views of the Department of Agriculture. I am very grateful for the thoughtful comments of Professors PETER MURRELL and WALLACE OATES, and the support of the Bureau of Business and Economic Research, University of Maryland.

1. In addition, the imposition of environmental regulations has often been suggested as a partial explanation for inflation in the U. S. and declines in productivity growth experienced by most industrialized countries in the 1970s.

pollution control measures should lead to a small but discernible effect on the balance of trade, but there are few studies to confirm this prediction.

The location-of-industry studies [LEONARD, 1988; PEARSON, 1987, 1985; WALTER, 1985] have explored the related ideas that stringent pollution control measures push industries out of the U.S. (the 'industrial-flight' hypothesis), and that less-developed countries compete to attract multinational industries by minimizing their own environmental policies (the 'pollution-haven' hypothesis). Their investigations, however, have been unable to find evidence in support of either hypothesis.

The present paper complements the results of the less rigorous location of industry studies by providing an empirical test of the hypothesis that stringent environmental policy has caused trade patterns to deviate in commodities produced by the world's 'dirty' industries.

The empirical tests are conducted using the cross-section Heckscher-Ohlin-Vanek (HOV) model of international trade. LEAMER [1984], BOWEN [1983] and others [MURRELL, 1990 and RYTERMAN, 1988] have popularized the application of this model to empirical tests of the sources of international comparative advantage. The basic HOV model is extended, in addition, to allow for non-homothetic preferences (NHP) and scale economies/product differentiation (EOS). Under all three specifications, two different approaches are taken to conduct the empirical tests. The first involves inclusion of a qualitative variable in the estimated equation to represent the stringency of pollution control measures. The second examines the signs of the estimated error terms when the variable measuring the stringency of a country's environmental policy is not included in the estimated equation.

It is found that the stringent environmental regulations imposed on industries in the late 1960s and early 1970s by most industrialized countries have not measurably affected international trade patterns in the most polluting industries. This result is consistent with and reinforces the results of the location-of-industry studies which use a very different empirical approach, but it may nevertheless be intuitively surprising to those who still fear the undesirable competitive effects of environmental policy.

THE EFFECTS OF DOMESTIC ENVIRONMENTAL POLICIES

Before proceeding with the empirical test, commodities whose production draws heavily on environmental resources – termed 'pollution-intensive' commodities – are defined.

II. DEFINITION OF POLLUTION-INTENSIVE COMMODITIES

A commodity's relative pollution intensity is defined in this study by the pollution-abatement costs incurred in its production in the

Table 1

I–O Industry	SITC	Description	Pollution Abatement Costs as Percentage of Total Costs
	Mining		
5	281	Iron ore, concentrates	2.03
6	283	Ores of nonferrous base metals	1.92
	Primary Nonferrous Metals		
38	681	Silver, platinum, etc.	2.05
38	682	Copper	2.05
38	683	Nickel	2.05
38	685	Lead	2.05
38	686	Zinc	2.05
38	687	Tin	2.05
38	689	Nonferrous base metals, n. e. s.	2.05
	Paper and Pulp		
24	251	Pulp and waste paper	2.40
24	641	Paper and paperboard	2.40
24	642	Articles of paper	2.40
	Primary Iron and Steel		
37	671	Pig iron	2.38
37	672	Ingots	2.38
37	673	Iron and steel bars	2.38
37	674	Universals, plates	2.38
37	675	Hoops and strips	2.38
37	676	Railway material	2.38
37	677	Iron and steel wire	2.38
37	678	Tubes and fittings	2.38
37	679	Iron, steel castings	2.38
	Chemicals		
27	513	Inorganic elements	2.89
27	514	Other inorganic chemicals	2.89
28	581	Plastic materials	2.36

United States. Such costs are reported by the U.S. Department of Commerce [1975] and the Environmental Protection Agency [1984]. KALT [1985] has taken these data for 1977 and matched them to sixty-four agricultural and manufacturing 2-digit I-O industries. These direct pollution abatement costs are then multiplied by the 1977 total expenditures I-O table to generate an estimate of total (direct and indirect) PACs per dollar of industrial output.

Commodities termed pollution-intensive are defined as the products of those industries whose direct and indirect abatement costs in the U.S. are equal to or greater than 1.85 percent of total costs. The cut-off of 1.85 percent is chosen because it results in a set of industries that are generally considered the most polluting (metals, chemicals, and paper industries) throughout the world[2]. Moreover, there is a considerable difference between the pollution-abatement costs in these industries and in those of the remaining group of industries.

In *Table 1,* these input-output industries which I have defined as pollution-intensive are matched to 3-digit SITC commodities and aggregated into five commodity groups including paper and pulp products (paper), mining of ores (mining), primary iron and steel (steel), primary nonferrous metals (nfmetals), and chemicals (chems). It is interesting to note at the outset the relatively small size of pollution abatement costs as a percentage of total costs in even the most highly regulated industries.

III. HECKSCHER-OHLIN-VANEK MODEL OF INTERNATIONAL TRADE

The HOV equations are a multi-factor, multi-commodity extension of the Heckscher-Ohlin (H-O) model of international trade. They have been used in three different ways. The factor content studies and cross-commodity regressions use measures of factor intensities and trade to infer factor endowments. The third methodology and the approach taken in this study, regresses trade in a specific commodity across countries on country characteristics, i.e., resource endow-

2. This cut-off does not include the petroleum industry. Petroleum is excluded because it is believed that the dynamics of this industry during this time (1975) were heavily influenced by extraordinary circumstances affecting the availability and processing of crude oil. LEONARD [1988] supports this view.

ments. In that resource endowments are the explanatory variables, such regressions reveal the direct influence of resources on trade in a specific commodity. Since this study seeks to reveal information on the most pollution-intensive commodities across countries, the cross-country analysis is chosen as the most appropriate approach.

A set of eleven resource endowments for the year 1975 is used to explain net exports of the most polluting industries under the HOV model[3]. These endowments are provided by LEAMER [1984] and include:

1. CAPITAL (CAP) Accumulated and discounted gross domestic investment flows since 1948, assuming an average life of 15 years.
2. LABOR 1 (LAB1) Number of workers classified as professional or technical.
3. LABOR 2 (LAB2) Number of literate nonprofessional workers.
4. LABOR 3 (LAB3) Number of illiterate workers.
5. LAND 1 (LND1) Land area in tropical rainy climate zone.
6. LAND 2 (LND2) Land area in dry climate zone.
7. LAND 3 (LND3) Land area in humid mesothermal climate zone (for example, California).
8. LAND 4 (LND4) Land area in humid microthermal climate (for example, Michigan).
9. COAL (COAL) Value of production of primary solid fuels (coal, lignite, and brown coal).
10. MINERALS (MINLS) Value of production of minerals: bauxite, copper, flourspar, ironore, lead, manganese, nickel, potash, pyrite, salt, tin, and zinc.
11. OIL (OIL) Value of oil and gas production.

The HOV model can be summarized by the following equations which explicitly incorporate this list of endowments:

$$N_{it} = CST_{i0} + b_{i1}V_{1t} + b_{i2}V_{2t} + \ldots + b_{i11}V_{11t} + \mu_{it} \quad (1)$$

where N_{it} are net exports of commodity i by country t; V_{kt} are endowments of resource k (k = 1...11) in country t; b_{ik} are the coefficients which indicate the total effect (production and consump-

3. Trade data for 1975 comes from United Nations' trade tapes.

tion) of an increase in a resource on net trade of a specific commodity; μ_{it} is the disturbance term, and; CST_{i0} is the equation's constant term. The constant term embodies one resource endowment or country characteristic, which all countries are assumed to possess identically and which has a non-zero mean value.

If the environmental endowment, measured by the stringency of environmental regulations[4], has an effect on trade patterns then the set of eleven endowments in equation (1) is incomplete. In this case, estimation of the HOV trade equations implies a specification error involving an omitted variable. Two approaches are taken to test the effect of the environmental endowment on trade patterns under the HOV model when cross-country quantitative data on the environmental endowment are not available. In the first, a qualitative variable is included in equation (1) to represent the omitted variable, and, in the second an omitted variable test is conducted.

IV.

1. *The HOV Model with Environmental Stringency*

To test the pollution-haven hypothesis under the first approach, the following equation is estimated under ordinary least squares (OLS):

$$N_{it} = CST_{i0} + b_{i1}V_{1t} + b_{i2}V_{2t} + \ldots + b_{i11}V_{11t} + b_{iE}D_{Et} + \mu_{it} \quad (2)$$

where D_{Et} is a qualitative variable measuring the stringency of pollution control measures in country t based on a 1976 UNCTAD survey [WALTER and UGELOW, 1979].

The degree of environmental stringency is measured on a scale from one (tolerant) to seven (strict); the mean score for developed

4. Although pollution emissions are a joint product of the production process, they can also be interpreted as an input in the production function because they can be viewed as one of the various uses of the environment [BAUMOL and OATES, 1988]. Since use of the environment is typically a public good, the environmental endowment has no price attached to it and will be used freely by industries until pollution control measures are instituted. Thus, in this study, a country's environmental endowment is measured by their stringency of pollution control measures.

THE EFFECTS OF DOMESTIC ENVIRONMENTAL POLICIES

Table 2

Index of the degree of Stringency of Environmental Policy
(7 = strict, 1 = tolerant)

Group A	Index	Group B	Index	Group C	Index
1 Austria	4	1 Chile	4	1 Colombia	5
2 Australia	5	2 Cyprus	1	2 Liberia	1
3 Belux	3	3 Israel	4	3 Nigeria	2
4 Denmark	5	4 Malta	1		
5 Finland	6	5 Singapore	6		
6 Germany	5	6 Spain	4		
7 Japan	7	7 Panama	4		
8 New Zeal.	5				
9 Nether.	5				
10 Norway	6				
11 Sweden	7				
12 UK	4				
13 USA	7				

Source: WALTER and UGELOW [1979].

countries is 6.1, while for developing countries it is 3.1. There are observations for 23 countries: 13 industrialized and 10 developing countries (see *Table 2*).

The results are presented in *Table 3* (absolute value of the t radio shown in parentheses beside the estimated regression coefficient). In no instance is the t ratio found to be statistically significant on the measure for the stringency of environmental policy in the five regressions of net exports of polluting industries.

2. *Omitted Variable Test*

A second approach to testing the effect of pollution control measures on trade patterns investigates the bias in the regression residuals when the variable representing countries' environmental endowments are not included in the HOV equations[5].

5. The idea for this methodology is attributable to RYTERMAN [1988]. RYTERMAN was able to show that technological flexibility is a significant variable in determining trade patterns between market economies and centrally planned economies.

Table 3

Variable Name	Mining ($R^2=0.99$)	Paper ($R^2=0.96$)	Chems ($R^2=0.93$)	Steel ($R^2=0.89$)	NFMetals ($R^2=0.92$)
	Equations (D. F. = 10)				
CAP	−192 (2.4)	177 (1.6)	583 (5.6)	1537 (2.6)	−89 (1.0)
LAB1	735 (1.9)	−267 (0.5)	981 (1.9)	−1434 (0.5)	−550 (1.2)
LAB2	−111 (3.2)	−25 (0.5)	−154 (3.5)	54 (0.2)	44 (1.1)
LAB3	−15 (0.6)	50 (1.5)	−49 (1.6)	84 (0.5)	69 (2.5)
LND1	385 (1.5)	278 (0.8)	521 (1.6)	237 (0.1)	−254 (0.9)
LND2	−104 (0.7)	−192 (1.0)	−31 (0.2)	503 (0.5)	−247 (1.5)
LND3	1295 (2.8)	100 (0.2)	−268 (0.5)	−2898 (0.9)	−414 (0.8)
LND4	435 (0.9)	6089 (9.2)	-2003 (3.2)	−1374 (0.4)	−589 (1.1)
COAL	−78 (0.6)	−110 (0.6)	−283 (1.6)	−83 (0.1)	88 (0.6)
MINLS	338 (2.0)	330 (1.4)	88 (0.4)	26 (0.1)	715 (3.7)
OIL	−30 (1.6)	−110 (4.3)	−20 (0.8)	−142 (1.0)	17 (0.8)
D	−10314 (0.3)	2454 (0.1)	−1531 (0.1)	98844 0.4)	48658 (1.3)
CST	−5669 (0.1)	−168370 (1.0)	−107110 (0.7)	−697020 (0.8)	−122980 (0.9)

Consider first a simple HOV equation with one known and one unknown independent variable. Let x_{t2} represent a factor endowment for country t. Under the null hypothesis that the environmental factor (x_{t3}) has no effect on the pattern of trade, the equation specifying net exports (N_t) may be written as:

$$N_t = \beta_1 + \beta_2 x_{t2} + \tilde{\mu}_t \qquad (3)$$

The alternative to the null hypothesis is represented by the following equation:

$$N_t = \beta_1 + \beta_2 x_{t2} + \beta_3 x_{t3} + \mu_t \qquad (4)$$

If equation (3) is correct, the least squares estimators of β_1 and β_2 using equation (3) will be unbiased and efficient for all sample sizes. If equation (4) is correct, then estimation of equation (3) will still generate an unbiased estimator of β_2 given the following assumption[6]:

6. KMENTA [1971] shows that while $\hat{\beta}_2$ is unbiased, var($\hat{\beta}_2$) is positively biased. Therefore, the usual tests of significance concerning β_2 are not valid since they will tend to accept the null hypothesis more frequently than is justified by the given level of significance.

THE EFFECTS OF DOMESTIC ENVIRONMENTAL POLICIES

A1: The omitted variable is not correlated with any of the included independent variables.

Given assumption A1, estimation of equation (3) when the omitted variable (x_{t3}) does not equal zero will not affect $\hat{\beta}_2$. Its presence will, however, be embodied in the constant and disturbance term. Solving for $\tilde{\mu}_t$, the following equation can be derived:

$$= \beta_3(x_{t3} - \overline{X}_3) + \mu_t \quad (5)$$

Under the null hypothesis that x_{t3} has no effect on the pattern of trade so that $\beta_3 = 0$, $\tilde{\mu}_t$ is a consistent estimator of μ_t. Under the alternative case where pollution control measures are expected to have an effect on the pattern of trade, so that $\beta_3 \neq 0$, then (given assumption A1) $\tilde{\mu}_t$ provides a consistent estimate of equation (5).

A methodology to test the effect of pollution control measures on the pattern of trade may now be presented. Under the alternative hypothesis that equation (4) is correctly specified and assuming it also has all the properties of the classical regression model, then the sign of μ_t is expected to be random. Therefore, the expected sign of $\tilde{\mu}_t$ in equation (5) is the same as that of $\beta_3(x_{t3} - \bar{X}_3)$. β_3 is expected to be negative if pollution control measures reduce net exports of pollution-intensive commodities. To determine the sign of $(x_{t3} - \bar{X}_3)$, consider the distribution of the stringency of environmental regulations, x_{t3}, over the world. Industrialized, high-income countries have environmental endowments greater than the population mean $\bar{X}_3$, and less-developed countries have environmental endowments less than the population mean. Thus, the pattern of signs of $\tilde{\mu}_t$ under the alternative hypothesis depends on the distribution of x_{t3} over countries. Given the distribution above, the proportion of error terms that are postive for developing countries is expected to be significantly greater than the proportion of error terms that are positive for industrialized countries.

Let T_n represent the true proportion of errors for countries in group n (where $n = 1$ corresponds to industrialized countries and $n = 2$ corresponds to developing countries). The null hypothesis (H_0) states that the proportion of errors that are positive is the same for both industrialized and developing countries. The alternative hypothesis (H_1) states that the proportion of such errors is greater for developing countries than for industrialized countries.

$$H_0: T_2 = T_1$$
$$H_1: T_2 > T_1$$

A nonparametric statistical procedure was chosen to conduct the statistical test because it requires few assumptions regarding the distribution of the error terms. Under the null hypothesis, the test statistic may be given as[7]:

$$A = \frac{R_2 - R_1}{[\hat{T} \times (1 - \hat{T})[(1/I \times J_2) + (1/I \times J_1)]]^{1/2}}$$

where $R_n = S_n/(i \times J_n)$ represents the proportion of estimated errors that are positive; 'I' equals the total number of commodity groups (= 5), J_n equals the total number of countries in country group n; and S_n equals the number of estimated error terms for countries in group n that are positive.

$\hat{T}$ is an estimate of the true proportion under the null hypothesis. The best estimate of the true population proportion is constructed by combining the observations for both industrialized and developing countries as follows:

$$\hat{T} = (S_1 + S_2)/(I \times (J_1 + J_2))$$

To perform the omitted variable test a set of 58 countries is arranged in three groups (see TAble 4). Group one consists of industrialized, high-income countries. Environmental regulatory costs in this group are predicted to generate a comparative disadvantage in the production of polluting commodities. Group two is composed of upper-income developing countries and semi-industrialized nations without a stringent environmental program in 1975[8]. Group three is composed of middle to low-income developing countries.

A summary of information on the estimated residuals when equation (1) is estimated using this set of 58 countries is shown in Table 5. It is not possible to reject the null hypothesis that $T_2 = T_1$ in the comparison of industrialized countries with any combination of the

7. See YAMANE [1967].

8. A review of international environmental policy [TOBEY, 1989] is used to specify those countries with and without enforced pollution control measures as of the mid 1970s.

THE EFFECTS OF DOMESTIC ENVIRONMENTAL POLICIES

Table 4

Country Observations

Country	GDP per capita[1]	Country	GDP per capita[1] (1975 constant U. S. $)	Country	GDP per capita[1]
Group One		Group Two		Group Three	
Australia	5919	Argentina	3159	Afghanistan	380
Austria	4994	Brazil	1978	Burma	312
Belux	5569	Chile	1834	Colombia	1596
Canada	6788	Costa Rica	1835	Dom Rep	1443
Denmark	5969	Cyprus	1811	Ecuador	1300
Finland	5192	Greece	3360	Egypt	929
France	5864	Hong Kong	2559	El Salvador	1005
Germany	5758	Ireland	3067	Ghana	952
Iceland	5201	Israel	4154	Honduras	871
Japan	4904	Italy	3870	India	472
Netherlands	5321	Malta	2154	Indonesia	536
New Zealand	4769	Mexico	2276	Jamaica	1763
Norway	5419	Panama	2026	Korea	1530
Sweden	6749	Peru	1860	Liberia	830
Switzerland	6082	Portugal	2397	Lybia	6680[2]
UK	4601	Singapore	2875	Malaysia	1532
USA	7132	Spain	4032	Mauritius	1260
AVERAGE	5661	Turkey	1738	Nigeria	1179
		Yugoslavia	1960[2]	Paraguay	1186
		AVERAGE	2567	Philippines	912
				Sri Lanka	661
				Thailand	930
				AVERAGE	1002[3]

[1] HESTON and SUMMERS [1984].
[2] 1977 GNP per capita, from World Bank [1979], *World Development Report*.
[3] Excluding Libya.

developing country groups. These results reinforce the earlier finding which used a qualitative variable to represent the environmental endowment and which also found no effect of pollution control measures on HOV trade patterns.

IV. EXTENSIONS TO THE HOV MODEL

This section specifies alternative trade models when two of the HOV assumptions are relaxed (see LEAMER s[1984] for a complete list of

JAMES A. TOBEY

Table 5

Positive Residuals

Country Group	Paper	Steel	Chems	NFMetals	Mining	S_n[1]	J_n[2]	R_n[3]	A[4]
One	7	9	5	8	11	40	17	0.47	–
Two	5	10	9	5	6	35	19	0.37	−1.32
Three	10	18	15	5	11	59	22	0.54	0.96
2 + 3	15	28	24	10	17	94	41	0.45	−0.15

[1] S_n is the number of errors for group n that are positive.
[2] J_n is the number of countries in group n.
[3] $R_n = S_n/(I \times J_n)$.
[4] 'A' is the test statistic computed using group one as the sample of industrialized countries compared against groups of developing countries ($T = 0.46$). An absolute value of 1.65 for the test statistic in the normal distribution corresponds to a probability of 95 percent.

necessary assumptions) and reports the empirical results when the above empirical tests are again performed on these models.

The first exension of the HOV model allows for non-homothetic preferences. The HOV model assumes identical homnothetic tates – meaning that individuals facing identical commodity prices will consume commodities in the same proportions. In this cross-section study, with countries at various levels of development, this assumption may not be completely reasonable. To allow for NHP I assume that consumption across countries is a linear function of population and national income. When the HOV model is modified to incorporate this assumption, per capita net exports (n_{it}) become a linear function of per capita resource endowments (v_{kt}) as given by the following equation:

$$n_{it} = b^*_{i0} + (\sum_{k=1}^{K} b_{ik} v_{kt}) \tag{6}$$

where $b^*_{iO} = -c_{iO}$, and c_{iO} is a parameter that relates consumption of commodity i in country t to country t's population. As before, b_{ik} indicates the total effect of an increase in a resource on net trade of a specific commodity.

The same set of empirical tests are conducted using this equation.

Without burdening the reader with additional tables, I simply report that WALTER and UGELOW's variable is not significant in any of the OLS regressions. Similarly, the statistical comparison of error terms under the omitted variable test does not support the hypothesis being tested.

The second extension of the HOV model emphasizes scale economies and product differentiation. All of the pollution-intensive commodity groups are associated with what are generally considered very large-scale production processes. Moreover, HUFBAUER [1970] has found the production of paper products to be subject to large economies of scale and the production of nonferrous metals to be subject to diseconomies of scale. Scale economies may therefore be important in determining international comparative advantage for these goods. If this is the case, developing countries, with small economies and limited infrastructure outside of major cities may be at a disadvantage in the production of these commodities. A model which allows for the fact that the production function for polluting commodities exhibits economies of scale is therefore tested.

I use a model which MURRELL [1990] derives and which follows HELPMAN and KRUGMAN [1985] closely. The set of assumptions used to generate this model are essentially the same as those of the previous HOV model except that product differentiation and economies of scale are introduced. Specifically, it is assumed that each good can be produced in an infinite nujmber of varieties. Each variety of a single good has the same production function, but such functions vary between goods. Furthermore, the production function for each variety exhibits economies of scale, at least at low levels of output.

With the introduction of economies of scale and product differentiation, the export of good i by country t, x_{it}, are specified as follows [MURRELL, 1990]:

$$x_{it} = \sum_{k=1}^{K} b^{*}_{ik} V_{kt}(1 - G_t/G_w) \tag{7}$$

where G_t is the national income of country t and G_w is total world income.

Equation (7) cannot be derived from the H-O theory and and the asterisks on the coefficients of the equation are a reminder that these coefficients are not equivalent to b_{ik} in the previous two models.

Again, the same set of empirical tests are conducted, this time using equation (7). Once again, WALTER and UGELOW's variable is not found significant in any of the five OLS regressions. In contrast, the test statistics comparing the sign of the estimated residuals of industrialized and developing countries are significant at the 95 percent level of confidence, but, because they are negative, they also fail to support the hypothesis being tested.

V. A FIXED-EFFECTS EMPIRICAL TEST

A reasonable explanation for the empirical results above may be that the magnitude of environmental expenditures incurred by the industrialized countries in the late 1960s and early 1970s were not sufficiently large to cause a noticeable effect on trade patterns between countries with and without environmental protection programs. The cross-section HOV model may not be sufficiently precise to identify these small changes in factor abundances and comparative advantage. Thus, the effect of domestic environmental policy on trade may be getting lost in the 'noise'. By examining the change in trade patterns before and after te introduction of environmental measures in the industrialized countries, one might be able to detect the hypothesized shifts in trade patterns in response to environmental policies that don't show up in the equations using data from a specific point in time. Such a methodology would also be effective in capturing the effect of environmental policy even if there was a significant lag in the impact of pollution controls on international competitiveness.

Although endowment data are only available fo the year 1975, most resource endowments change little over time. At least for the most polluting industries, one might argue that the most important endowment change over the period 1970 to 1984 was the increase in environmental regulations. Consider then a HOV model where the change in net exports over 1970–84 is linearly related to the change in factor endowments over the same period. Under a 'fixed-effects' specification, assume tht, except for the environmental endowment, the change in factor endowments equals zero. In this case, one is left with the following equations:

$$\Delta N_{it} = E_t + \mu_{it}$$

THE EFFECTS OF DOMESTIC ENVIRONMENTAL POLICIES

Table 6

Variable Name	Equations (D. F. = 22) Mining ($R^2=0.03$)	Paper ($R^2=0.0+$)	Chems ($R^2=0.05$)	Steel ($R^2=0.0+$)	NFMetals ($R^2=0.04$)
E	−54155 (1.1)	−2298 (0.1)	78007 (1.9)	49437 (0.4)	−65593 (1.1)

where ΔN_{it} are 1984 minus 1970 net exports of commodity i by country t. E_t is the WALTER and UGELOW [1979] measure of the degree of the stringency of environmental policy in 23 countries in 1977. Since these countries generally did not have enforced environmental programs in place by 1970, the level of environmental policy given by this index is a reasonable proxy for the change in environmental policy. Finally, μ_{it} are the random error terms.

The results of the OLS estimation of this model are shown in *Table 6*. If environmental policies reduce countries' international comparative advantage in the most pollution-intensive commodities, then the sign on the environmental endowment coefficient should be negative and significant. Only in the chemicals group does the significance of the coefficient approach a conventionally accepted level of confidence. The sign, however, is positive, and once again does not support the hypothesized impact of pollution control measures on trade patterns.

VI. CONCLUDING REMARKS

Several tests are undertaken under a variety of specifications, but in no case is there any evidence that the introduction of environmental control measures has caused trade patterns to deviate from the HOV predictions. This result is important in that it casts serious doubt on the 'balance-of-trade' argument against environmental control which, as mentioned above, can be a strong deterrent to the implementation of new or stronger pollution control measures. the test results also lend support to the less empirically rigorous location-of-industry studies which maintain that the world distribution of 'dirty' industries has not been affected by differing country levels of environmental stringency.

As already noted, a reasonable explanation for these empirical results may simply be that the magnitude of environmental expenditures in countries with stringent environmental policies are not sufficiently large to cause a noticeable effect. This seems like the most likely explanation. Other explanations can, however, be postulated and I offer two possibilities below.

The first relates to the validity of the HOV equations themselves. The accuracy of the cross-section HOV model was recently questioned by BOWEN et al. [1987] who shows that since this model makes no reference to factor input intensities, it is only a weak test of the H-O hypothesis. The stricter H-O hypothesis requires that factor supplies, magnitude of the difference in robustness and accuracy of the weak version vis-à-vis the strict version is not clear.

The second observation relates to the nature of the pollution-intensive commodity groups and violations of the assumptions of the HOV model. this model assumes that commodities move inernationally at zero cost of tansportation, and that there are no other impediments to trade. However, transportation costs, tariffs, and subsidies[9] are important considerations in these industries and may affect a country's composition of trade. These trade impediments are difficult to deal with at an empirical level since they are very difficult to measure for large sets of countries. However, if they are distributed across countries in the same pattern as environmental controls then they would interfere with the ability of the HOV model to pick up the effect of environmental policy.

9. Many countries with stringent pollution control measures have offered various subsidies to polluting industries which lessen the impact of pollution control measures on world trade patterns in these industries.

THE EFFECTS OF DOMESTIC ENVIRONMENTAL POLICIES

REFERENCES

BAUMOL, W. and OATES, W.: *The Theory of Environmental Policy,* Second Edition, NY: Cambridge University Press, 1988.

BOWEN, H.: 'Changes in the International Distribution of Resources and their Impact on U.S. Comparative Advantages', *Review of Economics and Statistics,* Vol. 65 (1983), pp. 402–414.

BOWEN, H.; LEAMER, E. and SVEIKAUSKAS, L.: 'Multicountry, Multifactor Tests of the Factor Abundance Theorem', *American Economic Review,* Vol. 77 (1987), pp. 791–809.

D'ARGE, R.: 'International Trade, Domestic Income, and Environmental Controls: Some Empirical Estimates', in: KNEESE, A. (ed.), *Managing the Environment: International Economic Cooperation for Pollution Control,* New York: Praeger, 1974, pp. 289–315.

KRUGMAN, P. and HELPMAN, E.: *Market Structure and Foreign Trade,* Cambridge: MIT Press, 1986.

HESTON, A. and SUMMERS, R.: 'Improved International Comparisons of Real Product and its Composition: 1950–1980', *Review of Income and Wealth,* Vol. 30 (1984), pp. 207–262.

HUFBAUER, G.C.: 'The Impact of National Characteristics and Technology on the Commodity Composition of Trade in Manufactured Goods', in: VERNON, RAYMOND (ed.), *The Technological Factor in International Trade,* NY: Columbia University Press, 1970.

KALT, J.P.: 'The Impact of Domestic Environmental Regulatory Policies on U.S. International Competitiveness', Energy and Environmental Policy Center, Discussion Paper Series, John F. Kennedy School of Government, Harvard University, 1985.

LEAMER, E.E.: *Sources of International Comparative Advantage: Theory and Evidence,* Cambridge: MIT Press, 1984.

LEONARD, H.J.: *Pollution and the Struggle for World Product,* Cambridge: Cambridge University Press, 1988.

MCGUIRE, M.: 'Regulation, Factor Rewards, and International Trade', *Journal of Public Economics,* Vol. 17 (1982), pp. 335–354.

MURRELL, P.: *The Nature of Socialist Economies: Lessons from East European Foreign Trade,* Princeton University Press, 1990.

OECD: *The Macro-Economic Impact of Environmental Expenditures,* Organization for Economic Cooperation and Development, Paris, 1985.

PEARSON, C.: *Down to Business: Multinational Corporations, the Environment and Development,* Washington, D.C.: World Resources Institute, 1985.

PEARSON, C. (ed.): *Multinational Corporation, the Environment and Development,* Washington, D.C.: World Resources Institute, 1987.

PETHIG, R.: 'Pollution, Welfare, and Environmental Policy in the Theory of Comparative Advantage', *Journal of Environmental Economics and Management,* Vol. 2 (1976), pp. 160–169.

ROBISON, D. H.: 'Industrial Pollution Abatement: The Impact on Balance of Trade', Unpublished manuscript, University of Maryland, 1986.

RYTERMAN, R.: *Technological Flexibility and the Pattern of East-West Trade*, Ph. D. Thesis, University of Maryland, 1988.

SIEBERT, H.: 'Environmental Quality and the Gains from Trade', *Kyklos*, Vol. 30 (1977), pp. 657–673.

TOBEY, J.: *The Impact of Domestic Environmental Policies on International Trade*, Ph. D. Dissertation, University of Maryland, 1989.

U.S. Department of Commerce, Bureau of the Census: 'Pollution Abatement Costs and Expenditures', Current Industrial Reports, Washington, D.C., 1975.

WALTER, I.: 'Environmentally Induced Industrial Relocation to Developing Countries', in: RUBIN, S. J. and GRAHAM, T. R. (eds.), *Environment and Trade*, Allanheld, Osmum, and Publishers, 1982, pp. 67–101.

WALTER, I. and UGELOW, J.: 'Environmental Policies in Developing Countries', *Ambio*, Vol. 8 (1979), pp. 102–109.

YAMANE, T.: *Statistics: An Introductory Analysis*, NY: Harper and Row, 1967, pp. 584–585.

SUMMARY

The premise that trade suffers from the imposition of environmental policy has a strong element of a priori plausibility, but, surprisingly, has little empirical support. The present paper provides an empirical test of the hypothesis that stringent environmental policy has caused trade patterns to deviate in commodities produced by the world's 'dirty' industries. The empirical tests are conducted using the cross-section Heckscher-Ohlin-Vanek (HOV) model of international trade. It is not found that the introduction of stringent environmental control measures has caused trade patterns to deviate from the HOV predictions. This result casts serious doubt on the balance of trade argument against the imposition of stronger environmental control.

THE EFFECTS OF DOMESTIC ENVIRONMENTAL POLICIES

ZUSAMMENFASSUNG

Die Behauptung, dass der Handel unter umweltpolitischen Auflagen leidet, scheint a priori zwar äusserst plausibel, findet jedoch überraschenderweise wenig empirische Unterstützung. Der vorliegende Artikel liefert einen empirischen Test, in dem die Hypothese aufgestellt wird, dass eine strenge Umweltpolitik eine Verlagerung der Handelsströme zugunsten der Güter bewirkt, welche von den «schmutzigen» Industrien in der Welt produziert werden. Die Tests werden unter Verwendung des Heckscher-Ohlin-Vanek (HOV) Querschnittmodells für den internationalen Handel durchgeführt. Das Ergebnis liefert keine Unterstützung der Hypothese. Dies lässt ernsthaften Zweifel daran aufkommen, ob Argumente gegen die Einführung strengerer Umweltkontrollen aus Gründen des Handelsbilanzgleichgewichts Gültigkeit besitzen.

RÉSUMÉ

Il apparaît plausible qu'une politique gouvernementale vis-à-vis l'environnement ait un impact négatif sur les échanges commerciaux. Mais on n'avait jamais mesuré réellement cet impact. Cet article présente un test empirique de l'hypothèse selon laquelle une politique environnementale contraignante conduit à des déviations dans la structure du commerce international en ce qui concerne les biens produits par les secteurs polluants de l'industrie mondiale. L'auteur a mené ce test grâce au modèle du commerce international de Heckscher-Ohlin-Vanek (HOV). Ce test ne permet pas de prouver que l'introduction de contrôles et de fortes contraintes sur l'environnement ait entraîné la structure du commerce international à dévier des prédictions du modèle HOV. Désormais, grâce à ce test, vouloir s'appuyer sur une soit disant dégradation du commerce international pour freiner la mise en place des contrôles de l'environnement apparaîtra comme de plus en plus difficile.

Part II
Trade Liberalization, Environmental Damage and Developing Countries

Trade Liberalization, Environment and Welfare

[13]

NORTH-SOUTH TRADE AND THE ENVIRONMENT*

BRIAN R. COPELAND AND M. SCOTT TAYLOR

A simple static model of North-South trade is developed to examine linkages between national income, pollution, and international trade. Two countries produce a continuum of goods, each differing in pollution intensity. We show that the higher income country chooses stronger environmental protection, and specializes in relatively clean goods. By isolating the scale, composition, and technique effects of international trade on pollution, we show that free trade increases world pollution; an increase in the rich North's production possibilities increases pollution, while similar growth in the poor South lowers pollution; and unilateral transfers from North to South reduce worldwide pollution.

I. INTRODUCTION

One of the most interesting developments in trade policy in recent years has been the emergence of trade liberalization as an environmental issue.[1] In addition to facing traditional protectionist pressures, recent initiatives such as the North American Free Trade Agreement and the Uruguay Round of GATT negotiations have been questioned on the grounds that they might increase pollution. This has led to much debate about the environmental consequences of free trade.

Proponents of freer trade argue that environmental quality is a normal good, and hence trade-induced income gains should create political demands for tougher environmental standards. Tougher standards should in turn bring forth cleaner *techniques* of production. Skeptics, however, point out that if production methods do not change, then pollution must rise as trade increases the *scale* of economic activity. Moreover, if environmental quality is a normal good, then less developed countries will adopt relatively low environmental standards. As a result, because of asymmetries in the world distribution of income, free trade may affect the *composition* of national output with many developing countries turning toward relatively pollution-intensive activities. Grossman and Krueger [1991] and others have recently begun to investigate the

* Early versions of this paper were presented at the Simon Fraser University and University of British Columbia joint seminar in international trade, the Midwest International Economics Meetings in Pittsburgh in October 1992 and at the NBER 1993 Summer Institute. We thank participants for their comments. We are also grateful to the referees for helpful suggestions. Copeland acknowledges support from a SSHRC research grant.

1. See Anderson and Blackhurst [1992] and Dean [1992] for useful surveys of the literature on trade and the environment.

The Quarterly Journal of Economics, August 1994

empirical significance of each of these effects, but the issue has received relatively little attention in the theoretical literature.

This paper takes a first step toward clarifying the theoretical issues by developing a simple static two-country general equilibrium model in which income-induced differences in environmental policy create incentives to trade. Using this framework, we first define the scale, technique, and composition effects,[2] and link their magnitudes to tastes, technologies, and endowments. We then use this decomposition to examine how pollution levels are affected by trade liberalization, exogenous increases in production capacity (scale-induced increases in income), and international transfers (redistributions of world income). We emphasize income effects because they determine the strength of the technique effect mentioned above, are tied to the scale of economic activity, and can determine how free trade affects the composition of national outputs and overall pollution levels.

Since the primary objective of the paper is to investigate factors determining the level and international incidence of pollution, we focus on positive rather than normative issues. As well, we simplify the analysis by assuming that the damage caused by pollution is confined to the country of emission.[3] As a consequence, it is perhaps wise to remind the reader at the outset that increases in pollution levels should *not* be viewed as equivalent to decreases in welfare. In fact, trade is always welfare-improving in our model, even when it raises pollution levels.

Our results indicate that increases in economic activity per se need not lower environmental quality because income effects can lead to the adoption of cleaner techniques of production. However, this conclusion must be tempered when we move to an open economy: we find that openness to international markets fundamentally alters the way in which income effects determine pollution levels. For example, in our model, economic growth[4] in autarky has no effect on pollution levels, but economic growth in a trading environment can raise pollution levels. Moreover, the distribution of growth across countries matters: growth in the rich North may

2. The "scale, technique, and composition effect" terminology has been employed by several authors, including Grossman and Krueger [1991], but explicit model-based definitions of these effects have yet to be presented.

3. Transboundary pollution is clearly an important issue, but its analysis is left to a companion paper [Copeland and Taylor 1993]. This allows us to abstract from problems of policy failure due to the lack of an international government, and frees us to concentrate on the transmission mechanisms linking trade and pollution.

4. By "growth" we mean the effect of once-for-all increases in technological capabilities or endowments.

increase pollution, while growth in the poor South lowers pollution. Freer trade, like growth, raises real incomes, but it also changes the composition of national output and hence alters both the incidence and level of pollution across countries. If the pattern of trade-induced specialization is driven only by differences in pollution policy, then aggregate world pollution may rise with trade.

The model that we develop has three key features designed to capture what we feel are the essentials. First, since most of the concern over the effect of international trade on environmental quality is motivated by international differences in pollution policy, we adopt a North-South framework in which there is a large income disparity across countries. To generate this disparity in income, we start with a model where countries differ only in the level of human capital per person.[5] As a result, income-induced differences in the level of pollution taxes are the sole determinant of trade flows. This permits an investigation of whether trade that is motivated by differences in environmental policy is inherently pollution-creating, and the simplicity thereby gained also allows us to decompose any change in pollution levels into scale, technique, and composition effects.

In reality, of course, trade is influenced by many conflicting factors. However, as a first step in understanding the interaction between trade and the environment, it is useful to isolate the impact of environmental standards on the pattern of trade.[6] To make inferences about the actual pattern of trade, one would have to weigh the influences derived from environmental policy against other determinants of trade. Current estimates of environmental control costs are relatively small [Dean 1992]. However, marginal control costs are in many cases higher than average costs, and this suggests that environmental control costs are likely to become an increasingly important influence on trade in the future.

Second, to provide a link between income levels and environmental policy, we assume that benevolent planning authorities in each country set pollution taxes to offset the marginal damage from

5. In Section VII of the paper we examine how differences in population density, country size, and physical carrying capacity of the environment can also affect trade flows.

6. This is a fairly standard methodology. For example, Staiger [1987] uses a similar model to investigate the effect of unionization on the pattern of trade, and assumes that differences in the scope of unionization are all that differentiate countries. Similarly, much of the early literature on increasing returns to scale abstracted from all other incentives to trade.

emissions. This assumption ensures that pollution is optimally provided in both autarky and trade and, moreover, that governments adjust pollution policy in response to changed economic circumstances such as growth or trade. While this may reflect an overly optimistic belief in the capabilities of government policy, it is the simplest way to capture the view that governments are responsive to the preferences of their citizens.

Finally, to capture the effect of differing standards of environmental protection on trade patterns, we adopt a many-good general equilibrium model based on Dornbusch, Fischer, and Samuelson [1977]. By adopting a general equilibrium approach, we ensure that the full impact of environmental policy can be traced through to its ultimate effects on factor markets, incomes, and trade flows. A many-good framework allows us to highlight composition effects. If, as we assume, industries differ in their pollution intensities, then changes in the composition of output arising from free trade will affect both national and world pollution levels.

Several previous studies [Baumol and Oates 1988; Pethig 1976; Siebert et al. 1980; McGuire 1982] have investigated the effects of pollution policy on the pattern of trade. Pethig [1976] extends the two-good Ricardian model to include pollution, and shows that if two countries are identical, except that they exogenously set different emission standards, then the country which allows a higher level of pollution emissions will export the pollution-intensive good. Siebert et al. [1980] and McGuire [1982] extend the analysis to the case of two primary factors. Pollution policy in all of these models, however, is exogenous. By endogenizing policy in the present paper, we explain the pattern of trade as a function of the underlying technology and endowments, rather than as merely reflecting exogenous policy differences. This allows us to examine explicitly the role that income differences may play in determining the pattern of trade. This issue, which is the subject of much policy debate, has not been addressed in previous formal models.[7]

Recent empirical work in the area is mixed. Grossman and Krueger [1991] examine data on air pollution levels in 43 developed and developing countries and conclude that pollution levels first

7. There is also a literature on optimal choice of pollution policy and trade policy in an open economy (see, for example, Markusen [1975], Baumol and Oates [1988], and Copeland [1994]). The focus of this literature is on the structure of the optimal policy for a single country, whereas in our paper we are concerned with how the choice of policies in two countries interact to determine the pattern of trade. Moreover, this literature has not examined how optimal pollution policy would differ systematically across countries that have different income levels.

rise and then fall with per capita income. Therefore, if trade liberalization raises incomes, it may also lower pollution levels. Low and Yeats [1992, p. 94] find that the share of world trade accounted for by pollution-intensive products has experienced a secular decline from 20.4 percent in 1965 to 15.9 percent in 1988; but the export share of such "dirty" goods has been increasing for many developing countries. In addition, Lucas, Wheeler, and Hettige [1992] find that although many developed countries are experiencing a fall in the pollution intensity of national product, this appears to be due to a change in the composition of output and *not* a movement toward cleaner production methods. These last two results suggest that international trade may be serving as a vehicle for dirty industry migration to less developed countries. While our model is highly stylized and abstracts from other important determinants of trade, it provides a useful starting point from which to interpret the earlier empirical work.

It is important, however, to recognize the limitations of our analysis. For example, openness to international markets may mean less developed countries gain access to better pollution abatement technology and to international capital markets. Our analysis limits the effects of openness to those arising from goods trade. As well, our conclusions follow from a decidedly stark model. While we are able to derive unambiguous answers to many questions and clearly identify the forces at work, there is much scope for future work aimed at relaxing some of our assumptions.

The remainder of the paper is organized as follows. Section II sets out our assumptions on preferences and technologies. A simple diagrammatic framework to analyze the equilibrium is developed in Section III. Section IV explores the relation between international trade and the level of pollution; we also derive the scale, technique, and composition effects at this point. The effects of economic growth and international transfers on pollution are investigated in Sections V and VI. Section VII considers some extensions of the model, and Section VIII concludes.

II. The Model

We consider a world with two countries: the highly developed North and the less developed South. Southern variables are indicated by an asterisk (*). There is a continuum of private consumption goods, indexed by $z \in [0,1]$, and one primary input, effective labor (to be described in more detail below). Pollution is

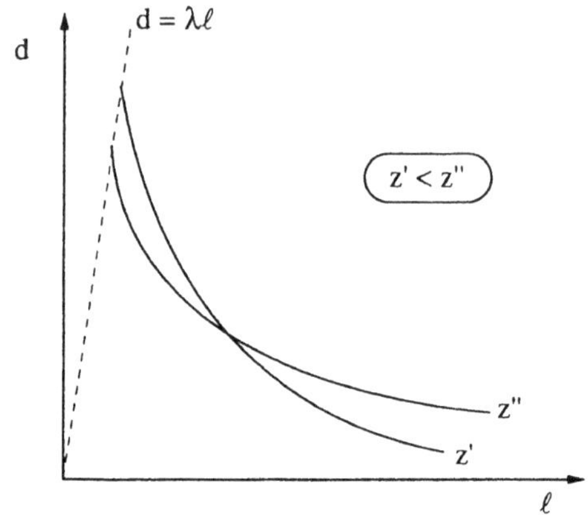

FIGURE I
Unit Isoquants for Two Industries, z' and z''
Industry z'' is more pollution intensive than industry z'.

produced jointly with consumption goods. We assume that the output (y) of good z can be written as a function of pollution discharge (d) and effective labor input (l).[8] To keep the model simple, we adopt the following functional form:

$$y(d,l;z) = \begin{cases} l^{1-\alpha(z)}d^{\alpha(z)} & \text{if } d \leq \lambda l, \\ 0 & \text{if } d > \lambda l, \end{cases} \tag{1}$$

where $\lambda > 0$ and $\alpha(z)$ is a parameter that varies across goods. We assume that $\alpha(z) \in [\underline{\alpha},\bar{\alpha}]$, with $0 < \underline{\alpha} < \bar{\alpha} < 1$.

Isoquants for two typical goods z' and z'' are illustrated in Figure I. For any given level of output of a good, a firm may choose among a continuum of production techniques, each of which generates different levels of pollution. By moving down and to the right along the isoquant, the firm adopts relatively cleaner technologies by abating pollution at the expense of more labor input. Note that the specification in (1) is analytically equivalent to treating pollution as an input that can be substituted for labor in the production of good z.[9] There is a limit to these substitution

8. This requires that the joint production technology satisfy certain regularity conditions. In the Appendix we show how equation (1) can be derived from a joint production technology.

9. The treatment of pollution as an input has been adopted by several others; see, for example, Pethig [1976], Siebert et al. [1980], and McGuire [1982].

possibilities, however, because output must be bounded above for a given labor input. Hence points above the line $d = \lambda l$ are not feasible.[10]

If firms were unregulated, they would have no incentive to abate pollution and would always choose a point along the line $d = \lambda l$ in Figure I. We assume throughout, however, that governments regulate pollution and that firms chose interior solutions where they engage in at least a small amount of abatement.[11] Consequently, if a pollution tax τ is imposed and w_e is the return to a unit of effective labor, the firm's labor/pollution combination that minimizes costs satisfy

$$\frac{w_e}{\tau} = \frac{1-\alpha(z)}{\alpha(z)}\frac{d}{l}. \tag{2}$$

An implication of (2) is that the share of pollution charges in the cost of producing good z is always $\alpha(z)$. As a result, we can order the goods in terms of increasing pollution intensity to obtain $\alpha'(z) > 0$.[12] Thus, in Figure I, if $z'' > z'$, the isoquants for good z'' are flatter than those for good z' along any ray through the origin: good z'' is always more pollution intensive than good z'.

The technologies embodied in (1) are available to both countries. The North-South distinction arises only from an assumed higher level of human capital in the North. Each worker in the North has effectiveness $A(h)$, where h is the level of human capital, and $A' > 0$. Each Southern worker has $h^* < h$ units of human capital, and hence supplies less effective labor than a Northern worker. For most of the paper we assume that each country has the same number of workers, L, so that the total supply of effective labor in the North is $A(h)L$, while that in the South is $A(h^*)L$.

Northern and Southern consumers have identical utility functions defined over consumption goods and pollution. To simplify matters, we assume that utility is strongly separable with respect to consumption and pollution, and we follow Dornbusch, Fischer, and Samuelson [1977] in assuming that the share of spending on each good is constant.

10. To see that this assumption puts an upper bound on production for given labor input, note that with $d \leq \lambda l$, we have $y \leq l^{1-\alpha}(\lambda l)^{\alpha} = l\lambda^{\alpha}$. The Appendix describes in more detail how this constraint arises naturally from an underlying abatement technology.

11. If the South's endowment of effective labor is not too small, then an interior solution will always obtain. See the Appendix for further details.

12. For simplicity, we assume that α is *strictly* increasing in z.

To specify how the damage caused by pollution affects utility, recall that we are concerned with pollution which has only localized effects. Suppose that individuals within a country live in identically sized communities, that pollution generated by one community affects only that community, and that sources of pollution are evenly spread throughout a community. Then pollution damage depends on both the pollution generated per individual, and the community's population density. If population density is very low, people are harmed mainly by their own pollution; but as communities get more crowded, individuals are affected by the pollution of others as well, and the harm caused by pollution rises. As well, if we increase population size but hold aggregate pollution and population density fixed (either by increasing the physical size of the country, or by creating another community distant from the others), then the harm caused by a given amount of aggregate pollution falls since each person is exposed to a smaller fraction of the total pollution.

A simple specification satisfying these requirements is given by

$$U = \int_0^1 b(z) \ln [x(z)]\, dz - \frac{\beta(L,\rho)D^\gamma}{\gamma}, \tag{3}$$

where $x(z)$ is consumption of good z, $b(z)$ is the continuum counterpart to the many-commodity budget share, and $\int_0^1 b(z)dz = 1$. The impact of pollution on utility is captured by $\beta(L,\rho)D^\gamma/\gamma$, where D is the total amount of pollution generated by the country where the individual lives, ρ is the community population density, $\partial\beta/\partial L < 0$, $\partial\beta/\partial\rho > 0$, and $\gamma \geq 1$. The assumption on γ ensures that the marginal willingness to pay for pollution reduction is a nondecreasing function of pollution levels.

Since our main objective is to focus on the effects of income-induced differences in pollution policy on the pattern of trade and environmental quality, in most of the paper we consider the case where all countries are identical in size and population density, and differ only in their per capita endowment of human capital. In this case, β is constant across countries, and to economize on notation, we drop the reference to the arguments of β. In Section VII we examine the more general case where L and ρ differ across countries.

III. North-South Trading Equilibrium

A. Exogenous Pollution Taxes

As a first step toward determining the equilibrium, suppose that North and South have imposed pollution taxes of τ and τ^* per unit of discharge. For concreteness, assume that $\tau > \tau^*$ on the basis of North's higher income (we later show when this holds in equilibrium). Then the unit cost functions derived from (1) and (2) can be written as

$$c(w,\tau;h,z) = \kappa(z)\tau^{\alpha(z)}[w/A(h)]^{1-\alpha(z)}, \tag{4}$$

where $\kappa(z) \equiv \alpha^{-\alpha}(1-\alpha)^{-(1-\alpha)}$ is an industry-specific constant, and w is the wage rate for raw labor. For given Northern and Southern taxes and wages, good z will be produced in the North if $c(w,\tau;h,z) \leq c(w^*,\tau^*;h^*,z)$; that is, if

$$\omega \equiv \frac{w}{w^*} \leq \frac{A}{A^*}\left(\frac{\tau^*}{\tau}\right)^{\alpha(z)/(1-\alpha(z))} \equiv T(z). \tag{5}$$

Conversely, good z will be produced in the South if $\omega \geq T(z)$. With $\tau > \tau^*$ and $\alpha'(z) > 0$, T must be decreasing in z: because of North's relatively higher pollution taxes, its cost advantage in producing good z declines as pollution charges become a larger fraction of total costs.

For any given relative wage rate, ω, the $T(z)$ locus determines a critical industry $\tilde{z}(\omega)$ such that goods in the interval $[0,\tilde{z})$ are produced at least cost in the North, while goods over $(\tilde{z},1]$ are produced at least cost in the South. That is, with $\tau > \tau^*$, the North produces the least pollution-intensive goods, while the South produces the most pollution-intensive goods.

B. Endogenous Pollution Taxes

To determine τ and τ^*, first consider a representative Northern consumer's problem. All consumers own one unit of labor and receive an equal share of the pollution taxes collected by their government. Each consumer takes as given prices, aggregate pollution (D), and his or her share of national income (I/L). The indirect utility function corresponding to (3) for a representative consumer is given by

(6)

$$V = \int_0^1 b(z) \ln [b(z)]\, dz - \int_0^1 b(z) \ln [p(z)]\, dz + \ln \left(\frac{I}{L}\right) - \frac{\beta D^{\gamma}}{\gamma}.$$

The government's problem is then to choose its pollution tax τ to maximize V taking as given consumer and producer behavior. We also assume that governments treat world prices as given when choosing their environmental policy. This means that governments do not attempt to use pollution policy to manipulate their terms of trade. There are two reasons why we think that this is the most reasonable assumption. First, in many countries pollution policy is set at the local and state or provincial level, while international trade policy is set by national governments. Any individual local regulator is unlikely to perceive significant international market power. Second, Article XX of the General Agreement on Tariffs and Trade (GATT) requires that countries abstain from using domestic health or environmental policies as disguised trade barriers. Since we wish to focus on the pattern of trade, and not on strategic trade policy, we assume that governments honor their GATT commitments.

Maximizing indirect utility with respect to τ, treating $p(z)$ as given, yields

$$\tau = -LV_D/V_I = \beta D^{\gamma-1}I, \tag{7}$$

using (3). The government simply sets the pollution tax equal to the marginal damage caused by pollution emissions. Similarly, South's tax is given by $\tau^* = \beta D^{*\gamma-1}I^*$. Pollution taxes are increasing in income since environmental quality is a normal good, and nondecreasing in the aggregate pollution level since the marginal rate of substitution between consumption and pollution is nondecreasing.

We now replace the $T(\cdot)$ schedule, which depends on exogenous pollution taxes, with a new schedule $S(\cdot)$, which reflects endogenous choice of taxes. To do so, we obtain an expression for τ/τ^* in terms of $\tilde{z}$, which we then substitute into (5).

To begin, our optimal tax rate calculations imply that

$$\frac{\tau^*}{\tau} = \frac{I^*}{I}\left(\frac{D^*}{D}\right)^{\gamma-1}, \tag{8}$$

which means that we now must solve for both income and pollution in terms of $\tilde{z}$. Let $\varphi(\tilde{z}) \equiv \int_0^{\tilde{z}} b(z)\,dz$ denote the share of world spending on Northern goods. Then balanced trade requires that

$$I = \varphi(\tilde{z})(I + I^*). \tag{9}$$

Aggregate Northern pollution, D, is the sum of pollution generated by the production of Northern output:

(10)

$$D = \int_0^{\tilde{z}} d(z)\,dz = \int_0^{\tilde{z}} \frac{[\alpha(z)p(z)y(z)]}{\tau}\,dz = \int_0^{\tilde{z}} \left[\frac{\alpha(z)b(z)(I + I^*)}{\tau}\right] dz.$$

The second equality follows from our Cobb-Douglas production functions (recall that $\alpha(z)$ is the share of pollution charges in the cost of good z) and from the zero profit conditions. The third equality follows from the definition of $b(z)$. Combining (9) and (10), we obtain

$$D = I\theta(\tilde{z})/\tau\varphi(\tilde{z}), \tag{11}$$

where $\theta(\tilde{z}) \equiv \int_0^{\tilde{z}} \alpha(z)b(z)dz$ is the share of Northern pollution charges in world income.[13] Now use the optimal pollution tax formula (7) to eliminate τ from (11), and do the same for the South to obtain expressions for pollution:

$$D = \left(\frac{\theta(\tilde{z})}{\beta\varphi(\tilde{z})}\right)^{1/\gamma} \quad \text{and} \quad D^* = \left(\frac{\theta^*(\tilde{z})}{\beta\varphi^*(\tilde{z})}\right)^{1/\gamma}, \tag{12}$$

where $\varphi^*(\tilde{z}) = 1 - \varphi(\tilde{z})$ is the share of world spending on Southern goods, and

$$\theta^*(\tilde{z}) = \int_{\tilde{z}}^1 \alpha(z)b(z)\,dz$$

is the share of Southern pollution charges in world income.

We can now return to (8) and use the balance of trade condition (9) and our expressions for pollution in (12) to obtain relative pollution taxes as a function of $\tilde{z}$:

$$\frac{\tau^*}{\tau} = \left(\frac{\theta^*(\tilde{z})}{\theta(\tilde{z})}\right)^{(\gamma-1)/\gamma}\left(\frac{\varphi^*(\tilde{z})}{\varphi(\tilde{z})}\right)^{1/\gamma} \equiv \zeta(\tilde{z}). \tag{13}$$

Finally, substituting (13) into (5) yields the result that North will

13. To see this, note that the share of Northern pollution charges in world income is $\tau D/(I + I^*)$, and use (10).

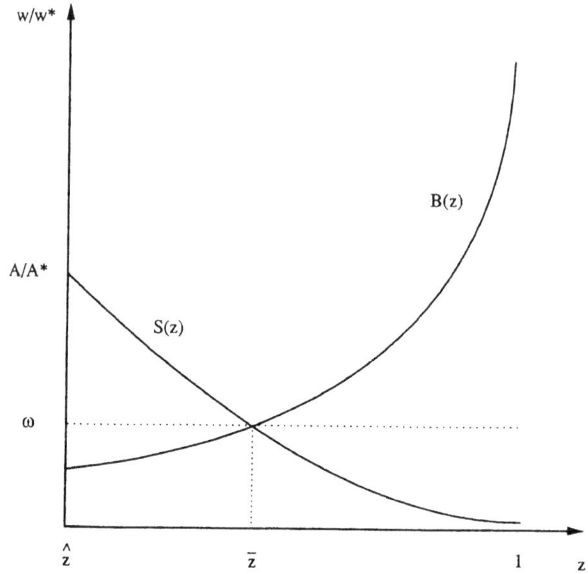

FIGURE II
Trading Equilibrium

produce all goods in the interval $[0,\tilde{z})$ if

$$\omega = \frac{A}{A^*}\,[\zeta(\tilde{z})]^{\alpha(\tilde{z})/(1-\alpha(\tilde{z}))} \equiv S(\tilde{z}), \tag{14}$$

provided that in equilibrium, $\tau > \tau^*$. The condition $\tau > \tau^*$ requires that $\zeta(\tilde{z}) < 1$. Thus, (14) is valid only for $\tilde{z} > \hat{z}$, where $\zeta(\hat{z}) \equiv 1$.[14] In this region S is decreasing in $\tilde{z}$;[15] we also have $S(\hat{z}) = A/A^*$, and $S(1) = 0$. The S schedule is plotted in Figure II.

To determine the equilibrium critical industry $\bar{z}$, we must combine $S(\tilde{z})$ with a balance of trade schedule that takes into account the resource constraints of the economy. Northern income is the sum of wages and pollution taxes (which are rebated to consumers). Hence

$$I = wL + \tau D. \tag{15}$$

14. Equation (14) is not valid outside this interval because the balance of trade condition (9) is constructed for the case where $\tau > \tau^*$. If $\bar{z} < \hat{z}$, we would have $\tau < \tau^*$, which is inconsistent with the pattern of trade implicit in (9). The case where $\tau \leq \tau^*$ is discussed briefly below.

15.

$$\frac{d \ln (S(\tilde{z}))}{d\tilde{z}} = \left[\frac{\alpha'}{(1-\alpha)^2}\right] \ln(\zeta) - \left[\frac{\alpha}{(1-\alpha)^2}\right]\left\{\frac{(\gamma-1)\theta'\theta(1)}{\gamma\theta^*\theta + \varphi'/\varphi\varphi^*}\right\} < 0, \text{ since } \zeta < 1.$$

Using (11) to eliminate D in (15), and rearranging yields

$$I = \frac{wL\varphi(\tilde{z})}{\int_0^{\tilde{z}} b(z)[1 - \alpha(z)]dz}. \tag{16}$$

Following similar steps to obtain an expression for Southern income, and substituting into (9), we can solve for the balance of trade schedule:

$$\omega = \frac{\int_0^{\tilde{z}} b(z)[1 - \alpha(z)]\, dz}{\int_{\tilde{z}}^1 b(z)[1 - \alpha(z)]\, dz} \equiv B(\tilde{z}). \tag{17}$$

Note that $B(0) = 0$, $B(1) = \infty$, and $dB/d\tilde{z} > 0$. The $B(\tilde{z})$ schedule is positively sloped because an increase in the range of goods produced in the North raises exports and lowers imports, and must be met with an increase in North's relative wages to maintain balanced trade.

If $B(\tilde{z})$ and $S(\tilde{z})$ intersect at some $\tilde{z} = \bar{z} > \hat{z}$, as shown in Figure II, they determine an equilibrium where North produces all of the relatively clean goods (i.e., all $z < \bar{z}$), and South produces all of the relatively pollution-intensive goods (all $z > \bar{z}$).[16] We now show that this pattern of trade must obtain if a Northern worker's human capital endowment is sufficiently large relative to that of a Southern worker.

PROPOSITION 1. There exists an equilibrium with $\tau > \tau^*$, where North produces all goods $z \in [0,\bar{z})$ and South produces all goods, $z \in (\bar{z},1]$ if and only if $A/A^* > \delta > 1$, where $\delta \equiv B(\hat{z})$.

Proof of Proposition 1. See Appendix.

The intuition for this result is straightforward. If North has a relatively high income, it chooses a higher pollution tax. Consequently, this forces all of the pollution-intensive industries to locate in the South. Conversely, all of the relatively clean industries locate in the North. However, as the statement of the proposition makes clear, this result is reliant on relative factor endowments being sufficiently different. If this is not the case, then B and S will not intersect over the range $z \in [\hat{z},1]$, and other outcomes are possible.

16. The case where the two curves do not intersect to the right of $\hat{z}$ is discussed below.

First, the roles of South and North may be reversed: if South is sufficiently well endowed with human capital relative to North (i.e., if $A/A^* < 1/\delta$), then $\tau^* > \tau$, and there will be an equilibrium where the pattern of trade is reversed and North produces all of the pollution-intensive goods. Second, if Southern and Northern human capital levels are similar (i.e., if $1/\delta \leq A/A^* \leq \delta$), then a factor-price equalization equilibrium will arise. The two countries will choose identical pollution taxes, and the returns to *effective* labor units will be equalized. The pattern of trade in goods will be indeterminate, but as long as $A/A^* > 1$, the North will be a net exporter of embodied labor services, while the South will be a net exporter of embodied pollution services. Since our primary interest in this paper is in the effect of significant income differences on linkages between trade and the environment, we limit our discussion to equilibria where North chooses a higher pollution tax than the South.

IV. Trade and Pollution

One of the central questions raised by many of those concerned about linkages between trade and the environment is whether trade is inherently pollution-creating. Since trade in our model is driven entirely by income-induced international differences in pollution policy, it provides a useful framework in which to examine this question. By comparing free trade pollution levels with those in autarky, we obtain

PROPOSITION 2. If the assumptions of Proposition 1 hold, trade always lowers the pollution level in the North, increases the pollution level in the South, and increases worldwide pollution.

Proof of Proposition 2. See Appendix.

To investigate the intuition behind Proposition 2, it is useful to decompose the change in pollution levels into the scale, technique, and composition effects. Totally differentiating (11) (evaluated at the equilibrium) yields

$$dD = \frac{\partial D}{\partial I}dI + \frac{\partial D}{\partial \tau}d\tau + \frac{\partial D}{\partial \bar{z}}d\bar{z}. \tag{18}$$

Similar decompositions can be carried out for Southern and World pollution.

The *scale effect* reflects the increase in pollution created by an increase in the level of economic activity in the relevant jurisdiction, holding constant the techniques of production and the composition of final output. For the North it is represented by the first term in (18). This effect must be positive, and in fact, pollution must rise in direct proportion to income if tastes are homothetic (implying an equal percentage increase in the demand for all goods), and if technologies exhibit constant returns to scale (ensuring that these increases in output are met by an equal percentage increase in labor input and pollution discharge). This is confirmed by differentiating (11):

$$(19) \qquad \frac{\partial D}{\partial I} = \frac{\theta(\bar{z})}{\tau\varphi(\bar{z})} > 0, \qquad \text{and} \qquad \frac{\partial D}{\partial I}\frac{I}{D} = 1.$$

Similarly, the scale effect in the South is positive and proportional to income.

The *technique effect* measures the change in aggregate pollution arising from a switch to less pollution-intensive production techniques, holding constant income and the range of goods produced. Since an increase in pollution taxes leads to the adoption of cleaner production methods, the technique effect, given by the second term in (18), must be negative:

$$(20) \qquad \frac{\partial D}{\partial \tau} = -\frac{I\theta(\bar{z})}{\tau^2\varphi(\bar{z})} < 0.$$

Similarly, $\partial D^*/\partial \tau^* < 0$. Moreover,

$$\frac{\partial D}{\partial \tau}\frac{\tau}{D} = \frac{\partial D^*}{\partial \tau^*}\frac{\tau^*}{D^*} = -1.$$

This follows directly from our assumptions on the substitution possibilities in production and consumption which imply that τD is constant when both I and $\bar{z}$ are held constant:

$$\tau D = \int_0^{\bar{z}} \tau d(z)\, dz = \int_0^{\bar{z}} \alpha(z)p(z)y(z)\, dz$$
$$= \int_0^{\bar{z}} \alpha(z)b(z)[I + I^*]\, dz = \int_0^{\bar{z}} \frac{\alpha(z)b(z)I}{\varphi(\bar{z})}\, dz.$$

The second equality holds because the elasticity of substitution in production is one, and the third holds because the elasticity of substitution in consumption is one. (The final equality follows from the balance of trade condition.) The preceding suggests that if the elasticities of substitution in production or consumption exceed one, we expect a larger technique effect, and if they are less than one, we expect a smaller technique effect.

Finally, the *composition* effect measures the change in pollution due to a change in the range of goods produced by a country. For the North this effect is captured by the third term in (18). Differentiation of (11) yields

$$\frac{\partial D}{\partial \bar{z}} = D\left[\frac{\theta'(\bar{z})}{\theta(\bar{z})} - \frac{\varphi'(\bar{z})}{\varphi(\bar{z})}\right] = \frac{Ib(\bar{z})}{\tau\varphi(\bar{z})^2}\int_0^{\bar{z}} [\alpha(\bar{z}) - \alpha(z)]b(z)\,dz > 0, \tag{21}$$

since α is increasing in z. Thus, pollution rises in response to an increase in the range of goods produced in the North, if income and pollution taxes are held constant. This is because marginal goods added to Northern production are more pollution intensive than the original goods. Allocating a given Northern labor force across a group of industries that has become, on average, more pollution intensive must raise Northern pollution.

In the South we obtain

$$\frac{\partial D^*}{\partial \bar{z}} = \frac{I^*b(\bar{z})}{\tau^*\varphi^*(\bar{z})^2}\int_{\bar{z}}^{1} [\alpha(z) - \alpha(\bar{z})]b(z)\,dz > 0.$$

The composition effect for the South due to an increase in $\bar{z}$ is also positive. However, note that in this case, an increase in $\bar{z}$ corresponds to a *decrease* in the range of products produced by the South. As $\bar{z}$ increases, South loses its cleanest industries, leading to an increase in average pollution intensity. With a given production capacity, overall pollution must rise. Conversely, the composition effect due to an *increase* in the range of industries produced by the South (*a* fall in $\bar{z}$) leads to a *decrease* in Southern pollution. Thus, the composition effect works to increase pollution in a country if it leads to an increase in the average pollution intensity of production (i.e., if dirty industries are attracted to a region or if clean industries leave), and it leads to a decrease in pollution if the average pollution intensity falls.

With these definitions in hand, we can now show that although international trade changes the range of goods produced in each country (a composition effect), increases real incomes (a scale effect), and creates incentives for governments to adjust their pollution taxes (a technique effect), the composition effect always dominates the other two effects. To examine the net result of these three effects, use (19)–(21) to rewrite (18) in percent change notation. Letting $\hat{D} = dD/D$, etc., this yields

$$\hat{D} = \hat{I} - \hat{\tau} + (\hat{\theta} - \hat{\varphi}), \tag{22}$$

where $\hat{I}$ is the scale effect, $-\hat{\tau}$ is the technique effect, and $\hat{\theta} - \hat{\varphi}$ is the composition effect.[17] The change in the pollution tax can be obtained from (7):

$$\hat{\tau} = (\gamma - 1)\hat{D} + \hat{I}. \tag{23}$$

Combining the above two expressions and rearranging yields

$$\hat{D} = -[(\gamma - 1)/\gamma](\hat{\theta} - \hat{\varphi}) + (\hat{\theta} - \hat{\varphi}). \tag{24}$$

The first term is the net result of the scale and technique effects. If $\gamma = 1$, this term disappears: the technique effect exactly offsets the scale effect. When $\gamma > 1$, pollution taxes respond more than proportionately to a change in income if pollution rises. As a result, the technique effect not only fully offsets the scale effect, but also offsets a fraction $(\gamma - 1)/\gamma$ of the composition effect. However, the composition effect must always dominate: from (24) we have

$$\hat{D} = (\hat{\theta} - \hat{\varphi})/\gamma. \tag{25}$$

Thus, while a larger γ dampens the magnitude of response of pollution to changes in the economy, the direction of the change is always determined by the sign of the composition effect $(\hat{\theta} - \hat{\varphi})$.

To understand why the composition effect dominates, it is useful to reinterpret trade in goods as implicit trade in factor services. The model behaves much like a two-factor Heckscher-Ohlin model with one factor in variable supply (pollution in our case) and one factor in inelastic supply (effective labor).[18] Hence by constructing pollution demand and supply, we can show that trade is driven by differences in relative factor supplies, and that when the South has an opportunity to trade, it can increase its gains from trade by accepting an increase in pollution.

Combining the optimal tax condition (7) and the economy's budget constraint (15) yields an expression for the inverse supply of pollution in the North:

$$\frac{\tau}{w_e} = \frac{\beta A(h) L D^{\gamma - 1}}{1 - \beta D^{\gamma}}, \tag{26}$$

where $w_e = w/A(h)$ is the return to a unit of effective labor. This is

17. Note that $\hat{\theta} = \theta' d\bar{z}/\theta$ and $\hat{\varphi} = \varphi' d\bar{z}/\varphi$. Also, note from (21) that $\hat{\theta} - \hat{\varphi} > 0$ for $d\bar{z} > 0$.

18. We are grateful to Alan Deardorff for suggesting this interpretation.

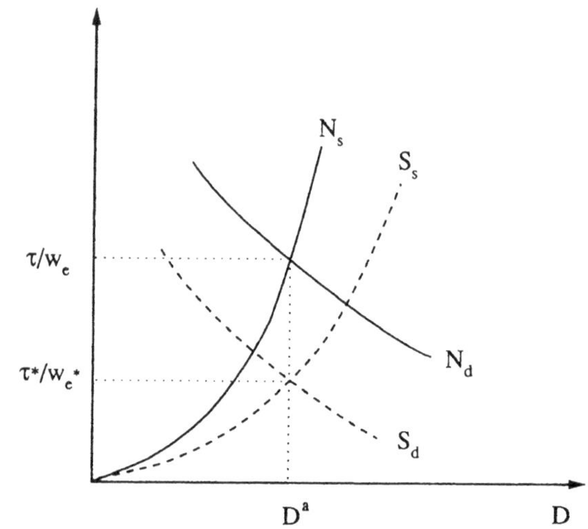

FIGURE III
Pollution Supply and Demand

plotted in Figure III and labeled N_s. The supply of pollution is increasing in τ/w_e since consumers are willing to accept increases in pollution if they are compensated with higher revenue from pollution taxes.

The derived demand for pollution in autarky (i.e., the pollution implicit in the demand for consumer goods) can be obtained by setting $\bar{z} = 1$ in (11), and combining with the economy's budget constraint to obtain

$$\frac{\tau}{w_e} = \frac{A(h)L\theta(1)}{D[1 - \theta(1)]}. \tag{27}$$

This is plotted as N_d in Figure III. As one would expect, the derived demand for pollution is decreasing in its relative price, τ/w_e.

Equating the demand and supply for pollution in the North yields the autarky factor price ratio (τ/w_e), and autarky pollution level,

$$D^a = \left(\frac{\theta(1)}{\beta}\right)^{1/\gamma}. \tag{28}$$

Note that a reduction in human capital shifts down both the demand and supply curves by the same proportion (as indicated by the two dashed lines S_s and S_d in Figure III). This leaves the pollution level unchanged, but reduces τ/w_e.[19] Since the South differs from the North only in that it has less human capital, we conclude that pollution is a relatively scarce input in the North prior to trade ($D^a/AL < D^a/A^*L$), and consequently, that pollution is relatively more costly for firms in the North than in the South ($\tau/w_e > \tau^*/w_e^*$).

This provides a basis for trade. North is willing to export effective labor services (embodied in goods) in return for imports of pollution services, and South is willing to do the reverse. Since trade increases the demand for pollution services in the South, and reduces the demand in the North, it reduces the gap between factor prices by raising τ^*/w_e^* and reducing τ/w_e. Since the supply curves are valid both in trade and autarky, we see from Figure III that trade must therefore increase pollution in the South (a movement up its pollution supply curve) and reduce pollution in the North (a movement down its supply curve). Increases in γ make the supply curves more inelastic, but the direction of the response is not altered, since trade is driven by pressures to reduce the gap in factor prices across countries.

The last result in Proposition 2 is that total world pollution rises with trade. The change in world pollution is the net result of the scale, technique, and composition effects in both countries. We have already shown that the composition effect dominates the scale and technique effects; and therefore to understand how world pollution responds to trade, we need to consider the strength of the two opposing composition effects.

Trade shifts some of the Northern labor force from dirty industries into clean ones, and shifts some of the Southern labor force from clean industries into dirty ones. To examine the consequences of these reallocations, consider the movement of one unit of Southern effective labor from a clean industry in the South (z') to a dirty industry in the South (z''). At the same time, shift one unit of Northern effective labor from a dirty industry in the North (z'') to a clean industry in the North (z'). The change in pollution in each country can be deduced from the local $d(z)/l(z)$ ratio. Using (2), we can infer that the induced change in pollution in the North is

$$\Delta d_N = \frac{d(z')}{l(z')} - \frac{d(z'')}{l(z'')} = \frac{w_e}{\tau}\left[\frac{\alpha(z')}{1-\alpha(z')} - \frac{\alpha(z'')}{1-\alpha(z'')}\right] < 0,$$

19. Pollution is not, however, independent of country size, since β depends on L. The effect of country size is discussed in Section VII.

since $\alpha(z') < \alpha(z'')$. A similar calculation for the South yields $\Delta d_S > 0$. Adding, to determine the net effect of this reallocation on world pollution, we obtain

$$\Delta d_N + \Delta d_S = \left[\frac{\alpha(z'')}{1-\alpha(z'')} - \frac{\alpha(z')}{1-\alpha(z')}\right]\left[\frac{w_e^*}{\tau^*} - \frac{w_e}{\tau}\right].$$

Since trade reduces but does not eliminate the gap between relative factor prices, we have $w_e^*/\tau^* > w_e/\tau$, and therefore $\Delta d_N + \Delta d_S > 0$. This combined world composition effect raises world pollution provided that factor prices are not equalized across countries.[20]

V. Trade, Pollution, and Economic Development

The previous section showed that opening a country up to trade affects both the level and distribution of world pollution. These results were driven mainly by changes in the location of production since the output-enhancing effects of trade were offset by changes in pollution policy. In the present section we focus on the effects of changes in production capacity on pollution, by examining the consequences of increases in human capital.

Let us first consider the effects of growth on pollution in autarky. An increase in the level of human capital stimulates pollution directly through the scale effect. In Figure III this corresponds to an outward shift in the demand for pollution. Because of higher income, the pollution supply curve shifts inward. This increases the τ/w_e ratio, but since the demand and supply for pollution are proportional to the economy's endowment of effective labor, the scale and technique effects exactly offset each other, leaving the level of pollution unaffected by economic growth. Note that there is no composition effect in autarky since tastes are homothetic.[21] The result that growth has no effect on pollution in autarky is specific to our assumptions on substitution possibilities, but it nevertheless provides a very useful benchmark. Any change in pollution induced by trade or growth in the open economy version of our model must be driven entirely by the opportunity to

20. As may be expected from our simple argument above, it is straightforward to show that if North and South are sufficiently similar so that pollution taxes are equalized by trade, then free trade has no effect on global pollution levels. However, trade will still alter the distribution of pollution across countries with the human-capital-rich country reducing its pollution level while the human-capital-poor country increases its pollution level.

21. If demand shifted to relatively clean goods (such as services) as income rose, then there would be a composition effect in autarky. We leave the investigation of nonhomothetic preferences for future work.

trade, and not by the simple effects of increases in the level of economic activity.

We next consider symmetric growth in the world economy. Suppose that there is equiproportionate, labor-augmenting technological progress. With $dA/A = dA^*/A^* > 0$, neither the $S(z)$ nor the $B(z)$ schedule is affected, and hence (referring to Figure II) ω and $\bar{z}$ are unchanged. Since $\bar{z}$ does not change, then from (12), pollution levels are unchanged. As in autarky, symmetric growth across countries increases the world's productive capacity and raises pollution through the scale effect, but this is just offset by the technique effect as pollution taxes respond to higher income levels. With equiproportionate growth in both countries the terms of trade remain constant—there is no reallocation of industries across countries, and hence no composition effect. World pollution remains constant.

Now consider asymmetric growth. Suppose that there is an increase in the level of human capital in the North, holding the level of Southern human capital constant. This shifts the $S(z)$ schedule upwards, while leaving $B(z)$ unaffected. From Figure II it is apparent that North's relative wage rises ($d\omega/dh > 0$), and the range of commodities produced in the North grows ($d\bar{z}/dh > 0$). The effect on Northern pollution is obtained by differentiating (12):

$$\frac{dD}{dh} = \frac{1}{\gamma}\left[\frac{b(\bar{z})D}{\theta(\bar{z})\varphi(\bar{z})}\int_0^{\bar{z}} b(z)[\alpha(\bar{z}) - \alpha(z)]\,dz\right]\frac{d\bar{z}}{dh} > 0, \tag{29}$$

since α is increasing in z. Northern pollution increases, even though the government has an opportunity to adjust the pollution tax rate.

To understand this result, recall that North's government adjusts the pollution tax so that the technique effect fully offsets the scale effect, and partially offsets the composition effect. That is, if $\bar{z}$ were held constant, pollution levels in the North would be unaffected by the increase in output generated by the increase in human capital. However, $\bar{z}$ cannot remain constant since the North's production of exportables and its demand for importables both rise. A fall in North's terms of trade is required to maintain balanced trade. This induces Southern industries to migrate to the North. Thus, the effect of growth on pollution is determined by the composition effect. This can be confirmed by referring to (21), and noting that the term in brackets in (29) is simply $\partial D/\partial \bar{z}$. Because the marginal Southern industries that move northward are more pollution intensive than existing Northern industries, the composition effect is positive, and Northern pollution rises.

To determine the effect of Northern growth on Southern pollution, differentiate (12):

$$\frac{dD^*}{dh} = \frac{1}{\gamma}\left[\frac{b(\bar{z})D^*}{\theta^*(\bar{z})\varphi^*(\bar{z})}\int_{\bar{z}}^{1} b(z)[\alpha(z) - \alpha(\bar{z})]\, dz\right]\frac{d\bar{z}}{dh} > 0.$$

Once again, the composition effect determines the direction of the change in pollution. An increase in $\bar{z}$ shifts South's least pollution-intensive industries to the North. As a result, the average pollution intensity in the South rises, and with a given labor force, this increases total pollution.

In contrast, economic development in the South lowers pollution in both countries. An increase in Southern human capital shifts down the $S(z)$ schedule in Figure II, and both ω and $\bar{z}$ fall. South's economy expands, but the marginal industries it attracts from the North are less pollution intensive than existing Southern industries. Hence the composition effect is negative, and Southern pollution falls. The composition effect in the North is also negative since the North loses its most pollution-intensive industries to the South; hence Northern pollution also falls.

To summarize, we have found that as rich countries get richer, world pollution increases, but as poor countries get richer, world pollution falls. The intuition for these surprising results can best be understood with the aid of Figure III. Growth increases a country's supply of effective labor, which raises its autarky τ/w_e ratio. When growth occurs in the North, the differences between the two countries are magnified. This widens the gap between both pre- and posttrade factor prices. But recall that it is the gap between posttrade factor prices that determines the strength of the overall world composition effect. A greater gap between factor prices means a greater difference in techniques across countries, and a greater increase in pollution arising from concentrating dirty industries in the lower income country. When growth occurs in the South, the opposite occurs. Factor supply ratios move closer together, shrinking the gap between factor prices. The world composition effect is muted, and hence pollution falls. Therefore, our results here provide a corollary to Proposition 2.

COROLLARY. The increase in pollution accompanying trade is greater, the greater are the differences across countries in human capital endowments.

VI. Transfers, Trade, and Pollution

In this section we consider the impact of an income transfer from North to South. In the basic Dornbusch-Fischer-Samuelson [1977] model, transfers have no real effects because there are identical homothetic preferences and no public goods. In the present model, transfers have real effects since they alter relative income levels, and hence relative pollution taxes. The transfer case is important to consider because unlike the asymmetric growth experiments conducted above, a transfer provides us with an example of a change in the world distribution of income that is not accompanied by changes in production capacity. Consequently, it allows us to focus on pure income effects. The study of transfers is also of interest because a theme in the recent literature on trade and the environment is that tied aid can be used to reduce pollution in the South. In this section we show that untied aid can accomplish the same objective.

To proceed, we derive a modified $S(\cdot)$ schedule that incorporates transfers. Once this schedule is constructed, we can again use Figure II to generate comparative static results. Let T be the value of the transfer (measured in terms of Northern labor), and let I and I^* be the level of income (excluding transfers) generated within each country. Then it is straightforward to show that pollution taxes are given by

$$(30) \qquad \tau = \beta D^{\gamma-1}(I - T) \qquad \text{and} \qquad \tau^* = \beta D^{*\gamma-1}(I^* + T).$$

Using a derivation analogous to that which led to (12), we obtain pollution levels:

$$(31) \quad D = \left(\frac{I\theta(\tilde{z})}{(I - T)\beta\varphi(\tilde{z})}\right)^{1/\gamma} \qquad \text{and} \qquad D^* = \left(\frac{I^*\theta^*(\tilde{z})}{(I^* + T)\beta\varphi^*(\tilde{z})}\right)^{1/\gamma}.$$

Combining (30) and (31) and letting

$$(32) \qquad h(T,\tilde{z}) = \frac{T}{\varphi(\tilde{z})(I - T)} > 0,$$

we can obtain an expression for the ratio of pollution taxes:

$$(33) \qquad \frac{\tau^*}{\tau} = \left(\frac{\theta^*(\tilde{z})}{\theta(\tilde{z})}\right)^{(\gamma-1)/\gamma}\left(\frac{\varphi^*(\tilde{z})}{\varphi(\tilde{z})} + h(T,\tilde{z})\right)^{1/\gamma} \equiv \zeta(\tilde{z},T).$$

Note that (33) differs from (13) only by the presence of the term $h(T,\tilde{z})$. It is easy to show that $\partial h/\partial T > 0$, $\partial h/\partial \tilde{z} < 0$, and $h(0,\tilde{z}) = 0$; and hence (33) reduces to (13) when there is no transfer. Also note that with Northern labor as the numeraire, h is a function of $\tilde{z}$ and T, but not of ω.

A modified $S(\cdot)$ schedule is obtained by substituting (33) into (4):

$$\omega = \frac{A}{A^*}\,[\zeta(\tilde{z},T)]^{\alpha(\tilde{z})/(1-\alpha(\tilde{z}))} \equiv S(\tilde{z},T). \tag{34}$$

Since h is decreasing in $\tilde{z}$, $S(\tilde{z},T)$ is also decreasing in z, provided that North remains the high income country after the transfer; i.e., provided that $I - T > I^* + T$. Also, since $h(0,\tilde{z}) = 0$, the modified $S(\tilde{z},T)$ schedule coincides with the original $S(\tilde{z})$ schedule for $T = 0$.

A transfer has no effect on $B(\tilde{z})$, but $S(\tilde{z},T)$ shifts up as T rises. Hence by interpreting the S schedule as a function of $\tilde{z}$ and T, we can use Figure II to conclude that a transfer raises both $\bar{z}$ and ω. The reasoning is straightforward. A transfer from North to South reduces North's relative income, and hence its relative pollution tax falls, rendering Northern industries more competitive. As a result, North attracts marginal industries from the South ($\bar{z}$ rises). This increases the relative demand for North's labor, pushing up its relative wage, but not by enough to offset the direct effect of the transfer.

Let us now consider the effects of the transfer on pollution. Define $\sigma(T) = (I - T)/(I + I^*)$ to be the share of income accruing to the North after the transfer is applied. We confine ourselves to the case where $\sigma(T) > 1$; that is, where North continues to be the relatively rich country. Note that a transfer must lower North's consumption share of world income; that is, $d\sigma/dT < 0$.[22] Using (31), Northern pollution can be written as

$$D(T) = \left(\frac{\theta(\bar{z})}{\beta\sigma(T)}\right)^{1/\gamma}.$$

Differentiating with respect to T shows that the transfer leads to an increase in North's pollution:

$$\frac{dD}{dT} = \frac{D}{\gamma}\left[-\frac{\sigma'}{\sigma} + \frac{\alpha(\bar{z})b(\bar{z})}{\theta}\frac{d\bar{z}}{dT}\right] > 0, \tag{35}$$

where $\sigma' \equiv d\sigma/dT$. North reduces its pollution tax in response to its

22. Since $\tau^*/\tau = (1 - \sigma)/\sigma$, we have $\sigma(T) = 1/(1 + \tau^*/\tau)$. Moreover, note that since $d\bar{z}/dT > 0$, we must have $d(\tau^*/\tau)/dT > 0$; and hence $\sigma'(T) < 0$. Note that this is not a partial derivative, as it includes both the direct and indirect effects of the transfer on σ.

lower disposable income, and this tends to increase pollution via the technique effect.[23] As well, the decline in North's pollution tax attracts marginal industries from the South, and since these new industries are relatively pollution intensive, the composition effect also tends to increase North's pollution.

Conversely, South's pollution falls in response to the transfer:

$$\frac{dD^*}{dT} = \frac{D^*}{\gamma}\left[\frac{\sigma'}{1-\sigma} - \frac{\alpha(\bar{z})b(\bar{z})}{\theta^*}\frac{d\bar{z}}{dT}\right] < 0. \tag{36}$$

In the South, disposable income increases, its pollution tax rises, and pollution falls from the technique effect. However, its marginal industries migrate to the North, and since these are relatively clean, the average pollution intensity of South's industries rises for given techniques. Consequently, Southern pollution should rise from the composition effect. However, as (36) shows, the direct effect of the pollution tax increase more than offsets this indirect composition effect: pollution falls in the South. Direct effects swamp indirect effects since the increase in the pollution tax affects the pollution intensity of all Southern industries, and all of these industries are more pollution intensive than the marginal ones given up.

Finally, we show that a small transfer must lower world pollution. Summing (35) and (36) and evaluating at $T = 0$ noting that at this point $\sigma(T) = \varphi(\bar{z})$ yields

$$\left.\frac{d(D + D^*)}{dT}\right|_{T=0} = \left(\frac{\sigma'}{\gamma}\right)\left[\frac{D^*}{1-\varphi(\bar{z})} - \frac{D}{\varphi(\bar{z})}\right] + \frac{\alpha(\bar{z})b(\bar{z})(I + I^*)}{\gamma}\left[\frac{1}{\tau} - \frac{1}{\tau^*}\right]\frac{d\bar{z}}{dT} < 0.$$

Putting the technique and composition effects from both countries together, world pollution must fall. This follows since the transfer raises pollution taxes in the most pollution-intensive country, and reduces the disparity in techniques used worldwide.[24]

23. Note that the technique effect is usually offsetting a scale effect, but that in this case there is no direct scale effect, since North's underlying production capacity is not affected by the transfer.

24. The effects of a transfer on pollution can be summarized by appealing to Figure III one last time. A transfer shifts out the donor's supply of pollution (since environmental quality is a normal good), and shifts in the recipient's supply function. This reduces the gap between autarky factor price ratios, reduces the incentives to trade to exploit differences in pollution policy, and thereby reduces world pollution. South to North transfers have opposite effects.

VII. Extensions

This section extends the model to examine the implications of cross-country differences in population density, climate, and other factors that affect the damage caused by pollution. These modifications would be an important preliminary step to empirically testing the model.

Consider the following specification for the utility function:

$$U = \int_0^1 b(z) \ln [x(z)]\, dz - \beta_0 \left[\frac{D}{L} g(\rho)\right]^{\gamma} \Big/ \gamma \tag{37}$$

where $\beta_0 > 0$ is a constant, and $g'(\rho) > 0$. This corresponds to setting

$$\beta(L,\rho) = \beta_0[g(\rho)/L]^{\gamma} \tag{38}$$

in (3). In this specification, increases in either pollution per capita or in population density (for given pollution levels) reduce utility by increasing the exposure of a typical person to pollution.

Let us now reconsider autarky pollution. Substituting (38) into (28) yields

$$\frac{D^a}{L} = \frac{(\theta(1)/\beta_0)^{1/\gamma}}{g(\rho)}. \tag{39}$$

If two countries have the same population density, then pollution per capita is the same across countries. This means that if we scale up the size of a country, by increasing both land mass and population proportionately, then aggregate pollution rises. This is a reasonable prediction for pollution that has localized effects. On the other hand, as population density increases, pollution per capita falls, since a given unit of pollution causes more damage in a more crowded environment.

Let us now consider trade. First, suppose that two countries differ only with respect to labor force size, but are otherwise identical in terms of population density and human capital. In this case, there is no basis for trade. The larger country is just a scaled-up version of the smaller, and relative factor supplies are identical. Not surprisingly, in a constant returns to scale world with equal relative factor supplies, autarky prices are identical, and free trade is identical to autarky. This is confirmed by substituting

(39) into (27) to obtain the autarky factor price ratio:

$$\frac{\tau}{w_e} = \frac{A(h)[\theta(1)^{\gamma-1}\beta_0]^{1/\gamma}g(\rho)}{1 - \theta(1)},$$

which is independent of L.

Next suppose that North and South are identical in all respects, except that North is more densely populated. Then from (26), (27), and (38), North's pollution supply curve will be to the left of South's, and hence the autarky τ/w_e ratio will be relatively higher in the North. Thus, in free trade the more densely populated country will export labor-intensive goods, while the less densely populated country will export pollution-intensive goods.

If countries differ both with respect to the level of human capital and population density, then the pattern of trade depends on the interaction between the two effects. If the human-capital-poor country is less densely populated than the rich country, then its tendency to specialize in pollution-intensive goods will be reinforced. However, if the poor country is more densely populated than the rich country, then its supply curve for pollution will shift inward, and the pattern of trade may be reversed, with the poor country exporting relatively clean goods.

Finally, suppose that two countries differ with respect to the carrying capacity of the environment, as determined by prevailing winds, ocean currents, soil conditions, and other factors. This may be captured by allowing the β function to differ across countries. Suppose that a given unit of pollution causes less damage at Home than abroad because of differences in the environment. Then for any given L and ρ, we have $\beta(L,\rho) < \beta^*(L,\rho)$. Consequently, if the countries are otherwise identical, Home's supply of pollution will be to the right of Foreign's, and hence Home exports pollution-intensive goods.

VIII. Conclusion

This paper has presented a simple model to examine how trade between two countries differentiated solely by income can affect environmental quality. Our most important results are that income gains arising from an opportunity to trade can affect pollution in a different way than income gains obtained through economic growth and, moreover, that economic growth has different effects on pollution in a free trade regime than in autarky.

If environmental policy is set optimally, then potential increases in pollution generated by economic growth in autarky can be prevented by a policy-induced switch to cleaner methods of production. Given our assumption on substitution possibilities in production and consumption, growth in autarky has a neutral effect on pollution: the technique effect fully offsets the scale effect.

However, international trade opens up a different channel that may nevertheless lead to an increase in world pollution. While trade, like growth, increases real incomes in both countries, it also creates a composition effect that is critical in determining the effect of trade on pollution. If differences in pollution taxes are the only motive for trade, and trade does not equalize factor prices, then a movement from autarky to free trade increases aggregate world pollution.

Composition effects also determine the impact of asymmetric economic growth on pollution in free trade. Even if, as in our model, the pollution-generating effects of symmetric growth across countries are exactly offset by stricter environmental policy, the migration of industries induced by asymmetric growth has important and interesting effects on pollution through the composition effect. Consequently, economic growth in the North has much different effects on the environment than economic growth in the South.

While our model is stylized and many of its particular results model-specific, much of the intuition springs from more general factor endowment considerations. Most of our results follow from just two suppositions: (1) trade has a tendency to reduce, but not fully eliminate, international differences in factor prices if countries are sufficiently different; and (2), in autarky, the relative price of pollution-intensive goods is higher in relatively high-income countries. The first of these suppositions is a quite general result. The second is much more tenuous, but it clearly holds in our simple model. In more general factor endowment models it may not. Nevertheless, the simple structure of our model is a virtue since it lays bare the basic relationships driving our results, and at once suggests extensions of the model that can only enhance our understanding of the relationship between pollution and international trade.

APPENDIX

A. Derivation of Equation (1) from a Joint Production Technology

The following is one way to motivate equation (1). Let l_y be the amount of effective labor used to produce good y. Since the analysis applies to any good, we suppress the index z to economize on notation. Assume that

$$y = \lambda^{\alpha} l_y, \tag{A1}$$

$$d_0(y) = \lambda^{(1-\alpha)} y = \lambda l_y, \tag{A2}$$

where d_0 is the amount of pollution produced in the absence of any abatement activity.

The firm has an abatement technology given by

$$A[l_a, d_0(y)] = d_0(y) - \left[\frac{\lambda^{\alpha-1} d_0(y)}{[d_0(y)/\lambda + l_a]^{1-\alpha}}\right]^{1/\alpha},$$

where l_a is the amount of effective labor assigned to abatement. Note that $A[0, d_0(y)] = 0$, and that $\partial A/\partial l_a > 0$, so that there is no abatement unless labor is allocated to it, and that an increase in labor assigned to abatement yields an increase in abatement. In addition, note that the abatement function is concave in l_a, and is asymptotic to $d_0(y)$, reflecting an assumption of diminishing returns to abatement activity.

Pollution discharged by the firm is equal to the unconstrained level of pollution, less the amount abated:

$$d(y, l_a) = d_0(y) - A[l_a, d_0(y)] = \left[\frac{\lambda^{\alpha-1} d_0(y)}{[d_0(y)/\lambda + l_a]^{1-\alpha}}\right]^{1/\alpha}. \tag{A3}$$

Using (A1) and (A2), we can rewrite (A3) as

$$d(y, l_a) = \left[\frac{y}{[l_y + l_a]^{1-\alpha}}\right]^{1/\alpha}. \tag{A4}$$

Letting $l = l_y + l_a$ be the total effective labor employed by the firm, we can rearrange (A4) to obtain

$$y = d^{\alpha} l^{1-\alpha}. \tag{A5}$$

Note that we require $l_a \geq 0$ and $l_y \geq 0$. Hence since $y = \lambda^{\alpha} l_y$, equation (A5) is valid only for $y \leq \lambda^{\alpha} l$, or equivalently, for $d \leq \lambda l$. Thus, output is not feasible for $d/l > \lambda$.

B. Conditions for an Interior Solution

To ensure an interior solution (i.e., that all firms engage in at least a small amount of abatement), we assume that $d/l < \lambda$ for all firms. Because Southern firms are the most pollution intensive, it is sufficient to ensure that this holds for the South. Using (2), we require that $\tau^*/w^* > \alpha(z)/[\lambda A^*(1 - \alpha(z))]$, for all z. Using the Southern version of (7) and (16) to eliminate τ^*/w^*, this is equivalent to requiring that

$$A^*L > \frac{\alpha(z)[\varphi^*(\bar{z}) - \theta^*(\bar{z})]}{\lambda\beta[1 - \alpha(z)]D^{*\gamma-1}\varphi^*(\bar{z})}, \quad \text{for all } z. \tag{A6}$$

But from Proposition 2, $D^* > D^a$, which implies that $\theta^*(\bar{z}) > \varphi^*(\bar{z})\theta(1)$. Hence we have

$$\frac{\varphi^*(\bar{z}) - \theta^*(\bar{z})}{D^{*\gamma-1}\varphi^*(\bar{z})} < \frac{1 - \theta(1)}{[\theta(1)/\beta]^{(\gamma-1)/\gamma}}. \tag{A7}$$

Using (A7) in (A6), and noting that $\alpha(z) < \bar{\alpha}$, we conclude that the following condition is sufficient to ensure that $d/l < \lambda$ for all z (in either country):

$$AL > A^*L > \frac{\bar{\alpha}[1 - \theta(1)]}{\lambda\beta^{1/\gamma}(1 - \bar{\alpha})\theta(1)^{(\gamma-1)/\gamma}}.$$

The following make the condition more likely to be satisfied: (1) an increase in β, which corresponds to an increase in the disutility of pollution; (2) an increase in A^*L, which increases the willingness to pay to control pollution; (3) an increase in λ, which is the unregulated d/l ratio; and (4) an increase in $\theta(1)$, which is a weighted average of the pollution share parameters α.

C. Proofs of Propositions

The following inequalities are useful:

$$\theta(\bar{z}) < \alpha(\bar{z})\varphi(\bar{z}), \tag{A8}$$

$$\theta^*(\bar{z}) > \alpha(\bar{z})\varphi^*(\bar{z}). \tag{A9}$$

$$\varphi(\hat{z}) > 1/2. \tag{A10}$$

The first two follow since α is increasing in z. The third follows from the definition of $\hat{z}$.

Proof of Proposition 1. (i) Sufficiency. B and S are both continuous. Also B is strictly increasing, and S is strictly decreasing for $z > \hat{z}$. Hence if $B(\hat{z}) < S(\hat{z}) = A/A^*$, they must intersect at some $z \in (\hat{z},1)$. (ii) Necessity. If $B(\hat{z}) > A/A^*$, then (17) and (14) cannot be solved for $\bar{z} > \hat{z}$. But for $\bar{z} \leq \hat{z}$, we have $I \leq I^*$, which is inconsistent with $\tau > \tau^*$ (and hence the construction of B and S is not valid). (iii) Finally, to show that $\delta > 1$, note that using (A8)–(A10), we have $\delta > \varphi(\hat{z})/\varphi^*(\hat{z}) > 1$.

QED

Proof of Proposition 2. Using a derivation similar to that which led to (12), we obtain an expression for autarky pollution levels:

$$D^a = D^{*a} = \left(\frac{\theta(1)}{\beta}\right)^{1/\gamma}.$$

Free trade pollution is given by (12). Subtracting yields

$$\text{(A11)} \qquad D - D^a = \beta^{-1/\gamma}\left[\left(\frac{\theta(\bar{z})}{\varphi(\bar{z})}\right)^{1/\gamma} - \theta(1)^{1/\gamma}\right].$$

Since $\theta(1) = \theta(\bar{z}) + \theta^*(\bar{z})$, and using (A8) and (A9), we have

$$\frac{\theta(\bar{z})}{\varphi(\bar{z})} - \theta(1) = \frac{\theta(\bar{z})\varphi^*(\bar{z}) - \varphi(\bar{z})\theta^*(\bar{z})}{\varphi(\bar{z})}$$

$$< \frac{\alpha(\bar{z})\varphi(\bar{z})\varphi^*(\bar{z}) - \varphi(\bar{z})\alpha(\bar{z})\varphi^*(\bar{z})}{\varphi(\bar{z})} = 0.$$

Hence $\theta(\bar{z})/\varphi(\bar{z}) < \theta(1)$. But since the inequality is preserved by a monotonic transformation, we conclude that $[\theta(\bar{z})/\varphi(\bar{z})]^{1/\gamma} < [\theta(1)]^{1/\gamma}$, and hence $D < D^a$.

Turning now to the South, a similar analysis yields

$$\text{(A12)} \qquad D^* - D^{*a} = \beta^{-1/\gamma}\left[\left(\frac{\theta^*(\bar{z})}{\varphi^*(\bar{z})}\right)^{1/\gamma} - \theta(1)^{1/\gamma}\right].$$

Proceedings as above, we have

$$\frac{\theta^*(\bar{z})}{\varphi^*(\bar{z})} - \theta(1) = \frac{\theta^*(\bar{z})\varphi(\bar{z}) - \varphi^*(\bar{z})\theta(\bar{z})}{\varphi^*(\bar{z})}$$

$$> \frac{\alpha(\bar{z})\varphi(\bar{z})\varphi^*(\bar{z}) - \varphi(\bar{z})\alpha(\bar{z})\varphi^*(\bar{z})}{\varphi^*(\bar{z})} = 0.$$

Using this inequality, it is straightforward to show that $D^* > D^{*a}$.

Finally, consider world pollution.[25] Define $r = 1/\gamma$, and $f(z) = [\theta(z)/\varphi(z)]^r + [\theta^*(z)/\varphi^*(z)]^r - 2[\theta(z) + \theta^*(z)]^r$. Summing (A11) and (A12), we see that proving that world pollution goes up is equiva-

25. We are grateful to Michele Piccione and Guofu Tan for help with this proof.

lent to showing that $f(\bar{z}) > 0$ for $\bar{z} > \hat{z}$, where, from (13), $\hat{z}$ is defined by

$$\text{(A13)} \qquad [\theta^*(\hat{z})/\theta(\hat{z})]^{1-r}[\varphi^*(\hat{z})/\varphi(\hat{z})]^r = 1.$$

Using (A8) and (A9), one can show that f is increasing in z. Hence to prove our result, we need only show that

$$\text{(A14)} \qquad f(\hat{z}) \geq 0.$$

Using (A13) to eliminate φ^*, (A14) is equivalent to (where unless otherwise indicated, all functions are evaluated at $\hat{z}$):

$$\text{(A15)} \qquad (\theta + \theta^*)/\varphi^r\theta^{1-r} \geq 2(\theta + \theta^*)^r.$$

Rearranging (A15) yields

$$\text{(A16)} \qquad (1 + \theta^*/\theta)^{1-r} \geq 2\varphi^r.$$

Using (A13) to eliminate θ^*/θ, (A16) is equivalent to

$$\text{(A17)} \qquad \varphi^{*s} + \varphi^s \geq 2\varphi^s\varphi^{*s},$$

where $s \equiv r/(1 - r)$. Hence to show (A14), we must establish (A17). But since $\varphi^{*s} + \varphi^s - 2\varphi^{s/2}\varphi^{*s/2} = [\varphi^{s/2} - \varphi^{*s/2}]^2 \geq 0$, and since $s \geq 0$, we have

$$\varphi^{*s} + \varphi^s \geq 2\varphi^{s/2}\varphi^{*s/2} \geq 2\varphi^s\varphi^{*s},$$

where the latter inequality follows since $\varphi^s\varphi^{*s} < 1$.

QED

UNIVERSITY OF BRITISH COLUMBIA

REFERENCES

Anderson, Kym, and Richard Blackhurst, eds., *The Greening of World Trade Issues* (London: Harvester Wheatsheaf, 1992).

Baumol, William J., and Wallace E. Oates, *The Theory of Environmental Policy* (Cambridge: Cambridge University Press, 1988; first edition: 1975).

Copeland, Brian R., "International Trade and the Environment: Policy Reform in a Polluted Small Open Economy," *Journal of Environmental Economics and Management,* XXVI (1994), 44–65.

Copeland, Brian R., and M. Scott Taylor, "Trade and Transboundary Pollution," Discussion Paper 93-46, Department of Economics, University of British Columbia, December 1993.

Dean, Judith M., "Trade and the Environment: A Survey of the Literature," in Patrick Low, ed., *International Trade and the Environment: World Bank Discussion Papers* (Washington, DC: World Bank, 1992).

Dornbusch, Rudiger, Stanley Fischer, and Paul A. Samuelson, "Comparative Advantage, Trade and Payments in a Ricardian Model with a Continuum of Goods," *American Economic Review,* LXVII (1977), 823–39.

Grossman, Gene M., and Alan B. Krueger, "Environmental Impacts of a North American Free Trade Agreement," NBER Working paper No. 3914, November 1991.

Low, Patrick, and Alexander Yeats, "Do 'Dirty' Industries Migrate?" in Patrick Low, ed., *International Trade and the Environment: World Bank Discussion Papers* (Washington, DC: World Bank, 1992).

Lucas, Robert E. B., David Wheeler, and Hermamda Hettige, "Economic Development, Environmental Regulation and the International Migration of Toxic Industrial Pollution: 1960–1988," in Patrick Low, ed., *International Trade and the Environment: World Bank Discussion Papers* (Washington, DC: World Bank, 1992).

Markusen, James R., "International Externalities and Optimal Tax Structures," *Journal of International Economics,* V (1975), 15–29.

McGuire, Martin C., "Regulation, Factor Rewards, and International Trade," *Journal of Public Economics,* XVII (1982), 335–54.

Pethig, Ruediger, "Pollution, Welfare, and Environmental Policy in the Theory of Comparative Advantage," *Journal of Environmental Economics and Management,* II (1976), 160–69.

Siebert, Horst, J. Eichberger, R. Gronych, and R. Pethig, *Trade and Environment: A Theoretical Enquiry* (Amsterdam: Elsevier/North-Holland, 1980).

Staiger, Robert W., "Organized Labor and the Scope of International Specialization," *Journal of Political Economy,* XCVI (1988), 1022–47.

JOURNAL OF ENVIRONMENTAL ECONOMICS AND MANAGEMENT 27, 163–184 (1994)

The Environment as a Factor of Production: The Effects of Economic Growth and Trade Liberalization[1]

RAMÓN LÓPEZ

Department of Agricultural and Resource Economics, University of Maryland, College Park, Maryland 20742

Received September 2, 1993; revised June 10, 1993

Economic growth and trade liberalization decrease the degradation of natural resources if and only if producers internalize their stock feedback effects on production. For environmental factors without stock effects on production, economic growth is necessarily detrimental if preferences are homothetic. In the non-homothetic case, the relationship between growth and pollution depends on the elasticity of substitution in production between conventional factors and pollution and on the relative degree of curvature of utility in income. The lower are the elasticity of substitution and relative curvature coefficient, the more likely it is that pollution increases with income. An inverted U-shaped relationship between pollution and income is obtained.

Trade liberalization leads to once-and-for-all efficiency gains as well as to dynamic gains. Empirical measurement of the static gains in most cases has been shown to be rather small. However, several empirical studies have concluded that the dynamic income gains leading to faster economic growth, even in the long run, are much larger than the static gains (Balassa [2], Kavoussi [10], and Ram [19]). These growth effects apparently arise from an acceleration of investment and an increase in the rate of adoption of new technologies that an export-oriented trade strategy seems to bring about.

Several authors have addressed different aspects of the relationships between environmental degradation and economic growth (Anderson [1], Uimonen and Whalley [26]). The connection between trade policies and the environment have also been the object of recent analysis (Sutton [25], Schuh [23], Lutz [16], Uimonen and Whalley [26]). In general there is very little agreement on the nature of the linkages among trade reform, growth, and environmental degradation.[2] This is not surprising in view of the complexity of the issues, given the large number of environmental factors that one can consider, and the variety of mechanisms by which growth, relative prices, and environmental change can interact.[3]

The objective of this paper is to reconsider the growth/trade policy/environment analysis but within a substantially more modest and limited framework:

[1]The author is grateful to two anonymous referees for helpful criticisms and suggestions.

[2]See Dean [5] for an excellent survey of this literature.

[3]Some authors have even questioned the relevance of the analysis because whatever the environmental effects are, the analysis needs to focus on the externality/public goods aspects of the environment. Since these issues have been thoroughly explored in the theoretical literature, it is argued that there is little new in the debate on growth/trade/environment relationships. See Uimonen and Whalley [26] for an analysis of these issues and for a discussion of why this simple Pigouvian view of the world needs to be qualified in important ways.

0095-0696/94 $6.00

(i) Instead of focusing on the interactions between economic growth and environmental developments we consider only a one-way connection from "growth" to environmental degradation. To do this we define growth consistently with the definition of national accounts that ignore changes in environmental factors. That is, we define growth as increases in the conventional factors of production and technological change. (ii) Instead of focusing on liberalization of trade at a world scale we only consider utilateral trade liberalization in a small open developing country, where liberalization is defined as a reduction in tariffs that protect the manufacturing sector. (iii) We try to provide a systematic analysis of polar cases using highly simplified models. The fact that we concentrate on polar cases and the simplistic nature of the models used obviously subtract "realism" from the exercise, but at the same time it may be useful to introduce a degree of systematicness to the analysis, and have the analysis serve as a departing point for considering more "realistic" aspects.

The idea is to reconsider the growth/trade policy/environment relationships using a neoclassical model that incorporates the more or less standard assumptions that have been most widely used in conventional general equilibrium and growth analyses. These assumptions include: (i) an aggregator function of capital (K), labor (L), and technology (t), $f(K, L, t)$, exists (in the conventional models this is called "output"), and (ii) the production technology exhibits constant returns to scale in the factors of production.[4]

The analysis focuses on exogenously determined growth rather than on endogenous growth. Although this assumption subtracts elegance from the analysis it does allow us to study the conditions under which economic growth could lead to stationary or decreasing levels of pollution. This issue is very important because if this is not the case, i.e., if pollution is ever increasing with economic growth, it is growth itself which would have to come to a stop. After all, our capacity, or, more generally, the world's capacity, to absorb pollution is limited. Once pollution levels approach the absolute tolerable limit (beyond which we all die), economic growth would not become feasible anymore. To put it in a less dramatic way, if pollution is constantly increasing as output expands, the rate of growth would eventually have to slow down and come to depend exclusively on non-neutral technological change that is "pollution saving." Consider, for example, the extreme case where the elasticity of substitution between conventional factors and pollution (considered as a factor of production) is about zero, i.e., the case of a Leontief technology. If this is the case, it can be shown that economic growth based on conventional factor expansion or even technical change that increases the efficiency of conventional factors would necessarily lead to everexpanding pollution levels regardless of the nature of preferences. Hence, if pollution tolerance is limited, the only possible outcome would be to eventually repress economic growth except when based on non-neutral technical change that is pollution saving. Thus, long-run economic growth would in this case come to depend exclusively on the rate of pollution-saving technical change.

We suggest that in the analysis of the impact of "growth" and trade policy on the environment there are two important distinctions to be made that may

[4]Practically all neoclassical growth models use these assumptions. The exception is the more recent "endogenous" growth literature (see Lucas [14] and Romer [20] among others). General equilibrium trade models traditionally use these assumptions as well. Examples are Johnson [9], Dornbusch [7], Razin and Svensson [21], and many others.

significantly alter the effects. On the one hand it is necessary to distinguish whether or not the natural resource has stock feedback productive effects. That is, whether the changes in the stock of the environmental factor play a role in output. Examples of environmental factors that have productive stock feedback effects are the forest resource, the fish stock, and agricultural soil quality. In these cases production can expand on the short run by more intense exploitation of the resource, but at the cost of a gradual reduction in the stock which eventually may decrease productivity in the respective industries. An important example where the productive stock feedback effects are negligible is air quality. Expansion of industrial production may increase air pollution, but greater air pollution is unlikely to significantly affect industrial production.[5] Moreover, at least on a local basis, the stock effect of air pollution is very short-lived. A reduction in emissions is likely to cause a fast recovery of air quality in the local (city) framework and thus the stock effect is quite negligible.[6]

A second essential distinction is whether producers and consumers internalize temporal and intertemporal externalities through private ownership, contractual community arrangements à la Coase or government policies. It turns out that the impact of economic "growth" and trade policy are crucially dependent on the internalization of the environmental effects by individual producers in the case where productive stock feedback effects are present.

The remainder of this paper is organized as follows: Section 1 considers the case of resources that exhibit little stock productive effects, while Section 2 discusses the opposite case. Section 3 is devoted to the relative price effects of trade liberalization, Section 4 considers available empirical evidence, and in Section 5 we state the conclusion and discuss policy implications of the analysis.

1. RESOURCES THAT DO NOT HAVE STOCK FEEDBACK EFFECTS IN PRODUCTION

Here we consider environmental resources as factors of production that may affect utility essentially through the flow effect. The environmental factor can recover quite rapidly as soon as its exploitation rate is reduced. There are no important stock accumulation effects. An example of this is air pollution. Air quality tends to improve very fast when the rate of air emissions is reduced. Moreover, air pollution does not have major directly negative effects on production although it does have a negative utility effect.[7]

We assume that the economy is composed of two sectors. Consistent with the conventional neoclassical assumption we assume that we can define an aggregator function of capital, labor, and technology for each industry of the form

$$f^i = f^i(K_i, L_i; t), \qquad i = 1, 2, \tag{1}$$

where K_i and L_i are capital and labor in industry i, respectively, and t is an index

[5] Air pollution, however, does have a negative direct effect on welfare, but not through income.

[6] This is ignoring global stock effects related to climatic warming and ozone depletion.

[7] In this section we only consider pollution externalities that affect consumers, but we do not consider production externalities that affect other producers. Since we use a representative firm approach this assumption is not very restrictive. Negative externalities can be simply represented as a lower "marginal product" of pollution in the production function of the representative firm.

of technology. The functions $f^i(\cdot)$ are assumed increasing and linearly homogenous in K_i and L_i. The functions $f^i(\cdot)$ are of course the production functions typically specified as independent of the environmental factors.

To consider the environment as a factor of production we simply extend (1) to specify that total industry output is also a function of the environmental factor of production,

$$y_i = G^i\left[f^i(K_i, L_i; t), x_i; \tau\right], \qquad i = 1, 2, \tag{2}$$

where y_i is output of industry i, x_i is the environmental factor used by industry i,[8] and τ is an index of technology. $G(\cdot)$ is increasing and concave in f^i and x_i. Technical change may generate changes in τ that could affect the marginal rate of substitution between the conventional factors f^i and the environmental factor x_i. Consistent with the conventional neoclassical specification of technology we assume that $G^i[\cdot]$ is also linearly homogenous in f^i and the level of air pollution, x_i. This implies that the macro production function $G^i[\cdot]$ is characterized by constant returns to scale in K_i, L_i, and x_i.

The specification (2) assumes weak separability between the conventional factors of production and the environmental factor. That is, the marginal rate of substitution between capital and labor is assumed independent of the level of pollution. This is quite consistent with the neoclassical specification. Weak separability as in (2) is a condition for the production function defined only in terms of conventional factors of production to make sense when factors other than the conventional ones change. Moreover, this assumption simplifies the algebra substantially by allowing the consideration of the interactions between one aggregate conventional factor and the environmental resource. The robustness of the results to relaxing this assumption will be discussed.

Assuming that the total capital and labor endowments are fixed and mobile across sectors, we can define a revenue function conditional on total level of pollution, x, as

$$\begin{aligned} &R[p; f(K, L, t), x, \tau] \\ &\quad \equiv \max_{K_i, x_i, L_i} \left\{ \sum_i p_i G^i\left[f^i(K_i, L_i; t), x_i; \tau\right] : \Sigma K_i = K \right. \\ &\qquad\qquad\qquad\qquad\qquad\qquad\qquad\qquad \Sigma L_i = L \\ &\qquad\qquad\qquad\qquad\qquad\qquad\qquad\qquad \left. \Sigma x_i = x \right\}, \end{aligned} \tag{3}$$

where p is a vector of output prices, K and L are total capital and labor endowments, $x \equiv \Sigma x_i$ is the total utilization of the environmental factor (i.e., the total level of air emissions), and $f(\cdot)$ is an aggregator of the total conventional factors of production. The revenue function is homogenous of degree one in p. We assume a small open economy, and thus the vector of prices p is fixed. Moreover, because of the constant returns to scale assumption $R(\cdot)$ is also linearly homogenous in K, L, and x. We note that in contrast with K and L, the total use of the environmental factor, x, is not fixed. In the absence of any internalization of the

[8]For the case of air as an environmental factor, x_i are air emissions produced by industry i.

environmental externality, presumably firms would use x_i until its marginal product is zero. If the air quality effects are internalized (through policy), firms would be forced to pay a price for their emissions. In either case as long as prices paid by firms are identical, we can use well-known aggregation theorems to define $R(\cdot)$ in terms of x rather than of the individual x_i.

Apart from being a factor of production, x has a direct effect on the societal welfare function, $\mu(\cdot)$. We assume that $\mu(\cdot)$ is a function of total consumption of goods and of x. Total expenditures in goods, in turn, is assumed equal to the revenue. The welfare function is then increasing and concave in R and decreasing and concave in x. Thus, the indirect welfare function (conditional on a certain level of x) is

$$\mu = \mu[R[p; f(K, L; t), x; \tau], x, p]. \tag{4}$$

Maximization of $\mu(\cdot)$ with respect to x yields the optimal level of air emissions under the assumption that the air quality externality is completely internalized. The first-order condition of such maximization is

$$R_3(\cdot) = -\mu_2(\cdot)/\mu_1(\cdot), \tag{5}$$

where $\mu_1(\cdot)$ and $\mu_2(\cdot)$ stand for the marginal utility of the consumer good and emissions, respectively, and $R_3 \equiv \partial R/\partial x$.

1.1. The Case Where Polluters Do Not Pay or Pay a Constant Price

Here we consider the case where firms pay a constant (marginal) price for pollution which can be equal to zero. Thus we assume a per unit pollution price equal to q, which is fixed by the government independently of changes in consumers' willingness to accept pollution. This may happen because of government failure to adjust the pollution price to reflect its social marginal cost or because preferences are such that the ratio $-\mu_2/\mu_1$ does not change (which is of course a very special case). Given a fixed price q for pollution, producers would now maximize profit by

$$R_3(\cdot) = q, \tag{6}$$

and, hence, totally differentiating (6) with respect to x and f,

$$\frac{dx}{df} = -\frac{R_{32}}{R_{33}},$$

which is necessarily positive by concavity of R ($R_{33} < 0$) and by the fact that R_{32} is positive because of linear homogeneity of R in f and x.

In general, without constant returns to scale, R_{32} is positive under the plausible assumption of cooperant factors of production, i.e., that the marginal product of one factor increases when the level of the other factor rises. Thus, the level of pollution emissions necessarily rises with growth in conventional factors of production. This result is not dependent on the constant returns to scale assumption. Furthermore, it can be easily seen that an increase of any conventional factor of production (say K) or technology t will have an unambiguously positive effect on air pollution even if the separability assumption is not imposed. All that matters is that the marginal revenue product of x be increasing in the conventional factor that expands. Linear homogeneity of R in f and x implies that the marginal revenue $R_3(\cdot)$ is homogeneous of degree 0 and hence can be expressed as a function of the x/f ratio. Hence, (6) can be written as

$$\frac{x}{f} = g(p, q, \tau) > 0, \tag{6'}$$

where $g(\cdot)$ is a positive function. From (6') it is clear that the factor ratio x/f is fixed for given p, q, and τ. Hence, any increase in $f(\cdot)$, whether originated in increasing levels of factor endowments or technical change t, will be followed by a proportional increase in air pollution. The assumed fixity of q is here the key assumption which we relax in the ensuing sections.

1.2. The Case Where Polluters Pay the True Social Marginal Cost of Pollution and Preferences Are Homothetic

Here we allow the price of pollution to be endogenous, equal to the social marginal cost of pollution, i.e., $q = -\mu_2/\mu_1$. This implies that as pollution increases q will be adjusted. For illustrative purposes we use the most common assumption about preferences, homotheticity. Given constant returns to scale in production and homothetic preferences the first-order conditions (5) can be written as

$$\begin{aligned} R_3\left[p; 1, \frac{x}{f(\cdot)}\right] &= -\frac{\mu_2[1, x/R[p, f(\cdot), x; \tau]]}{\mu_1[1, x/R[p, f(\cdot), x; \tau]]} \\ &= -\frac{\mu_2\left[1, (x/f)\dfrac{1}{R(p, 1, x/f; \tau)}\right]}{\mu_1\left[1, (x/f)\dfrac{1}{R(p, 1, x/f; \tau)}\right]} \equiv \psi\left[p, \frac{x}{f}, \tau\right], \end{aligned} \tag{7}$$

where $\psi(\cdot)$ is a well-defined function. Note that the constant returns to scale assumption implies that $R_3(\cdot)$ is homogenous of degree zero in x and $f(\cdot)$. Hence, $R_3(\cdot)$ is a function of the x/f ratio. Similarly, the assumption of homothetic preferences also implies, without loss of generality, that $\mu(\cdot)$ is linearly homogenous and, hence, that the right-hand side of (7) can also be written as a function of the ratio x/f.

Thus, from (7) we can solve for the x/f ratio as

$$\frac{x}{f(K, L; t)} = \phi(p; \tau) > 0, \tag{8}$$

where $\phi(p)$ is some function of the vector of output prices. To see the effect of f on x we do not require any specific knowledge of the function $\phi(p)$ except that it is positive. This is enough to allow us to know that an increase in $f(\cdot)$, whether caused by an expansion of conventional factors or by technical change t, will necessarily cause the level of emissions x to proportionally increase. What happens is that under homothetic preferences the socially optimum price of pollution, q, is in fact constant because it only depends on the x/f ratio, which is, in turn, also constant. Apart from homothetic preferences and constant returns to scale in production, this result depends on exogenously given output prices.

Thus, homothetic preferences imply that pollution is ever increasing with economic growth even if government policies are efficient and set the price of pollution to truly reflect its social marginal cost. The implication of this is that in the long run, growth in the absence of pollution-saving technical change would have to stop. The capacity of people and of the ecosystem to absorb pollution is limited, and, thus, as pollution levels approach the maximum tolerable limits economic growth would have to stop. Positive rates of economic growth in the long run would be limited by the rate of environmentally biased technical change. Another possibility is of course that preferences become non-homothetic as x reaches a certain level. This case is analyzed below.

Differentiating (8) with respect to time and assuming that factors are paid their marginal value products, we obtain

$$\hat{x} = s_k \hat{K} + s_L \hat{L} + A + \eta, \tag{9}$$

where ^ indicates rate of growth, and s_k is the share of capital and s_L the share of labor in total revenue, $A \equiv f_t/f$ is the rate of a (conventional) factor enhancing technical change, and $\eta \equiv \phi_t/\phi$ is the rate of bias in technical change between x and f. A negative value for η reflects technical change that is environmentally saving and $\eta > 0$ implies a conventional factor saving technical change. The coefficient A is of course non-negative under normal conditions. That is, technical change, if anything, increases the efficiency of the conventional factors of production, $A \geq 0$.

From (9) it is clear that growth based on capital accumulation or increased employment necessarily causes increases in pollution if preferences are homothetic. If growth is based purely on technological change the effect on pollution would be ambiguous. To the extent that technical change is environmentally saving, i.e., $\eta < 0$, the net effect will depend on the strength of this effect relative to $A > 0$.[9]

The positive relationship between factor endowments and pollution is robust to the assumption of weak separability between conventional factors of production and pollution to the extent that the capital/labor ratio is constant as in the long-run neoclassical growth model. Without imposing separability it can be shown

[9]The cost of pollution controls for firms in industrialized economies has been shown to be very small, less than 1% of total costs (Low [13]). Hence, one would expect that the research and development efforts of the private sector in developed countries (the originator of most new technologies) to generate environmentally saving innovations are not likely to be large. Given the small private cost share of pollution controls, environmental saving technical change is not likely to generate very significant increases in profits for firms, while the large costs of conventional factors, particularly labor, imply that the bulk of the research effort in the private sector is likely to continue to be oriented to conventional factor saving technical change. All this implies that the factor A in (9) is still very large, while η may not yet be sufficient to induce a negative $\dot{x}$ even if growth were entirely based on technological change.

that (7) implies

$$\frac{x}{L} = \psi(p, K/L, \tau, t) > 0, \tag{10}$$

where $\psi(\cdot)$ is some positive function. In this case a simultaneous increase in K and L that preserves the capital labor ratio will unambiguously increase pollution x. That is, as in the neoclassical growth model, steady-state factor ratios do not change (unless non-neutral technical change occurs); this is true for the pollution/labor and pollution/capital ratios. Therefore, any increase in factor endowments will necessarily imply a corresponding increase in the third factor of production, x.

If growth is originated in both conventional factor accumulation and productivity growth, the possibility of a net negative value for x is even more remote. In summary, growth based on factor expansion and/or neutral technical change necessarily increases pollution if preferences are homothetic. Homothetic preferences impose a unitary income elasticity on the environmental goods. This could be a good approximation within certain income ranges. Eventually, however, as pollution and income increase, the environment could become a luxury good and thus the homotheticity assumption would no longer be a good approximation. We relax the homotheticity assumption below.

1.3. Non-Homothetic Preferences

If preferences are non-homothetic the effect of growth on pollution is naturally ambiguous. To the extent that the income elasticity of the environmental good is sufficiently larger than one, pollution does not necessarily increase with factor accumulation or neutral technological change. Totally differentiating (5) with respect to x and f,

$$\left(R_{33}\mu_1 + R_3^2\mu_{11} + R_3\mu_{12}\right) dx + \left(R_{32}\mu_1 + R_2R_3\mu_{11} + R_2\mu_{21}\right) df = 0. \tag{5'}$$

From the second-order conditions of maximization of (4) it follows that the first bracketed left-hand-side term in (5′) should be negative. Therefore, the effect of f on x critically depends on the sign of $B \equiv R_{32}\mu_1 + R_2R_3\mu_{11} + R_2\mu_{21}$. In particular, pollution will be increasing (decreasing) in f if B is positive (negative). Assuming separability of preferences between x and R, it follows that $\mu_{21} = 0$, in which case the condition for x to be increasing in f is[10]

$$\frac{R_{32}}{R_2}\mu_1 + R_3\mu_{11} > 0.$$

The above condition can be rewritten as

$$\frac{fR_{32}}{R_2} > -\frac{\mu_{11}}{\mu_1}R\frac{R_3 f}{R}.$$

[10]This assumption does not change the qualitative nature of the results. It only facilitates the interpretation of the ensuing results and allows us to relate them to well-understood coefficients.

Defining the relative slope coefficient $-\mu_{11}R/\mu_1 \equiv a$ (which is known as the coefficient of relative risk aversion in the context of uncertainty or more generally the Frisch coefficient) and $R_3 f/R \equiv s_f$ as the share of all non-environmental factors in national income, we have that

$$\frac{dx}{df} \gtrless 0 \quad \text{if} \quad \frac{fR_{32}}{R_2}\frac{1}{s_f} \gtrless a \tag{11}$$

We note that $a = \bar{a}(f, x(f)) = a(f)$. That is, the Frisch coefficient is a function of f once the optimal value of x is used (the optimal x is a function of f as well as other exogenous variables).

In order to shed some light on the implications of the above condition we postulate a CES specification for the revenue function R,

$$R = A(p, \tau)[\gamma_2 f^{\rho} + \gamma_3 x^{\rho}]^{1/\rho},$$

where $A(\cdot)$ is a general linearly homogenous function of p and increasing in τ, and γ_2, γ_3 and ρ are coefficients. Using the CES specification we obtain that condition (11) is equivalent to

$$\frac{dx}{df} \gtrless 0 \quad \text{if} \quad 1 - \rho \gtrless a(f). \tag{12}$$

Now, the left-hand side of the second inequality in (12) can be related to the elasticity of substitution between pollution and non-pollution inputs, σ. For the CES specification it is clear that $\rho = (\sigma - 1)/\sigma$, and therefore the above condition becomes

$$\frac{dx}{df} \gtrless 0 \quad \text{if} \quad \frac{1}{\sigma} \gtrless a(f). \tag{13}$$

That is, the effect of factor expansion on pollution depends on two critical parameters, the elasticity of substitution in production between pollution and non-pollution inputs, and the relative degree of curvature of the utility function in income. The smaller the technical substitution possibilities between pollution and non-pollution inputs and the smaller the "degree of relative risk aversion" the more likely is that pollution will increase with growth even if preferences are non-homothetic. If, for example, $\sigma = 0$, pollution would always be increasing regardless of the degree of non-homotheticity of preferences.

The intuition behind this result is clear: Economic growth increases the value of the environment for consumers. If this increased value is manifested in the market, firms will have to pay an increasing price for pollution. A higher elasticity of substitution in production between conventional inputs and pollution implies that for firms it is less costly to reduce pollution by substituting it for more conventional inputs. That is, firms need to spend less conventional inputs to reduce pollution in response to a higher pollution price when σ is high than when it is low. Or equivalently, just a small increase of the price of pollution will be enough to induce firms to reduce it by a large extent. The lower is σ the greater the price increase would have to be (and the more costly for firms) to achieve similar pollution reductions. The coefficient a, on the other hand, shows how the marginal utility of income declines as income expands. Hence, a high level of a implies that consumers would be willing to give up a proportionally greater additional (potential) income as they become richer in order to buy a better environment. Thus, if a is large the pollution price that consumers will demand will increase much more as income increases than if a is small, and vice versa. At the extreme if $a = 0$ (utility is linear in income) then the price of pollution would be constant as income expands and pollution would thus permanently increase with economic growth. Empirical measures of the coefficient a are commonly available from the economics under uncertainty literature. The coefficient of relative risk aversion typically ranges between one and two. This would imply that pollution would cease to increase with income only if σ is greater than 0.5. The coefficient a is not, however, likely to be independent of economic growth. We now turn to this issue.

The effect of f on $a(\cdot)$ becomes crucial in determining the effect of economic growth on pollution. Under the assumption of separability between income and pollution in the utility function it can be shown that

$$a'(f) = -\left(R_2 + R_3\frac{dx}{df}\right)\left[a\left(\frac{\mu_{11}}{\mu_1} + \frac{\mu_{111}}{\mu_{11}}\right) + \frac{\mu_{11}}{\mu_1}\right].$$

The term $R_2 + R_3(dx/df)$ is the net effect of factor accumulation on income including the direct and indirect effect via changes in pollution. This effect has to

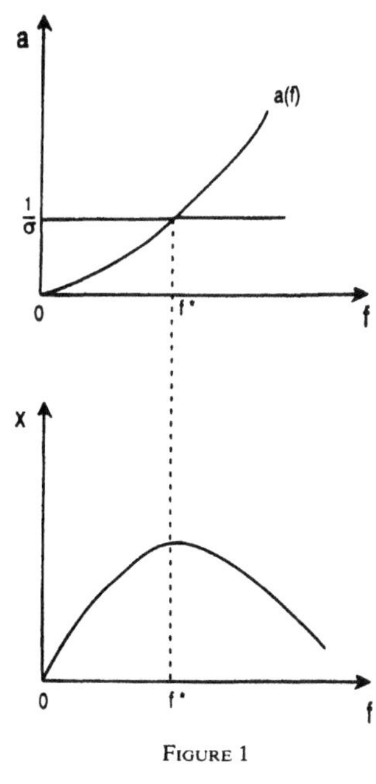

FIGURE 1

be positive (otherwise no factor accumulation would take place). Also we assume that utility is strictly concave in income and thus $\mu_{11} < 0$. Thus, unless third-order effects are very strongly positive (i.e., $\mu_{111} > 0$ and large) the Frisch coefficient is likely to be increasing in factor accumulation, $a'(f) > 0$.

The upper graph in Fig. 1 shows the relationship between a and f. In the area above the $1/\sigma$ line we have that $a > 1/\sigma$, and hence x is decreasing in f. In the area below the $1/\sigma$ line x is increasing in f because $a < 1/\sigma$. At point f^* we have $1/\sigma = a$, and hence at that level x is not affected by $f(dx/df = 0)$. The lower graph shows the implied relationship between x and f. Thus, if $a'(f) > 0$, we obtain the inverted U-shaped relationship between income and pollution that has been frequently discussed in the literature.[11] Grossman and Krueger [8] have, in fact, empirically confirmed such relationship for certain urban air pollutants.[12]

2. RESOURCES THAT HAVE STOCK FEEDBACK PRODUCTIVE EFFECTS

Here we consider resources that have both flow and stock effects on production. Also it is assumed that the stock of resources does not directly enter into the utility function. The effect of the resource stocks on utility occurs exclusively via the level of income. We will consider here only the effects of changes in the conventional factors of production (and of t). Here we ignore τ, but all the caveats about τ discussed in Section 1 apply. We consider an economy composed of two sectors, a primary sector that uses natural resources as a factor of production and the rest of the economy that does not use natural resources that have stock feedback productive effects. We illustrate the analysis here using biomass as a natural resource and referring to the primary sector as "agriculture."[13] We will use as an example the case of agriculture in tropical areas, where productivity greatly depends on the stock of natural biomass.[14]

Agriculture production under shifting cultivation in tropical areas is dependent not only on the cultivated land area (i.e., the amount of deforestation) but also on the stock of forest (biomass) itself because soil quality and fertility are dependent on an adequate stock of forest or biomass.[15] This permits us to write the production function in agriculture as

$$y^{\mathrm{A}} = F^{\mathrm{A}}(K^{\mathrm{A}}, L^{\mathrm{A}}, z, s), \tag{14}$$

where y^{A} is agricultural output, z is cultivated land, and s is the stock of forest or

[11]Note that income R monotonically increases with f. Therefore, an inverted U-shaped relation between x and f also implies the same relation for x and R.

[12]Also see The World Bank [27].

[13]Note that we are not really assuming that only agriculture uses environmental resources with a stock effect. We are simply referring to "agriculture" as all sectors that use these resources.

[14]The ensuing model can easily be adapted to analyze renewable natural-resource-based sectors other than agriculture.

[15]The level of forest itself plays an important role in preventing flooding and soil erosion. Also in the context of shifting cultivation the fertility of the land periodically cleared for cultivation depends on the forest density. For details on the stock/flow effects see López and Niklitschek [12]. Another example is in the context of soil conservation. Agriculture output depends on both the extent of soil loss (the flow) and on soil depth (the stock of the resource) (McConnell [17]).

biomass. $F^{\mathrm{A}}(\cdot)$ is thus increasing and concave in the four factors of production. Moreover, we also assume that $F^{\mathrm{A}}(\cdot)$ exhibits constant returns to scale in the four factors of production.[16]

For a given total availability of land the stock of biomass depletion is proportional to the level of cultivated area.[17] Hence, assuming that the natural rate of biomass growth is $\alpha > 0$ and that biomass extraction is βz, where β is a positive constant, the time evolution of the stock of biomass is

$$\dot{s} = \alpha s - \beta z.$$

The revenue function for an economy composed of two sectors, agriculture and the rest of the economy, under the assumption of weak separability between the conventional and the environmental factor can be written as[18]

$$R = R[p_{\mathrm{A}}, p_{\mathrm{N}}; f(K, L), z, s; t], \tag{15}$$

where p_{A} is the price of the agricultural good, p_{N} is the price of the non-agricultural output, K, L are the total resource endowments of capital and labor in the economy, and t is an index of technical change.

We assume that the non-agricultural sector is also characterized by constant return to scale, and, hence, $R(\cdot)$ is linearly homogenous in f, z, and s. Also $f(\cdot)$ itself is homogenous of degree one in K and L. Given that only agriculture uses the environmental factor we have that

$$R_{14} \equiv \frac{\partial^2 R}{\partial p_{\mathrm{A}} \partial z} > 0, \qquad R_{24} < 0, \qquad R_{15} > 0, \qquad R_{25} < 0.$$

The socially optimal level of z would then be determined by

$$\max_{z} \int_0^{\infty} R(p_{\mathrm{A}}, p_{\mathrm{N}}; f(K, L), z, s) e^{-rt}\, dt \tag{16}$$

$$\text{s.t.} \quad \dot{s} = \alpha s - \beta z$$

$$s(0) = \bar{s}_0,$$

where r is the discount rate and $s(0)$ is the initial level of biomass stock. The

[16] The assumption of constant returns to scale in all factors including the stock of the resource was tested by Lópex [11] for agriculture in the Ivory Coast. He could not reject this hypothesis, finding that the estimated returns to scale fluctuated between 0.92 and 1.01.

[17] The larger the cultivated area the shorter the fallow periods and, hence, the shorter the period allowed for regeneration of the forest.

[18] Here, for notational simplicity, we are ignoring the factor x used in the non-manufacturing sector. This does not, however, affect any of the results below.

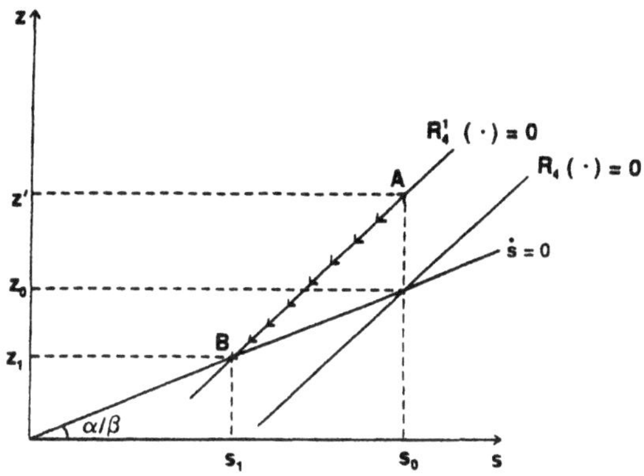

FIGURE 2

first-order necessary conditions are

$$
\begin{aligned}
&\text{(i)}\ R_4(\cdot) = \lambda,\\
&\text{(ii)}\ \dot{\lambda} = (r - \alpha)\lambda - R_5(\cdot),\\
&\text{(iii)}\ \dot{s} = \alpha s - \beta z,\\
&\text{(iv)}\ s(0) = \bar{s}_0;\ \lim_{t\to\infty} e^{-rt}\lambda(t)s(t) = 0,
\end{aligned}
\qquad (17)
$$

where λ is the current value co-state variable measuring the shadow value of s.[19]

First we consider the case when individual producers do not internalize the stock effect of the resource on society's wealth. This may happen when the stock of biomass is under public or common property and the community, for whatever reason, has not developed the necessary contractual arrangements that would have led to a solution like (17). We first analyze a polar case where producers totally ignore the shadow value of biomass in their decisions. That is, they behave as if $\lambda = 0$, and hence (ii) Eq. 17 would not form part of the solution and (iii) in Eq. 17 will simply take the role of an accounting identity. Thus, the effect of economic "growth" is in this case entirely ruled by the condition $R_4(\cdot) = 0$.

Figure 2 considers the effect of an increase in f for the case when the initial equilibrium is stable. Before f increases the stock of biomass is s_0 and the cultivated area is z_0. A rise in f will increase the marginal revenue product of cultivated land for any given level of the stock. Hence, the $R_4 = 0$ schedule will shift upward. This will cause an instantaneous increase in the area cultivated to z', which, in turn, will cause the stock s to decline. As s is reduced the marginal revenue product of cultivated land is gradually reduced, thus causing z to decline. This process is shown by the arrow line. The new steady state will occur at a lower stock and service flow of the resource. That is, under stability, capital expansion or

[19] An additional assumption is that $r > \alpha$.

more generally, an increase in the conventional factors of production, will necessarily cause a higher rate of biomass depletion.[20]

Next we examine the other polar case, where individual producer decisions take full account of the social value of the stock of biomass. In this case the behavior of the system is ruled by the complete system of Eq. (17). First we consider the steady state; i.e., we assume $\dot{\lambda} = \dot{s} = 0$. In this case we have

$$R_4\left(p_A, p_N; f(K,L), \frac{\alpha}{\beta}s^*, s^*, t\right) = \frac{1}{r-\alpha}R_5(\cdot), \tag{18}$$

where s^* is the steady-state level of biomass stock. Individual producers fully consider the social shadow price of the stock of biomass (the right-hand side of (18)), and also they are fully aware that in the long run the flow of resource extraction is proportional to the long-run level of the stock; in the long run $z = (\alpha/\beta)s^*$.

Under constant returns to scale both $R_4(\cdot)$ and $R_5(\cdot)$ are homogenous of degree 0 in f, z, and s, and, hence, (15) can be expressed as

$$R_4\left[p_A, p_N; \frac{f(K,L)}{s^*}, \frac{\alpha}{\beta}, 1, t\right] = \frac{1}{r-\alpha}R_5\left[p_A, p_N; \frac{f(K,L)}{s}, \frac{\alpha}{\beta}, 1, t\right]. \tag{19}$$

Thus, (19) can be solved for f/s^*,

$$\frac{f(K,L)}{s^*} = \varepsilon\left(p_A, p_N, \frac{\alpha}{\beta}, \frac{1}{r-\alpha}, t\right) > 0, \tag{20}$$

where $\varepsilon(\cdot)$ is some unspecified function of the exogenous variables. Since $\varepsilon(\cdot) > 0$ we have that the optimal long-run level of the stock of biomass, s^*, is necessarily increasing in $f(\cdot)$ and, therefore, in K and L. That is, in contrast with the case when producers do not internalize the biomass externality, now deforestation will decrease as economic growth takes place.

An expansion in the level of conventional factors of production increases the value of biomass as a factor of production. The marginal productivity of the resource extracted from the forest also increases, and hence producers would like to extract more biomass from the forest. However, producers are aware that in order to extract a greater flow of resources from the forest stock in a sustainable basis they need to allow the stock of biomass to expand. In contrast with the previous case, now individual producers have incentives to increase the stock because they will directly benefit from their investment in the resource stock. In the previous polar case, because of lack of private property or lack of adequate contractual arrangements, an individual producer may not necessarily benefit in the long run by investing in the resource stock and hence has no incentives in allowing the stock of biomass to expand. This is the crucial difference between the two polar cases.

[20]The unstable case occurs when the slope of the $R_4 = 0$ schedule is flatter than the $\dot{s} = 0$ schedule. In this case an increase in f will lead to complete extinction of the resource.

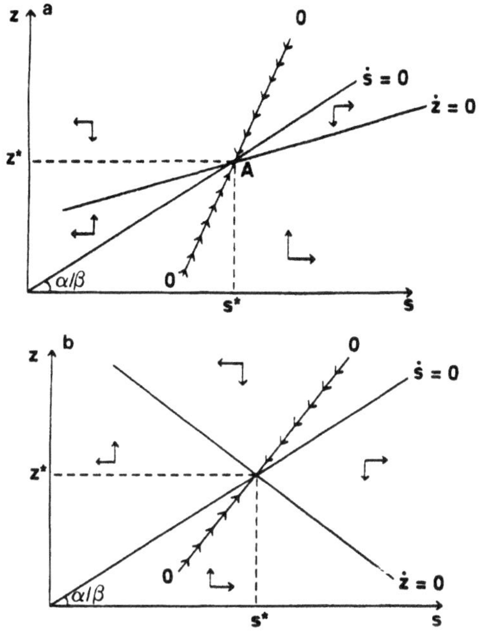

FIGURE 3

The dynamic of the system can be represented by the following two differential equations derived from (17):

$$\text{(i)}\ \dot{z} = \frac{1}{R_{44}}[(r-\alpha)R_4(\cdot) - R_5(\cdot) - R_{45}(\alpha s - \beta z)]$$

$$\text{(ii)}\ \dot{s} = \alpha s - \beta z. \tag{21}$$

From (21) we obtain the slopes of the $\dot{z} = 0$ and $\dot{s} = 0$ schedules. The slope of the $\dot{s} = 0$ schedule is positive with slope α/β (Fig. 3). The slope of $\dot{z} = 0$ may be positive or negative, but stability requires that its slope be less than the slope of the $\dot{s} = 0$. Figure 3a shows the case when the slope of the $\dot{z} = 0$ schedule is positive and Fig. 3b shows it when it is negative. Also Figs. 3a and 3b show with the arrows the motion of the system in the neighborhood of the steady state shown by the points A in the figures. Stability thus requires that the adjustment, shown as line 00 in Fig. 3, be steeper than the $\dot{s} = 0$ schedule.

Figure 4 shows the adjustment toward equilibrium when $f(\cdot)$ increases. A rise in f will not affect the $\dot{s} = 0$ schedule. Since we know from (20) that the new steady state occurs at a higher s, it is clear that the schedule $\dot{z} = 0$ must shift to the right (from $\dot{z} = 0$ to $\dot{z}' = 0$ in Fig. 4). The adjustment path from the old steady state A to the new one at C is depicted by the arrow line BC. That is, first the rate of extraction is reduced from z^* to z_1 and then gradually increases to the new steady-state level $z^{*\prime}$, which is above the original extraction level z^+.

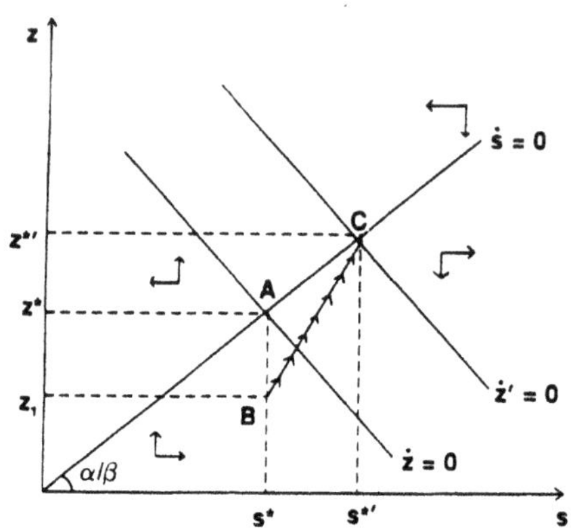

FIGURE 4

We have so far considered two polar cases of resource control, namely, where the stock effect is not considered at all in producers' decisions and, alternatively, when the complete shadow value of the resource stock is considered in the allocation decisions. In cases where the resource is privately owned the second polar case would be valid. There are, however, important examples, particularly in LDCs, where natural resources are owned in communal form rather than individually. In this case it is most likely that neither of the two polar cases analyzed would be entirely appropriate.[21]

Thus if λ^a is the actual value of the resource stock considered by producers, then $\lambda^a = \Omega\lambda$, where $\Omega < 1$. If the Ω coefficient does change with f, i.e., if the actual distortion does change with economic growth, one would expect that the analysis of the second polar case to be valid for this intermediate situation. If, however, Ω does change with growth, the analysis would become more complicated. Presumably, if $\Omega'(f) > 0$, that is, if growth induces a greater resource control, the result of increased resource conservation as growth occurs would be reinforced. If $\Omega'(f) < 0$, on the other hand, the net effect of growth on the resource stock would be ambiguous. In general, unless economic growth causes an increase in the rate of distortion affecting resource valuation, resource degradation will decrease with growth.

So far we have assumed that growth is based on factor expansion or technical change that increases the effective availability of factors of production to the primary or agricultural sectors. If growth is, however, based on technological change that is biased against the primary sector (and toward, for example, the

[21]A recent study by López [11] using data for the Côte d'Ivoire has empirically tested the hypothesis that social controls in the context of communal ownership are sufficient to induce individual producers to fully internalize the value of the resource stock in their decisions. López found that although the communities do exert some control on individual producers, these controls are far from being sufficient to cause optimal allocation. The biomass stock is overexploited although some internalization of the stock value does occur. López found that on average producers consider about 30% of the social value of the resource stock in their decisions, i.e., the value of λ actually considered is about one-third of the true λ in (17).

manufacturing and service sectors) then it may cause a decrease of the value of the environmental resources used by the primary sectors. Following the logic of the previous model, this type of growth would thus increase (rather than decrease) resource degradation in the primary sector. Casual empiricism suggests that as countries get richer the primary sector of the economy shrinks relative to the other sectors. This does not imply, however, that the primary sector shrinks in absolute terms. On the contrary, the primary sectors' absolute levels apparently continuously increase with growth due to an expanded availability of conventional factors in efficiency units. Thus, it appears that under efficient social natural resource valuation, economic growth is likely to decrease resource degradation in the primary sectors. Growth, so dominated by technical change that is biased against the primary sectors that it causes an absolute shrinking of the primary sectors' effective availability of conventional factors, does not seem consistent with the historical experience.

3. THE RELATIVE PRICE EFFECTS OF TRADE LIBERALIZATION

Here we consider the effects of trade liberalization on the environment in a typical developing country. We focus on the effects that take place through the changes in relative prices as well as through the static income effect induced by trade liberalization.[22] We assume that the economy is small and open. It produces two tradable outputs, an agricultural good which is exportable and a manufactured good which is a substitute for imports. It is assumed that production of manufacturing is more intensive in the pollution input than agriculture. That is, the pollution/output ratio is higher in manufacturing than in agriculture.[23]

The pollution effect at the consumer level has not received nearly as much attention in the literature as the production-generated pollution. However, consumption pollution appears to be quite important, particularly in the consumption of durable (manufactured) goods. Pollution from the operation of cars, refrigerators, air conditioners, etc., appears to be a major source of air contamination in many middle- and high-income countries. On the other hand, consumption of food and other agricultural products does not appear to be as nearly as polluting as the manufactured good. Thus, for consumption pollution we focus on pollution generated by industrial goods.

We assume that initially the manufacturing import substitution sector is protected to the detriment of the agricultural-export-oriented sector. We assume that neither the production nor the consumption air pollution externalities are internalized. The revenue function for this economy is thus

$$R = R(p_{\mathrm{A}}, 1 + m, f(K, L), x_1), \tag{22}$$

[22]See Chapter 16 in Baumol and Oates [3] for an analysis of environmental protection programs for the international competitiveness of countries undertaking such programs and for the analysis of pollution that can be transported internationally.

[23]This assumption is reasonable for air pollution but is less clear for water pollution. Agricultural fertilizers and pesticides can be a major source of water contamination. Nonetheless, it appears that at least for developing countries, industrial waste per unit of output tends to be much higher than agricultural waste.

where we normalize the world price of the manufactured good to 1, m is the *ad valorem* tariff rate, $(1 + m)$ is therefore its domestic price, p_A is the price of the agriculture good, and x_1 is now production pollution. As before, constant returns to scale implies that $R(\cdot)$ is linearly homogenous in $f(\cdot)$ and x_1, and $R_i > 0$ for $i = 1, 2, 3, 4$.

Moreover, the nature of the general equilibrium Rybczynski relationship implies that if agriculture production is less pollution intensive than manufacturing, then $R_{14} < 0$ and $R_{24} > 0$. If the price of pollution is q (if no pollution controls exist $q = 0$), firms will choose x, so that

$$R_4(\cdot) = q.$$

Differentiating this with respect to x_1 and m we obtain

$$\frac{dx_1}{dm} = -\frac{R_{24}}{R_{22}} > 0. \tag{23}$$

That is, trade liberalization, i.e., a reduction in m, necessarily decreases production pollution.

To consider consumption pollution we need to incorporate the consumption sector in a general equilibrium framework. We define $x_2 = x_2(c_2)$, with $x_2'(c_2) > 0$ as consumption pollution. The level of x_2 is an increasing function of the consumption of the manufactured good c_2. The (dual) expenditure function is

$$E = E(p_A, 1 + m; \mu, x_1 + x_2(c_2)), \tag{24}$$

which is increasing and concave in p_A and $1 + m$ and increasing in μ. $E(\cdot)$ is of course also increasing in $x_1 + x_2$. The economy-wide budget constraint implies that

$$E(p_A, 1 + m; \mu, x_1 + x_2(c_2)) = R(p_A, 1 + m; f, x_1) + m[E_2(\cdot) - R_2(\cdot)]. \tag{25}$$

Next, to specify the consumption of the manufactured good, c_2, we can use Shephard's lemma,

$$c_2 = E_2(p_A, 1 + m; \mu, x_1 + x_2(c_2)). \tag{26}$$

By differentiating (25) and (26) using (23) it can be shown that the effect of a decrease in m is to increase the consumption of the manufactured good. This, in turn, would cause an increase in consumer-originated pollution.

Thus, the net effect of trade liberalization on pollution is ambiguous. Lowering protection reduces production-generated pollution but at the same time increases consumer-generated pollution. The strength of the production effect will depend on the supply elasticity of the manufactured good and on the pollution intensiveness of manufacturing production. Empirical studies suggest (Michaely *et al.* [18]) that the manufacturing sector has a large degree of flexibility to respond to decreased protection. Thus, the level of economic activity in manufacturing tends to be only slightly affected by trade liberalization in most cases. Moreover, given that developing countries tend to have relatively more lenient environmental regulations than developed countries, it is likely that trade liberalization would bring about changes in the composition of industrial output toward more polluting-intensive activities. Thus, one would expect that the effect of decreased industrial protection will cause a relatively minor reduction in production-generated pollution.

The consumption effect is likely to be greater. The consumption effect depends on the demand elasticity for the manufacturing goods and on the degree to which pollution increases by an expansion in the consumption of industrial goods. Demand for manufactured goods in developing countries appears to be very elastic with respect to both price and income. Hence, the decrease in price of import substitutes and increase in income associated with trade liberalization is likely to cause a large expansion in demand for manufactured goods, particularly automobiles and other durables. The experience of certain Latin American countries is illustrative. After a period of adjustment, trade liberalization has been followed by a strong expansion in the demand for durables. In Chile, for example, after the trade reform of 1975, the automotive park increased almost three times in six years in part because of the drastic reduction in the domestic price of motor vehicles. Thus, it appears that the consumption effects of trade reform are likely to dominate the production effects causing a net increase in air pollution.

Finally, we consider the effect of trade liberalization on deforestation. If there is no internalization of the stock effect of biomass and assuming that agriculture is a more intensive user of biomass than manufacturing, the effect of trade liberalization on the stock of forest biomass is unambiguously negative. A decrease in protection of manufacturing in this case causes a flow of capital and labor toward agriculture, which now is relatively more competitive. This, in turn, increases the marginal value product in the biomass extracted from the forest (i.e., increases the marginal value product of cultivated land), inducing greater deforestation.[24]

If farm producers do internalize the stock value of the forest, trade liberalization induces an increase in the forest stock. The effect of a reduction in m on agriculture is entirely captured by an increase in f. As m is reduced factor returns in the manufacturing sector temporarily fall, thus inducing capital and labor to flow from industry to agriculture, thus increasing f in agriculture. From this point the analysis is, therefore, identical to the growth effect in Section 2. The net effect is to increase the long-run forest stock. The key thing to understand is that the complete effect of a reduction in m is through an expansion in the $f(\cdot)$ for agriculture.

4. EMPIRICAL EVIDENCE

Empirical evidence for the effect of growth and the trade regime on environmental degradation is quite scarce. Two recent studies have focused on air pollution generated in the manufacturing sector using developing and developed country data for 1960–1988 (Lucas *et al.* [15], Birdsall and Wheller [4]). Both studies conclude that toxic intensity of GDP (i.e., air pollution emissions/GDP) does not decline with income.

[24]See López and Niklitschek [12] for details about the adjustment dynamics in this case.

Lucas *et al.* finds that pollution intensity remained constant throughout the sixties, independent of income. During the seventies and eighties the pollution-intensity effect of income is on average also zero or rather negligible. However, the effect of income on pollution intensity tends to be negative in more open countries while it is positive in closed economies. Even in the most open countries, however, the absolute level of pollution increases with income despite the fact that pollution intensity declines. These effects are quantitatively more important during the eighties than in the seventies. In fact, the strength of the openness effect in the eighties is more than twice the effect in the seventies. Thus, the findings of these analyses are quite consistent with the theoretical results obtained assuming homothetic preferences. A problem with these studies, however, is that they are not based on actual measures of air pollution but rather on estimated virtual indicators. These indicators were calculated using the U.S. pollution coefficients for several industrial branches. The authors then used these industrial branch coefficients to calculate an aggregated measure of emissions based on the weight that each industrial branch has in each county over the period of analysis. This effectively implied that the calculated changes in air emissions only reflect changes in the composition of industrial output, i.e., whether "dirty" industries increase or decrease their share versus "clean" industries.

The study by Grossman and Krueger [8], by contrast, uses actual city measures of various air pollutants in several cities around the world. They econometrically estimated a reduced form relationship between pollution levels and per capita income. They found an inverted U-shaped relationship with pollution increasing up to a per capital income of about U.S. $5000 and gradually declining beyond that level. This would be consistent with our analysis based on non-homothetic preferences. It is not clear whether this relationship is valid for air pollutants other than those considered by Grossman and Krueger. Steer [24], for example, using analyses prepared for the World Development Report 1992 [27], reports a similar relationship for sulfur dioxide concentrations, but total per capita carbon emissions are reported to be ever increasing with income. Similarly, recent estimates for the United States suggest that urban waste has been increasing at more than 7% per annum over the last two decades (Schmidheiny [22]). That is, urban waste has been increasing at more than twice the rate of GDP growth.

5. CONCLUSIONS

The major implication of the previous analysis is that the effects of economic growth and relative price changes on the environment critically depend on the nature of the resource stock effects on production and/or whether individual producers internalize such stock effects. It is shown that for resources that have a productive stock feedback effect, economic growth and trade liberalization in a typical developing country decrease degradation in both the short and the long run if individual producers internalize the stock effect. This is valid whether the internalization is induced by government policy, contractual arrangements among producers, or individual private property. On the other hand, the effects of economic growth and trade liberalization on the resource stock are unambiguously negative if individual producers do not internalize the productive stock effects of the resource. The effect of trade liberalization is dependent on three assumptions, namely, that initially the manufacturing sector is protected vis-à-vis the primary sectors, that the productive stock effects of the resource occur entirely in the primary sectors, and that the productive sector is characterized by a constant returns to scale technology.

For environmental factors that do not have stock effects on production (i.e., air quality), economic growth originated by the accumulation of conventional factors or conventional technological change is necessarily detrimental whether or not individual producers (are forced to) consider the environmental externality if preferences are homothetic. Moreover, policies (i.e., trade policy, price policy, taxation of pollution, etc.) can affect pollution intensity (pollution per capita or per unit of capital) in a once-and-for-all form but will not affect the relationship between pollution change and (conventional) factor accumulation. The elasticity of environmental degradation with respect to factor accumulation is identical in the long run whatever the policy mix if preferences are homothetic. In the absence of environmentally biased technical change the elasticity is equal to one. Obviously, pollution cannot expand forever, and, hence, either preferences become non-homothetic at a certain level of income and pollution and/or growth decelerates or even stops.

If preferences are non-homothetic, however, the relationship between growth and pollution becomes non-linear. It has been shown that such a relationship depends on two key parameters, the elasticity of substitution in production between conventional factors and pollution on the one hand, and the relative degree of curvature of utility in income (the "relative risk-aversion" coefficient). The lower is the elasticity of substitution and relative curvature coefficient, the more likely it is that pollution increases with income. It is shown that under certain conditions an inverted U-shaped relationship between pollution and income can be derived in the non-homothetic case. That is, we have derived a theoretical justification for the inverted U-shaped reduced form relationship between pollution and income which has been so prominent in the literature.

The effect of trade liberalization on environmental factors that do not have stock production effects has been shown in general to be ambiguous. In a typical developing country the manufacturing sector is protected, while agriculture is implicitly taxed. Trade liberalization thus reduces protection to manufacturing, increasing incentives for agriculture. If manufacturing is more pollution-intensive than agriculture, it follows that production pollution will fall due to the fact that the composition of production shifts toward agriculture after trade is liberalized. Consumption pollution, however, is likely to expand if the pollution intensity at the consumer level of manufactured goods is greater than that of the agricultural goods. Thus, the net effect will depend on the relative strength of the production vis-à-vis the consumption effect.

REFERENCES

1. D. Anderson, Economic growth and the environment, Paper prepared for the 1989 Royal Dutch/Shell Group Planning Scenarios, London (1990).
2. B. Balassa, Development strategies and economic performance, *in* "Development Strategies in Semiindustrialized Economies" (B. Balassa, Ed.), Oxford Univ. Press, London (1982).
3. W. Baumol and W. Oates, "The Theory of Environmental Policy," Cambridge Univ. Press, New York (1988).

4. N. Birdsall and D. Wheeler, Openness reduces industrial pollution in Latin America: The missing pollution haven effect, Paper presented at the Symposium on International Trade and the Environment, The World Bank, Nov. (1991).
5. J. Dean, Trade and the environment: A survey of the literature, Mimeo, School of Advanced International Study, John Hopkins University, Apr. (1991).
6. A. Dixit and V. Norman, "Theory of International Trade," Cambridge Univ. Press, Cambridge, MA (1980).
7. R. Dornbusch, "Open Economy Macroeconomics," Basic Books, New York (1980).
8. G. Grossman and A. Krueger, Environmental impacts of a North American free trade agreement, Unpublished paper, Nov. (1991).
9. H. Johnson, Towards a general theory of the balance of payments, *in* "International Trade and Economic Growth" (H. Johnson, Ed.), Allen & Unwin, London (1958).
10. R. Kavoussi, Export expansion and economic growth: Further empirical evidence, *J. Develop. Econom.* **14**, 241–250 (1984).
11. R. López, Resource degradation and agricultural productivity in poor tropical areas: The effectiveness of community controls of common property resource, Unpublished, University of Maryland, College Park (1992).
12. R. López and M. Niklitschek, Dual economic growth in poor tropical areas, *J. Develop. Econom.* **36**, 189–211 (1991).
13. P. Low, Trade measures and environmental quality: Implications for Mexico's exports, Paper presented at the Symposium on International Trade and the Environment, The World Bank, Nov. (1991).
14. R. Lucas, On the mechanics of economic development, *J. Monetary Econom.* **22**, 3–42 (1988).
15. R. E. B. Lucas, D. Wheeler, and H. Hettige, Economic development, environmental regulation and the international migration of toxic industrial pollution: 1960–1988, Paper presented at the Symposium on International Trade and the Environment, The World Bank, Nov. (1991).
16. E. Lutz, Agricultural trade liberalization, price changes and environmental effects, *Environ. Resource Econom.* **2**, 79–89 (1992).
17. K. McConnell, An economic model of soil conservation, *Amer. J. Agr. Econom.* **65**, 83–89 (1983).
18. M. Michaely, D. Papageorgiou, and A. Choksi, "Liberalizing Foreign Trade: Lessons of Experience in the Developing World," Blackwell, Oxford (1991).
19. R. Ram, Exports and economic growth: Some additional evidence, *Econom. Develop. Cultural Change* **33**, 415–425 (1985).
20. P. Romer, Increasing returns and long-run growth, *J. Polit. Economy* **94**, 1002–1037 (1986).
21. A Razin and L. Svensson, An asymmetry between imports and export taxes, *Econom. Lett.* **13**, 33–57 (1983).
22. S. Schmidheiny, "Changing Course: A Global Business Perspective on Development and the Environment," MIT Press, Cambridge, MA (1992).
23. E. Schuh, International economic policies and sustainable development, Paper presented at the Workshop on the Economics of Sustainable Development, Washington, DC (1990).
24. A. Steer, The environment for development, *Finance Develop.*, June 18–21, (1992).
25. J. Sutton, Ed., "Agricultural Trade and Natural Resources: Discovering the Critical Linkages," Rieumer, Boulder/London (1988).
26. P. Uimonen and J. Whalley, Trade and environment, Unpublished, The World Bank (1991).
27. World Bank "World Development Report 1992," Oxford Univ. Press, New York (1992).

[15]

North–South Trade and the Global Environment

By GRACIELA CHICHILNISKY *

Differences in property rights create a motive for trade among otherwise identical regions. Two regions with identical technologies, endowments, and preferences will trade if one, the South, has ill-defined property rights on environmental resources. Trade with a region with well-defined property rights transmits and enlarges the problem of the commons: the North overconsumes underpriced resource-intensive products imported from the South. This occurs even though trade equalizes all prices, of goods and factors, worldwide. Taxing the use of resources in the South is unreliable as it can lead to more overextraction. Property-rights policies may be more effective. (*JEL* A13, F10, F02, K11, O10, Q20)

Why has the global environment emerged as a North–South issue? There is widespread concern about international problems such as acid rain, global warming, biodiversity, and the preservation of the world's remaining rain forests. In June 1992, one hundred nations agreed at Rio de Janeiro to consider a treaty linking environmental policy to economic issues of interest to industrial and developing countries, such as the remission of international sovereign debt and transfer of technology.

In order to develop adequate environmental policies one needs to understand the connection between markets and the environment. Why do developing countries tend to specialize in the production and the export of goods which deplete environmental resources such as rain forests (see Chichilnisky and Geoffrey Heal, 1991)? Do they have a comparative advantage in "dirty industries," and if so, does efficiency dictate that this advantage should be exploited? Is it possible to protect resources without interfering with free markets? Are trade policies based on traditional comparative advantages compatible with environmental preservation?

This paper proposes answers to these questions. It does so by studying patterns of North–South trade in a world economy where the North has better-defined property rights for environmental resources than the South. Property rights have been neglected in the literature on the economics of environment and trade, although they have been recognized as important in other areas of resource allocation (Ronald Coase, 1960; Harold Demsetz, 1967; Jon S. Cohen and Martin Weitzman, 1975). The paper analyzes the interactions between property rights and international trade. It considers a trade model with two countries (North and South), two goods, and two factors, which extends that of Chichilnisky (1981, 1985, 1986; Chichilnisky and Heal, 1987). The environment, which is one of the factors of production, is owned as unregulated common property in the South, and as private property in the North.

Section IV of the paper considers a general completely symmetric case: a world economy consisting of two identical countries, both with the same inputs and outputs, and with the same endowments, technologies, and preferences. The two countries engage in free trade in unregulated and competitive

*Department of Economics, Stanford University, Stanford, CA 94305, and Columbia University. Research support from the U.S. National Science Foundation Grant No. 92-16028, Stanford Institute for Theoretical Economics, (SITE), and Monti di Paschi di Siena is gratefully acknowledged. This paper appeared as Technical Report No. 31 of SITE, in October 1991. I thank Joshua Gans, Geoffrey Heal, Christopher Stone, Wallace Oates, and anonymous referees for helpful comments and suggestions.

markets. The countries differ only in the pattern of ownership of an environmental resource used as an input to production. I consider this case to demonstrate that lack of property rights alone can create trade, and that trade itself can exacerbate the common-property problem. No trade is necessary for efficiency when the two countries are identical, yet trade occurs when they have different property-rights regimes. In this context I establish two general propositions. First, the country with ill-defined property rights overuses the environment as an input to production, and these ill-defined property rights by themselves create a motive for trade between two otherwise identical countries. Second, for the country with poorly defined property rights, trade with a country with well-defined property rights increases the overuse of resources and makes the misallocation worse, transmitting it to the entire world economy. Trade equalizes the prices of traded goods and of factors worldwide, but this does not improve resource allocation. In the resulting world economy, resources are underpriced; there is overproduction by one country and overconsumption by the other. These results have been extended to a dynamic context in Chichilnisky (1993c).

Section V of the paper explores more specific cases. Its purpose is to evaluate policies to check environmental overuse: taxes and property-rights policies. Here, in contrast with Section IV, I allow a realistic asymmetry between the North and the South. The South's resources are produced now either using capital or using labor from a subsistence sector. This labor is not directly traded in the market or employed in other sectors. Subsistence labor is only engaged in the extraction of the environmental resource, which is traded in exchange for capital-intensive goods. In this context I show that taxes on the use of environmental resources in the South are generally unreliable at deterring overextraction. Taxes can force lower-income harvesters to work harder and extract more resources to meet their consumption needs. Taxes can therefore lead to more rather than less extraction of the resource. Therefore, property-rights policies may be preferable in the South as a way of correcting environmental overuse. Examples of such policies are discussed.

Property rights can affect market behavior in many ways. Here I focus on their impact on the supply of resources; these are price-dependent, with their supply curves derived rigorously from micro foundations. I establish that with ill-defined property rights the supply of resources is more price-responsive than it is when property rights are well defined. This price responsiveness is crucial in determining the patterns of international trade; at each price the South offers more resources than the North, leading to apparent comparative advantages in resource-intensive products. This parallels the results of the original North–South model (Chichilnisky, 1981, 1985, 1986), where the price responsiveness of labor supply—called there abundance of labor—played an equally important role in determining the terms of trade and the welfare results from exports of labor-intensive products.

These results offer a new perspective on a current debate, initiated in 1992 by Lawrence Summers, a World Bank economist, about whether developing countries have a comparative advantage in "dirty industries" (see e.g., *The Economist*, 8 February 1992, Vol. 322, p. 66). If so, the argument goes, is it not efficient that they specialize in "dirty industries" and environmentally intensive production?

One response to this is that the apparent comparative advantages may not be actual comparative advantages, an issue which this paper addresses rigorously. They may derive neither from a relative abundance of resources nor from differences in productivity or preferences, not even from lower factor prices, but rather from historical and institutional factors: the lack of property rights for a common-property resource. In this context the South produces and exports environmentally intensive goods to a greater degree than is efficient, and at prices that are below social costs. This happens even if all factor prices are equal across the world, all markets are competitive, and the two regions have identical factor endowments, preferences and technologies. Under those conditions the trade patterns which emerge are inefficient for the world economy as a whole, and for the developing countries themselves. Developing countries are not made better off by specializing in "dirty industries," nor is the world better off if they do.

I. Empirical Motivation: Property Rights, Trade Patterns, and Taxes

The problems described in this paper appear when societies that are still in transition between agricultural and industrialized economies trade with societies already industrialized. Many traditional societies had well developed systems for inducing cooperative outcomes in the use of shared resources. Laws to protect the citizens' property rights in running water were in operation in the United Kingdom in the Middle Ages. Japan had well developed systems for the management of traditional communal lands (*Iriaichi*). Other examples are the communal-field agriculture in the Andes and in medieval England, and the successful sea-tenure systems in Bahia, Brazil, before the arrival of outsiders (see Daniel Bromley, 1992). These traditional systems, however, appear to lapse in the period of transition between agricultural and industrial economies.

Today many environmental resources are unregulated common property in developing countries. Examples are rain forests, which are used for timber or destroyed to give way to the production and export of cash crops such as coffee, sugar, and palm oil. Other examples include grazing land, fisheries, and aquifers, which by the nature of things must usually be shared property even when the land covering the aquifer is privately owned (see Partha Dasgupta, 1992). These are common-property resources whose ownership is shared with future generations. They are typically used as inputs to the production of goods that are traded internationally.

Recent studies show that 90 percent of all tropical deforestation is for the agricultural use of forests, particularly for the international market (C. S. Binley and Jeffrey R. Vincent, 1990; Torsten Amelung, 1991; Edward Barbier et al., 1991; W. F. Hyde and D. H. Newman, 1991). The Korup National Park between Cameroon and Nigeria, at 60 million years old, one of the oldest rain forests in the world and one of the richest in biodiversity, is exploited as an unregulated common-property resource for the production of palm oil, trapping, and other forest products sold in the international market (H. J. Ruitenbeck, 1990). So is the Amazon basin, which is cleared and used as a source of land for the production of cash crops, such as soy beans and coffee, for the international market.

In the now industrialized countries communal land was frequently observed prior to industrialization. Industrialization in England was preceded by the "enclosure" (privatization) of common lands (Cohen and Weitzman, 1975). Now, however, industrial countries have much better defined property rights for their resources than do developing countries. The United States has property-rights regimes for petroleum. These include laws to prevent the overexploitation of common-property resources such as the Conally "Hot Oil Act" of 1936 and "unitization" laws (Steven McDonald, 1971). Water, however, is still treated as common property in parts of Texas and California, leading to misallocation. Japan is well known for its protection of property rights in environmental resources, including even sunlight. Germany recently initiated a parallel system of national accounts which records the depreciation of environmental assets, effectively treating the accounting of national property on the same basis as that of private property. Indeed, the proposal to update all national accounting systems so that they record the depreciation of environmental assets (see Dasgupta and Heal, 1979) is a move toward treating national property on the same accounting basis as private property.

Although today's differences in property rights between industrial and developing countries are easily observed, only tentative explanations can be offered. It is known that the overexploitation of "the commons" emerges from noncooperative situations, or overuse by "free riders" (Dasgupta and Heal, 1979). Cooperative outcomes in the use of communal property resources, such as shared bodies of water, fisheries, and forests, are achieved through the enforcement of punishment and rewards within a stable group, the members of which share a common land site for many generations. One observes a "repeated game" which enforces cooperative outcomes without the need for formally defined individual property rights (Bromley, 1992).

In the period of industrialization, these age-old institutions cease to work, because small and stable populations become large and transient, so that cooperative solutions are more difficult to enforce. This may be why those societies that have completed the process of industrialization rely instead on formal property rights rather than on tradition and custom. The problems described in this paper appear because the South is still in transition, but it trades with already industrialized economies.

Patterns of trade in environmental resources can defy common wisdom. Small countries such as Honduras, with scarce forest resources, export wood to the United States, which has some of the largest forests in the world. Honduras's hardwood (e.g., mahogany) forests have been recently nationalized and are treated as unregulated common property, with no accounting of the depreciation of the forest as an asset, while the United States has better-defined property rights. Currently about two-thirds of Latin American exports are resources, and an even larger proportion holds for Africa. Many of these are produced from common-property sources: Korup National Park and the Amazon are valuable biodiversity reservoirs which are being destroyed in part for the production of export cash crops such as palm oil, soy beans, and coffee. These crops are exported to industrial countries with much higher agricultural productivity and with larger endowments of agricultural land. The puzzle is how to explain such patterns of trade. The exporters do not have a technical advantage in the sense of Ricardo, since their labor is not more productive, and it is unlikely that they have a comparative advantage in the sense of Heckscher-Ohlin either.

These issues are analyzed in Section IV, which establishes that, due to differences in property rights, the countries will trade following the empirically observed patterns of trade just discussed. Since under these conditions markets do not allocate resources efficiently, Section V examines policies to check environmental overuse: taxes and changes in property rights. In Section V, I introduce a realistic difference between the North and the South. In the North, resources are extracted using capital. In the South, resources are extracted either by using capital as in the North, or by using labor from a subsistence sector consisting of workers for whom there is no formal labor market. These workers extract environmental resources from the common-property pool such as a forest. Their labor is not traded directly: they use it to extract resources which are traded for capital-intensive goods at market prices. Workers employed in this fashion exist today in parts of Paraguay, Argentina, and Brazil; they are employed in a so-called "piecemeal" fashion, usually in environmentally related sectors such as timber and agriculture, and are unemployable in other sectors because of their lack of formal education. Workers who extract wood and trappings from common-property land, such the Korup rain forest in Nigeria, appear to conform to this pattern (see Ruitenbeck, 1990), and so do those who extract rubber in the Amazon. Such patterns also appear within firms: much of the Amazon's land is treated as unregulated common property by firms which buy forest products from their employees in a piecemeal fashion, at market prices. This specification also has some points in common with the formulation of abundant labor in Chichilnisky (1981, 1986), and it fits well with the results of empirical studies of subsistence labor in agriculture in Latin American countries, such as Thomas Schweigert's (1993) research on Guatemalan agriculture.

The first policy considered in Section V is a tax which the South levies on the use of environmental resources, the revenues of which are spent on the capital-intensive good. The intention is to raise the producer's costs and to deter its use of environmental resources. In this context I show that taxes will not always work as intended. As taxes decrease the demand for resources, the harvesters receive lower prices for their products. This can force the harvesters to work harder and lead them to extract more rather than less of the resources, a possibility which is explored rigorously in this paper (Proposition 2; see also World Bank [1992]). For this reason, taxes in the South are generally ineffective and can be unreliable: when the workers' demand for marketed goods is relatively inelastic, taxes can lead to more extraction of resources, defeating their original purpose (Proposition 3).

II. The North–South Model

Following Chichilnisky (1981, 1985, 1986), consider a model with two goods, two inputs, and two countries, similar to that of Heckscher Ohlin, except that here the supplies of inputs are price-dependent. For example, the supply of resources is $E^s = E^s(p_E)$, where p_E is the price of the resource E. The model for one region is as follows. Capital (K) and the environmental resource (E) are used to produce two goods, A and B: one good, B, is more intensive in the use of the environmental resources than the other, A, which is more capital-intensive.[1] Production exhibits constant returns to scale; a concave utility function $U(A, B)$ is postulated. Both E and K are supplied by continuous supply functions $E = E(p_E)$ and $K = K(r)$, where p_E is the price of the environmental resource, and r is the rental of capital. E is extracted from a resource pool using an input x which has opportunity cost q; this cost q is endogenously derived in Proposition 2 and Appendix C, as are all other prices and quantities, in a general-equilibrium fashion. To show that the results are robust under different model specifications, the input used to extract E is taken to be quite general in this model: it can be capital (as in Section IV, Theorem 1), subsistence labor, or either of the two (as in Section V, Propositions 2 and 3). The supply of the environmental resource E is formally derived in Proposition 1, where it is shown to vary systematically with the property rights of the resource pool. Since endowments, technologies, and preferences are defined, all ingredients of a general-equilibrium model are provided. A one-region competitive equilibrium is a price vector $\mathbf{p}^*$ at which each of the four markets (for A, B, E, and K) clears.

The two-region model (North–South) is defined as usual by considering two one-region models together and, to allow for international trade, by relaxing the hypothesis that each commodity market (for A and B) clears in each region to require instead that the world markets for A and B must clear. Input markets clear in each country because, as is standard in international trade, the factors of production (K and E) are only traded domestically. Appendix B provides a set of equations and computes an equilibrium of the North–South model, which is shown to be unique in Appendix C.

The model differs from earlier versions of the North–South model (Chichilnisky, 1981, 1985, 1986) in that in those versions all goods were privately owned, and the supply functions of the endowments were exogenously given. Here, instead, the supply of input E is derived explicitly from microeconomic behavior and is shown to depend on the property-rights regime. There is, however, an unexpected similarity with the original North–South model: the crucial role played by the responsiveness of resource supplies to their price. With common-property regimes, more is supplied at any given price than is supplied with private-property regimes (Proposition 1). Since at each price the quantity supplied under common property exceeds that supplied under private property, resources appear to be more "abundant" with common property. A similar responsiveness of supplies, but of labor instead of resources, appears as a

[1]This is a standard assumption in trade theory: it means that the production of good B requires a higher ratio of input K than does the production of good I. This is formalized in Appendix B.

crucial parameter in Chichilnisky (1981, 1986): it measures "labor abundance" in the South and determines whether the country will benefit from increasing its exports of labor-intensive goods or not.

III. Property Rights and the International Supply of Resources

Property rights act on the market in many complex ways. Here I identify a simple but critical way in which property rights enter in a general-equilibrium trade model and propose a transparent and general explanation of how they determine the patterns of trade and the welfare of the traders. *The two regions are assumed to differ solely in their property rights for a pool of resources from which one input to production is extracted.* For example, the property rights on forests from which wood and pulp are produced are different in the North and the South.

How do property rights affect trade? Tracing the impact of property rights is nothing more and nothing less than a comparative-statics exercise: the comparison of a world equilibrium in which both regions have well-defined property rights with a second world equilibrium in which the South does not.[2] In principle, this could be a complex undertaking. However, when property rights involve solely an input of production as they do here, their effects can be summarized in a simple fashion: by their impact on resources supplied. Indeed, Proposition 1 below establishes that, for each price of the resource, more is supplied under unregulated common property than under private property. Therefore the comparative-statics exercise need only compare a world where the two countries have the same supply curve for resources with another world where the South has a different supply curve than the North: it supplies more at each price.

In practice, therefore, one compares the equilibrium of a market with two identical traders to the equilibrium of another market in which the traders are identical *except* for their supply of resources. In the first equilibrium both countries have the identical *private-property supply curve* $E^{P}(p_E)$. In the second, the South has, instead, a *common-property supply curve* $E^{C}(p_E)$, which prevails with ill-defined property rights. The North has one supply curve throughout, which arises with well-defined property rights. Why are the two curves different in the South?

Under unregulated[3] common-property regimes the harvester's cost of extracting an additional unit of E is relatively low. It merely reflects the opportunity costs of the inputs used to extract the resources: in the case of a fishery, the costs incurred in catching; and in the case of an aquifer, the costs incurred in obtaining the water. These costs do not reflect the full impact on other users of one individual's use of the resource pool. In the case of the fishery or a forest, each unit extracted decreases the stock available to others and increases their extraction costs. This could eventually lead to the depletion of the stock. In a private-property regime matters are different. Externalities are fully internalized so that the cost to a harvester of extracting the resource reflects fully the costs this imposes on the extraction by others and could increase rapidly with the level of extraction (Dasgupta and Heal, 1979 Ch. 3).

In its simplest possible form, the argument is that with private property the efficient harvester equates the relative prices of inputs and outputs to the *marginal* productivity. Instead, with common property and with many producers, the relative prices are often equated to *average* productivity. If production has decreasing returns to scale,

[2]At the second world equilibrium prices are distorted, since one of the traders, the South, does not satisfy the marginal optimality conditions (Proposition 1 below and Appendix A); therefore although the first world equilibrium is a competitive equilibrium, the second is a general equilibrium but is not a competitive equilibrium.

[3]I consider here unregulated common property, which is also called "open access"; it must be differentiated from regulated common property.

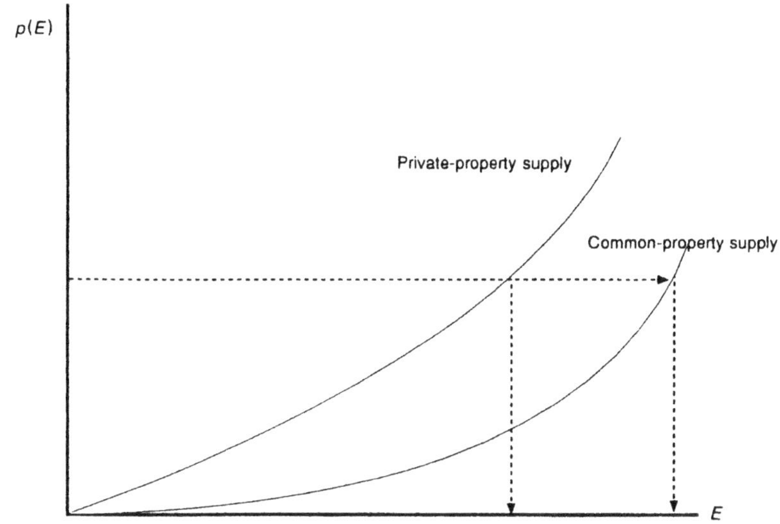

FIGURE 1. AT EACH PRICE, THE COMMON-PROPERTY SUPPLY EXCEEDS THE PRIVATE-PROPERTY SUPPLY.

then average productivity is always larger than marginal productivity, so that at the same prices there is always an incentive to produce more under common-property regimes. This argument is actually valid much more generally: it is true for any finite number of harvesters and without invoking marginal and average costs; under general conditions it leads to the following proposition, which is rigorously established in Appendix A within a Nash equilibrium framework.

PROPOSITION 1: *The common-property supply curve for the resource lies below the private-property supply curve, so that under common-property regimes, more is supplied at any given price. Both supply curves are increasing functions of resource prices.*

(Proposition 1 is illustrated in Figure 1.)

It is worth emphasizing that this proposition does not depend on what input is used for extracting the resource: for example the input used could be either capital or labor. Indeed, both inputs are considered in the paper. The difference of supplies with private and common property regimes has substantial practical implications. It leads by itself to different concepts of comparative advantages and of gains from trade. These are crucial to current policy because they clarify whether developing countries have a comparative advantage in environmentally intensive exports and, if so, whether such advantage should be exploited.

IV. Property Rights, Comparative Advantages, and Gains from Trade

The completely symmetric case of the North–South model is utilized in this section because it shows very clearly the role of property rights in determining patterns of trade. The comparative advantages of nations with price-dependent endowments are defined as follows: region S is said to have a *comparative advantage* in the production of good B which is intensive in the use of the input E, when for each price p_E the supply of E relative to that of K in region S is larger than the corresponding supplies in region N. *Actual comparative advantages* rely on the private-property supply curve for E, which internalizes all the externalities that each unit of extraction has on others.

This is the supply curve corresponding to points in the economy's efficient frontier.

It is worth noting that this definition of comparative advantage, while rather natural, differs from classical ones. This must be the case because Ricardian comparative advantages cannot exist in a world where countries have identical technologies, as considered here. Nor can Heckscher-Ohlin comparative advantages be well defined here, since the endowments of factors are price-dependent, so at different prices the countries can exhibit different Heckscher-Ohlin advantages, measured as the relative endowments of production.

A correct understanding of the comparative advantages of developing countries is, as already pointed out, a substantial policy concern. To examine the matter it will prove useful to consider *apparent comparative advantages*. These are defined in the same manner as actual comparative advantages, but using for each price the supply curve corresponding to the prevailing property regimes in each region, which in the South corresponds to the case in which some externalities are not internalized. Apparent comparative advantages of the South reflect its institutional constraints, in this case inadequate property rights, which may hinder the attainment of full optimality. A market response by the South to these institutional constraints leads it to behave as if it has a comparative advantage even if it does not. When institutional constraints are binding, apparent comparative advantages prevail; observers could then attribute to developing countries a comparative advantage in exporting environmentally intensive products which they do not actually have.

It must be noted that here the two regions are identical except for property rights, so that neither region has a comparative advantage over the other. However, Proposition 1 established that the South, with ill-defined property rights, exhibits an *apparent* comparative advantage in the production of the resource-intensive good. This is because at each price the South supplies more resources than does the North, so its resources appear to be "more abundant."

Theorem 1 below uses another useful concept, *gains from trade*, which are measured as usual by the increase of utility $U(A,B)$ associated with a move from autarky (i.e., where each country maximizes utility within its own production possibility set) to a world equilibrium. Again it is useful to differentiate between apparent and actual gains from trade in the South. *Apparent gains from trade* are computed by comparing welfare in a model where the production possibility sets emerge from common-property supply curves. *Actual gains from trade* are defined, instead, by using the private-property supply curve. The weaker the property rights in the South, namely, the less the production externalities are internalized, the larger will be the divergence between its common-property and private-property supply curves, and between the apparent and actual production possibilities.[4] Thus the weaker the property rights in the South, the larger will be the divergence between its apparent and its actual gains from trade.

The following theorem shows that trade by a region with ill-defined property rights with another with well-defined rights leads to apparent comparative advantages when none exist, and to apparent gains but actual losses from trade. It is established for two identical regions with the same technologies and preferences, both using the same technology to extract resources E using capital K, $E = F(K)$; the initial endowment of capital $\bar{K}$ is the same in the two regions. The theorem compares two equilibria: one in which both countries have the same property rights (private property) over the resource pool, with another in which the South has common property. The model is formally defined in Appendix B; the theorem and its corollary are proved in Appendix C.

THEOREM 1: *Consider the North–South model in which both regions have identical*

[4]The North–South model has one parameter (α, a real number), which can be used to represent the degree of internalization of property rights (see Appendixes A and B).

technologies, the same homothetic preferences, and the same endowment of inputs $\bar{K}$. (a) The model as defined in Appendix B has at most one competitive equilibrium. (b) If the pool from which the environmental resource is extracted is unregulated common property in the South, then the South exhibits apparent comparative advantages in environmentally intensive goods even though neither region has any (actual) comparative advantage over the other. (c) At a world equilibrium the two regions trade, and the South exports environmentally intensive goods at a price that is below social cost. The equilibrium is not Pareto efficient. (d) Trade makes things worse, in the sense that the overuse of the resource increases as the South moves from autarky to trade. Furthermore, trade leads to lower resource prices worldwide. (e) The South shows apparent gains from trade, even though it has no actual gains from trade. It extracts more environmental resources, and it produces and exports more environmentally intensive goods than is Pareto efficient.

Note that the environmental overuse described in Theorem 1 is induced by a competitive market response. There is no regulation in either country, and all markets are free and competitive.

COROLLARY 1: *Trade between the North and the South leads to the equalization of the prices of all traded goods and of all inputs of production, and in particular to the equalization of the price of environmental inputs in the two regions. However prices for environmentally intensive goods are below social costs. At a competitive equilibrium the South uses more environmental resources and produces and exports more environmentally intensive goods than the North, and more than is Pareto optimal.*

This corollary calls attention to the possibility that the overexporting of environmentally intensive goods from developing countries, such as mineral by-products, wood products, or cash crops, may not be due to the fact that the production costs are lower in the South than in the North, as is sometimes thought. For example, under unregulated common-property regimes for environmental resources, a country such as Mexico would export environmentally intensive agricultural products, or products produced from "dirty industries," even if its forest land, clean air, and machinery were as expensive as they are in the industrial countries and even if it had the same technologies and preferences. Equalizing factor prices through the international market does not resolve the problem of overuse of environmental resources.

V. Environmental Policies

Since unregulated competitive markets do not lead to efficient allocations with ill-defined property rights, the task of this section of the paper is to analyze policies that could correct the problem of environmental overuse, focusing first on taxes. Taxes will be considered in a general-equilibrium framework, tracing their full incidence on all prices and quantities worldwide. This approach captures the impact of taxes in an economy where income effects prevail, a case particularly relevant to developing countries.

A realistic asymmetry is introduced between the North and the South in this section. In the South the environmental resource E is extracted either using capital as in Section IV above or, alternatively, by workers from a subsistence sector. These workers do not sell their labor directly in the marketplace. Instead, they use their labor to extract the resource, which they exchange for capital-intensive goods in the marketplace. This specification is less symmetric than that of Section IV. It captures a stylized fact in developing countries where many markets, including labor markets, are less developed than in industrial countries; empirical motivation for this was provided in Section I. Proposition 3 will contrast the effects of taxes within these two alternative specifications of the process for extracting E in the North and the South. The economy of the North remains as in Section IV.

A. *Lower Resource Prices Can Lead to More Extraction: The Opportunity Cost of Subsistence Labor*

Does the South extract more or less resources after taxes? This is studied rigorously in the next subsection and in Appendix C. Taxes alter extraction because they induce price changes. Here I trace how this occurs. In particular, I show how resource extraction changes with the opportunity costs of the inputs that are used to extract the resources.

No matter what input is used (labor or capital), and no matter what the property-rights regime, in this model the supply of the resource E always increases when the relative price of outputs to inputs increases (Appendix A). However, in a market economy the cost of an input is its opportunity cost, and this typically changes along with the price of the resource itself. The relevant issue is therefore whether the opportunity cost of the inputs relative to that of the resource increases.

What are the opportunity costs of inputs? How are they affected by resource prices? There is a simple answer when capital is employed to extract the resource: the opportunity cost then equals the rental on capital (r), and r varies across the equilibria of the model in a well-specified fashion: it is inversely related to the price of the resource [Appendix B, equation (3)].

A difficulty arises when E is extracted instead by subsistence workers. Since by definition no formal market exists for subsistence labor, market wages, which would be the natural proxy for the opportunity cost of labor, are not available. It is nevertheless possible to deduce implicitly the opportunity cost q of subsistence workers' time, to explore how this changes with the prices of the produced goods, and to see how this affects the extraction of resources. Proposition 2 shows how. Its formulation opens up a whole range of issues which are unobservable in a partial-equilibrium formulation, and which are useful for understanding the behavior of resource markets with low-income populations. It formalizes the intuition that a drop in the price of a resource can force lower-income harvesters to work harder and extract more resources in order to meet their consumption needs. Discussions about this phenomenon appear in the World Bank's 1992 *World Development Report*, without any formal analysis.

Assume that the harvesters' endowments consist solely of their labor input ($\bar{x} = 24$ hours a day). A harvester trades his harvest of resources E for the good A at competitive market prices. Each harvester has strictly concave increasing utility function $u_i(A, \bar{x} - x_i)$, which increases in leisure $(\bar{x} - x_i)$ and in consumption (A). The harvester's problem is

$$(1) \qquad \max_{x_i} \left[u_i(A, \bar{x} - x_i) \right]$$

subject to

$$p_A A = p_E E^C(x_i)$$

For each p_A and p_E, the solution $E^C(x_i)$ is the optimal quantity extracted by the harvester, where p_A and p_E are determined by the market in a general-equilibrium fashion. Proposition 1 (proved in Appendix A) explains the quantity of resource extracted in a different manner: it shows that it depends on resource prices p_E and on the opportunity cost of labor, q. In a general-equilibrium world these two ways of explaining extraction must tally: this observation allows one to derive rigorously the opportunity cost q of a worker's labor (which was previously treated as an exogenous parameter) endogenously, as a function of the prices p_A and p_E. This derivation proves that, as is intuitively obvious, q equals the rate of substitution between leisure and consumption of A [see Appendix C equation (C7)]. Recall that the "terms of trade" between leisure and consumption are determined by the competitive market, because the market determines the price of the good A and the price of the good E which is exchanged for A by the harvester. Therefore the market determines implicitly the opportunity cost of subsistence labor, q.

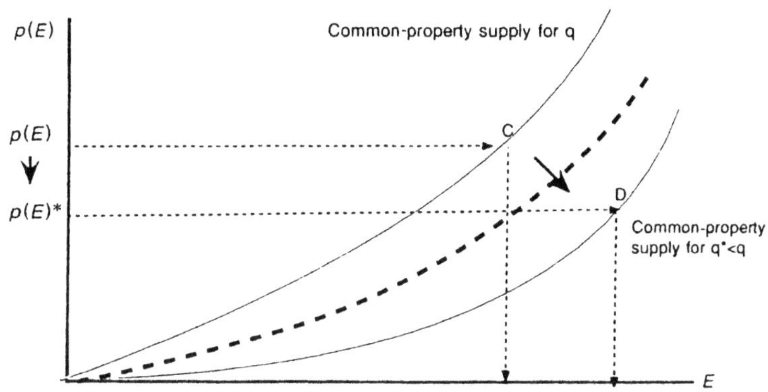

FIGURE 2. THE COMMON-PROPERTY SUPPLY CURVE SHIFTS WITH DROPS IN THE OPPORTUNITY COST OF THE INPUT USED IN EXTRACTING THE RESOURCE, q.

Note: As established in Proposition 2, the equilibrium level of output of E increases as $p(E)$ drops to $p(E)^*$, because the corresponding opportunity cost drops to q^*.

Consider now a North–South model as defined in Section II but with the addition indicated above. E is supplied by the type of harvesters just defined: they own only labor, extract and trade the resource E for the good A, and their utilities have elasticity of substitution $\sigma < 1$. I call this *the North–South model with a subsistence sector*. The following proposition studies the consequences of a drop in resource prices; its proof is in Appendix C.

PROPOSITION 2: *Under the assumptions made above, a drop in the price of resources leads to a drop in the opportunity cost of labor of the subsistence worker in the South. At the new, lower resource prices, more effort is applied by the harvester, and more resources are extracted.*

(Proposition 2 is illustrated in Appendix Fig. C1.)

Why do lower resource prices lead to more extraction? One explanation is that harvesters have relatively inelastic demand for the marketed good A. If so, as the relative price of the resource falls, the proportion of total expenditure spent on A rises, and the quantity of resources extracted must increase, because each unit of the resource brings now lower revenue. Here I do not assume this inelastic behavior of demand: I prove that it arises naturally from utility maximization on the part of the harvester when the harvester's utility u_i has an elasticity of substitution σ less than 1 (Appendix C). This result is useful in practice because the condition $\sigma < 1$ is plausible and rather general: for example, with constant-elasticity-of-substitution (CES) utilities, $\sigma < 1$ is always satisfied when the indifferences of u_i do not intersect the axis (see Hal Varian, 1992 pp. 19–20), which is a standard case. Note however that the proof of Proposition 2 applies to a general class of concave utilities with $\sigma < 1$ and does not require that u_i be CES or any other functional form.

The result in Proposition 2 has useful implications under more general conditions as well. It highlights the weakness of any policy that leads to a drop in resource prices in lower-income countries: as prices drop, by continuity, harvesters with relatively low elasticity of substitution do not decrease their extraction very much. Lower resource prices are therefore ineffective at deterring overextraction.

The proposition also highlights the crucial role of the opportunity costs of labor in determining the extraction of resources. This is of practical interest because the opportunity cost of subsistence labor q could be regarded as a policy variable: this opportunity cost could be increased by providing productive job opportunities for subsistence workers outside the environmental sector. The general point is that any policy that increases the opportunity cost of subsistence labor could have beneficial environmental effects. Figure 2 illustrates how: at each resource price, a lower opportunity cost q leads to a shift in the supply curve for resources as illustrated (and established rigorously in Appendix C). Under the conditions, lower resource prices lead to an even lower opportunity cost of labor, and the ratio of output to input prices q/p_E actually *increases*. Because of this, at lower resource prices the subsistence harvesters extract more resources than they did before. In Figure 2 this is shown as a move from point C to D.

In summary, in lower-income regions a drop in the price of resources can lead to more poverty, and this in turn can lead to more extraction. A policy that induces lower resource prices does not provide an effective way of checking environmental overuse. This provides a key to the following results on taxes.

B. *Taxes in the South*

The next proposition shows that the results of taxing the use of the resource could be just the opposite of what is expected if all prices are allowed to adjust to their new market-clearing levels: taxes could lead to more extraction. Intuitively this occurs because the resource is extracted by lower-income subsistence workers whose demand for consumption goods is somewhat inelastic. The trade literature has not covered this case, which is implicit in the discussions of the World Bank's 1992 *World Development Report* with respect to the effects of poverty on the environment. Exploring this possibility requires tracing all impacts of taxes on prices, quantities, and income, a somewhat complex task.[5] Most of the international trade literature on taxation uses a partial-equilibrium framework. However, some of the most important effects of taxes in developing countries are income effects, and these cannot be examined properly in a partial-equilibrium.

For example, corrective tariffs and subsidies in a partial-equilibrium framework have been studied in Dixit and Norman (1980). However, as in all partial-equilibrium analysis, these results occur in a world where the terms of trade and all factor prices remain fixed throughout. Consider for example a standard policy of taxing the use of the common-property resource in order to restrict its use. When prices remain fixed, such a tax has the effect of deterring use. The tax increases the relative price of the resource, and this leads to less use of it as an input.

It is not always realistic to assume that prices remain fixed after taxes. Taxes alter income and therefore alter demand and hence prices. The classical works of Abba Lerner (1936) and Lloyd Metzler (1949) analyzed tariffs on traded goods which have general-equilibrium effects on the terms of trade of the trading regions. I shall consider here, instead, a tariff which is levied domestically on the use of the resource E which is a (nontraded) input to production.

The complexity of tracing the effects of taxes on all prices and quantities is alleviated by an unusual feature of the North–South model which makes it particularly useful for this purpose: it has an explicit analytic solution, which is obtained by solving a second-order equation in the terms of trade, from which all other endogenous variables are determined explicitly. This

[5]In their *Theory of International Trade* (Section 2, Policy Responses to Distortions and Constraints"), Avinash Dixit and Victor Norman (1980 p. 176) state: "Having examined the terms of trade and interpersonal distribution at some length, we now put them aside by assuming a *small one-consumer economy* [i.e., partial-equilibrium analysis]. This is done in order to highlight the new questions that are raised by the presence of further constraints on policy. It is not in principle difficult to combine everything into a grand model, but its algebraic complexity obscures all economic understanding."

procedure was introduced in Chichilnisky (1981, 1986) and is the methodology that is used in establishing Proposition 3 below.

The relative price of exports and imports of the South, p_B/p_A ($=p_B$ since $p_A=1$) are called the South's *terms of trade*.

PROPOSITION 3: *Consider the North–South model with a subsistence sector in the South which extracts the resource E from a common-property pool. The North has well-defined property rights. Assume further that a unit tax T is imposed on the producers in the South for their use of the resource E as an input of production: all producers pay* p_E+T *per unit of the input E. Furthermore, assume that the tax revenues increase the domestic demand for the product that does not use the environmental resource E intensively, namely, for the good A. Then the tax always leads to:*

(i) *a decrease in the price of the resource E,*
(ii) *a drop in the South's terms of trade* p_B,
(iii) *an increase in the extraction of the resource E in the South, and*
(iv) *an increase in its exports of the environmentally intensive good B for some parameter values.*[6]

If the South produces E using capital, the tax leads also to (i), (ii), and (iv), but instead of (iii) to

(iii)′ *a drop in the extraction of the resource E in the South.*

(See Appendix C for the proof.)

An intuitive explanation for this proposition is as follows. A unit tax T on the use of the resource E is collected from the producers who use E as an input. The tax proceeds TE are allocated to increasing the demand of the non-resource-intensive sector, A, giving the tax the best opportunity to work in the intended direction, namely, reducing the demand for resource-intensive products. The relative price of the environmentally intensive good B then drops; this is (ii). The drop in demand for B leads to a decreased demand, and a lower price, for the resource E; this is (i). Therefore, after taxes, the price of resources, E, is lower.

Consider first the case when the harvesters use subsistence labor as an input. If the resource E is extracted by the subsistence sector, then after taxes the price of E is lower and the supply of E is higher (this follows from Proposition 2); this is (iii).

The second case is when E is extracted using capital as an input. Since p_E is lower after taxes, the cost of capital r is higher: these two variables are always inversely related across equilibria [see equations (B1) in Appendix B]. Since the opportunity cost of the harvesters' labor is higher and output prices are lower after taxes, the supply of the environmental resource decreases; this is (iii)′.

Finally the exports of B increase after the increase in p_E if and only if price effects dominate; when income effects dominate then exports decrease (see also Chichilnisky, 1981, 1986); this is (iv).

VI. Conclusions: Property Rights and North–South Trade

Differences in property-rights regimes for environmental resources can account for some puzzling aspects of the patterns of trade between the North and the South. The problems analyzed in this paper arise when societies which are in transition from agricultural to industrial economies, such as the South today, trade with already industrialized societies. The South exports environmentally intensive goods even if it is not well endowed with them. The South overproduces, and the North overconsumes, even if trade equalizes all traded goods and all factor prices worldwide.

I have discussed several environmental policies. Section V examined tax policies in the South and established that they are not always reliable. When environmental resources are extracted using subsistence labor, taxes can lead to more extraction. I

[6]Formally, exports increase if and only if the condition $c_2/D<2p_Ep_B$ is satisfied, a condition which is shown to be satisfied precisely when "income effects dominate" (see the penultimate paragraph of Appendix C).

showed that anything that decreases the price of the resource can increase poverty and lead to more extraction, an observation which was made in the World Bank's 1992 *World Development Report*. Taxes can have this effect, because they can decrease the demand for environmental goods, which are a main source of income for the subsistence sector.

A main argument in favor of property-rights policies is that once these have been implemented, no market intervention is needed. Consider, for example, any policy which improves the property of Amazonian small farmers, such as rubber-tappers. This will change the supply function of Amazonian resources as shown in Proposition 1, reducing output at each price. In turn this will change the computation of comparative advantages and of gains from trade from agricultural exports based on deforestation of the Amazon. Production patterns shift, and export patterns will reflect more fully the social cost of deforesting the Amazon.

Examples of such property-rights approaches are provided by recent agreements involving debt-for-nature swaps (Ruitenbeck, 1990). Another example is provided by recent agreements between the United States pharmaceutical industry and Costa Rica. The spearhead of this project is a pair of ingenious efforts to exploit the forests to obtain medicinal products.[7] A Costa Rican research institute (INBIO) is prospecting for promising plants, microorganisms, and insects to be screened for medical uses by Merck and Company, the world's largest drug company. Merck, in turn, is supporting the prospecting effort financially and will share any resulting profits with Costa Rica. Thus Costa Rica has acquired property rights over the "intellectual property" embodied in the genetic information within its forests. A similar initiative was taken by a small Californian company, Shaman Pharmaceuticals, which is tapping the expertise of traditional healers, "Shamans" or medicine people, in various parts of the tropics (see Chichilnisky, 1993a). The company intends to promote the conservation of the forests by channeling some of its profits back to the localities whose medicine people provided the key plants. The theory behind both ventures is that everybody wins: the world gets new drugs, the pharmaceutical companies earn profits, and people in the localities are justly compensated for their "intellectual property" and their conservation and collection efforts.[8]

Similar examples hold for land resources. Recently the government of Ecuador allocated a piece of the Amazon the size of the state of Connecticut to its Indian population, a clear property-rights policy.[9] Under the conditions examined here, this policy should lead to a better use of the forest's resources and to a more balanced pattern of trade between Ecuador and the United States.[10]

However, property rights change slowly because they require expensive legal infrastructure and enforcement. Poor countries may find themselves unable to implement such policies quickly. The improvement of property rights of indigenous populations in developing countries, which house most of the world's population, should nevertheless

[7]The plans were described at a symposium held in January 1992 at Rockefeller University, organized jointly by the Rain Forest Alliance, and the New York Botanical Garden's Institute of Economic Botany (see e.g., the report in *Science Times*, science supplement to *The New York Times*, 28 January 1992, p. C1).

[8]Examples of successful medical discoveries from rain forests and other natural sources include widely used medicines such as aspirin, morphine, quinine, curare, the rosy periwinkle used to treat childhood leukemia and Hodgkin's disease, and (more recently) taxol.

[9]Indian groups will gain title to land in Pastaza Province, a traditional homelands area covering 4,305 square miles in eastern Ecuador. Ecuador's move is part of a wider trend in the Amazon basin. Achuar, Shiwiar, and Quiche Indians will soon administer an area where population density averages five people per square mile.

[10]In fact, forest and other environmental assets have public-good aspects, which have not been covered here. Markets with public goods have different behavior and require a different treatment. For example, Lindahl prices or particular distributions of endowments are needed for efficiency (see Chichilnisky et al., 1993).

be considered a major policy goal.[11] There is a small but apparently growing trend of this type in Brazil, Bolivia, Columbia, Ecuador, French Guyana, and Venezuela.[12] Property-rights policies, either through government action or preferably through private enterprise, as in the examples offered here, provide a hopeful foundation for resolving some North–South environmental issues. Improving property rights should also lead to better, more balanced income patterns, since one of the most direct causes of poverty in the developing countries is the lack of entitlements for land and environmental resources such as clean water (Dasgupta, 1992). Similarly, as I have shown here, poverty can prevent environmental policies based on taxation from having their intended effects. Poverty and environmental overuse have a common root, and both are at the core of the North–South environmental dilemma.

Inexpensive environmental resources are a main source of environmental overuse. The statement that resources are overconsumed is practically equivalent to the statement that they are underpriced. Environmental overuse does not occur solely because the locals overconsume their resources, but because they export these resources to a rich international market at prices that are below social costs. This is why the global environmental issue is inextricably connected with North–South trade. The South overproduces, and the North overconsumes. The international market transmits and enlarges the externalities of the global commons. No policy that ignores this connection can work.

Appendix A: Resource Extraction and Property Rights

The Nash Equilibrium of the Harvester Extraction Problem with Unregulated Common-Property Resources.—The extraction of the input E is carried out by N "harvesters" of an unregulated common-property pool, indexed $i = 1,\dots,N$. Let x_i be the input of harvester i, and let $x = \sum_{i=1}^{n} x_i$. All harvesters are identical and interchangeable, so that the total harvest can be expressed as a function $E = F(x)$ of the total input. Assume also that all harvesters are symmetric, so that each harvester obtains as its output a fraction of the total output equal to the fraction that it supplies of the total input, formally, $E_i = F(x)(x_i/x)$. This insures uniqueness of the solutions. These are all standard assumptions (Dasgupta and Heal, 1979). Each harvester chooses its input level x_i to maximize the value of its share of outputs net of costs, $p_E E_i(x_i) - qx_i$, taking as given p_E, q, and the input levels of others, x_j for $j \neq i$. Here p_E is the market-induced price of the resource, and q is the "opportunity cost" of the input x_i; both q and p_E are endogenously determined in Appendixes B and C along with all other prices in a general-equilibrium fashion.

[11] Judge Alvaro Eduardo Junqueira declared that a shipload of mahogany sold by C&C Industria e Comercio was illegally felled and stolen from Indian reserves in the Amazon region, and he ordered the immediate seizure of thousands of cubic meters of mahogany bound to London. Tradelink, the London-based timber agent, stated that they will cease purchasing wood from C&C Industria e Comercio if the theft is confirmed (see *Financial Times*, 29 October 1993, pp. 1, 34). The matter is causing embarrasement for Britain's Timber Trade Federation: Britain imports about half of Brazil's entire mahogany exports.

[12] In the last three years, the Governments of Ecuador, Columbia, and Venezuela have restricted most of their Amazon areas as national parks or Indian reserves, as have Brazil and Bolivia, and France has made plans to protect a third of French Guyana. Last year, a coalition of Amazon Indians and foreign and local environmentalists confronted U.S. oil companies to induce them to abandon plans for extracting oil in Ecuador's Amazon (see J. Kane, 1993). Ecuador, one of South America's poorest countries, draws currently about $50 million yearly in revenues from oil exports. In the highlands of Ecuador, Indian groups have expressed similar resistance to export-oriented farming. José Maria Cabascango, leader of Indigenous Nationalities of Ecuador which is said to represent the nation's estimated two million Indians, states: "We should only produce food for our own consumption. The Amazon region has a very fragmented ecology and to continue colonization would destroy it" (see e.g., *New York Times*, 6 September 1992, p. L10. Similar concerns were expressed by Antonio Macedo, Coordinator of the National Council of Rubber-Tappers of the Amazon, of Cruzeiro do Sul, Acre, Brazil, in a recent interview at Columbia University, 7 December 1992. A recent article in the *The New Yorker* (Kane, 1993) highlights the practical issues involved.

$F(0)=0$, $F'(x)>0$, and $F(x)$ is strictly concave, so there are strictly diminishing returns, arising perhaps from the application of increasing amounts of variable input x to a fixed body of land or water, and this insures existence of solutions. This models a Nash equilibrium pattern of use of an unregulated common-property resource, which is unique under the symmetry conditions.

PROOF OF PROPOSITION 1: The marginal product of input is $F'(x)$. The average product is $F(x)/x$, and by strict concavity $F(x)/x > F'(x)$. Look first at marginal products. The private-property marginal product of the input is denoted $\mathrm{MP^P}$, and the common-property marginal product is $\mathrm{MP^C}$. Now, $\mathrm{MP}_i^{\mathrm{C}} = d/dx_i[x_i F(x)]$ equals $d/dx_i[x_i F(x_i + x_{-i})]/(x_i + x_{-i})$ where $x_{-i} = \sum_{j \neq i} x_j$. Hence, under the assumptions,

$$\begin{aligned}\mathrm{MP}_i^{\mathrm{C}} &= F(x)/x + x_i\{[xF'(x) - F(x)]/x^2\}\\ &= F(x)/x\\ &\quad + (x_i/x)[F'(x) - F(x)/x].\end{aligned}$$

Note that the analysis provided here is independent of the number of harvesters as long as there is more than one $(N>1)$. As $N \to \infty$, $x_i/x \to 0$, and the common-property marginal product becomes the average product. In this limiting case we recover the well-known result that harvesters equate input prices to average return rather than to marginal product, the basis of the "tragedy of the commons." Since $\mathrm{MP}_i^{\mathrm{P}} = F'(x)$,

$$\begin{aligned}\mathrm{MP}_i^{\mathrm{P}} - \mathrm{MP}_i^{\mathrm{C}} &= F'(x) - F(x)/x\\ &\quad - (x_i/x)[F'(x) - F(x)/x]\\ &= [F'(x) - F(x)/x][1 - x_i/x]\\ &< 0.\end{aligned}$$

Therefore the common-property marginal product is lower than the private-property one. The private-property supply curve E^{P}, is obtained by equalizing the opportunity cost q with the value of $\mathrm{MP}_i^{\mathrm{P}}$, $q = p_E \mathrm{MP}_i^{\mathrm{P}}$, and the common-property supply curve E^{C} is obtained by equating $q = \mathrm{MP}_i^{\mathrm{C}} p_E$: both supply functions of E as a function of p_E are parameterized by the opportunity cost q of the input x_i.

The last task is to show that, with both private- and common-property regimes, both supply curves increase with the price of the resource E at any given q. For simplicity in the rest of this proof I use E_i to indicate either the common-property supply curve or the private-property supply curve, because the argument that follows applies to both. For each p_E, the harvester's objective is to find x_i which optimizes

$$p_E E_i(x_i) - qx_i. \tag{A1}$$

For each fixed q, the solution to this problem, denoted $x_i(p_E, q)$, is an increasing function of p_E: as the market price of E increases, the marginal productivity of x_i which maximizes the objective function of the harvester must satisfy $p_E(\partial E_i/\partial x_i) = q$. For each p_E and q, this maximization problem defines $E_i = E_i(x_i(p_E, q))$. Note that, for a given q, as p_E increases (A1) implies that $\partial E_i/\partial x_i$ must decrease. The concavity of E_i implies then that the optimal level of input $x_i(p_E, q)$ increases with p_E for any given q (i.e., $\partial x_i/\partial p_E > 0$). Therefore for any given q *the supply curve $E_i(x_i)$ is always increasing in the resource's price p_E*.

Appendix B: Formulation of the North–South Model

Consider a Heckscher-Ohlin formulation of two competitive economies trading with each other, except that factor endowments in the two countries are not fixed, but variable, depending on factor prices. This follows Chichilnisky (1981, 1985, 1986, 1990, 1993b) but differs from these works because they considered privately owned goods only. Variable factors are crucial in the consideration of property rights: Proposition 1 showed that at each price the supply of resources under common-property regimes is larger than with private property, a characterization which requires price-dependent endowments. This paper considers simple production functions with constant returns to scale; the model and its results have been extended to a variety of utility demand specifications, to Cobb-Douglas and CES production functions, and to economies with increasing returns (Chichilnisky, 1993b). Specify first one economy: the South. It produces goods A and B using two inputs, E and K. I consider a fixed-proportions technology in each sector, although there is substitution of factors at the aggregate level. This is because changes in factor prices lead to changes in factor endowments and so to changes in the composition of output and the factor intensity of final production. This could not happen in a Heckscher-Ohlin model, but *can* happen here because factor supplies vary with prices (see also Chichilnisky, 1986).

Production is specified by $B^S = E^B/a_1 = K^B/c_1$, and $A^S = E^A/a_2 = K^A/c_2$, where the superscript S denotes supply and superscripts A and B denote sectors, and where a_1, a_2, c_1, and c_2 are input–output coefficients. $E^S = E^B + E^A$ varies with prices, and so does $K^S = K^B + K^A$. The good B is more resource-intensive than A so that $D = (a_1c_2 - a_2c_1) > 0$. The following equations identify an equilibrium. First, with zero profits in the production of A and B,

(B1) $$p_A = a_1 p_E + c_1 r$$
$$p_B = a_2 p_E + c_2 r$$

or

$$p_E = \frac{p_B c_2 - c_1}{D} \qquad r = \frac{a_1 - p_B a_2}{D}$$

where p_A and p_B are the prices of A and B, respectively, p_E is the price of E, and r is the rental on capital, K. Consider next the exogenously given supply functions for the inputs E and K. It was established in Proposition 1 (see Appendix A) that the supplies of the environmental resource E increase with p_E/q, where q is the opportunity cost of the input used in extracting E. To simplify the computation of solutions consider a simple form of the supply function:

(B2) $$E^S = \alpha p_E/q + E^0 \qquad \alpha > 0.$$

The variable q in (B2) takes different values depending on the input used to extract E: q is r when E is produced from capital K; when E is produced from subsistence labor, p_B is an appropriate proxy for q. Note that when the supply function has the form in (B2) the slope α represents the property-rights regimes for the pool from which E is extracted: as established in Proposition 1 (proof in Appendix A), the supply of E has a larger slope when resources are common property and a smaller one in the case of private property, quite independently of which input is used to extract E. The assumptions made on the property-rights regimes of the economies of the North and the South made in Section III translate therefore into: $\alpha(\mathrm{N}) < \alpha(\mathrm{S})$ and $\alpha(\mathrm{S})$ large, where the letters in parentheses denote the North and the South. The supply for capital is similarly

(B3) $$K^S = \beta r + \bar{K}$$

where $\beta \geq 0$; everything that follows applies for $\beta = 0$ as well (i.e., when K^S is a constant $\bar{K}$). In equilibrium all markets clear:

(B4) $$E^S = E^D \qquad K^S = K^D$$

(B5) $$E^D = E^B + E^A = B^S a_1 + A^2 a_2$$
$$K^D = K^B + K^A = B^S c_1 + A^S c_2$$

where superscript D denotes demand. When the extraction of E uses capital, $K^D = K^B + K^A + K^E$,

(B6) $$B^S = B^D + X_B^S$$
$$A^S = A^D + X_A^D$$

where X_B^S and X_A^D denote exports of B and imports of A, respectively, and

(B7) $$p_B X_B^S = p_A X_A^D$$

(i.e, the value of exports equals the value of imports). The North is specified by a set of equations similar to equations (B1)–(B7) with the same technology parameters and the same capital supply functions, but with different α's (i.e., different supply functions for environmental resources E), as explained in the paragraph following (B2), and discussed in Section III. The two supply functions are now denoted $E^S(S)$ and $E^S(N)$. In a world equilibrium, the prices of the traded goods (A and B) are equal, and exports match imports:

$$\text{(B8)} \qquad p_A(N) = p_A(S)$$

$$p_B(N) = p_B(S)$$

$$X_A^S(N) = X_A^D(S)$$

$$X_B^S(S) = X_B^D(N)$$

where the terms in parentheses, (S) and (N), indicate the North and South, respectively. Since the economies are identical except for property rights, in the two regions there are nine exogenous parameters: a_1, a_2, c_1, c_2, β, $\bar{K}$, E^0, and $\alpha(N)$ and $\alpha(S)$. I add a price-normalization condition $p_A = 1$ and obtain a total of 26 independent equations, (B1)–(B7) for the North and for the South, plus (B8) and $p_A = 1$.[13] There are in total 28 endogenous variables, 14 for each region: p_A, p_B, p_E, r, E^S, E^D, K^S, K^D, A^S, A^D, B^S, B^D, X_B^S, and X_A^D, so the system is underdetermined so far up to two variables, which reflects the fact that demand has not been specified yet. I consider a demand specification which leads to simple analytics (more general utility functions can be considered at the cost of more computation). In each region consider the utility function:

$$\text{(B9)} \qquad U(A,B) = B + k \qquad \text{if } A \geq A^{D*}$$

where $k > 0$, and

$$U(A,B) = B + \gamma A \qquad \text{otherwise}$$

[13] Walras's law assures market-clearing in one of the markets whenever all other markets clear, thus reducing the number of equations presented here by one.

where $\gamma = k/A^{D*} > 0$. For $p_B > 1/\gamma$, agents demand A^{D*} so by choosing k and γ in U appropriately, one may assume:

$$\text{(B10)} \qquad A^D(N) = A^{D*}(N)$$

$$A^D(S) = A^{D*}(S).$$

Thus, I have a system of 28 equations on 28 variables, depending on nine exogenous parameters, and the model is now fully specified. The economies of the two regions are identical except for the parameters $\alpha(N)$ and $\alpha(S)$ which depend on the property rights for the common-property resource in each region. I shall say that property rights are better defined in the North when $\alpha(N) < \alpha(S)$; both countries have the same property right when $\alpha(N) = \alpha(S)$. Note that by inverting equations $E^S = a_1 B^S + a_2 A^S$ and $K^S = c_1 B^S + c_2 A^S$ one obtains

$$\text{(B11)} \qquad B^S = (c_2 E - a_2 K)/D$$

$$A^S = (a_1 K - c_1 E)/D$$

where as before $D = a_1 c_2 - a_2 c_1 > 0$. When the extraction of E uses capital, K in the two equations in (B11) is replaced by $K - K^E$.

Appendix C: Proofs of the Results

Proof of Uniqueness of a Competitive Equilibrium.—The North–South model defined in Appendix B has at most one competitive equilibrium for any parameters $\alpha(S)$ and $\alpha(N)$ representing the structure of property rights in the two regions. In the following, the supply function of resources in (B2) is $E = \alpha p_E / p_B + E^0$, which, as discussed in the paragraph following (B2), corresponds to the case in which E is extracted using subsistence labor, as in Section V. Similar computations obtain when E is extracted using capital (K) as an input; in this latter case, q is replaced by r in (B2) and $K^D = K^S = K^A + K^B + K^E$, where $F(K^E) = E$

(see Proposition 1). From (B8) and (B10),

$$\text{(C1)} \quad A^{D*}(S) - A^{S}(N) = A^{S}(N) - A^{D*}(N).$$

Now rewrite (C1) as a function of one variable only, p_B. Substituting equations (B1)–(B8) and (B11) into (C1), one obtains:

$$\text{(C2)} \quad p_B^2[\psi(S) + \psi(N)] + p_B[A^{D*}(S) + A^{D*}(N) + \Gamma(S) + \Gamma(N)] - [\rho(S) + \rho(N)] = 0$$

where

$$\psi = \beta a_1 a_2 / D \qquad \rho = \alpha c_1^2 / D^2$$

and

$$\Gamma = (1/D)\left[c_1 E^0 - \alpha_1 \bar{K} + (1/D) \times (\alpha c_1 c_2 - \beta a_1 a_2)\right].$$

Equation (C2) is a quadratic equation in p_B which has at most one positive root, because the constant term is negative. Therefore there is at most one equilibrium price p_B^*. From p_B^* one obtains in each country the equilibrium levels of all other variables: p_E^* and r^* from (B1), E^{S*} and K^{S*} from (B2) and (B3), B^{S*} and A^{S*} from (B11), X_A^{D*} from (B10), and A^{D*}, A^{S*}, and X_B^{S*} from (B7) and (B8), so the (unique) full equilibrium of the North–South model is computed.

PROOF OF THEOREM 1:

The completely symmetric case of the North–South model is utilized here because it shows very clearly the role of property rights in determining patterns of trade. Here, the two regions are identical except for property rights: same inputs K and E, same produced goods A and B, same production functions for A and B, and same preferences. In the two regions E is produced by harvesters using an exogenous, fixed endowment of capital $\bar{K}$ as an input, where $\bar{K}$ is the same in the two regions, and using the same production technology f: $K \to E$ (see Proposition 1). The South extracts E from an unregulated common-property pool, and the North does so under private-property regimes. The market-clearing condition for K is $K^D = K^A + K^B + K^E = \bar{K}$, where $F(K^E) = E$ as derived in Proposition 1. In sum, the two regions are identical, but the South's supply of E is given by the common-property supply curve $E^C(p_E)$ while the North's is given by the private-property supply curve $E^P(p_E)$ (see Appendix A). At each price vector, the supply of E in the South exceeds that of the North (see Proposition 1; proof in Appendix A).

Consider now a world equilibrium commodity price vector $\mathbf{p}_w^*$; at the equilibrium, factor prices p_E^* and r^* are the same in the two regions because the two regions have the same technologies (i.e., the same a_1, a_2, c_1, and c_2), and by the zero-profit conditions on the production of A and B given in (B1). However, the South supplies more environmental resources than the North by Proposition 1. By inverting the two linear equations $E^S = a_1 A^S + a_2 B^S$ and $K^S - K^E = c_1 B^S + c_2 A^S$ one obtains

$$B^S = \frac{c_2 E - a_2(K - K^E)}{D}$$

which increases with E because $D > 0$. It follows that at $\mathbf{p}_w^*$ the South produces a larger amount of the traded good B than does the North; intuitively this is a consequence of the fact that B is intensive in the input E, which is more abundant in the South.

When the two regions have the same homothetic utilities, since at $\mathbf{p}_w^*$ the two regions face the same relative prices for goods A and B, the North and the South demand goods for A and B in the same proportions. Since in equilibrium the supply of B in the South is proportionately larger, when the international markets clear, the South must export B, and the North must import B; that is, the South is an exporter of environmentally intensive goods at the world equilibrium.

Next I establish formally the intuitively obvious proposition that in the move from autarky to trade, the South produces more resources. First I establish that from autarky to trade the relative price of the environmentally intensive good B must increase from the autarchic level in the South. To establish this, I show that, in autarky, the relative price p_B/p_A (recall $p_A = 1$), must be larger in the North than it is in the South, that is, in autarky,

$$(C3)\quad (p_B/p_A)(\mathrm{N}) > (p_B/p_A)(\mathrm{S}).$$

This is also intuitively obvious because preferences are the same in both countries, and the South has an institutional comparative advantage in B. Formally, it is seen as follows. It is known that *at any given price* the South produces more B than the North because of common-property regimes (Proposition 1). If, in contradiction with (C3) $(p_B/p_A)(\mathrm{N}) < (p_B/p_A)(\mathrm{S})$, then this effect is emphasized according to Proposition 1 and equations (B1), and therefore in autarky the South supplies more B than the North. But preferences are assumed in this theorem to be homothetic, so that if $(p_B/p_A)(\mathrm{N}) < (p_B/p_A)(\mathrm{S})$, in autarky the North consumes proportionately more B than the South. This contradicts the assumption that the two countries are both in an autarchic equilibrium: they are identical, but the South produces proportionately more B than the North, and it consumes proportionately less than the North. Therefore, in one of these countries the market for B must fail to clear, a contradiction. Since the contradiction arises from negating (C3), inequality (C3) must hold.

Now it is straightforward to show that a move from autarky to trade leads to a world price of B that is higher than the autarky price was in the South (i.e., that $p_B^* > (p_B/p_A)(\mathrm{S})$. Assume not; then, by the above,

$$(C4)\quad (p_B/p_A)(\mathrm{N}) > (p_B/p_A)(\mathrm{S}) > p_B^*.$$

Since preferences are homothetic, (C4) implies that the proportion of goods B/A consumed in both countries increases after trade. However, the proportion of goods B/A produced in both countries decreases, because as p_B decreases, so does p_E, while r increases [equation (B1)], so that the harvesters extract less E, and the B good, which is E-intensive, is produced in smaller quantities while the A good is produced in higher quantities.

As shown above, (C4) implies that at a trade equilibrium the proportion B/A in which goods are produced decreases in both countries with respect to autarky, while the proportion B/A in which goods are consumed increases in both countries. This implies that markets cannot clear at the trade equilibrium when (C4) is satisfied, a contradiction. Therefore at a world equilibrium it must be true that $p_B^* > (p_B/p_A)(\mathrm{S})$ as I wished to prove. Similarly I have proved that p_B^* is lower than the autarky price in the North, $p_B/p_A(\mathrm{N})$.

Having proved that p_B/p_A increases in the South from autarky to trade, it follows immediately that the extraction of E increases in the South after trade. As the price of the environmentally intensive good B increases from autarky to trade, the price E must increase, and the rental on capital r, which moves in the opposite direction to p_E, decreases [see equations (B1)]. Therefore, after trade, the harvesters face lower opportunity costs for their input, K, and higher prices for the output, E. They therefore harvest more (see the proof of Proposition 1 in Appendix A), and the extraction of E increases.

Since the two countries are identical except for property rights, when the two have well-defined property rights they do not trade (i.e., the result is autarky). By the first theorem of welfare economics, when $K^S = \bar{K}$ the private-property competitive equilibrium is Pareto efficient, and as proved above in this appendix, it is unique. Since as seen in the previous paragraph the South produces more E when it moves from autarky to trade, at a trade equilibrium (with common property) its production of E is larger than is Pareto efficient. Its equilibrium price is lower than in autarky (i.e., when both countries have well-defined property rights), since $p_B^* < (p_B/p_A)(\text{N})$.

PROOF OF COROLLARY 1:

The fact that factor prices in the two regions are equalized at a competitive equilibrium follows immediately from equations (B1), which shows that the factor prices are determined by the traded-goods prices p_A and p_B and by the technical coefficients a_1, c_1, a_2, and c_2, which are identical in equilibrium in the two regions.

PROOF OF PROPOSITION 2:

The resource E is supplied to the market by harvesters as specified in Appendix A. The harvesters own only their input $\bar{x}$ of labor, they exchange their harvest of E for A, and they have utilities $u_i(A, \bar{x} - x_i)$ which depend on consumption of A and on leisure, with elasticity of substitution between leisure and consumption, $\sigma < 1$. Consider the harvester's optimization problem:

$$\text{(C5)} \quad \max\left[u_i(A, \bar{x} - x_i)\right]$$

$$\text{subject to } p_A A = p_E E(x_i)$$

where $E(x_i) = E^C(x_i)$ is as defined in Proposition 1. At each relative market price p_E/p_A the harvester chooses x_i so that

$$\text{(C6)} \quad (p_E/p_A)E_i'(x_i) = \left[\partial u_i/\partial(\bar{x} - x_i)\right]/\left[\partial u_i/\partial A\right].$$

The solution to (C6) is denoted $x_i(p_E, p_A)$. The opportunity cost of the input q must satisfy

$$\text{(C7)} \quad (p_E/p_A)E_i'(x_i) = q$$

so that by (19),

$$q(p_E, p_A) = \left[\partial u_i/\partial(\bar{x} - x_i)\right]/\left[\partial u_i/\partial A\right].$$

That is, *the opportunity cost $q(p_E, p_A)$ of x_i is the ratio of the marginal utility of leisure and the marginal utility of consumption*, as stated in Section IV-A.

In (C7), q appears explicitly as a function of p_A and p_E. Using (C7) one can now explore how the extraction of the resource E changes with its price p_E, and how the opportunity cost q of the input x_i, varies across equilibria. First recall that the workers' elasticity of substitution between leisure and consumption, which measures precisely how substitutable one good (A) is for the other (leisure, $\bar{x} - x_i$), is assumed to be less than 1, that is

$$\sigma = \frac{\partial\left(\dfrac{A}{\bar{x} - x_i}\right)}{\partial\left(\dfrac{p_A}{q}\right)}\left[\frac{\dfrac{p_A}{q}}{\dfrac{A}{\bar{x} - x_i}}\right] < 1$$

(Varian, 1992 p. 44). This implies immediately, by definition, that as the relative price of A increases, leisure decreases. This in turn implies that extraction has increased. Figure C1 illustrates this fact: as the relative price of A increases, the proportion of consumption of A and of leisure must go down by a smaller proportion, because $\sigma < 1$. The vertical segment between the two indifference surfaces in Figure C1 represents the change in prices, while the part of this segment indicated with Δ, which indicates the change in the proportion of consumption of A and of leisure, is smaller, leading to less leisure after the price of A increases.[14] More effort x_i is applied, and therefore there is more extraction of E as the price p_E drops. Note that the utilities used here are quite general, requiring only continuity, strict concavity, and $\sigma < 1$. For example, with CES utility functions (which are not required here),[15] the assumption $\sigma < 1$ simply means that the indifference surfaces of a worker's utility do not cross the axis, which is a standard assumption.

[14] For example, if utilities are Cobb-Douglas, one obtains the limiting case of constant supply of the resource E as p_E/p_A decreases.

[15] CES utilities are of the form $u(A, \bar{x} - x) = [dA^\rho + e(\bar{x} - x)^\rho]^{1/\rho}$, and their elasticity of substitution is $\sigma = 1/(1 - \rho)$ (see Varian, 1992).

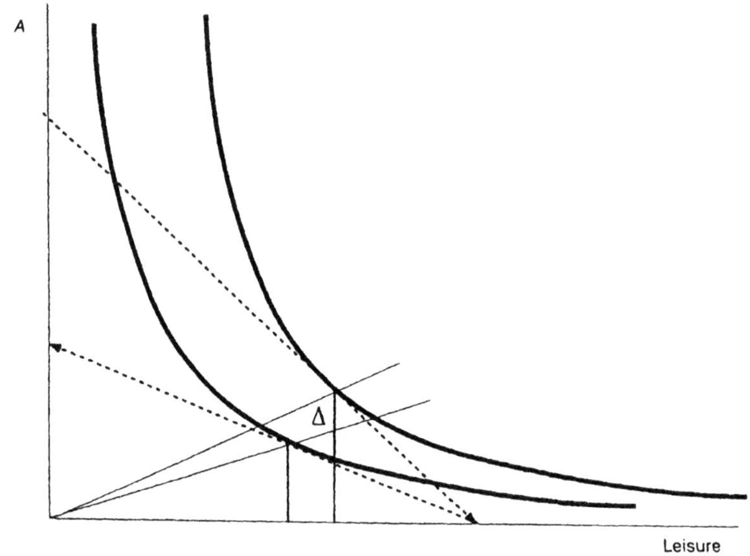

FIGURE C1. THE HARVESTER MAXIMIZATION PROBLEM

Notes: The curves represent indifferences of the harvester between consumption of A and leisure. The two dashed lines represent budget lines at different prices. They converge to a point on the horizontal axis which is the harvester's initial endowment of labor. With harvesters owning only labor, and with elasticity of substitution less than 1, as the relative price of resources increases (the price of A increases) leisure decreases, and more is harvested.

The last task is to explain Figure 2, which indicates how a decrease in opportunity cost of labor increases extraction. First note that the opportunity cost of the input x_i decreases with p_E: as p_E/p_A decreases, the quantity of $x_i(p_E, p_A)$ supplied increases (as in Fig. C1), so that the supply of the resource $E = E(x_i(p_E, p_A))$ also increases. By the concavity of the production function for E, this implies that as p_E/p_A drops, the derivative $E_i'(x_i(p_E, p_A))$ must also drop. Since p_E/p_A decreases and $E_i'(x_i)$ has not increased, the opportunity cost q defined in (C7), $q(p_E, p_A) = (p_E/p_A)E_i'(x_i)$ must have decreased as well. As the relative price of the resource p_E decreases, the opportunity cost of labor q drops, and the supply curve of resources shifts as was indicated in Figure 2.

PROOF OF PROPOSITION 3:

Consider a unit tax T on the use of the resource E in the South, which increases the value of demand for A, $A^{D*}(S)$, by TE^* (recall that $p_A = 1$). I shall now consider the cross-equilibria relationship between p_B and $A^{D*}(S)$ to determine the changes in prices of the resource-intensive good A in a new equilibrium, following the tax. From (C2), by the implicit-function theorem, across equilibria,

$$\text{(C8)} \quad \frac{\partial p_{B^*}}{\partial A^{D*}(S)}$$

$$= \frac{-p_{B^*}}{2p_B[\Psi(S)+\Psi(N)]+\Gamma(S)+\Gamma(N)+A^{D*}(S)+A^{D*}(N)}$$

which, when $\alpha(S)$ is sufficiently large, is always negative [see (C2) and also Chichilnisky, 1986 p. 15]. Now, by assumption, the tax proceeds lead to a higher level of demand for the capital-intensive good A in equilibrium, A^{D*}. Therefore by (C8) the tax leads to a drop in the equilibrium price p_B^* of the resource-intensive good, B.

Finally, when $c_2/D < 2p_E/p_B$ and α is large, the equilibrium level of exports of B increases as their price p_B drops since $X^S_B(S) = B^S - B^D = B^S - (p_E E + rK - A^{D*})/p_B$ so that

$$\text{(C9)} \quad X^S_B(S)$$

$$= \frac{c_2 E - a_2 K}{D} - \frac{p_E E + rK - A^{D*}}{p_B}$$

$$= \left(\frac{\alpha c_1}{D^2 p_B}\right)\frac{c_2 - c_1}{p_B} + \left(\frac{\beta a_1}{D^2}\right)\frac{a_2 - a_1}{p_B}$$

$$+ \frac{c_1 E^0 - a_1 \bar{K}}{D p_B} + \frac{A^{D*}(S)}{p_B}$$

and thus,

$$\text{(C10)} \quad \frac{\partial X^S_B}{\partial p_B} = \frac{\alpha c_1}{D^2 p_B^2}\left(\frac{2c_1}{p_B} - c_2\right) + \frac{\beta a_1}{D^2 p_B^2}$$

$$+ \frac{a_1 \bar{K} - c_1 E^0}{p_B^2} - \frac{A^{D*}(S)}{p_B^2}$$

(see also Chichilnisky, 1981, 1986). When α is large, (C10) implies that $\partial X^S_B/\partial p_B$ has the sign of $2c_1/p_B - c_2$, which is equal to that of $c_2/D - 2p_E/p_B$ by (B1). Since by assumption $c_2/D < 2p_E/p_B$, (C10) is negative; therefore taxes lead to a lower p_B and to an increase in exports $X^S_B(S)$. Notice that when α is large, c_2/D is the term representing the supply (B^S) response to the change in terms of trade p_B, while $2p_E/p_B$ is the demand response to p_B. Therefore the inequality $c_2/D < 2p_E/p_B$ implies that an increase in the price of B leads to a larger increase in the demand for B than in supply of B, a situation which is described by stating that "income effects dominate" in the market for B. The rest of the proof follows from Proposition 2.

To simplify computations, in this proof I have taken utility functions which effectively make the demand for A in each region an exogenously chosen parameter at an equilibrium [see equation (B10)]. This follows Chichilnisky (1981, 1986, 1993b), where it is also shown that the results generalize to more general utilities and demand functions. This procedure allows one to explore the effect of a tax which unequivocally increases the demand for non-resource-intensive goods, the most favorable conditions for the tax to work in the intended direction. Proving the results under such assumptions gives a stronger result than if demand for the resource-intensive goods also increased after taxes.

REFERENCES

Amelung, Torsten. "Tropical Deforestation as an International Economic Problem." Unpublished manuscript presented at the Egon-Sohmen Foundation Conference on Economic Evolution and Environmental Concerns, Linz, Austria, 30–31 August 1991.

Barbier, Edward B.; Burgess, J. C. and Markandya, Anil. "The Economics of Tropical Deforestation." *AMBIO*, April 1991, *20*(2), pp. 55–58.

Binkley, C. S. and Vincent, Jeffrey R. "Forest Based Industrialization: A Dynamic Perspective." World Bank (Washington, DC) Forest Policy Issues Paper, 1990.

Bromley, Daniel W., ed. *Making the commons work*. San Francisco: ICS Press, 1992.

Chichilnisky, Graciela. "Terms of Trade and Domestic Distribution: Export-Led Growth with Abundant Labour." *Journal of Development Economics*, April 1981, *8*(2), pp. 163–92.

______. "International Trade in Resources: A General Equilibrium Analysis." *Proceedings of the American Mathematical Society*, 1985, *32*, pp. 75–125; reprinted in Robert McElvey, ed., *Environmental and natural resource mathematics*. Providence, RI: American Mathematical Society, 1985, pp. 75–125.

______. "A General Equilibrium Theory of North–South Trade," in Walter P. Heller, Ross M. Starr, and David A. Starrett, eds., *Essays in honor of Kenneth Arrow*,

Vol. 2: Equilibrium analysis. Cambridge: Cambridge University Press, 1986, pp. 3–56.

______. "On the Mathematical Foundations of Political Economy." *Contributions to Political Economy*, 1990, *9*, pp. 25–41.

______. "Biodiversity and Property Rights in the Pharmaceutical Industry." Case study, Columbia University School of Business, 1993a.

______. "Traditional Comparative Advantages vs. External Economies of Scale." Report to the Economic Commission for Latin America and the Caribbean, Project on Trade Liberalization in the Americas, United Nations, New York, 1993b; *Journal of International Comparative Economics* (forthcoming).

______. "North–South Trade and the Dynamics of Renewable Resources." *Structural Change and Ecnomic Dynamics*, December 1993c, *4*(2), pp. 219–48.

Chichilnisky, Graciela and Heal, Geoffrey M. *The evolving international economy*. Cambridge: Cambridge University Press, 1987.

______. *Oil in the international economy*. Oxford: Clarendon, 1991.

Chichilnisky, Graciela; Heal, Geoffrey M. and Starrett, David. "International Markets with Emission Permits: Equity and Efficiency." Working paper, Stanford Institute for Theoretical Economics, December 1993.

Coase, Ronald H. "The Problem of Social Cost." *Journal of Law and Economics*, October 1960, *3*, pp. 1–44.

Cohen, Jon S. and Weitzman, Martin L. "A Marxian Model of Enclosures." *Journal of Development Economics*, February 1975, *1*(4), pp. 287–336.

Dasgupta, Partha. *The control of resources*. Cambridge, MA: Harvard University Press, 1992.

Dasgupta, Partha and Heal, Geoffrey M. *Economic theory and exhaustible resources*. Cambridge: Cambridge University Press, 1979.

Demsetz, Harold. "Towards a Theory of Property Rights." *American Economic Review*, May 1967 (*Papers and Proceedings*), *57*(2), pp. 347–57.

Dixit, Avinash and Norman, Victor. *Theory of international trade*. Cambridge: Cambridge University Press, 1980.

Hyde, W. F. and Newman, D. H. "Forest Economics in Brief—With Summary Observations for Policy Analysis." Unpublished manuscript (draft report), Agricultural and Rural Development, World Bank, Washington, DC, 1991.

Kane, Joe. "Letter from the Amazon." *New Yorker*, 27 September 1993, *69*(31), pp. 54–79.

Lerner, Abba P. "The Symmetry Between Import and Export Taxes." *Economica*, August 1936, *3*(11), pp. 306–13.

McDonald, Steven L. *Petroleum conservation in the United States: An economic analysis*. Baltimore, MD: Johns Hopkins University Press, 1971.

Metzler, Lloyd. "Tariffs, the Terms of Trade, and the Distribution of National Income." *Journal of Political Economy*, February 1949, *57*(1), pp. 1–29.

Ruitenbeck, H. J. "The Rainforest Supply Price: A Step Towards Estimating a Cost Curve for Rainforest Conservation." Development Research Programme Working Paper No. 29, London School of Economics, 1990.

Schweigert, Thomas. "Commercial Sector Wages and Subsistence Sector Labor Productivity in Guatemalan Agriculture." *World Development*, January 1993, *21*(1), pp. 81–91.

Varian, Hall. *Microeconomic analysis*, 3rd Ed. New York: Norton, 1992.

World Bank. *World development report: Development and the environment*. Oxford: Oxford University Press, 1992.

[16]

ELSEVIER Journal of International Economics 44 (1998) 181–209

Journal of INTERNATIONAL ECONOMICS

Open access renewable resources: Trade and trade policy in a two-country model

James A. Brander[a,*], M. Scott Taylor[b]

[a]Faculty of Commerce, 2053 Main Mall, University of British Columbia, Vancouver, BC V6T 1Z2, Canada

[b]Department of Economics, University of British Columbia, Vancouver, BC V6T 1Z1, Canada

Accepted 27 March 1997

Abstract

This paper develops a two-good, two-country model with national open access renewable resources. We derive an appropriate analog of "factor proportions" for the renewable resource case and link it to trade patterns and to the likelihood of diversified production. The resource importer gains from trade. However, a diversified resource exporting country necessarily suffers a decline in steady state utility resulting from trade, and may lose along the entire transition path. Thus the basic "gains from trade" presumption is substantially undermined by open access resources. Tariffs imposed by the resource importing country always benefit the resource exporter, and may be pareto-improving. © 1998 Elsevier Science B.V.

Keywords: International trade policy; Renewable resources

JEL classification: F10; Q20

1. Introduction

There are at least two important connections between international trade policy and renewable resource management One connection is the concern that trade liberalization may lead some countries to excessively exploit their renewable

*Corresponding author. Tel.: +1 604 8228483; fax: +1 604 8228477; e-mail: brander@nervana.commerce.ubc.ca

PII S0022-1996(97)00029-9

resources, leading to long-run losses.[1] A second connection arises from suggestions that trade sanctions might reasonably be linked to resource management practices. Specifically, it has been suggested that weak resource management regimes confer the equivalent of an export subsidy on producers and should therefore be subject to countervailing duties under international trade law.[2]

There has, however, been relatively little formal economic analysis addressing such concerns. In an early step towards such analysis, Brander and Taylor (1997a) consider the case of a small open economy with an open access renewable resource. That paper obtains the striking result that if the small open economy has a comparative advantage in the resource good and remains diversified in production after trade, then its steady-state utility is necessarily reduced by trade.

In this paper we attempt to take another significant step forward in understanding the relationship between trade policy and renewable resource management. We wish to go beyond the small country case and allow the world price of the resource good to be endogenously determined within the model. This is important as it allows us to examine how one country's trade and resource management practices affect resource stocks and welfare elsewhere in the world. In this context, we examine the determinants of trade patterns, the welfare effects of opening trade, and the positive and normative consequences of tariffs and export taxes.

The simplest model for investigating these issues is a two-country model in which each country is similar to the small country considered in Brander and Taylor (1997a). Each country is endowed with a renewable resource stock and labour, and may produce the resource good and/or a numeraire good which we refer to as manufactures. The renewable resource is subject to domestic open access (i.e. foreigners cannot use the resource) and has a dynamic structure of the classic Schaefer (1957) type.

Using this model we are able to obtain several interesting results. First, we are able to find an analog of "factor proportions" for the case of a renewable resource model. We are then able to link trade patterns to relative factor service flows, deriving a result similar in structure to the Heckscher-Ohlin theorem. In addition, we show that sufficient similarity across countries in this ratio of factor proportions ensures diversified production and factor price equalization in steady state.

We also show that the resource abundant country necessarily suffers a reduction

---

[1]For example, Brown (1995) discusses the Ivory Coast and the Philippines, both of which dramatically increased harvesting and exporting of forest products in the 1970s, substantially depleted their forest stocks, and now have much lower levels of earnings from their forest resources. In the Ivory Coast, this was a major factor contributing to the approximate 50% decline in per capita real income that occurred between 1980 and 1994.

[2]There is an active literature in law and political science on the linkage between trade sanctions and environmental policies. Good examples include Reichert (1996) and Yechout (1996). These papers provide a balanced overview of how GATT and the WTO might seek to deal with issues related to resource management and environmental damage.

in its steady state utility as a result of trade if it is diversified in the trading steady state. Moreover, if the resource exporter is always diversified during the transition from autarky to the trading steady state, then it also loses at every point along the transition path. The basic intuition underlying these results arises from the negative externality associated with harvesting open access resources. An open access resource is one lacking property rights, so all producers can use the resource "freely", and do not face the full cost of stock depletion. The primary cost of stock depletion is that harvesting becomes more costly in the future (e.g. it is more costly to catch fish if the fish stock is largely depleted and more costly to harvest timber once the large trees have been cut). Because of this negative externality, there is over-harvesting even in autarky, and opening trade increases the cost of this externality for the resource good exporter.

The mechanism by which these welfare effects arise derives from the interaction of terms of trade effects and resource depletion. More specifically, under autarky, the resource abundant country has a larger resource stock and a lower relative price of the resource good. When trade opens, consumers in the resource poor country have an incentive to import the resource good, leading the resource abundant country to increase its harvesting (for export). This causes depletion of the resource stock in the resource abundant country and, as its resource stock falls, the labor cost of producing the resource good rises, causing a gradual increase in the price of the resource good. Because the resource stock is an open access resource, there are no direct factor returns to the resource stock and, in addition, potential profits are fully dissipated by entry. The only income is labour income, and the real value of this income falls as the price of the resource good rises.

Therefore, a resource abundant country may suffer long run losses from trade. This provides some rationale for concerns about the long run impact of trade liberalization on countries where renewable resources are an important part of the export sector but where property rights over the resources are incomplete. Our analysis of policy shows that an import tariff imposed by the country importing the resource good raises the steady state utility of the resource exporter, and may be pareto-improving. This result lends some support to the argument in favour of linking tariffs or other trade sanctions to resource management practices. In addition we show that export taxes on the resource good increase the steady state resource stock in the resource exporting country but reduce the importing country's stock. The resource exporter necessarily gains from a small export tax, while the importer loses. In effect, tariffs or other trade restrictions can act as a "second-best" policy to reduce the negative consequences of the open access externality.

The assumption that resources are subject to open access may seem extreme. In practice, renewable resources often have partially controlled access. For example, many fisheries are regulated. However, excessive use and rent dissipation still occurs. In particular, restrictions on fishing time and numbers of boats have led to larger boats and more intensive fishing per unit of time, and direct catch limits have been hard to monitor and enforce. Rent dissipation and overuse in other renewable resources (such as forests, wildlife and soil) may be less severe than in fishing, but are still major problems in much of the world. As long as property rights are incomplete, even if they are not totally absent, the basic insights of our analysis will have relevance.

This work draws on traditional (Ricardian and factor proportions) trade theory, and on the theory of renewable resources. Suitable background for the trade theory component of our analysis is available in standard references such as Dixit and Norman (1980) or Ethier (1984). Papers focusing on trade and growth such as Srinivasan and Bhagwati (1980) and Deardorff (1973) also provide useful comparative background. As for the renewable resource component, our paper builds on the classic work of Schaefer (1957) and Gordon (1954), and much of the analytical background to our paper is set out in the comprehensive overview of "bioeconomics" provided by Clark (1990). Other valuable overviews include Munro and Scott (1985) and Neher (1990). The literature on trade in renewable resources is relatively modest in scope. The review article by Kemp and Long (1984) contains some material on renewable resources, and early papers dealing with trade and renewable resources include McRae (1978), Markusen (1976) and Scott and Southey (1969). A related recent paper is Lopez (1994).

There has been extensive recent analysis of the relationship between trade and the environment, including Barrett (1994), Copeland and Taylor (1994, 1995) and Rauscher (1993). Valuable overviews of international resource management problems are provided in books by Pearce and Warford (1993) and Cooper (1994). Overall, however, we view this paper, along with Brander and Taylor (1997a), as a substantial departure from existing themes in the literature. Also, in a tangentially related paper, (Brander and Taylor, 1997c) we combine closed-economy renewable resource dynamics with Malthusian population dynamics to explain the economic rise and fall of Easter Island.

An apparently closely related paper is Chichilnisky (1994), in which one country (the "South") has incomplete property rights and the other (the "North") has complete property rights. That paper demonstrates, using a static framework, that the free trade equilibrium is not pareto-efficient.[3] It is important to note, however, that the actual proofs of propositions do not provide a formal welfare comparison of autarky and free trade. In contrast, in this paper we do formally compare free trade and autarky, showing conditions under which the resource exporting country loses from trade in steady state and along the transition path.

The analysis in our paper has a connection to the literature on "trade and distortions" associated particularly with Bhagwati and Ramaswami (1963), and

[3]The same basic result is also reported in Chichilnisky (1991). Chichilnisky (1993) carries out a similar analysis for the dynamic case. In Brander and Taylor (1997b) we also consider a model in which one country has an open access resource and the other does not, but have a different specification and obtain different results from those of Chichilnisky (1991, 1993, 1994).

the formal structure of the second-best problems arising from trade liberalization is similar to the structure in the literature on "immiserizing growth" as represented by Bhagwati (1958); Johnson (1967) and Brecher and Choudri (1982). In the distortions literature, an ordering of policy interventions is provided for each type of distortion. In our model, the "first-best" policy is to eliminate the distortion of incomplete property rights at source, as in the distortions literature. However, the ordering of second-best policies does not carry over to our model, as our dynamic structure goes beyond the static models considered in the distortions literature.

Section 2 of the paper sets out the basic autarky model incorporating renewable resources, following the development in Brander and Taylor (1997a). Section 3 then extends the model to the two- country case and demonstrates the central normative and positive properties of trade in this setting. Section 4 and Section 5 consider possible trade policy interventions and Section 6 considers possible extensions and generalizations. Section 7 contains concluding remarks.

2. General equilibrium with a renewable resource: autarky

2.1. Renewable resource growth

As in Brander and Taylor (1997a) it is necessary to begin by describing the basic structure of renewable resource growth. Each country has a resource stock. Focusing on just one country for now, referred to as the "domestic" country, its resource stock at time t is denoted $S(t)$. The natural growth of the resource, denoted G, is a function of the existing stock. The change in the stock at time t is the natural growth rate $G(S(t))$, minus the harvest rate, $H(t)$. Dropping the time argument for convenience yields

$$dS/dt = G(S) - H. \tag{1}$$

We use a specific functional form for G, given by

$$G(S) = rS(1 - S/K). \tag{2}$$

This functional form for $G(S)$ is the logistic function. It is widely used in the analysis of renewable resources and is perhaps the simplest empirically plausible functional form for biological growth in a constrained environment. The variable K, referred to as the "carrying capacity", is the maximum possible size for the resource stock. If $S=K$, further growth cannot occur. The variable r is the "intrinsic" or "uncongested" growth rate. Proportional growth rate $G(S)/S$ would be approximately equal to r if congestion were negligible in the sense that carrying capacity were large relative to the current stock.

2.2. Production and supply

Each country produces and consumes two goods. H is the harvest of the renewable resource, and M is some other good which might be thought of as manufactures. Good M is treated as a numeraire whose price is normalized to 1. In addition to resource stock S, there is only one other factor of production, labour, L. Manufactures are produced with constant returns to scale using only labour. By choice of units, one unit of labour produces one unit of good M. As the price of M is 1, it follows that labour's value of marginal product in manufacturing is 1. We assume that labour markets are perfectly competitive, thus the wage in manufacturing is 1. We also assume that harvesting is carried out according to the Schaefer harvesting production function.

$$H^S = \alpha S L_H \tag{3}$$

where H^S is the harvest supplied by producers. (The superscript S stands for "supply".) L_H is the amount of labour used in resource harvesting and α is a positive constant. Letting $a_{LH}(S)$ represent the unit labour requirement in the resource sector, Eq. (3) implies that $a_{LH}(S) = L_H/H^S = 1/(\alpha S)$. Note that $a'_{LH}(S) < 0$: unit labour requirements rise as the resource stock falls. Production in both sectors is carried out by profit-maximizing firms operating under conditions of free entry. Thus the price, p, of the resource good must equal its unit cost of production.

$$p = wa_{LH} = w/(\alpha S) \tag{4}$$

where w is the wage. Condition Eq. (4) incorporates the open-access assumption, because it means that labour costs are the only explicit cost of production. There is no explicit rental cost for using S. Labour is mobile between the two sectors. Thus if manufactures are produced, the wage must be 1, and Eq. (4) becomes

$$p = 1/(\alpha S). \tag{4a}$$

2.3. Ricardian temporary equilibrium

A representative consumer is endowed with one unit of labour and is assumed to have instantaneous utility given by the following Cobb-Douglas utility function

$$u = h^{\beta} m^{1-\beta} \tag{5}$$

where h represents individual consumption of the resource good, m is individual consumption of manufactures, and taste parameter β is strictly between 0 and 1. The consumer maximizes utility at each moment in time subject to an instantaneous budget constraint $ph + m = w$. This maximization yields demand functions $h^D = w\beta/p$ and $m^D = w(1-\beta)$, using superscript D to represent demand. Total domestic demand is just L times individual demand.

$$H^D = w\beta L/p\ ;\ M^D = w(1-\beta)L. \tag{6}$$

Rearranging the left hand expression in Eq. (6), the inverse demand for the resource good can be written as

$$p = w\beta L/H^D. \tag{7}$$

On the production side, at a moment in time the resource stock is fixed, and the economy is Ricardian. The full employment condition defines the temporary Ricardian production possibility frontier (PPF) and is given by $H^P\ a_{LH}(S)+M=L$. The temporary equilibrium harvest can be determined by setting the supply price given by Eq. (4) equal to the demand price given by Eq. (7) (i.e. by setting supply equal to demand). This yields

$$H = \alpha\beta LS. \tag{8}$$

Note that the temporary equilibrium harvest is an increasing linear function of the stock. The equilibrium output of M is $M=(1-\beta)L$, hence fraction β of the labour force is employed in the resource sector.

2.4. An autarkic steady-state

The temporary equilibrium is like a standard Ricardian equilibrium. However, there is no guarantee that the harvest will equal the underlying biological growth rate of the resource. If, for example, the temporary equilibrium harvest, H, exceeds biological growth G, then the stock diminishes as time proceeds. As a result, labour productivity in the resource sector falls. (From Eq. (3)) the average and marginal product of labour is αS, which obviously falls as S falls.) The Ricardian PPF, which has harvest intercept αLS, then pivots inward, leading to a new temporary equilibrium, as illustrated in Fig. 1.

A steady state emerges when the stock has evolved to a level at which $H(S)$ as given by Eq. (8) is equal to $G(S)$ as given by Eq. (2). Setting these equal yields

$$\alpha\beta LS = rS(1 - S/K) \tag{9}$$

One solution to Eq. (9) occurs when $S=0$. Thus $S=H=0$ is a possible (and miserable) steady state. If S is not zero, we obtain the solution

$$S_A = K(1 - \alpha\beta L/r) \tag{10}$$

where S_A stands for the autarkic steady state resource stock. The resource dynamics associated with convergence to a steady state are illustrated in Fig. 2. This figure illustrates a situation in which the initial stock level, S_0, implies a harvest $H(S_0)$ in excess of natural growth $G(S_0)$. Thus the stock shrinks toward its autarkic steady state level S_A.

The autarkic steady state harvest, denoted H_A, is obtained by substituting Eq. (10) into Eq. (8).

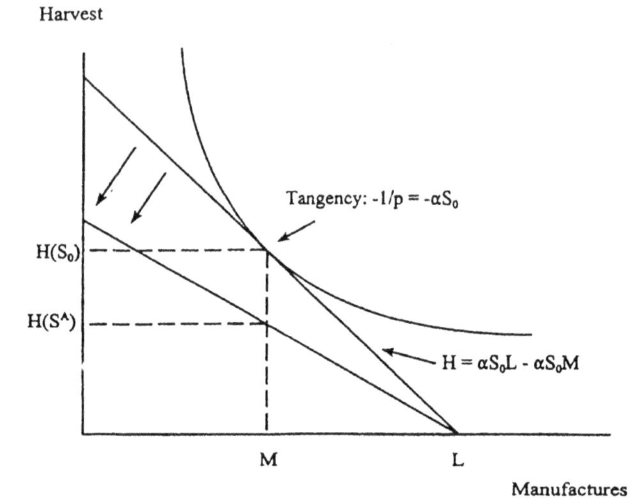

Fig. 1. Temporary equilibrium dynamics.

$$H_A = \alpha\beta LK(1 - \alpha\beta L/r) \tag{11}$$

As shown in Brander and Taylor (1997a), a positive steady state solution exists if and only if

$$r/L > \alpha\beta \tag{12}$$

in which case the solution is globally stable (for $S_0 > 0$). If Eq. (12) is not satisfied, the resource will be extinguished and the unique steady state is $S = H = 0$. To appreciate the meaning of Eq. (12) note (from Eq. (2)) that r is proportional to G, the instantaneous growth rate of the resource. Thus r is a measure of the service flow from the resource stock, and the ratio r/L measures the relative factor service

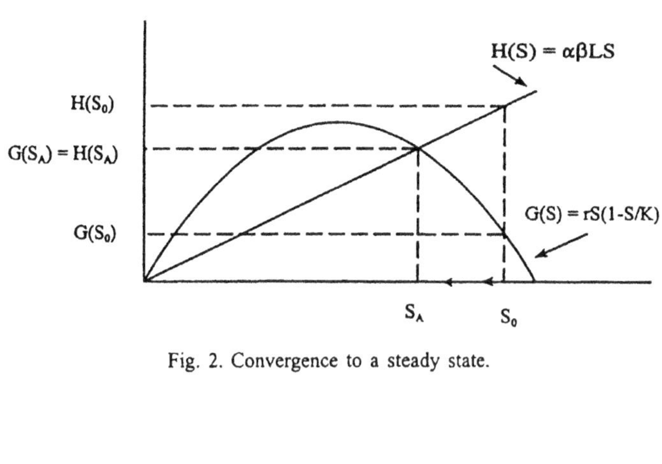

Fig. 2. Convergence to a steady state.

flow. Expression Eq. (12) can then be interpreted as saying that a positive steady state exists only if "factor proportion" r/L implies sufficient resource abundance.

3. A two-country model of international trade

We now consider trade between two countries that are identical except for factor proportions. In particular, each country has a renewable resource that is subject to open access by residents of that country only. We therefore abstract from the international open access problem. The international aspect of open access is interesting and important, but the case of nationally controlled open access resources is much more empirically significant.[4] Both goods may be traded, but labour is immobile across countries.

As suggested earlier, a useful measure of comparative advantage is given by factor proportion ratio r/L. We refer to the countries as "foreign" and "domestic" and use asterisks to denote foreign variables. For concreteness, we take the foreign country to be relatively resource abundant and the domestic country to be labour abundant.[5]

$$r^*/L^* > r/L \tag{13}$$

We assume that the parameters are such that each country has a positive steady state resource stock in autarky (i.e. expression Eq. (12) holds for each country), and then consider trade.

3.1. The positive analysis of trade

A central feature of trade is that wages and resource stocks must be equalized (in or out of steady state) whenever each country produces both goods, as expressed in Proposition 1.

Proposition 1: If each country remains diversified in production after trade, then
(i) (factor price equalization, FPE) the wage must be equal to 1 in each country ($w = w^* = 1$), *and*

[4] In a recent comprehensive review of international fisheries research conducted by the U.N. Development Program, the Commission of European Communities, the World Bank, and the Food and Agriculture Organization of the U.N, the authors conclude that "Although states have largely ended international open access through the extension of jurisdiction, most still allow *free and open access* to their domestic fisheries." (original emphasis) World Bank (1992); (p14). Accordingly we take domestic open access as our working hypothesis.

[5] While we focus on cross-country differences in r/L as the central asymmetry between countries, differences in other parameters such as α (harvesting efficiency) and K (carrying capacity) would also have interesting consequences.

(ii) (resource stock equalization, RSE) each country will have the same resource stock ($S=S^*$).

Proof: (i) If each country is diversified, then each produces some manufactures, where the marginal value product of labour is 1, which implies that the wage is 1. (ii) From expression Eq. (4) and from (i), it follows that $p_T=a_{LH}=a^*_{LH}$, where p_T is the world price of the resource good. Then, as $a_{LH}=1/(\alpha S)$, while $a^*_{LH}=1/(\alpha S^*)$, it follows that $S=S^*$.

We now provide a brief heuristic description of the dynamic transition that occurs when trade opens using the relative supply and demand curves shown in Fig. 3. The demand for the harvest good relative to manufactures (H^D/M^D) is easily obtained from expression Eq. (6) as $\beta/((1-\beta)p)$. This relative demand is common to both countries and therefore to the world, and it applies both in and out of steady state. As shown by the line labelled RD in Fig. 3, this relative demand is a downward sloping function of relative price, p.

For each country, the relative supply curve at a point in time is a typical Ricardian relative supply curve, consisting of a horizontal segment and a vertical segment. Given a resource stock of size S, a country will specialize in manufactures if $p<1/(\alpha S)$, and the relative (and absolute) supply of the resource good would be zero. Thus the relative supply curve is vertical at zero for $p<1/(\alpha S)$. For $p>1/(\alpha S)$, a country would specialize in the resource good, implying an infinite relative supply, whereas the relative supply could be anything between 0 and infinity if $p=1/(\alpha S)$. The relative supply curve is therefore horizontal at $p=1/(\alpha S)$.

As trade opens, we assume each country is at its autarkic steady state. As the

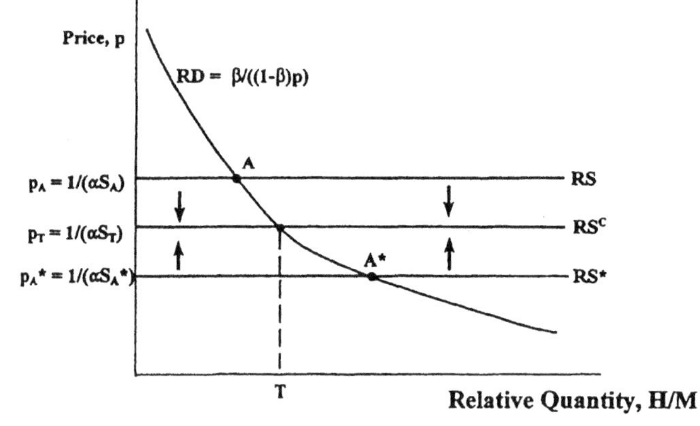

Fig. 3. Relative demand and supply under autarky and free trade.

foreign country has the higher autarky resource stock, the relative supply curves for the two countries are as shown in Fig. 3. RS is the initial relative supply curve for the domestic country and RS* is the relative supply curve for the foreign country. The autarky price and output are indicated by point A for the domestic country and point A^* for the foreign country. As trade opens, domestic consumers have access to lower prices from foreign resource good suppliers, implying that the foreign country will begin to export the resource good while the domestic country exports manufactures. Labour exits from the domestic resource sector, harvesting falls, and the domestic stock begins to rebuild, causing relative supply curve RS to shift down, as illustrated by the arrows in Fig. 3. The foreign country goes through the converse adjustment.

When trade opens, there are incipient profits available in the resource sector, inducing a shift of labour into that sector. Either all labour flows into the resource sector, or output rises sufficiently to bring the world price down to p_A^* at some production configuration short of full specialization. In either case, harvesting rises in the foreign country, the foreign stock starts to decline, and relative supply curve RS* starts to shift up, as indicated. These movements in the two relative supply schedules continue until a new steady state is reached (as shown more formally in Section 3.3).

At a diversified trading steady state, the two countries must have equal resource stocks, denoted S_T, and therefore have common relative supply curve RS^C, which has its horizontal segment at world price $p_T = 1/(\alpha S_T)$. At this world price, Fig. 3 implies that relative demand in each country is given by T. The foreign country produces to the right of T and exports the resource good, while the domestic country produces to the left of T and exports manufactures.

In Fig. 3 we have presumed that both countries remain diversified in steady state. However, if the world demand for the resource good is very high (i.e. if β is large) or if countries differ substantially in factor proportions, then the foreign country might specialize in the resource good in steady state. The key difference in diagrammatic terms is that the adjustment in Fig. 3 ends before domestic and foreign supply curves become coincident. In the specialized case, the world price of the resource good lies above the relative supply curve of the foreign country and coincides with the horizontal portion of the domestic relative supply curve. The foreign country specializes in resource good production, while the domestic country is diversified. The configuration where the foreign country specializes in production of the resource good is the only possibility for specialization, as stated and proven in Proposition 4.

In this paper we focus on the diversified case. The specialized case is of some interest, but we view it as less empirically relevant and, given space constraints, we do not pursue it here. Proposition 4 states precisely when specialization and diversification will occur. We now demonstrate the properties of the trading state more formally, starting with our analog of the Heckscher-Ohlin theorem linking trade patterns to factor endowments.

Proposition 2: *In a diversified trading steady state, the resource abundant country must export the resource good. The labour abundant country must export manufactures (the labour intensive good).*

Proof: From expression Eq. (8) we have $H^D = L\alpha\beta S$ and $H^{D*} = L^*\alpha\beta S^*$. Recalling from Proposition 1 that $S = S^*$, it follows that $H^D/H^{D*} = L/L^*$. A steady state requires $H^S = G$ and $H^{S*} = G^*$. Therefore $H^S/H^{S*} = G/G^* = r/r^*$. We then obtain $(H^D/H^S)/(H^{D*}/H^{S*}) = (L/r)/(L^*/r^*) > 1$, or $H^D/H^S > H^{D*}/H^{S*}$. The material balance condition given by $H^D + H^{D*} = H^S + H^{S*}$ then implies that $H^D > H^S$. Thus the labour abundant country consumes more of the resource good than it produces and must import it. It follows that the resource abundant country must export the resource good.

Proposition 2 provides a formal statement and algebraic proof of the key point that follows from Fig. 3. Namely, as in standard factor proportions models, relative resource abundance determines autarky relative prices, which in turn predict the direction of trade. Unlike standard factor proportions models, however, the mechanism by which this occurs is that production reallocations across countries cause resource stocks to be equalized. Proposition 3 establishes the natural intuition about post-trade resource stock and price levels (as illustrated in Fig. 3).

Proposition 3: *In a diversified trading steady state, (i) the common post-trade resource stock in each country, denoted S_T, lies between the autarky and steady state stock sizes, and (ii) the post-trade world price of the resource good lies between the autarky prices.*

Proof: (i) By material balance, $H^D + H^{D*} = G(S_T) + G^*(S_T)$ or, using Eq. (8) and Eq. (2),

$$\alpha S_T(\beta(L + L^*)) = rS_T(1 - S_T/K) + r^*S_T(1 - S_T/K). \tag{14}$$

Rearrangement of Eq. (14) yields a solution for the diversified steady state stock in each country.

$$S_T = K[1 - (L + L^*)\alpha\beta/(r + r^*)] > 0. \tag{15}$$

Comparing expression Eq. (15) with expression Eq. (10) completes the proof.

(ii) Diversification of production implies (using Eq. (4a)) that $p = 1/(\alpha S)$ and $p^* = 1/(\alpha S^*)$ before trade, and also that $p_T = 1/(\alpha S_T)$ after trade. Using part i) then implies $p > p_T > p^*$, as was to be shown.

Propositions 1, 2, and 3, and Fig. 3 presume that both countries remain diversified in production after trade. Whether diversification occurs in steady state depends on the similarity across countries in factor proportions and the strength of tastes for the resource good, as follows from Proposition 4.

Proposition 4: *(i) Neither country can specialize in manufactures.*

(ii) A necessary and sufficient condition for the post-trade pattern of production to be diversified in both countries is

$$[(L^*/r^*)]/[(L+L^*)/(r+r^*)] > \beta. \tag{16}$$

(iii) If Eq. (16) fails to hold, then the foreign (resource abundant) country will specialize in production of the resource good and the domestic country will be diversified. This is the only specialization possibility.

Proof: See Appendix A.

The left hand side of expression Eq. (16) is a measure of the similarity of factor proportions across countries. If the countries are identical up to scalar multiples (i.e. $r=\delta r^*$ and $L=\delta L^*$ for some $\delta>0$) then $r/L=r^*/L^*$ and condition Eq. (16) reduces to $1>\beta$, which is true by model construction. Thus, by continuity sufficient similarity in factor proportions implies that Eq. (16) must be satisfied, which in turn implies that diversification (and therefore FPE) follow.

We can increase the difference in factor proportions while maintaining our relative factor abundance ranking by increasing L/r or decreasing L^*/r^*. In either case, Eq. (16) is more likely to be violated. In addition, increases in β (reflecting the world taste for the resource good) make Eq. (16) more likely to be violated. If Eq. (16) is violated, then factor prices will not be equalized by trade and the foreign country will specialize in production of the resource good in steady state. In effect, Proposition 4 points out that the possibility of FPE depends both on relative resource endowments and on tastes, as in conventional factor proportions theory. (A standard reference on FPE is Dixit and Norman (1980), but see Deardorff (1994) for some new results and a recent perspective.)

Although the model is Ricardian at each point in time the positive steady state properties of the model are surprisingly similar to standard factor proportions models. A measure of relative resource abundance determines "comparative advantage", and trade flows are reliably predicted by this measure. Moreover, if the countries are sufficiently similar in factor proportions, then trade will bring about diversified production and FPE.

3.2. Normative steady state implications of trade

Despite the similarities between our renewable resource model and standard factor proportions models, we can now establish a result that contrasts sharply with the basic normative insight associated with the theory of comparative advantage.

Proposition 5: Comparing a diversified trading steady state with autarky,
(i) trade causes steady state utility to fall in the resource-abundant country, and
(ii) trade causes steady state utility to rise in the labour-abundant country.

Proposition 5 can be readily seen diagrammatically, as shown in Fig. 4. The foreign country has autarky consumption possibilities given by its PPF, $H^{D*}a^*_{LH}(S^*_A)+M^*=L^*$ (noting that $H^{D*}=H^{S*}$ under autarky and letting S^*_A be the foreign autarky steady state resource stock). After trade, the foreign country must consume on a budget line running through the production point with slope equal to the world terms of trade. This is its post-trade steady state PPF. The equation of this line is $H^{D*}a^*_{LH}(S_T)+M^*=L^*$. Because $S_T<S^*_A$ (from Proposition 3), it follows that the post-trade PPF lies inside the autarky consumption (and production) possibility frontier, except at the corner where $M^*=L^*$.

As autarky consumption lies outside the post-trade consumption possibility set, foreign steady state utility must be strictly lower in the trading steady state than under autarky. One way of seeing that foreign utility must fall in the move from autarky to a trading steady state is to observe that, relative to autarky, foreign nominal income stays constant (at L^*), the price of manufactures stays constant (at 1), and the price of the resource good rises (from Proposition 3). Therefore, the representative foreign consumption bundle must shrink and foreign utility must fall. The home country undergoes a mirror-image change in its fortunes. The

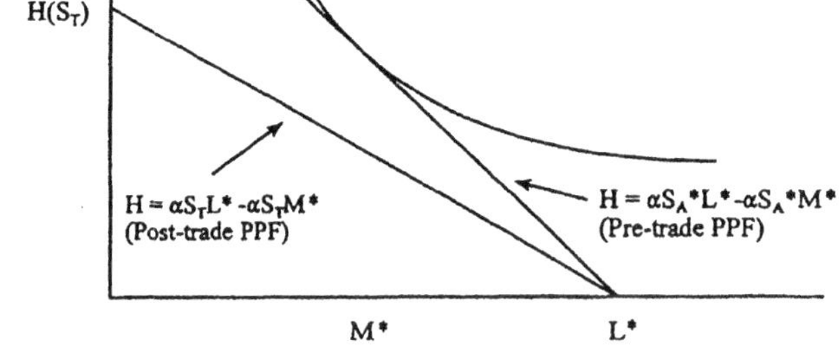

Fig. 4. Losses from trade for resource exporter.

reasoning is identical as for the foreign country, except that, as $S_T > S_A$, the home country experiences steady-state gains from trade. From its point of view, nominal (labour) income and the price of manufactures are the same as in autarky, while the price of the resource good is lower.

The only way the foreign country could take advantage of terms of trade effects and experience steady state gains from trade would be if it could specialise in the resource good and experience an increase in the wage. However, specialisation will only occur if Eq. (16) is violated (i.e. if the difference between foreign and domestic relative resource abundance is sufficiently great).

Proposition 5 is the analog to the result in Brander and Taylor (1997a) that a resource abundant small open economy that remains diversified after trade has a lower steady-state utility level after trade than in autarky. Taken together, Brander and Taylor (1997a) and Proposition 5 weaken the gains from trade presumption for trade based on the exploitation of a renewable resource under conditions of incomplete property rights. This can be seen as a "second-best" problem. Because open access creates a market failure, there is no presumption that removing another distortion (prohibitions on trade) will necessarily improve welfare.

3.3. Normative analysis of transitional dynamics

We now consider the welfare properties of the dynamic transition from autarky to the new post-trade steady state. Even when trade leads to diversified production and lower steady state utility for the foreign country, it may provide utility gains during the transition period. This seems an important qualification to our analysis, but we show that there are reasonable conditions under which the foreign country loses at every point on the transition path as well as in steady state.

The key to understanding this possibility follows from the intuition regarding terms of trade and resource depletion effects. If the foreign country remains diversified throughout the transition process then utility would be lower at each point in time in trade than in autarky, because of ongoing resource depletion effects. The aggregate present value of foreign welfare would then necessarily be reduced by trade, regardless of the discounting rule used.

One condition underlying transitional losses from trade for the foreign country is

$$L^* > \beta(L + L^*) \tag{17}$$

Rearranging Eq. (17) yields $(1-\beta)(L+L^*)>L$. Wage rates w and w^* cannot be less than 1. Therefore,

$$(1 - \beta)(wL + w^*L^*) > L \tag{17a}$$

However, it follows from the right hand expression in Eq. (6) that world demand for manufactures is precisely the left hand side of expression Eq. (17a). Therefore, world demand exceeds L. But L is the maximum amount of manufactures that can be produced in the domestic country even if all domestic labour is devoted to manufactures. It follows that the foreign country must in this case (i.e. if Eq. (17) holds) produce some manufactures and have a wage equal to 1 at every point on the transition path. Condition Eq. (17) also implies that Eq. (16) holds and therefore insures convergence to a diversified steady state.

Now consider what happens when trade opens. As established in Section 3, expression Eq. (10) implies that the initial resource stock is higher in the foreign country than in the domestic country. Furthermore, foreign and domestic wages equal 1. We can then infer from Eq. (4a) that the supply price of the resource good in the foreign country must be less than the supply price in the domestic country. Therefore, the domestic country cannot sell the resource good, as it will be undercut by foreign producers, so it must specialize in manufactures and produce a harvest of zero. The foreign country remains diversified, and the wage remains at 1 in both countries. As long as $S^*>S$, the domestic harvest remains zero, and the evolution of the domestic stock (from Eq. (1)) is given by

$$dS/dt = rS(1 - S/K) > 0 \tag{18}$$

To obtain the corresponding equation for the foreign country, we need to determine its harvest. This can be done by finding the labour allocated to harvesting. With the (specialised) domestic country producing amount L of manufactures, and with world demand for manufactures given by $(1-\beta)(L+L^*)$ (from Eq. (17a) with $w=w^*=1$), it follows that foreign production of manufactures is $(1-\beta)(L+L^*)-L$. This must also be the amount of foreign labour devoted to manufacturing, so the amount of foreign labour left over for harvesting is $L^*-[(1-\beta)(L+L^*)-L]=\beta(L+L^*)$. Using Eq. (3), we can then observe that the foreign harvest is $H^*=\alpha\beta(L+L^*)S^*$. Therefore, from Eq. (1), the differential equation governing the evolution of the foreign stock (for $S^*>S$) is

$$dS^*/dt = r^*S^*(1 - S^*/K) - \alpha\beta(L + L^*)S^* \tag{19}$$

We could integrate Eq. (18) and Eq. (19) to provide explicit solutions for the trajectory of foreign and domestic stocks. It is easier, however, to draw inferences directly from Eq. (18) and Eq. (19). From Eq. (18), recalling that $S<K$ as trade opens, we can infer that S approaches and gets arbitrarily close to K as time proceeds. To interpret Eq. (19) recall (from Eq. (8)) that under autarky $r^*S^*(1-S^*/K)=\alpha\beta L^*S^*$. Therefore Eq. (19) must be negative as trade opens. Thus, immediately upon the opening of trade, S starts to grow and S^* starts to fall.

As S grows, eventually one of two things must happen. Either S must get arbitrarily close to K (as implied by Eq. (18)), or it must equalize with S^*. Meanwhile, S^* would continue to fall either until it reached the stabilizing value implied by Eq. (19), which is $K[1-\alpha\beta(L+L^*)/r^*]<K$, or until it equalized with S. Given that $S^*>S$ initially, S and S^* must equalize at some finite time. When S

and S^* do equalize, differential Eq. (18) and Eq. (19) cease to govern the further evolution of the stocks. We denote this time when S and S^* equalize as t_e.

Throughout this entire time up to t_e foreign utility is falling. To see this recall that the foreign country remains diversified throughout the process. (This is ensured by condition Eq. (17).) Therefore its wage remains at 1 and its total income is L^*. The price of manufactures remains stable at 1. The world price of the resource good is determined by the foreign supply price, as only the foreign country produces the resource good. This price starts at the foreign autarky level then rises as the foreign stock declines. Therefore, the foreign country has a stable nominal income and a steadily increasing real cost of consumption, implying that its utility falls at each point along the transition until $S=S^*$ at time t_e.

Once the two resource stocks equalize, they can never differ from each other again. Any incipient deviation of S from S^* would lead to an instantaneous flood of labour into the resource sector of the country with the marginally higher stock. The speed of this production "correction" is instantaneous, whereas stock adjustment occurs in real time (i.e. comparatively slowly). Thus stock deviations can never get started because they are instantaneously swamped by production adjustments.

The two stocks evolve in tandem toward the steady state value S_T given by Eq. (17). The dynamic behaviour of the stocks after time t_e (i.e. when $S=S^*$) is given by

$$dS/dt = rS(1 - S/K) - \alpha L_{HS} = dS^*/dt = r^*S^*(1 - S^*/K) - \alpha L_H^* S^* \quad (20)$$

Given condition Eq. (17), the two countries must both be diversified when stocks are equalized. Therefore wages are equal to 1 and (from Eq. (17a)) world demand for manufactures is $(1-\beta)(L+L^*)$. Total labour devoted to manufactures must be precisely the same quantity. The remaining amount of labour, $\beta(L+L^*)$, must equal $L_H + L_H^*$. Using Eq. (20) and this market-clearing condition allows us to solve for the labour allocations in each country during this phase of the transition. These are given by

$$L_H = (1/2)[[(r - r^*)/\alpha](1 - S/K) + \beta(L + L^*)] \quad (21)$$

$$L_H^* = (1/2)[[(r^* - r)/\alpha](1 - S^*/K) + \beta(L + L^*)] \quad (22)$$

where $S=S^*$. These allocations apply at each point in time from t_e forward along the transition path.

We can now solve for the transition path of either country's resource stock over the remaining interval of the transition period. Substituting Eq. (21) into Eq. (20) and rearranging shows that the evolution of the domestic resource stock from its position at $t=t_e$ is given by:

$$dS/dt = \tfrac{1}{2}[(r + r^*)S(1 - S/K) - \alpha\beta(L + L^*)S] \quad (23)$$

The solution to Eq. (23) shows that the domestic stock converges monotonically to steady state stock S_T (given in Eq. (17)), as does the foreign stock (substituting Eq. (22) into Eq. (20)). We have already determined that the foreign country has a declining instantaneous utility everywhere along the first part of its transition path towards the trading steady state (i.e. for $t<t_e$). We have now shown that over the rest of the transition the foreign stock must move monotonically toward $S_T<S_A^*$. Therefore, the foreign stock is less than its autarky level throughout the entire transition period, and the world price of the resource good, which equals $1/(\alpha S^*)$ must always exceed the foreign autarky price. Foreign nominal income is steady at L^*, and the price of manufactures is steady at 1. Thus foreign utility must be lower at every point along the transition path. Parallel reasoning implies that the home country gains during the transition. Proposition 6 summarizes this discussion.

Proposition 6: If condition Eq. (17) holds ($L^*>\beta(L+L^*)$), then foreign utility is lower at every point along the transition from autarky to free trade than in autarky. Conversely, domestic utility is higher at every point along the transition than in autarky. Therefore, for any plausible discounting procedure, foreign welfare is reduced by trade and domestic welfare is increased by trade.

If condition Eq. (17) does not hold, then the foreign country may gain, depending on parameter values, along some interval of the transition path, even if the steady state is ultimately diversified. In such a case discount rates and adjustment speeds would be important in determining an overall welfare result. Specifically, a high discount rate would tend to reduce the present discounted value of losses from trade and could even cause net discounted benefits from trade for the country exporting the resource good. What happens is that this country may specialize in the resource good as trade opens, driving wages above 1, and earn gains from trade in the early stages of adjustment (i.e. until its resource stock has depleted sufficiently). Similarly, slow adjustment speeds improve the prospects for a resource exporting country to experience increases in the discounted value of welfare arising from the opening of trade.

Furthermore, if the steady state is specialized, the foreign country may gain from trade along the transition and in steady state. Nevertheless, Propositions 5 and 6 taken together do provide a serious caveat to the "trade lifts all boats" hypothesis when open access renewable resources are present.

4. Trade policy

We now consider possible interventions. There are many policies that might be considered. Rather obviously, the "first-best" policy would be to solve the open access market failure by establishing some system of appropriate property rights or by using an appropriate harvesting tax. By hypothesis, however, this is either impossible or very costly, leading to a search for alternative policy instruments. Given the policy-level debate over resource management and trade policy, the natural first step is to consider a small import tariff on resource good imports by the domestic country. In addition, as many resource exporting countries argue that export taxes are really tools of resource management, we will also consider a small export tax by the resource exporter.

We restrict attention to comparative steady state analysis with diversified production. As we introduce policy, we need to distinguish between steady state domestic and foreign stock levels. We now use S and S^* to refer to the post-trade steady state resource stocks. Similarly, p and p^* will refer to post-trade steady state prices in the two countries.

We are interested in how a domestic tariff on the resource good will affect steady state stocks, harvests, prices, and utility levels. The basic methodology is that we imagine an initial tariff of 0, then consider the introduction of a marginal specific tariff, τ. To carry out the associated comparative analysis we need to see how various endogenous magnitudes must change so as to maintain the steady state material balance requirement, while also maintaining temporary equilibrium requirements for profit-maximization under free entry. In addition, perfect competition implies that domestic and foreign prices differ only by the amount of the tariff, implying that $p=p^*+\tau$.

The steady state material balance requirement is based on based on setting expression Eq. (1) to 0 for each country. Thus harvesting in each country must equal that country's resource growth in steady state. As world demand of the resource good $(H+H^*)$ must equal the world harvest, expression Eq. (24) follows from Eq. (6) and Eq. (2).

$$\beta I/p + \beta I^*/p^* = rS(1 - S/K) + r^*S^*(1 - S^*/K) \tag{24}$$

With $w=w^*=1$, domestic nominal income I is simply $L+\tau Z$, where Z is imports, and foreign nominal income is L^*. Noting that production is diversified in both countries, we have $p=1/(\alpha S)$ and $p^*=1/(\alpha S^*)$. Making these substitutions, Eq. (24) can be rewritten as

$$\begin{aligned} A(S, S^*; \tau) &= \beta(L + \tau Z)\alpha S + \beta L^*\alpha S^* - rS(1 - S/K) - r^*S^*(1 - S^*/K) \\ &= 0 \end{aligned} \tag{25}$$

Also, the condition $p=p^*+\tau$ becomes $1/(\alpha S)=1/(\alpha S^*)+\tau$, or

$$B(S, S^*; \tau) = 1/(\alpha S) - 1/(\alpha S^*) - \tau = 0 \tag{26}$$

Expressions Eq. (25) and Eq. (26) form a two-equation simultaneous system that must be maintained across comparative steady states. We can solve for the comparative steady state effects $dS/d\tau$ and $dS^*/d\tau$ by totally differentiating this two equation system and using Cramer's rule to find:

$$dS/d\tau = (-A_\tau B_{S*} + A_{S*}B_\tau)/D \quad (27)$$

$$dS^*/d\tau = (-A_S B_\tau + A_\tau B_S)/D \quad (28)$$

where subscripts represent partial derivatives, and $D = A_S B_{S^*} - A_{S^*} B_{S^*} > 0$. Proposition 7 follows.

Proposition 7: Starting from free trade ($\tau=0$), a marginal import tariff imposed by the domestic (labour abundant) country on imports of the resource good will have the following effects.

(i) The domestic steady state resource stock will fall and the foreign steady state resource stock will rise ($dS/d\tau < 0$ *and* $dS^*/d\tau > 0$).

(ii) The domestic steady state price of the resource will rise and the foreign steady state price of the resource good will fall ($dp/d\tau > 0$ *and* $dp^*/d\tau < 0$).

(iii) Foreign steady state utility rises and domestic steady state utility may either rise or fall.

Proof: See Appendix A.

There are two surprising results given in Proposition 7. First, even though the world price of the resource good falls and the resource exporter suffers a terms of trade loss, the resource exporter gains (in steady state). The exporter gains because, when the world price falls, the foreign stock rebuilds to make harvesting a break-even activity again, and this has the effect of expanding its consumption possibilities set. Second, the home country may lose from the tariff even though it "benefits" from a terms of trade improvement. The potential domestic loss stems from the fact that the domestic relative price of the resource good rises. A higher domestic price for the resource leads to additional harvesting and to a lower steady state resource stock. The domestic PPF pivots in from this effect. The domestic country could still gain, however, because it also receives tariff revenue. Thus it is quite possible that both countries may gain (in steady state) from such a tariff, and this possibility can be verified using specific numerical examples.

5. An export tax

We now consider the imposition of an export tax by the exporter of the resource good (i.e. by the foreign country). Let the export tax be denoted by τ^*. As before, the domestic and foreign prices must differ by the amount of the tax; that is, $p = p^* + \tau^*$. Expression Eq. (24) applies here as well: total consumption of the resource good must equal total production of the resource good. In this case, however, domestic income is simply L, while foreign income is $L^* + \tau^* Z$, because the foreign government collects the revenue associated with an export tax. Our two-equation system becomes:

$$A(S, S^*; \tau^*) = \beta L\alpha S + \beta(L^* + \tau^* Z)\alpha S^* - rS(1 - S/K) - r^*S^*(1 - S^*/K) = 0 \tag{29}$$

$$B(S, S^*; \tau^*) = 1/\alpha S - 1/\alpha S^* - \tau^* = 0 \tag{30}$$

Totally differentiating this two equation system with respect to S, S^*, and τ^* yields

$$\mathrm{d}S/\mathrm{d}\tau^* = (-A_{\tau^*}B_{S^*} + A_{S^*}B_{\tau^*})/D \tag{31}$$

$$\mathrm{d}S^*/\mathrm{d}\tau^* = (-A_s B_{\tau^*} + A_{\tau^*}B_S)/D \tag{32}$$

Proposition 8: *Starting from a position of free trade, a marginal export tax has the following steady state effects.*

(i) The domestic resource stock falls and the foreign resource stock rises ($\mathrm{d}S/\mathrm{d}\tau^*<0$ *and* $\mathrm{d}S^*/\mathrm{d}\tau^*>0$).

(ii) The domestic price of the resource good rises while the foreign price falls ($\mathrm{d}p/\mathrm{d}\tau^*>0$ and $\mathrm{d}p^*/\mathrm{d}\tau^*<0$).

(iii) Domestic steady state utility falls and foreign steady state utility rises.

Proof: See Appendix A.

The domestic country loses from the export tax because the tax raises the world relative price of the resource good and this leads to further stock depletion at home. The foreign country gains from the export tax because the tax depresses its relative producer price of the resource good and this leads to stock rebuilding.

The central insight in both Propositions 7 and 8 is that any marginal policy intervention away from "laissez faire" that raises the relative price of the resource good in a particular country will, taken by itself, tend to create losses for that country via resource depletion effects. If that country is the recipient of revenues from the policy instrument, these losses may be partially or even more than offset by those revenues. Conversely, a country where the relative price of the resource good is depressed by a policy instrument will tend to gain from the resulting resource accumulation, and these gains may be augmented by any revenues flowing directly from the policy instrument itself.

It is difficult to rank alternative policies, but some rankings can be inferred. For the resource abundant or "foreign" country, tax instruments can be ranked as follows. The first-best policy would be a production tax that offsets the externality, and an export tax that allows it to optimize with respect to terms of trade effects. (However, if one country sought to use its market power, the other country might be expected to object or to retaliate.) The second best policy for this country is an

202 J.A. Brander, M. Scott Taylor / Journal of International Economics 44 (1998) 181–209

export tax alone, and the third best policy is an import tariff imposed by the other country. For the domestic country, rankings are more difficult to establish, but it certainly prefers to levy its own import tariff rather than have the foreign country tax exports.

6. Extensions and generalizations

The model and analysis in this paper contain a number of limitations. First, the analysis is based on specific functional forms for utility, production, and for resource growth. While the functional forms are not unreasonable, obviously the generality of the analysis is limited. If we attempt to replace these specific forms with general functions, then we can no longer carry out the analysis using explicit closed-form solutions and must adopt a different approach. The easiest approach is to use diagrams that exploit whatever properties are imposed on the three basic functional relationships in the model. It is possible to develop an understanding of how the generalized case would work by building up the generalization in steps.

The easiest generalization is the harvest function $G(S)$. The natural approach is to replace the logistic form given by expression Eq. (2) with a general compensatory (i.e. bent-over) growth function with the properties that $G(0)=0$, $G(K)=0$ for some $K>0$, and $G''(S)<0$ for S between 0 and K. This generalization does not affect the Ricardian temporary equilibrium (shown in Fig. 1) in any way. The autarkic steady state is very similar to the situation illustrated in Fig. 2, except that growth function $G(S)$ need not have such a regular shape. It must, however, be concave and single-peaked and would have an interior steady state provided that r exceeds $\alpha\beta L$, where r is defined as the limit of $G(S)/S$ as S approaches 0.

Now consider two countries which have the same growth functions but different levels of L (causing r/L to differ across the countries). The country with the higher L will have the steeper harvest function, and will therefore have the lower autarky steady state stock, and the higher price. Opening trade will cause the resource abundant country to export the resource good, depleting its resource stock, until resource stocks in the two countries equalize. The main positive and normative properties of the model are unchanged by this generalization. If the growth function were not compensatory (bent-over) then the model could behave very differently, but the compensatory assumption is very plausible for renewable resources.

The next step is to generalize the harvest production function given by Eq. (3). A natural generalization would be to allow the harvest production function to show constant returns to labour, but variable (and probably decreasing) returns to S. This harvesting production function would be written as $H^P=Lf(S)$ where $f'(S)>0$ and $f''(S)<0$. In this case, the temporary equilibrium remains Ricardian, as in Fig. 1. In Fig. 2 the only change is that the harvest function becomes a concave increasing function, rather than a linear increasing function. We can compare two countries with different values of L, draw the two harvest functions, and proceed as before. The algebraic analysis becomes much more cumbersome (and less instructive) than with specific forms, but the basic structure of the analysis remains unchanged.

The third line of generalization concerns utility. The natural step here is to replace the Cobb-Douglas form with a general homothetic utility function. The harvest function is again an increasing function of the resource stock and the analysis proceeds much as before, although the possibility of multiple steady states arises. Some restrictions would be required to obtain a unique steady state. For non-homothetic utility the analysis becomes quite intractable as income effects can have a major impact on the pattern of trade. Countries at different levels of real income may have different relative demands for the two products and this may muddy the link between cost-based comparative advantage and trade patterns.

Overall, we feel comfortable in asserting that the basic structure of our model is not an artifact of particular functional forms, as the basic results hold given fairly standard (but still strong) "regularity" conditions on the three central functional relationships. This should not be a surprise as both the intuition and the diagrammatic structure of the analysis seem to follow from relatively general economic principles. However, we do not wish to overstate the case, as the formal analysis using general forms is very awkward and we acknowledge that our paper might be viewed only as an example at this stage.

There are other extensions and generalization that would be natural to consider. For example, we have not considered capital markets. If private agents (or governments) could take the proceeds from temporary resource rents earned in trade and invest these proceeds in an alternative asset such as physical capital or claims on future consumption, then the consumption path of private agents would be smoother than predicted here. However, the absence of capital markets is not critical for our results. The key problem is the externality created by open access. Opening capital markets does not reduce a marginal agent's incentive to move into harvesting when presented with a higher price for the product, nor does it eliminate the negative production externality created when this agent's harvesting lowers the common stock of the resource.

7. Concluding remarks

This paper examines trade flows, gains and losses from trade, and the effects of trade policy in a two-good, two-country model in which one of the goods derives from harvesting an open access renewable resource. We are able to define an appropriate notion of factor proportions based on the ratio of the intrinsic growth rate of the resource to labour. We show that this ratio determines comparative advantage and the direction of the trade flow. The country with the higher ratio is effectively "resource abundant" and exports the resource good. Sufficient similarity across countries in factor proportions ensures diversified production in steady state and factor price equalization.

To the extent that the model captures an element of real trade flows, it suggests that incomplete property rights in renewable resource sectors undermine the presumption that trade liberalization is necessarily welfare-improving. Thus the claim that some countries are induced to over-exploit their renewable resources because of trade liberalization appears to have some merit. We find that the resource exporter must have lower steady state utility in a diversified trading steady state than in autarky, and in some cases will have lower instantaneous utility at every point along the transition path as well. Conversely, the resource importer always gains from trade. Furthermore, we have shown that diversified production is necessarily the result of trade if countries are sufficiently similar.

Our analysis stands as a marked counterpoint to the recent literature on trade and growth. In, for example, Baldwin (1992); Grossman and Helpman (1991) and Taylor (1994), trade liberalization may enhance welfare through dynamic effects on capital accumulation or on research and development. We abstract from such considerations, but clearly they are important, and we have no wish to understate them. However, renewable resource dynamics are also important and abstracting from them may lead to a rather optimistic assessment of the dynamic effects of trade liberalization.

As for our analysis of trade policy, we found that an import tariff that acts as a "countervail" to inadequate resource management practices may improve the steady state utility of both trade partners. Export taxes by resource exporters raise resource stocks in the exporting country and serve a conservationist end, but they reduce resource stocks elsewhere and lower utility in the importing country. Overall, while there are various modifications to the paper that could be carried out, we believe that our structure provides a simple and flexible framework for examining some of the important policy issues associated with resource management and international trade. Here we have focused on one important concern that has received relatively little attention in the formal literature on international trade despite its significant practical importance: incomplete property rights in renewable resource sectors. While we are convinced that none of our results is sufficient reason to abandon ongoing trade liberalizations around the world, we are equally convinced that trade liberalization is a two-edged sword for a country with a comparative advantage in renewable resources and weak property rights in those sectors.

Acknowledgements

We thank Rob Feenstra and two anonymous referees for very helpful comments. We also thank Brian Copeland, Guofu Tan, Gordon Munro, Philip Neher, seminar participants in several locations, and other colleagues who made suggestions.

Financial support from the Social Sciences and Humanities Research Council of Canada, the Canadian Institute for Advanced Research, the Killam Trusts, the Network Centre of Excellence for Sustainable Forestry Management, and the UBC Centre for International Business Studies is gratefully acknowledged.

Appendix A

Proofs of Propositions

Proof of Proposition 4

(i) Consider the possibility that the labour abundant country specializes in manufactures. In this case its wage is 1. Over time, its resource stock grows to K. Thus the implicit cost of producing the resource good is $a_{LK}(K)$. In the other (foreign) country the resource good is being produced. The foreign wage must be at least 1 (depending on whether manufactures are also being produced) and the stock must be less than K. Therefore the cost of production (and world relative price) must be $w^*a^*_{LK}(S_T)>a_{LK}(K)$. This implies that the (domestic) labour abundant country would certainly produce the resource good, contradicting the initial hypothesis. By similar reasoning, the resource abundant country cannot specialize in the manufacturing good either.

(ii) To demonstrate (ii) precisely requires a substantial amount of detailed algebra that we judge to be a poor use of space, so we report only the basic method of proof here. It is necessary to show that Eq. (16) is necessary and sufficient for diversification. To show necessity, assume diversification. Foreign demand for labour in the resource sector is given by $L^*_H=H^{P*}a^*_{LH}=G^*(S_T)a^*_{LH}=r^*S_T(1-S_T/K)(1/\alpha S_T)$, where S_T, the common steady state stock, is given by Eq. (15). Simplifying this expression and imposing the condition that labour used in the resource sector cannot exceed total labour in the country yields expression Eq. (16). To show sufficiency, we assume that specialization occurs, note that $S^*=K(1-L^*\alpha/r^*)$ in this case, invoke overall material balance, and show that the inequality in Eq. (16) must run the other way. Thus, if Eq. (16) is satisfied, diversification is the only possibility.

(iii) The proof of part (ii) implies that if inequality Eq. (16) is not satisfied, then the resource abundant country specializes in the production of the resource good. Together with (i) this proves (iii).

Proof of Proposition 7

(i) First we calculate the various components in comparative steady state expressions Eq. (27) and Eq. (28).

$$A_S = \beta L\alpha - r(1 - 2S/K),\ A_{S*} = \beta L^*\alpha - r^*(1 - 2S^*/K),$$
$$A_\tau = \beta\alpha SZ,\ B_S = -1/(\alpha S^2),\ B_{S*} = 1/(\alpha S^{*2})$$

and $B_\tau = -1$.

Substituting the necessary partial derivative expressions into D yields

$$D = A_S B_{S*} - A_{S*} B_S$$
$$= (\beta L\alpha - r(1 - 2S/K))/\alpha S^2 + (\beta L^*\alpha - r^*(1 - 2S^*/K))/(\alpha S^{*2}) \quad \text{(A1)}$$
$$= [\beta L\alpha - r(1 - S/K) + \beta L^*\alpha - r^*(1 - S^*/K)]/\alpha S^2 + r + r^*)/(\alpha KS) \quad \text{(A2)}$$
$$= (r + r^*)/(\alpha KS) > 0 \quad \text{(A3)}$$

In moving from Eq. (A1) to Eq. (A2) we have made use of the fact that $S = S^*$ at $\tau = 0$. In moving from Eq. (A2) to Eq. (A3) we have used expression Eq. (25).

With $D > 0$, we can sign comparative steady state effects $dS/d\tau$ and $dS^*/d\tau$ by evaluating the numerators in expressions Eq. (27) and Eq. (28). Define N as the numerator of expression Eq. (27) and N^* as the numerator of expression Eq. (28). The sign of comparative static effect $dS/d\tau$ is therefore given by the signs of N. $N = A_{S*}B_\tau - A_\tau B_{S*} = -(\beta L^*\alpha - r^*(1 - S^*/K) + r^*S^*/K) - \beta\alpha SZ/(\alpha S^{*2})$.

In order to simplify N we note that $S = S^*$ at $\tau = 0$. We can also use the fact that domestic imports, Z, must be the difference between foreign production and foreign consumption, implying that $Z = r^*S^*(1 - S^*/K) - \beta\alpha L^*S^*$. Substituting Z into our expression for N and rearranging yields $N = [\beta^2\alpha L^* - \beta\alpha L^*] + r^*(1 - 2S^*/K) - \beta r^*(1 - S^*/K)$. The term in square brackets is obviously negative, since $\beta < 1$. The remaining terms can be written as $r^*[(1 - 2S^*/K) - \beta(1 - S^*/K)]$. We therefore need to show that the expression inside the square brackets is negative. Recalling that $S^* = S_T$ at $\tau = 0$, we can use Eq. (15) to substitute for S^* in this expression in square brackets. We can think of this expression as a function of β and write it as follows: $\phi(\beta) = (L + L^*)\alpha\beta/(r + r^*) - 1/(2 - \beta)$. We wish to show that $\phi(\beta) < 0$ for all relevant values of β.

To see this, note that $\phi(0) = -1/2 < 0$ and $\phi(1) = \alpha(L + L^*)/(r + r^*) - 1 < 0$ (using Eq. (12) for both countries with $\beta = 1$). Thus ϕ must be negative at the endpoints of the region $\beta \in [0,1]$. It can then be shown that $\phi'(\beta) > 0$ if $\phi(\beta) > 0$. To see this note that $\phi'(\beta) = \alpha(L + L^*)/(r + r^*) - 1/(2 - \beta)^2$. We then observe that $\phi'(\beta)$ must have the same sign as $\beta\phi'(\beta) = \alpha\beta(L + L^*)/(r + r^*) - \beta/(2 - \beta)^2$. But, if $\phi(\beta) \geq 0$, then $\beta\phi'(\beta)$ must be positive also, as $\beta/(2 - \beta)^2 < 1/(2 - \beta)$ for all $\beta \in (0,1)$. Therefore, if $\phi(\beta)$ is non-negative, then $\phi'(\beta)$ is positive. It follows that if $\phi(\beta)$ were zero or positive for any $\beta < 1$, then it would be impossible for $\phi(1)$ to be negative. This is a contradiction, as $\phi(1)$ must be negative. It follows that $\phi(\beta)$ must be negative for all permissible values of β, which proves the result.

We now show that $dS^*/d\tau > 0$. Sign $(dS^*/d\tau) =$ sign $[A_\tau B_S - A_S B_\tau] =$ sign

$[-\beta SZ/S^2+\beta L\alpha-r(1-2S/K)]=\text{sign }[(1-\beta)Z/S+rS/K]>0$. In moving to the last equality we have used the fact that $\beta L\alpha-r(1-S/K)=Z/S$, as domestic imports, Z, equal the difference between domestic consumption (given by $\alpha\beta LS$) and domestic production (given by $rS(1-S/K)$).

(ii) follows immediately from (i).

(iii) Since all individuals are identical, we can examine the welfare effects on a representative consumer with an endowment equal to that of the whole economy. Straightforward substitution of the foreign counterpart to Eq. (6) into the aggregate version of utility function Eq. (5) yields the aggregate indirect utility function for the foreign country:

$$U^* = \gamma I^* p^{*^{-\beta}} \tag{A4}$$

where $\gamma=\beta^{\beta}(1-\beta)^{1-\beta}$ and $I^*=L^*$. Taking the derivative of U^* with respect to τ yields

$$dU^*/d\tau = -\gamma p^{*^{-\beta}}\beta(L^*/p^*)dp^*/d\tau > 0 \tag{A5}$$

It is easily seen that expression Eq. (A5) is positive, as $dp^*/d\tau<0$ from part (ii) of the proposition.

Domestic indirect utility can be written as $U=\gamma Ip^{-\beta}$ where $I=L+\tau Z$. Differentiating U with respect to τ then yields

$$dU/d\tau = \gamma p^{-\beta}(Z-(\beta I/p)dp/d\tau) \tag{A6}$$

There are two effects of a tariff on domestic utility. There is a positive effect arising from tariff revenue, but a negative effect associated with the increase in the domestic price of the resource good. We have established by simulation that either of these effects may dominate. Therefore, there are cases in which both countries experience steady state gains from trade.

Proof of Proposition 8

(i) The proof is almost identical to the proof of part (i) of Proposition 7.

(ii) This follows from (i), since $p=1/(\alpha S)$ and $p^*=1/(\alpha S^*)$.

(iii) Domestic welfare is given by $U=\gamma p^{-\beta}I$ where $I=L$. Hence

$$dU/d\tau^* = \gamma p^{-\beta}\beta(L/p)(dp/d\tau^*) < 0 \tag{A7}$$

using the fact that $dp/d\tau^*>0$ from part (ii). Foreign welfare is given by Eq. (A4) where $I^*=L^*+\tau^*Z$. Substituting this for I^*, differentiating with respect to τ^*, and rearranging yields

$$dU^*/d\tau^* = \gamma p^{*^{-\beta}}(Z-I^*\beta/p^*)(dp^*/d\tau^*) > 0. \tag{A8}$$

The fact that $dU^*/d\tau^*>0$ follows from the result of part (ii) that $dp^*/d\tau^*<0$.

References

Baldwin, R., 1992. Measurable dynamic gains from trade. Journal of Political Economy 100, 162–174.

Barrett, S., 1994. Strategic environmental policy and international trade. Journal of Public Economics 54, 325–338.

Bhagwati, J., 1958. Immiserizing growth: a geometrical note. Review of Economic Studies 25, 201–205.

Bhagwati, J., Ramaswami, V.K., 1963. Domestic distortions, tariffs, and the theory of optimum subsidy. Journal of Political Economy 71, 44–50.

Brander, J.A., Taylor, M.S., 1997a. International trade and open access renewable resources: the small open economy case, Canadian Journal of Economics, forthcoming.

Brander, J.A., Taylor, M.S., 1997b. Trade between consumer and conservationist countries, Resource and Energy Economics 30, 526–552.

Brander, J.A., Taylor, M.S., 1997c. The simple economics of Easter Island: a Ricardo-Malthus model of renewable resource use, American Economic Review, forthcoming.

Brecher, R.A., Choudri, E.U., 1982. Immiserizing investment from abroad: the Singer-Prebisch thesis reconsidered. Quarterly Journal of Economics 97, 181–190.

Brown, L.R., 1995. Nature's limits. In: Brown, L.R., et. al. (Eds.), State of the World 1995, Norton, New York, pp. 3–20.

Chichilnisky, G., 1991. Global environment and North–South trade. Asian Journal of Economics and Social Studies 10, 185–201.

Chichilnisky, G., 1993. North–South trade and the dynamics of renewable resources. Structural Change and Economic Dynamics 4, 219–248.

Chichilnisky, G., 1994. North–South trade and the global environment. American Economic Review 84, 851–874.

Clark, C.W., 1990. Mathematical bioeconomics: The optimal management of renewable resources, 2nd ed., Wiley, New York.

Cooper, R.N., 1994. Environment and resource policies for the world economy, Brookings Institution, Washington, D.C.

Copeland, B.R., Taylor, M.S., 1994. North–South trade and the environment. Quarterly Journal of Economics 109, 755–787.

Copeland, B.R., Taylor, M.S., 1995. Trade and trans-boundary pollution. American Economic Review 85, 716–737.

Deardorff, A.V., 1973. The gains from trade in and out of steady-state growth. Oxford Economic Papers 25, 173–191.

Deardorff, A.V., 1994. The possibility of factor price equalization, revisited. Journal of International Economics 36, 167–175.

Dixit, A., Norman, V., 1980. The theory of international trade: a dual general equilibrium approach, Cambridge University Press, Cambridge.

Ethier, W.J., 1984. Higher dimensional issues in trade theory. In: Jones R.W., Kenen, P., (Eds.), Handbook of International Economics, Vol. 1, North Holland, Amsterdam, pp. 131–184.

Gordon, H.S., 1954. The economic theory of a common property resource: the fishery. Journal of Political Economy 62, 124–142.

Grossman, G.M., Helpman, E., 1991. Innovation and Growth in the Global Economy, MIT Press, Cambridge, Mass.

Johnson, H.G., 1967. The possibility of income losses from increased efficiency or factor accumulation in the presence of tariffs. Economic Journal 77, 151–154.

Kemp, M.C., Long, N.V., 1984. The role of natural resources in trade models. In: Jones R.W., Kenen, P.B. (Eds.), Handbook of International Economics, Vol. 1, (North-Holland, Amsterdam) pp. 367–417.

Lopez, R., 1994. The environment as a factor of production: The effects of economic growth and trade liberalization. Journal of Environmental Economics and Management 27, 163–184.
Markusen, J., 1976. Production and trade from international common property resources. Canadian Journal of Economics 9, 309–319.
McRae, J., 1978. Optimal and competitive use of replenishable natural resources by open economies. Journal of International Economics 8, 29–54.
Munro, G.R., Scott, A.D., 1985. The economics of fisheries management. In: Kneese, A.V., Sweeney, J.L. (Eds.), Handbook of natural resource and energy economics, vol. 2, North-Holland, Amsterdam, pp. 623–676.
Neher, P., 1990. Natural resource economics: conservation and exploitation, Cambridge University Press, Cambridge.
Pearce, D.W., Warford, J., 1993. World without end: Economics, environment and sustainable development, Oxford University Press, Oxford.
Rauscher, M., 1993. On ecological dumping . Oxford Economic Papers 46, 822–840.
Reichert, W.M., 1996. Resolving the trade and environmental conflict: the WTO and NGO consultative relations. Minnesota Journal of Global Trade 5, 219–246.
Scott, A.D., Southey, C., 1969. The problem of achieving efficient regulation of a fishery. In: Scott, A.D. (Ed.), The economics of fishery management: A symposium, Institute of Animal Resource Ecology, University of British Columbia, Vancouver, B.C., pp. 47–59.
Schaefer, M.B., 1957. Some considerations of population dynamics and economics in relation to the management of marine fisheries. Journal of the Fisheries Research Board of Canada 14, 635–647.
Srinivasan, T.N. Bhagwati, J.N., 1980. Trade and welfare in steady state. In: Chipman J., Kindleberger, C. (Eds.), Flexible exchange rates and the balance of payments, North-Holland: Amsterdam, pp. 341–353.
Taylor, M.S., 1994. 'Once-off' and continuing gains from trade. Review of Economic Studies 61, 589–601.
World Bank, 1992, A study of international fisheries research, in collaboration with the United Nations Development Programme, the Commission of the European Communities, and the Food and Agriculture Organization of UN, World Bank, Washington, D.C.
Yechout, P.J., 1996. In the wake of Tuna II: new possibilities for GATT-compliant environmental standards. Minnesota Journal of Global Trade 5, 247–275.

Review of Development Economics 1(3), 324–336, 1997

Export Bans, Environmental Protection, and Unemployment

*Judith M. Dean and Shubhashis Gangopadhyay**

Abstract

This study investigates the case for an export ban on intermediate goods which generate environmental damage. Since export restrictions on intermediates have long been advocated as a method of stimulating domestic industries in developing countries, we consider whether the case for an export ban is strengthened or weakened by the presence of unemployment in the industrial sector. We find that, in the short run, an export restriction worsens unemployment, thus weakening the case for a ban. In the long run, however, the results are reversed. If the environmental problem is severe, unemployment has a negligible impact on the case for an export ban.

1. Introduction

During the Uruguay Round, much pressure was put on the GATT (now WTO) to explicitly introduce environmental concerns as legitimate grounds for trade intervention. Some argued that production of some traded goods generates domestic and/or global environmental damage, and that trade restraints are a good method of reducing that damage. A familiar example of this is the advocacy of import restrictions on tropical timber if an exporting country does not manage its forests sustainably.[1]

Indonesia imposed a ban on the export of logs in 1985, in an attempt to spur the growth of domestic wood processing industries (Braga, 1992; Barbier et al., 1995). Although logging is not the main cause of deforestation in Indonesia, many environment advocates saw the export ban as an appropriate policy to reduce the environmental damage ensuing from deforestation. As is well known, restricting exports is not a first-best policy to address environmental damage, nor to increase output in the industrial sector. These two goals require two separate policy tools: a domestic tax which internalizes the value of the negative externality into the costs of the environmentally damaging production process, and a subsidy to output in the sector to be expanded. However, an export restriction on an intermediate good (such as a ban on log exports) could be seen as a good second-best policy choice, particularly for developing countries which face unemployment problems in urban/industrial areas. Such a ban would presumably both reduce output of the intermediate export good, lowering environmental damage, and stimulate growth in processing industries by lowering the cost of the intermediate input.

Is there a case for an export ban as a second-best policy tool to address environmental damage? If so, is this case strengthened by the presence of unemployment? Many

*Dean: SAIS, Johns Hopkins University, 1740 Massachusetts Avenue NW, Washington, DC 20036, USA. Tel: 202-663-5686; Fax: 663-7718; Email: jdean@jhu.edu Gangopadhyay: Indian Statistical Institute, Delhi Centre, 7.S.J.S. Sansanwal Marg, New Delhi 110016, India. Email: shub@isid.ernet.in. We thank Bee Aw, Rick Bond, Brian Copeland, Kala Krishna, Will Martin, Charles Pearson, James Riedel, and Alan Strout for very helpful comments. We also thank those at the Midwest International Economics Meetings, November 1994, the Northeast Universities Development Conference, November 1995, the economics seminars at SAIS and Rutgers University, and two anonymous referees. Finally, we thank Lina Zenni and Pablo Zoido-Lobaton for excellent graphics.

recent studies have investigated the environmental implications of trade policy.[2] Early studies, such as those of Baumol and Oates (1988) and Krutilla (1991), examined the case of a large country whose production generates environmental damage. Assuming the combination of an optimal tariff and an optimal environmental tax are not feasible, these studies showed the nature of the second-best tariff (environmental tax) which could be used to address both distortions.

Copeland (1994) and Beghin et al. (1994) considered the environmental repercussions of piecemeal trade reform. Copeland examined small changes in trade barriers (pollution taxes) in an economy characterized by many trade barriers and many pollutants, and established sufficient conditions for these changes to be welfare-improving. Beghin et al. extended this to include consumption pollution, and to allow for changes in production methods in response to various domestic policies designed to address pollution.

In all these studies only final goods were considered, and the effect of environmental damage was confined to a direct reduction in welfare through the utility function. In addition, the focus was on developing optimal export taxes, or optimal changes in export taxes. Because countries often choose blunt instruments, such as export bans, as second-best policy tools, Dean (1995) examined the case for an export ban on a good whose production generates environmental damage. She argued that with sufficiently severe environmental damage, the second-best export tax could indeed be a ban. However, use of such a blunt instrument creates an unnecessary tradeoff between raising national welfare and achieving the environmental objective. Even if the ban raises welfare relative to free trade, it is likely to be inadequate to reduce output to an environmentally sustainable level.

This paper considers whether the case for an export ban as an environmental policy is strengthened when there is unemployment in the industrial sector.[3] We consider a three-good model in which environmental damage arises from the production of intermediate goods, but directly lowers the productivity of an input in another sector. This better captures the nature of some environmental damage, such as soil erosion from deforestation, which affects downstream users. It also allows us to consider the possibility that the byproduct distortion of an export restriction may correct an unemployment problem in the processing industry which uses the intermediate good. We develop expressions for the optimal export tax to correct environmental damage (in the absence of a first-best policy), and from this derive the case for an export ban. We then consider how the optimal export tax changes in the presence of both unemployment and environmental damage, and whether this weakens or strengthens the case for an export ban. Throughout the discussion we use tropical timber as an example of an export good which generates environmental damage.

We find that an export ban on the intermediate good aggravates urban unemployment in the short run, thus weakening the case for the ban as an environmental policy. This is because the ban actually widens the wage gap between the rural and urban sectors, inducing increased migration to the urban sector. In the long run, however, this result is reversed. Provided the sector experiencing environmental damage is relatively labor-intensive, an export ban reduces the rural–urban wage gap, decreasing unemployment. Since agriculture is typically more labor-intensive than logging, this suggests that the case for an export ban may indeed be stronger than it first appears. However, as environmental damage becomes more severe, the impact of export restrictions on unemployment diminishes. Hence the presence of unemployment, in either the long or short run, would have a negligible impact on the case for an export ban.

2. The Model

Consider a small country producing logs (X), agriculture (Y), and processed wood products (Z). Goods X and Y are produced in the rural sector, using land (T) and labor (L). The production of logs damages the land (e.g. causes soil erosion), lowering the productivity of land in agriculture:

$$X = X(L_x, T_x), \tag{1}$$

$$Y = Y(L_y, g(X)T_y). \tag{2}$$

ASSUMPTION 1. *$g(0) = 1$, $g'(X) < 0$, $g''(X) = 0$ and $0 < g(X) \leqslant 1$ for all $X \geqslant 0$.*

Good Z is produced in the urban sector, using labor, logs, and capital. The stock of capital (K) is fixed, and is fully employed in Z:

$$Z = Z(L_z, X_z, \overline{K}). \tag{3}$$

All sectors are perfectly competitive and characterized by constant returns to scale. For the Y sector, scale is measured by an equiproportionate increase in labor and land measured in efficiency units, i.e. $g(X)T_y$. For the Z sector, given the presence of fixed K, a proportionate increase in labor and logs increases output less than proportionately. Good Z is the *numéraire* commodity, with $P_z \equiv 1$.

All factors are paid the value of their marginal products. However, we assume that the labor market is characterized by unemployment of the Harris–Todaro (1970) type. Rural sector wages (w_r) are flexible, but urban wages ($\overline{w}$) are fixed above market-clearing. Migration between sectors takes place until the expected wage in the urban sector equals the actual wage in the rural sector:

$$\overline{w} = w_r(1 + \mu), \tag{4}$$

where $\mu = L_u/L_z$, L_u are the unemployed, and μ is the rate of unemployment in the urban sector. With fixed stocks of labor and land, we have:

$$L_x + L_y + L_z(1 + \mu) = \overline{L}, \tag{5}$$

$$T_x + T_y = \overline{T}. \tag{6}$$

The negative externality generated by log production implies that Y producers maximize the following expression:

$$P_y Y(L_y, g(X)T_y) - w_r L_y - rT_y,$$

where r is the rental on land. For an interior solution it is necessary that

$$P_y Y_2 = r/g(X),$$

where Y_2 is the marginal product of land measured in efficiency units. Thus, the production decisions of the Y producer would change even if P_y, r, and w_r were held constant, if the production of logs were to change.

Logs and agricultural output are exported in exchange for processed wood imports, at fixed international prices. The producer price for log exports (P_x) differs from the world price (P_x*) by the size of any export taxes and/or production taxes:

$$P_x = P_x^*(1 - t) - \tau, \tag{7}$$

where t is an *ad valorem* export tax and τ is a specific tax on output. Trade is balanced, with

$$P_x{}^*X^e + P_y{}^*Y^e = P_z{}^*Z^m$$
$$X^e = X - X_z$$
$$Y^e = Y - Y^d \tag{8}$$

where superscripts "e" and "m" refer to exports and imports, respectively, and superscript "d" refers to domestic demand. Domestic demand for goods Y and Z is a function of the prices of Y and Z and national income.

3. Short-Run Analysis of an Export Ban

In the short run, the allocation of land between X and Y in the rural sector is given: T_x is specific to X and T_y is specific to Y. With this simplification, the previous model may be represented by:

$$P_y Y_L - \left[P_x{}^*(1-t) - \tau\right]X_L = 0, \tag{9}$$

$$Z_L - \overline{w} = 0, \tag{10}$$

$$Z_X - P_x{}^*(1-t) = 0, \tag{11}$$

$$\overline{w}L_z - \left[P_x{}^*(1-t) - \tau\right]X_L(\overline{L} - L_x - L_y) = 0, \tag{12}$$

where an uppercase subscript refers to the partial derivative of a function with respect to that variable (e.g. $Y_L = \partial Y/\partial L_y$).

Let the expenditure function E represent the minimum expenditure on Y and Z necessary to attain utility level U. Then:

$$E(P_y,\, 1,\, u) = \min(P_y Y^d + Z^d) \tag{13}$$

such that $u(Y^d, Z^d) = U$. With $E(\cdot)$ equal to national income,

$$E(\cdot) = P_y Y + Z + \left[P_x{}^*(1-t) - \tau\right](X - X_z) + tP_x{}^*(X - X_z) + \tau(X - X_z). \tag{14}$$

Totally differentiate (14) and define the change in welfare as $dW = E_u du$. With some simplification, making use of equations (9)–(12), the change in welfare may be expressed as:

$$dW = P_y Y_L\{dL_x + dL_y + (1+\mu)dL_z\} + P_y Y_2 g_X T_y dX$$
$$+\, tP_x{}^*dX + \tau dX - tP_x{}^*dX_z. \tag{15}$$

Suppose that the only distortion to be corrected is the environmental damage generated by log production. Since there is no unemployment, the first term of (15) drops out. Assuming no export tax, solve (15) for $dW/d\tau$. Setting this equal to zero yields the optimal production tax to address environmental damage:

$$\tilde{\tau} = -P_y Y_2 g_X T_y. \tag{16}$$

This is the standard result, that the tax on X production should equal the value of the marginal environmental damage (MED) created by X production in the Y sector. Implementation of this tax would reduce production of X to the environmentally sustainable level.[4]

As is well known, the *ad valorem* export tax which would maximize welfare in this case would be smaller than $\tilde{\tau}/P_x{}^*$. Assuming no production tax, solve (15) for dW/dt. Setting this equal to zero yields:

$$\tilde{t} = \left(\tilde{\tau}/P_x^*\right)\left[\varepsilon_x X/\left(\varepsilon_x X - \eta_x X_z\right)\right] \tag{17}$$

where $\varepsilon_x = (tdX/Xdt) < 0$ and $\eta_x = (tdX_z/X_z dt) > 0$.

Since the export tax shifts sales of X to the home market, it lowers the domestic price of X and encourages its use in the wood processing industry. This shift of sales is a byproduct distortion which lowers welfare. Hence, $\tilde{t} < \tilde{\tau}/P_x^*$. Let the right side of (17) be the "adjusted value of marginal environmental damage" (AMED) which prevails in free trade.

The results in (16) and (17) can be used to show that there is a case for an export ban as a tool to correct the environmental externality. Figure 1 graphs the optimal export tax ($\tilde{t}$) in relation to the optimal production tax ($\tilde{\tau}/P_x$) where the latter is in *ad valorem* terms. Since ($\tilde{\tau}/P_x$) equals the MED sustained in free trade, and $\tilde{t}$ equals the AMED, they are both positive functions of $|g_x|$. Thus, the greater the rate at which environmental damage grows with output of X, the greater is MED in free trade, and the higher both $\tilde{\tau}$ and $\tilde{t}$ must be. For some $|g_x| > 0$, the first-best production tax is $\tilde{\tau}_2 = t_p$, where t_p is a prohibitive export tax. This implies that a prohibitive export tax achieves the environmental objective: it reduces logging output to the sustainable level by internalizing the costs of damage to land productivity. However, t_p clearly exceeds the export tax which would maximize welfare, $\tilde{t}_2$. For a higher value of $|g_x|$, $\tilde{t} = t_p$, and the prohibitive export tax maximizes welfare. However, t_p then is clearly inadequate to achieve the environmental objective, since $t_p < \tilde{\tau}_3$.

Let $(t_p - \tilde{t})$ represent the marginal loss from implementing a ban instead of an optimal export tax. This is shown by the bold line between t_p and $\tilde{\tau}_3$. Recall that $\tilde{\tau}$ equals the value of the MED in free trade. For low values of $|g_x|$, such that $0 < \tilde{\tau} < \tilde{\tau}_1$, the marginal welfare loss from a ban exceeds the MED sustained in free trade. However, for higher $|g_x|$, such that $\tilde{\tau}_1 < \tilde{\tau} < \tilde{\tau}_3$, the marginal loss from a ban is lower than the MED in free trade. Thus, the higher is $|g_x|$, the more likely the ban is to raise welfare. However, it is also more likely that the ban will be inadequate to achieve the environmental goal.

In the presence of unemployment, the optimal production tax and the optimal export tax must be revised. Again using (15), we have:

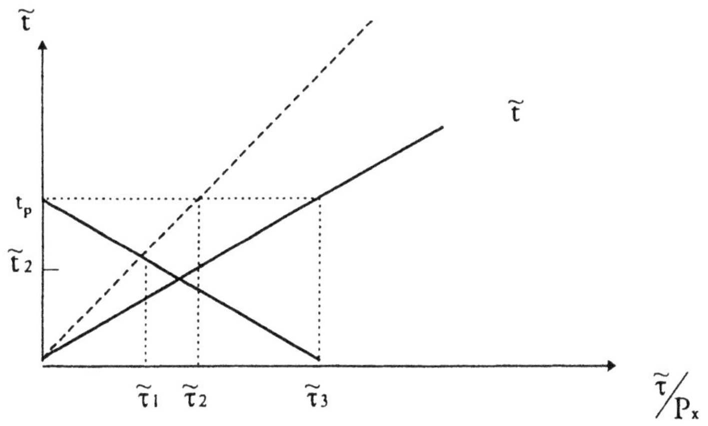

Figure 1. The Case for an Export Ban

$$\tilde{\tau}' = -P_y Y_{2} g_x T_y + P_y Y_L \left(\varepsilon_{\mu\tau} L_z \mu / \varepsilon_x X\right), \tag{16'}$$

$$\begin{aligned} \tilde{t}' = &\left(\tilde{\tau}'/P_x\right)\left[\varepsilon_x X / \left(\varepsilon_x X - \eta_x X_z\right)\right] \\ &+ P_y Y_L \left[\varepsilon_{\mu t} L_z \mu / \left(\varepsilon_x X - \eta_x X_z\right)\right], \end{aligned} \tag{17'}$$

where $\varepsilon_{\mu\tau} = \tau d\mu/\mu d\tau$ and $\varepsilon_{\mu t} = t d\mu/\mu dt$.

Stability of the labor market in this model requires that $(1 - \eta_L) > 0$, where η_L is the elasticity of the rural labor demand curve with respect to a change in the rural wage. If $\eta_L < 0$, the demand curve for rural labor slopes downward and stability is guaranteed. For $\eta_L < 0$, the impact of the environmental externality on labor productivity in agriculture must not be too large (see the Appendix). A sufficient condition for $\eta_L < 0$ is that:

$$\left(\partial Y_L / \partial L_y\right) - \left(\partial Y_L / \partial L_x\right) = Y_{LL} - \left(\partial Y_L / \partial L_x\right) < 0. \tag{18}$$

Equation (18) implies that the movement of a worker from X to Y production will on net reduce the marginal productivity of labor in Y. That is, the direct effect on marginal productivity of labor in Y of moving a worker from X to Y (the first term) exceeds the indirect effect via increased agricultural land productivity (the second term).

Proposition 1. *In the presence of unemployment, the optimal production tax is* less than *the value of marginal environmental damage which prevails in free trade, if (18) holds.*

Proof. We know $dL_z/d\tau = 0$. Thus:

$$\begin{aligned} d\mu/d\tau &= -\left(1/L_z\right)\left[\left(dL_x/d\tau\right) + \left(dL_y/d\tau\right)\right] \\ &= \left(\alpha\eta_L - 1\right)^{-1}\left[\left(L_x/L_z P_x\right)\eta_{LX}\left(1 - \partial Y_L/\partial L_X Y_{LL}\right)\right] \end{aligned}$$

where $\alpha = (L_x + L_y)/L_z(1 + \mu)$ and $\eta_{LX} = w_T \partial L_x / L_x \partial w_r < 0$. If (18) holds, $\eta_L < 0$ and the bracketed term is negative. Therefore, $d\mu/d\tau > 0$. Thus, $\varepsilon_{\mu\tau} > 0$, and by (16'), $\tilde{\tau}' < -P_y Y_{2} g_x T_y$. □

Proposition 1 implies that the production tax to correct for environmental damage aggravates unemployment if (18) holds. Clearly a tax on production of X will reduce the demand for workers in X but leave the price of logs as inputs unchanged. As long as (18) holds, moving workers from X to Y will depress the rural wage. The bracketed term shows the net change in demand for rural labor (for a given w_r) for a change in the price of X. If (18) holds, this is negative, implying an excess supply of labor at the original wage. This excess supply will be larger, the more elastic the demand for labor in X, and the smaller the impact of the externality on labor productivity in agriculture. The inverse of $(\alpha\eta_L - 1)$ gives the percentage change in the rural wage for a change in excess demand for rural labor. The fall in the rural wage implies a positive expected wage differential between urban and rural sectors. To bring about equilibrium (equation (4)), the unemployment ratio must rise to offset the fall in w_r.

PROPOSITION 2. *In the presence of unemployment, the optimal export tax will be* less than *the adjusted marginal environmental damage which prevails in free trade, if (18) holds, and if* η_x *is sufficiently small.*

PROOF.

$$d\mu/dt = P_x^*(\alpha\eta_L - 1)^{-1}\{[(L_x/L_z P_x)\eta_{LX}(1-(\partial Y_L/\partial L_x Y_{LL})] + (1+\mu)(Z_{LX}/|Z|L_z)\}$$

where $|Z| = (Z_{LL} Z_{XX} - Z_{LX}^2)$. If (18) holds, as before $\eta_L < 0$ and the first term in brackets on the right side is positive. The second term is equal to $(1 + \mu)(dL_z/dtL_z)$ and is positive. Now we know from (10) that $dL_z/dt = -(Z_{LX}/Z_{LL})(dX_z/dt)$, since $d\overline{w} = 0$. Assuming $-(Z_{LX}/Z_{LL}) < 1$, the size of the second term in brackets will depend upon η_x. Clearly if $\eta_x = 0$, the second term is zero, the bracketed term is negative, and $d\mu/dt > 0$. Given values for η_{LX} and for the size of the externality, there exists some value of $\eta_x = \eta_x^*$ such that for all $0 \leq \eta_x < \eta_x^*$, the bracketed term is negative and $d\mu/dt > 0$. For those cases, $\varepsilon_{\mu t} > 0$, and by (17′), $\tilde{t}' < \{(\tilde{\tau}'/P_x)[\varepsilon_x X/(\varepsilon_x X - \eta_x X_z)]\}$. Therefore, by Proposition 1, $\tilde{t}' < \{-(P_y/P_x)Y_2 g_x T_y[\varepsilon_x X/(\varepsilon_x X - \eta_x X_z)]\}$. □

As with a production tax, the export tax causes a net drop in demand for rural labor at a given w_r. Counteracting this is a drop in "supply" of labor to the rural sector; i.e. given μ and w_r, urban employment rises. Since the export tax implies a fall in the price of logs as an input into Z, this raises labor productivity at the margin in Z, absorbing some displaced workers from X, at the given w_r. However, the extent of this effect is limited by the fact that, with a fixed minimum wage, employment in Z can only rise by a fraction of the increase in demand for logs as inputs into Z. Therefore, for low values of the elasticity of demand for logs as inputs, the increased employment in Z will be too small to prevent the rural wage from falling relative to the urban wage. The unemployment ratio will then rise.

From Proposition 1, we see that in the presence of unemployment, the optimal production tax must be reduced below the level which corresponds to the MED prevailing in free trade. This itself implies a reduction in the optimal export tax such that it falls below the AMED. Proposition 2 shows that this latter result is unlikely to be reversed, despite the fact that an export tax stimulates the processing sector. Unless the elasticity of demand for logs as inputs is large, the export tax will also reduce the rural wage, increasing urban migration and unemployment. Hence, its optimal level will indeed remain below AMED.

Figure 2 shows the implications of Propositions 1 and 2 for the case for an export ban. As before, $\tilde{\tau}$ equals the MED which prevails in free trade, and $\tilde{t}$ equals the AMED. With unemployment, the optimal export tax must fall below AMED. This is shown by $\tilde{t}'$. It would now require a higher $|g_x|$ in free trade, such that $\tilde{\tau} = \tilde{\tau}_3'$, for an export ban to maximize welfare. This implies that there is now a larger range of $|g_x|$ in free trade, such that $0 < \tilde{\tau} < \tilde{\tau}_1'$, over which a ban would be welfare-reducing. Hence, in the short run the existence of unemployment has weakened, the case for an export ban as a second-best tool for environmental problems.

It should be noted, however, that the worse the environmental problem is in free trade, the less export restrictions actually affect unemployment. The faster environmental damage grows with output (the larger is $|g_x|$), the greater the positive impact of moving a worker from X to Y on labor productivity in Y. A small increase in the

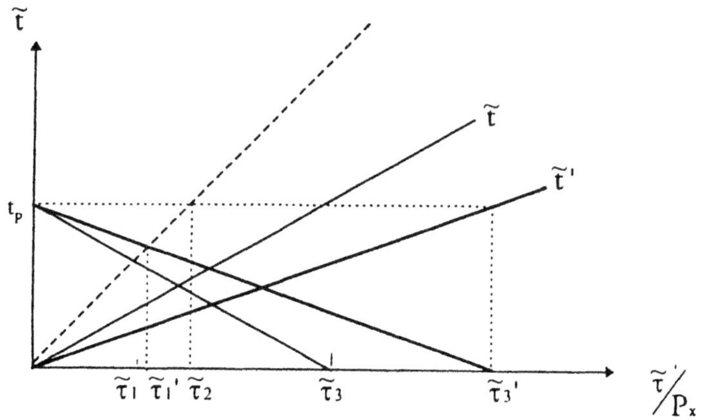

Figure 2. Short Run: Unemployment and the Export Ban

production tax (export tax) on X will, therefore, create *less* excess supply of labor in the rural sector (and less downward pressure on the rural wage), the higher the value of $|g_x|$ in free trade. Thus, $\varepsilon_{\mu\tau}$ and $\varepsilon_{\mu t}$ fall with a rise in $|g_x|$, and the importance of adjusting export restrictions due to unemployment diminishes. For severe enough environmental problems, then, the presence of an unemployment problem has a negligible effect on the case for an export ban.

4. Long-Run Analysis of an Export Ban

In the long run, all factors are mobile, and thus land can also be shifted between the logging and agricultural sectors. We continue to assume (simplistically) that environmental damage comes from a single source: production of the intermediate, logs, generates environmental damage by reducing the productivity of land in the agricultural sector. Thus, moving both land and labor from logging to agriculture is assumed to reduce environmental damage as long as logging output falls. This is true even if the land is cleared for use in agriculture.[5]

With all factors mobile, the model in section 2 may be written using the familiar Jones (1965) notation. Suppose there is no export restriction. Then, the reduced form model is:[6]

$$\theta_{Lx}\hat{w}+\theta_{Tx}\hat{r}=-\hat{\tau}\left(\tau/P_x\right), \tag{19}$$

$$\theta_{Lx}\hat{w}+\theta_{Ty}\hat{r}-\theta_{Ty}\rho\hat{X}=0, \tag{20}$$

$$\lambda_{Tx}\hat{X}+\lambda_{Ty}\hat{Y}+\partial_T\left(\hat{w}-\hat{r}\right)+A\rho\hat{X}=0, \tag{21}$$

$$\lambda_{Lx}\hat{X}+\lambda_{Ly}\hat{Y}-C\hat{w}-\partial_L\left(\hat{w}-\hat{r}\right)-B\rho\hat{X}=0, \tag{22}$$

where $A=\lambda_{Ty}\theta_{Ly}(\sigma_y-1)$, $B=\lambda_{Ly}\theta_{Ty}(\sigma_y-1)$, $C=\lambda_{Lz}(1+\mu)$, and $\rho=\hat{g}/\hat{X}$. The circumflex represents percentage change. θ_{ij} is the share of input i in the unit cost of output j; λ_{ij} is the proportion of the total stock of i used in producing j; σ_j is the elasticity of substitution of land for labor in industry j. Using these definitions, $\partial_L = \lambda_{Lx}\theta_{Tx}\sigma_X + \lambda_{Ly}\theta_{Ty}\sigma_y$ and $\partial_T = \lambda_{Tx}\theta_{Lx}\sigma_X + \lambda_{Ty}\theta_{Ly}\sigma_y$.

Equations (19) and (20) express changes in input prices as functions of changes in the production tax, assuming world prices of goods are constant. Changes in environmental damage are captured by $\rho < 0$. This elasticity measures the sensitivity of agricultural land productivity to a change in the output of logs. Equations (21) and (22) express changes in input usage in relation to changes in outputs, assuming factor endowments are constant.

Assumption 2. *Y is more labor-intensive than X.*

For stability of the system, an increase in the production tax on X should lower the output of X. Under Assumption 2, this will occur if the determinant of the system, $|D|$, is negative;[7] that is:

$$|D| = |\theta||\lambda| + \rho\left[|\theta|(\lambda_{Ly}A + \lambda_{Ty}B) - \theta_{Ty}E - \theta_{Ty}\theta_{Tx}\lambda_{Ty}C\right] < 0, \quad (23)$$

where:

$$E = (\partial_T\lambda_{Ly} + \partial_L\lambda_{Ty}) > 0,$$

$$|\theta| = \theta_{Ty} - \theta_{Tx} < 0,$$

$$|\lambda| = \lambda_{Tx}\lambda_{Ly} - \lambda_{Ty}\lambda_{Lx} > 0.$$

Proposition 3. *In the presence of unemployment, the optimal production tax is* greater than *the value of marginal environmental damage which prevails in free trade, if (23) holds.*

Proof. Solving (19)–(22) for $\hat{w}/\hat{\tau}$ yields:

$$\hat{w}/\hat{\tau} = -(\tau/P_x)\theta_{Ty}\left[|\lambda| + \rho(\lambda_{Ly}A + \lambda_{Ty}B) - E\right]/|D|.$$

By (23), $[|\lambda| + \rho(\lambda_{Ly}A + \lambda_{Ty}B)] > 0$. Since $\theta_{Ty} > |\theta|$, then also by (23), the sum in brackets is positive. Since $|D| < 0$, $\hat{w}/\hat{\tau} > 0$. From (4) we know that (holding $\overline{w}$ constant) $\varepsilon_{\mu\tau} = -\hat{w}(1 + \mu)/\mu\hat{\tau}$. Therefore, $\varepsilon_{\mu\tau} < 0$, and by (16′), $\tilde{\tau}' > -P_yY_2g_xT_y$. □

Proposition 3 implies that the short-run result found in Proposition 1 is reversed in the long run. In the short run an increase in the production tax lowers the rural wage. In a Harris–Todaro labor market this increases unemployment. Here an increase in the production tax raises the rural wage and therefore lowers unemployment. According to the Stolper–Samuelson theorem, we should expect this result. A fall in the price of X relative to Y will create an expansion of the relatively labor-intensive sector, an excess demand for labor, and an increase in the rural wage. This creates a wage differential in favor of the rural sector, generating reverse migration and a fall in unemployment.

However, from (19) and (20) we have:

$$(\hat{P}_x - \hat{P}_y) = |\theta|(\hat{w} - \hat{r}) + \theta_{Ty}\rho\hat{X}. \quad (24)$$

Equation (24) is the usual expression for the Stolper–Samuelson theorem with an additional term reflecting the negative externality. Given Assumption 2, we know $|\theta| <$ 0. However, with $\rho < 0$, the second term on the right side of (24) works against the first term. If X production falls, this tends to raise the marginal productivity of land in the rural sector, increasing its value relative to labor. As is shown in the Appendix, however, the stability of the system ($|D| < 0$) is sufficient for the usual Stolper–Samuelson result to occur.

If there is no production tax, the reduced-form model becomes (19′), (20), (21), and (22′):

$$\theta_{Lx}\hat{w} + \theta_{Tx}\hat{r} = \hat{t}, \tag{19'}$$

$$\lambda_{Lx}\hat{X} + \lambda_{Ly}\hat{Y} - C\hat{w} - \partial_L(\hat{w} - \hat{r}) - B\rho\hat{X} = -C\left[\left(1 - \theta_{Xz}\right)/\theta_{Lz}/\right]\varepsilon_z\hat{t} \tag{22'}$$

where:[8]

$$\hat{t} = d(1-t)/(1-t),$$

$$\varepsilon_z = \hat{Z}/\hat{t} = -\eta_x + \theta_{Lz}\,\sigma_z/\left(1 - \theta_{Kz}\right) < 0.$$

Again for stability of this system, we would want an export tax to reduce output of X on net. Because the export tax on X does stimulate demand for X as an input into Z, the condition for net X production to fall as a result of the tax is more stringent than in the case of the production tax. Given that (23) holds, a sufficient condition for this to occur is $-\varepsilon_z \leqslant \theta_{Lz}/1 - \theta_{Xz}$.

Proposition 4. *In the presence of unemployment, the optimal export tax is* greater than *the adjusted value of marginal environmental damage prevailing in free trade, if (23) holds and* $-\varepsilon_z \leq \theta_{Lz}/(1 - \theta_{Xz})$.

Proof. Solving the model for $\hat{w}/\hat{t}$ yields:

$$\hat{w}/\hat{t} = \theta_{Ty}\left\{|\lambda| + \rho\left[\left(\lambda_{Ly}A + \lambda_{Ty}B\right) - E - \theta_{Tx}\lambda_{Ty}C\varepsilon_z\left(1 - \theta_{Xz}/\theta_{Lz}\right)\right]\right\}/|D|.$$

By (23), we know that $|D| < 0$, and the sum of the first three terms in the numerator is positive. If $-\varepsilon_z \leqslant \theta_{Lz}/(1 - \theta_{Xz})$, then by (23), the numerator must be positive. Thus, $\hat{w}/\hat{t} < 0$. Using (4) and the definition of $\hat{t}$, $\varepsilon_{\mu t} = -\hat{\mu}/\hat{t} = \hat{w}(1 + \mu)/\mu\hat{t} < 0$. Thus, by (17′), $t' > (\bar{\tau}'/P_x)\ [\varepsilon_x X/(\varepsilon_x X - \eta_x X_z)]$, and by Proposition 3, $\bar{t}' > \{-(P_y/P_x)Y_2 g_x T_y\ [\varepsilon_x X/(\varepsilon_x X - \eta_x X_z)]\}$. □

Here again, an export tax causes X production to fall and Y production to expand. However, the expansion of the Z sector reduces the extent to which the X sector shrinks. This implies a smaller relative expansion of Y, and hence a smaller excess demand for labor in the rural sector.[9] The impact on the rural wage via the Stolper–Samuelson mechanism is, therefore, smaller. However, the export tax on X will still reduce the rural wage, and thereby unemployment, as long as it causes X production to fall.

The implications of these results for the case for an export ban can be seen in Figure 3. By Propositions 3 and 4, the optimal export tax must exceed AMED. Thus it must rise in relation to the MED prevailing in free trade. This is shown by $\bar{t}''$. It would now require a lower $|g_x|$ in free trade, such that $\bar{\tau} = \bar{\tau}_3''$, for an export ban to maximize welfare. As a result, there is now a smaller range of $|g_x|$ in free trade, corresponding to $0 < \bar{\tau} < \bar{\tau}_1''$, over which a ban would be welfare-reducing. Therefore, the case for an export ban is actually stronger in the long run, in the presence of unemployment.

As in the short-run case, however, the impact of an export restriction (or a production tax) on unemployment diminishes as $|g_x|$ rises. It can be shown that $\partial\varepsilon_{\mu\tau}/\partial\rho > 0$ and $\partial\varepsilon_{\mu t}/\partial\rho > 0$. This is because (as noted above) the existence of the environmental externality works against the Stolper–Samuelson result. A fall in X production raises the marginal productivity of land in Y. This tends to diminish the extent of the typical outcome—an excess supply of land and excess demand for labor. Thus, the beneficial impact of each of these taxes on unemployment diminishes as $|\rho|$ increases. For a

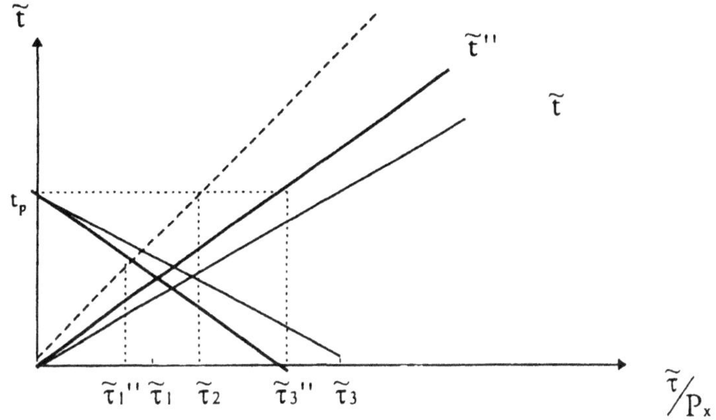

Figure 3. Long Run: Unemployment and the Export Ban

sufficiently severe environmental damage problem, then, unemployment has a negligible effect on the long-run case for an export ban.

5. Conclusions

It has been suggested that an export restriction may be a useful second-best tool for developing countries facing both environmental damage generated by production of some export goods, and unemployment in the industrial sector. If the export good is an intermediate (such as logs), an export restriction will both reduce environmental damage and stimulate local processing industries by decreasing the price of the intermediate good.

Because countries often choose blunt instruments as second-best policy tools, this study investigated the case for an export ban as environmental policy, in the presence of unemployment. A three-sector model was developed in which production of an intermediate good export was assumed to generate environmental degradation. However, this degradation was assumed to reduce the productivity of an input in another sector. The urban import-competing processing sector was characterized by unemployment of the Harris–Todaro type. Within this framework, we characterized the optimal export tax to address environmental damage (in the absence of a first-best policy), and from this derived the case for an export ban. We then considered how the optimal export tax changed in the presence of unemployment, and whether this strengthened or weakened the case for an export ban.

In the short run, both production taxes and export taxes were shown to reduce rural wages, aggravating the unemployment problem rather than improving it. Hence, the optimal export tax was reduced, for any given level of environmental damage in free trade. This weakened the case for an export ban, since it raised the minimum level of environmental damage in free trade required for an export ban to be welfare-improving.

This result was reversed in the long run. Provided that environmental damage affected the relatively labor-intensive sector, the usual Stolper–Samuelson result occurred. Export taxes on the intermediate good tended to expand output of the relatively labor-intensive sector, bidding up rural wages. Hence, export restrictions tended to alleviate urban unemployment. This called for a higher optimal export tax, for any given level of environmental damage in free trade. This also strengthened the case for an export ban, since it reduced the minimum level of environmental damage in free trade required for an export ban to be welfare-improving.

Finally, the impact of export restrictions on unemployment (positive or negative) was shown to diminish as the severity of the environmental problem increased. Dean (1995) had argued that for very severe environmental damage in free trade, an export ban would raise welfare, but would be inadequate to reduce output to an environmentally sustainable level. Our results suggest that the presence of unemployment would do little to change this result.

Appendix

Necessary and Sufficient Condition for Labor Market Stability

The elasticity of demand for rural labor with respect to the rural wage, w_r, is:

$$\eta_L = \left[X_{LL}Y_L + Y_{LL}X_L - X_L(\partial Y_L/\partial L_X)\right] / X_{LL}Y_{LL}(L_X + L_Y). \tag{A1}$$

For stability in the labor market, an increase in the wage must cause an excess supply of rural labor. Given the Harris–Todaro condition in (4), we know that with no change in $\overline{w}$, the elasticity of labor supply to the rural sector (i.e. reverse migration) is 1. Therefore, the necessary condition for stability is $(1 - \eta_L) > 0$. A sufficient condition for stability to hold is $\eta_L < 0$. Given diminishing marginal returns to labor in X and in Y, $\eta_L < 0$ if

$$-(X_{LL}Y_L + Y_{LL}X_L) > -X_L(\partial Y_L/\partial L_X). \tag{A2}$$

A sufficient condition for (A2) is (18).

Derivation of the Stolper–Samuelson Result

We know that:

$$(\hat{P}_x - \hat{P}_y) = |\theta|(\hat{w} - \hat{r}) + \theta_{Ty}\rho\hat{X}. \tag{24}$$

To solve for $\hat{X}$, subtract (22) from (21):

$$\hat{X} = \left[-E(\hat{w} - \hat{r}) - \lambda_{Ty}C\hat{w}\right] / \left[|\lambda| + (\lambda_{Ly}A + \lambda_{Ty}B)\right], \tag{A3}$$

where E, C, A, and B are defined as in the text. Substitute (A3) into (24) and simplify:

$$\begin{aligned}(\hat{P}_x - \hat{P}_y)/(\hat{w} - \hat{r}) &= \left\{|\theta||\lambda| + \rho\left[|\theta|(\lambda_{Ly}A + \lambda_{Ty}B) - \theta_{Ty}E - \theta_{Ty}\theta_{Tx}\lambda_{Ty}C\right]\right\} \\ &\quad \div \left[|\lambda| + (\lambda_{Ly}A + \lambda_{Ty}B)\right] \\ &= |D| / \left[|\lambda| + (\lambda_{Ly}A + \lambda_{Ty}B)\right].\end{aligned} \tag{A4}$$

The expression in (A4) is negative if $|D| < 0$, i.e. if (23) holds.

References

Anderson, K. and R. Blackhurst (eds), *The Greening of World Trade Issues*, Ann Arbor: University of Michigan Press, 1992.

Barbier, E., Bockstaal, N., Burgess, J., and Strand, I., "The Linkages Between the Timber Trade and Tropical Deforestation Indonesia," *World Economy* (1995):411–40.

Baumol, W. and W. Oates, *The Theory of Environmental Policy*, Cambridge: Cambridge University Press, 1988.

Beghin, J., D. Roland-Holst, and D. van der Mensbrugghe, "Trade and Pollution Linkages: Piecemeal Reform and Optimal Intervention," manuscript, 1994.

Bovenberg, A. L. and R. A. deMooij, "Environmental Levies and Distortionary Taxation," *American Economic Review* 94 (1994):1085–9.

Braga, C. P., "Tropical Forests and Trade Policy: The Cases of Indonesia and Brazil," in P. Low (ed.), *International Trade and the Environment*, World Bank Discussion Paper 159, 1992.

Chao, C. and E. Yu, "Content Protection, Urban Unemployment and Welfare," *Canadian Journal of Economics* 93 (1993):481–92.

Copeland, B., "International Trade and the Environment: Policy Reform in a Polluted Small Open Economy," *Journal of Environmental Economics and Management* 26 (1994):44–65.

Dean, J., "Trade and the Environment: A Survey of the Literature," in P. Low (ed.), *International Trade and the Environment*, World Bank Discussion Paper 159, 1992.

———, "Export Bans, Environment, and Developing Country Welfare," *Review of International Economics* 3 (1995):319–29.

Harris, J. and M. Todaro, "Migration, Unemployment, and Development: A Two Sector Analysis," *American Economic Review*.

Jaffe, A., S. Peterson, P. Portnoy, and R. Stavins, "Environmental Regulation and the Competitiveness of US Manufacturing," *Journal of Economic Literature* 33 (1995):132–63.

Jones, R., "The Structure of Simple General Equilibrium Models," *Journal of Political Economy* 73 (1965):557–72.

Krutilla, K., "Environmental Regulation in an Open Economy," *Journal of Environmental Economics and Management* 20 (1991):127–42.

Low, P. (ed.), *International Trade and the Environment*, World Bank Discussion Paper 159, 1992.

Notes

1. Braga (1992) discussed a proposal by the European Parliament, which would impose annual quotas on exports of tropical hardwood to the EU. Exporters with "sustainably"-managed forests would be given larger quotas.
2. See Dean (1992), Low (1992), Anderson and Blackhurst (1992), and Jaffe et al. (1995).
3. In a similar spirit, Bovenberg (1994) investigates whether or not environmental tax revenues could be used to decrease other distortionary taxes.
4. The calculation of an environmentally sustainable rate of X production would require a dynamic model. Assuming that this rate can be determined, there should be a corresponding optimal level of annual X output. The static model used here focuses on the first-best production tax to achieve this optimal level of output.
5. A more complex model would take into account the optimal forest stock, recognizing that depletion of the forest stock below that level would lead to additional environmental problems. It would also account for other types of environmental damage, generated by agricultural production itself, which might be as or more serious than those from deforestation.
6. The "w" refers to rural wage w_r. The subscript is dropped throughout this section.
7. The necessary condition for $|D| < 0$ is $-|\theta||\lambda| > \rho\,[\cdot]$.
8. This definition of $\hat{t}$ implies that an increase in the export tax corresponds to $\hat{t} < 0$.
9. One can show that the response of rural wages to price changes (24) will diminish by the extent to which the Z sector expands.

Freer Trade and Pollution Havens

[18]

ELSEVIER Journal of Public Economics 56 (1995) 55–77

JOURNAL OF PUBLIC ECONOMICS

Competition in regional environmental policies when plant locations are endogenous[1]

James R. Markusen[a,b,*], Edward R. Morey[a], Nancy Olewiler[c]

[a]*Department of Economics, University of Colorado, Boulder, CO 80309-0256, USA*
[b]*NBER, 1050 Massachusetts Av., Cambridge, MA 02139, USA*
[c]*Simon Fraser University, Burnaby, British Columbia V5A 1S6, Canada*

Received October 1992, final version received October 1993

Abstract

A two-region model is presented in which an imperfectly competitive firm produces a good with increasing returns at the plant level. Production of the good causes local pollution. The firm decides whether to maintain plants in both regions, serve both regions from a single plant or shut down. If the disutility of pollution is high enough, the two regions will compete by increasing their environmental taxes (standards) until the polluting firm is driven from the market. Alternatively, if the disutility from pollution is not as great, the regions will usually compete by undercutting each other's pollution tax rates.

Key words: Environmental policy; Tax competition; Plant location

JEL classification: H7; Q2; R3

1. Introduction

There are at least two conceptually distinct types of environmental problems that can play a significant role in interregional and in international policy. One problem is transfrontier pollution such as acid rain, and global

* Corresponding author.

[1] Earlier versions of this paper were presented at a meeting of the Canadian Association of Environmental Economists, September 1991, at the Allied Social Sciences meetings, New Orleans, January 1992, and the NBER Summer Institute, August 1992.

SSDI 0047-2727(94)01419-0

warming. Transfrontier pollution has attracted considerable attention, and a rapidly increasing amount of economic analysis.

A second and to some extent overlapping problem involves strictly *local pollution* externalities, but involves interregional and international considerations insofar as the location of production is endogenous. As environmental issues have moved to the forefront of public debate, regional politicians ambivalently worry that imposing stricter environmental standards will drive industry from their region, while strongly believing that highly polluting plants, although sometimes necessary, should only be located in someone else's region. These issues are now receiving considerable attention from an international perspective. The Canadian–U.S. Free Trade Agreement, the debate on North American free trade, and the completion of the internal market for the European Economic Community are forcing politicians to confront these issues. For example, some US and Canadian groups are worried that free trade will mean the movement of many of their plants to Mexico in order to take advantage of the cost savings afforded by lower environmental standards in Mexico.

Alternatively, if the disutility from pollution is sufficiently high, each region will want the polluting firm to produce only in the other region. In this case, the regions might bid up each other's environmental standards until the firm is driven from business. This can happen even though both regions would be better off if the firm operates a plant in one of the regions, and the region without the plant compensates the region with the plant for the pollution they experience. This is the case of NIMBY (Not in my back yard). For example, no one wants a hazardous waste site in their region, but we are collectively better off with one, than without one.[2]

In a previous paper (Markusen, Morey, Olewiler, 1993), hencforth MMO), we address the issue of plant endogeneity in a two-region model that involves two polluting firms choosing plant locations: location decisions that are influenced by the environmental policy of one region (the other region is passive). That model, which involves increasing returns to scale at the plant level, produces results that differ dramatically from those obtained from more traditional competitive models using Pigouvian marginal analysis.[3] We show in MMO that regional welfare functions exhibit large discontinuities at critical levels of the environmental policy variables when plant location decisions are endogenous.

The purpose of the present paper is to turn our attention to the governments themselves, and consider the fact that the governments of two

[2] Mitchell and Carson (1986) consider the locating of such facilities in a model that emphasizes aversion to risk taking. There is no interregional competition in their model.

[3] Examples of General equilibrium models with trade and pollution include Pethig (1976), Asako (1979), and Merrifield (1988). These models assume pure competition and constant returns to scale and thus are able to use marginal analysis. There is a literature on imperfect competition and pollution that examines policies, but does so in models without trade. Examples include Misiolek (1980) and Copeland (1991).

regions can compete in terms of their environmental policies. Our work builds on the literature on tax competition among governments. In the part of this literature most relevant to our work, capital and goods, but not individuals, are mobile across regions.[4] In most of the tax competition literature, taxes are used to generate the revenues to provide public goods. Jurisdictions desire to attract industry and the resulting competition typically results in lower tax rates and the underprovision of public goods.[5] See, for example, Arnott and Grieson (1981), Wilson (1985, 1986), Mintz and Tulkens (1986), Wildasin (1988, 1989), and several papers in a special issue of Regional Science and Urban Economics edited by Wildasin and Wilson (1991). These papers all model the 'rationale' which motivates destructive tax competitions. Mintz and Tulkens, in addition, explicitly consider the resulting non-cooperative equilibrium as the result of a game between the regions. Mintz and Tulkens use the Nash equilibrium concept with tax rates as the strategic variable.

There are a few papers that look specifically at environmental quality and government competition (Cumberland, 1979, 1981; Oates and Schwab, 1988). Both assume pure competition. Neither explicitly models the game between the governments. Cumberland considers environmental standards, rather than taxes, and argues that regions are likely to compete by relaxing standards to attract industry. He concludes that this competition will result in too low a level of environmental quality. He does not consider the NIMBY possibility. Oates and Schwab consider the joint determination of a tax rate on capital (to finance public goods), and the appropriate level of environmental quality. The *n* regions in their model do not compete directly in terms of either tax rates or environmental standards. Like the models cited above, the tax on capital is used to raise revenue and is distortionary. The nature of the *tax competition* in their model is a capital relocation externality; i.e. when capital is mobile, regions realize that as they level taxes to finance local public goods, capital will move to untaxed regions. The result is too few public goods and too low a level of environmental quality relative to a first-best optimum. Strategic behavior is not modelled.[6]

[4] Along another vein, Tiebout (1956) generated a government competition literature where people are mobile and *vote with their feet*. In this literature, governments compete to provide a mix of public goods that maximizes households' utility. The resulting equilibria are efficient.

[5] Because the focus of these articles is on the provision of public goods, and not negative externalities, a NIMBY case where tax rates are bid up cannot arise.

[6] There are several recent papers examining strategic behavior among government regulators of pollution (See Hoel, 1991; Dockner and Long, 1991; Folmer et al., 1991). In each paper, government behavior is modeled as a cooperative or non-cooperative game when there is transboundary (global) pollution. Papers by Barrett (1994), Rauscher (1991), and Ulph (1992) consider other aspects of imperfect competition with non-cooperative government environmental policies. Barrett shows how strategic (rent shifting) motives influence policies, while Rauscher and Ulph focus on quantity standards versus pollution taxes. The potential impact of government decisions on industrial structure and plant location are not examined in any of these papers.

In this paper, we assume a single, imperfectly-competitive firm producing some product X with increasing returns to scale. The X firm may choose to build plants in both regions, a plant in only one of the regions, or not produce at all. The existence of shipping costs between regions is responsible for the fact that the firm may choose plants in both regions despite increasing returns to scale. Pollution is generated as a by-product of the production of X, but this pollution does not cross regional borders. There is also a competitive Y industry in each region. The Y industry does not pollute. The issue addressed is thus trans-border competition in environmental policies, not transfrontier pollution.

Each government's decision criteria is to maximize their region's consumer surplus from the consumption of X and Y, plus tax revenue, minus the region's disutility from pollution.[7] These regional goals conflict. The resulting competition between the two governments is modelled as a two-stage non-cooperative game. In the first stage of the game, the two governments simultaneously set the values of environmental policy variables. These are interpreted as pollution taxes throughout the analysis, but they could also be thought of as regulatory variables that impact on the firm's marginal cost (e.g., requiring cleaner fuel or other more expensive inputs). In the second stage, the firm chooses one of four configurations of plants: a plant in both regions, referred to as (1,1), a single plant in Region A, denoted (1,0), a single plant in Region B, denoted (0,1), or zero plants, denoted (0,0). The game is solved backwards in the usual fashion. The second stage is solved first in two steps. We first solve for the firm's maximum profits given the levels of the pollution taxes and given a particular configuration of plants. We then solve for the firm's choice of plant locations given the tax levels. In the first stage of the game, we solve for the two governments' non-cooperative equilibrium levels of pollution taxes using a Nash (best response) solution concept.

The increasing-returns and discrete-choice aspects of the problem make it an interesting one, but unfortunately greatly add to its analytical complexity. In particular, the traditional reaction-curve analysis that allows the Nash equilibrium to be expressed as a fixed-point of some mapping is of little use here. There are large discontinuities in tax reaction curves as the firm changes the number/location of its plants, and the relationship between the discontinuities in the two countries is very sensitive to parameter values. The lack of continuity eventually led us to abandon the traditional ap-

[7] For simplicity, we assume that the ownership of the firm is widely distributed throughout the 'world' so that the firm's profits are not taken into consideration in regional welfare. Because our industry is non-competitive, the optimal pollution tax is not equal solely to the marginal disutility from pollution, but is more complex as will be shown later in the paper. Thus, there may be tax revenue in excess of total pollution disutility.

proach. We are able to show the range of parameter values which support a particular equilibrium, and the critical combination of parameters that cause us to move from one equilibrium to another. But we resort to examples in order to illustrate the welfare losses from non-cooperative behavior, and do not attempt to provide an exhaustive characterization of all possible equilibria.

2. The effect of taxation on the number and location of plants

This section develops the model and solves for the equilibrium configuration of plants as a function of the two countries' tax rates. As noted earlier, the four possible equilibria are (1,1), (1,0), (0,1) and (0,0).

The two regions are assumed to be absolutely identical in all respects. The resulting symmetry aids us greatly in obtaining simple expressions for solutions. An individual consumer in each region has the utility function

$$U = \alpha C_x - (1/2)C_x^2 - \gamma(X_d + X_e) + C_y \tag{1}$$

where C_x and C_y are per capita consumption levels of X and Y respectively. $X = (X_d + X_e)$ is the total domestic production of X. X_d denotes production sold domestically and X_e denotes production that is exported. Assume one unit of pollution is produced in a region for each unit of X produced in that region. Thus γ is the marginal disutility of pollution to a consumer. Let N denote the total number of individuals in a region. Each individual views the total level of pollution in his or her region as exogenous, and in the absence of a pollution tax, or regulation, this externality will, ceteris paribus, lead to a market failure. Note that the system is also distorted by the market power of the X firm. To help simplify notation, we will normalize N at $N = 1$.

An individual is assumed to own L units of labor, and the production function for Y is simply $Y = L_y$ where L_y is the labor allocated to Y production out of the endowment of L units of labor. Y or L is numeraire (if the price of Y equals 1, then the price of L must equal one), and p_x denotes the price of X in terms of Y or L. There is no pollution associated with the production of Y. The X firm produces with a constant marginal cost m and with fixed costs as discussed below.

Let t denote the pollution tax levied on the production of X that is sold domestically, and let t_e denote the pollution tax that is levied on the production of X that is exported. The tax rate t_e can be thought of as the sum of the domestic pollution tax t plus a supplemental tax or subsidy, e, on export sales; i.e., $t_e = t + e$. Assume no other taxes. Allowing a region to differentiate between production for local consumption and exports gives each region greater flexibility, than would a single pollution tax, to address jointly the pollution and market power distortions in a world where plant locations are endogenous.

Assume tax revenues are redistributed equally among all individuals. An individual's budget constraint is thus given by

$$L + tX_{\mathrm{d}} + t_{\mathrm{e}}X_{\mathrm{e}} = p_x C_x + C_y \tag{2}$$

Maximizing (1) subject to (2) yields the very simple linear demand function

$$p_x = \alpha - C_x \tag{3}$$

Profits, before fixed costs, for the X producer from production for sale within a region ($C_x = X_{\mathrm{d}}$) (recall N is normalized at $N = 1$) are given by

$$(\alpha - X_{\mathrm{d}})X_{\mathrm{d}} - mX_{\mathrm{d}} - tX_{\mathrm{d}} \tag{4}$$

Since an increase in the marginal cost m is equivalent to a decrease in α in this formulation, we will simplify notation from here on by setting $m = 0$. Maximizing (4) with respect to X_{d} yields the firm's optimal supply.[8]

$$X_d = (\alpha - t)/2 \tag{5}$$

When the firm considers export sales, there is an equation similar to (4) but with t_{e} and an additional term for exporting costs: sX_{e}, where s is per-unit transportation cost. The supply function for exports (recall that populations are identical) is thus

$$X_{\mathrm{e}} = (\alpha - s - t_{\mathrm{e}})/2 \tag{6}$$

Let $\pi(i, j)$ denote the profits of the firm in market structure $(i, j) \in \{1, 0\}$. Let subscripts a and b denote regions A and B respectively. Let G denote the plant-specific fixed cost and F the firm-specific fixed cost. Inserting (5) and (6) into the profit equations, the maximized values of profits under each market structure are given by

$$\pi(1, 1) = [(\alpha - t_{\mathrm{a}})^2 + (\alpha - t_{\mathrm{b}})^2]/4 - 2G - F \tag{7}$$

$$\pi(1, 0) = [(\alpha - t_{\mathrm{a}})^2 + (\alpha - s - t_{\mathrm{ae}})^2]/4 - G - F \tag{8}$$

$$\pi(0, 1) = [(\alpha - s - t_{\mathrm{be}})^2 + (\alpha - t_{\mathrm{b}})^2]/4 - G - F \tag{9}$$

and $\pi(0, 0) = 0$.

For a given set of tax rates, the firm will choose that configuration of plants that maximizes its profits. This configuration can be found by using equations (7)–(9) and $\pi(0, 0)$ to determine maximum profits, at the given tax rates, for each of the four possible configurations. Said loosely, the firm

[8] We assume throughout (and specify in the examples) that L is sufficiently large such that consumers are able to pay for the X produced at the implied price. Resources used for fixed costs may come from the 'outside world'.

will choose the (1,1) configuration, rather than (1,0) or (0,1), when t_e and s are large (exports are less attractive as t_e and/or s increases); t is small (production for local consumption becomes less attractive as t increases); and G is small (a second plant becomes less attractive as G increases). The firm will choose not to operate, (0,0), given sufficiently large values of G and F. For example, (1,1) at $t = t_e = 0$ corresponds to a situation where plant-specific costs are low relative to the size of the market (α) and low relative to shipping costs (s) so that the X producer prefers to bear the fixed cost of an additional plant relative to the unit shipping cost. Horstmann and Markusen (1992) analyzes these determinants of market structure in more detail. Note that the firm's choice of plant locations does not directly depend on the disutility from pollution, γ (the demand price is independent of γ).

The next step is to determine each region's choice of tax rates. Before determining the non-cooperative equilibrium tax rates that will result when plant locations are endogenous across regions, we derive, as a pedagogic device to help determine the actual equilibrium, each region's optimal tax rates under the artificial assumption that plant locations are exogenous. These tax rates are set ignoring the strategic nature of the competition between the regions, and, since they are set to equate the marginal benefits and costs from pollution and market power, can be interpreted as the Pigouvian tax rates. They are therefore the optimal *non-strategic Pigouvian* tax rates. For brevity, we will refer to them as the *non-strategic* tax rates and identify them with the superscript η; i.e. t^η and t_e^η.

3. Regional social welfare and optimal taxes for exogenous plant locations: The optimal non-strategic tax rates

Substituting equations (2) and (3) into (1) and multiplying by N (normalized to $N = 1$) gives social welfare for the region.

$$W = U = (1/2)C_x^2 + (t - \gamma)X_d + (t_e - \gamma)X_e + L \tag{10}$$

If one plant is operating in each region, (1,1), $C_x = X_d$ and $X_e = 0$ (if we let X_m equal imports of X, $X_m = 0$ as well). Welfare of each region is thus

$$W(1,1) = (1/2)X_d^2 + (t - \gamma)X_d + L \tag{11}$$

Under asymmetric plant configurations, (1,0) or (0,1), Region A's welfare equations are

$$W_a(1,0) = (1/2)X_d^2 + (t_a - \gamma)X_d + (t_{ae} - \gamma)X_e + L \tag{12}$$

$$W_a(0,1) = (1/2)X_m^2 + L \tag{13}$$

where X_m is equal to the exports of Region B.

Now consider the optimal taxes for a region *assuming* exogenous plant locations. Begin by considering the plant configuration (1, 1). To obtain the non-strategic pollution tax for a (1, 1) market structure differentiate (11) with respect to t and set the derivative equal to zero.

$$\frac{\mathrm{d}W(1,1)}{\mathrm{d}t} = (X_{\mathrm{d}} + t - \gamma)\frac{\mathrm{d}X_{\mathrm{d}}}{\mathrm{d}t} + X_{\mathrm{d}} = 0 \qquad \frac{\mathrm{d}X_{\mathrm{d}}}{\mathrm{d}t} = -\frac{1}{2} \tag{14}$$

where the second equation is derived from (5). Substituting the second equation of (14) into the first and using (5), we get the non-strategic tax formula

$$t^{\eta} = \alpha/3 + 2\gamma/3 \tag{15}$$

Substituting (15) into (5), we get X^{η} and substituting X^{η} and t^{η} into (11), we get welfare under the (1, 1) market structure, denoted W^{η}.

$$X^{\eta} = (\alpha - \gamma)/3 \tag{16}$$

$$W^{\eta}(1,1) = (\alpha - \gamma)^2/6 + L \tag{17}$$

Next, consider the taxes that the government of Region A will set on pollution associated with production for domestic consumption and for export, given the exogenous configuration of plants (1, 0). Assume that the firm is able to price discriminate between the regional markets (prices can be set independently in A and B). Referring to welfare in Eq. (12), we see that the derivative with respect to t is the same as (14), and so Region A will set $t = t^{\eta}$ as in the case of market structure (1, 1). To determine t_{e}^{η}, differentiate (12) with respect to t_{ae} to obtain

$$\frac{\mathrm{d}W_{\mathrm{a}}(1,0)}{\mathrm{d}t_{\mathrm{ae}}} = (t_{\mathrm{ae}} - \gamma)\frac{\mathrm{d}X_{\mathrm{e}}}{\mathrm{d}t_{\mathrm{e}}} + X_{\mathrm{e}} = 0 \quad \frac{\mathrm{d}X_{\mathrm{e}}}{\mathrm{d}t_{\mathrm{ae}}} = -\tfrac{1}{2} \tag{18}$$

where the second equation follows from (6). Substituting the second equation of (18) into the first and using (6), we get the non-strategic export tax formula

$$t_{\mathrm{e}}^{\eta} = (\alpha - s + \gamma)/2 \qquad \text{where} \qquad (t_{\mathrm{e}}^{\eta} - \gamma) = (\alpha - s - \gamma)/2 \tag{19}$$

Therefore, each region will set $t = t^{\eta}$ and $t_{\mathrm{e}} = t_{\mathrm{e}}^{\eta}$ if they ignore the strategic interactions. Substituting (19) into (6) we get the non-strategic export function

$$X_{\mathrm{e}}^{\eta} = (\alpha - s - \gamma)/4 \qquad \text{where} \qquad (t_{\mathrm{e}}^{\eta} - \gamma)X_{\mathrm{e}}^{\eta} = (\alpha - s - \gamma)^2/8 \tag{20}$$

For the remainder of the paper, we will assume parameterizations of the model such that $(\alpha - s - \gamma)$ is positive. Elaborating, $(\alpha - s - \gamma) > 0$ implies that pollution is not so bad that the export tax is prohibitive (of course, fixed costs may imply negative profits such that the firm does not enter); if the firm does choose to export, the tax revenues from exports minus the disutility from pollution on those exports, $(t_e^\eta - \gamma)X_e^\eta$, is positive.

To get social welfare for Region A with plant configuration (1, 0) at tax rates (t^η, t_e^η), equation (12) indicates that we simply add the right-hand equation of (20) to (17).

$$W_a^\eta(1,0) = (\alpha - \gamma)^2/6 + (\alpha - s - \gamma)^2/8 + L > W^\eta(1,1) \tag{21}$$

Equation (21) and its right-hand inequality indicate that, if the firm chooses only a single plant at the non-strategic tax rates, the region that gets the plant is better off than if the firm chooses two-plants. When Region A gets the sole plant at (t^η, t_e^η), it realizes the same welfare benefit from domestic sales that it does in the (1, 1) configuration, but, in addition, it captures the benefit of tax revenue in excess of the disutility of pollution on export sales.

If there is just one plant, the region which does not get the plant realizes the welfare level shown in Eq. (13), where $X_{bm} = X_{ae}$. Region B's welfare in (1, 0) at (t^η, t_e^η) is

$$W_b^\eta(1,0) = (\alpha - s - \gamma)^2/32 + L < W^\eta(1,1) < W_a^\eta(1,0) \tag{22}$$

Thus *if* plant configuration (1, 0) or (0, 1) is chosen by the X producer at (t^η, t_e^η), the region that does not get the plant does worse than the region that does, and worse than in market structure (1, 1). The country without the plant receives no tax revenue net of pollution disutility, and receives a lower consumer surplus from X due to the higher price caused by the transport cost.

A final point to note is that we can substitute the formulae for t^η and t_e^η in (15) and (19) respectively into the profit functions (7) and (8). Some manipulation will yield the result that

$$\pi^\eta(1,1) - \pi^\eta(1,0) = (\alpha - \gamma)^2/9 - (\alpha - s - \gamma)^2/16 - G \tag{23}$$

It is clear that, for given values of α, s, and γ (subject to our earlier restriction that $(\alpha - s - \gamma) > 0$), *there necessarily exist values of G such that the case in which one plant is chosen and the case in which two plants are chosen at the non-strategic tax rates both occur*. As we increase G beginning at $G = 0$, two plants are chosen, then (23) equals zero at some value of $G > 0$ (the firm is indifferent between one and two plants), and one plant is chosen for still higher values of G.

4. Non-cooperative environmental policy equilibria: Three cases

Depending on the values of the parameters, a number of different types of non-cooperative equilibria can occur.

4.1. Case I: More plants, too much pollution

For Case I, initially assume the firm will choose one plant at $t^{\eta} = t_a = t_b$, $t_e^{\eta} = t_{ae} = t_{be}$. Said loosely, Case I assumes that pollution is not 'too bad' and that plant-specific cost (G) is large relative to the shipping cost s.

Let $\pi^{\eta}(1,0)$ denote the profits of the X producer when it locates its single plant in Region A, given that A maintains its non-strategic tax rates. In terms of this notation, the initial assumption of Case I is that $\pi^{\eta}(1,0) > 0$ ((8) is positive at (t^{η}, t_e^{η})), and

$$\pi^{\eta}(1,0) > \pi^{\eta}(1,1) \quad \text{implying} \quad (\alpha - \gamma)^2/9 - (\alpha - s - \gamma)^2/16 - G < 0$$

where the second inequality follows from (23).

If both countries impose taxes of t^{η} and t_e^{η}, the firm will service one region by exports. Assume without loss of generality that the firm produces for both regions from a single plant in Region A. Region A earns the welfare level given in equation (21) and Region B earns the welfare level given in Eq. (22). Region A's welfare is significantly higher than Region B's. This situation cannot be a Nash equilibrium of our simple game. Region B can under-cut Region A's tax schedule by an arbitrarily small amount, and given these new rates, the X producer will switch to Region B. Equations (12), (13), (15) and (19) can be used to demonstrate that Region B has improved its welfare by this small tax under-cutting. Thus (1, 0) with tax schedule (t^{η}, t_e^{η}) cannot be an equilibrium.

Proposition 1. If one plant is chosen at t^{η}, t_e^{η}, this situation cannot be a Nash equilibrium because there is an incentive for the region without the plant to undercut.

The under-cutting process must continue over some finite interval. The under-cutting process may be terminated either by the governments, or by the firm switching to two plants. Referring to equations (12) and (13), the welfare of the region with the plant must decrease (as taxes deviate more from their non-strategic levels) and the welfare of the region without the plant must increase (its consumer surplus must increase as its import price falls with the fall in the other region's export tax) as the under-cutting continues.

Eventually we may have an equilibrium at a (t, t_e) combination with plant locations $(1, 0)$ or $(0, 1)$ if (12) equals (13), and if it continues to be the case that $\pi(1, 0)$ or $\pi(0, 1)$ exceeds $\pi(1, 1)$. We will not develop this possibility in detail, but instead concentrate on the case when, as the under-cutting proceeds, we arrive at (t, t_e) values such that $\pi(1, 0)$ or $\pi(0, 1) < \pi(1, 1)$ and the firm switches to one plant in each country.

Note that there is a discrete change in a region's incentive to under-cut when taxes fall to the level that supports two plants. Above these tax rates, a region is engaged in under-cutting to move itself away from the situation of having no plant, importing at high cost and receiving no tax revenue. When the taxes fall to the critical levels necessary to support $(1, 1)$, each country has one plant and further under-cutting would be for the purpose of gaining the additional tax revenue from export sales, but at the expense of higher pollution levels.

We propose the following as a possible equilibrium. Under-cutting occurs until each region's export tax reaches the level $t_e^\epsilon = \gamma$, such that each region is indifferent to having production for export. Second, each region's domestic tax is cut until the X producer is just indifferent to maintaining two plants and switches to $(1, 1)$. This tax rate, which we will denote by t^ϵ is found by setting equation (7) equal to (8), letting $t_e = \gamma$ and solving.

$$t^\epsilon \equiv \alpha - ((\alpha - s - \gamma)^2 + 4G)^{1/2} \tag{24}$$

Several things can be deduced at this proposed equilibrium. First, neither region has an incentive to lower its export tax further to induce the firm to shut its other plant because the added pollution will outweigh the tax revenue. Second, neither region has an incentive to raise its export tax since this has no effect (there are no exports in $(1, 1)$). Third, neither region has an incentive to lower its domestic tax because this is already below t^η: if the firm chooses one plant at (t^η, t_e^η) and then the export taxes are lowered, it must be the case that the domestic taxes are then lowered to induce the firm to maintain two plants. Fourth, profits of the X producer are clearly positive at the proposed equilibrium and the producer is willing to maintain two plants by definition of t^ϵ.

Two additional conditions must be established to prove that there is non-cooperative equilibrium at $(t^\epsilon, t_e^\epsilon)$. At the proposed equilibrium, neither region must have an incentive to raise its domestic tax to drive the plant out. Let $W^\epsilon(1, 1)$ be the welfare level a country enjoys when $t = t^\epsilon$, $t_e = t_e^\epsilon$. Let $W_a^\epsilon(0, 1)$ be the welfare enjoyed by Region A if A then raised taxes to drive out the local plant, B's taxes remaining constant. $W_b^\epsilon(1, 0)$ is similarly defined. The necessary condition for the region with a plant not to want to shed its plant is that $W^{\epsilon}(1,1) > W_a^{\epsilon}(0,1) = W_b^{\epsilon}(1,0)$. A *sufficient* condition for this is that $t^{\epsilon} \geqslant \gamma$.[9]

Sufficient conditions for a (1, 1) equilibrium at $(t^{\epsilon}, t_e^{\epsilon})$ are thus summarized as follows where the superscript ϵ denotes the non-cooperative equilibrium tax rates.

Proposition 2. If one is plant chosen at (t^{η}, t_e^{η}) *and if* $t^{\epsilon} \geqslant \gamma$, *market structure* (1, 1) *is a non-cooperative equilibrium with tax rates* $t_a^{\epsilon} = t_b^{\epsilon} = t^{\epsilon}$ *(defined in* (24)), $t_{ae}^{\epsilon} = t_{be}^{\epsilon} = \gamma$.

It is easy to find parameterizations of the model such that the conditions of Proposition 2 hold, and thus (1, 1) is an equilibrium market structure at $t = t^{\epsilon}$ (given by (24)), and $t_e = t_e^{\epsilon} = \gamma$. Table 1 gives such a parameterization and associated results (indeed, $t^{\epsilon} < \gamma$ in Table 1, emphasizing that $t^{\epsilon} \geqslant \gamma$ is sufficient but not necessary).

Result 1 in Table 1 indicates that t^{η} and t_e^{η} can significantly exceed t^{ϵ} and t_e^{ϵ}. The direct profit calculating in Result 2 indicates that the firm will operate only one plant at (t^{η}, t_e^{η}). Result 3 indicates that the example satisfies the welfare condition of Proposition 2, implying that at (1, 1) with tax rates $(t^{\epsilon}, t_e^{\epsilon})$, neither region can do better by raising its tax sufficiently to drive out the plant and import instead. Result 4 implies that neither country can do better by lowering its export tax to induce the firm to shut its other plant: the additional tax is outweighed by the disutility of additional pollution. Thus the two countries have no incentive to deviate from tax rates $(t^{\epsilon}, t_e^{\epsilon})$. Result 5 of Table 1 indicates that the firm also has no incentive to deviate from two plants. Thus (1, 1) is a Nash equilibrium.

Table 1 then presents some welfare effects. Welfare for each region is presented under the arbitrary assumption that the one plant is in Region A, (1, 0), rather than (0, 1) at tax rates (t^{η}, t_e^{η}). Equivalent figures for the (0, 1) market structure are found by simply reordering the two regions. The welfare numbers at the bottom of Table 1 indicate that the combined welfare level of the two regions is 4.4% higher with (1, 0) than with (1, 1) (the two identical utility functions are additive). But the higher aggregate welfare with (1, 0) is very unevenly distributed. Region A gets both the tax

[9] If $t^{\epsilon} \geqslant \gamma$, the country loses the non-negative excess of tax revenue over the disutility of pollution plus loses consumer surplus from the higher import price if it drives the plant out.

The last condition is more subtle. Each country must not have an incentive to induce the X producer to close its foreign plant through some combined policy of raising its domestic pollution tax above t^{ϵ} (where $t^{\epsilon} < t^{\eta}$), compensated for by a sufficient lowering of its export tax below t_e^{ϵ}. We can show that this last condition need not be specified as an additional assumption (i.e., it is implied by the other assumptions). This is demonstrated in a short appendix to the paper.

Table 1
One plant chosen at the non-strategic tax rates

A numerical example of a non-cooperative equilibrium with plant locations (1, 1) at $t^{\epsilon}_{a} = t^{\epsilon}_{b} = t^{\epsilon} \equiv \alpha - ((\alpha - s - \gamma)^2 + 4G)^{1/2} < t^{\eta}$, $t^{\epsilon}_{ae} = t^{\epsilon}_{be} = \gamma < t^{\eta}_{e}$

Parameterization
$s = \gamma = 1$, $\alpha = 8$, $G = 3.6$, $F = 4$, $L = 16$
These parameter values imply the following results:
(1) $t^{\epsilon} = 0.901 < t^{\eta} = 3.33$, $t^{\epsilon}_{e} = 1 < t^{\eta}_{e} = 4.0$
(2) $\pi^{\eta}(1,1) = -0.296 < \pi^{\eta}(1,0) = \pi^{\eta}(0,1) = 0.102$
(3) $W^{\epsilon}(1,1) = 21.947 > W^{\epsilon}_{a}(0,1) = W^{\epsilon}_{b}(1,0) = 20.500$
(4) $(t^{\epsilon}_{e} - \gamma) = 0$
(5) $\pi^{\epsilon}(1,1) = \pi^{\epsilon}(0,1) = \pi^{\epsilon}(1,0) = 14.000 > 0$

Welfare implications

	At the non-strategic tax rates	The non-cooperative equilibrium
Market structure and taxes	(1, 0) at (t^{η}, t^{η}_{e})	(1, 1) at $(t^{\epsilon}, t^{\epsilon}_{e})$
Welfare of Region A	28.712	21.947
Welfare of Region B	17.125	21.947
Sum of A and B	45.837	43.894
X producer's profits	0.102	14.000
Total pollution	3.835	7.099

revenue in excess of pollution disutility $((t^{\eta} - \gamma) > 0)$ and the consumer surplus gain from a lower price for X. Thus Region B has an incentive to under-cut Region A's taxes. The result, for the parameterization of Table 1, is a Nash equilibrium (1, 1) at $(t^{\epsilon}, t^{\epsilon}_{e})$ with Region A doing worse and Region B doing better than at (1, 0).[10]

We emphasize that the non-strategic tax rates are not in general a Pareto optimum for the two regions, nor is the number of plants in this outcome necessarily optimal. In the example of Table 1, the two regions can cooperatively achieve a Pareto improvement over the non-strategic outcome in one of two ways: (1) both regions can agree to set prohibitive export taxes and set their domestic taxes as close as possible to (or at) t^{η} subject to the firm breaking even with two plants, or (2) Region A can set $t = t^{\eta}$ and lower its export tax below t^{ϵ}_{e} to take into account the consumer surplus generated in B by its export to B, plus A makes a transfer payment to B. The first option (giving two plants) is better given the parameterization of Table 1, but higher plant-specific fixed costs make the one-plant option preferred.

Finally, we emphasize that such an outcome is much more general than

[10] Note that there is no suggestion that this is a unique Nash equilibrium given the assumptions of Proposition 2.

this simple example suggests. To recap, the equilibrium illustrated by the example in Table 1 occurs whenever (23) and (8) are both positive (one plant is chosen at the non-strategic tax rates), and (24) exceeds γ (regions do not have the incentive to force the plant out at $(t^{\epsilon}, t^{\epsilon}_{e})$). These restrictions are mutually consistent for a wide range of parameter values, roughly speaking situations in which G is relatively large and γ is relatively small.

4.2. Case II: Correct number of plants, too much pollution

In this section, we assume that the X producer will choose two plants at tax rates (t^{η}, t^{η}_{e}). Specifically, and with reference to equation (23), parameters are chosen such that

$$(\alpha - \gamma)^2/9 - (\alpha - s - \gamma)^2/16 - G > 0 \tag{25}$$

We can move from Case I to Case II simply by lowering G (plant scale economies become less important), and indeed that is what we will do in the numerical example of Table 2.

The fact that in Case II the firm chooses two plants at the non-strategic tax rates does not imply that (1, 1) is an equilibrium at (t^{η}, t^{η}_{e}). One region may wish to under-cut on its export tax to induce the firm to shut its foreign plant, if the resulting increase in tax revenue exceeds the added disutility of pollution. Note that in an initial configuration of (1, 1), neither region has an incentive to cut its domestic tax below t^{η}, since that will have no effect on the firm's location decisions. Also note that by inequality (22), neither region has an incentive to raise its domestic tax to induce the firm to shut its local plant.

Thus to determine whether there is a noncooperative (1, 1) equilibrium at (t^{η}, t^{η}_{e}) we need only examine a region's incentives to cut its export tax below t^{η}_{e}. To determine this, set $t_a = t_b = t^{\eta}$ and solve for the value of t_{ae} that makes the firm indifferent between (1, 1) and (1, 0); specifically, substitute t^{η} from equation (15) into (7) and (8) for t_a and t_b, and set (7) equal to (8). Rearranging one obtains

$$(\alpha - s - t_{ae})^2/4 = (\alpha - \gamma)^2/9 - G \tag{26}$$

Region A has an incentive to deviate to this lower export tax t_{ae} if and only if $t_{ae} > \gamma$ (tax revenue per unit of export production exceeds the disutility of pollution). Substitute γ for t_{ae} in equation (26). The value of t_{ae} that solves (26) will exceed γ if and only if

$$(\alpha - \gamma)^2/9 - (\alpha - s - \gamma)^2/4 - G < 0 \tag{27}$$

If the inequalities in (25) and (27) both hold (and $\pi(1, 1) > 0$), then two plants will be chosen at the non-strategic tax rates, but these tax rates cannot be an equilibrium. Each region has an incentive to deviate by cutting its export tax. *It should be clear that values of G must exist such that both the inequalities (25) and (27) hold simultaneously.*

Proposition 3. If G is chosen such that (25) *and* (27) *both hold at* (t^η, t_e^η), *two plants are chosen, but the non-strategic tax rates cannot be an equilibrium.*

Assume that (25) and (27) both hold. Suppose A begins the process by deviating to the value of t_{ae} given in (26). The firm shuts its plant in B and supplies both regions from its plant in A. B initially enjoys a lower level of consumer surplus because its price for X is higher and B loses its tax revenue $(t^\eta - \gamma)X^\eta$.[11]

Region B should now cut its domestic tax by a small bit to regain a plant to supply for domestic consumption. The added consumers' surplus and tax revenues will more than offset the disutility from the resulting pollution. Region B should in turn cut its export tax to capture A's market, provided $(t_{be} - \gamma)$ remains positive. The under-cutting continues in this manner, with each region in turn cutting its domestic tax and cutting its export tax to capture the foreign market. This process comes to an end when there is no incentive to capture the other region's market; i.e., when there is no longer an incentive to get the firm to shut its foreign plant. This occurs when the export tax is driven down to $t_e = \gamma$. Given this export tax, a country sets its domestic tax as high as possible without loosing its domestic market. Thus its domestic tax t^ϵ is given by the same *formula* (although it does not have the same *value*) given in (24).

Proposition 4. If two plants are chosen at (t^η, t_e^η) *((25) holds), and if* (27) *holds as well, a non-cooperative equilibrium configuration of plants is* (1, 1) *with both countries having domestic taxes of* $t_a = t_b = t^\epsilon$ *(defined in* (24)) *and export taxes of* $t_e^\epsilon = \gamma$.

Table 2 presents an equilibrium in which the configuration of plants is (1, 1) at the nonstrategic tax rates, but in which tax competition drives the two regions' tax rates down below t^η, to the rates indicated in Proposition 4. The parameterization differs from that of Table 1 only in that G is lowered to 3.0. Result 1 of Table 2 indicates that the parameters satisfy both the inequalities (25) and (27), so that two plants are chose but that each country

[11] It can be shown using (26) that $t_{ae} > t^\eta - s$. Because switching to one plant saves the firm the fixed cost G, Region A does not have to cut its export tax so far that the export tax in A is less that the domestic tax in B by the amount of the transport cost. Thus when the firm switches to one plane in A, the price of X in B rises.

Table 2
Two plants chosen at the non-strategic tax rates

A numerical example of a non-cooperative equilibrium with the configuration of plants (1, 1) at $t_a^\epsilon = t_b^\epsilon = t^\epsilon \equiv \alpha - ((\alpha - s - \gamma)^2 + 4G)^{1/2} < t^\eta$, $t_{ae}^\epsilon = t_{be}^\epsilon = \gamma < t_e^\eta$

Parameterization

$s = \gamma = 1, \quad \alpha = 8, \quad G = 3, \quad F = 4, \quad L = 16$

These parameter values imply the following results:

(1) $(\alpha - \gamma)^2/9 - (\alpha - s - \gamma)^2/16 - G = 0.194 > 0$
$(\alpha - \gamma)^2/9 - (\alpha - s - \gamma)^2/4 - G = -6.56 < 0$

(2) $t^\epsilon = 1.07 < t^\eta = 3.33, \quad t_e^\epsilon = 1 < t_e^\eta = 4.0$

(3) $\pi^\eta(1, 1) = 0.904 > \pi^\eta(1, 0) = 0.702$

(4) $W^\eta(1, 1) = 24.165 > W^\epsilon(1, 1) = 22.077$

(5) $(t^\epsilon - \gamma) = 0.07 > 0, \quad (t_e^\epsilon - \gamma) = 0$

(6) $\pi^\epsilon(1, 1) = \pi^\epsilon(0, 1) = \pi^\epsilon(1, 0) = 14.0 > 0$

Welfare implications

	At the non-strategic tax rates[a]	The non-cooperative equilibrium
Market structure and taxes	(1,1) at (t^η, t_e^η)	(1, 1) at $(t^\epsilon, t_e^\epsilon)$
Welfare of Region A	24.165	22.077
Welfare of Region B	24.165	22.077
Sum of A and B	48.330	44.154
X producer's profits	0.904	14.000
Total pollution	4.670	6.926

[a] Note that this is also a Pareto Optimal outcome; i.e. $t^* = t^\eta$ and $t_e^* = t_e^\eta$.

has an incentive to deviate from (t^η, t_e^η) by lowering its export tax to induce the firm to shut its foreign plant. Result 2 states that the Nash equilibrium tax rates are $t^\epsilon = 1.07$ and $t_e^\epsilon = 1.0$. Result 3 verifies that the firm earns higher profits as a consequence of choosing two plants at the non-cooperative tax rates, while Result 4 verifies that the two regions lose as a result of this competition. Result 5 notes that each region earns a surplus of tax revenue over the disutility of pollution on production for domestic consumption at the Nash equilibrium, and verifies that export taxes are set such that there is no equivalent surplus on (potential) exports, so that neither region has an incentive to under-cut. Result 6 of Table 2 notes that the firm is indifferent between one and two plants at the non-cooperative equilibrium.

The welfare implications of noncooperative equilibrium are summarized relative to the (1, 1) configuration of plants with tax rates t^η. This is done at the bottom of Table 2. Tax competition reduces the welfare of the two regions by almost 10% and significantly increases the profits of the firm. Total pollution is 48% higher at the Nash equilibrium than with non-strategic taxes. It should also be noted that the non-strategic tax rates are Pareto optimal in this case (they maximize the sum of Region A and Region

B's welfare).[12] Note that, unlike in Case I, neither region has to make a side-payment to maintain this Pareto Optimal cooperative equilibrium, each just needs to agree to impose the non-strategic tax rates.

Note that there is a certain continuity between Cases I and II. We move between the cases simply by lowering G, and therefore plant scale economies, making two plants more attractive. We could also move from Case I to Case II by lowering γ, which would lower the non-strategic tax rates, effectively making the market bigger and encouraging the firm to choose the high fixed-cost option of two plants. The *formulae* for the non-cooperative tax rates are also the same in the two cases: the export tax is set at the disutility of pollution and the domestic tax is then raised as far as possible such that the firm does not close the local plant. But the *value* of the non-cooperative domestic tax is different in the two cases, since the values of the parameters are necessarily different.

As was true with Case I, the outcome in Case II is supported by a much greater range of parameter values than is obvious from the numerical example of Table 2. The inequalities in Result 1 of Table 2 (plus the restriction that $\pi^{\eta}(1, 1) > 0$), hold for a wide range of 'intermediate' values for G. Much lower values of G support $(1, 1)$ at the non-strategic tax rates, but a region would have to cut its export tax so much to induce the firm to shut its other plant, that it is not worthwhile to do so. In this case ((25) holds but (27) does not), the non-strategic rates are Nash equilibrium rates.

4.3. *Case III: Too few plants, too little pollution*

Our third and final case focusses on the NIMBY possibility, in which neither region will accept a plant in a non-cooperative equilibrium but in which a cooperative equilibrium, with one plant, can achieve a higher level of joint welfare. In this situation pollution is sufficiently high, and plant-specific fixed costs are sufficiently high, that neither region wants a plant in

[12] This last point not withstanding, note in Tables 1 and 2 that the sum of welfare (which is defined exclusive of the X producer's profits) and profits is larger at the Nash equilibrium that at $t = t^{\eta}$. The reason is that, from a 'world' point of view, the two regions are over-taxing the firm by ignoring the contribution of its profits to welfare. If each region took profits into account, tax rates would be substantially lower and could possibly be negative. The equilibrium tax rates would still be driven down by the existence of tax competition. The incentive to gain tax revenue by inducing the firm to shut its foreign plant still exists. Furthermore, equilibrium tax rates may remain too high from the 'world' point of view. For example, if each region held 50% equity in the firm, an action by Region A that reduces the profits of the firm by \$1 only reduces the equity income of Region A by \$0.50 (instead of \$0.00 in our formulation) so the tendency to over tax persists. This result is analogous to those derived in the tax competition literature without trade. See, for example, Mintz and Tulkens (1986), Oates and Schwab (1988) and Wildasin (1988, 1989).

their region, but pollution is not so bad that it is collectively best that X is not produced.

Suppose that we raise the plant-specific costs and the disutility of pollution sufficiently (relative to their levels in the two previous sections) such that the firm chooses only one plant at zero taxes and indeed loses money with two plants at zero taxes. In order to provide a straightforward illustration of NIMBY, we will in fact chose parameters such that the firm just breaks even with one plant if the country with the plant sets its export tax at the disutility of pollution, γ, and sets its domestic tax at zero: $t = 0$, $t_e = \gamma$.

Under these assumptions, one plant is chosen if both countries set their taxes at $t = 0$, and $t_e = \gamma$, so let us propose this as an equilibrium. With $t = 0$ and $t_e = \gamma$, equations (12) and (13) give us the welfare expressions for Regions A and B, assuming arbitrarily that A gets the plant.

$$W_a(1,0) = (1/2)X_d^2 - \gamma X_d + L \qquad W_b(1,0) = (1/2)X_e^2 + L \qquad (t_e = \gamma) \tag{28}$$

$(1,0)$ cannot be an equilibrium at these taxes if $W_a(1,0)$ is greater than or less than $W_b(1,0)$. If $W_a > W_b$, then B will have an incentive to lower its domestic tax by a small amount to attract the plant, and under-cutting proceeds until the welfare in the region with the plant and the region without the plant are equal. The equilibrium will entail positive production.

NIMBY may arise when $W_a(1,0) < W_b(1,0)$ at these taxes. In that case, Region A has an incentive to deviate by raising its domestic and/or export taxes to drive the plant to B. Thus the proposed outcome cannot be a Nash equilibrium. Suppose A raises its taxes and drives the plant to B. B knows that if it raises its taxes, the plant will now be driven out completely since it cannot profitably return to A. NIMBY is thus the equilibrium if B would rather not have X produced at all than have it produced domestically at $t = 0$, and $t_e = \gamma$ (note that the appendix demonstrates that a region cannot do better than this by raising its domestic tax and lowering its export tax such that the firm's profits remain zero). With reference to (28), and recalling that $X = \alpha/2$ from (5) at $t = 0$, NIMBY then occurs when the sum of the first two terms of (28) are negative at $t = 0$ and $t_e = \gamma$ $(t_e - \gamma = 0)$.

$$\alpha^2/8 - \gamma\alpha/2 = \alpha/2(\alpha/4 - \gamma) < 0 \tag{29}$$

Proposition 5. Choose G such that the firm just breaks even with one plant at $t = 0$, $t_e = \gamma$. Then $(0,0)$ is a non-cooperative equilibrium if $\alpha/4 < \gamma$.

Table 3 presents an example in which the non-cooperative equilibrium is $(0,0)$ but in which it is also true that the sum of the welfare levels in the two regions is higher if one of the regions will accept a plant at taxes $t = 0$, $t_e = \gamma$ (these taxes are not Pareto optimal: joint welfare could be further improved

Table 3
A numerical example of an non-cooperative equilibrium with no plants, (0, 0)

Parameterization
$s = 1$, $\alpha = 8$, $\gamma = 2.1$, $G = 18.0025$, $F = 4$, $L = 16$
These parameter values imply the following results:
(1) $X = 4.0$, $X_e = 2.45$, at $t = 0, t_e = \gamma$
(2) $\pi(1, 0) = \pi(0, 1) = 0$ at $t = 0, t_e = \gamma$
(3) $\pi(1, 1) < 0$ at all non-negative tax rates ($\pi(1, 1) = -11.75$ at $t = t_e = 0$)
(4) $\alpha/4 = 2 < \gamma = 2.1$

Welfare implications

	Pareto-preferred outcome	The non-cooperative equilibrium
Market structure and taxes	$(1, 0)$ at $(t = 0, t_e = \gamma)$	$(0, 0)$ at $(t^* > 0, t_e^* > \gamma)$
Welfare of Region A	15.600	16.000
Welfare of Region B	19.001	16.000
Sum of A and B	34.601	32.000
X producer's profits	0.000	0.000
Total pollution	6.450	0.000

with a lower export tax and higher domestic tax). This case is quite the opposite of Case I. As in Case I, a transfer payment is needed to achieve a Pareto preferred outcome, but the direction of the transfer is now opposite to that of Case I. Here it is the region *without* the plant that must pay the region with the plant to achieve the cooperative outcome. We also have the opposite results to Case I with respect to both the numbers of plants and the level of pollution. Here we have two few plants and too little pollution at the Nash equilibrium.

To recap the relationship among our three cases, consider beginning with a parameter that supports Case II. We move to Case I simply by raising the plant-specific cost G. We then move to Case III by raising G further, and by raising γ as well.

5. Summary and conclusions

A two-region model is developed where a firm can locate plants in one, both or neither region, and where production from the plant(s) causes local pollution. In this world, the two governments compete in terms of the environmental policies. The model differs significantly from the Pigouvian tradition of marginal analysis in competitive models by assuming production with increasing returns to scale and shipping costs between regions. The single firm chooses between the high fixed-cost option of having plants in both of two regions, versus the high variable-cost option of serving both markets from a single plant. There are large jumps in a region's welfare at critical levels of policy variables where the firm switches the number and location of its plants. In addition to concerning itself with the traditional price and output decisions of the firm, policy must also address discrete-choice problems such as whether to (1) attract a plant to the region, (2) expel a plant due to its environmental externality, and (3) induce the firm to close its foreign plant and serve that foreign market by exports from its local plant.

In this context, pollution taxes affect the firm's choice and therefore regional welfare in two ways. First, generally higher taxes in both regions are, from the firm's point of view, a contraction in effective demand. Thus the firm may shift away from the high fixed-cost option of two plants to the high-variable cost option of a single plant. Second, relatively lower taxes in one region may induce the firm to move its single plant to that region, and/or close its plant in the other region.

Our Case I focusses more on the first effect. In Case I, when both regions impose their individually optimal non-strategic taxes (taxes that are optimal assuming that market structure remains fixed with plants in both regions), the firm chooses a single plant. We then show that the region that does not get the plant has an incentive to cut its taxes, and a tax competition results. A Nash equilibrium with taxes lower than their non-strategic values results, and that equilibrium may either have a single plant or plants in both countries. We presented a numerical example of the latter, in which tax competition results in more plants and pollution.[13]

Our Case II focusses more on the second effect of taxes. In this case when both regions impose their non-strategic taxes, the firm continues to choose two plants. But both regions may have an incentive to under-cut in order to induce the firm to close its foreign plant, if the added tax revenue from export sales exceeds the disutility of added pollution. We derive sufficient conditions for under-cutting to occur and then solve for the non-cooperative equilibrium tax rates. An equilibrium is reached with plants in both regions, but at tax levels lower than the non-strategic levels. The non-cooperative outcome in this case has the right number of plants, but too much pollution.

Our Case III focuses on the NIMBY possibility, in which the Nash equilibrium involves no production of X and no pollution. Yet the joint welfare of the two regions is higher if one of them will accept a plant, an outcome that can be supported by an appropriate transfer payment from the region without the plant. Case III is in a sense opposite to Case I in two respects: in the former, (1) there are too few plants and too little pollution

[13] Again, this result compares the number of plants at the non-cooperative equilibrium versus the number that are chosen by the firm at the non-strategic rates. It is not clear without further analysis that the non-cooperative equilibrium has too many plants relative to some cooperative outcome that the two counties could achieve given their limited set of instruments.

at the Nash equilibrium instead of too many and too much, and (2) the transfer payment must be from the region without the plant to the region with the plant rather than the other way around as in Case I.

We showed that the three cases are related to one another through the initial values of parameters, and in particular we focussed on the size of fixed costs and the disutility of pollution. Beginning at an 'intermediate' value of G and a relatively low value of γ, we have Case II. We can then move to Case I simply by raising the fixed cost G. From Case I, we can move to Case III by raising G further, and by raising the disutility of pollution, γ.

Acknowledgment

Markusen's portion of this research was financed by NSF grant number SES-9022898.

Appendix

The purpose of this appendix is to demonstrate the assertion made in Cases I and II of Section 4 that a region cannot improve its welfare (at the proposed (1, 1) equilibrium) by induced the firm to shut its other plant by a combination of raising its domestic tax and lowering its export tax (we proved in the text that neither of these things individually are welfare improving). The effect of a small lowering of the export tax and an increase in the domestic tax in Region A that leaves the firm indifferent between (0, 1) and (1, 0) can be divided into the usual marginal effect plus the impact effect of a sudden discrete change in the level of exports (initially zero at the proposed equilibrium). In Cases I and II, $(t_e - \gamma) = 0$ initially, so the impact effect is zero.

Consider then the marginal effect of raising t and lowering t_e. Intuitively, this does not seem to make sense since raising the domestic tax generates a loss of consumer surplus while the combined effects of the two tax changes may leave pollution and tax revenue roughly unchanged.

Note from (8) that profits for the firm with one plant in Region A, (1, 0), can be written as

$$\pi = X_d^2 + X_e^2 - G - F \tag{A1}$$

The minimum amount Region A can lower t_e for a given increase in t without the firm switching to (0, 1) is given by setting the total differential of (A1) equal to zero.

$$2[X_d(\mathrm{d}X_d/\mathrm{d}t)\,\mathrm{d}t + X_e(\mathrm{d}X_e/\mathrm{d}t_e)\,\mathrm{d}t_e] = 0 \qquad \mathrm{d}X_i/\mathrm{d}t_i = -1/2 \tag{A2}$$

Substituting the right-hand equation ($i = \mathrm{d}, \mathrm{e}$) into the left, this condition becomes

$$\mathrm{d}t_e = -(X_d/X_e)\,\mathrm{d}t \tag{A3}$$

The effect of the proposed scheme on welfare is given by

$$\mathrm{d}W = \left[[X_d + (t-\gamma)]\frac{\mathrm{d}X_d}{\mathrm{d}t} + X_d\right]\mathrm{d}t + \left[(t_e - \gamma)\frac{\mathrm{d}X_e}{\mathrm{d}t_e} + X_e\right]\mathrm{d}t_e \tag{A4}$$

Now replace $\mathrm{d}t_e$ with (A3) and replace $\mathrm{d}X_i/\mathrm{d}t_i$ with $-1/2$. Finally, divide through by $\mathrm{d}t > 0$. (A4) becomes

$$\mathrm{d}W_a/\mathrm{d}t = -(X_d/2) - (t-\gamma)(1/2) + (t_e - \gamma)(1/2)(X_d/X_e) \tag{A5}$$

In Cases I and II of Section 4, $(t_e - \gamma) = 0$ and $(t - \gamma) > 0$ initially, so the whole expression in (A5) is negative. At the proposed (1, 1) equilibrium in both cases, Region A cannot improve its welfare by a combined policy of raising its domestic tax and lowering its export tax in order to induce the X producer to shut its plant in Region B. (Note that the argument cannot be reversed to conclude that the domestic tax should be lowered and the export tax raised: at (1, 1) initially, raising t_e has no effect on exports and the domestic tax is already lower than its optimal value.)

References

Asako, K., 1979, Environmental pollution in an open economy, Economic Record 55, 359–367.

Arnott, Richard and Ronald E. Grieson, 1981, Optimal fiscal policy for a state or local government Journal of Urban Economics 9, 23–48.

Copeland, Brian R., 1991, Taxes versus standards to control pollution in imperfectly competitive markets, mimeo, presented at the Canadian Resource and Environmental Economics Study Group Annual Meeting, Guelph, Ontario, September 1991.

Cumberland, John H., 1979, Interregional pollution spillovers and consistency of environmental policy, in: H. Siebert et al., eds., Regional evironmental policy: The economic issues (New York Univeristy Press, New York), 255–281.

Cumberland, John H., 1981, Efficiency and equity in interregional environmental management, Review of Regional Studies 2, 1–9.

Barrett, Scott, 1994, Strategic environmental policy and international trade, Journal of Public Economics 54, 325–338.

Dockner, Engelbert J. and Ngo Van Long, 1991, International pollution control: cooperative versus non-cooperative strategies, mimeo, presented at the Canadian Resource and Environmental Economics Study Group Annual Meeting, Guelph, Ontario, September 1991.

Folmer, Henk, Pierre Mouche and Shannon Ragland, 1991, International environmental problems and interconnected games, mimeo, presented at the Conference of Environmental and Resource Economists, Stockholm, Sweden, June 1991.

Hoel, Michael, 1991, Global environmental problems: the effects of unilateral actions taken by one country, Journal of Environmental Economics and Management 20, 55–70.
Horstmann, I.J. and James R. Markusen, 1992 Endogenous market structure in international trade, Journal of International Economics 32, 109–129.
Markusen, James R., Edward R. Morey and Nancy Olewiler, 1993, Environmental policy when market structure and plant locations are endogenous, Journal of Environmental Economics and Management 24, 69–86.
Markusen, James R., 1975, Cooperative control of international pollution and common property resources, Quarterly Journal of Economics 89, 618–632.
Merrifield, John D., 1988, The impact of selected abatement strategies on transnational pollution, the terms of trade and factor rewards: a general-equilibrium approach, Journal of Environmental Economics and Management 15, 259–284.
Mintz, Jack and Henry Tulkens, 1986, Commodity tax competition between member states of a federation: equilibrium and efficiency Journal of Public Economics 29, 133–172.
Misiolek, Walter S., 1980, Effluent taxation in monopoly markets, Journal of Environmental Economics and Management 7, 103–107.
Mitchell, Robert Cameron and Richard T. Carson, 1986, Property rights, protest, and the siting of hazardous waste facilities, American Economic Review 76, No. 2, 285–290.
Oates, Wallace E. and Robert M. Schwab, 1988, Economic competition among jurisdictions: efficiency enhancing or distortion inducing?, Journal of Public Economics 35, 333–354.
Pethig, R., 1976, Pollution, welfare, and environmental policy in the theory of comparative advantage, Journal of Environmental Economics and Management 2, 160–169.
Rauscher, Michael, 1991, Foreign trade and the environment, in: Horst Siebert (ed.), Environmental scarcity: the international dimension (J.C.B. Mohr, Tubingen).
Tiebout, Charles M., 1956, A pure theory of local expenditures, Journal of Political Economy 64, 416–424.
Ulph, Alastair 1992, The choice of environmental policy instruments and strategic international trade, in: R. Pething (ed.), Conflicts and cooperation in managing environmental resources, (Springer-Verlag, Berlin).
Wildasin, David E., 1988, Nash equilibria in models of fiscal competition, Journal of Public Economics 35, 229–240.
Wildasin, David E., 1989 Interjurisdictional capital mobility: fiscal externality and a corrective subsidy, Journal of Urban Economics 25, 193–212.
Wildasin, David E. and John Douglas Wilson (eds.), 1991, Theoretical issues in local public economics, Regional Science and Urban Economics (special issue) 21, 317–528.
Wilson, John D., 1985, Optimal property taxation in the presence of interregional capital mobility, Journal of Urban Economics, 17, 73–89.
Wilson, John D., 1986, A theory of interregional tax competition, Journal of Public Economics 19, 296–315.

[19]

Trade Policy and Industrial Pollution in Latin America: Where Are the Pollution Havens?

NANCY BIRDSALL AND DAVID WHEELER

It is commonly assumed by economists and environmentalists alike that greater economic "openness" will lead to increased industrial pollution in developing countries. This paper challenges the "pollution haven" hypothesis, arguing that liberalization of trade regimes and increased foreign investment in Latin America have not been associated with pollution-intensive industrial development. From case studies and econometric evidence, we conclude that protected economies are more likely to favor pollution intensive industries, while openness actually encourages cleaner industry through the importation of developed-country pollution standards.

Introduction

The prevailing assumption is that free trade will increase environmental degradation in developing countries. Among environmentalists, one common concern is that liberalized trade regimes and market-driven exchange rates, by increasing the incentive for export, will lead to greater exploitation of natural resources such as native forests. A second concern, and the one we explore in this paper, is that free trade will increase industrial pollution in developing countries, through displacement of dirty industries from developed countries with stricter environmental regulation, and through competitive pressure on developing countries to reduce further their environmental standards.

The question we address is simple: among countries of Latin America, has greater "openness," defined in terms of trade regimes and foreign investment, in fact been associated with pollution-intensive industrial development? More generally, are open economies more likely to be so-called pollution havens?

There are at least three reasons to expect higher pollution intensity (i.e., more pollution per unit of output) in developing countries. First, environmental amenities are normal goods; higher income in the developed countries produces greater demand for clean air and water. Similarly, at lower levels of income and higher discount rates, income gains and jobs may be more valued relative to health and other costs of

---

Nancy Birdsall is Director and David Wheeler is Senior Economist in the Country Economics Department at the World Bank.

Journal of Environment & Development 2,1 (Winter 1993).

pollution. Second, the relative costs of monitoring and enforcing pollution standards are higher in developing countries, given scarcity of trained personnel, difficulty of acquiring sophisticated equipment, and the high marginal costs of undertaking any new governmental activity when the policy focus is on reducing fiscal burdens. Third, growth in developing countries is associated with a shift out of agriculture into industry with rapid urban growth and heavy investment in urban infrastructure; this is more likely to imply increasing levels of pollution for each unit of output. In developed countries, by contrast, growth is associated with a shift out of industry into services, and thus with decreasing levels of pollution for each unit of output. These structural differences are consistent with differences in comparative advantage and would be reinforced by free trade.

For these reasons, rising pollution intensity in developing countries could simply reflect differences across countries in the social cost comparative advantage of different mixes of polluting activities.[1] Many economists subscribe to this view, arguing that free trade and increased openness should not be resisted even if they increase environmental problems in developing countries.

There are two problems with this common wisdom, however (if not with the general conclusion about support for openness). First, if the social costs of pollution are not appropriately reflected in current environmental standards in developing countries, then freer trade could increase those social costs, possibly even eclipsing the conventional economic gains of openness. Though secondary instruments to address the pollution problem could be designed (rather than using trade policy, which would increase economy-wide distortions), the failure to use such secondary instruments in the first place implies they are not easy to design or implement. Furthermore, if free trade increases pollution in developing countries, total world pollution may rise. This could impose additional costs on developed countries if some polluting activities have negative transnational externalities.

Second, the premise—that freer trade and more open economies will lead to more environmental degradation—may be wrong in itself. From a policy point of view, this would mean that an important argument in favor of more openness is being overlooked, and that the potential for a happy marriage of economists and environmentalists is being lost.[2]

The question of what effect openness has on the extent of industrial pollution in developing countries is, of course, an empirical one. In the rest of this paper, we suggest why the effect may be negative (i.e., benign) rather than positive; and present some qualitative evidence for one country (Chile) that tends to support the likelihood of a negative relationship. We then use new estimates of pollution intensity for Latin American industry during the period 1960-1988 to show that (1) the pollution intensity of industry grew more slowly in higher-income countries, and has generally grown more slowly where income growth was more rapid; (2) the slower growth of pollution intensity in relation to income growth was attenuated in the 1970s and 1980s compared to the 1960s—consistent with the possibility that dirty industries grew slightly more in Latin America than they would have once Organization for Economic Cooperation and Development (OECD) environmental standards began tightening in the early 1970s; and (3) most importantly, the more open the economy the less pollution-intensive its pattern of industrial development—so that any "displacement" of dirty industries from OECD to Latin America is associated with protectionist and not open economies.

How Free Trade Could Reduce Industrial Pollution

Industrial pollution at the country level can be decomposed as follows:

Industrial Pollution/GDP = [Output (Q) of industry/GDP] ×
[Q (dirty industries) / Q (all industries)] ×
[Pollution from dirty industries / Q (dirty industries)].

The first term (or "development effect") measures the tendency for the industrial and urban share to be increasing in the product of developing countries. The second term (or "composition effect") measures the effect of distribution among industries whose pollution intensity differs greatly (e.g., petrochemicals and cement vs. beer). The third term (or "process effect") measures the extent to which polluting industries reduce or fail to reduce emissions. The degree of openness could affect the size of any of these terms. We concentrate on possible pollution reduction from composition and process effects.

First, labor is relatively more plentiful in developing countries; there is also evidence that more capital-intensive sectors are more pollution-intensive. As Kosmo[3] demonstrates for Turkey, protection therefore tends to bias industrial composition toward pollution intensity.[4]

Second, exports must often meet product standards higher than those of the producing country. To the extent that clean products require clean processes, an export-oriented economy will have cleaner processes for some industries. In Chile, the need to maintain access to industrial countries' markets for fruit and vegetable exports was a consideration in the country's decision to invest in a new sewage collection system. To ensure the sanitary quality of these food exports, it was essential to stop using raw wastewater in their production.[5] Katz[6] refers to two other examples for Chile: the fishmeal industry is treating its effluents to eliminate bacterial contamination of its product; and the pulp and paper industry has had to treat its effluents and change some of its processes to eliminate trace amounts of dioxin.

Third, foreign investors may simply impose a common international emission standard wherever they invest. Multinational corporations may face high costs in implementing different business practices (different pollution standards) in different settings. High costs could come in the form of stockholder pressure not to "exploit" populations of poor countries by using dirty processes; in the form of stockholder pressure to avoid liability for damages;[7] or in the form of costs associated with retraining managers and changing familiar production processes. Low[8] suggests that the costs to industrial firms of clean technology and processes are now small in the U.S. (less than 1 percent of total costs); for new investments by firms that maintain some production in several countries, the business and information costs of differentiating in different settings could easily exceed any direct cost advantage of dirtier production.[9]

Fourth, openness and resulting competitive pressure will increase investment in the latest technology, all other factors remaining the same. To the extent that the newest and most efficient technology embodies cleaner processes, this will reduce overall emissions.[10]

Fifth, if the costs of being clean are low for new investment but high for retrofitting, then a higher overall growth rate is likely to induce cleaner processes. This is independent of but complementary to the possibility that the more efficient technology embodies cleaner processes.

The first point above suggests a benign compositional impact for openness: the comparative advantage of developing countries is actually with labor-intensive industries that are intrinsically less polluting. The second and third points rely on a process effect, i.e., the possibility that irrespective of local demand for pollution control and short-run local comparative advantage, openness would induce industries in developing countries to adopt cleaner processes. The fourth and fifth points also rely on process effects, though in both cases those effects are fully consistent with long-run comparative advantage. Openness, by increasing competitive pressures, would accelerate investment in new technologies, which tend to be cleaner because they are imported from countries with higher pollution standards. Such new technologies are also generally more efficient in terms of overall factor productivity, even if not perfectly suited to the factor proportions of a particular developing country. In addition, openness, through its effect on growth, would increase the rate of retirement of older, dirtier equipment and processes.

Note that of the five potentially beneficial effects of openness (beneficial in the simple sense of reducing pollution intensity), only one works through a shift in the composition of industry (the composition effect); the others affect the cleanliness of the process in given industries (the process effect). This distinction is important for assessing the relevance of the empirical work reported in the section on cross-country evidence.

The Chile Case[11]

Chile provides a useful example of a country with limited or no controls on industrial emissions, and openness to trade and foreign investment. Is Chile a "pollution haven"?

The former military government that assumed power in 1973 established an economic system based on limited intervention by government in markets and on export-led growth under a liberalized trade regime. Barriers to foreign investment were eliminated; import restrictions were eliminated and tariffs reduced to their current low of about 15 percent. Restrictions on industry for environmental reasons were presumably not considered; they would have been seen as discouraging growth and as an example of a potentially welfare-reducing intervention by government in the affairs of the market.

The democratic government that assumed power in 1990 has announced its intention to address the country's environmental problems, and is exploring alternative instruments for control of industrial air and water pollution. However, current responsibilities are widely diffused among various agencies, and the legislative and regulatory arrangements and capacity for enforcement of any policies or programs that might be desirable will take time to be put in place.

The most visible immediate environmental problem is air pollution in Santiago; after Mexico City, Santiago has the most polluted air in the world, due in part to a recurring thermal inversion layer that traps pollutants. This problem has demanded the attention of the new government, which has so far responded with short-term emergency measures, including restrictions on vehicle use during periods of high pollution. The visibility of the air pollution problem and the need for recurrent imposition of emergency measures have put environmental problems, especially air and water pollution, high on the public agenda. For this reason if for no other, industry executives anticipate that the government will eventually impose emissions and ambient standards;

their chief concern is not whether such standards will be imposed, but how and at what level.

Thus Chile represents a case study of an open economy with virtually nonexistent pollution standards, in which, however, there is a credible threat of future imposition of standards.

We have only anecdotal evidence on the behavior of industrial firms in Chile with respect to pollution. That evidence suggests, however, that the situation is not consistent with the notion that Chile has become a pollution haven—either by attracting multinational companies seeking a cost advantage because standards are low, or by leading to even weaker government enforcement of any existing standards in order to attract more foreign investment through regulatory competition.

For example, several representatives of the largest and apparently most profitable pulp and paper and petrochemical firms report they do not know the extra costs they incur in the form of "cleaner" equipment; they invest in modern, efficient, clean equipment—as a package. In some cases they accept higher costs to reduce emissions and ensure that the exported product meets foreign standards; for example, paper produced with chlorine will have traces of dioxin and cannot be exported to Germany. But even where product standards can be met with dirty processes, the fact that the newest technology is clean dominates any search for lower costs. Representatives of large multinational firms with operations in Chile report that, in any event, they face pressure from shareholders in Europe to avoid polluting the environment in developing countries.[12] In contrast, state-owned enterprises that enjoy relative monopoly positions within Chile and have access to government subsidies to shield them from international competition are the dirtiest polluters; the state-owned copper company is an example.

Government and industry representatives report that industry itself is prodding the government to establish pollution standards, and that through the industry association, firms are sponsoring development of self-regulating standards. Scarsborough[13] points out that, in the face of the threat of future regulation, the least-cost way for the industrial sector to respond is to urge the government to adopt a mutually negotiated set of standards; this is particularly attractive to the larger cleaner firms, as it would permit them to eliminate local cost competition from dirtier firms.[14] For multinational firms the least-cost way to meet the threat is to adopt the standards prevailing in their home countries.

A stylized summary of the effect of openness on the intensity of industrial pollution in Chile, abstracting from the effects of economic growth per se on pollution, would thus be as follows. Openness to foreign investment and the absence of barriers to technology imports encourage multinational companies to invest in Chile, and ensure that domestic producers will have to compete with them. Industry is, in effect, pushed toward exceeding local standards because cleanliness is embodied in newer equipment, processes, and/or the shareholder effect. The larger, often multinational, firms then attempt to reduce local competition by encouraging the government to introduce or raise standards. The threat of future regulation may reinforce the process, but may not actually be necessary to it.

The overall effect is that openness in Chile is associated with, if not contributing to, the opposite of a pollution haven effect—perhaps even implying higher standards than are actually efficient given social preferences in Chile.[15]

Cross-Country Evidence

The Chile evidence refers entirely to the "process" effect in the three-part decomposition set out above. We now turn to evidence regarding the "composition effect" in Latin America, i.e., the trend in the mix of "dirty" vs. "clean" industries. Our database is a pooled cross section of time series for 25 Latin American countries during the period 1960-1988. We estimate an equation that describes the relationship between changes in pollution intensity and three variables: per capita income, growth of per capita income, and the degree of openness. We use the results to test three hypothesized effects: The positive income elasticity of environmental protection, which should reduce pollution intensity at higher incomes (ceteris paribus); the displacement effect of stricter OECD regulation, which should raise pollution intensity for Latin America after the early 1970s; and the compositional impact of openness, which should affect the pollution intensity of more open economies (ceteris paribus).

Wheeler and colleagues in the World Bank have constructed indices of the toxic intensity of industries per dollar of output in the U.S. for all four-digit industries on the International Standard Industrial Classification.[16] Their estimates are based on a sample of 15,000 industrial plants in 1987, formed by merging output data from the U.S. Census of Manufactures with pollution data from the Toxic Release Inventory (TRI) of the U.S. Environmental Protection Agency. TRI reports releases of 320 toxic substances into the air, water, and as underground and solid waste. Three indices are constructed, which incorporate different assumptions about the health and other risks of various toxic

Table 1

DETERMINANTS OF POLLUTION INTENSITY GROWTH, 1960S THROUGH 1980S, 25 COUNTRIES OF LATIN AMERICA

Variable	Parameter Estimate	t-statistic
INTERCEP	0.437405	3.105
NAS	0.043748	2.588
PCGR	3.331180	2.989
LINC	-0.081427	-3.382
PCGRD70	-4.454373	-3.276
PCGRD80	-6.009647	-2.519
LINCD70	0.023213	3.780
LINCD80	0.025131	4.411
PGRD70	0.144721	0.440
PGRD80	1.268344	1.868
R-square 0.6055		
Adj R-sq 0.4575		

NOTES: Dependent Variable: Toxic intensity growth rate, from log regression. Independent Variables: **NAS** = Dummy variable for non-Andean South American countries. **LINC** = Log of per capita income in the decade's initial year (thus represents 1960s in the results). **PCGR** = Per capita income growth rate for the decade (from log regression) (thus represents 1960s in the results). **PCGRD70** = PCGR × Dummy variable for the 1970s. **PCGRD80** = PCGR × Dummy variable for the 1980s. **LINCD70** = LINC × Dummy variable for the 1970s. **LINCD80** = LINC × Dummy variable for the 1980s. **PGRD80** = PCGR × Dummy variable for the 1980s × Dollar openness index. **PGRD70** = PCGR × Dummy variable for the 1970s × Dollar openness index.

emissions; the results reported below use one index but are not sensitive to the index used.[17]

The measures of toxic intensity are applied to the mix of industrial outputs for the 25 Latin American countries, using data reported in the United Nations *Industrial Statistics Yearbooks*. This yields an annual index of pollution intensity for each country. The index is of course related solely to the mix of industries, and not to unobserved and unmeasured differences in technologies and enforcement standards.[18]

Table 1 reports the results from a pooled regression of pollution intensity change over three decades—the 1960s, 1970s and 1980s—on three sets of variables: the log of per capita income at the beginning of each decade, representing the initial level of per capita income; the growth of per capita income in each decade; and, for each decade, the interaction of per capita income growth with an openness index developed by David Dollar[19] for the World Bank's 1991 *World Development Report*.[20]

The results for initial per capita income are consistent with a positive income elasticity of environmental protection. The negative and statistically significant coefficient on LINC indicates that pollution intensity growth is lower (although still positive) at higher levels of per capita income in all three decades. The significant, positive dummy variable interactions for the 1970s and 1980s (LINCD70 and LINCD80) show that the positive income elasticity of environmental protection was somewhat attenuated in the 1970s and 1980s, compared to the 1960s. One interpretation for the attenuation of the benign income effect in the later decades is a displacement of dirtier industry to Latin America after OECD environmental regulation (which began to take hold in the early 1970s) became stricter. Any such displacement effect, however (i.e., higher growth or more entry of polluting industries in Latin America than there might otherwise have been) was not itself associated with the degree of openness to trade of the different economies—as will be seen below.

The effects of per capita income growth (as opposed to initial income level) are also fundamentally benign. A positive effect of income growth on pollution intensity in the 1960s (PCGR) appears to have been more than offset in the 1970s and 1980s (PCGRD70, PCGRD80). In fact, as shown below in Figure 1, the overall effect of income growth was negative on growth of pollution intensity in the open economies.

This effect of openness is the critical result. The positive interaction of Dollar's index with income growth for the 1980s (PGRD80) indicates that openness to trade is systematically associated with less pollution intensity growth (the more positive the index, the more closed the economy). The implied intensity elasticity of income growth was much higher in relatively closed economies (i.e., those with high numerical rankings on the index). The coefficient for the interaction of the openness index with income growth for the 1970s (PGRD70) shows a similarly positive effect of openness, though it is not statistically significant.

Figure 1 is designed to illustrate the regression results. It shows how predicted pollution intensity changes as income, growth, and the Dollar index vary independently across their full range of values in the data set.[21] The effect of initial income level on pollution intensity can be seen in Figure 1 by comparing the bars in the low-, middle-, and high-income panels. Pollution intensity growth was the fastest for those countries that were initially the poorest. For example, the predicted pollution intensity growth for slow-growing closed economies in the 1970s is 11.5 percent (low); 5.1 percent (middle); 1.1 percent (high). In

Figure 1

Rates of Annual Growth in Pollution Intensity:
25 Countries of Latin America

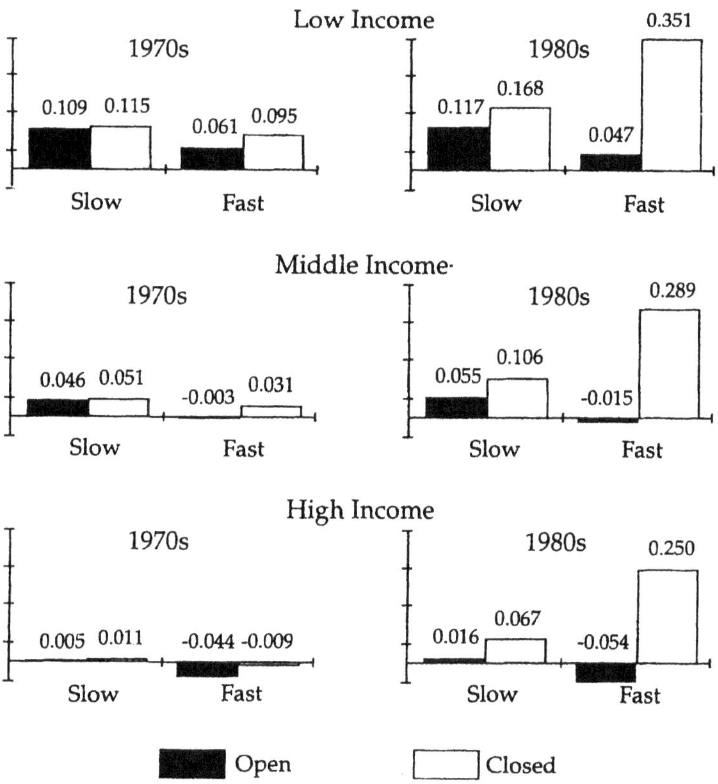

the 1980s, it is 16.8 percent (low); 10.6 percent (middle); 6.7 percent (high). In every case, the predicted transition is toward lower intensity growth rates at higher incomes. Indeed, the prediction for fast-growing open economies is negative intensity growth rates at high incomes.

Similarly, faster growth is associated with less pollution intensity growth—as can be seen by comparing the slow vs. fast groups in each panel. The exception is closed economies in the 1980s, where pollution intensity growth was the greatest.

By looking at equivalent cells for the 1970s and 1980s, we can gauge the apparent size of a possible displacement effect. Most paired cells suggest the possibility of progressive displacement from OECD environmental regulation—typical Latin American pollution intensity growth was higher in the 1980s. Again the exception is made by the fast-growing open economies. At low, middle, and high incomes, they show lower rates of pollution intensity growth in the 1980s compared to the 1970s.

More generally, the effect of openness is clearly a major reduction in the growth of pollution intensity during the 1980s, particularly for fast-growing economies where sectoral shares in total output can change rapidly. For low-income, fast-growing economies, switching from closed to open status is predicted to decelerate pollution intensity growth from 35.1 percent annually to 4.7 percent. In middle-income, fast-growing economies, the predicted change is from 28.9 percent to negative 1.5 percent.

Conclusions

This paper began by asking: among countries of Latin America, has greater "openness," defined in terms of trade regimes and foreign investment, been associated with pollution-intensive industrial development? *Our evidence suggests the opposite conclusion—openness encourages cleaner industry.* Anecdotal evidence from Chile suggests several reasons why the elimination of barriers to importation of new technology and to foreign capital may lead to importation of industrialized country pollution standards. Once these higher standards are introduced (and despite the fact that they may be too high from the point of view of local demand for environmental quality), the larger multinational firms are likely to push for enforcement so as to reduce the cost advantage of smaller local firms. The econometric evidence, though at best exploratory, suggests that over the last two decades, the more open economies have ended up with a cleaner set of industries. This is consistent with a growing literature suggesting that it is capital- and materials-intensive industries that have both enjoyed protection and have been heavy polluters.

Our evidence is also consistent with the possibility of displacement: pollution intensity grew more rapidly in Latin America as a whole after rather than before 1970—as OECD environmental regulation became stricter. This effect is not, however, associated with more trade openness. Instead, it is possible that as OECD countries shifted out of dirtier industries, the protectionist countries of Latin America shifted in. We conclude, in short, that "pollution havens" can be found, but not where they have generally been sought. They are in protectionist economies.

Endnotes

INFORMATION AND ACKNOWLEDGMENTS: We are grateful to Charles Blitzer, John Briscoe, John Dixon, and Robert Schneider for useful comments on our earlier draft. We also gratefully acknowledge the collaboration of the Center for Economic Studies, U.S. Bureau of the Census. The views expressed are those of the authors and should not be attributed to the World Bank, its Board of Directors, its management, or any of its member countries.

1. Judith Dean, "Trade and the Environment: a Survey of the Literature," paper prepared for the *World Development Report 1992*, mimeo, April, 1991.

2. This is more than a philosophical issue. Some groups of environmentalists may continue to resist through political channels a free trade agreement between the United States and Mexico, for fear of the environmental effects. Similarly, the agreement is resisted by groups that fear a loss of jobs in the U.S. if firms move south to avoid environmental standards in the U.S. Some of the resistance to this and future free trade agreements could arise because of incorrect predictions about the actual links between free trade and environmental standards.

3. M. Kosmo, "Economic Incentives and Industrial Pollution in Developing Countries," Environment Department Division Working Paper No. 1989-2, World Bank, 1989.

4. For evidence that import substitution policies in Turkey led to inefficient and material and energy-intensive activities, see Anne Krueger and Baron Tuncer, "Empirical Test of the Infant Industry Argument," World Bank, 1982.

5. World Bank, *World Development Report: Environment and Development* (New York: Oxford Union Press, 1992): .100.

6. Ricardo Katz, "Urban Air Pollution and Standards. The Case of Mexico City and Santiago," paper prepared for the World Bank, May-June 1991.

7. Changes in the chemical industry following the Bhopal incident provide evidence of this phenomenon. See Cornelius C. Smith, "Bhopal Aftermath: Union Carbide Rethinks Safety," *Business and Society Review*, 75 (Fall 1990).

8. Patrick Low, "Trade Measures and Environmental Quality: The Implications for Mexico's Exports," mimeo, June 1991.

9. For further discussion that there was no evidence of environmentally induced industrial relocation or foreign investment patterns — apparently due to such countervailing factors as poor labor quality, high transport costs and political risks in settings with laxer standards, see Ingo Walter, "Environmentally Induced Industrial Relocation to Developing Countries," in Seymour J. Rubin and Thomas R. Graham, eds., *Environment and Trade: The Relation of International Trade and Environmental Policy* (Totowa, NJ: Allanheld, Osumun, 1982): 67-101. See also World Resources Institute, "Improving Environmental Co-operation: The Roles of Multinational Corporations and Developing Countries," World Resources Institute, 1984

10. If the new technology has higher operating costs, its effectiveness may still depend on regulatory pressure or penalties.

11. This section relies heavily on Erik Scarsborough, "The Environmental Effects of Macroeconomic and Sectoral Policy in Chile and Peru," World Bank, draft, October 1991; and on discussions between one of the authors and Scarsborough while working jointly on a study of the effects of macroeconomic and sectoral policies on environmental problems in Chile.

12. The manager of a large pulp and paper plant in Chile was quoted recently in the *New York Times* (November 10, 1991, p. E6) as conceding that the investment in pollution control by his company was not to abide by Chilean law, but rather to be able to sell his pulp in Europe, where Green movements have persuaded many governments to impose high import tariffs on pulp made with a process that creates chlorine gas as a byproduct.

13. Scarsborough, "Environmental Effects."

14. A similar pattern occurred in the baby food industry in at least one developing country. The Swiss multinational Nestle, once it began adhering to WHO marketing guidelines for infant formula and was losing market share in Indonesia, put heavy pressure on the Indonesian government to force all baby food manufacturers, domestic and foreign, to follow WHO guidelines. We are grateful to John Briscoe for pointing out this good analogy.

15. There may still, of course, be a problem of small U.S. firms that go just south of the border to avoid U.S. environmental or occupational health and safety standards. The evidence in the third section suggests that even given this phenomenon, more open economies have cleaner industries.

16. See Paul Martin, David Wheeler, Mala Hettige, et al., "The Industrial Pollution Projection System: Concept, Initial Development, and Critical Assessment," World Bank, 1991.

17. For evidence that all simple correlations between indices are above .94, see Robert Lucas, David Wheeler, and Mala Hettige, "Economic Development, Environmental Regulation, and the International Migration of Toxic Industrial Pollution: 1960-1988," World Bank, 1991.

18. In addition, as Lucas et. al. (1991) note, to apply the U.S. intensities to other countries requires the assumption that the pollution intensity of different products within an industry group is similar or that the mix of products within each industry group is similar across countries; and the assumption that emissions are related to output, not to value added, as in fact seems reasonable.

19. David Dollar, "Outward Orientation and Growth: An Empirical Study Using a Price-Based Measure of Openness," World Bank, 1990.

20. The openness index ranks countries from one to seven with respect to openness. Economies with rank one are the most open.

21. The ranges are as follows:
Income: High ($3000 (US 1987), Middle ($1500), Low ($500);
Income growth: Fast (6%), Slow (1%);
Dollar index value: Open (1), Closed (5).

[20]

ELSEVIER

Journal of Development Economics
Vol. 52 (1997) 65–82

JOURNAL OF
Development
ECONOMICS

The environment and welfare implications of trade and tax policy

Hiro Lee [a], David Roland-Holst [b,c,d]

[a] Nagoya University, Nagoya, Japan
[b] OECD Development Centre, Paris, France
[c] CEPR, London, UK
[d] Mills College, Oakland, CA, USA

Received 15 October 1994

Abstract

Developing countries with comparative advantage in dirty industries face the risk of environmental degradation unless appropriate policies are implemented. Using applied general equilibrium analysis, we examine how trade influences the environment and assess the welfare and environmental implications of alternative pollution abatement policies for Indonesia. Our results indicate that unilateral trade liberalization by Indonesia would increase the ratio of emission levels to real output for almost all major pollution categories. More importantly, when tariff removal is combined with a cost-effective tax policy, the twin objectives of welfare enhancement and environmental quality improvement appear to be feasible. This sheds new and positive light on the role of trade in sustainable development.

JEL classification: F13; O53; Q28; Trade and environment; Pollution; Indonesia; Applied general equilibrium model

1. Introduction

International trade can exert an important influence on the environment via its effects on the composition of domestic production activities. Countries with less stringent environmental regulations may have comparative advantage in dirty industries. This leads to the export of 'pollution services' embodied in goods made with technologies that do not meet the environmental standards of the importing

PII S0304-3878(96)00439-7

countries. In the course of trade, one observes pollution being transferred across a life cycle from more to less advanced nations. A number of empirical studies (e.g. Grossman and Krueger, 1992; Hettige et al., 1992; Lucas et al., 1992) have shown an inverse U-shaped relationship between GDP per capita and industrial pollution intensity. [1] The normal good characteristic of environmental quality, relatively high costs of monitoring and enforcing pollution standards, and an increase in output shares of manufactures during industrialization are some of the major factors leading to relatively high pollution levels per unit of output in developing countries (Birdsall and Wheeler, 1992).

Although there has been intense pressure from environmentalists and some policy makers to include environmental standards in trade agreements, economists have long argued that trade is not the root cause of environmental damage. Low and Safadi (1992) suggest that freer trade may provide benefits to the environment through its effects on resource allocation and income levels. Lucas et al. (1992) find that among developing countries, the more closed economies experienced very rapid shifts toward toxic-intensive structures in the 1970s and 1980s. This is because import-substituting industrialization protected mainly capital- and pollution-intensive sectors. Using partial equilibrium analysis, Anderson (1992) shows that even if a country has comparative advantages in the production of pollution-intensive goods, free trade would still raise welfare unambiguously, so long as an optimal pollution tax is introduced. Thus, previous studies suggest that trade does not necessarily lead to degradation of national environment, trade policy is never the first-best policy to remedy environmental problems, and an efficient environmental policy is one which would equalize marginal social costs and benefits of production. [2]

The objective of this paper is to show empirically that a combination of trade liberalization and a cost-effective tax policy would not only raise the country's welfare, but it can also improve the environmental quality. We use applied general equilibrium analysis to examine the environmental implications of trade and tax policies in Indonesia. This is a country well suited to our analysis because it has comparative advantages in dirty industries and its trade has historically conferred asymmetric environmental effects, inducing a net transfer of environmental costs from its trading partners, particularly Japan.

In Section 2, we present some statistics on the embodied pollution service trade between Indonesia and Japan during 1965–1990. Section 3 describes the two-country calibrated general equilibrium (CGE) model used in this study, followed

[1] Hettige et al. (1992) and Lucas et al. (1992) suggest that the declining portion in the inverse U-shaped relationship is due solely to a shift from industry to services and not a result of a shift toward a less toxic mix of manufacturing output.

[2] See Dean (1992) for a survey of literature on trade and the environment. O'Connor (1994) reviews the recent Asian Pacific experience. A survey of Indonesia's trade and adjustment policies can be found in Roland-Holst (1992).

by the appraisal of the environmental implications of Indonesia's trade liberalization in Section 4 and the evaluation of the welfare effect of pollution abatement by alternative instruments in Section 5. Conclusions are summarized in Section 6.

2. International trade and patterns of effluent transfer

This section offers some historical evidence on how international trade influences the transfer of environmental effects. We introduce the concept of embodied effluent trade (EET) to capture the idea that traded commodities embody an environmental service, i.e. the amount of pollution emitted when goods are produced domestically. If countries impose different environmental costs on pollution, then the ability to pollute becomes a source of comparative advantage. One would thus expect to see a pattern with relatively high EET in exports from countries with low environmental standards and relatively low EET in their imports, while the opposite would prevail in countries with higher environmental standards. This is indeed the case for trade between Indonesia and Japan, which exhibits a striking imbalance in EET.

The database on the Industrial Pollution Projection System of the World Bank is used to measure domestic effluent intensities in production. It provides emission levels per unit of output for a variety of pollutants at a four digit ISIC level of sectoral detail for US manufacturing. [3] The data are then mapped to four-digit output share data for Indonesia and Japan, computed from a 128-sector bilateral input–output table constructed by the Institute of Developing Economies (1991), to obtain weighted emission intensities for the 19 sectors of the model. [4] Table 1 presents the results of this conversion for Indonesia. [5]

As the database is limited to industrial pollution, agriculture and services are omitted from the effluent database. Since environmental damages related to agriculture and forestry, such as soil erosion and loss of soil fertility from deforestation are particularly important for Indonesia, their omission would understate the pollution content of domestic production. Of the remaining 17 sectors, petroleum, mining, lumber and wood, pulp and paper, industrial chemicals,

[3] See Martin et al. (1991) and Wheeler (1992).

[4] Such detailed emission intensities are at the moment only available for US manufacturing sectors, obliging us to apply them to both Indonesia and Japan. The 19 sectors are (1) agriculture, forestry and fishing, (2) petroleum, (3) mining, (4) processed food, (5) textiles, (6) lumber and wood products, (7) pulp and paper products, (8) industrial chemicals, (9) other chemicals, (10) plastics, (11) non-metallic mineral products, (12) steel, (13) nonferrous metals, (14) metal products, (15) machinery and precision instruments, (16) electrical machinery, (17) transport equipment, (18) other manufactures, and (19) services.

[5] The results for Japan are similar to those for Indonesia although there are some differences in the emission intensities at the 19-sector level of disaggregation between the two countries because of different output shares at the four-digit ISIC level.

Table 1
Sectoral effluent intensities in Indonesia (tons/year/$million unless indicated otherwise)

	PARTIC [a]	*SO2*	*NO2*	*LEAD*	*VOC*	*CO*	*BOD* [b]	*SS*	*TOX* [c]	*METAL*
1 Agriculture	n.a.	n.a.	n.a.	n.a.	n.a.	n.a.	n.a.	n.a.	n.a.	n.a.
2 Petroleum	5.36	16.28	3.47	6.54	1.60	0.65	0.48	0.58	1.15	0.06
3 Mining	4.19	20.12	1.65	0.40	2.05	19.76	8.17	117.64	4.05	2.79
4 Processed food	0.53	0.63	1.84	0.02	0.37	0.51	7.55	1.95	0.29	0
5 Textiles	0.40	2.83	4.91	0.00	1.20	0.93	0.02	0.03	1.49	0.07
6 Lumber and wood products	4.15	1.42	3.10	0.00	4.19	5.33	0	0	2.05	0.02
7 Pulp and paper	1.35	13.37	5.41	0.69	2.85	7.72	9.9	39.91	3.1	0.02
8 Industrial chemicals	0.61	4.09	3.95	0.03	4.15	5.60	9.41	21.09	13.57	0.08
9 Other chemicals	0.50	5.50	2.69	0.10	2.58	3.30	2.54	0.72	1.7	0.02
10 Plastics	0.14	1.36	40	0.00	4.52	0.12	0	0	3.39	0.09
11 Non-metallic mineral products	4.71	6.90	7.62	0.29	0.54	1.38	0	0	1.54	0.38
12 Steel	1.61	4.42	1.99	6.11	1.05	15.27	0.02	12.41	3.47	1.86
13 Non-ferrous metals	4.12	20.36	1.54	0.00	2.08	21.00	8.67	125.23	4.23	2.97
14 Metal products	0.25	0.17	0.82	0.22	4.23	0.09	0.55	11.71	2.08	0.3
15 Machinery & precision instruments	0.68	0.37	0.28	0.20	0.83	0.10	0	0	0.71	0.11
16 Electrical machinery	0.05	0.17	0.10	0.15	2.04	0.12	0	0.02	0.82	0.14
17 Transport equipment	0.15	0.09	0.06	0.00	0.85	0.02	0	0.01	0.5	0.02
18 Other manufactures	0.26	0.22	0.07	0.00	4.12	0.03	0	0	1.23	0.27
19 Services	n.a.	n.a.	n.a.	n.a.	n.a.	n.a.	n.a.	n.a.	n.a.	n.a.

[a] Air pollutants: particulates (*PARTIC*), sulfur dioxide (*SO2*), nitrogen dioxide (*NO2*), lead (tons/year/$billion), volatile organic compounds (*VOC*), carbon monoxide (*CO*).
[b] Water pollutants: biochemical oxygen demand (*BOD*), suspended solids (*SS*).
[c] Toxic pollutants/all media: total toxic release (*TOX*), bioaccumulative metals (*METAL*).
Sources: Martin et al. (1991), Wheeler (1992), and authors' calculations.

non-metallic minerals (consisting of cement and stone products), steel, and nonferrous metals may be regarded as pollution-intensive sectors. For example, petroleum has high effluent intensities of particulates, SO_2, NO_2, and lead, while mining and nonferrous metals have high emission coefficients on particulates, SO_2, carbon monoxide, the two water pollutants (biochemical oxygen demand and suspended solids), and the two toxic pollutants (total toxic release and bioaccumulative metals).

Let ε_{ih} denote sectoral effluent intensities of pollutant h. To measure average effluent levels embodied in tradeable commodities, the acute human toxic linear (AHTL) index developed by Wheeler (1992) is used. The AHTL index is a weighted average of various effluents with weights representing their human health risk. The index of sectoral effluent output is defined as

$$e_i = \frac{\varepsilon_{i,A}}{\sum_i \varepsilon_{i,A} q_i}, \tag{1}$$

where $\varepsilon_{i,A}$ is the sectoral AHTL emission rate per unit of output in US manufacturing and q_i is sector i's share in total domestic output. If these indices are multiplied by 1985 US sectoral output shares, they sum to unity. For any other country, such a sum measures the effluent potential of domestic output in units relative to the United States. In 1985, for example, Japanese output shares give a value of $E_q = \sum_i e_i q_i = 0.86$, indicating that, under the same technologies, the effluent intensity of Japanese domestic production would be 14% below that of the United States by this index. The comparable figure for Indonesia is 2.45. Thus E_q serves as an index of aggregate effluent levels for a given composition of domestic production. As the structure of the economy shifts toward relatively cleaner activities, such as services, this index will decline. It is unaffected by the absolute level of output, but simply allows comparison across countries of one representative unit of domestic product.

In light of differing environmental standards in the two countries, the disparity in E_q is likely to be greater than the indices would indicate. Japan's effluent controls are more stringent than those of the US, and thus the compositional index for the former is likely to overstate Japanese effluent levels. Likewise, Indonesia's environmental controls are weaker than the reference country, so its actual effluent levels are underestimated by E_q.

This measure can also be used to evaluate the implicit effluent content of trade. The indices

$$E_x^f = \sum_i e_i x_i^f \tag{2}$$

and

$$E_m^f = \sum_i e_i m_i^f \tag{3}$$

measure the embodied effluent content of exports and imports, respectively; x_i^f

Table 2
Trends in embodied effluent content of exports and imports [a]

	1965	1970	1975	1980	1985	1990	Average
Indonesia							
Exports to							
Japan	11.32	11.45	15.34	13.43	11.77	10.41	12.29
Rest of world	7.28	6.49	14.14	12.20	10.59	7.23	9.66
Imports from							
Japan	2.10	2.17	2.03	1.80	1.99	1.67	1.96
Rest of world	2.29	2.73	2.79	4.44	4.16	3.34	3.29
Effluent trade ratio (E_x / E_m)							
Japan	5.38	5.29	7.57	7.47	5.93	6.24	6.31
Rest of world	3.18	2.38	5.06	2.75	2.54	2.17	3.01
Japan							
Exports to							
Indonesia	2.10	2.17	2.03	1.80	1.99	1.67	1.96
Rest of world	1.75	1.62	1.69	1.60	1.52	1.54	1.62
Imports from							
Indonesia	11.32	11.45	15.34	13.43	11.77	10.41	12.29
Rest of world	4.09	3.87	7.63	8.86	7.39	4.78	6.10
Effluent trade ratio (E_x / E_m)							
Indonesia	0.19	0.19	0.13	0.13	0.17	0.16	0.16
Rest of world	0.43	0.42	0.22	0.18	0.21	0.32	0.30

[a] These indices measure embodied effluent content of exports and imports relative to the emission intensity of overall US domestic output. Values greater than unity imply that the country's overall exports by destination or imports by origin are more pollution-intensive than the US output.
Sources: Wheeler (1992), United Nation's COMTRADE database, and authors' calculations based on Eq. (2) and Eq. (3) in the text.

and m_i^f are the sectoral shares of exports to destination f (f = bilateral partner, rest of world (ROW)) and the sectoral shares of imports from origin f. If E_x^f exceeds unity, for example, the composition of the country's existing exports represents (in their production) a higher level of pollution per unit than that of the representative output in the United States. Values less than unity mean that the country's overall exports are 'cleaner' than overall US domestic output.

The indices E_x and E_m thus measure the embodied effluent trade for a given composition of exports and imports per unit of trade. E_x and E_m for Indonesian–Japanese bilateral trade and their trade with the rest of the world are presented in Table 2. These estimates were constructed for the 1965–1990 period at five-year intervals, with detailed trade data from the United Nation's COMTRADE tables. The ratios of E_x to E_m are also given in the table. [6]

[6] The pollution content of US exports and imports has been estimated by Walter (1973). He estimated environmental-control loadings entering US trade flows and found that the pollution content of US exports exceeded that of imports in 31 out of 78 sectors in 1971.

The most arresting feature of Table 2 is the imbalance in direct EET between the two trading partners. Over the last two and a half decades, Indonesia's production for export to Japan has been about six times more effluent intensive than have Japanese exports to Indonesia. In a long-term situation of relatively balanced bilateral trade, this implies a sustained and significant transfer of environmental costs from Japan to Indonesia. Although the trend in recent years has reduced this disparity, it is still quite significant.

These results are even more striking when compared to each country's trade with the rest of the world. Indonesia's imports from Japan are about half as effluent intensive as what it buys from other countries and its exports to Japan are about 30% as effluent intensive as other countries' exports to Japan. Trade between countries at different stages of modernization has long exhibited hierarchical properties which are correlated with technology levels and environmental effects.

Given that the effluent indices are derived assuming US technology and environmental standards, economic structure alone could explain Indonesia's higher pollution intensities in production, both for domestic and foreign consumption. There are significant differences in sectoral and trade structure between the two countries. Indonesia's heavy export dependence on petroleum (64% of total exports in 1985) is the dominating factor for its high effluents embodied in overall exports. On average, the petroleum sector has been responsible for more than 50% of Indonesia's industrial emissions and about 90% of the EET in exports. Lumber and wood and nonferrous metals have each accounted for between 3 and 4% of the effluents embodied in exports. [7] By contrast, except for steel, Japan's exports are concentrated in sectors with low pollution intensities, resulting in low effluents embodied in its exports. Thus, the composition of output in Indonesia is substantially more pollution intensive than that in Japan. [8]

3. Two-country CGE model for Indonesia and Japan

Calibrated general equilibrium models have been increasingly used as tools for detailed empirical analysis of the long-run implications of economic policy. They

[7] Because log exports were banned in 1985, the production and exports of wood products have increased sharply. In our industrial classification, logging is included in agriculture where no emission data are incorporated. Thus, a shift in exports from logs to lumber and wood products would also raise the value of embodied effluent content of Indonesian exports although the export ban could slow deforestation.

[8] Since the US effluent coefficients are applied to Indonesia and Japan, differing levels of technology and environmental regulations between the two countries do not affect our results. If country-specific data were available, the results would have yielded even larger asymmetries. There are significant technological disparities between the two countries in a variety of industrial activities, with Japan's environmental regulation being more stringent than Indonesia's.

have been used extensively in general equilibrium assessments of CO_2 abatement policies (e.g. Burniaux et al., 1992; Jorgenson et al., 1992; Perroni and Rutherford, 1993; OECD, 1994). Because a CGE model can distinguish dirty industries and capture a variety of indirect effects, such as interindustry and trade linkages, it is well suited to analyzing the impact of trade and tax policy on the environment and economic welfare.

The Indonesia–Japan CGE model is calibrated to the 1985 social accounting matrix (SAM) of the two countries. [9] An important feature of this model is its endogenous specification of domestic supply, demand, and bilateral trade for the two countries at the sectoral level. This is particularly important for Indonesia as its bilateral trade with Japan as a percentage of the total trade was 47% for exports and 21% for imports in the base year. While trade between the two countries is modeled endogenously, we assume that their individual trade flows with the rest of the world (ROW) are each governed by the small country assumption. [10] The resulting six sets of sectoral trade flows are then directed by two endogenous price systems (Indonesia–Japan imports and exports), and four exogenous price systems (Indonesia–ROW and Japan–ROW imports and exports).

As has been employed in many other CGE models, a differentiated product specification is used for the demand and supply for tradeable commodities. Domestic demand is a CES composite of goods differentiated by origin. For each product category,

$$D_i = \bar{A}_{D_i}\left[\sum_k \beta_i^k \left(D_i^k\right)^{(\sigma_i - 1)/\sigma_i}\right]^{\sigma_i/(\sigma_i - 1)} \quad (4)$$

where k = {Indonesia, Japan, ROW}. D_i^k consists of domestic goods, imports from the bilateral trading partner, and imports from ROW, σ_i is elasticities of substitution among D_i^k, and $\bar{A}_{D_i}$ and β_i^k are intercept and share parameters. Similarly, domestic production is supplied to differentiated destinations (domestic market, exports to bilateral partner, and exports to ROW), which is specified as a CET composite:

$$S_i = \bar{A}_{S_i}\left[\sum_k \delta_i^k \left(S_i^k\right)^{(\lambda_i + 1)/\lambda_i}\right]^{\lambda_i/(\lambda_i + 1)} \quad (5)$$

where λ_i is elasticities of transformation among S_i^k, and $\bar{A}_{s_i}$ and δ_i^k are intercept and share parameters.

[9] See Lee and Roland-Holst (1993b) for a complete set of equations describing the model.

[10] Lee and Roland-Holst (1993a) treat Japan as a large country so as to affect prices in the ROW market. For the moderate trade flow adjustments for Japan described in this study, however, the small country assumption makes almost no change in the results of simulation experiments.

Every sector is characterized by constant returns to scale and perfect competition. [11] The production function is given by

$$S_i = \min\{CES(L_{D_i}, K_{D_i}; \phi_i), V_{1i}/a_{1i}, \ldots, V_{ni}/a_{ni}\}, \tag{6}$$

where L_{D_i} and K_{D_i} are labor and capital demands, ϕ_i is the elasticities of substitution between labor and capital, a_{ji} is input–output coefficients, and $V_{ji} = a_{ji}S_i$ is demand for intermediate good i in sector j. The zero-profit condition implies

$$(1 - t_{S_i})P_{S_i} = AC_i, \tag{7}$$

where P_{S_i} and AC_i are prices and average costs of composite supply. [12]

Ad valorem tax rates on supply, t_{S_i}, are the sum of ad valorem indirect taxes, t_{X_i}, and ad valorem effluent taxes:

$$t_{S_i} = t_{X_i} + \sum_h \tau_{ih}\varepsilon_{ih}, \tag{8}$$

where τ_{ih} are excise taxes on emissions (\$/ton of pollutant h).

We assume both countries have a fixed aggregate stock of domestic productive capital which is mobile between sectors, while the economy-wide average rental rate adjusts to equate aggregate capital demand to the fixed total supply. We also assume that labor in both countries is mobile between sectors, but the total labor supply is specified as a function of the wage rate and household income. In the product markets, prices are normalized by a fixed numéraire chosen to be the GDP price deflator. Finally, we assume that the real exchange rate is flexible while the current account balances for the two countries are fixed at the baseline values. [13]

Sectoral emission levels by pollutant and destination of supply are computed as

$$EMI_{ih}^k = \varepsilon_{ih} P_{S_i}^k S_i^k. \tag{9}$$

The matrix of effluent intensities by sector and type of pollutant, $\{\varepsilon_{ih}\}$, forms the basis for calculating environmental effects resulting from policy changes, such as tariff liberalization and effluent taxes. A limitation of this approach at the moment is that there is no scope for technical substitution within sectors, and thus emissions are proportional to output regardless of relative prices and differential effluent taxes. The main advantage of this approach over previous modeling with these coefficients is the general equilibrium nature of the simulations, which allow

[11] While varying returns to scale does affect the magnitude of impact of trade and tax policies, the key results of this paper are robust and not affected by different specifications on market conduct (e.g. oligopolistic behavior) and returns to scale.

[12] The composite supply price is given by $P_{S_i}S_i = \Sigma_k P_{S_i}^k S_i^k$.

[13] Since there are no assets in the model, the real exchange rate is the relative price of tradeables to nontradeables.

Table 3
Aggregate results of Indonesia's tariff liberalization (percentage changes)

	Indonesia	Japan
Real GDP	0.87	0.00
EV income	0.53	0.03
Wage rate	1.10	0.05
Employment	1.87	0.00
Rental rate on capital	3.31	0.04
Real exchange rate	5.26	−0.07
Total imports	5.81	0.14
Total exports	5.72	−0.07

for changing composition of domestic output, a large medium-term source of pollution mitigation. [14]

4. Trade and domestic pollution in Indonesia

The two-country CGE model is used to assess the linkage between trade and the environment by removing Indonesia's nominal tariffs on all imports. Table 3 summarizes the aggregate results. The tariff removal leads to an increase in Indonesia's real GDP by 0.87% and economy-wide employment by 1.87%. Equivalent variation (EV) income, which measures the change in real consumer purchasing power, rises by less than the increase in real GDP because of a fall in the bilateral terms of trade with Japan. [15] The wage rate and the rental rate on capital both increase, but the latter increases more because an increase in labor supply in response to higher wages raises the marginal productivity of capital. Indonesia's tariff removal induces real rupiah depreciation and the subsequent increase in its exports. It has a negligible effect on the Japanese economy, with all aggregate measures changing by a small fraction of one percent.

Trade liberalization leads to dramatic shifts in the composition of Indonesia's sectoral trade and output that are driven by sharp changes in relative prices. It induces an expansion of output in petroleum and mining, lumber and wood, nonferrous metals, and services. [16] The real rupiah depreciation leads to increased demand for Indonesian exports in most of the major sectors. [17] Results for Japan are again small, except for adjustments in bilateral trade with Indonesia. There is

[14] Compare to e.g. Anderson (1992) and ten Kate (1993).

[15] The terms of trade with the rest of the world are unaffected because of the small country assumption.

[16] The sectoral results are available upon request from the authors.

[17] The sectors that experience a fall in exports (pulp and paper, non-mineral metallic products, steel, and metal products) have small export shares.

Table 4
Changes in emission levels by destination of supply: Indonesia [a]

	Absolute changes [b]				Percentage changes			
	(1) Domestic	(2) Japan	(3) ROW	(4) Total	(5) Domestic	(6) Japan	(7) ROW	(8) Total
PARTIC	773	2298	2297	5369	0.89	4.94	7.40	3.27
SO2	2461	7146	6338	15945	1.04	5.01	7.23	3.41
NO2	−209	1443	1619	2853	−0.24	4.89	6.96	2.04
LEAD	1.17	2.54	2.23	5.94	1.57	4.79	7.02	3.73
VOC	−599	747	1029	1178	−1.15	5.07	7.80	1.47
CO	−778	1112	1307	1641	−1.20	6.71	9.49	1.73
BOD	−657	536	608	487	−0.83	6.43	8.66	0.51
SS	−1497	5094	3973	7571	−0.76	7.66	11.71	2.55
TOX	−368	649	951	1232	−0.89	5.46	9.38	1.95
METAL	−62	137	106	181	−0.91	6.99	9.80	1.83
AHTL index	−0.10	1.17	1.56	2.64	−0.16	5.16	8.76	2.64

[a] Changes in emission levels of pollutant embodied in output supplied to different destination resulting from unilateral tariff liberalization by Indonesia.
[b] Absolute changes in thousand tons of pollutant except the AHTL index.

some shift of resources toward Japanese export sectors and a slight diversion of import demand in response to the rupiah depreciation.

While removing tariff protection leads to expanded trade and greater economy-wide efficiency, in the absence of new technologies it entails an increase the total emission levels. Tables 4 and 5 report the effects on emission levels of each

Table 5
Changes in emission levels by destination of supply: Japan [a]

	Absolute changes [b]				Percentage changes			
	(1) Domestic	(2) Indonesia	(3) ROW	(4) Total	(5) Domestic	(6) Indonesia	(7) ROW	(8) Total
PARTIC	−1058	51	−49	−1057	−0.08	2.82	−0.07	−0.08
SO2	−3619	83	−147	−3683	−0.10	1.58	−0.07	−0.09
NO2	−520	84	−38	−473	−0.03	2.97	−0.04	−0.03
LEAD	−0.96	0.01	−0.05	−1.00	−0.09	0.70	−0.06	−0.09
VOC	−417	83	−72	−406	−0.03	2.77	−0.06	−0.03
CO	−2111	50	−221	−2282	−0.06	0.67	−0.08	−0.06
BOD	−495	25	−46	−517	−0.02	1.05	−0.07	−0.02
SS	−9796	126	−638	−10309	−0.09	0.75	−0.12	−0.09
TOX	−550	56	−72	−565	−0.04	1.45	−0.06	−0.03
METAL	−276	9	−30	−297	−0.06	1.00	−0.08	−0.06
AHTL index	−0.64	0.08	−0.12	−0.69	−0.03	1.11	−0.05	−0.03

[a] Changes in emission levels of pollutant embodied in output supplied to different destination resulting from unilateral tariff liberalization by Indonesia.
[b] Absolute changes in thousand tons of pollutant except the AHTL index.

pollutant embodied in domestic output supplied to different destination (domestic market, bilateral partner, and ROW). Given the extensive compositional shifts in production that occur in response to trade liberalization in Indonesia, emissions from the production of goods supplied domestically increase for three pollutants (particulates, SO_2, and lead) while those decrease for the other pollutants (column (1) of Table 4). In percentage terms, these changes are relatively small (column (5)). Trade expansion would, however, increase emissions quite substantially from the production of goods that are exported to both Japan and the rest of the world for all pollution categories included in the study (columns (2)–(3), (6)–(7)). The net effect is an increase in the emission level of all the pollutants generated from total output (columns (4), (8)). Table 5 reports the effects on emissions from output produced in Japan resulting from Indonesia's tariff removal, which are significantly smaller than those in Indonesia in percentage terms.

The result that trade liberalization leads to higher pollution levels is not surprising because it leads to an increase in real output. A more interesting result is that it leads to an increase in the relative output shares of dirty industries, causing higher average pollution intensities for almost all major pollution categories. The only exception is biochemical oxygen demand (water pollution) whose emission level rises by a smaller percentage (0.51%) than the increase in real output. For all other pollutants, the percentage change in emission levels (1.43–3.73%) exceeds the percentage change in real output, resulting in higher emission intensities.

5. Relative cost of alternative trade and tax policies in curtailing pollution

For Indonesia, the emission results of Section 4 amplify the policy challenge of addressing the environmental consequences of trade-based economic growth. If the marginal social damage caused by an increase in emissions of a particular pollutant is known, then in the absence of other distortions in the economy an optimal policy would be the imposition of an effluent tax which would internalize the social damage (Pigou, 1920). However, true marginal damage is unknown, and reliable estimates on marginal damage functions associated with externalities are unavailable. This is an important direction for future research as economic accounting of environmental costs and benefits would be essential for comprehensive integration of economic and environmental policies. [18]

Since the uncertainties on marginal benefits of pollution abatement would make the calculation of an optimal tax rate impossible, our approach is to set a particular level of emission target and assess empirically the relative cost of alternative

[18] For a survey of this kind of environmental valuation, see O'Connor (1992).

instruments that achieve the target. [19] In the first three experiments, we evaluate the cost of mitigating emissions of various pollutants by 5% using three policy instruments: an export tax, sector-specific effluent taxes, and a uniform effluent tax. [20] Different abatement targets have also been tried, but the relative efficiency of these instruments were not affected by the choice of abatement targets. No taxes are levied on the agricultural or service sector because no emission data are incorporated for these sectors. An AHTL (human health risk index) tax is equivalent to a set of taxes on the major air pollutants (particulates, SO_2, NO_2, lead, volatile organic compounds, and carbon monoxide) which act to reduce the AHTL index by 5%. In the fourth experiment, the combination of a uniform effluent tax and tariff removal is simulated to evaluate whether it is possible to increase real output and reduce emissions at the same time. While these experiments were conducted for each pollutant, for simplicity we only report the aggregate results for SO_2 and the AHTL index in Table 6. [21]

In the first experiment, an export tax is chosen as a policy instrument because in Indonesia exports are on average considerably more pollution intensive than goods supplied domestically (Section 2). Since the root cause of the pollution problem is production (regardless of destination), however, the imposition of a tax only on exports would be less efficient than a tax on output supplied domestically and exported. Columns (1a) and (1b) of Table 6 indicate that the cost of achieving the emission target with an export tax, in terms of lost real GDP or EV income, is highest among the three policy instruments. The reduction in total exports is partly offset by a large real depreciation of the rupiah but is still over 10% of the baseline quantity. The sharp contraction of trade causes additional reduction in real GDP and EV.

In experiment 2, sector-specific effluent taxes are levied to lower SO_2 emissions or the AHTL index by 5% in every sector. [22] While effluent taxes are imposed on all output regardless of destination, an enforcement of the same abatement target in all industrial sectors imposes an extremely high cost on some. This is clearly illustrated in Table 7, which summarizes the sector-specific SO_2

[19] An optimal rate of effluent tax would equalize marginal damage and marginal abatement cost of 1 ton of pollutant. On the cost side, Hartman et al. (1994) provide comprehensive estimates on abatement of 7 air pollutants for 37 US manufacturing industries.

[20] Since our primary objective is the evaluation of the combined effects of trade liberalization and cost-effective tax policy, we limited the number of tax instruments to three. For evaluation of alternative policy instruments, such as pollution abatement and control expenditure (PACE) equalization tax and the polluter-pay principle, see Low (1992) and Low and Safadi (1992).

[21] SO_2 is chosen because it is a pollutant that is known to adversely affect local environmental conditions, including acidification of soils and water and corrosion of materials.

[22] Sector-specific taxes required to mitigate emissions by 5% will lead to the same results regardless of the pollutant chosen except for the effluent tax results, which depend upon the effluent intensities of the pollutant in different sectors.

Table 6
Aggregate results for alternative trade and tax policies (percentage changes)

	Export tax [a]		Sector-specific effluent taxes [b]	Uniform effluent tax [c]		Uniform tax and liberalization [d]	
	(1a)	(1b)	(2)	(3a)	(3b)	(4a)	(4b)
	SO_2	AHTL		SO_2	AHTL	SO_2	AHTL
Real GDP	−1.65	−2.26	−1.22	−0.56	−0.54	0.30	0.33
EV income	−1.18	−1.67	−1.14	−0.34	−0.45	0.25	0.14
Employment	−3.07	−3.99	−2.46	−0.15	−0.97	1.82	0.92
Wage rate	−2.53	−3.57	−2.16	−1.15	−1.09	0.03	0.14
Rental rate on capital	−5.75	−7.68	−5.46	−2.49	−2.78	0.80	0.56
Real exchange rate	17.67	24.70	4.81	3.61	3.54	9.02	9.03
Total imports	−11.87	−15.58	−1.94	−1.45	−1.47	4.20	4.09
Total exports	−10.87	−14.25	−2.26	−2.15	−1.64	3.31	3.81
SO_2 emissions	−5.00	−6.42	−5.00	−5.00	−3.74	−2.03	−0.61
AHTL index	−3.98	−5.00	−5.00	−3.44	−5.00	−1.10	−3.07

[a] (1a) export tax to cut SO_2 emissions by 5%; (1b) export tax to lower the AHTL index by 5%.
[b] Sector-specific effluent taxes to lower SO_2 emissions or the AHTL index by 5% in every sector.
[c] (3a) uniform effluent tax to cut SO_2 emissions by 5%; (3b) uniform effluent tax to lower the AHTL index by 5%.
[d] (4a) combination of (3a) and tariff removal; (4b) combination of (3b) and tariff removal.

taxes required to achieve alternative emission targets within each sector. These taxes approximate the marginal cost of mitigating SO_2 emissions compared with the baseline levels for each sector. [23] SO_2 abatement costs in metal products, transport equipment, and other manufactures are found to be more than 400 times those in industrial chemicals. Thus, regulation which would require every sector to cut emissions by the same proportion would be highly inefficient.

Given the large disparity in marginal abatement costs, a uniform effluent tax would significantly reduce the costs of achieving a given emission curtailment target (experiment 3). The cost of cutting SO_2 emissions by 5% in terms of a loss in real GDP under a uniform tax is less than half (0.56 vs. 1.22%) compared with sector-specific taxes (Table 6, columns (2) and (3a)). Under this scheme each sector will abate SO_2 until the marginal abatement cost is equal to the uniform tax

[23] These are not directly comparable with the econometric estimates on US sectoral marginal abatement costs by Hartman et al. (1994). As in other CGE models, our estimates take into account input–output linkages but are based on the database of the benchmark year (1985) and the embedded model structure.

Table 7
Summary of SO_2 tax results under alternative emission targets ($/ton of SO_2 at 1985 prices and 1985 exchange rate)

Sector-specific taxes	Emission reductions compared with the baseline				
	1%	3%	5%	7%	10%
1 Agriculture	n.a.	n.a.	n.a.	n.a.	n.a.
2 Petroleum	1.05	3.07	5.01	6.87	9.50
3 Mining	1.16	3.39	5.51	7.52	10.34
4 Processed food	30.20	89.87	148.59	206.40	291.49
5 Textiles	3.65	10.83	17.85	24.71	34.70
6 Lumber and wood	14.21	42.00	68.96	95.09	132.75
7 Pulp and paper	0.70	2.05	3.36	4.61	6.39
8 Industrial chemicals	0.22	0.60	0.93	1.20	1.48
9 Other chemicals	4.27	12.64	20.78	28.69	40.14
10 Plastics	11.63	34.85	58.05	81.25	116.12
11 Non-metallic mineral products	5.89	16.85	26.79	35.78	47.65
12 Steel	3.55	10.40	16.90	23.07	31.70
13 Nonferrous metals	0.34	0.99	1.61	2.19	3.02
14 Metal products	89.25	262.54	429.05	588.94	816.70
15 Machinery and precision instruments	17.64	52.66	87.35	121.71	173.03
16 Electrical machinery	47.47	139.98	229.23	315.23	438.08
17 Transport equipment	87.66	259.92	428.18	592.51	831.85
18 Other manufacturing	90.97	270.54	446.95	620.20	874.09
19 Services	n.a.	n.a.	na.	n.a.	n.a.
20 Weighted average [a]	1.79	5.27	8.62	11.85	16.46
21 Uniform tax	0.74	2.19	3.61	4.99	7.02

[a] The sectoral SO_2 emission shares are used for the weights.

rate. Thus, the industrial chemical and nonferrous metal sectors will abate more than 10% of SO_2, pulp and paper over 5%, and petroleum and mining between 3 and 5% (Table 7). Many high abatement cost sectors will not abate any SO_2 emissions at all. The uniform tax rate required to achieve a given target is also substantially lower than the emission weighted average of the sector-specific taxes (Table 7, rows 20 and 21).

While a uniform effluent tax will tend to minimize the cost of a given mitigation target, those sectors with low marginal abatement cost would bear much of the cost in terms of loss in real output. A system of tradeable emission permits is an alternative cost-effective instrument to a uniform tax, but which can be more supportive to equity issues. Under this system a fixed number of permits to emit a specified quantity of the pollutant is issued to emitters. Those firms or sectors with low abatement cost can sell permits to those with high abatement cost at a market-clearing permit price, thereby receiving compensation for further abatement in emissions. The equilibrium permit price is determined by demand and supply of permits, which should equal the uniform tax rate required to achieve the same emission curtailment target. In the absence of transaction costs and regulatory distortions, a uniform tax and tradeable emission permits would both achieve a given level of environmental quality at minimum cost. [24]

In the final experiment, the same uniform tax scheme implemented in the third experiment is combined with the removal of all tariffs. This experiment is conducted to illustrate a critical point that the combination of trade liberalization and a cost-effective emission abatement instrument can lead to both an improvement in welfare (in terms of real GDP or EV) and a reduction in pollution (Table 6, columns (4a) and (4b)). This is possible because the benefits of tariff removal are greater than the cost of cutting pollution by the magnitude which more than offsets pollution induced by trade liberalization. The twin objectives of a welfare improvement and an emission curtailment can be achieved under a range of ex ante abatement targets for each pollutant. For SO_2, for example, the implementation of an ex ante abatement target of between 3.2 and 7.4% by a uniform tax, combined with complete tariff removal, will lead to realization of both objectives. It should be recalled that no pollution externalities have been introduced in our model because of the uncertainties regarding marginal damage. In the presence of externalities, therefore, the net social benefits of the combined policy would be even greater than our estimates would suggest.

6. Conclusions

Indonesia's historical trade orientation has been environmentally asymmetric, effecting significant transfers of pollution services from its trading partners, particularly Japan, to the domestic economy. While trade liberalization would improve Indonesian real income, it would also raise the emission level of major industrial pollutants. In light of this tradeoff between outward-oriented industrialization and the environment, we have assessed the relative cost of curtailing pollution with a variety of instruments, including export taxes, sector-specific effluent taxes, and uniform effluent taxes. In addition, a combination of uniform tax and tariff removal is simulated to examine the possibility of lowering domestic emissions and raising material welfare simultaneously.

Our simulation results indicate that a uniform effluent tax is the most cost-effective instrument in abating SO_2 emissions. This result holds for abatement of other industrial pollutants and for different abatement targets. Neither the imposition of an export tax, nor uniform emissions reduction with sector-specific taxes are recommended as an alternative policy. Pollution abatement using these instru-

[24] Hahn and Stavins (1992) point out that these incentive-based approaches are not well suited when there are political and technological constraints. For example, source-specific standards may be more appropriate for highly localized pollution problems with nonlinear damage functions. It is beyond the scope of this study, however, to incorporate such additional features as emission source type and political constraints.

ments would result in a loss of real GDP that is significantly greater than achieving the same target using a uniform effluent tax.

The most important result of this paper is that it is possible to abate industrial pollution while maintaining or even increasing real output when uniform taxation is combined with trade liberalization. In other words, trade liberalization should not be discouraged because of its environmental effects, and environmental taxation need not be contractional if distortions can be removed elsewhere. While the present model does not incorporate the benefits of reduced pollution in the utility function or EV calculation, their inclusion would only strengthen our conclusion.

Acknowledgements

Research was conducted under the auspices of the OECD Development Centre's 1993–1995 research programme on Sustainable Development, Environment, Resource Use, Technology and Trade and CEPR's research project on Market Integration, Regionalism and the Global Economy. Funding from the Japan Foundation Center for Global Partnership (CGP) and the Permanent Delegation of the Netherlands to the OECD is gratefully acknowledged. We thank Sebastian Dessus, David O'Connor, David Turnham, Dominique van der Mensbrugghe, and anonymous referees for their helpful comments. The opinions expressed here are those of the authors and should not be attributed to their affiliated institutions.

References

Anderson, K., 1992, Effects of trade and environmental policies on the environment and welfare, in: K. Anderson and R. Blackhurst, eds., The greening of world trade issues (University of Michigan Press, Ann Arbor).

Birdsall, N. and D. Wheeler, 1992, Trade policy and industrial pollution in Latin America: Where are the pollution havens? in: P. Low, ed., International trade and the environment, Discussion Paper 159 (World Bank, Washington, DC).

Burniaux, J.M., G. Nicoletti and J.O. Martins, 1992, GREEN: A global model for quantifying the costs of policies to curb CO_2 emissions, OECD Economic Studies 19, 49–92.

Dean, J.M., 1992, Trade and the environment: A survey of the literature, in: P. Low, ed., International trade and the environment, Discussion Paper 159 (World Bank, Washington, DC).

Grossman, G.M. and A.B. Krueger, 1992, Environmental aspects of a North American Free Trade Agreement, Working Paper 644 (Centre for Economic Policy Research, London).

Hahn, R.W. and R.N. Stavins, 1992, Economic incentives for environmental protection: Integrating theory and practice, American Economic Review, Papers and Proceedings 82, 464–468.

Hartman, R.S., D. Wheeler and M. Singh, 1994, The cost of air pollution abatement, Mimeo. (Policy Research Department, World Bank, Washington, DC).

Hettige, H., R.E.B. Lucas and D. Wheeler, 1992, The toxic intensity of industrial production: Global patterns, trends, and trade policy, American Economic Review, Papers and Proceedings 82, 478–481.

Institute of Developing Economies, 1991, International input–output table: Indonesia–Japan, 1985 (IDE, Tokyo).
Jorgenson, D.W., D.T. Slesnick and P.J. Wilcoxen, 1992, Carbon taxes and economic welfare, Brookings Papers on Economic Activity: Microeconomics, 393–431.
Lee, H. and D. Roland-Holst, 1993a, Cooperation or confrontation in US–Japan trade? Some general equilibrium estimates, Irvine Economics Paper 92-93-08 (University of California, Irvine, CA).
Lee, H. and D. Roland-Holst, 1993b, International trade and the transfer of environmental costs and benefits, Technical Paper 91 (OECD Development Centre, Paris).
Low, P., 1992, Trade measures and environmental quality: The implications for Mexico's exports, in: P. Low, ed., International trade and the environment, Discussion Paper 159 (World Bank, Washington, DC).
Low, P. and R. Safadi, 1992, Trade policy and pollution, in: P. Low, ed., International trade and the environment, Discussion Paper 159 (World Bank, Washington, DC).
Lucas, R.E.B., D. Wheeler and H. Hettige, 1992, Economic development, environmental regulation and the international migration of toxic industrial pollution: 1960–1988, in: P. Low, ed., International trade and the environment, Discussion Paper 159 (World Bank, Washington, DC).
Martin, P., D. Wheeler, M. Hettige and R. Stengren, 1991, The industrial pollution projection system: Concept, initial development, and critical assessment, Mimeo. (World Bank, Washington, DC).
O'Connor, D., 1992, Measuring the costs of environmental damage: A review of methodological approaches with an application to Bangkok, Thailand, Mimeo. (OECD Development Centre, Paris).
O'Connor, D., 1994, Managing the environment with rapid industrialisation: Lessons from the East Asian experience, Development Centre Studies (OECD, Paris).
OECD, 1994, Policy response to the threat of global warming, Working Party No. 1 Report of the Economic Policy Committee, ECO/CPE/WP1(94)5 (OECD, Paris).
Perroni, C. and T. Rutherford, 1993, International trade in carbon emission rights and basic materials: General equilibrium calculations for 2020, Scandinavian Journal of Economics 95, 257–278.
Pigou, A.C., 1920, The economics of welfare (Macmillan, London).
Roland-Holst, D., 1992, Stabilization and structural adjustment in Indonesia: An intertemporal general equilibrium analysis, Technical Paper 83 (OECD Development Centre, Paris).
ten Kate, A., 1993, Industrial development and the environment in Mexico, Working Paper 1125 (Policy Research Department, World Bank, Washington, DC).
Walter, I., 1973, The pollution content of American trade, Western Economic Journal 11, 61–70.
Wheeler, D., 1992, The economics of industrial pollution control, Industry Series Paper 60 (Industry and Energy Department, World Bank, Washington, DC).

Part III
Trade and Transboundary Pollution

Non-cooperative Analyses of Transborder Pollution and Trade Policy

[21]

Journal of International Economics 5 (1975) 15–29. © North-Holland Publishing Company

INTERNATIONAL EXTERNALITIES AND OPTIMAL TAX STRUCTURES

James R. MARKUSEN*

University of Western Ontario, London, Ont., Canada

Received July 1973, revised version received October 1974

This paper develops a model of two trading countries which are related by a bilateral production externality. Necessary conditions which must characterize an optimal tax structure from the point of view of one country are solved for and interpreted. Second, the model serves as a vehicle to extend the theory of corrective taxation in the case where only one policy instrument is available to deal with several distortions simultaneously. It is pointed out that the ranking of alternate second best tax structures typically depends upon which good is imported and which good is exported.

1. Introduction

Interest in externalities, distortions, and the theory of corrective taxes has been stimulated by a wide range of issues. Of particular interest to the theory of international trade are developments which suggest the possibility of externalities that are international in scope. A good deal of attention, for example, has recently been devoted to issues of international pollution and the depletion of international common property resources. Canada is concerned with formulating policies to discourage U.S. industrial pollution of Lake Erie and waste dumping in the Atlantic. United States East Coast fishermen are concerned that their government adopt policies to discourage foreign fishing in certain areas and to prevent further mercury pollution of ocean waters. Similarly, articles by Alan Williams (1966) and Michael Connally (1970 and 1972) have considered externalities arising from interregional and international public goods.

The difference between these problems and the usual types of externality situations typically encountered in the microeconomic literature is due simply to the sharply limited ability of one government to intervene in the internal affairs of another country. One country cannot tax foreign producers, for example, but if the country has monopoly power in trade, it can generally influence foreign production by changing world commodity prices.

This paper will develop a model of two countries in a trading relationship.

*The author wishes to express his appreciation to James E. Anderson, John G. Riley, and James R. Melvin for helpful comments and suggestions. The author is also grateful to an unknown referee for the proof given in footnote 1.

The model will attempt to incorporate the underlining similarities of a wide range of problems characterized by externalities between national and regional decision making bodies. Specifically, the model assumes that we are dealing with a situation in which one country is affected by an eyesore type pollution externality (it does not affect production functions) generated by the domestic and foreign production processes. The special case in which the externality is purely domestic will always be implicit in the analysis and will be referred to from time to time.

In the model, a national government undertakes the responsibility to maximize a social welfare function. It is assumed that the only tool available to this government is a tax structure, composed of production, consumption, and trade taxes (tariffs and subsidies). The economic problem is to solve for and interpret a set of necessary conditions which must be satisfied by an optimal tax structure which will maximize social welfare.

The second purpose of the paper is to use this model to develop and apply recent work on distortions and optimal tax structures when the first best optimum cannot be attained. The theory of the second best has demonstrated that if an uncorrected distortion exists in one sector, then the usual optimizing rules for the remaining sectors will generally no longer produce an optimal allocation. The existing distortion will define a new set of 'second best' optimizing conditions for the economy [see Lipsey–Lancaster (1956) and Davis–Whinston (1965)]. This theory has recently been developed in an open economy framework by Bhagwati and Ramaswami (1963), Bhagwati, Ramaswami and Srinivasan (1969), Kemp and Negishi (1969), and Vandendorpe (1972).

The model developed here will serve as a vehicle to discuss a situation where only one policy instrument is available to deal with several distortions simultaneously. This extends the work of Vandendorpe, in particular. Several situations in which first best solutions are unavailable due to institutional constraints are considered. Tariffs, for example, are becoming relatively fixed in the short run under a series of international agreements. Alternations in existing tariffs may not only violate these agreements, they also invite retaliation. Production taxes, on the other hand, seem to be politically difficult to institute. Second best tax structures in the presence of these constraints will be developed and compared to the first best solutions. Ranking of alternate second best tax structures will also be discussed and it will be pointed out that this ranking will generally depend upon which goods are imported and which goods are exported. A simple numerical example concludes the paper.

2. First best optimal tax structure

We begin by postulating a simple two-commodity, two-country model, and employ an algebraic technique developed by Vandendorpe (1972). The model is presented in such a way that generalization to the n-commodity case is straightforward as the interested reader may note from the Vandendorpe paper.

We assume that there is one eyesore type pollutant (it does not affect production functions) which is produced in some single valued functional relationship to the domestic and foreign production of one consumption good. There is no possibility of substitution among inputs or outputs such that the amount of pollution resulting from a given level of production can be varied. It is assumed that this pollution and the disutility associated with it are flows and that no stocks of pollution accumulate.

We assume that both countries produce and trade two goods (X_0, X_1), and that pollution is a function of the domestic and foreign production of good X_1. We let S denote pollution and letting superscripts denote countries (the domestic economy is country A), we write:

$$S = S(X_1^A, X_1^B), \qquad S_1 = \frac{\partial S}{\partial X_1^A}, \qquad S_2 = \frac{\partial S}{\partial X_1^B}, \tag{1}$$

where S is assumed to be additive. The special case in which the externality is purely domestic is given by $S_2 = 0$ in (1). The general case can be modified to this special case by setting $S_2 = 0$ in the optimal tax formulas derived throughout the paper.

Assume that we can specify the efficient aggregate transformation function for the domestic and foreign economies which produce two goods from factors in completely inelastic supply as either of the following:

$$F^i(X_0^i, X_1^i) = 0 \qquad \text{or} \qquad X_0^i = T^i(X_1^i), \qquad i = \text{A, B}, \tag{2}$$

where partial derivatives will be denoted F_j^i and T_j^i, respectively. Strictly convex technology will be assumed throughout the paper.

The domestic government is assumed to implement a social welfare function which lump sum redistributes income such that we can express the welfare of the country as some function of the total quantity of each good consumed and pollution. It is assumed that pollution can be characterized as a pure international public 'bad'. Letting C_i's represent the aggregate domestic consumption of good X_i^A, domestic welfare is given by

$$W = W(C_0, C_1, S) \qquad \text{or} \qquad C_0 = M(C_1, S, W), \tag{3}$$

where W_j and M_j will represent partial derivatives with respect to the jth argument.

Three price ratios, giving the price of X_1 in terms of X_0 will be utilized in the course of the paper. q will refer to the domestic consumer price ratio, p to the domestic producer price ratio, and p^* will denote the world price ratio. The domestic tariff rate will be given by θ, the consumption subsidy rate by σ, and the production tax rate by τ. X_0 is used as numéraire in both countries and it is assumed that no taxes are placed on this commodity. The price relationships are

$$p^*(1+\theta) = p(1+\tau) = q(1+\sigma). \tag{4}$$

For convenience, we assume that the foreigner does not have and will not institute taxes. It is sufficient for the conclusions of this paper to simply assume that the foreigner will not change his existing taxes in response to changes in domestic taxes (i.e., no retaliation), but the added assumption that these taxes equal zero simplifies notation.

The balance of payments constraint for the domestic economy will be written

$$e_0+p^*e_1 = 0, \qquad e_j = (X_j^{\mathrm{A}}-C_j), \qquad j = 0, 1, \tag{5}$$

that is, the sum of domestic excess supplies at world prices (in terms of X_0) for all commodities must equal zero.

If a unique foreign offer is associated with every world price ratio, the balance of payments constraint allows us to specify the world price ratio as a function of the domestic excess supply of one commodity only.

$$p^* = E(e_1), \qquad \mathrm{d}p^* = E_1\mathrm{d}e_1. \tag{6}$$

Similarly, Vandendorpe derives from (2) and (3) the following supply and demand relationships:

$$\mathrm{d}X_1^i = R_1^i\mathrm{d}p^i, \qquad \text{where } R_1^i = (-T_{11}^i)^{-1}, \qquad i = \mathrm{A}, \mathrm{B}, \tag{7}$$

$$\mathrm{d}q = D_1\mathrm{d}C_1+D_2\mathrm{d}S, \qquad \text{where } D_i = (-M_{1i}), \qquad i = 1, 2. \tag{8}$$

Both relations hold in the absence of distortions other than those considered. The second relation, however, only holds in a neighborhood about the optimum, where $\mathrm{d}W = 0$.

Differentiating the transformation function given in (2) above and dividing by F_0^i gives

$$\mathrm{d}X_0^i+F_1^i/F_0^i\,\mathrm{d}X_1^i = \mathrm{d}X_0^i+p^i\,\mathrm{d}X_1^i = 0, \qquad i = \mathrm{A}, \mathrm{B}, \tag{9}$$

where $p^{\mathrm{B}} = p^*$ by assumption.

We can also differentiate the social welfare function given in (3) and divide by W_0 to obtain an expression for the change in social welfare in terms of consumption good C_0 (alternatively, the change in real income in terms of C_0),

$$\frac{dW}{W_0} = dC_0 + W_1/W_0\, dC_1 + W_s/W_0\, dS = dC_0 + q\, dC_1 + q_s\, dS, \tag{10}$$

where q_s is the social marginal rate of substitution between pollution and X_0.

We now wish to make several substitutions. First we replace dC_0 and dC_1 in (10) by $dX_0^A - de_0$ and $dX_1^A - de_1$, respectively.

$$\frac{dW}{W_0} = dX_0^A - de_0 + q\, dX_1^A - q\, de_1 + q_s\, dS. \tag{11}$$

Second, we replace de_0 and dX_0^A by the expressions derived from differentiation of the balance of payments constraint (5) and from (9), respectively.

$$\frac{dW}{W_0} = e_1\, dp^* + (p^* - q)\, de_1 + (q - p)\, dX_1^A + q_s\, dS. \tag{12}$$

This equation, except for the term $q_s\, dS$, is identical to the one derived by Vandendorpe.

Now we totally differentiate (1) and replace dX_1^B by the transformation given in (7),

$$dS = S_1\, dX_1^A + S_2 R_1^B\, dp^*. \tag{13}$$

Suppose, that we now wish to solve for the optimal production tax and tariff holding the consumption tax (arbitrarily) equal to zero. In this case, (4) tells us that $(p^* - q) = -p^*\theta$ and $(q - p) = p\tau$. Substituting (13) into (12) and replacing dp^* by $E_1\, de_1$ as given in (6), (12) becomes:

$$\frac{dW}{W_0} = (e_1 E_1 + q_s S_2 R_1^B E_1 - p^*\theta)\, de_1 + p\tau\, dX_1^A + q_s S_1\, dX_1^A. \tag{14}$$

An interior optimum requires that this expression be zero for all differentials of e_1 and X_1^A. This requirement yields the following set of necessary conditions for an interior optimum:

$$\theta = \frac{e_1}{p^*} E_1 + \frac{q_s S_2}{p^*} R_1^B E_1, \tag{15}$$

$$\tau = -\frac{q_s S_1}{p}.$$

Eq. (15) suggests that the optimum can be achieved by a producer's tax on X_1^A and an appropriate trade tax together with some system of lump sum transfers. The producer's tax on X_1^A equals $-q_s S_1/p$. This tax is positive since q_s is assumed to be negative ($W_s < 0$). This relationship can also be written as $q + q_s S_1 = p$, which illustrates that this tax is a simple joint product optimality condition. Producers receive a price p per unit of production equal to the sum of the social values of the joint products produced, C_1 and S. One unit of X_1^A produced yields one unit of C_1 and S_1 units of S.

An examination of the optimal tariff formula given in (15) reveals that $e_1 E_1/p^*$ is simply the well known optimal tariff formula for the two-good case [see, for example, Graaff (1949)]. This term reduces (if X_1 is imported) to the reciprocal of the foreign elasticity of supply in the two-good case. This term is positive if X_1 is imported and negative if X_1 is exported (an export tax). In both cases, the effect is the same; the domestic price ratio of importables in terms of exportables is raised relative to the world price ratio.

The second term in (15), $q_s S_2 R_1^B E_1/p^*$, is the component of the optimal tariff which results from the existence of the foreign pollution externality. We would expect this term to be positive (q_s and E_1 are negative). This term does not change signs depending on whether X_1 is the domestic import or export good. Once again, the effect on foreign production is the same in either case. Ceteris paribus, $q_s S_2 R_1^B E_1/p^*$, raises the import tariff (when X_1 is imported), driving down the world price of X_1 relative to X_0 (given the usual elasticity conditions for a tariff to improve the terms of trade). If X_1 is exported, this term lowers the export tax, ceteris paribus, lowering the foreign price of X_1 relative to X_0.

This tax rate and others derived later is logically restricted to values greater than minus one. This condition will always be satisfied given the assumption of interior solutions made throughout the paper. Admitting the possibility of corner solutions (specialization in some activity) implies the need for certain restrictions on the functions given in (7) and (8). These restrictions, in turn, would imply restrictions on the optimal tax formulas, thereby guaranteeing tax rates greater than minus one.

Finally, the optimal trade tax in the presence of foreign pollution involves the derivative of world price with respect to domestic excess supply. This implies that if the victimized country faces a foreign offer surface which is infinitely elastic (the domestic economy has no monopoly power in trade) this derivative, and hence the tax itself, is equal to zero. Both components of the optimal trade tax tend to zero as the foreign offer surface becomes infinitely elastic. If the economy cannot affect world prices, then it cannot affect the foreigner's production (given the assumption of strictly convex technology).

It is well known that the first best optimum can be achieved in this type of problem provided that any two sets of taxes (plus lump sum transfers) are available. When tariffs are constrained to equal zero, for example, a tax regime involving consumption and production taxes exists which will satisfy the necessary conditions for a first best optimum. This optimum involves equating the marginal social rate of substitution in consumption (MRS) to the marginal social rate of transformation in production (MRT) to the foreign social rate of transformation through trade (FRT); i.e., a first best optimum is characterized by MRS = MRT = FRT. Two taxes are sufficient to satisfy these equations provided, of course, that the existing distortions are only between and not within sectors.

In this general equilibrium model, it is generally impossible to predict the effect of these taxes on consumption and production quantities even in the two-good case. The first difficulty is that the optimal tax formulas are only equilibrium conditions that give us little information as to the magnitudes of the optimal taxes. Secondly, if X_1 is the import good, the optimal tariff tends to raise the producer price of X_1 relative to X_0, while the optimal production tax tends to lower that same relative price. Third, consumers' marginal rates of substitution generally depend on the flow of pollution, and therefore on domestic and foreign producer prices. The direction of variable change in response to these taxes will depend upon the technology of the economy, the social welfare function, and the foreign offer surface. The appendix gives a numerical example of the effect of different tax regimes on welfare and on production and consumption variables.

3. Second best tax structures – Consumption taxes only

We now consider a situation in which tariffs are fixed by international agreement and production taxes cannot be instituted for political reasons. For added convenience, we assume that these taxes are identically zero. The problem is to solve for a set of necessary conditions which must be satisfied by an optimal consumption tax structure.

The constraints on production taxes and tariffs imply that the necessary conditions for a social optimum given in (15) cannot be satisfied, except by pure chance. Consumption taxes could be used to produce either MRS = MRT or MRS = FRT but generally not both. The second best solution, however, will generally dictate that neither equation be satisfied.

Tariffs and production taxes equal to zero imply an equality between world prices and domestic producer prices. This in turn implies $\mathrm{d}p = \mathrm{d}p^*$, which yields the following relationship:

$$\mathrm{d}X_1^{\mathrm{A}} = R_1^{\mathrm{A}}\,\mathrm{d}p = R_1^{\mathrm{A}}\,\mathrm{d}p^* = R_1^{\mathrm{A}}E_1\,\mathrm{d}e_1. \tag{16}$$

From (4) above, we have $p^* = p = q(1+\sigma)$. This implies that $(p^*-q) = q\sigma$, and that $(q-p) = -q\sigma$. We can now write (12) as

$$\frac{\mathrm{d}W}{W_0} = (e_1E_1 + q\sigma - q\sigma R_1^{\mathrm{A}}E_1 + q_sS_1R_1^{\mathrm{A}}E_1 + q_sS_2R_1^{\mathrm{B}}E_1)\,\mathrm{d}e_1. \tag{17}$$

An interior optimum requires that (17) be zero for all differentials of e. This necessary condition can be solved for the optimal consumption tax,

$$\sigma = \frac{e_1 E_1 + q_s S_1 R_1^A E_1 + q_s S_2 R_1^B E_1}{q(R_1^A E_1 - 1)}. \tag{18}$$

If X_1 is an import good, (18) has the following sign:

$$\sigma = \frac{(+)+(+)+(+)}{(-)} < 0. \tag{19}$$

The optimal consumption tax is positive (the optimal subsidy is negative) in the case of an import. The first term in the numerator and the denominator relate to the domestic economy's monopoly power in trade. These would be the only terms present if there were no externality. The second two additive terms in the numerator result from the presence of the pollution externality. Both of these terms tend to raise the optimal consumption tax. The effect is to discourage consumption of both domestic and foreign X_1, tending to drive down the world price (equal to domestic producer price) of X_1 relative to X_0. Finally, given the assumption of an interior solution, it can be shown that (18) will always satisfy the condition that $\sigma > -1$.[1] If X_1 is the export good, (18) has the following sign:

$$\sigma = \frac{(-)+(+)+(+)}{(-)}. \tag{20}$$

In the absence of the externality, the optimal consumption tax on the export good would be negative (the optimal consumption subsidy would be positive). But the components of the consumption tax due to the presence of the externality, remain positive. The relative magnitudes of the 'monopoly power' and 'externality' components of tax will determine whether the tax is positive or negative.

As a final point, we note from (18) that all components of the optimal consumption tax depend upon the existence of monopoly power in trade. Under this tax regime, both domestic and foreign producer prices are equal to world prices. If the domestic economy cannot influence world prices, then it cannot influence either domestic or foreign production of X_1 and optimal consumption taxes equal zero.

4. Second best tax structures – Tariffs only

If the domestic economy has constraints placed both upon its use of consumption and production taxes or on its use of consumption taxes and tariffs, the

[1]Since $p^* = q(1+\sigma)$, the σ in (18) can be reformulated as $\sigma = -N/\{p^*(1-R_1^A E_1)+N\}$, where $N = e_1 E_1 + q_s S_1 R_1^A E_1 + q_s S_2 R_1^B E_1$. When $e_1 < 0$ (X_1 is imported), $N > 0$ and clearly $\sigma > -1$.

problem becomes more difficult than the second best problem just considered. The reason for this is that welfare and consumer prices are a function not only of consumption, but also of pollution and hence a function of domestic and foreign production. In this section we will consider a situation in which consumption and production taxes are arbitrarily constrained to equal zero. The problem is to derive a set of necessary conditions which must be satisfied by an optimal tariff structure.

The requirement that domestic production and consumption prices be equal implies that $\mathrm{d}p = \mathrm{d}q$. Using (7) and (8) we can express $\mathrm{d}q$ as follows:

$$\mathrm{d}q = \mathrm{d}p = D_1\,\mathrm{d}C_1 + D_2\,\mathrm{d}S = (R_1^{\mathrm{A}})^{-1}\,\mathrm{d}X_1^{\mathrm{A}}. \tag{21}$$

Using the total differential of $\mathrm{d}S$ given in (13), we have

$$(1 - R_1^{\mathrm{A}}D_2S_1)\,\mathrm{d}X_1^{\mathrm{A}} = R_1^{\mathrm{A}}D_1\,\mathrm{d}C_1 + R_1^{\mathrm{A}}D_2S_2\,\mathrm{d}X_2^{\mathrm{B}}. \tag{22}$$

Replacing $\mathrm{d}C_1$ in (22) by $\mathrm{d}X_1^{\mathrm{A}} - \mathrm{d}e_1$ gives

$$(1 - R_1^{\mathrm{A}}D_2S_1 - R_1^{\mathrm{A}}D_1)\,\mathrm{d}X_1^{\mathrm{A}} = -R_1^{\mathrm{A}}D_1\,\mathrm{d}e_1 + R_1^{\mathrm{A}}D_2S_2\,\mathrm{d}X_2^{\mathrm{B}}, \tag{23}$$

$$\mathrm{d}X_1^{\mathrm{A}} = \frac{(-R_1^{\mathrm{A}}D_1 + R_1^{\mathrm{A}}D_2S_2R_1^{\mathrm{B}}E_1)\,\mathrm{d}e_1}{(1 - R_1^{\mathrm{A}}D_2S_1 - R_1^{\mathrm{A}}D_1)} = (\mathrm{A})\,\mathrm{d}e_1.$$

Substituting (23) into the welfare differential given in (12) and noting that $(q-p) = 0$ and $(p^* - q) = -p^*\theta$ gives

$$\frac{\mathrm{d}W}{W_0} = (e_1E_1 - p^*\theta + q_sS_1(\mathrm{A}) + q_sS_2R_1^{\mathrm{B}}E_1)\,\mathrm{d}e_1. \tag{24}$$

Setting (24) equal to zero for all values of $\mathrm{d}e_1$ yields the optimal tariff,

$$\theta = \frac{e_1}{p^*}E_1 - \frac{q_sS_1R_1^{\mathrm{A}}D_1}{p^*(1 - R_1^{\mathrm{A}}D_2S_1 - R_1^{\mathrm{A}}D_1)} + \frac{q_sS_1R_1^{\mathrm{A}}D_2S_2R_1^{\mathrm{B}}E_1}{p^*(1 - R_1^{\mathrm{A}}D_2S_1 - R_1^{\mathrm{A}}D_1)} + \frac{q_sS_2R_1^{\mathrm{B}}E_1}{p^*}. \tag{25}$$

One sign in (25) is not strictly determined, that is the sign of D_2 which depends upon the particular form of the social welfare function chosen. Assuming for the moment that this term is negative, (25) has the following sign when X_1 is imported:

$$\theta = (+)-(+)+(-)+(+) = (+)-(+)+(+),$$

where the second equality comes from the fact that the last two terms can be merged into a positive term.

The first of the additive terms in (25) is simply the reciprocal of the foreign elasticity of supply, the standard two-good optimal tariff in the absence of externalities. This term is positive in the import case and negative in the export case as always. The second additive term is negative regardless of whether X_1 is the import or export good. This term is due to the existence of domestic pollution; it tends, ceteris paribus, to lower the optimal import tariff or raise the optimal export tax relative to the foreign elasticity of supply (demand). A constant elasticity of supply foreign offer curve is sufficient for this to cause an absolute decrease (increase) in the optimal tariff (export tax).

The third additive term in (25) is derived from the fact that consumer's marginal rate of substitution between C_0 and C_1 may depend upon the total flow of pollution. If consumers substitute C_1 for C_0 as the flow of pollution increases ($D_2 < 0$) then a decrease in the import tariff on X_1 will cause an increase in foreign production of X_1 and pollution. This will cause domestic consumers to substitute C_1 for C_0 which will put an upward pressure on the price and production of X_1 in both countries. The negative sign of this term reflects this fact. The opposite is true, of course, when ($D_2 > 0$). If the social welfare function is such that the marginal rate of substitution is independent of the flow of pollution, then this third term is identically zero. In any event, there does not seem to be any reasonable assumption we could make a priori about the sign of D_2.

The fourth additive term in (25) is due to the existence of the foreign pollution externality. This term is identical to the corresponding term in the first best optimal tariff given in eq. (15). This term is positive regardless of whether X_1 is the import or export good. In either case the effect is the same, the world price of X_1 is driven down relative to the price of X_0 (subject to the elasticity condition that a tariff improve the terms of trade).

Disregarding the third additive term in (25) (being agnostic about its sign), the optimal second best tariff formula sets the domestic marginal social rate of substitution in consumption (equal to the private marginal rate of transformation in domestic production) at a level less than the marginal social rate of transformation through foreign trade (MRS < FRT). The basic point (in the case of X_1 imported) is that, in the absence of a domestic production tax on X_1, the gains of exploiting monopoly power in trade can only be bought at the expense of an increase in domestic production of X_1 and pollution.

All terms, with the exception of the second term, depend upon the existence of monopoly power in trade. But even in the absence of monopoly power, a tariff can always affect domestic price ratios and hence domestic production. In the absence of influence over world prices, (25) is reduced to the second additive term, which implies an import subsidy or an export tax on X_1 to drive the domestic price of X_1 down in terms of X_0.

As a final point, we note that the second and third components of the optimal tariff depend upon the magnitude of the second partials of the transformation function. The reason for this is that we are introducing a second distortion into the system to compensate for existing distortions. The 'benefits' of compensating for the existing distortions must be weighed against the 'costs' of introducing the additional distortion. In our case, a tariff structure can be used to decrease pollution at the expense of a reduction in commodity consumption. This commodity cost of a given reduction in pollution in our second best problems will depend upon the properties of the production and consumption sets.

5. Second best tax structure – Production tax only

An optimal second best production tax can be derived in the same manner as the optimal second best tariff. Therefore, we will describe it only briefly. Making use of the equality $dp^* = dq$, eqs. (6) and (8) give

$$D_1\,dC_1 + D_2\,dS = E_1\,de_1, \tag{26}$$

$$dC_1 = D_1^{-1}E_1\,de_1 - D_1^{-1}D_2S_1\,dX_1^A - D_1^{-1}D_2S_2R_1^BE_1\,de_1,$$

$$dC_1 = \frac{(D_1^{-1}E_1 - D_1^{-1}D_2S_1 - D_1^{-1}D_2S_2R_1^BE_1)de_1}{(1+D_1^{-1}D_2S_1)} = (G)\,de_1.$$

The relevant welfare differential is given by

$$\frac{dW}{W_0} = (e_1E_1 + (p^*-p))\,de_1 + (q-p)\,dC_1 + q_s\,dS. \tag{27}$$

Noting that $(p^*-p) = (q-p) = p\tau$, appropriate substitutions give us the optimal production tax formula.

$$\tau = \frac{e_1E_1 + q_sS_1 + q_sS_1G + q_sS_2R_1^BE_1}{-p(1+G)}. \tag{28}$$

We run into the same problem in regard to the sign of D_2 as we did deriving the optimal tariff formula. Assuming that its sign is either zero or negative is overly sufficient to ensure that (G) is positive. Domestic demand and world excess demand rise and fall together when $q = p^*$. (28) has the following sign when X_1 is imported and exported, respectively,

$$\tau = \frac{(+)+(-)+(-)+(+)}{(-)}, \quad X_1 \text{ imported,}$$

$$\tau = \frac{(-)+(-)+(-)+(+)}{(-)}, \quad X_1 \text{ exported.}$$

The first of the four additive terms in the numerator is what we can call the terms of trade or monopoly power component of the tax which we have seen before. The second component is recognized as the first best optimal production tax formula. The third component derives from the indirect effect of changes in world prices on domestic production. The fourth term is the now familiar component relating to foreign pollution. This term always contributes to lowering the tax (toward subsidizing production) in order to reduce foreign production. We note that in the absence of monopoly power in trade, that E_1 becomes zero, leaving us with $\tau = -q_s S_1/p$. Eliminating monopoly power eliminates the foreign sector distortion, of course, and leaves us with a first best solution.

6. Ranking alternate tax structures

This paper has considered a situation in which there are two distortions in the system, such that MRS $\neq$ MRT $\neq$ FRT. Both distortions still exist, of course, for the special case in which foreign pollution is dropped from the model.

The mathematics has confirmed the conclusions of Bhagwati, Ramaswami, and Srinivasan (1969) and Kemp and Negishi (1969) that second best taxes generally exist which produce an allocation superior to free trade. However, some of the second best taxes derived here contain components of opposite algebraic signs, such that a particular optimal second best tax may, by chance, equal zero. This confirms the conclusions of Bhagwati et al. that a particular second best tax may not exist which is superior to free trade.

Assuming for the moment that $D_2 = 0$, it is useful to break each of our second best taxes down into three components: a terms of trade (monopoly power) component, a domestic production component, and a foreign production component. The signs of each of these components can be summarized by table 1.

Even when we ignore cross effects, we see that of six possible situations, a consumption tax when X_1 is imported is the only second best tax of unambiguous sign (and hence unambiguously superior to free trade). If foreign pollution is dropped from the model (and, therefore, column 3 of table 1) we can add to this list the second best tariff and the second best production tax when X_1 is exported. But when X_1 is exported the sign of the optimal consumption tax is ambiguous. Given distortions in the system, a particular second best tax may or may not be unambiguous in sign depending on which good is imported and which good is exported.

In the general case, however, the fact that a particular second best tax has an unambiguous sign cannot be used to infer that this tax will produce an allocation superior to that produced by an alternate tax of ambiguous sign. It is not possible to rank second best taxes in the general case. Such a ranking must depend upon the sizes and directions of the distortions in the system. Even though a ranking can be worked out in a specific problem (such as that considered in the appendix), the above suggests that it is likely that such a ranking would change if the import and export goods were switched.

As a final point, it should be mentioned that a definite ranking does emerge if we drop monopoly power from the model, reducing our problem to a simple domestic distortion similar to that considered by Bhagwati and Ramaswami (1963). In this case, a production tax represents a first best solution and is therefore superior to any other single tax. A consumption tax, on the other hand, cannot influence either world prices or domestic production. In the absence of monopoly power, the optimal consumption tax is unambiguously zero. At the same time, the optimal tariff is always non-zero, being negative when X_1 is imported and positive when X_1 is exported. This implies that a tariff exists which is superior to free trade while free trade is necessarily superior to any (non-zero) consumption tax.

Table 1
Sign components of optimal second best taxes.

	Terms of trade component	Domestic production component	Foreign production component
		X_1 imported	
Consumption tax	(+)	(+)	(+)
Production tax	(−)	(+)	(−)
Tariff	(+)	(−)	(+)
		X_1 exported	
Consumption tax	(−)	(+)	(+)
Production tax	(+)	(+)	(−)
Tariff	(+)	(+)	(−)

Appendix

The purpose of this appendix is to give a simple numerical example of how alternate tax regimes affect the level of social welfare and the equilibrium values of the system variables. A series of experiments have demonstrated to me that the results of table 1 are quite sensitive to parameter values and therefore should be regarded as an example only. In particular, the relative efficiency of the different second best tax structures should not be regarded as independent of the particular functional forms chosen.

The results of table 1 are generated by a two-good general equilibrium model given by the following equations:

$$W = C_0 + 40C_1^{\frac{1}{2}} - S,$$

$$F(X_0^A, X_1^A) = 200 - X_0^A - \tfrac{1}{4}(X_1^A)^2 = 0,$$

$$S = X_1^A + X_1^B,$$

$$e_0 = \frac{1}{20}e_1^2.$$

Finally, it is assumed that X_1^B is linear in $-e_1$ and that $\partial X_1^B/\partial e_1 = -1$. Table 2 ranks the taxes according to their efficiency in this particular example.

Table 2

Variable	First best optimum	Consumption tax only	Production tax only	Tariff only	No taxes
W	353.11	348.11	329.88	319.48	302.30
p^*	1.48	1.51	2.59	2.47	2.61
p	2.45	1.51	3.09	2.70	2.61
q	3.45	3.50	2.59	2.70	2.61
C_0	154.71	153.16	39.94	70.35	56.06
C_1	33.61	32.65	58.10	54.87	57.76
X_0	194.71	198.82	190.42	192.71	193.11
X_1	4.60	2.43	6.19	5.40	5.25
e_0	40.60	45.66	150.48	122.36	137.05
e_1	−29.00	−30.22	−51.81	−49.47	−52.51

Since X_1 is imported, the consumption tax drives down the world price ratio which reduces foreign pollution and exploits monopoly power in trade. Secondly, the consumption tax drives down domestic producer price of X_1 which reduces domestic pollution. We should not expect the consumption tax to do as well if X_1 were the export good, however. As pointed out in the body of the paper, if X_1 were the export good, the monopoly power and pollution components of the optimal tax would have opposite signs. Pollution reduction in that case could only be bought at the expense of the gains from exploiting monopoly power in trade, and, therefore, the ranking might well change.

The optimal production tax generates a welfare level superior to the tariff but inferior to the consumption tax. In this example, the optimal production tax is negative (a production subsidy). Reduction of foreign pollution and exploitation of monopoly power in trade are bought at the expense of increasing domestic pollution. If X_1 were exported, a positive tax would reduce domestic pollution and exploit monopoly power in trade at the expense of increasing foreign pollution.

The welfare level in the presence of the second best tariff is the lowest of all the tax regimes (the no tax welfare level is presented for comparison). Foreign pollution reduction and exploitation of monopoly power in trade are purchased at the expense of an increase in the domestic production of X_1 and hence domestic pollution. If X_1 were exported, domestic pollution reduction and exploitation of monopoly power in trade could be obtained only at the expense of increasing foreign production of X_1 and pollution.

References

Bhagwati, J., 1971, The generalized theory of distortions and welfare, in: Trade, balance of payments and growth: Essays in honor of Charles P. Kindleberger (North-Holland, Amsterdam).

Bhagwati, J. and V.K. Ramaswami, 1963, Domestic distortions, tariff, and the theory of optimum subsidy, Journal of Political Economy 71, 44–50.

Bhagwati, J., V.K. Ramaswami and T.N. Srinivasan, 1969, Domestic distortions, tariffs, and the theory of optimum subsidy, Journal of Political Economy 77, 1005–1010.

Connally, M., 1970, Public goods, externalities, and international relations, Journal of Political Economy 78, 279–290.

Connally, M., 1973, Trade in public goods: A diagrammatic analysis, Quarterly Journal of Economics 342, 61–78.

Davis, O.A. and A.B. Whinston, 1965, Welfare economics and the theory of the second best, Review of Economic Studies 32, 1–14.

Graaff, J. Van de, 1949, On optimal tariff structures, The Review of Economic Studies 17, 47–59.

Kemp, M.C. and T. Negishi, 1969, Domestic distortions, tariffs and the theory of the optimum subsidy, Journal of Political Economy 77, 1011–1013.

Lipsey, R.G. and K. Lancaster, 1956, The general theory of the second best, Review of Economic Studies 24, 11–32.

Vandendorpe, A.L., 1972, Optimal tax structure in a model with traded and non-traded goods, The Journal of International Economics 2, 235–256.

Williams, A., 1966, The optimal provision of public goods in a system of local government, Journal of Political Economy 74, 18–33.

[22]

Cross-border externalities and trade liberalization: the strategic control of pollution

RODNEY D. LUDEMA University of Western Ontario
IAN WOOTON University of Western Ontario and CEPR

Abstract. We examine international trade in a commodity whose production creates a negative externality for the importing country; and we consider the nations' strategic policy choices, when they can restrict trade, and when they are bound by a free-trade agreement. When pollution-abatement technology is available, the exporting country induces its adoption, despite national indifference to the externality, in order to reduce the tariff. In a free-trade agreement, environmental policy is used to exploit monopoly power in trade. An alternative policy instrument, a process standard is introduced. National competition in controlling emissions leads to very restrictive anti-pollution measures.

Externalités trans-frontières et libéralisation du commerce international: le contrôle stratégique de la pollution. Les auteurs examinent le commerce international d'un bien dont la production engendre un effet externe négatif pour le pays importateur. Ils considèrent les choix de stratégies politiques pour ces nations quand elles peuvent restreindre le commerce et quand elles sont liées par un accord de libre échange. Quand une technolgie qui réduit la pollution est disponible, le pays exportateur promeut son adoption, même s'il est indifférent par rapport à l'effet externe, de façon à réduire le droit de douane. Dans le cadre d'un accord de libre-échange, la politique environnementale est utilisée pour exploiter un pouvoir de monopole dans le commerce. On introduit un instrument de rechange de politique publique, des normes appliquées au processus de production. La concurrence nationale pour le contrôle des émissions va tendre à engendrer la mise en place de mesures anti-pollution fort strictes.

I. INTRODUCTION

The environmental consequences of trade liberalization have recently become a

We are grateful to workshop participants at ITAM, the University of Pittsburgh, the University of Western Ontario, the Mid-West International Trade Meetings at Michigan State University, the Norwegian School of Economics and Business Administration, and the Canadian Economics Association Meetings in Charlottetown for their comments and suggestions on earlier drafts of this paper. Particular thanks are due to John Chilton and to two anonymous referees. Any remaining errors are entirely our responsibility. We would like to thank the Donner Canadian Foundation and the Ford Foundation for financial support.

Canadian Journal of Economics Revue canadienne d'Economique, XXVII, No. 4
November novembre 1994. Printed in Canada Imprimé au Canada

0008-4085 / 94 / 950–66 $1.50

topic of much public debate, although the mechanisms that link the volume of international trade and the rate of environmental degradation are seldom adequately explained. Part of the problem is that the environmental problems that are faced are extremely varied both in character and severity, and it is futile to attempt to provide a single remedy for all of them. For example, atmospheric pollution is produced by and affects all countries; therefore the appropriate solution must be on a global scale, as is, for example, the Montreal Protocol. In constrast, industrial production in a country that, say, pollutes the waterways of its downstream neighbour calls for a more local remedy, such as a bilateral or regional pact. We have chosen to address an example of the latter problem and examine the relationship between trade liberalization and the level of pollution. Specifically, we wish to establish the extent to which environmental policies can become strategic trade policy instruments. We further wish to determine the likely effects on the environment of regional integration, in which formal trade barriers are eliminated. We consider, in particular, the replacement of the tariff by a process standard and investigate the subsequent impact on production and on the environment.

A venerable topic in public finance theory is the question of the most appropriate intervention in a market characterized by negative externalities in production (see, e.g., Pigou 1932, Baumol and Oates 1975). The first-best policy is a tax on the externality itself or, if there are no means to reduce the level of the externality per unit of production (such as pollution abatement techniques), a tax on production will serve the same purpose. But there are circumstances in which the choices available to the social planner are circumscribed; the particular case that we address is when the good is traded internationally.

Suppose that an individual country produces and exports a good whose production process results in a negative externality for the consumers in the importing country, though none of the firms nor consumers (nor their representatives) in the exporting nation cares about the externality. In such circumstances a production or an externality tax cannot be directly implemented by the government of the importing country, since the firms are outwith its tax jurisdiction, and it will not be willingly imposed on the importer's behalf by the exporting nation. If, as we assume in this paper, the countries behave non-cooperatively, then the importer is reduced to finding some other policy in order to limit the externality.[1]

Of all the feasible policies available to the consuming country's government, a tariff on imports of the good produced by the offending country will be nationally optimal. That is, no other feasible policy, such as a domestic production subsidy or a consumption tax, will be superior to a discriminatory tariff, given this extraterritoriality (Markusen 1975a). This justification for a tariff reinforces the familiar, beggar-thy-neighbour motive for trade restriction. Thus the non-cooperative trade-policy equilibrium is affected by the presence of the externality. Consequently,

1 Ludema and Wooton (1993) examine the form that such a cooperative agreement might take when the countries have private information regarding the costs of abatement activity and the disutility arising from the externality.

while the foreign country has no interest in pollution abatement as an end in itself, it might choose to use environmental policy as a means to influence its gains from trade. Further, it is no longer clear that multilateral trade liberalization is an appropriate goal of international negotiations, as the externality is to some degree regulated by the trade barriers. Therefore some new policy instrument, directed at the externality, may have to be introduced in order to guarantee welfare gains from trade liberalization.

We look at the appropriate policies for the (socially planning) governments of the importing and exporting countries, both when the countries are free to impose taxes on trade and when they are constrained by a free-trade agreement. We focus on a two-country model, in order to rule out the possibility that any environmental standard might be circumvented by the simultaneous export of 'dirty' goods (that is, those that generate large amounts of externality in their production) to some third country and the import of 'clean' (that is, low externality) products from that nation. For ease of exposition, we shall occasionally refer to the externality as 'pollution' or 'emissions,' though these terms are relevant only for specific examples of a more general problem.

In section II, we consider the case in which the externality is produced in fixed proportions to output of the good. We demonstrate that, in the Nash equilibrium, both countries impose tariffs in an attempt to exploit their monopoly power in trade, but that the equilibrium tariff of the importing country will be higher than it would otherwise be as a result of the externality, with the end result that the externality is always overcorrected. When, in section III, technology to abate the externality is introduced, we find that the exporting country will choose to impel its firms to adopt these techniques (or, in the appendix, that the government decides to pay for their use) and thereby limit the output of the externality. This is not a magnanimous gesture to the citizens of the other country, but rather a means of capturing a larger share of the gains from trade. Thus while trade instruments can be used to pursue environmental goals, so too might environmental policy be used to gain an advantage in international trade.[2]

Section IV looks at the outcome when a free-trade agreement (eliminating trade taxes) is reached between the two countries. Despite its own lack of concern, the exporter will tax the externality, since doing so (again, indirectly) permits it to exploit its monopoly power of trade in the absence of an export tax. The importing country, which cares about the externality, is unable (even indirectly) to limit its output, however, raising concerns that the economic integration will be accompanied by increased levels of pollution. In section V, the environmental lobby's fears are assuaged by the introduction of a process standard, limiting sales in a market to goods produced using 'clean' processes. Such policies are the focus of recent debates in the GATT, where the question has arisen as to whether trade restrictions imposed on the basis of production process, rather than type of finished product,

2 The focus on the terms-of-trade effects distinguishes our paper from other strategic models of environmental policy, for examples, Markusen (1975b), Copeland (1989), and Conrad and Scott (1988).

are consistent with the principle of non-discrimination. We examine the interaction of the externality tax and the process standard and show that, in the trading equilibrium, the process standard will always be binding. Competition between the two governments to restrict pollution and exploit monopoly power will result in highly restrictive policies and very low levels of both pollution and trade.

II. A MODEL OF TRADE WITH A CROSS-BORDER EXTERNALITY

1. Structure of the model

We adopt a very simple structure for the market for the good. There are two countries: the home country, H, and the foreign country, F. All consumption takes place in H, while production occurs in both countries.

Let x be the quantity of the good that is traded. Country H's demand for imports is a linear function of its consumer price, p. Hence the inverse import demand curve is

$$p = a - bx. \tag{1}$$

The good is produced in perfectly competitive markets. The foreign inverse supply curve is linear in the foreign price, q:

$$q = f + gx, \tag{2}$$

where the domestic import price of x is the foreign price augmented by any (specific) import tariff, r, and export tax, s.[3] Let the aggregate trade tax, $t \equiv r + s$. Thus:

$$p = q + t. \tag{3}$$

Suppose that foreign production results in an externality at the fixed level $\bar{m}$ per unit of output.[4] Home production of the good is assumed to create no externality. That is, for each unit of the good that is produced in F, the marginal utility from the creation of the externality is $-\bar{m}$. This is assumed to be constant, and hence the total cost (in terms of utility) from emissions of the externality amounts to $\bar{m}x$. Home-country welfare, u, is the sum of consumer surplus, domestic producer surplus, and tariff revenue *less* the externality.[5]

3 Since our model is partial equilibrium, similar to that of Snape (1991), the two countries must use different instruments in the tax-setting game: H, the importer, uses a tariff; while F, the exporting nation, must use an export tax. The model could be readily recast in general equilibrium terms, in which countries could as easily use tariffs, due to Lerner symmetry. Trade taxes are equivalent to production taxes here, but this is solely an artefact of the lack of foreign consumers.

4 We consider the possibility of pollution abatement technology in the next section.

5 The additive separability of the home utility function follows the assumption that this is a *pure* (that is, non-pecuniary) externality. We simply define the externality in terms of utility units. The restrictive assumption being made is that the externality is a constant fraction of output This affects only the results of section III and the appendix.

Using equation (1) and normalizing autarky welfare to zero, welfare in H can be written as

$$u(x, r, m) = \frac{bx^2}{2} + (r - \bar{m})x. \tag{4}$$

Foreign-country welfare, v, is the sum of foreign producer surplus and production-tax revenue and, using equation (2), may therefore be written as

$$v(x, s) = \frac{gx^2}{2} + sx. \tag{5}$$

We have purposely excluded from our framework three of the main ingredients that might have been expected to form part of a general model: foreign consumption of the good; foreign consumption of the externality; and home production of the externality. If each government were to use its optimal *domestic* policies, the inclusion of any of these components would have no substantive effect on our results. Specifically, foreign consumers would be insulated from the effects of any production or externality taxes by the appropriate consumption subsidy; damage to the foreign country from the foreign-produced externality would be corrected by a suitable externality tax; while a home externality tax would deal with any home-produced externality. In each case the remedy is domestic, whereas our concern is with cures for *international* problems.

We have chosen to use such a restrictive model in order to demonstrate our results as clearly as possible. For example, in the absence of foreign consumers, tariffs and export taxes are equivalent to taxes on foreign production, and therefore trade policy instruments are 'first best' in the absence of pollution abatement technology. Thus, when we show (below) that the non-cooperative use of trade taxes in the presence of a negative cross-border externality results in overcorrection of the externality, we are doing so in a context that would otherwise be quite favourable to the use of tariffs as environmental policy. Similarly, the absence of foreign environmental concerns means that the foreign government would have no domestic need for an externality tax. Consequently, our demonstration (in section III, below) that the foreign government would wish to use an externality tax to reduce the home incentive to use tariffs is done in a context in which externality taxes would not otherwise be used.

2. Equilibrium

Equilibrium output can be determined by solving equations (1), (2), and (3) for x:

$$x = \frac{B}{b}\{A - t\}, \tag{6}$$

where $A \equiv (a - f)$ and $B \equiv b/(b + g)$.

Now consider the countries' choices of trade taxes. Let each country maximize national utility by setting its optimal tax rate, given the tax level of the other country.[6] This yields the reaction functions of the two countries:

$$r(s, m) = \frac{D(A - s)}{(1 + D)} + \frac{\bar{m}}{(1 + D)},$$
$$s(r) = \frac{B(A - r)}{(1 + B)} \tag{7}$$

where $D \equiv 1 - B$. The Nash equilibrium is the solution of these simultaneous equations:

$$r^N = \frac{D}{2}\{A - \bar{m}\} + \bar{m},$$
$$s^N = \frac{B}{2}\{A - \bar{m}\}. \tag{8}$$

The total (Nash-equilibrium) taxes on the good are

$$t^N = \frac{A + \bar{m}}{2}, \tag{9}$$

and the Nash-equilibrium output is

$$x^N = \frac{B}{2b}\{A - \bar{m}\}. \tag{10}$$

Let w be the sum of national welfare levels; that is, $w \equiv u + v$. A Pareto-efficient combination of taxes will maximize w. If the countries behave cooperatively, we would expect such optimally chosen taxes, but in the non-cooperative environment that we are considering, this *world optimum* provides purely a reference point for comparison. In the present setting, w is maximized when aggregate trade taxes, $t^* \equiv (s^* + t^*)$, equal the size of the externality. That is, the world optimum is achieved when $t^* = \bar{m}$. This forces the consumer fully to take into account the increased levels of emissions that would be associated with further imports (and hence production) of the good. This level of trade taxes therefore achieves the standard closed-economy optimum in which consumers are made fully to internalize the externality.

Now consider whether the world optimum will be achieved in the Nash equilibrium. The Nash-equilibrium aggregate tax level coincides with the optimum only when $A = \bar{m}$, which, from equation (10), implies $x^N = 0$. That is, except in the circumstance in which the tax wars result in autarky and consequently there is foreign production of neither the good itself nor the externality, the aggregate taxes on trade in the Nash equilibrium will exceed those of the world optimum.

6 In a political context, for example, Hillman and Ursprung (1991), the objective functions may be more complex.

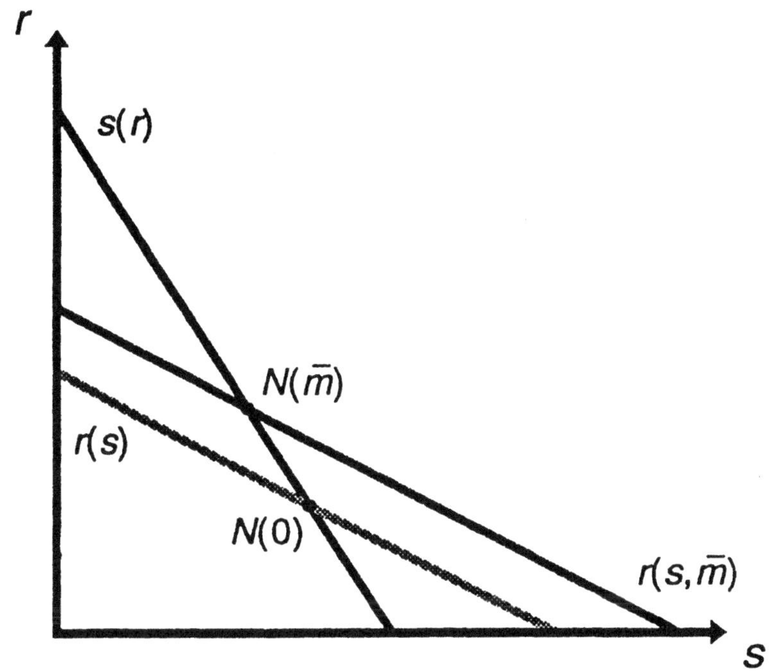

FIGURE 1

These results are illustrated in figure 1. In the absence of any externality (that is, $\bar{m} = 0$) the reaction curves for home and foreign countries are $r(s)$ and $s(r)$, respectively, with the Nash equilibrium occurring at $N(0)$. This outcome is purely a result of the familiar terms-of-trade argument for unilateral taxes on trade. The existence of an externality gives the government of H an additional incentive to restrict trade, but has no direct effect on the actions of uncaring F. Consequently, H's reaction curve shifts out and a new Nash equilibrium is attained at $N(\bar{m})$. The export tax declines while the import tariff increases, undoubtedly lowering welfare in F. The aggregate tax t^* increases but, from equation (9), by less than the full amount of the externality. The presence of the externality results in a diminished volume of trade: as has been noted, a sufficiently large externality ($\bar{m} \geqq A$) will lead to autarky.

III. EXTERNALITY ABATEMENT TECHNOLOGY

Now suppose that the externality produced per unit of the good can be reduced by abatement technology to a level m, where $m \leqq \bar{m}$. Thus the abatement per unit of production would be $(\bar{m} - m)$. Let the per-unit cost of achieving this be $c(m)$;

where $c(\bar{m}) = 0$, $c' \leqq 0$, $c'' \geqq 0$.[7] A firm producing x units of output will therefore spend $c(m)x$ on pollution abatement. The firm can be induced to reduce its rate of pollution either through a tax on the externality or by a subsidy on abatement expenditures. We consider the case of tax in this section, leaving discussion of a subsidy to the appendix.

We assume that that tax/tariff game now takes on a two-stage timing structure. Specifically, let the foreign government choose its environmental policy prior to playing the trade-tax game with the home country. As is standard in games of this type, while the foreign country's externality tax is applied first, it is done in full knowledge of the structure of the second stage of the game. This sequence of policy decisions might be justified on the basis that a pollution tax involves investment by the foreign producers in abatement equipment, and hence their response to such a tax is 'slower' than to trade taxes.[8]

Let e be a specific tax on a firm's production of the externality, such that the firm that produces output level x and emits mx of the externality must pay emx in pollution taxes. Thus the total costs to the firm of pollution are its expenditures on abatement and the taxes it must pay on the remaining emissions; that is, $\{c(m) + em\}x$. For any positive x, firms therefore choose m so as to minimize the *per-unit* costs of abatement, $c(m) + em$.[9] We define $k(e)$ to be the minimum per-unit costs associated with the pollution tax, that is $k(e) \equiv \min\{c(m) + em\}$, and we define $m(e)$ to be the firm's cost-minimizing level of emissions, where $c'(m) = -e$. Hence the private marginal cost of the firm is augmented by $k(e)$.

Import demand is not directly affected by this foreign policy and continues to be represented by equation (1). The foreign supply curve shifts back, however, owing to the additional marginal costs in production:

$$q = f + k(e) + gx. \tag{11}$$

Home and foreign prices continue to differ by the size of the trade taxes, as in equation (3). Welfare in H now depends on the actual emission level that is achieved:

$$u(x, r, e) = \frac{bx^2}{2} + \{r - m(e)\}x. \tag{12}$$

Foreign welfare now has an additional component: the revenue from the externality tax. Recognizing that the externality is now a function of country F's pollution tax, national welfare can be written

$$v(x, s, e) = \frac{gx^2}{2} + \{s + em(e)\}x. \tag{13}$$

7 While costs are increasing in the level of abatement ($\bar{m} - m$), they are linear in the quantity of the good produced, holding constant the emission rate, m. Thus we are assuming that there are no economies of scale in pollution abatement.

8 This is not a Stackelberg leadership game in trade taxes, because the foreign government is free to change its export tax in the second stage. We allow pre-commitment only in environmental policy. Without this two-stage structure, the foreign government would set the externality tax to zero, and the analysis would follow that of section II.

9 We assume that taxes and tariffs must be applied uniformly across firms.

Equilibrium output is the solution to equations (1), (11), and (3):

$$x = \frac{B}{b}\{A - k(e) - t\}. \tag{14}$$

Comparing equations (6) and (14), we see that, for the same level of aggregate trade taxes, the introduction of an externality tax has lowered output.

The reaction functions become

$$\begin{aligned} r(s) &= \frac{D\{A - k(e) - s\}}{(1 + D)} + \frac{m(e)}{(1 + D)} \\ s(r) &= \frac{B\{A - k(e) - r\}}{(1 + B)} - \frac{em(e)}{(1 + B)}. \end{aligned} \tag{15}$$

Finding the Nash equilibrium:

$$\begin{aligned} r^N &= \frac{D}{2}\{A - k(e) - (1 - e)m(e)\} + m(e) \\ s^N &= \frac{B}{2}\{A - k(e) - (1 - e)m(e)\} - em(e). \end{aligned} \tag{16}$$

The aggregate (Nash) taxes on trade are

$$t^N = \frac{A - k(e) + (1 - e)m(e)}{2}, \tag{17}$$

and the Nash-equilibrium output is

$$x^N = \frac{B}{2b}\{A - k(e) - (1 - e)m(e)\}. \tag{18}$$

Now substitute this into equation (13) and differentiate in order to determine the foreign government's optimal externality tax. Simplifying, using equation (16), yields

$$\frac{du}{de} = \frac{2b + g}{b + g}\,\frac{\{1 + c'(m)\}}{c''(m)}\,x^N. \tag{19}$$

This expression has critical values at $c'' = \infty$ and at $e^* = 1$. Thus in the Nash trade-tax game, the foreign country will have set an externality tax of unity, forcing the foreign firms to internalize fully the pollution.[10]

In order to understand this outcome, consider the foreign government's behaviour in the second stage of the game. The externality tax has had two effects: the first is in having induced firms to spend resources on emission control; while

10 Note that $e^* = 1$ is the rate of taxation that is optimal for the world (i.e., Pareto efficient) in free trade, when $t = s = 0$. If the externality was not linear in foreign output, then e^* (the optimal pollution tax from the perspective of the foreign government) would not be unity.

the second effect is that the private marginal costs of foreign production have been raised through the penalization of production of the remaining pollution. The latter outcome means that the externality tax acts in large part as a production tax which, in the model in question, is identical to an export tax. So in the second stage of the game, in which m is set and the abatement expense, $c(m)$, is a sunk cost, e and s are perfect substitutes, the 'effective' export tax being $s + em$. This implies that the foreign government can pre-commit e to any level that it wishes in the first stage of the game, and s can be chosen to bring the effective tax to its optimal level.[11]

Why does F use a combination of direct export taxation and a tax on the externality? As has been shown above, the existence of the externality makes the home country more aggressive in its tariff-setting behaviour. The externality tax has the advantage over the export tax of lowering m and thereby moderating the home country's trade tax.[12]

IV. EXTERNALITY TAXES WITH A FREE-TRADE AGREEMENT

Now restrict the import tariff and export tax to zero, as would be required by a free-trade agreement. We assume that the only instrument available is the externality tax of the foreign government. In such a case: equation (1) represents import demand; equation (11) represents foreign supply; and home and foreign prices are equated; that is,

$$p = q. \tag{20}$$

Home and foreign welfare are (respectively)

$$u(x, e) = \frac{bx^2}{2} - m(e)x \tag{21}$$

$$v(x, e) = \frac{gx^2}{2} + em(e)x. \tag{22}$$

Equilibrium output is determined from the solution of equations (1), (11), and (20):

$$x = \frac{B}{b}\{A - k(e)\}. \tag{23}$$

11 This raises the question as to whether or not e^* is a 'time-consistent' policy, meaning that the foreign government would have no incentive to alter e^* (if it could) in the last stage of the game. The perfect substitutability of e for s in the last stage ensures that F will have no incentive to abandon e^* in order to wage the trade war more effectively. Another issue is whether F would wish to forsake e^* if, for some reason, a single firm failed to abate its pollution in the first stage. While this issue could be critical in a world of few firms (e.g., that of Conrad 1993), it cannot be adequately addressed in this model, since we treat firms as atomistic price takers. The reason F uses e in the first stage is to reduce the aggregate externality (which, in turn, moderates H's tariff), and it imposes s or e in the second stage in order to raise the world price of x. Since the effect of a single firm on the aggregate externality and on the world price of x is negligible, there is an inconsistency between the optimal policy for a single firm and that for the market as a whole. For this reason we have assumed that all taxes are applied uniformly across firms and we abstract from any strategic behaviour on the part of firms.

12 This is similar to the strategic enhancement of the environment discussed in Copeland (1989).

Maximizing foreign welfare through the choice of the optimal externality tax yields an implicit expression for e^*:

$$e^*m^* = \frac{\{B - \rho(e^*)\}\{A - c(m^*)\}}{1 + B - \rho(e^*)}, \tag{24}$$

where $m^* \equiv m(e^*)$ and $\rho(e)$ is the elasticity of response in abatement level m with respect to changes in the rate of externality tax e; that is,

$$\rho(e) = -\frac{e}{m(e)} m'(e). \tag{25}$$

Two points can be made here. First, e^* does not generally coincide with the world optimum level of tax ($e^* = 1$). This is because the foreign country is not imposing the externality tax in order to quell the production of a noxious substance (or the like), but is doing so for the purely selfish motive of exploiting its monopoly power in trade. Second, $em(e)$ is the effective export tax arising from the use of the externality tax. The optimal level (from equation (24)) is lower than the export tax that the foreign country would unilaterally impose:

$$s(r)|_{r=0} = \frac{BA}{(1 + D)}, \tag{26}$$

if it were not constrained from doing so. The first-best policy for a country that wishes to manipulate its terms of trade is, of a course, the tariff. As such an instrument is unavailable because of the free-trade agreement, the externality tax is a second-best policy. It is inferior to the tariff in that it induces firms to spend resources on pollution abatement (a worthless, but costly, activity to the citizens of F), and so the externality tax will be imposed at a lower effective level than that of the optimal tariff.

V. EFFECTS OF A HOME-COUNTRY PROCESS STANDARD

The outcome so far for the home country is that, under a free-trade agreement, it has lost any influence over the level of the externality, through relinquishing its import tariff, as well as having no means of retaliating against the behaviour of the foreign country. Thus the free-trade agreement would likely be opposed both by protectionists and the environmental lobby.[13] Consider another policy, in the context of a free-trade agreement, that appears designed to assuage the fears of the latter group and may go a long way towards satisfying the first as well: a *process standard* imposed by the home country on goods sold on its domestic markets. Note that this is not a regulation on the characteristics of the final product, but rather is a constraint on the way in which it is manufactured. Thus the standard

13 The countries might bargain over setting externality taxes in their negotiations for the free-trade agreement. We discuss the nature of such an agreement in Ludema and Wooton (1993).

does not accord equal treatment to like goods and is therefore probably in violation of GATT rules as currently written.

Let this process standard take the form of an upper bound on the level of externality produced per unit of the good manufactured. We assume that the government of H can determine which products exceed this limit and prevent them from entering the country, while goods that satisfy the standard are imported without further restriction. Let z denote the process standard, in which commodities meeting this standard involve per-unit production of the externality that is no greater than this limit. The process standard will be ineffective if it exceeds $\bar{m}$, the pollution level of firms that take no abatement measures. If the standard is binding, foreign firms will reduce their emissions rate to z and incur the additional per-unit cost $c(z)$, provided that the marginal cost $f + c(z)$ of production does not exceed the market price. Hence, as long as $a - f - c(z) > 0$, there will be trade.

If the foreign country has access to an externality tax, then process standards above m^* will not be binding. This is because the unconstrained optimal externality tax e^* induces firms to choose m^*, which more than satisfies the process standard. This is represented by point A in figure 2. Hence, if we let $e(z)$ denote the best response of the foreign country to process standard z, then $e(z) = e^*$, for all $z \geqq m^*$. In other words, when the home country introduces an ineffectual policy, F's best response is to ignore it and continue to follow what continues to be its optimal tax policy.

For process standards tighter than m^*, that is, $z < m^*$, there are two possibilities. Either the foreign country can choose an externality tax that will induce exactly the same level of m as z, or it can choose an externality tax that will not have any effect upon firms' choices of m. If it does the former, it chooses $e(z)$ so that $m(e(z)) = z$. Letting $m^{-1}(z)$ be the inverse of $m(e)$ gives

$$e(z) = m^{-1}(z). \tag{27}$$

Such a choice is represented by point B in figure 2.

If F chooses its tax so that it has no effect on firms' choices of m, it is essentially using the externality tax solely as a trade-policy instrument. Its optimal choice, in this case, is to set e such that ez is equal to its optimal export tax. Doing so gives

$$e(z) = \frac{B\{A - c(z)\}}{z(1 + B)} > 0, \qquad \text{for } x \geqq 0, \tag{28}$$

which is respresented by point C in figure 2.

It is clear that for $z < m^*$ (but not too small), F will choose to follow (27) over (28). As z approaches m^*, $m^{-1}(z)$ becomes arbitrarily close to e^*; whereas the expression in (28) does not, as long as $\rho^* > 0$. Given the continuity of the welfare functions, this implies that for some (perhaps small) range of process standards, F will choose a tax that induces exactly the standard imposed by H.

The best-response externality tax of F is therefore represented by the three line segments shown in figure 3 as $e(z)$.

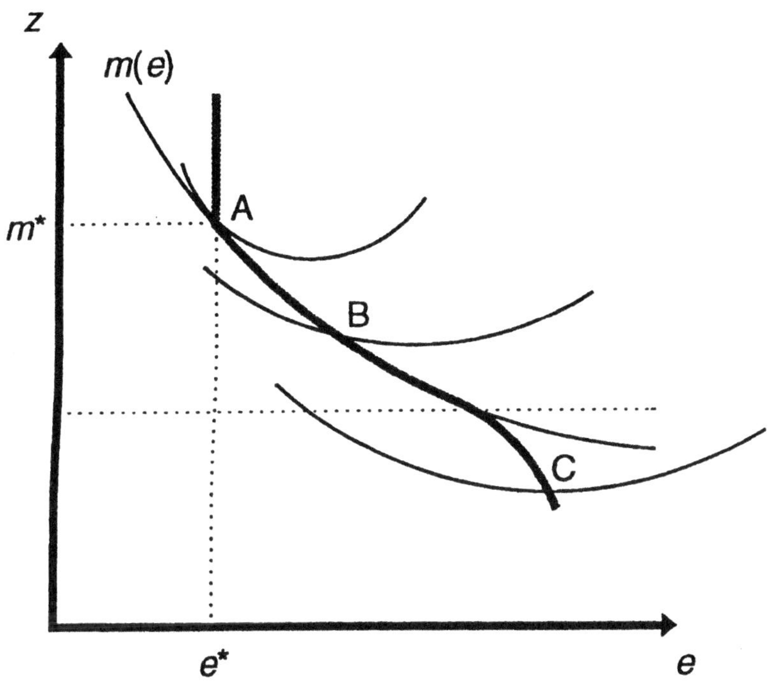

FIGURE 2

The home government chooses its optimal process standard given the externality tax set by the foreign government. A binding process standard will always be chosen. To see this, suppose that the government of H was contemplating setting $z = m(e)$ as a best response to e, where $m(e)$, as before, is the firms' cost-minimizing choice. The home government cannot gain by raising z above $m(e)$, since the process standard would not bind. But the home government can gain by lowering z below $m(e)$. For a binding process standard, home welfare is given by

$$u(x, z) = \frac{bx^2}{2} - zx, \tag{29}$$

where

$$x = \frac{B}{b}\{A - c(z) - ez\}. \tag{30}$$

Differentiating equation (29) yields

$$\frac{\partial u}{\partial z} = (bx - z)\frac{\partial x}{\partial z} - x.$$

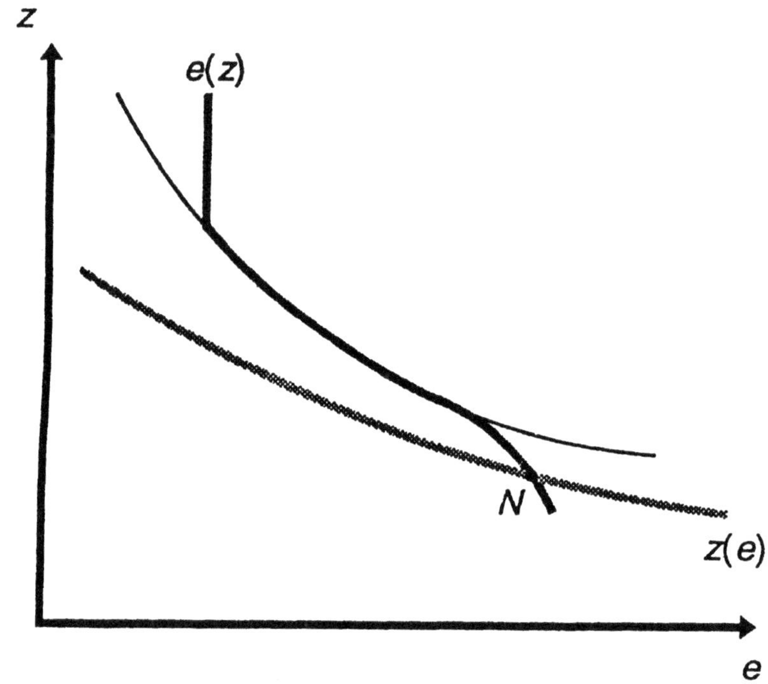

FIGURE 3

Now, $\partial x/\partial z = 0$, when evaluated at $z = m(e)$. Thus, as long as there is trade (i.e., $x > 0$), H can gain by tightening its process standard so that it binds.[14]

For $z < m(e)$, the first-order condition for maximization of home welfare is given implicitly by

$$z = \left\{B + \frac{1}{c'(z) + e}\right\} \{A - c(z) - ez\} > 0, \qquad \text{for } x \geqq 0. \tag{31}$$

The home country's best-response process standard satisfies equation (31); it is shown on figure 3 as the locus $z(e)$.

The Nash equilibrium N is at the intersection of $e(z)$ and $z(e)$. It can be shown that the Nash-equilibrium externality tax is strictly greater than unity, the rate in the world optimum. Thus we have the somewhat ironic result that competition between countries in controlling emissions leads to more restrictive measures than they would choose cooperatively.

14 The magnitude of the gain from lowering z for a given x is of the first order, whereas the loss from the decline in x, given z near $m(e)$, is of the second order.

VI. CONCLUSION

We have examined a non-cooperative game between two countries. The production of the good in the foreign country generates an externality that hurts only the residents of the home country. Thus the home country has two incentives to restrict imports: to improve its terms of trade and reduce the externality. We have shown that in a non-cooperative game there is an incentive for the foreign country to commit to imposing a tax that fully internalizes the externality, not because it cares about the pollution (which it does not), but because doing so will reduce the aggressiveness of the other country's tariff setting. In a free-trade agreement, where trade restrictions are proscribed, the importing country may introduce a process standard. The resulting equilibrium will be characterized by very restrictive anti-pollution measures, since the pollution policies of both countries are used to influence their terms of trade.

Our results have some relevance for the question as to why free-trade agreements are made in the first place. Without pollution and in the absence of international transfers, there is nothing to guarantee that a move to free trade will be Pareto improving, since the international distribution of gains between the nations may well be asymmetric, to the point where some countries lose from the trade liberalization. Nevertheless, it is often argued in policy circles that the costs of concessions made by an individual country in lowering its import barriers may well be more than compensated by the benefits from the reciprocal tariff reductions made by its trading partners, so that each country gains without the need to implement international transfers. The more similar are the countries, in terms of their size and stage of development, the stronger this argument: bilateral trade flows will be closely balanced and the terms-of-trade effects will be quantitatively close.

When countries markedly differ in size or development, the gains from bilateral trade liberalization will, in all likelihood, be quite asymmetrically distributed, the smaller country benefiting both from eliminating its own trade barriers and from the concessions made by its much larger trading partner, while the latter gives up the exercise of its monopoly power with little in return. In the absence of international transfers, it then seems unlikely that large, developed countries would be inclined (on purely economic grounds) to form free-trade agreements with smaller countries. If a small country's production activities are the source of a negative externality, however, then it has something to offer its larger trading partner in order to induce it into a free-trade agreement, namely, measures to restrict pollution.

APPENDIX

We now consider the case in which the government reimburses firms for their externality expenditures. So, by setting the subsidy per unit $y = c(m)$, the foreign government effectively chooses the level of externality per unit of production $m(y)$, but it will not affect the firms' marginal costs and hence the supply curve of the good will not shift. Ordinarily this would imply that the subsidy to pollution abatement is not equivalent to the pollution tax. In the presence of the second-stage tax/tariff game, however, we shall establish that they are indeed equivalent.

National welfare must take into account the production of the externality and the cost of the pollution abatement activity:

$$u(x, r, y) = \frac{bx^2}{2} + \{r - m(y)\}x \tag{A1}$$

$$v(x, s) = \frac{ex^2}{2} + (s - y)x. \tag{A2}$$

Equilibrium output is again determined from equations (1), (2), and (3); hence x is as in equation (6), and the reaction functions are

$$\begin{aligned} r(s) &= \frac{D(A - s)}{(1 + D)} + \frac{m(y)}{(1 + D)} \\ s(r) &= \frac{B(A - r)}{(1 + B)} + \frac{y}{(1 + B)}. \end{aligned} \tag{A3}$$

The Nash equilibrium tariffs are

$$\begin{aligned} r^N &= \frac{D}{2}\{A - y - m(y)\} + m(y), \\ s^N &= \frac{B}{2}\{A - y - m(y)\} + y. \end{aligned} \tag{A4}$$

Aggregate trade taxes in the Nash equilibrium are

$$t^N = \frac{A + y + m(y)}{2}, \tag{A5}$$

and the Nash-equilibrium output is

$$x^N = \frac{B}{2b}\{A - y - m(y)\}. \tag{A6}$$

Now determine the optimal subsidy. Differentiating foreign welfare (equation (A2)) with respect to the subsidy rate yields

$$\begin{aligned} \frac{dv}{dy} &= \{2b + e\}x^N \frac{dx^N}{dy}, \text{ where} \\ \frac{dx^N}{dy} &= -\frac{B}{2b}\left\{1 + \frac{dm}{dy}\right\} = 0. \end{aligned} \tag{A7}$$

This has exactly the same outcome as in the externality-tax sample. To see that this is the case, compare the Nash-equilibrium output levels for the subsidy on abatement (equation (A6)) with those for an externality tax (equation (18)). Note that $k(e) = em(e) + c(m)$. If the abatement costs instead were covered by a subsidy, that is, $c(m) = y$; then the two equations coincide. As both output and the level of emissions are identical in the two cases, so too are the welfare levels of the countries. Thus a pollution tax, e, and a subsidy on abatement, y, that induce the same level of emissions, m, will generate identical trade-tax-setting behaviour. Hence the optimal subsidy must reduce emissions by the same amount as a 100 per cent tax rate would.[15]

REFERENCES

Baumol, William J., and Wallace E. Oates (1975) *The Theory of Environmental Policy* (Englewood Cliffs, NJ: Prentice Hall)

Copeland, Brian (1989) 'Strategic enhancement and destruction of fisheries and the environment in the presence of international externalities.' Discussion Paper No. 89-12, University of British Columbia

Conrad, Jon M., and Anthony D. Scott (1988) 'Transfrontier pollution: cooperative and non-cooperative solutions.' Discussion Paper No. 88-30, University of British Columbia

Conrad, Klaus (1993) 'Taxes and subsidies for pollution-intensive industries as trade policy.' *Journal of Environmental Economics and Management* 25, 121–35

Hillman, Ayre L., and Heinrich Ursprung (1992) 'The influence of environmental concerns on the political determination of international trade policy.' In *The Greening of World Trade Issues*, ed. Kym Anderson and Richard Blackhurst (New York: Harvester-Wheatsheaf)

Ludema, Rodney D., and Ian Wooton (1993) 'International cooperation on trade and environmental policy: cross-border externalities with asymmetric information.' CSIER Working Paper No. 9301C, University of Western Ontario

Markusen, James R. (1975a) 'International externalities and optimal tax structures.' *Journal of International Economics* 5, 15–29

— (1975b) 'Cooperative control of international pollution and common property resources.' *Quarterly Journal of Economics* 89, 618–32

Pigou, A.C. (1932) *The Economics of Welfare* (London: Macmillan)

Snape, Richard (1992) 'The environment, international trade, and competitiveness.' In *The Greening of World Trade Issues*, ed. Kym Anderson and Richard Blackhurst (New York: Harvester-Wheatsheaf)

Uimonen, Peter, and John Whalley (1992) *Trade and Environment* (Washington, DC: Institute for International Economics)

15 In the case of the pollution tax, $e^* = 1$, and for the subsidy, $e^* = 0$, with the same expense on pollution control and the identical effective export tax. Hence the outcomes are identical.

[23]

Trade and Transboundary Pollution

By BRIAN R. COPELAND AND M. SCOTT TAYLOR*

This paper examines how national income and trading opportunities interact to determine the level and incidence of world pollution. We find that (i) free trade raises world pollution if incomes differ substantially across countries; (ii) if trade equalizes factor prices, human-capital-abundant countries lose from trade, while human-capital-scarce countries gain; (iii) international trade in pollution permits can lower world pollution even when governments' supply of permits is unrestricted; (iv) international income transfers may not affect world pollution or welfare; and (v) attempts to manipulate the terms of trade with pollution policy leave world pollution unaffected. (*JEL* F10, H41, Q28)

There is growing concern over the effects of international trade on the global environment. While traditional opposition to free trade focused on potential job losses and wage reductions, environmentalists have recently turned the pro-free-trade case on its head by arguing that, even if trade liberalization succeeds in raising incomes and consumption, this will only lead to more pollution.

Economists have responded by pointing out that the national income gains brought about by freer trade will increase the demand for environmental quality, make new investment in pollution abatement affordable, and generate much-needed government revenues for enforcement of environmental regulations. In fact, recent empirical work by Gene M. Grossman and Alan B. Krueger (1993) suggests that income gains can have a significant effect on some types of pollution emissions.

It is clear that both sides may be at least partially right. Trade may tend to increase world pollution by raising the scale of economic activity and by providing added incentives for polluting industries to locate in countries with low environmental standards. Conversely, the income gains created by trade may increase the pressure for tougher environmental regulation and enforcement. In this paper we develop a very simple model to investigate these issues. We assume that global environmental quality is a pure public good whose supply responds endogenously to trade-induced changes in relative prices and incomes, and we use the model to explore how welfare and pollution levels are affected by free trade in goods and pollution permits, by international income transfers, and by international agreements limiting or reducing pollution emissions. Our model is designed to highlight income effects, since these are central to the arguments put forward on both sides of the debate.

The model builds on our earlier work (Copeland and Taylor, 1994), where we studied trade in a world where environmental quality is a *local* public good (pollution damage is confined to the emitting country). In that paper, we developed a static two-country general-equilibrium model with a

*Department of Economics, University of British Columbia, Vancouver, BC Canada V6T 1Z1. Copeland's portion of this research was funded by a grant from SSHRC. Earlier versions of this paper were presented at the Midwest International Economics Meetings, the Third Canadian Conference on Resource and Environmental Economics, the winter meetings of the Econometric Society, the NBER 1994 Summer Institute, and in seminars at UBC and the University of Victoria. We thank participants for their comments. We are also grateful for helpful comments from Jim Brander, Satya Das, Mick Devereux, David Donaldson, and three anonymous referees.

continuum of goods differing in their pollution intensity of production. Countries differed only in their endowment of the one primary factor (human capital); and we studied only the case in which this difference was large. Governments set pollution policy endogenously, and because environmental quality is a normal good, the higher-income country had tougher environmental regulations. We found that free trade shifted pollution-intensive production to the human-capital-scarce country and raised world pollution. Nevertheless, there was no market failure because pollution stayed within the country of origin and governments regulated pollution optimally. Consequently, trade always increased welfare.

In the present paper, global environmental quality is a *pure* public good (or equivalently, pollution is a pure public bad): all countries are equally exposed to a given unit of pollution, regardless of its source. The pollutants we have in mind feature prominently in much of the debate over global warming, depletion of the ozone layer, and biodiversity. The welfare effects of trade in this case are fundamentally different. If pollution is a pure public bad, the relocation of pollution-intensive industries to countries with less stringent environmental protection may increase the exposure of home residents to pollution, and this works against standard gains from trade. Because pollution crosses borders, uncoordinated regulation of pollution at the national level does not eliminate all market failures, and consequently free trade need not raise welfare.

In addition to allowing for transboundary pollution, we depart from our earlier work in several other significant ways. We allow for an arbitrary number of countries, and we consider two cases: one with a large number of countries (where no country perceives a terms-of-trade effect from changes in its environmental policy) and one with a small number of countries (where terms-of-trade motivations for environmental policy cannot be ignored). This allows us to isolate the effects of terms-of-trade motivations for pollution policy from purely environmental motives. Finally, we study equilibria where factor prices are equalized by trade (FPE equilibria), as well as specialized equilibria. This allows us to examine how inequalities in the international distribution of income influence the effects of trade on the environment.

The bulk of the paper focuses on the case with a large number of countries. Each government sets a national pollution quota and implements it with marketable permits, treating the rest of the world's pollution as given. We find a Nash equilibrium in pollution levels, examine the effects of liberalizing trade in goods, and analyze various proposals for reducing world pollution. Within this context we obtain several interesting results.

First, if human-capital levels differ substantially across countries, then a movement from autarky to free trade raises world pollution. In contrast, if all countries have similar human-capital levels, then world pollution does not rise with trade. When countries are very different, trade does not equalize factor prices, and consequently pollution permit prices are lower in human-capital-scarce countries. "Pollution havens" are created by trade as the most pollution-intensive industries shift to countries with weak environmental regulations. This tends to raise world pollution above autarky levels. On the other hand, if countries are sufficiently similar, then trade equalizes pollution-permit prices, and the pollution-haven effect is eliminated.

Second, we find that the human-capital-abundant countries lose from trade and the human-capital-scarce countries gain from trade when regions have similar (but still different) income levels in autarky. As we show, lower-income countries have a strategic advantage when setting pollution levels in a free-trade regime, and this allows them to increase their income and pollution at the expense of richer countries.

Third, we find that when free trade in goods raises world pollution, allowing for international trade in pollution permits can lower global pollution. This result holds even when countries are not restricted in the number of permits they issue. This is because free trade in permits equalizes pollution-permit prices and eliminates the pollution-haven effect.

Fourth, we show that untied international transfers of income lower the recipient's pollution but raise the donor's. In an FPE equilibrium, the donor's welfare may be no lower after the transfer than before. This result underscores the potential importance of income effects in analyzing global pollution reform.

Finally, when we move to the case with a small number of countries, we find that the flavor of most of our results carries over; although terms-of-trade motivations for pollution policy reduce the strategic advantage of low-income countries, increase the pollution produced by the high-income North, and render income transfers from North to South welfare-reducing for the donor and welfare-enhancing for the recipient.

While there is an extensive literature on transboundary pollution, there is little work examining the interaction among pollution, income levels, and the pattern of trade in a general equilibrium setting (see Judith M. Dean [1992] for a survey). Optimal unilateral and multilateral approaches to transboundary pollution have been addressed in a number of papers (see in particular James R. Markusen [1975a, b]), but this literature is mainly concerned with how to regulate pollution and not with the interaction among income levels, pollution policy, and trade. Markusen (1975b) also considered a noncooperative Nash equilibrium in pollution levels between governments, but the pattern of trade was exogenous. Rodney D. Ludema and Ian Wooton (1994) have recently extended this work, but confine their attention to strategic trade policy issues. Michael Rauscher's (1991) work is closest in spirit to ours: he uses a two-country general-equilibrium model with no goods trade, but capital is mobile and responds to differences in environmental regulations. He finds that increased capital mobility leads to a pollution reduction in at least one country but has ambiguous welfare effects. In contrast, we adopt a multi-good, many-country trading model. This allows us to analyze linkages between trade patterns and pollution levels, and also to contrast FPE equilibria with specialized equilibria and to compare pure goods trade with trade in pollution permits.

The remainder of the paper proceeds as follows. In the first six sections of the paper we assume that the number of countries is large, and hence terms of trade motivations for pollution policy can safely be ignored. Sections I and II detail the model's assumptions and derive the equilibrium conditions. Section III examines autarky, and Section IV considers the effects of trade on welfare and pollution levels. We examine various approaches to pollution policy reform in Section V and study the effects of untied income transfers in Section VI. Section VII reconsiders our earlier results when the number of countries is small, and Section VIII presents our conclusions.

I. The Model

We consider a world economy consisting of two regions (North and South), each composed of many countries: n in the North and n^* in the South. All countries within a region are identical. Countries differ across regions only in their endowments of the one primary factor, effective labor, which is supplied inelastically. Effective labor can be thought of as the product of the number of workers and an efficiency index determined by the level of human capital. Since the number of individuals per country plays no independent role in our analysis, we normalize the population of each country to 1.[1] Consequently, international differences in effective labor endowments reflect differences in human capital. Each Northern country has L units of effective labor, and each Southern country has L^* units. We assume $L > L^*$ so that Northern countries are human-capital-abundant relative to Southern countries.

[1] In section 7 of Copeland and Taylor (1994) we consider an extension of the model in which factors such as country size, population density, and the environment's absorptive capacity allow these two components of effective labor to have different effects. We have not adopted this extension here, given the complications of transboundary pollution.

There is a continuum of private consumption goods, indexed by $z \in [0,1]$. Pollution is produced jointly with consumption goods, but the output (y) of a consumption good z can be written as a function of pollution emissions (e) and labor input (ℓ).[2] To keep the model simple, we adopt the following functional form:

$$(1) \quad y = f(e, \ell; z) = \begin{cases} \ell^{1-\alpha(z)} e^{\alpha(z)} & \text{if } e/\ell \le \lambda \\ 0 & \text{if } e/\ell > \lambda \end{cases}$$

where $\lambda > 0$, and $\alpha(z) \in (0,1)$ is a parameter varying across goods. Because pollution is a by-product of production, output must be bounded above for any given labor input. This constraint is most easily captured by the requirement $e \le \lambda \ell$ since this ensures that $y \le \lambda^{\alpha} \ell$.

Private firms must obtain permits to emit pollution. Letting τ denote the price of a permit, and w the return to a unit of effective labor, the unit-cost function corresponding to (1) is

$$(2) \quad c(w, \tau; z) = \kappa(z) \tau^{\alpha(z)} w^{1-\alpha(z)}$$

where $\kappa(z) \equiv \alpha^{-\alpha}(1-\alpha)^{-(1-\alpha)}$ is an industry-specific constant.[3] Since the share of pollution charges in the total cost of producing good z is $\alpha(z)$, we can easily rank goods in terms of pollution intensities so that $\alpha'(z) > 0$. High-z goods are more pollution-intensive than low-z goods at all factor prices.

Northern and Southern consumers have identical utility functions defined over consumption goods and aggregate world pollution. Pollution is a pure public bad: consumers in all countries are harmed by the pollution released from any one country. To simplify matters we assume that pollution affects only the level of utility and plays no role in determining consumer choice among goods. For tractability, we follow Rudiger Dornbusch et al. (1980) and impose constant budget shares; hence,

$$(3) \quad U = \int_0^1 b(z) \ln[x(z)]\, dz - \beta \left(\sum_{i=1}^{n+n^*} E_i \right)^{\gamma} \Big/ \gamma$$

where β and γ are positive constants, E_i is the total amount of pollution emitted by country i, $x(z)$ is consumption of good z, and $b(z)$ is the budget-share function satisfying $\int_0^1 b(z)\, dz = 1$. We assume that $\gamma \ge 1$, to ensure that the marginal willingness to pay for pollution reduction is a nondecreasing function of pollution levels.

II. Pollution Supply

There are three types of decision-makers: governments, producers, and consumers. We abstract from all income distributional issues and assume that the government chooses policy to maximize the utility of the representative consumer. Governments move first and set national pollution quotas. Next, consumers and producers maximize utility and profits, treating prices and pollution as given. Finally, markets clear.

We consider a noncooperative Nash equilibrium with each government treating the rest of the world's pollution as given when choosing its own pollution quota E_i. Pollution targets are implemented with a marketable permit system: the government of country i issues E_i pollution permits, each of which allows a (local) firm to emit one unit of pollution. The permits are auctioned off to firms, and all revenue is given to consumers via lump-sum transfers.[4]

[2] This requires that the technology satisfy certain regularity conditions. In Copeland and Taylor (1994), we show how (1) can be derived from a joint production technology.

[3] We assume an interior solution, but one always obtains if effective labor endowments are not too small. See Copeland and Taylor (1994) for further details.

[4] This is equivalent to assuming that the aggregate pollution target is implemented with a pollution tax whose revenues are rebated to consumers.

We begin with the production sector. Given goods prices $p(z)$, and the government's allotment of pollution permits, profit-maximizing firms maximize national income and, hence, implicitly solve

$$G(p, E_i, L_i) = \max_{\{\ell(z), e(z)\}} \left\{ \int_0^1 p(z) f[e(z), \ell(z); z] \, dz \right\}$$

subject to

$$\int_0^1 e(z) \, dz = E_i$$

$$\int_0^1 \ell(z) \, dz = L_i.$$

For given $p(z)$, the market price of a pollution permit in country i can be obtained as

$$\tau_i = \partial G / \partial E_i$$

which measures the marginal cost to the economy of reducing pollution.

Consumers maximize utility, given prices and pollution levels. Let I_i denote national income of country i [in equilibrium $I_i = G(p, E_i, L_i)$]. Then the indirect utility function corresponding to (3) for the representative consumer in country i is given by

$$(4) \quad V = \int_0^1 b(z) \ln[b(z)] \, dz - \int_0^1 b(z) \ln[p(z)] \, dz + \ln(I_i) - \beta \left(\sum_{j=1}^{n+n^*} E_j \right)^{\gamma} \Big/ \gamma.$$

Each government chooses its pollution target E_i to maximize the utility of its representative consumer, treating the pollution level of all other countries as fixed. For country i the first-order condition implies

$$(5) \quad \tau_i = -V_E / V_I + \int_0^1 m_i(z) \frac{dp(z)}{dE_i} \, dz$$

where $m_i(z)$ is net imports of good z. Equation (5) tells us that the pollution target should be chosen so that the equilibrium permit price (the marginal cost of pollution abatement) is equal to the marginal benefit from lower pollution, measured by marginal damage (V_E / V_I) plus an indirect terms-of-trade effect.

When the number of countries is large, no individual government can have a significant effect on its terms of trade. Consequently, the final term in (5) tends to zero as n and n^* increase. In contrast, each country retains an incentive to control its pollution even as the number of countries grows large. The intuition for this result is as follows. Start from an existing equilibrium with $n + n^*$ countries each contributing to global pollution, and add another country. On impact, this extra country adds to the stock of world pollution. Since the marginal damage from pollution is rising in global pollution levels, this extra pollution *increases* the incentive of each existing country to control its own pollution. Hence as n and n^* grow large, each country retains an incentive to limit its contribution to global pollution.[5]

Until Section VII, we assume that the number of countries is large enough so that no government will perceive any terms-of-trade benefit from manipulating pollution policy. With this assumption, each government chooses its target so that the equilibrium permit price is equal to marginal damage:

$$(6) \quad \tau_i = -V_E / V_I = \beta \left(\sum_{j=1}^{n+n^*} E_j \right)^{\gamma - 1} I_i.$$

[5]For a proof of this assertion see footnote 25 in Section VII. This result, which applies to public bads, is in fact just the mirror image of the typical (voluntary provision) public-goods problem. In the public-goods case, the addition of further agents increases the quantity of the public good on impact and reduces the incentive of each agent to provide the public good. The key difference between public bads and goods is that the impact effect of another agent in the public-bads case is to *lower* the utility of all others, thus raising the marginal benefit of controlling the public bad; whereas in the public-goods case, adding an extra agent *raises* the utility of others, thus reducing the marginal benefit of contributing to the public good.

Permit prices are increasing in income since environmental quality is a normal good,[6] and nondecreasing in the aggregate pollution level since the marginal willingness to pay for pollution reduction is nondecreasing.

To generate a relationship between relative factor prices (τ_i / w_i) and pollution supply, note that national income is the sum of labor income and returns from pollution permits:

$$(7) \qquad I_i = w_i L_i + \tau_i E_i .$$

Combining (6) with (7), letting $E^w \equiv \Sigma_j E_j$ denote world pollution, yields country i's inverse pollution supply curve:

$$(8) \qquad \rho_i \equiv \frac{\tau_i}{w_i} = \frac{\beta L_i (E^w)^{\gamma - 1}}{1 - \beta E_i (E^w)^{\gamma - 1}} .$$

Since all countries within a region are identical, it is clear from (8) that their pollution supply curves are identical. In equilibrium (autarky or free trade), all countries within a region attain the same level of utility and emit the same amount of pollution.

III. Autarky Equilibrium

The (derived) demand for pollution in autarky arises from the demand for goods whose production creates pollution. Recalling that $\alpha(z)$ is the share of pollution charges in the cost of production, we have

$$(9) \qquad \tau_i e_i(z) = \alpha(z) p_i(z) y_i(z) = \alpha(z) p_i(z) x_i(z) = \alpha(z) b(z) I_i$$

where $e_i(z)$ is the number of pollution permits needed to produce autarky consumption $x_i(z)$. Integrating over all goods and using (7) yields the derived demand for pollution:

$$(10) \qquad \rho_i \equiv \frac{\tau_i}{w_i} = \frac{\bar{\theta} L_i}{E_i [1 - \bar{\theta}]}$$

where $\bar{\theta} \equiv \int_0^1 \alpha(z) b(z) dz$ is the share of pollution-permit revenue in national income. Equating country i's pollution demand (10) and supply (8) yields its best response to foreign pollution:

$$(11) \qquad E_i (E^w)^{\gamma - 1} = \bar{\theta} / \beta .$$

Solving the system (11) simultaneously for all i yields autarky pollution levels:

$$(12) \qquad E_i^a = \left(\frac{\bar{\theta}}{\beta (n + n^*)^{\gamma - 1}} \right)^{1/\gamma} \equiv E^a .$$

World pollution in autarky is obtained by summing (12) over all countries:

$$(13) \qquad E^{aw} = \left(\frac{(n + n^*) \bar{\theta}}{\beta} \right)^{1/\gamma}$$

Autarky pollution is independent of the level of human capital, and hence all countries generate the same amount of pollution. A larger production capacity created by higher human-capital levels increases the demand for pollution permits (a scale effect), but the ensuing higher income reduces the amount of pollution the population is willing to supply, leading to a higher pollution-permit price and cleaner techniques of production. As in Copeland and Taylor (1994), these scale and technique effects exactly offset each other in autarky, leaving pollution independent of the level of human capital.

On the other hand, changes in the number of countries do affect pollution. On impact, an increase in the number of countries raises world pollution. This increases marginal damage and raises the marginal benefit of controlling pollution. In response,

[6] The optimal permit supply problem depends on *aggregate* income, reflecting our decision to abstract from income distributional issues by assuming a representative agent. If instead pollution permits were given to firms (rather than auctioned), and if the government placed different weights on labor income and pollution-permit rents collected by firms, then the supply of pollution would depend on distributional weights.

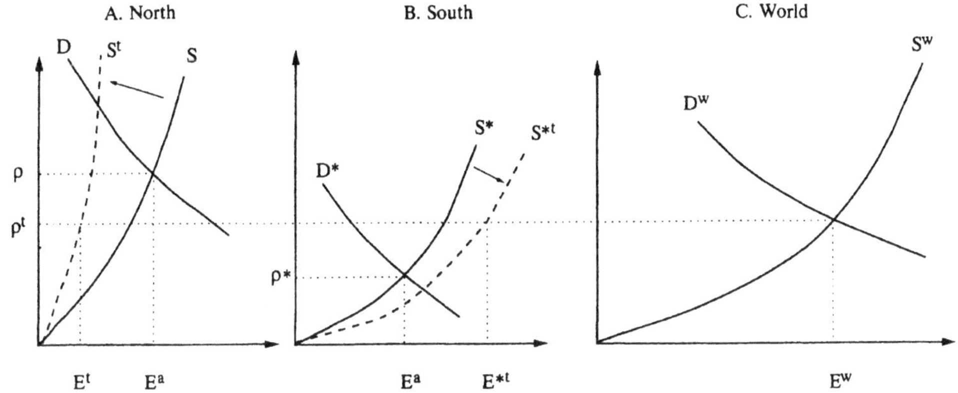

FIGURE 1. POLLUTION DEMAND AND SUPPLY

each country cuts back its pollution [from (12), an individual country's pollution is declining in $n+n^*$], but not by enough to prevent global pollution from rising [from (13), world pollution is increasing in $n+n^*$].

While pollution levels are the same across countries, the relative price of pollution permits differs: since $L > L^*$, we have $E^a/L < E^a/L^*$, and hence pollution permits are relatively scarce (and expensive) in the North. This is illustrated in Figure 1, which plots a Northern and a Southern country's pollution demand (D) and supply (S) [using equations (8) and (10)], parameterized by the equilibrium autarky pollution level of the rest of the world. Because of its higher income, Northern demand for pollution is higher, and its supply lower, than in the South. Consequently, $\rho^a > \rho^{a*}$, and this provides the basis for trade.

IV. Trading Equilibrium

If countries have sufficiently similar effective labor endowments, factor prices will be equalized by trade; conversely, if endowments are sufficiently different, trade will not equalize factor prices.[7] Since these two types of equilibria have very different implications, we consider both cases.

A. *Factor Prices Equalized*

First consider the FPE case. With equal factor prices the exact pattern of commodity trade is indeterminate,[8] but we can obtain results on the pattern of trade in factor services. Moreover, because supply curves of countries within a region are identical, all countries within a region will produce the same amount of pollution and attain the same income level in free trade. Consequently, we omit individual country subscripts, except in cases where there may be some ambiguity. Thus, for example, E is the amount of pollution produced by a typical Northern country. Asterisks denote corresponding Southern-country variables.

Since $\tau = \tau^*$ in a FPE equilibrium, we conclude from (6) that $I = I^*$, and hence $wL + \tau E = wL^* + \tau E^*$. Rearranging yields

$$(14) \qquad L - L^* = \rho(E^* - E)$$

where $\rho \equiv \tau / w$. By definition we have $L >$

[7] The conditions which generate each type of equilibrium are discussed in the Appendix.

[8] This is a standard feature of trade models in which the number of goods exceeds the number of factors. See, for example, Dornbusch et al. (1980).

L^*, and hence $E^* > E$; more pollution is generated by Southern countries. Moreover, since $I = I^*$ and preferences over goods are homothetic, each country consumes a fraction $1/(n+n^*)$ of the world's (embodied) pollution and effective labor services. Hence each Northern country is a net exporter of $n^*(L - L^*)/(n+n^*)$ units of effective labor services, and each Southern country is a net exporter of $n(E^* - E)/(n+n^*)$ units of pollution services.

Equilibrium pollution levels can be obtained by equating world demand and supply for pollution services.[9] Denote world magnitudes with a superscript "w", and use the same argument that led to (10) to obtain the world demand for pollution:

$$\rho = \frac{\bar{\theta}L^{w}}{(1-\bar{\theta})E^{w}}. \tag{15}$$

Next, invert (8), sum, and rearrange to obtain world supply:

$$\rho = \frac{\beta L^{w}(E^{w})^{\gamma-1}}{n+n^* - \beta(E^{w})^{\gamma}}. \tag{16}$$

Equating demand and supply yields world pollution in the FPE equilibrium:

$$E^{w} = \left(\frac{(n+n^*)\bar{\theta}}{\beta}\right)^{1/\gamma}. \tag{17}$$

Comparing (17) with (13), and using (12) and (14), we have shown the following.

PROPOSITION 1: *In an FPE equilibrium, trade raises the level of pollution generated by each Southern country, lowers the pollution level generated by each Northern country, and leaves world pollution unaffected.*

Figure 1 illustrates the effects of trade on pollution. In Figure 1A and 1B, we depict the autarky ("a") and trading ("t") equilibria for typical Northern and Southern countries. Figure 1C illustrates the trading equilibrium with aggregate world demand and supply. Trade eliminates the gap between Northern and Southern pollution permit prices. Northern countries move down their supply curves as the relative price of a pollution permit drops, while Southern countries move up their supply curves. In addition, each Northern country's supply curve shifts inward in response to the net increase in foreign pollution,[10] while each Southern supply curve shifts outward in response to the net decrease in pollution from the rest of the world. Consequently, pollution must fall in the North and rise in the South. As is apparent from the diagram, the elastic supply of pollution and the pollution spillovers tend to reinforce the production shifts that trade creates in a standard Heckscher-Ohlin model.

Aggregate world pollution is unaffected by trade for essentially the same reason that pollution is independent of the level of human capital in autarky. Trade leads to real income changes which generate offsetting scale and technique effects. In addition, trade generates a composition effect, as the relatively pollution-intensive industries on average shift to the South from the North. Nevertheless, when factor prices are equalized by trade, the techniques of production are identical across countries, and hence shifting production across regions has no effect on pollution emissions.

Although trade does not affect the level of global pollution, it nevertheless has interesting welfare effects. These can be investigated with the aid of Figure 2. Since the world pollution level is unaffected by trade, we can draw an Edgeworth box with dimensions equal to the world supply of pollution

[9] This aggregation is possible because factor prices are equalized by trade and tastes are homothetic over private consumption goods.

[10] The net result of Southern pollution increases and other Northern reductions leaves a typical Northern country facing more foreign pollution. The shift in the supply curve can be obtained from (8): we have $\partial\rho_i/\partial E_j > 0$ for $j \neq i$ since an increase in foreign pollution raises the marginal damage from domestic pollution.

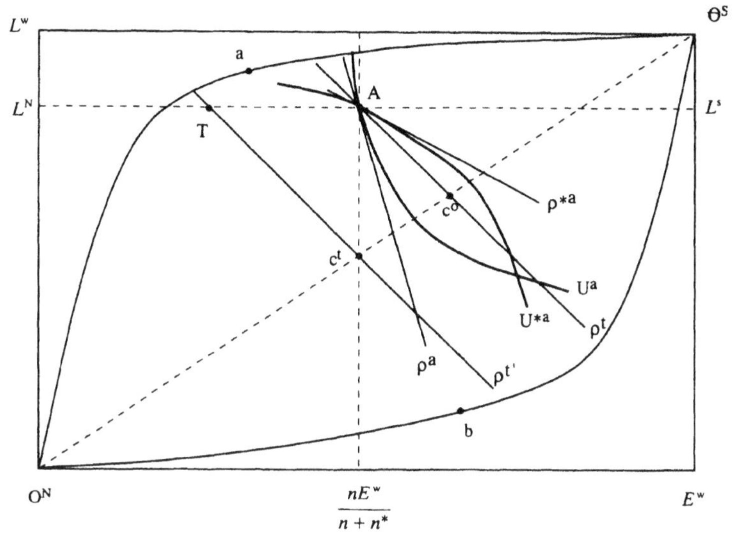

FIGURE 2. GAINS AND LOSSES FROM TRADE

E^w and effective labor L^w. Let L^N denote North's aggregate endowment of effective labor. Then the autarky factor supply point is at A, since North produces a share $n/(n+n^*)$ of pollution in autarky (recall that autarky pollution levels are identical across countries). Now consider an *integrated equilibrium* where factor supplies are fixed but freely mobile across countries. This yields some equilibrium $\rho = \tau/w$, and a production locus $y(z)$. If we now divide the world factor supplies between the two regions and allow free trade in goods but not in factors, then, as in Avinash Dixit and Victor Norman (1980), we can find the set of factor allocations where trade in goods alone can replicate the integrated equilibrium. This set is the interior and boundary of the area $O^N aO^S bO^N$. Outside of this area, the full-employment conditions for countries in at least one of the regions cannot be satisfied at the factor price and output vector of the integrated equilibrium.[11]

[11] In Dixit and Norman's analysis, the boundaries of the integrated equilibrium region are piecewise linear, with the slope of each piece being the factor-input ratio of each good. With a continuum of goods, the boundary is smooth, and the slope at each point is the factor-input ratio for some good z.

Because of constant returns to scale, we can think of each consumer as buying a bundle of factor services and using the bundle to produce consumption goods.[12] Hence we can draw indifference curves with re-

[12] If consumers have a factor service bundle of (E, L), utility is given by

$$\tilde{U}(E,L) = \max\left\{\int_0^1 b(z)\ln(f[e(z),\ell(z);z])\,dz - \beta(E^w)^\gamma/\gamma\right\}$$

subject to

$$\int_0^1 e(z)\,dz = E$$

$$\int_0^1 \ell(z)\,dz = L$$

where consumers treat world pollution E^w as fixed. Solving, we obtain

$$\tilde{U}(E,L) = K + \bar{\theta}\ln E + (1-\bar{\theta})\ln L - \beta(E^w)^\gamma/\gamma$$

where K is a constant. This analysis (i.e., the equivalence of buying goods and factor services) is valid as long as all goods are produced by firms facing the same factor prices.

spect to factor services. Moreover, we can aggregate preferences because all individuals within a region have identical incomes and homothetic preferences over goods. This allows us to draw an indifference curve in Figure 2 which represents "Northern utility." In autarky, Northern consumers collectively face the budget constraint labeled ρ^a, and their indifference curve is tangent to this line at point A. Southern consumers face the budget constraint ρ^{*a} and must also be at point A. Potential gains from trade lie within the lens-shaped area bounded by the two indifference curves. If pollution were unaffected by trade, the equilibrium free-trade factor-price ratio would generate a budget constraint through point A (labeled ρ^t), and because preferences over goods are identical and homothetic, the equilibrium consumption point would be at c^0. In this hypothetical case, all countries necessarily gain from trade.

Although global pollution is not affected by trade, pollution levels within each country do respond to trade. Southern countries increase their pollution, and Northern countries reduce their pollution. This corresponds to a leftward movement along the line $L^N L^S$ to point T. Because pollution permits generate income, this change in the *distribution* of pollution-generating activities has the same effect on the North as a transfer of some of its earning potential to the South. The free-trade budget constraint is thus $\rho^{t'}$, and the free-trade consumption point is at c^t.[13]

Several results are immediately apparent from this analysis. First, Southern countries must always gain from trade. World pollution is not affected by trade, and so welfare is affected only by the change in real income. If factor supplies stayed constant before and after trade, then the standard gains-from-trade results would apply. Since the South also generates a greater share of the world's pollution after trade, it realizes additional income gains from its expanded supply of pollution permits.

PROPOSITION 2: *In the FPE equilibrium, Southern countries always gain from trade.*

Whether or not the North gains from trade depends on how much the South increases its pollution as a result of trade. If pollution supplies did not change, the North would gain from access to the South's relatively cheaper (in autarky) pollution-intensive production. However, the North is harmed by South's increase in pollution. As Northern countries cut back on their pollution in response to increased pollution from the South, their collective budget constraint shifts down. In fact, as shown, the North's free-trade budget constraint, $\rho^{t'}$, must lie outside the lens-shaped area, and hence Northern countries lose from trade.

PROPOSITION 3: *Each Northern country is worse off in free trade than in autarky.*

(See Appendix A for the proof.)

The North loses from trade because without any global agreements, Southern countries have a strategic advantage: their lower income allows them to commit to higher pollution levels with the opening of trade. Northern countries can respond either by accepting more global pollution or by cutting back on their own pollution and allowing their incomes to fall. In our model, the reduction in pollution by Northern countries is exactly enough to maintain global pollution at its autarky level. In a more general model, Northern countries may choose a different income/pollution tradeoff. But the central point remains: the increased pollution emanating from the South reduces the gains from trade for the North, and this effect can be strong enough to make the North lose from trade.

This suggests that there are strong incentives for the North to link environmental agreements to free-trade agreements. As noted above, if the South were prevented from increasing its pollution, then the North would always gain from trade. Thus, the North has an incentive to link a free-trade

[13] The slopes of $\rho^{t'}$ and ρ^t are equal because A and T are both within the FPE region. The equilibrium consumption point must be at c^t because with identical homothetic preferences and identical incomes, the North consumes a fraction $n/(n+n^*)$ of the world's factor services.

agreement with an agreement that freezes pollution at its pre-trade levels, whereas the South has an incentive to oppose this.

PROPOSITION 4: *As compared with unconstrained free trade, each Northern country would gain from an agreement that freezes pollution in each country at its pre-trade levels, and each Southern country would lose from such an agreement.*

Note that global pollution levels are unaffected by such an agreement—the issue here is a conflict over who generates the pollution. For a given level of global pollution, the right to pollute is a valuable asset, and each country can gain if it obtains a greater share of this asset. Since free trade allows the South to exploit its strategic advantage, the North has an incentive to place restrictions on its ability to do so, either by opposing free trade or by insisting that a trade agreement be linked to an environmental agreement.

B. *Factor Prices Not Equalized*

If factor prices are not equalized by trade, Northern countries specialize in human-capital-intensive goods, and Southern countries specialize in pollution-intensive goods. Given our ordering on $\alpha(z)$ there will exist some $\bar{z}$ such that goods on the interval $[0, \bar{z})$ are produced in the North, and goods on the interval $(\bar{z}, 1]$ are produced in the South. To determine the equilibrium, we follow Dornbusch et al. (1980), and solve for the marginal good. As in the FPE case, all countries within a region will attain the same outcome, and we omit country subscripts. Aggregate Northern and Southern variables are denoted with superscripts N and S; hence, for example, $L^N = nL$.

Since the marginal good is produced at equal cost in both regions; we have $c(w, \tau; h, \bar{z}) = c(w^*, \tau^*; \bar{z})$, or equivalently, using (2),

$$(18) \qquad \omega \equiv \frac{w}{w^*} = \left(\frac{\tau^*}{\tau}\right)^{\alpha(\bar{z})/[1-\alpha(\bar{z})]}$$

To eliminate τ^*/τ from the above, note that North's share of world income equals the share of world spending on Northern goods:

$$(19) \qquad I^N = \varphi(\bar{z})(I^N + I^S)$$

where $\varphi(\bar{z}) \equiv \int_0^{\bar{z}} b(z)\,dz$ is the North's share of world income. Using (6) and (19), we have $\tau^*/\tau = n\varphi^*(\bar{z})/n^*\varphi(\bar{z})$ where $\varphi^*(\bar{z})$ is the South's share of world income. Substituting into (18) yields the following:[14]

$$(20) \qquad \omega = \left(\frac{n\varphi^*(\bar{z})}{n^*\varphi(\bar{z})}\right)^{\alpha(\bar{z})/[1-\alpha(\bar{z})]} \equiv T(\bar{z}).$$

To obtain another equation linking ω and $\bar{z}$, note that income is the sum of wages and pollution-permit revenue, and pollution-permit revenue is the sum of fees paid by all producers. In the North, we have

$$(21) \qquad \tau E^N = \int_0^{\bar{z}} \alpha(z) b(z) I^w\,dz = \frac{I^N \theta(\bar{z})}{\varphi(\bar{z})}$$

where the last step uses (19) and where $\theta(\bar{z}) \equiv \int_0^{\bar{z}} \alpha(z) b(z)\,dz$ is the share of Northern pollution charges in world income. Now use (21) to eliminate pollution charges in (7), do the same for the South, substitute into (19), and simplify to obtain:

$$(22) \qquad \omega = \frac{n^*L^*}{nL}\left[\frac{\int_0^{\bar{z}} b(z)[1-\alpha(z)]\,dz}{\int_{\bar{z}}^1 b(z)[1-\alpha(z)]\,dz}\right] \equiv B(\bar{z}).$$

Jointly solving (22) and (20) determines the equilibrium.

[14] This analysis is valid only if $\tau > \tau^*$, since otherwise we are in the FPE case. Thus we must have $n\varphi^*(\bar{z}) < n^*\varphi(\bar{z})$; or letting $\varphi(\hat{z}) \equiv n/(n+n^*)$, we require $z > \hat{z}$.

PROPOSITION 5: *If trade does not equalize factor prices, then (i) global pollution is higher in free trade than in autarky; (ii) pollution in the North falls with trade; and (iii) pollution in the South rises with trade.*

(See Appendix A for the proof.)

In contrast to the FPE case, free trade increases global pollution in a specialized equilibrium.[15] As before, the supply response to the factor-price movements created by trade leads to reduced pollution in the North and increased pollution in the South. However, since the gap between factor prices is not fully eliminated, the South has relatively lower pollution-permit prices than the North. Consequently, the marginal good is produced with more pollution-intensive techniques in the South than in the North. Since the most pollution-intensive industries shift to the country with the lowest pollution-permit price, the increase in pollution generated by the South is less than the fall in the North.[16]

C. *Trade in Pollution Permits*

As in the Heckscher-Ohlin model, trade in goods in our model is an indirect way of allowing countries to trade factor services. We now consider the effects of allowing direct trade in pollution services when governments agree that a permit issued by one country can be used by a firm that wants to emit pollution in any country.

In the FPE equilibrium, trade in goods and trade in factors are perfect substitutes: allowing trade in pollution permits has no effect on production, incomes, pollution, or welfare. This is a standard result in factor-proportions models—the only difference is that, in our case, the supply of the tradable factor is endogenous. Despite the fact that pollution permits are potential revenue-generators for governments, opening up international trade in pollution permits does not create an incentive to increase their supply beyond the levels of the pure goods-trading equilibrium. This is because pollution is a pure public bad. Since the harm suffered from pollution by the permit-issuing country is independent of the location of production, the income/pollution trade-off is not affected by making permits tradable when factor prices are equalized by goods trade alone.

In the specialized production equilibrium, trade in goods and trade in permits are no longer perfect substitutes. Consider an equilibrium with free trade in goods and then allow pollution permits to be freely traded internationally. Arbitrage equalizes the price of pollution permits across countries, and the zero-profit conditions ensure that τ/w is equalized. Consequently, the FPE equilibrium conditions apply. Since opening up the pollution permit market to international trade induces an FPE equilibrium, pollution must fall.

PROPOSITION 6: *Suppose factor prices are not equalized by goods trade. Then if countries allow pollution permits to be tradable internationally (without any global agreement to restrict their supply), global pollution will fall (relative to the pure goods trade level).*

When pollution-permit prices differ across countries and goods are freely tradable, there is an incentive to shift the most pollution-intensive production to countries with the lowest pollution-permit prices. This composition effect tends to increase world pollution because production techniques are dirtier in countries with low permit prices. Allowing trade in permits equalizes permit prices, ensures that production techniques are identical across countries, and thus eliminates the "pollution haven" effect.

[15] The intuition is similar to that for proposition 2 of Copeland and Taylor (1994), where we provide a detailed explanation based on the scale, technique, and composition effects.

[16] A general welfare result for the non-FPE case corresponding to Propositions 2 and 3 has thus far eluded us. It is, however, possible to derive some limited results. For example, at the borderline between FPE and non-FPE, Propositions 2 and 3 hold; as well, if $n^* = 1$, the South must always gain in the non-FPE case.

V. Reform of Pollution Policy

In autarky, there are two distortions: relative goods prices differ across countries, and the international externality leads to excessive global pollution. Thus far, we have considered the effects of eliminating the trade distortion, while leaving the pollution distortion unresolved. We now consider the effects of various proposals to control world pollution.

A. *Global Reform*

We begin by briefly discussing the first best. Since environmental quality is an international public good, it is clear that global pollution levels are Pareto inefficient in a Nash equilibrium. The Samuelson condition for efficient public-goods provision requires that permit prices (the marginal pollution-control cost) be equalized across countries, and set equal to the global sum of marginal damages; that is, for any country j,

$$(23) \qquad \tau_j = \tau \equiv -\sum_{i=1}^{n+n^*} \left(V^i_{E_i} / V^i_{I_i}\right) = \beta (E^{\mathrm{w}})^{\gamma-1} I^{\mathrm{w}}.$$

Combining (23) with (15) yields the optimal global pollution level:[17]

$$(24) \qquad \tilde{E}^{\mathrm{w}} = \left(\frac{\bar{\theta}}{\beta}\right)^{1/\gamma}$$

which is less than autarky and free-trade global pollution levels, as one would expect.

Implementation of the first best is straightforward in theory, but difficult in practice. For example, governments could agree to issue a fixed number of internationally tradable pollution permits. Moreover, since permits generate income, negotiations to divide the initial allocation of permits across countries can take the place of explicit international side payments. Alternatively, the permits need not be tradable, but since efficiency requires that their price be equalized, they must be allocated across countries in a manner that is consistent with factor-price equalization. In this case, explicit international transfer payments may be required to support some points on the Pareto frontier.

In practice, large changes in pollution may not be politically feasible. Instead, international agreements often require only small reductions in the target variable. In our model, it is easy to show that equiproportionate reductions in pollution by all countries will be Pareto-improving as long as global pollution exceeds the optimum, and that repeated application of the equiproportionate reduction rule will eventually implement a point on the Pareto frontier. In a more general model, the path to the Pareto frontier may not be so simple. But the main point remains: application of standard results from public finance implies that either radical or gradual multilateral reductions in pollution, perhaps combined with international transfers of income, can achieve a first-best allocation.

B. *Regional Reforms*

In reality, any multilateral agreement requiring pollution reductions by *all* countries may be difficult to achieve. Some pollution agreements, such as the Montreal protocol, require pollution reductions by only the major polluting countries. To examine the effect of these limited agreements, suppose all countries in the North agree to reduce their pollution by the same small amount while the South commits to freezing its pollution at current levels. For simplicity, we focus on the FPE case.

First consider the effect on the welfare of a typical Northern country whose indirect utility is given by (4). Using the zero-profit conditions and (2) we have $p(z) = c(z) = \kappa(z)\rho^{\alpha(z)}w$, and using (7) we have an ex-

[17]Note that the optimal level of global pollution is independent of any distributional weights on country utilities. This follows from our assumption that pollution is strongly separable from consumption in the (homothetic over goods) utility function.

pression for income. Substituting these into (4) and rearranging, we obtain the following expression for Northern country i's indirect utility:

$$(25)\quad V^i = K + \ln(L+\rho E) - \bar{\theta}\ln(\rho) - \beta(E^w)^\gamma/\gamma$$

where K is a constant. Totally differentiating, and noting that each individual country i has chosen its pollution level so that $dV^i/dE_i = 0$, yields

$$(26)\quad dV^i = \left[\frac{\rho E}{L+\rho E} - \bar{\theta}\right]\hat{\rho} - \beta(E^w)^{\gamma-1}\sum_{j\neq i} dE_j.$$

To simplify, let $M = E^w/(n+n^*) - E$ denote a Northern country's net imports of embodied pollution services in the FPE equilibrium. Then, after some manipulation, we obtain:[18]

$$(27)\quad dV^i = \frac{\rho E}{L+\rho E}\left[\frac{nM}{E^w} - (n-1)\right]\hat{E}.$$

As (27) illustrates, a cut in pollution by the North has two effects on Northern welfare. First, since world pollution is reduced, the relative price of pollution permits rises ($\hat{\rho} > 0$). Since each Northern country is a net importer of pollution services ($M > 0$), this worsens Northern countries' terms of trade. Although no individual country perceives a terms-of-trade effect from cutting its own pollution, when the coalition of all Northern countries cuts pollution, the terms-of-trade effect is multiplied n-fold and is therefore significant.

If there were only one Northern country ($n = 1$), then the terms-of-trade deterioration would be the only effect of a unilateral pollution cut,[19] and that country would have an incentive to *increase* its level of pollution in order to improve its terms of trade. With n countries, however, each country benefits from the reduction in pollution by the other pollution-cutting countries. This is the second term in (27), and it provides a counterbalance to the terms-of-trade effect. To determine the net effect, substitute for M in (27). Northern countries gain from a cut in Northern pollution provided that

$$\left[\frac{n}{n+n^*} - (n-1)\right]E^w < nE$$

which is true for $n \geq 2$. Once there are at least two Northern countries, the benefits of partially correcting the international pollution externality more than offset the terms-of-trade deterioration, and the North has a collective incentive to cut its pollution.

Let us now consider the effects of the North's cut in pollution on the South. Since Southern countries are net exporters of pollution services, they stand to reap a terms-of-trade gain as the relative price of pollution-intensive goods rises. Moreover, the South benefits from a cleaner environment. Hence, the South must gain from a cut in pollution by the North.

For similar reasons, a small cut in pollution by a coalition of all the Southern countries must also benefit the South: their terms of trade improve, and each Southern country benefits from the pollution cuts carried out by the other Southern countries. The North also gains from a pollution reduction by the South, despite a terms-of-trade deterioration. Totally differentiating (25), and

[18] Since $I = I^*$ in the FPE equilibrium, we have $(L^w + \rho E^w) = (n+n^*)(L+\rho E)$. Combining this with (15) yields $\bar{\theta} = \rho E^w/[(n+n^*)(L+\rho E)]$. Substituting this into (26), using (17) to eliminate E^w, and noting that $dE_j = dE$ for all Northern j, and $dE_j = 0$ for Southern j, yields

$$dV^i = \frac{\rho}{L+\rho E}[-M\hat{\rho} - (n-1)\,dE].$$

Finally, noting from (15) that $\hat{\rho} = -\hat{E}^w = -(nE/E^w)\hat{E}$, we obtain (27).

[19] Since we are starting at a Nash equilibrium, where each country sets its pollution level optimally, there is no first-order benefit to a country from its own pollution reduction.

noting from (16) that $\hat{\rho} = -\hat{E}^w$ (where $\hat{E}^w$ is the change in world pollution due to the South's cut), the effect on a typical Northern consumer in country i is

$$dV^i = \left[-\frac{\rho E}{L + \rho E} + \bar{\theta} - \beta(E^w)^\gamma \right] \hat{E}^w.$$

As long as world pollution is above the global optimum (i.e., as long as $E^w > [\bar{\theta}/\beta]^{1/\gamma} = \tilde{E}^w$), Northerners must gain from a fall in Southern pollution.

These results have several interesting implications for policy. First, since one region's reduction in pollution always benefits the other, each region has an incentive to offer a cash payment to the other in return for a reduction in pollution; however, net exporters of pollution services have a stronger incentive to do this. Second, a net exporter of pollution services stands to gain from its own region's cut in pollution. This means that selfish interests of pollution-intensive countries need not necessarily be in conflict with global environmental quality. Finally, the use of pollution policy by a coalition of countries to improve its terms of trade can be Pareto improving in some cases. If the pollution-intensive countries tighten their pollution regulations, they benefit through improved terms of trade, and their trading partners benefit from improved environmental quality.

It is, however, important to keep in mind that these results require that those countries not cutting pollution must commit to freezing pollution at its current level. Moreover, each country would prefer to be in the group subject to the freeze rather than in the group actually reducing emissions. Hence while the cuts are "unilateral," a multilateral treaty must be in force to restrict opportunistic behavior.

VI. Transfers

Because global pollution levels are inefficient at the Nash equilibrium, coalitions of countries have incentives to pay their trading partners to reduce pollution. Therefore a transfer tied to pollution reduction can lead to a Pareto improvement. In this section, we consider the effects of *untied* transfers. If there is no externality, then in a standard two-country trade model with identical homothetic tastes, a transfer leaves world prices unaffected and must harm the donor country. This result requires that, on impact, the transfer not directly affect the supply side of the model. In our case, however, the supply side of the model is affected, since pollution supplies respond to income changes. Despite this complication, we will show that a transfer has no real effects even if tastes are neither identical nor homothetic.

We consider only the FPE case. Let labor be the numeraire, and suppose a Northern country gives a transfer T to a Southern country.[20] Each country chooses its pollution level based on (6), where income is interpreted as being net of the transfer. Using a derivation similar to that which led to (8), the pollution supply of country i is given by

$$(28) \quad E_i = \frac{\rho - \beta(E^w)^{\gamma-1}(L_i + T_i)}{\rho\beta(E^w)^{\gamma-1}}$$

where $T_i = -T$ for the donor, $T_i = T$ for the recipient, and $T_i = 0$ for other countries.

Summing over all countries, we find that world pollution supply is unaffected by the transfer.[21] With FPE, both countries face the same income/pollution trade-off at the margin. Consequently, one country's marginal increase in pollution exactly offsets the other's reduction.

Perhaps more surprisingly, incomes are also unaffected by the transfer. The donor issues enough new pollution permits to bring its income back to where it was prior to the transfer. Similarly, the recipient's cut in pollution reduces its net income back to

[20] The same analysis applies if a coalition of Northern countries gives transfers to a group of Southern countries.

[21] In contrast, when factor prices are not equalized by trade, one can show that a transfer from Northern to Southern countries lowers world pollution.

its pre-transfer level. From (28), we have $\Delta E_i = -\Delta T_i / \rho$, and since $I_i = L_i + \rho E_i + T_i$, we have $\Delta I_i = 0$.

Since global pollution and each country's income are unaffected by the transfer, goods prices are also unaffected, and there is no effect on welfare in either country. The only effect of a transfer is to change the location of pollution emissions: the donor becomes more pollution-intensive, and the recipient becomes less pollution-intensive. To summarize, we have shown the following.

PROPOSITION 7: *In an FPE equilibrium, an income transfer between countries (i) raises pollution in the donor country, (ii) lowers pollution in the recipient country, (iii) has no effect on global pollution, and (iv) has no effect on welfare in either country.*

These surprising results are more general than might be thought, and they are quite closely related to Warr's theorem in public finance (Peter G. Warr, 1983). Warr shows that the private provision of a public good, and the welfare levels of the providers, are unaffected by income transfers among agents. Warr's result and ours do not rely on identical or even homothetic tastes;[22] they do, however, require that each individual face the same trade-off between private-goods consumption and public-goods consumption at the margin. In our context, agents (nations) contribute to a pure public bad (pollution), and each makes a positive contribution; but more importantly, each faces the same trade-off between private goods and pollution abatement in any FPE equilibrium. Consequently, income transfers have no effect on any agent's welfare.

VII. Terms-of-Trade Effects

Up until now, we have assumed that no individual country has an incentive to use its pollution policy to improve its terms of trade. In this section, we relax this assumption and allow each country to account explicitly for terms-of-trade effects when choosing its pollution quota.

We consider only the FPE case. Each country i chooses its own pollution E_i to maximize (25), treating foreign pollution $(E^w_{-i} \equiv E^w - E_i)$ as given, subject to the market-clearing condition (15), which can be rewritten as

$$(29) \qquad \rho \equiv \frac{\bar{\theta} L^w}{(1-\bar{\theta})(E^w_{-i} + E_i)}.$$

The first-order condition for country i's optimal choice is

$$(30) \quad \rho + V_E^i / V_I^i - M_i(\partial \rho / \partial E_i) = 0$$

where M_i is net imports of embodied pollution services. Using (29) to solve for $\partial \rho / \partial E_i$, and rearranging, we can write (30) as

$$(31) \quad \rho - \beta(E^w)^{\gamma-1} I_i - \frac{\theta_i - \bar{\theta}}{E^w} I_i = 0$$

where $I_i \equiv L_i + \rho E_i$ is national income of country i, and $\theta_i \equiv \rho E_i / I_i$ is the share of pollution-permit income in country i's national income (recall that $\bar{\theta}$ is the share of pollution charges in world income). Equation (31) differs from (6) only by the presence of the final term, which represents the terms-of-trade effect. Taking account of terms-of-trade effects tends to increase the marginal benefit of polluting for the North

[22] The following argument demonstrates that we do not require homotheticity or identical preferences. See also the proof of Warr's result in Theodore C. Bergstrom et al. (1986). With FPE and constant returns to scale, consumers can be thought of as purchasing embodied factor services (see footnote 11), and therefore the utility of a donor can be written as $V(\rho, I_0 + \rho E^w, E^w)$, where $I_0 = L - T - \rho E_{-i}$, E_{-i} denotes foreign pollution, and where we can think of the government as choosing E^w, subject to $E^w \geq E_{-i}$. The first-order condition is $\rho = -V_E / V_I \equiv \phi(\rho, I_0, E^w)$. If the South adjusts its pollution to fully offset the transfer (i.e., if $\Delta E^* = -\Delta T / \rho$), then $\Delta I_0 = 0$. Moreover, $\phi(\rho, I_0, E^w)$ is unchanged. Consequently, North's optimal choice of E^w (and hence E_i) is unchanged. Thus, if all other countries adjust their pollution to fully offset the transfer, the remaining country's optimal response is to do the same. Finally, since all real incomes and trade-offs are unaffected, the aggregate demand for pollution services is unaffected, and hence the equilibrium price ρ is also the same as before.

(a net importer of pollution services with $\theta < \bar{\theta}$) and tends to reduce it for the South (a net exporter with $\theta^* > \bar{\theta}$).

To find the new global pollution level, sum (31) over all countries, rearrange, and obtain (17): the level of world pollution is unaffected by the recognition of terms-of-trade effects! Moreover, using (15), we conclude that the equilibrium level of ρ is also unaffected. These two results might appear to be artifacts of our Cobb-Douglas specification, but they are not. In fact, they require only that aggregate demand and supply for pollution services be independent of the world distribution of income.

PROPOSITION 8: *Assume FPE, constant-returns-to-scale technologies which are identical across countries, and identical preferences which are homothetic over goods for any given level of world pollution. Consider two regimes: one where countries ignore terms-of-trade effects when choosing pollution levels, and the other where countries do take into account terms-of-trade effects. Then the equilibrium level of world pollution is the same in the two regimes.*

(See Appendix A for the proof.)

The intuition for this result is as follows. Notice from (30) that the introduction of terms-of-trade effects means that the net marginal benefit of polluting shifts up by $M\partial\rho/\partial E$ for a pollution importer, and down by $M^*\partial\rho/\partial E^*$ for a pollution exporter. But since these terms represent pure transfers of income, they must always sum to zero. Hence, on impact, the aggregate net marginal benefit of polluting (i.e., the aggregate "supply" of pollution) is unaffected by the introduction of terms-of-trade effects. If preferences are identical and homothetic over goods for given levels of global pollution, the ensuing income redistribution will also have no effect on the aggregate demand for pollution. Consequently, with both demand and supply unaffected, so too is world pollution.

This is quite a striking result because it tells us that global pollution levels will be unaffected if nations manipulate pollution policy to gain a terms-of-trade advantage. While this is quite surprising, it does rely heavily on our assumption that global pollution affects all countries equally. If instead we were to assume that creating emissions within a country also leads to additional local effects, then the result would not hold. That is, like Warr's theorem, Proposition 8 relies on the purity of the public bad or good.

Even though terms-of-trade effects have no aggregate effect on pollution, country-specific levels are affected. Using $I_i = L_i + \rho E_i$ in (31), we find

$$(32)\quad E_i = \frac{\rho E^w - L_i\left[\beta(E^w)^\gamma - \bar{\theta}\right]}{\rho\left[1+\beta(E^w)^\gamma - \bar{\theta}\right]}.$$

Using (32) and (17), the difference between Northern and Southern pollution is

$$(33)\quad E^* - E = \frac{L - L^*}{\rho}\left[\frac{(n+n^*-1)\bar{\theta}}{1+(n+n^*-1)\bar{\theta}}\right] > 0.$$

As before, Southern countries produce more pollution than Northern countries in free trade. Moreover, Propositions 2 and 3 continue to hold: the South must always gain from trade, and the North must always lose (see the Appendix). Despite these similarities, it is straightforward to show that the gap between Northern and Southern pollution is smaller in (33) than in (14). Consequently, the North does not cut its pollution with the opening of trade by as much as before, and the South increases its pollution by less. As a result, the North's free-trade income is higher, and the South's is lower, when terms-of-trade effects are not ignored.

We previously noted that South's low income gives it a strategic advantage in the pollution game since it can credibly commit to polluting more with the opening of trade. Our analysis here reveals that being a net importer of pollution services gives the North a strategic advantage in the interaction over terms-of-trade effects: the North's incentive to improve its terms of trade allows it to commit credibly to pollute more, and this makes the South less aggressive in increasing its pollution. In terms of the graph shown in Figure 2, when terms-of-trade effects were ignored, the free-trade equilibrium was at point T; once countries actively manipulate the terms of trade, the new equilibrium point must be to the right of point T.

It is apparent that the relative strengths of these two strategic effects determine the division of the gains from trade. As mentioned earlier, the strategic advantage of a low income always dominates in our formulation, to leave the North worse off in trade. Since this result is likely to be model-specific, it is useful to examine how the strengths of the two opposing effects are determined. Since market size is an obvious determinant of the strength of terms-of-trade effects, let us consider the effects of increasing the number of countries, holding the ratio of Northern to Southern countries (n/n^*) fixed:

PROPOSITION 9: *Let $n^* = kn$, where k is a constant. Let V^{T} and V^{A} denote Northern utility in free trade and autarky. Then $d(V^{\mathrm{T}} - V^{\mathrm{A}})/dn < 0$, and $d(V^{*\mathrm{T}} - V^{*\mathrm{A}})/dn > 0$, when terms-of-trade effects are not ignored by countries when choosing pollution policy; when terms-of-trade effects are ignored, $d(V^{\mathrm{T}} - V^{\mathrm{A}})/dn = d(V^{*\mathrm{T}} - V^{*\mathrm{A}})/dn = 0$.*

(See Appendix A for the proof.) Proposition 9 follows because the North, as a pollution importer, gains a strategic benefit as terms-of-trade effects become stronger. Terms-of-trade effects strengthen as the number of countries shrinks, and consequently, Northern losses from trade decrease. Conversely, Southern gains from trade rise with the number of countries because terms-of-trade motivations diminish in importance, and hence the strategic advantage of low income is enhanced.

A further implication of this analysis is the following.

PROPOSITION 10: *The North prefers a regime that allows pollution policy to be used as an instrument of trade policy, whereas the South prefers that such actions be banned.*

This proposition suggests that GATT Article XX outlawing environmental policy as disguised trade policy works in favor of lower-income nations. A regime that removes the ability of net importers of pollution services to manipulate their terms of trade via pollution policy puts them at a strategic disadvantage relative to net exporters. Such a rule strengthens the South's commitment to pollute more in free trade, and this shifts the ownership of the world's pollution services to the advantage of the South. Again, what is at issue here is the division of the right to pollute across countries, since global pollution is unaffected.

A final interesting change created by terms-of-trade effects is that the normative part of the neutrality result on transfers (Proposition 7) now fails.[23] Consider the effect of a transfer T from a Northern country to a Southern country. It is straightforward to show that, as before, the transfer does not affect the level of world pollution. The welfare effects, however, are different. In the large-country case, we had $dE/dT = 1/\rho$, and hence the North's real income was unaffected by the transfer (since $dI/dT = \rho\, dE/dT - 1 = 0$). In the present case, we have [differentiating (31), and noting that ρ and E^{w} stay constant]:

$$\frac{dE}{dT} = \frac{1}{\rho} - \left[\frac{I}{\rho(n+n^*-1)\bar{\theta}+\theta}\right]\frac{d(\theta-\bar{\theta})}{dT} < \frac{1}{\rho}.$$

Once again, North's pollution response is dampened by its recognition of terms-of-trade effects. Moreover, since $dE < dT/\rho$, the North must lose from a transfer to the South. The intuition for this result is evi-

[23] Many other authors have noted that Warr's result relies on each agent valuing his or her contribution to the public good only so far as it contributes to the aggregate quantity of the public good. Once terms-of-trade effects are allowed, this requirement is no longer met.

dent once we recall that the incentive to exploit terms-of-trade effects increases in the relative difference between countries. Since income is the only fundamental difference between countries, an income-disparity-reducing transfer from the North to the South tends to reduce the motive to use pollution to manipulate the terms of trade. [In terms of equation (31), the absolute value of $\theta - \bar{\theta}$ falls with the transfer.] This reduces the North's incentive to raise its pollution level to compensate for the income-reducing effects of the transfer, and similarly dampens the South's pollution reduction.

In summary, the analysis of strategic trade-policy motives for pollution policy has allowed us to generate several new and interesting results. In particular it has highlighted the strategic advantage gained by a net importer of pollution services and has shown that the key qualitative implications of our model are not sensitive to the recognition of terms-of-trade effects.[24] Moreover, substituting (17) into (31), we see that, as $n + n^*$ gets large, the terms-of-trade effect, $[\theta_i - \bar{\theta}]/E^w$, approaches zero, while the marginal disutility of increased pollution, $\beta(E^w)^{\gamma-1}$, gets large.[25] Thus, as $n + n^*$ gets large, the model of this section converges to our earlier specification.

[24] Moreover, as before, the North would prefer to commit to autarky pollution levels prior to trade, whereas the South would not (Proposition 4). The effects of pollution reform in Section V are only slightly different since each country has internalized its own terms-of-trade effect. If $n = n^* = 1$, no country has an incentive to make a unilateral reduction, since countries are initially at a Nash equilibrium. However, when there is more than one country of each type, the effects of pollution reduction by a coalition of countries are essentially the same: there is no first-order benefit or cost from the terms-of-trade effects of one's own reduction, but as before, each country in the coalition is affected by the terms-of-trade consequences of pollution reduction by all other members of the coalition, and also by the environmental benefits.

[25] The terms-of-trade effect $[\theta_i - \bar{\theta}]/E^w$ approaches zero as n approaches infinity because E^w is increasing in $n + n^*$, and $0 \le \theta_i \le 1$. Using (17) in (31), the marginal disutility of increased pollution is then $\beta[(n+n^*)\bar{\theta}/\beta]^{(\gamma-1)/\gamma}$. This increases with $n + n^*$ since $\gamma \ge 1$.

VIII. Conclusion

This paper has examined the effects of trade and environmental policy on trade flows, pollution levels, and welfare. To focus on income effects, we have eliminated all motives for trade except those arising from income-induced differences in attitudes toward the environment. In addition we have modeled global pollution as a pure public bad where a country's physical size, population density, or weather pattern has no bearing on its exposure to global pollution. A resolution of the debate over the effects of trade on the environment must of course examine the interaction among all of the many motives for trade and must consider how local and global pollution interact with each country's physical environment to generate the true impact of pollution. Nevertheless, while our model is very simple and stylized, we think it raises several interesting issues worthy of future examination.

First, we find that the pre-trade world distribution of income determines how trade will affect the environment. If the world distribution of income is highly skewed, then free trade harms the global environment; but if countries have relatively similar incomes, then free trade has no adverse effect on the environment. Second, we find that, because lower-income countries have a strategic advantage in setting pollution levels in a free-trade regime, they have an incentive to delay international pollution negotiations until after multilateral trade liberalization has been achieved. Third, we find that reductions in pollution by a coalition of countries may be Pareto improving, and that income transfers tied directly to pollution reduction can be welfare-enhancing. Untied transfers, however, may have no effect on global pollution levels, on prices, and most surprisingly, on either country's welfare. Finally, we find that many of these results continue to hold when countries use pollution policy to manipulate their terms of trade. However, terms-of-trade motivations for pollution policy do lessen the strategic advantage of lower-income countries.

Overall, our results underline the importance of endogenizing pollution policy within a general-equilibrium framework. While a complete resolution of the debate over the effects of trade on the environment must await further study and more general models, we have shown that income effects created by income transfers or by trade in goods or pollution permits have important and often surprising effects on pollution, trade flows, and welfare levels. Competitive trade theory is replete with examples of surprising results created by general-equilibrium income effects. Our contribution has been to show that these same income effects may also play a large role in determining how international trade affects the global environment.

Appendix A: Proofs of Propositions

PROOF OF PROPOSITION 3:

Denote free trade variables with T and autarky variables with A. Then using (4), and the fact that E^{w} is not affected by trade, we have

$$\text{(A1)}\quad V^{T}-V^{A}=\int_{0}^{1}b(z)\ln\left[\frac{I^{T}/p^{T}(z)}{I^{A}/p^{A}(z)}\right]dz$$

$$=\ln\left(\frac{L+\rho^{T}E^{T}}{L+\rho^{A}E^{A}}\right)\left(\frac{\rho^{A}}{\rho^{T}}\right)^{\bar{\theta}}.$$

Derivation of (A1) also uses (7) and the fact that $p(z)=c(z)=\kappa(z)\rho^{\alpha(z)}w$, where $\kappa(z)$ is an industry-specific constant. Let $s\equiv\bar{\theta}/(1-\bar{\theta})$. Then from (10) and (16), we have

$$\text{(A2)}\quad \rho^{A}E^{A}=sL$$

$$\rho^{T}E^{w}=sL^{w}.$$

Dividing these expressions and noting that $E^{w}=(n+n^{*})E^{A}$ [from (17) and (12)], we obtain

$$\text{(A3)}\quad \frac{\rho^{A}}{\rho^{T}}=\frac{(n+n^{*})L}{L^{w}}.$$

Inverting (8), evaluating at free trade, and rearranging yields

$$\text{(A4)}\quad E^{T}=\frac{E^{w}}{\beta(E^{w})^{\gamma}}-\frac{L}{\rho^{T}}.$$

Hence using (17), (A2), and (A4), we have

$$\text{(A5)}\quad \rho^{T}E^{T}+L=sL^{w}/(n+n^{*})\bar{\theta}.$$

Now substitute (A5), (A2), and (A3) into (A1), and noting that $\bar{\theta}(1+s)=s$, simplify to obtain

$$\text{(A6)}\quad V^{T}-V^{A}=\ln\left(\frac{L^{w}}{(n+n^{*})L}\right)^{1-\bar{\theta}}<0$$

since $L^{w}=n^{*}L^{*}+nL<(n+n^{*})L$. Similarly, $V^{T*}-V^{A*}>0$ since $(n+n^{*})L^{*}<L^{w}$.

PROOF OF PROPOSITION 5:

Use (6) to eliminate permit prices from (23) and (24), to obtain:

$$\text{(A7)}\quad E^{N}(E^{N}+E^{S})^{\gamma-1}=\frac{n\theta(\bar{z})}{\beta\varphi(\bar{z})}$$

$$E^{S}(E^{N}+E^{S})^{\gamma-1}=\frac{n^{*}\theta^{*}(\bar{z})}{\beta\varphi^{*}(\bar{z})}.$$

Dividing yields $E^{*}=E^{S}/n^{*}>E^{N}/n=E$ in trade, that is,[26]

$$\text{(A8)}\quad \frac{E^{*}}{E}=\frac{\theta^{*}(\bar{z})/\varphi^{*}(\bar{z})}{\theta(\bar{z})/\varphi(\bar{z})}>1.$$

[26] To confirm the inequality, note that because α is increasing in z, we have

$$\theta^{*}(\bar{z})>\int_{\bar{z}}^{1}\alpha(\bar{z})b(z)\,dz=\alpha(\bar{z})\varphi^{*}(\bar{z})$$

$$\theta(\bar{z})<\int_{0}^{\bar{z}}\alpha(\bar{z})b(z)\,dz=\alpha(\bar{z})\varphi(\bar{z}).$$

Using these inequalities in (A8) yields the result.

World pollution is determined by added the expressions in (A7) and solving

$$\text{(A9)} \quad E^{\text{N}} + E^{\text{S}} = \left(\frac{n^*\theta^*(\bar{z})/\varphi^*(\bar{z}) + n\theta(\bar{z})/\varphi(\bar{z})}{\beta} \right)^{1/\gamma}.$$

Subtract (13) from (A9) to obtain

$$E^{\text{N}} + E^{\text{S}} - E^{\text{aw}} = \left(\frac{n^*\theta^*(\bar{z})/\varphi^*(\bar{z}) + n\theta(\bar{z})/\varphi(\bar{z})}{\beta} \right)^{1/\gamma} - \left(\frac{(n+n^*)\bar{\theta}}{\beta} \right)^{1/\gamma} > 0.$$

The result follows since the first term is increasing in z and equals the second term for $\varphi = n/(n+n^*)$; but $\varphi > n/(n+n^*)$ since $I > I^*$ in the non-FPE equilibrium.

PROOF OF PROPOSITION 8:

By constant returns to scale and FPE, the utility function can be written as $V(\rho, I^i, E^{\text{w}})$, using an argument similar to that in footnote 12. By homotheticity, $V^i = \psi(\rho, E^{\text{w}})I^i$, for some function ψ. Using Roy's identity, the aggregate demand for pollution services is

$$\text{(A10)} \quad E^{\text{w}} = -\sum_i (\psi_\rho/\psi)I^i = -I^{\text{w}}(\psi_\rho/\psi) = -(L^{\text{w}} + \rho E^{\text{w}})(\psi_\rho/\psi).$$

The first-order condition for country i's supply of pollution is

$$\text{(A11)} \quad -M^i(\partial\rho/\partial E^i) + \rho + (\psi_E/\psi)I^i = 0$$

where M^i is i's net imports of pollution services. Summing over i (noting that $\Sigma_i M^i = 0$ and that, with FPE, $\partial\rho/\partial E^i = \partial\rho/\partial E^j \; \forall i, j$) yields:

$$\text{(A12)} \quad (n+n^*)\rho + (\psi_E/\psi)(L^{\text{w}} + \rho E^{\text{w}}) = 0.$$

The level of ρ and E^{w} are determined by (A10) and (A12). If terms-of-trade effects are ignored, the term $-M^i(\partial\rho/\partial E^i)$ drops out of (A11), but this has no effect on (A12) or (A10). Hence the same equations (A10) and (A12) determine E^{w} in each regime.

PROOF OF PROPOSITION 9:

From the proof of Proposition 3, we have $V^{\text{T}} - V^{\text{A}} = \ln(H)$, where

$$H \equiv \left(\frac{L + \rho^{\text{T}}E^{\text{T}}}{L + \rho^{\text{A}}E^{\text{A}}} \right) \left(\frac{\rho^{\text{A}}}{\rho^{\text{T}}} \right)^{\bar{\theta}} = \left[\frac{L + s(nL + n^*L^*)}{L + s(n+n^*)L} \right] \left[\frac{(n+n^*)L}{nL + n^*L^*} \right]^{s/(1+s)}$$

using an argument similar to that in the proof of Proposition 3, but using (32) instead of (A4). Hence, letting $n^* = kn$, we now have $d(V^{\text{T}} - V^{\text{A}})/dn = d(\ln H)/dn = k_1(L^* - L) < 0$, where $k_1 > 0$. For the South, the roles of L^* and L are reversed, and we have $d(V^{*\text{T}} - V^{*\text{A}})/dn > 0$. For the case in which terms-of-trade effects are ignored, the result follows from (A6), which is independent of n, once n/n^* is held constant.

PROPOSITION A1: *The South gains from trade, and the North loses from trade, under the assumptions of Section VII (i.e., FPE and that countries take into account terms-of-trade effects when setting pollution quotas).*

PROOF:

For the South, the argument behind Proposition 2 still works. For the North, referring to the proof of Proposition 9, note that $H = 1$ for $L = L^*$, and H is increasing in L^*. Hence $H < 1$ for $L^* < L$, and therefore $V^{\text{T}} - V^{\text{A}} = \ln(H) < 0$ for $L^* < L$.

APPENDIX B: CONDITIONS FOR FACTOR-PRICE EQUALIZATION

To determine the boundary between the FPE and non-FPE cases, start in an equilibrium where factor prices differ, and consider the effects of increasing L^*/L. This increases $B(z)$ for all z, but does not affect $T(z)$. As L^*/L rises, there is a point at which $B(z)$ and $T(z)$ intersect at $z = \hat{z}$. At this point, $\omega = 1$, and factor prices just equalize. Define

$$\delta \equiv \frac{\int_0^{\hat{z}} b(z)[1-\alpha(z)]\,dz}{\int_{\hat{z}}^1 b(z)[1-\alpha(z)]\,dz}.$$

Using (22) and (20), we have $B(\hat{z}) = T(\hat{z})$ when $n^*L^*\delta / nL = 1$, since by definition, $n^*\varphi(\hat{z}) = n\varphi^*(\hat{z})$. Thus we have a non-FPE equilibrium for $nL/n^*L^* > \delta$. By symmetry, if we reverse the roles of North and South, we will also have a non-FPE equilibrium if $n^*L^*/nL > \delta$, or if $nL/n^*L^* < 1/\delta$. For intermediate values of nL/n^*L^*, factor prices are equalized.

PROPOSITION B1: *Factor prices are equalized if and only if* $1/\delta \le nL/n^*L^* \le \delta$. *If* $nL/n^*L^* > \delta$, *then* $\tau > \tau^*$, *and the North specializes in relatively clean goods, while the South specializes in pollution-intensive goods. If* $nL/n^*L^* < 1/\delta$, *then* $\tau < \tau^*$, *and the North specializes in pollution-intensive goods, while the South specializes in clean goods.*

REFERENCES

Bergstrom, Theodore C.; Blume, Lawrence and Varian, Hal R. "On the Private Provision of Public Goods." *Journal of Public Economics*, February 1986, *29*(1), pp. 25–49.

Copeland, Brian R. and Taylor, M. Scott. "North–South Trade and the Environment." *Quarterly Journal of Economics*, August 1994, *109*(3), pp. 755–87.

Dean, Judith M. "Trade and the Environment: A Survey of the Literature," in Patrick Low, ed., *International trade and the environment.* World Bank Discussion Papers, Washington, DC: World Bank, 1992, pp. 15–28.

Dixit, Avinash and Norman, Victor. *Theory of international trade.* Cambridge: Cambridge University Press, 1980.

Dornbusch, Rudiger; Fischer, Stanley and Samuelson, Paul A. "Heckscher-Ohlin Trade Theory with a Continuum of Goods." *Quarterly Journal of Economics*, September 1980, *95*(2), pp. 203–24.

Grossman, Gene M. and Krueger, Alan B. "Environmental Impacts of a North American Free Trade Agreement," in Peter Garber, ed., *The Mexico–U.S. free trade agreement.* Cambridge, MA: MIT Press, 1993, pp. 13–56.

Ludema, Rodney D. and Wooton, Ian. "Cross-Border Externalities and Trade Liberalization: The Strategic Control of Pollution." *Canadian Journal of Economics*, November 1994, *27*(4), pp. 950–66.

Markusen, James R. "International Externalities and Optimal Tax Structures." *Journal of International Economics*, February 1975a, *5*(1), pp. 15–29.

______. "Cooperative Control of International Pollution and Common Property Resources." *Quarterly Journal of Economics*, November 1975b, *89*(3), pp. 618–32.

Rauscher, Michael. "National Environmental Policies and the Effects of Economic Integration." *European Journal of Political Economy*, 1991, *7*(3), pp. 313–29.

Warr, Peter G. "The Private Provision of a Public Good Is Independent of the Distribution of Income." *Economics Letters*, 1983, *13*(2/3), pp. 207–11.

Trade Restrictions and Coordination of Environmental Policy

[24]

ELSEVIER Journal of Public Economics 59 (1996) 17–32

JOURNAL OF PUBLIC ECONOMICS

Should a carbon tax be differentiated across sectors?

Michael Hoel

Department of Economics, University of Oslo, P.O. Box 1095 Blindern, N-0317 Oslo, Norway

Received May 1993; final version received September 1994

Abstract

If some, but not all, countries are cooperating to reduce CO_2 emissions, one could make the following argument: a high carbon tax for carbon intensive tradeable sectors in the cooperating countries will reduce the production of goods from these sectors, and therefore CO_2 emissions, in the cooperating countries. However, this will to a large extent be counteracted by increased production of such goods in the countries that have no climate policy. And since it is only *total* CO_2 emissions from *all* countries that are relevant for the climate, there is no point in a policy that simply relocates CO_2 emissions from the cooperating countries to the countries that have no climate policy. According to this line of reasoning, carbon intensive tradeable sectors should thus face a lower carbon tax than other sectors of the economy.

This paper shows that a carbon tax should *not* be differentiated across sectors in the economy, provided one can use import and export tariffs on all traded goods. It is also shown that such a differentiation of carbon taxes is optimal for the cooperating countries if they are prevented from using tariffs on the traded goods. However, informational or political factors constraining the use of tariffs are likely also to constrain the possibility of differentiating carbon taxes between sectors.

Keywords: Climate policy; Carbon tax; Tariffs

JEL classification: F02; F13; H21; H23; Q28; Q48

1. Introduction

Should a carbon tax be differentiated across sectors? The answer that follows from standard welfare theory is no: all users of carbon should face

SSDI 0047-2727(94)01490-6

the same carbon tax, as the environmental (i.e. climate) externality of using carbon is independent of where it is used. However, the answer is not so obvious in a situation where there is an incomplete international climate agreement. If some, but not all, countries are cooperating to reduce CO_2 emissions, one could make the following argument: a high carbon tax for carbon intensive tradeable sectors in the cooperating countries will reduce the production of goods from these sectors, and therefore CO_2 emissions, in the cooperating countries. However, this will to a large extent be counteracted by increased production of such goods in the countries that have no climate policy. And since it is only *total* CO_2 emissions from *all* countries that are relevant for the climate, there is no point in a policy that simply relocates CO_2 emissions from the cooperating countries to the countries that have no climate policy. According to this line of reasoning, carbon intensive tradeable sectors should thus face a lower carbon tax than other sectors of the economy. Arguments of this type have been made by, for example, the Commission of the European Communities (1991).

Limited participation in a climate agreement seems to be quite likely during the next decade or so. As long as there is no international law to force countries to participate in an international climate agreement, each country may have an incentive to be a free rider, i.e. to stay outside the agreement instead of participating in it. If the country stays outside the agreement, it can enjoy (almost) the same benefits of reduced emissions as if it participates in the agreement, while it does not bear any of the costs of reducing emissions. This free rider incentive remains even if the agreement is such that all countries are better off with the agreement than without: a country may be better off participating in an agreement than it would be without any agreement. But it will usually be even better off if the other countries cooperate, while it itself stays outside the agreement and pursues its self-interest.

The issue of free riding has been studied in more detail by, for example, Barrett (1994a), Bauer (1993), Carraro and Siniscalco (1993) and Hoel (1992). These studies demonstrate that in spite of the free rider incentive, a stable coalition of cooperating countries may exist. The coalition is stable in the sense that it is not in the self-interest of any country to break out of the coalition. One reason why such a stable coalition may exist is that each potential defector knows that if it breaks out of the coalition, the optimal response of the remaining countries will be to increase their emissions, which will hurt the defector more than the costs it saves by defecting. However, most of the studies mentioned above argue that for problems such as the climate problem, the number of countries in a stable coalition is likely to be very small. Moreover, total emissions from all countries will not be much lower than they are in the non-cooperative equilibrium.

The Rio Convention on Climate Change does not give the signatories any explicit quantitative commitments for greenhouse gas emissions. It seems plausible, however, that some form of agreement will be reached during the next decade. At least initially, the free rider problem makes it very unlikely that all countries will participate in such an agreement. Nevertheless, it may be possible to reach an agreement between a larger number of countries than the number corresponding to the stable coalition of the type mentioned above. One reason why countries may commit themselves to cooperating is the fact that decisions of greenhouse gas emissions, and of whether or not to participate in an international agreement, may be frequently revised. These decisions may therefore be treated as a repeated game. It is well known from the literature on game theory that it may be possible to sustain tacit cooperation as a perfect equilibrium of a non-cooperative (infinitely) repeated game; see, for example Barrett (1994a) and Torvanger (1993) for a discussion in the context of international environmental agreements. The fact that decisions about greenhouse gas emissions are frequently repeated may thus solve the free rider problem. However, as repeated games of this type have multiple equilibria, the coordination problems of reaching a Pareto-optimal equilibrium are large. Obviously, these coordination problems are larger the larger the number of countries involved. It therefore seems likely that only a subset of all countries will commit themselves to cooperation. The issue of whether a carbon tax should be differentiated across sectors when a climate agreement is incomplete is therefore a highly relevant issue.

The starting point of the paper is a situation in which a group of countries, e.g. the EU or the OECD countries, have committed themselves to cooperate. These countries are assumed to coordinate their policies in a way that maximizes the sum of welfare for the whole of this group. Henceforth, this group of countries is called the home country. The remaining countries in the world act independently and in pure self-interest, each of them taking total greenhouse gas emissions, as well as international prices of all traded goods, as given. We treat these latter countries as an aggregate group, and call the group the foreign country.

A relatively general model of the economy in the home country is given in Section 2. Outputs and inputs of all goods (including fossil fuels) must belong to a given production possibility set. Welfare depends on the consumption of all goods, as well as total CO_2 emissions. Since the environmental (= climate) effect of CO_2 emissions depends on the sum of emissions form *all* countries, it is *total* CO_2 emissions, and not only emissions from the home country, that affect welfare in the home country. Emissions in the foreign country will generally depend on the international prices of several goods, in particular on the prices of fossil fuels and of energy intensive traded goods. As international prices generally depend on the net import vector of the home country, foreign emissions will also depend on the net import vector of the home country. This relationship must be taken into consideration in the optimization problem of the home country.

The conditions for optimal consumption and production in the home country are derived in Section 2. In Section 3 it is shown how this social optimum may be implemented in a competitive economy. An important conclusion is that the carbon tax should be the same for all domestic users of fossil fuels, i.e. both for consumers and for all sectors using fossil fuels as an input in production. The possible effect of domestic consumption and production of traded goods on foreign emissions should be taken care of via tariffs on the traded goods, i.e. as a tax or subsidy on net imports or net exports.[1]

A somewhat simplified version of the general model is presented in Section 4, where we derive optimal carbon taxes under the assumption that tariffs for some reason or other are constrained to be zero. In this case the carbon tax on fossil fuels used as inputs should in general differ across sectors. A discussion of the main results, as well as key assumptions, is given in Section 5.

2. The optimal consumption and production pattern

The consumption vector of the home country is $\boldsymbol{c} = (c_0, c_1, \ldots, c_n)$, where c_0 is the consumption of fossil fuels (treated as an aggregate). Welfare (W) is equal to the utility of the consumption vector minus the environmental costs of total emissions (from *all* countries), denoted by z:

$$W = U(\boldsymbol{c}) - E(z) . \tag{1}$$

The consumption vector $\boldsymbol{c}$ will typically consist of both tradeable and non-tradeable goods. Among the non-tradeable goods we may include various types of labour, which are measured negatively, so that U is increasing in all its variables.

Total emissions come from domestic consumption of fossil fuels (c_0), domestic use of fossil fuels as inputs into production, denoted v, and foreign emissions, denoted $\boldsymbol{e}$:

$$z = c_0 + v + e . \tag{2}$$

Net imports are given by the vector $\boldsymbol{m}$, so the domestic net output vector is

[1] A similar result was first derived by Markusen (1975) in the context of a somewhat less general model.

$y \equiv c - m$. For all non-traded goods $m_i = 0$ by definition, i.e. $y_i = c_i$ for all non-traded goods. The vector y will typically have both positive and negative elements. For instance, if good ℓ is some type of (non-tradeable) labour, we have $m_\ell = 0$ and $y_\ell = c_\ell < 0$.

In most analyses one is only interested in the net outputs of the goods, and not gross outputs and inputs. In such cases the net output set can be specified by a transformation function of the type $\varphi(y) \leq 0$, where φ is increasing in each y_i [with efficient net outputs satisfying $\varphi(y) = 0$]. In the present case, however welfare depends not only on the net outputs of all goods, but also on the total amount of fossil fuels used as inputs, due to their environmental impact. We therefore want to use a specification of the economy's technology which keeps track of fossil fuel inputs in production, i.e. of v. For each value of v there is a feasible set of net outputs of all goods. This may be specified by a transformation function of the type $F(y, v) \leq 0$, where F is increasing in each y_i. The derivative F_v captures the effect of using more fuel inputs in production. As long as fuel input is lower than the value which is efficient in the absence of environmental externalities, an increase in fuel use will increase the economy's ability to produce output, i.e. $F_v < 0$.[2]. Since efficiency implies $F(y, v) = 0$, and $y = c - m$, we thus have the following equation describing efficient combinations of net outputs of all goods and fossil fuel inputs in production:

$$F(c - m, v) = 0 . \tag{3}$$

Our goods are indexed so that the first $1 + \eta (\leq n)$ goods are traded goods. We denote the international prices of these goods, which may depend on net imports, by $p(m) = (p_0(m), p_1(m), \ldots, p_\eta(m))$. Assuming balanced trade, we thus have

$$p(m)m = \sum_{i \leq \eta} p_i(m)m_i = 0 . \tag{4}$$

Balanced trade is defined as the current account being equal to zero. This means that our framework does not rule out capital movements. Denoting a given physical stock of a capital good by x_k, and the use of this capital good as an input in domestic production by v_k, we have net output given as $y_k = x_k - v_k$. From the equation $y_k = c_k - m_k$ we thus have $v_k + c_k = x_k + m_k$. In other words, the more capital is used domestically as an input in production or directly as consumption, the more capital must be imported.

Finally, foreign carbon emissions are assumed to depend on net imports via the effect of net imports on international prices:

$$e = e(m) = f(p(m)) . \tag{5}$$

[2] More precisely, $F_v < 0$ for $v < v^*(y)$, where $v^*(y)$ is the value of v which solves $\min_v F(y, v)$. Notice also that the relationship between $\varphi(y)$ and $F(y, v)$ is given by $\varphi(y) = \min_v F(y, v)$.

In the simplest case in which $\partial p_i / \partial m_j = 0$ for $i \neq j$, and $\partial p_j / \partial m_j > 0$, the sign of $\partial e / \partial m_j$ is equal to the sign of $\partial f / \partial p_j$. If j is an energy intensive good, we would expect $\partial f / \partial p_j > 0$, i.e. an increased international price for such a good increases foreign production and therefore foreign emissions. The opposite is true for a good which uses little or no fossil fuels: an increased international price will increase foreign production of this good, and thus reduce foreign production of other goods, which are more energy intensive. In this latter case we therefore have $\partial f / \partial p_j < 0$ and $\partial e / \partial m_j < 0$. Capital may be an example of such a good. With a fixed (short-run) global stock of capital, increased import of capital must reduce the foreign use of capital (via the price, i.e. the interest rate). This tends to reduce foreign production of all or at least most goods, with the consequence that foreign emissions decline.

The social optimum is defined as the vector $(\boldsymbol{c}, \boldsymbol{m}, v)$ which maximizes (1) subject to (2)–(5) and $m_j = 0$ for all non-traded goods.

Straightforward calculation yields the following conditions for a social optimum (using the notation $U_i = \partial U / \partial c_i$, $F_i = \partial F / \partial (c_i - m_i)$, etc.)[3]

$$\frac{U_0 - E'}{U_i} = \frac{F_0}{F_i}, \quad i = 1, \ldots, n, \tag{6}$$

$$\frac{-F_v}{F_i} = \frac{E'}{U_i}, \quad i \neq 0, \tag{7}$$

$$\frac{p_0 + T_0}{p_i + T_i} = \frac{(U_0 - E') - E'e_0}{U_i - E'e_i}, \quad i = 1, \ldots, \eta, \tag{8}$$

where

$$T_j = \sum_i m_i \frac{\partial p_i}{\partial m_j}, \quad j = 0, 1, \ldots, \eta. \tag{9}$$

Eqs. (6) are simply the standard requirement 'MRS = MRT' (marginal rate of substitution equal to marginal rate of transformation), with the environmental externality included in the MRS between fossil fuels and any other good.

Given (6), Eq. (7) is one equation. It states that the marginal cost of reducing emissions (in terms of good i) should be equal to the marginal environmental cost of emissions (measured in terms of good i).

The terms T_j defined by (9) measure the terms of trade effect of an increase of the import of good j. In the simplest case in which $\partial p_i / \partial m_j = 0$ for $i \neq j$, and $\partial p_j / \partial m_j > 0$, it is clear from (9) that T_j is positive for imported goods ($m_j > 0$) and negative for exported goods ($m_j < 0$). For the more

[3] In this and the next section, Σ_i is shorthand for $\Sigma_{i=0}^{n}$.

general case in which $\partial p_i / \partial m_j \neq 0$, there is no such simple relationship between the signs of T_j and m_j.

Eqs. (8) show the relationship between the MRS in consumption and international prices. If foreign emissions were independent of all imports, i.e. all $e_i = \partial e / \partial m_i = 0$, it follows from (8) that the MRS between two goods should be equal to the international price ratio after correcting for terms of trade effects. In other words, it is not the ratio between the two *prices* that is relevant, but the ratio between the two marginal import costs. When foreign carbon emissions depend on the size of the home country's imports, the MRS must be adjusted for this externality before it is equated to the ratio between marginal import costs. Instead of simply being the ratio of the marginal utilities of two goods, the adjusted MRS is the ratio between marginal utilities minus the marginal environmental costs of the foreign increase in emissions caused by increased imports of the two goods.

Eqs. (6)–(8) consist of $n + \eta + 1$ independent equations [after inserting the T_j's from (9)]. Together with the four equations (2), (3), (4) and (5), and the $n - \eta$ equations $m_j = 0$ for the non-traded goods, we thus have $2n + 5$ equations determining the $2(n + 1) = 2n + 2$ variables $(\boldsymbol{c}, \boldsymbol{m})$ as well as the three variables v, e and z.[4]

3. Implementation

In this section we shall see how the social optimum described in Section 2 may be achieved in a competitive economy.

Consider a common carbon tax θ for all users, and import tariffs (or export subsidies) t_j for each traded good, given by

$$\theta = E' \frac{p_i + t_i}{U_i}, \quad i \neq 0, \tag{10}$$

$$\begin{aligned} t_j &= T_j + \theta e_j, \quad &&\text{for } j \leq \eta, \\ t_j &= 0, &&\text{for } j > \eta, \end{aligned} \tag{11}$$

where T_j as before is defined by (9). The import tariff/export subsidy t_j on good j changes the price facing both consumers and producers from p_j to $p_j + t_j$. If t_j is positive, it is an import tariff or an export subsidy, depending

[4] Although the optimization of (1) subject to (2)–(5) will (almost always) have a unique solution, there may be several equilibria satisfying Eqs. (2)–(8). However, to simplify our discussion, we assume that the properties of the functions included in our analysis imply that there is a unique equilibrium satisfying these equations.

on whether good j is an imported or an exported good. Similarly for t_j negative: it is an import subsidy (for $m_j > 0$), or an export tax (for $m_j < 0$).

Consider first consumers, who will face the price vector $(p_0 + \theta + t_0, p_1 + t_1, \ldots, p_n + t_n)$.[5] The consumers' optimal consumption vector thus satisfies

$$\frac{U_0}{U_i} = \frac{p_0 + \theta + t_0}{p_i + t_i}, \quad i = 1, \ldots, n .$$

which together with (10) and (11) gives

$$\frac{U_0}{U_i} = \frac{p_0 + t_0}{p_i + t_i} + \frac{E'}{U_i}, \quad i = 1, \ldots, n ,$$

or

$$\frac{U_0 - E'}{U_i} = \frac{p_0 + t_0}{p_i + t_i}, \quad i = 1, \ldots, n . \tag{12}$$

It is thus clear that $(p_i + t_i)/U_i$ is independent of i for $i \neq 0$, so that the choice of i in (10) is arbitrary.

Consider next producers. For given prices and tariffs, they maximize $(p_0 + t_0)x - (p_0 + t_0 + \theta)\nu + \Sigma_{i>0}(p_i + t_i)y_i = \Sigma_i (p_i + t_i)y_i - \theta\nu$ subject to $F(y, v) = 0$. This gives

$$\frac{F_0}{F_i} = \frac{p_0 + t_0}{p_i + t_i}, \quad i = 1, \ldots, n , \tag{13}$$

$$\frac{-F_\nu}{F_i} = \frac{\theta}{p_i + t_i}, \quad i = 1, \ldots, n . \tag{14}$$

Combining (12) and (13) immediately gives the optimality condition (6). Moreover, using (10) we may rewrite (14) as

$$\frac{-F}{F_i} = \frac{E'}{U_i}, \quad i \neq 0 , \tag{15}$$

which is equivalent to the optimality condition (7).

From (10) and (12) we have

$$\frac{(U_0 - E') - E'e_0}{U_i - E'e_i} = \frac{(U_0 - E')\left(1 - \dfrac{\theta e_0}{p_0 + t_0}\right)}{U_i\left(1 - \dfrac{\theta e_i}{p_i + t_i}\right)} . \tag{16}$$

[5] Notice that all prices p_i are endogenously determined in the competitive equilibrium. The prices of the traded goods are given by the functions $p_i(\boldsymbol{m})$, while the prices of the non-traded goods are given by the equilibrium conditions $m_i = c_i - y_i = 0$.

Inserting (11) and (12) into the r.h.s. of this expression yields

$$\frac{U_0 - E' - E'e_0}{U_i - E'e_i} = \frac{p_0 + T_0}{p_i + T_i}, \quad \text{for } i = 1, \ldots, \eta, \tag{17}$$

which is equivalent to our optimality condition (8).

We have thus shown that the competitive equilibrium with the tax/tariff structure defined by (10)–(11) is equivalent to the social optimum derived in Section 2.

The interpretation of (10) is that the carbon tax is equal to the marginal environmental cost of carbon emissions measured in money: E' is the marginal environmental cost measured in utility, while $(p_i + t_i)/U_i$ is dollars per unit utility (for good i). $E'(p_i + t_i)/U_i$ is thus a monetary measure of the marginal environmental cost of carbon emissions.

The tariff t_j consists of two terms. The first term (T_j) measures the terms of trade effect of an increase in imports of good j. The second term (θe_j) measures the value of the change in foreign emissions as a consequences of a marginal increase in imports of good j. Since neither T_j nor e_j are unambiguously signed, the sign of t_j is also indetermined. Typically, the vector $(t_0, t_1, \ldots, t_\eta)$ will have some negative and some positive elements.

An important special case of our general model is the case in which all $\partial p_i/\partial m_j$ are close to zero. This will typically occur if the group of cooperating countries is small compared with the rest of the world. In this case it is clear from (9) that all T_j will be close to zero. Notice also that even if all $\partial p_i/\partial m_j$ are close to zero, the derivatives $e_j = \Sigma_i\, \partial f/\partial p_i \cdot \partial p_i/\partial m_j$ need not be 'small', since some or all $\partial f/\partial p_i$ may be large. Assume, for example, that a doubling of the domestic consumption of a good j, with a corresponding increase in imports, only increases the world market price of this good by, say, 1%. In this case the terms of trade effect is negligible. Although a 1% price change will only change foreign emissions by a small amount in percent of world emissions, this emission change may be large relative to the emissions of the home country. In this case $\partial f/\partial p_j$ will thus be 'large', so that we cannot set $e_j = 0$ for this good even if all T_j's may be approximated by zero.

If all T_j's are (approximately) zero, the sign and magnitude of the optimal import tariff t_j on good j will only depend on the sign and magnitude of e_j for this good, cf. (11). As mentioned previously, we would expect that e_j is positive for an energy-intensive good, e.g. that increased import (or reduced export) of such a good will increase foreign emissions. Such a good should thus have a positive import tariff, i.e. an export subsidy if this good is exported by the home country. For goods that use little or no fossil fuels in their production, on the other hand, we would expect e_j to be negative, thus implying an import subsidy or an export tax. We argued earlier that capital may be an example of a good with $e_j < 0$. If this is the case, the net import of capital should be encouraged by a capital import subsidy/export tax. The interpretation of this is that increased import of capital reduces the foreign use of capital. This tends to reduce foreign production of all or at least most goods, with the consequence that foreign emissions decline.

4. A second-best optimum

In this section we consider a second-best optimum in which tariffs of the type discussed in the previous section are ruled out. A further discussion of such a restriction is given in the concluding section.

In order to simplify the analysis somewhat, we restrict ourselves to the special case mentioned above in which we may set $T_j = 0$ for all j. More precisely, we assume that

(a) all international prices are fixed,
(b) all goods are tradeable, and
(c) there is no domestic production of fossil fuels.

Assumptions (a) and (b) simplify the analysis significantly, as the only consumer price that is endogenous in this case is the consumer price of fossil fuels. Assumption (c) could easily be disposed of, but makes notation somewhat simpler.

Let $\tilde{y} = (y_1, \ldots, y_n)$ denote the vector of net outputs of the n non-fuel goods. Instead of only considering aggregate fuel input use as we did in the previous section, we now distinguish between fuel used in the production of different goods. This vector of fuel use is denoted by $\boldsymbol{v} = (v_1, \ldots, v_n)$. The consumption vector is, as before, given by $\boldsymbol{c} = (c_0, c_1, \ldots, c_n)$. Net imports of the $n + 1$ goods are thus given by[6]

$$m_0 = c_0 + \sum_i v_i ; \qquad m_i = c_i - y_i , \quad \text{for } i > 0 . \tag{18}$$

As before, foreign emissions are given by $e(m_0, m_1, \ldots, m_\eta)$.

The government of the home country wishes to choose carbon tax rates $(\theta_0, \boldsymbol{\theta}) = (\theta_0, \theta_1, \ldots, \theta_n)$ to maximize welfare given by (1). To give a precise formulation of this optimization problem it is useful first to define the indirect utility function V and the profit function π. The price vector facing households is $(p_0 + \theta_0, p_1, \ldots, p_n)$. Since all international prices are assumed fixed, the indirect utility function is defined by

$$V(\theta_0, I) = \max U(c_0, \boldsymbol{c})$$
$$\text{s.t.} (p_0 + \theta_0)c_0 + \sum_i p_i c_i \leq I , \tag{19}$$

[6] In this section, Σ_i is shorthand for $\Sigma_{i=1}^{n}$.

where I is household income. The function V has the following properties:

$$\frac{\partial V}{\partial c_0} = -c_0\lambda\,; \qquad \lambda \equiv \frac{\partial V}{\partial I}\,. \tag{20}$$

The profit function is given by

$$\pi(\boldsymbol{\theta}) = \max \sum_i p_i y_i - \sum_i (p_0 + \theta_i)\nu_i\,, \tag{21}$$

where the vector $(\boldsymbol{y}, \boldsymbol{v})$ is constrained by the set of feasible technologies. The profit function has the properties

$$\frac{\partial \pi}{\partial \theta_i} = -\nu_i\,. \tag{22}$$

Finally, household income consists of profits plus reimbursed tax revenue, i.e.

$$I = \pi(\boldsymbol{\theta}) + \theta_0 c_0(\theta_0, I) + \sum_i \theta_i \nu_i(\theta_i)\,. \tag{23}$$

Using the expressions above, the welfare level W may now be written as

$$W = V(\theta_0, I) - E(c_0(\theta_0, I) + \sum_i \nu_i(\boldsymbol{\theta}) + e(c_0(\theta_0, I) + \sum_i \nu_i(\boldsymbol{\theta}), c_1(\theta_0, I) - y_1(\boldsymbol{\theta}), \ldots, c_n(\theta_0, I) - y_n(\boldsymbol{\theta})))\,. \tag{24}$$

In the Appendix it is shown that the emission taxes that maximize W are given by

$$\theta_0 = \frac{E'}{\mu} \cdot \left[1 + e_0 + \frac{\sum_i e_i \left(\frac{\partial c_i}{\partial \theta_0}\right)_{u=\bar{u}}}{\left(\frac{\partial c_0}{\partial \theta_0}\right)_{u=\bar{u}}} \right] \tag{25}$$

and

$$\theta_j = \alpha_j \cdot \frac{E'}{\mu} \cdot \left[1 + e_0 + \frac{\sum_i e_i \left(-\frac{\partial y_i}{\partial \theta_j}\right)}{\sum_i \frac{\partial \nu_i}{\partial \theta_j}} \right], \tag{26}$$

where

$$\alpha_j = \frac{\theta_j \sum_i \frac{\partial \nu_i}{\partial \theta_j}}{\sum_i \theta_i \frac{\partial \nu_i}{\partial \theta_j}} . \tag{27}$$

Consider first the term E'/μ. The term E' is the marginal environmental cost in terms of utility, and μ is the marginal welfare increase (i.e. increase in $U - E$) from a hypothetical transfer of money to the households. The term E'/μ thus measures the marginal cost of CO_2 emissions in money terms.

The term e_0 measures the change in foreign emissions per unit increase in domestic emissions, so that $1 + e_0$ gives the direct effect on global emissions per unit increase of domestic fossil fuel use. The terms $(E'/\mu)(1 + e_0)$ in (25) and (26) thus give the marginal environmental cost of the direct effect of increasing domestic fuel use. In addition to this direct effect, global emissions may be affected indirectly via changes in net imports of non-fuel goods. These indirect effects are captured in the last terms of (25) and (26).

Consider the last term of (25). The derivatives in this term are compensated demand derivatives. The denominator is the compensated direct price derivative of the demand for fossil fuels, and is thus negative. The numerator measures the effect of a compensated increase in the consumer price of fossil on foreign emissions, via the effects such a price increase has on the consumption of all other goods. This numerator can clearly not be unambiguously signed.

Consider next the last terms of (26). The denominator in this term for sector j measures the change in total fuel input in all sectors as a consequence of a rise in the price of fuel in sector j. Although it seems most likely that these denominators are negative, the opposite cannot be ruled out. The numerator of the last term of (26) for sector j is the effect on foreign emissions, via the effects on net outputs of all goods, of a rise in the price of fuel in sector j. This numerator cannot be unambiguously signed. Moreover, it is clear that the last term of (26) will generally differ between sectors, implying different optimal carbon taxes for different sectors. (Notice that *if* the last term in the square brackets of (26) was the same for all j, then all $\alpha_j = 1$, so that the optimal carbon tax would be equal for all sectors.)

It follows from the discussion above that even with the simplifications we have made, the optimal carbon taxes will in general differ across sectors. Moreover, unlike the optimal tariffs in the first-best optimum in the absence of terms of trade effects, there is no simple relationship between the sign and size of e_j and the optimal carbon tax for sector j.

Consider finally the case in which not only tariffs are ruled out, but in which one also for some reason must have the same carbon tax on all industries using fossil fuels as inputs. Assume, however, that the carbon tax may be differentiated between households and producers. In this case the government of the home country wishes to choose the two carbon tax rates (θ_0, θ) to maximize welfare given by (1). Compared with expression (24) above for total welfare, the only change is that a single carbon tax θ takes the place of the carbon tax vector $\boldsymbol{\theta}$. In the appendix it is shown that (25) remains valid, while the only change in (26) is that the subscript j must be omitted, and that α_j is replaced by 1. For this case it is thus clear that the optimal carbon tax facing households will usually differ from the carbon tax rate facing industry. However, the difference between the two tax rates is not unambiguously signed.

5. Discussion

The analysis above shows that as long as tariffs (i.e. taxes or subsidies on imports and exports) may be optimally chosen, the carbon tax should be equal for all users of fossil fuels. If, however, tariffs are ruled out, it is optimal for the cooperating countries to differentiate the carbon tax across sectors. Even for the simple model of Section 4, the determination of optimal carbon taxes was quite complex. There is no simple relationship between, for example, fossil fuel intensity or the effect on foreign emissions on the one hand and the optimal carbon tax on the other hand.

It is difficult to find good reasons for ruling out the use of tariffs. One argument could be that quite a substantial amount of information is needed to calculate optimal tariffs. However, it is clear from Section 4 that the information requirement needed for calculating optimal carbon taxes with zero tariffs is considerable larger than the information required for calculating optimal tariffs. Limited information about characteristics of the economy is thus not a reason to differentiate carbon taxes across sectors instead of supplementing a uniform carbon tax with tariffs.

Trade policy arguments could be made against import and export taxes/subsidies. However, similar arguments could also be made against differentiating taxes (in this case carbon taxes) across sectors. Moreover, the non-cooperating countries are not in a very strong position to argue against tariffs that might hurt them. The justification for the tariffs is after all an attempt to avoid excessive carbon emissions from the non-cooperating countries. Any non-cooperating country which claims to be adversely affected by the tariffs can avoid the tariffs by participating in the climate agreement instead of being a free rider. Provided a free riding country becomes no worse off it if joins the cooperating group, then it would be without *any* agreement, there seems little reason to have much sympathy for complaints from this country about being adversely affected by the tariffs.

Tariffs are generally not permitted according to trade agreements such as GATT, NAFTA, etc. It is not clear whether exceptions from this general rule may be made when there are good environmental reasons for imposing such tariffs. The use of trade restrictions is explicitly permitted under the Montreal Protocol on Substances that Deplete the Ozone Layer, although the GATT Secretariat has voiced its opposition to such use of trade restrictions; see Barrett (1994c) for a further discussion. Different tax treatment of different industries is also restricted under most trade agreements. A differentiated carbon tax may thus be equally difficult to impose as tariffs. As shown in Section 4, an optimal policy may therefore consist of one carbon tax rate for direct consumption of fossil fuels, and one rate for the use of fossil fuels as imputs in production. As long as this latter rate is uniform across industries, the differentiation between households and industries will probably not violate any trade agreements.

One limitation of our analysis is that the cooperating coalition was exogenously given. However, the use of tariffs or a differentiated carbon tax might affect which countries choose to join a coalition. This has been studied by Barrett (1994b), who shows that trade restrictions may help deter free riding, and thus make the coalition of cooperating countries larger. The free rider deterrence may be different for a uniform carbon tax combined with tariffs, on the one hand, and a differentiated carbon tax, on the other hand. A careful analysis of this issue is, however, beyond the scope of the present paper.

The analysis has focused on the climate problem. However, the qualitative results are relevant also for other international environmental problems. For several such problems the policies of a group of countries that reduce their emissions will also affect the international prices of traded goods. This may in turn affect production and consumption patterns, and thereby emissions, in other countries. Whenever there are international spillovers of harmful emissions, this should be taken into consideration by the countries that have an explicit environmental policy. Optimal environmental policies for such problems will consist of a combination of emission taxes and tariffs (positive or negative) on imports and exports for those traded goods whose prices may affect harmful emissions from countries which have no explicit environmental policy.

Acknowledgements

Financial support from the Research Council of Norway, the Nordic Council of Ministers, and the European Communities' Environment programme is gratefully acknowledged. I am grateful to Elin Halvorsen for useful assistance, and to Rolf Golombek for useful discussions of the topic. Two anonymous referees have given helpful comments on an earlier version of the paper.

Appendix: Derivation of Eqs. (25) and (26)

The lagrangian corresponding to the maximization of W [given by (24)] subject to (23) is[7]

$$\begin{aligned} L = {} & V(\theta_0, I) - E(c_0(\theta_0, I) + \sum_i \nu_i(\boldsymbol{\theta}) \\ & + e(c_0(\theta_0, I) + \sum_i \nu_i(\boldsymbol{\theta}), c_1(\theta_0, I) - y_1(\boldsymbol{\theta}), \ldots, c_n(\theta_0, I) - y_n(\boldsymbol{\theta}))) \\ & + \mu[\pi(\boldsymbol{\theta}) + \theta_0 c_0(\theta_0, I) + \sum_i \theta_i \nu_i(\theta_i) - I] . \end{aligned} \tag{28}$$

The first-order conditions for the maximization problem are

$$\frac{\partial L}{\partial I} = \lambda - E' \cdot \left[(1 + e_0) \frac{\partial c_0}{\partial I} + \sum_{i>0} e_i \frac{\partial c_i}{\partial I} \right] + \mu \left[\theta_0 \frac{\partial c_0}{\partial I} - 1 \right] = 0 , \tag{29}$$

$$\frac{\partial L}{\partial \theta_0} = -\lambda c_0 - E' \cdot \left[(1 + e_0) \frac{\partial c_0}{\partial \theta_0} + \sum_{i>0} e_i \frac{\partial c_i}{\partial \theta_0} \right] + \mu \left[c_0 + \theta_0 \frac{\partial c_0}{\partial \theta_0} \right] = 0 , \tag{30}$$

$$\frac{\partial L}{\partial \theta_j} = -E' \cdot \left[(1 + e_0) \sum_i \frac{\partial \nu_i}{\partial \theta_j} - \sum_i e_i \frac{\partial y_i}{\partial \theta_j} \right] + \mu \sum_i \theta_i \frac{\partial \nu_i}{\partial \theta_j} = 0 . \tag{31}$$

Multiplying (29) by c_0 and adding it to (30) yields

$$\begin{aligned} & -E' \cdot \left[(1 + e_0) \left(\frac{\partial c_0}{\partial \theta_0} + c_0 \frac{\partial c_0}{\partial I} \right) + \sum_{i>0} e_i \left(\frac{\partial c_i}{\partial \theta_0} + c_0 \frac{\partial c_i}{\partial I} \right) \right] \\ & + \mu \theta_0 \left[\frac{\partial c_0}{\partial \theta_0} + c_0 \frac{\partial c_i}{\partial I} \right] = 0 . \end{aligned} \tag{32}$$

The compensated demand derivatives are given by (for all i)

$$\left(\frac{\partial c_i}{\partial \theta_0} \right)_{u = \bar{u}} = \frac{\partial c_i}{\partial \theta_0} + c_0 \frac{\partial c_i}{\partial I} . \tag{33}$$

[7] As in Section 4, Σ_i is shorthand for $\Sigma_{i=1}^{n}$. Nevertheless, where it would be meaningful to take the sum over all $i = 0, 1, \ldots, n$, we have explicitly written which i's are included in the summation operator.

Dividing (32) through by the compensated demand derivatives for fuels immediately gives us Eq. (25).

It follows from the definition of α_j [given by (27)] that Eq. (31) may be rewritten as

$$-E' \cdot \left[(1 + e_0) \sum_i \frac{\partial \nu_i}{\partial \theta_j} - \sum_i e_i \frac{\partial y_i}{\partial \theta_j} \right] + \mu \frac{\theta_j}{\alpha_j} \sum_i \frac{\partial \nu_i}{\partial \theta_j} = 0 . \tag{34}$$

Dividing (34) through by $\Sigma_i(\partial v_i / \partial \theta_i)$ immediately gives us Eq. (26).

If we add the restriction $\theta_j = \theta$ for all $j \neq 0$, (31) is replaced by

$$\frac{\partial L}{\partial \theta} = -E' \cdot \left[(1 + e_0) \sum_i \frac{\partial \nu_i}{\partial \theta} - \sum_i e_i \frac{\partial y_i}{\partial \theta} \right] + \mu \theta \sum_i \frac{\partial \nu_i}{\partial \theta} = 0 . \tag{35}$$

Dividing (35) through by $\Sigma_i(\partial v_i / \partial \theta)$ immediately gives us Eq. (26) without the subscript j and with α_j replaced by 1.

References

Barrett, S., 1994a, Self-enforcing international environmental agreements, Oxford Economic Papers 46 (October, Supplementary Issue) 878–894.

Barrett, S., 1994b, Trade restrictions in international environmental agreements, mimeo, London Business School and Centre for Social and Economic Research on the Global Environment.

Barrett, S., 1994c, Climate change policy and international trade, Mimeo, London Business School and Centre for Social and Economic Research on the Global Environment.

Bauer, A., 1993, International cooperation over environmental goods, Mimeo, University of Munich.

Carraro, C. and D. Siniscalco, 1993, Strategies for the international protection of the environment, Journal of Public Economics 52, 309–328.

Commission of the European Communities, 1991, A community strategy to limit carbon dioxide emissions and improve energy efficiency, Communication from the Commission to the Council, SEC (91) 1744 final, Brussels, 14 October 1991.

Hoel, M., 1992, International environment conventions: The case of uniform reductions of emissions, Environmental and Resource Economics 2, 141–159.

Markusen, J.R., 1975, International externalities and optimal tax structures, Journal of International Economics 5, 15–29.

Torvanger, A., 1993, Efficient contracts in a game of nations pursuing greenhouse gas emissions abatement, CICERO Working Paper 93:3, Center for Climate and Energy Research, Oslo.

[25]

ELSEVIER

Resource and Energy Economics 19 (1997) 345–361

RESOURCE and ENERGY ECONOMICS

The strategy of trade sanctions in international environmental agreements

Scott Barrett*

London Business School, Sussex Place, Regent's Park, London NW1 4SA, UK

Received 1 March 1996; revised 1 January 1997

Abstract

This paper analyzes the links between policies aimed at supplying a global public good and international trade in segmented markets. I find that the credible threat to impose trade sanctions may be capable of sustaining full cooperation in the supply of the public good, provided the sanctions are accompanied by a minimum participation clause which serves to coordinate government behavior. In equilibrium, trade is not restricted. But if the threat to impose sanctions were not allowed by the rules of the game, supply of the public good would be Pareto-inefficient. © 1997 Elsevier Science B.V.

Keywords: Trade sanctions; International environmental agreements; Minimum participation clause

1. Introduction

If countries interact only in providing a global public good, such as protection of the ozone layer, then cooperation in the supply of this good can only be sustained by a self-enforcing international environmental agreement (IEA) if the threat of failing to provide the good in the event that others do

* Corresponding author: Tel.: +44 171 2625050 x3398; fax +44 171 7247875; e-mail sbarrett@lbs.lon.ac.uk

PII S0928-7655(97)00016-X

not do so is credible. But since such punishments hurt signatories to an IEA as well as non-signatories, substantial punishments are unlikely to be credible, and free-riding is thus unlikely to be deterred.[1]

When countries interact in other spheres, however, the strategy space for punishing non-cooperation can be expanded. Indeed, supply of a global public good will typically be automatically linked to international trade. If signatories to an IEA reduce their pollution emissions, for example, comparative advantage in the pollution-intensive industries is likely to shift to non-signatories, with the consequence that global emissions fall by less than the reduction undertaken by signatories—a phenomenon known as 'leakage.' The cooperating countries can correct for leakage by imposing the appropriate border tax adjustment.[2] But signatories to an IEA may wish to impose harsher trade measures, for if trade restrictions harm non-signatories to an IEA more than signatories, then they may prove more effective at deterring free-riding than the threat to increase emissions.

The Montreal Protocol on Substances that Deplete the Ozone Layer is a famous example of an IEA which bans trade between signatories and non-signatories (in the substances controlled by the treaty, hereafter referred to as CFCs, and in the products containing and made using CFCs). According to the chief US negotiator at the Montreal Protocol talks (Benedick, 1991), the sanctions were expected 'to stimulate as many nations as possible to participate in the protocol, by preventing non-participating countries from enjoying competitive advantages and by discouraging the movement of CFC production facilities to such countries.' But the sanctions did more than just plug the trade leak. They were, in Benedick's words, 'critical, since they constituted the only enforcement mechanism in the protocol.' The trade sanctions in the Montreal Protocol were thus intended to deter free-riding. Though a counterfactual is lacking, and so the effectiveness of the trade sanctions cannot be tested empirically, it is remarkable that the agreement has not suffered from any significant free-riding, despite demanding very substantial abatement by signatories.

This paper is a preliminary inquiry into the implications of sustaining international cooperation in the supply of a global public good when countries are also engaged in trade. The paper is 'preliminary' in that it develops a highly stylized model, one which links a model of international environmental cooperation, constructed in the manner of Barrett (1992, 1994a); Carraro and Siniscalco (1993, 1994); and Hoel (1992), with a model of international trade,

[1] In Barrett (1994a), I show that when supply of the public good is isolated from all other affairs, a self-enforcing IEA will typically be unable to sustain full cooperation. This is true whether the game is modelled as a stage game—the approach followed in this paper—or as a repeated game in which the equilibrium must be renegotiation-proof.

[2] For analyses of border tax adjustments in the context of transboundary pollution, see Markusen (1975) and Hoel (1996).

fashioned after the work by Brander (1981); and Brander and Krugman (1983)[3]. Though one might explore linkages between transboundary pollution and trade generally, I consider only trade in goods that are directly linked to the environmental problem (e.g., trade in CFCs). This would seem natural, given that trade restrictions may be required in any event to correct for leakage and that the trade sanctions in the Montreal Protocol are limited to the CFC and related industries. The (partial equilibrium) model of intra-industry trade used here assumes that imperfectly competitive firms produce an identical product but segment their markets.[4] This also seems appropriate, given that the Montreal Protocol restricts trade in bulk CFCs (a homogenous good) manufactured by an oligopolistic industry.[5] However, I must emphasize that other approaches might be taken and that the results obtained here are unlikely to hold generally, especially as I employ very simple functional relationships.

Though I cannot claim generality, the analysis presented here does offer some striking insights into the strategy of employing trade sanctions in IEAs: I find that the credible threat of imposing trade sanctions may be sufficient to deter free-riding completely; that sanctions must be accompanied by a minimum participation clause if they are to be incentive compatible; and that there may exist circumstances in which some countries would want to impose sanctions while others would oppose their use.

Section 2 sets out the basic model and solves for the non-cooperative and full cooperative outcomes. Section 3 solves for the self-enforcing IEA with and without trade sanctions and analyzes these solutions. Section 4 concludes with a brief discussion of the policy implications.

2. Environmental policy and trade in segmented markets

This section sets up the basic model and analyzes two different stage games. In both, governments move first by choosing the abatement levels which their firms must meet, while firms move last by simultaneously choosing their segmented outputs. The difference between the games is that governments behave non-cooperatively in the first but cooperate fully in the

[3] Cesar and de Zeeuw (1994) and Carraro and Siniscalco (1994) also examine linkages between international environmental protection and some other interaction, but neither of these papers consider trade linkages.

[4] An alternative approach would have been to assume that countries specialize in producing differentiated products, and that trade arises from the desire by consumers for variety. See Helpman and Krugman (1985).

[5] The Montreal Protocol also restricts trade in products containing CFCs (like refrigerators), and these are plainly not bulk items. The treaty includes provisions for restricting trade in products made using CFCs (including certain computer technologies), but these have never been implemented.

second. The solutions to these games provide useful benchmarks but they are also needed to solve the richer games analyzed in Section 3.

3.1. Firm choices

There are N symmetric countries and N symmetric firms. A single firm resides in each of the N countries and firm location is fixed. Each firm produces a joint product: a homogeneous traded good and transboundary pollution. Inverse demand in country i is $p(x^i) = 1 - x^i$, where x^i is consumption of the good in country i. Firm j's costs are $C(x_j, q_j) = \sigma q_j x_j$, where x_j is total output by firm j and $q_j \in [0,1]$ is the abatement standard for firm j. Firm j takes q_j as given and so takes unit costs as given and constant. Transport costs are zero. Emissions by firm j are $x_j(1 - q_j)$. If abatement is maximal, emissions are thus zero. If no abatement is undertaken, emissions are equal to output.[6]

Firms choose their outputs for each market simultaneously. Specifically, firm j takes its own abatement standard and the segmented outputs of other firms as given and chooses a quantity to produce and ship to market i, x_j^i, so as to maximize

$$\pi_j = \sum_{i=1}^{N} \left(1 - x^i - \sigma q_j\right) x_j^i \tag{1}$$

The first order conditions (for an interior solution) require

$$1 - x^i - \sigma q_j - x_j^i = 0 \qquad \forall i, j \tag{2}$$

It is easy to confirm that Eqs. 2 are also sufficient and that the solution is unique. In this paper I only consider cases in which firms produce positive quantities in equilibrium. Conditions in Eqs. 2 can be rewritten as

$$N(1 - \sigma q_j) - 2x_j - x_{-j} = 0 \tag{3a}$$

$$N(N-1)\left(1 - \sigma \overline{q_{-j}}\right) - N x_{-j} - (N-1)x_j = 0 \tag{3b}$$

$\forall j$, where $x_j = \sum_{i=1}^{N} x_j^i$, $x_{-j} = \sum_{l=1, l \neq j}^{N} x_l$, and $\overline{q_{-j}} = \sum_{l=1, l \neq j}^{N} q_l/(N-1)$. x_{-j} is thus rest-of-the-world output and $\overline{q_{-j}}$ is the average abatement level for countries other than j.

3.2. The equilibrium in unilateral policies

Government j's net benefits are the sum of firm j's profits and the consumer surplus realized by the citizens of j, less the environmental damage

[6] It is only necessary to assume that emissions are proportional to output, for one can always normalize such that emissions are equal to output when abatement is nil.

suffered by country j. Pollution is assumed to be a pure public bad and aggregate emissions are given by $\Sigma_{i=1}^{N} x_i(1-q_i)$. Marginal environmental damage for each country is a constant, ω. Given the demand specification, consumer surplus for country j is $(x^j)^2/2$. If governments do not cooperate, then in Stage 1 government j will take the abatement standards of other countries as given and choose $q_j \in [0,1]$ to maximize

$$\Pi_j = \pi_j + (x^j)^2/2 - \omega\left[\sum_{i=1}^{N} x_i(1-q_i)\right] \tag{4}$$

subject to Eqs. 3a and 3b, where π_j is given by Eq. 1. The Kuhn–Tucker conditions require

$$\frac{\partial \Pi_j}{\partial q_j} - \lambda_j \leq 0, \left(\frac{\partial \Pi_j}{\partial q_j} - \lambda_j\right) q_j = 0, \quad q_j \geq 0 \tag{5a}$$

$$q_j \leq 1, \qquad \lambda_j(1-q_j) = 0, \lambda_j \geq 0, \tag{5b}$$

where λ_j is a multiplier and

$$\frac{\partial \Pi_j}{\partial q_j} = (\omega - \sigma)x_j - \frac{\sigma x_j(N-1)}{(N+1)} - \frac{\sigma x^j}{(N+1)} + \frac{\omega\sigma N\left[(1-q_j)N - \left(1-\overline{q_{-j}}\right)(N-1)\right]}{(N+1)} \tag{6}$$

Since the constraints are linear, we know that the constraint qualification is satisfied. Sufficiency, however, cannot be guaranteed and so care must be taken to ensure that the necessary conditions do indeed identify the maximum.

The first term in Eq. 6 is the direct effect of a change j's abatement standard on country j's net benefits. It says that if country j's marginal benefit of abatement, ω, exceeds (is less than) its marginal cost of abatement, σ, then j should impose the maximal (minimal) abatement standard.

The last three terms in Eq. 6 arise because each government anticipates how its choice of an abatement standard affects firm output decisions in Stage 2. The second term in Eq. 6 indicates that a weaker abatement standard shifts industry profits toward the home firm, while the third term shows that a weaker standard also increases domestic consumer surplus. Strategic behavior by governments toward firms thus commends the setting of a weaker abatement standard under imperfect competition of the type modelled here[7]. In other words, taking this strategic effect into account, in some cases country j will choose $q_j = 0$ even when $\omega > \sigma$.

[7] See also Barrett (1994b); Kennedy (1994). For surveys of this literature, see Ulph (1994); and Xing and Kolstad (1996).

As the problem is symmetric, q_j and $\bar{q}_{-j}$ will be equal in equilibrium and the last term in Eq. 6 will thus be non-negative. A tighter abatement standard reduces industry output and hence reduces global emissions by more than the direct effect captured by the first term in Eq. 6, and so the last term in Eq. 6 commends the setting of a stronger abatement standard. Notice, however, that this term drops out if an emission standard can be chosen directly by governments.

Proposition 1. *Denote the equilibrium in unilateral policies* q^u. *Then:*

$$q^u = \begin{cases} 0 \text{ if } \omega \leq \dfrac{\sigma(2N+1)}{(1+\sigma)(N+1)} \\[2ex] \dfrac{[\omega(N+1)-\sigma(2N+1)]+\sigma\omega(N+1)}{\sigma[\omega(N+1)-\sigma(2N+1)]+\sigma\omega(N+1)} \text{ if } \omega \in \left[\dfrac{\sigma(2N+1)}{(1+\sigma)(N+1)}, \dfrac{\sigma(2N+1)}{(N+1)}\right] \\[2ex] 1 \text{ if } \omega \geq \dfrac{\sigma(2N+1)}{(N+1)} \end{cases} \tag{7}$$

for $\omega/\sigma > (2N^3+1)/2N^2(N+1)$; *and* $q^u = 0$ *otherwise.*

Proof: See Appendix.

If our concern is with the supply of a global public good, N will be large. Proposition 1 tells us that, in this case, every country will undertake zero abatement in equilibrium for $\omega < \sigma$. This inequality, however, is only a sufficient condition. $q^u = 0$ is also an equilibrium if $\omega > \sigma$ and $\omega \leq 2\sigma/(1+\sigma)$, while $q^u = 1$ is an equilibrium only for $\omega \geq 2\sigma$. If N is sufficiently large, the incentive to weaken abatement standards in order to shift industry profits home dominates all other effects.[8]

3.3. The full cooperative outcome

If the governments cooperate fully in Stage 1, government j will choose $q_j \in [0, 1]$ to maximize $\Pi^c = \Sigma_{i=1}^N \Pi_i$, while recognizing that firm behavior is given by Eqs. 3a and 3b. The Kuhn–Tucker conditions will be analogous to

[8] As N becomes large, the effect on consumer surplus vanishes. The last term in Eq. 6 commends a strong abatement standard even for N large but the profit-shifting motive dominates. It may seem that the profit-shifting motive should vanish as N increases. However, though an increase in N increases competition, it also increases the size of the market which one's own firm can serve.

Eqs. 5a and 5b and so need not be written down. Differentiation yields:

$$\frac{\partial \Pi^c}{\partial q_j} = N\left[(N\omega - \sigma)x + \frac{\sigma x(N-1)}{(N+1)} - \frac{\sigma xN}{(N+1)} + \frac{\omega\sigma(1-q)N^2}{(N+1)}\right] \tag{8}$$

where x is the output of each firm and q is the abatement standard imposed by each government. The first term in Eq. 8 is the direct effect of the choice of abatement standard. Under full cooperation this effect commends maximal (minimal) abatement if $\omega N > \sigma$ ($\omega N < \sigma$). The latter three terms reflect the strategic effect of abatement choice. These terms are similar to the ones appearing in Eq. 6 with the exception of the first term which is positive in Eq. 8. In contrast to the equilibrium in unilateral policies, full cooperation demands that countries strengthen their abatement standards to increase aggregate industry profits.

Proposition 2. *Denote the full cooperative abatement level* q^c. *Then:*

$$q^c \begin{cases} = 0 \text{ if } \omega N \le \dfrac{\sigma(N+2)}{(1+\sigma)(N+1)} \\ = \dfrac{[\omega N(N+1) - \sigma(N+2)] + \sigma\omega N(N+1)}{\sigma[\omega N(N+1) - \sigma(N+2)] + \sigma\omega N(N+1)} \textit{ if } \\ \qquad \omega N \in \left[\dfrac{\sigma(N+2)}{(1+\sigma)(N+1)}, \dfrac{\sigma(N+2)}{(N+1)}\right] \\ = 1 \text{ if } \omega N \ge \dfrac{\sigma(N+2)}{(N+1)} \end{cases} \tag{9}$$

for $\omega N/\sigma > (N+2)/2(N+1)$; *and* $q^c = 0$ *otherwise.*

Proof: See Appendix.

Consider again the case where N is large. Full cooperation will then require that q^c be maximal for $\omega N > \sigma$. However, minimal abatement is group rational only for $\omega N \le \sigma/2$ or $\omega N > \sigma/2$ and $\omega N \le \sigma/(1+\sigma)$. Under full cooperation there is thus an incentive for governments collectively to impose strong abatement standards.

4. The self-enforcing IEA with trade in segmented markets

This section modifies the rules of the game to allow for partial cooperation in an IEA, with and without trade sanctions.

4.1. The self-enforcing IEA under free trade

The game is modelled as follows: in Stage 1, countries choose simultaneously whether or not to be signatories to an IEA; in Stages 2 and 3, respectively, signatories and non-signatories choose their abatement standards; and in the final stage of the game, firms choose their segmented outputs. Since the last stage of the game was solved in Section 2.1, we need only solve here for the first three stages of the game.

Let k denote the number of signatories ($N-k$ is thus the number of non-signatories). Since the solution for non-signatories will be symmetric, and since symmetric signatories will choose a common abatement level, we can rewrite Eqs. 2 as

$$N-(N-k+1)x_n - kx_s - \sigma q_n N = 0 \tag{10a}$$

$$N-(N-k)x_n - (k+1)x_s - \sigma q_s N = 0 \tag{10b}$$

where x_s and x_n are the output levels of firms located in signatory and non-signatory countries and q_s and q_n are the abatement levels chosen by signatories and non-signatories, respectively.

Non-signatories behave non-cooperatively and so they each solve the problem formulated in Section 2.2. In general, non-signatory behavior will be influenced by choice of q_s. Hence, given the sequential nature of the game, signatories may choose q_s so as to alter the behavior of non-signatories to their own advantage. The analytical complications of such strategic behavior can be avoided, however, if we restrict the parameter space such that $q_n = 0$ is a dominant strategy.

Lemma. If

$$\frac{\omega}{\sigma} \leq \frac{(2N^2-1)}{2N(N+1)} \tag{11}$$

then $q_n = 0$ is a dominant strategy.

Proof. See Appendix.

For global environmental problems (that is, for N 'large'), Eq. 11 will hold if the marginal cost of abatement for each country is greater than the associated marginal benefit.

Signatories are assumed to choose q_s to maximize their collective payoff, $\Pi^s = k\Pi_s$, where Π_s is the payoff of a representative signatory (that is, q_s is assumed to be group rational). If Eq. 11 is satisfied, so that $q_n = 0$ is a dominant strategy, then the net marginal benefit of abatement for signatories will be

$$\frac{\partial \Pi_s}{\partial q_s} = (k\omega - \sigma)x_s + \frac{\sigma x_s(2k-N-1)}{(N+1)} - \frac{\sigma k x_s}{(N+1)} + \frac{\omega\sigma kN[1-q_s(N-k+1)]}{(N+1)} \tag{12}$$

It is easy to confirm that Eq. 12 reduces to Eq. 8 for $k = N$. The direct effect of choosing q_s requires that q_s be maximal provided $\omega k > \sigma$ and minimal for $\omega k < \sigma$. When k is 'small' ('large'), the strategic effect of the choice of an abatement standard on firm profits will commend the setting of 'weak' ('strong') standards by signatories. The other two strategic effects are as described previously.

Proposition 3. *Suppose Eq. 11 holds. Then, in equilibrium*, $q_n = 0$ *and*

$$q_s = \begin{cases} 0 & \text{if } \dfrac{\omega k}{\sigma} \le f(k) = \dfrac{(2N+2-k)}{(N+1)(\sigma+1)} \\[2ex] \dfrac{N[\omega k(N+1)(\sigma+1) - \sigma(2N+2-k)]}{\sigma\{2\omega kN(N+1)(N-k+1) - \sigma[k^2+2N(N-k+1)^2]\}} & \text{if } \dfrac{\omega k}{\sigma} \in [f(k), g(k)] \\[2ex] 1 & \text{if } \dfrac{\omega k}{\sigma} \ge g(k) = \left| \dfrac{N(2N+2-k) - \sigma[k^2+2N(N-k+1)^2]}{N(N+1)[1-\sigma(2N-2k+1)]} \right| \end{cases} \tag{13}$$

for $\omega k/\sigma > [k^2 + 2N(N-k+1)^2]/2N(N+1)(N-k+1)$.

Proof. The proof is analogous to the proofs to Propositions 1 and 2.

Notice that Proposition 3 only solves for q_s when the second order conditions hold. When these conditions do not hold, the solution will require either $q_s = 0$ or $q_s = 1$, depending on k. The full solution is quite messy, and it is best to calculate which of these values really does maximize Π^s.

We have so far solved for x_n and x_s as a function of q_n and q_s; restricted the parameter space such that $q_n = 0$ is a dominant strategy; and solved for q_s as a function of k. All that remains to be solved is the Stage 1 game, which determines the equilibrium value of k. Denote this value k^*. k^* must satisfy:

$$\Pi_s(k^*) \ge \Pi_n(k^*-1) \quad \text{and} \quad \Pi_n(k^*) \ge \Pi_s(k^*+1) \tag{14}$$

If Eq. 14 is satisfied, and if each country chooses to be a signatory or a non-signatory taking as given the labels (s or n) worn by the other countries, then no country can gain by unilaterally deviating from k^*.

4.2. Strategic trade sanctions in IEAs

It is an easy matter to solve for the behavior of signatories and non-signatories if trade sanctions are a given. With trade between signatories and non-signatories banned, non-signatories will play q^u, as solved in Section 2.2, but with $N-k$ substituted for N. Since, with trade sanctions, non-signatories cannot affect the output of signatory firms, and since non-signatories also take the abatement standards of signatories as given, non-signatories make their abatement choices independently of the choices of both signatory governments and signatory firms. Restrict the parameter space such that $q_n = 0$ will be an equilibrium for all feasible k. Then signatories cannot influence the abatement choices of non-signatories or the output choices of non-signatory firms. Signatories will thus play q^c, as solved in Section 2.3, but with k substituted for N.

More difficult is determining the stage at which the decision to invoke tradesanctions is made, and by which countries this decision is made. I propose the following game structure: in Stage 1, all countries decide whether the treaty is to employ trade sanctions and, if so, under what conditions; in Stage 2, countries choose simultaneously whether to be a signatory or a non-signatory; in Stages 3 and 4, respectively, signatories and non-signatories choose their abatement standards; and in the final stage of the game, firms choose their segmented outputs.

Stage 1 is not fully specified: I have not outlined how the decision to employ trade sanctions is to be taken (whether by consensus, majority voting, etc.), and a further complication is that, in general, no party knows in Stage 1 whether it will be a signatory or a non-signatory in equilibrium (only the equilibrium number of signatories can be anticipated in Stage 1). However, we shall see that, in the vast majority of cases examined, decisions taken in Stage 1 will be unanimous. In most cases, it will not be necessary to specify Stage 1 any further.

4.3. Simulation results

Solving analytically for the self-enforcing IEA under the two different regimes will plainly be difficult, even for this simple linear model. Since the model is so special anyway, it seems more sensible to solve it numerically. I limit the range of parameter values such that all firms produce positive quantities of the good. I also restrict the parameter space such that zero abatement is a dominant strategy for non-signatories whether or not trade is restricted and abatement in the full cooperative outcome is maximal (i.e., $q^c = 1$).

Consider, to begin, the equilibrium as $\omega \to 0$. Provision of the public good in this case has a negligible effect on the payoffs. So any IEA with trade sanctions will principally impact on the gains from trade (arising from inter-firm competition). For signatories, the gains from trade increase in k, and so trade sanctions in this case exhibit a kind of increasing returns. Accession to the IEA with trade sanctions would clearly not be in the interests of any country provided $k < N/2$, for the acceding country would suffer a significant loss in the gains from trade. By contrast, once at least half of all countries are in the agreement, accession would prove attractive to every country, taking the labels of all other countries (signatory or non-signatory) as given. So there will exist two equilibria, one in which every country is a non-signatory and one in which every country is a signatory. Provided ω, though 'small,' is positive, the latter equilibrium will be preferred by all countries.

How can signatories ensure that this preferred equilibrium is realized? This is a coordination problem, and an easy one at that. All that is required is a clause in the IEA saying that the agreement would not be 'binding' on parties (in the legal sense) until at least k^+ countries had acceded to it. In the present game, this minimum participation level would be specified by the agreement in Stage 1. Then, provided $k < k^+$, no country could lose by acceding. By the assumption that a country will accede if it is not made worse off, we therefore know that the equilibrium number of signatories must be at least as large as k^+. But once $k = k^+$, we know that every non-signatory is better off acceding to the agreement when ω is 'small.' Hence, appropriate choice of a minimum participation level ensures that the Pareto efficient outcome will be selected in equilibrium.

Trade sanctions are also tied to a minimum participation clause in the Montreal Protocol[9]. To become binding on parties (in the legal sense), the agreement would have to be ratified by at least 11 countries accounting for at least two-thirds of the 1986 level of global consumption of the controlled substances. As noted by Benedick (1991): 89–90), 'In effect, to become binding, the protocol would have to be ratified by the US and at least four of the six other large consumer countries... or by the US and the [European Community] as a unit.' Moreover, according to Benedick (1991), the intention of the minimum participation clause was to 'provide a sufficient critical mass to increase the pressure on any potential large holdouts to join the treaty.' While the trade sanctions in the Montreal Protocol almost certainly violate the multilateral trading rules, no country has complained officially about them. This hints that, as in the above example, support for the trade sanctions in this agreement has been universal.[10]

Figs. 1a,b illustrate the self-enforcing IEA under the free trade and trade sanctions regimes, respectively, assuming $\omega = 0.01$, $\sigma = 0.0125$ and $N = 10$. With trade sanctions prohibited (Fig. 1a), the self-enforcing IEA consists of $k^* = 3$ signatories, each of which undertakes 100% abatement (that is, $q_s(3) = 1.0$). Signatories earn a payoff of $\Pi_s(3) = 0.411$, which is higher than the payoff they would receive if there were no agreement ($\Pi^u = 0.405$); non-signatories, however, free ride and receive a higher payoff, $\Pi_n(3) = 0.433$. Under the trade sanctions regime (Fig. 1b), and with $k^+ = 5$, participation in the IEA requiring $q_s = q^c = 1$ is full, and each country earns a payoff equal to $\Pi_s(10) = \Pi^c = .484$. Since this payoff is greater than the payoffs both signatories and non-signatories would receive in the absence of trade sanctions, the

[9] Black et al. (1992) offer an alternative explanation for such a clause.

[10] This support has undoubtedly been helped by the use of side payments.

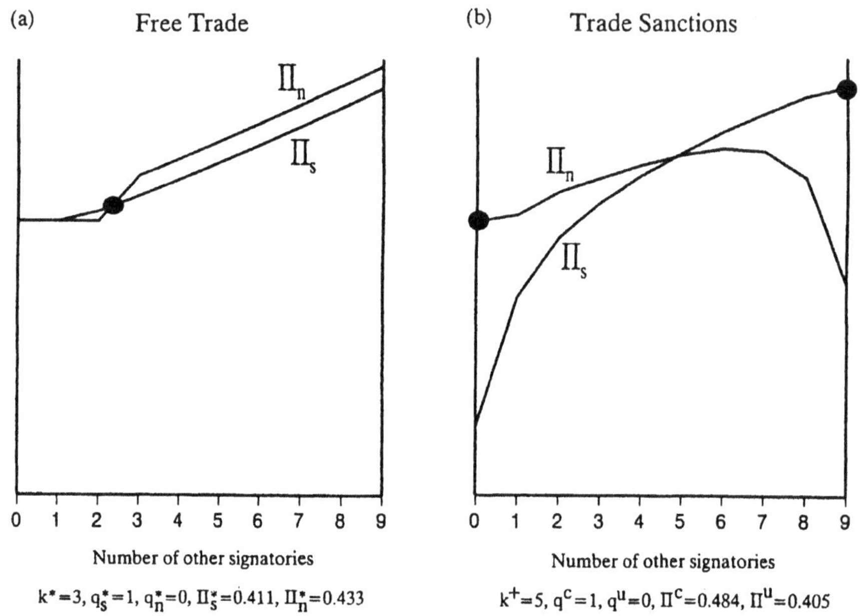

Fig. 1. Self-enforcing IEAs — $\omega = 0.01$, $\sigma = 0.0125$.

equilibrium IEA would specify the use of trade sanctions (provided this were permitted by the rules of the game), a minimum participation clause of $k^+ = 5$, and an abatement level of $q_s = 1$.

Notice that full cooperation is sustained as an equilibrium in Fig. 1b by the credible threat to impose sanctions. In equilibrium, trade is never restricted.

In Figs. 2a,b ω is even smaller than in Figs. 1a,b. So the qualitative result for the IEA with trade sanctions is the same. However, the ratio ω/σ is much smaller in Figs. 2a,b, and as a consequence k^* is much larger in Fig. 2a than in Fig. 1a. Because k^* is relatively large in Fig. 2a, and because σ is large relative to ω in this figure, non-signatories (free-riders) do better in the free trade regime than they would in the regime with trade sanctions. The question of whether trade sanctions should be allowed may thus spark a conflict in this case, though because of the weak specification of Stage 1 I cannot say how this conflict might be resolved.

In Figs. 3a,b, σ is also large relative to ω, and this explains why k^* is large. Unlike the earlier cases, however, ω is relatively large, and this changes the nature of the interactions in the sanctions regime. In Fig. 3b, there are three equilibria. When k is small, non-signatories do better than signatories because of the trade ban. When k exceeds 5, however, the payoffs of non-signatories start to fall because of the sanctions. Signatories do not

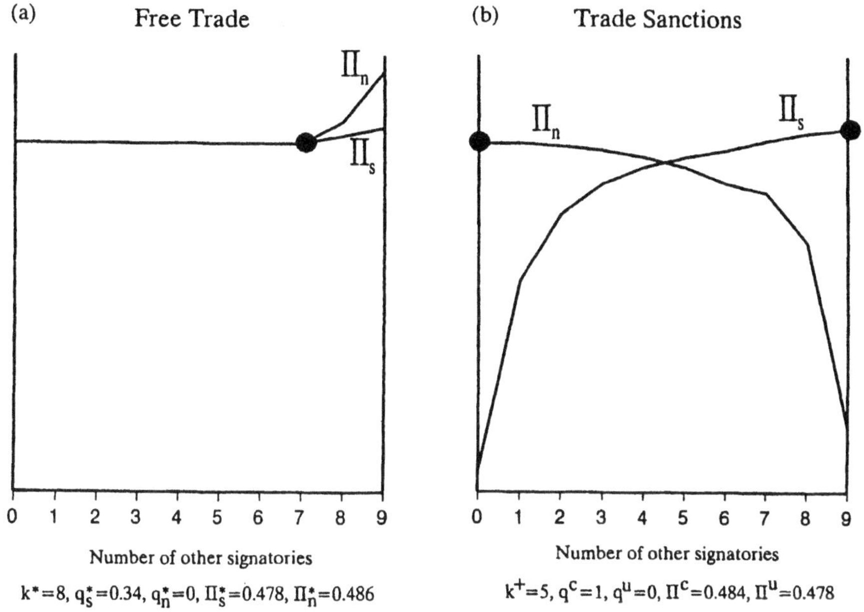

Fig. 2. Self-enforcing IEAs — $\omega = 0.002$, $\sigma = 0.0125$.

undertake any abatement until $k = 7$, at which level signatories play $q_s(7) = 0.95$. This abatement increases the payoff to non-signatories and the respective payoff curves cross at this participation level. For higher levels of k, the payoff to non-signatories falls as the effects of the trade ban bite harder. and joining the agreement becomes attractive once again for $k = 9$.

Finally, in Figs. 4a,b ω is quite large, while σ is small relative to ω. As a result, k^* is quite small. Unlike the earlier cases, the payoff to non-signatories increases over most of the range. As k increases, the gain to free-riding exceeds the loss in the gains from trade until $k = 9$. However, for $k \geq 7$, non-signatories do better by signing the agreement and abating their emissions completely. This is because, in doing so, they are permitted to trade within a larger market.

5. Policy implications

The trade sanctions in the Montreal Protocol might be viewed with some alarm, in so far as they violate the non-discrimination provisions of the GATT/WTO. When looked at in isolation, sanctions are indeed welfare-reducing (globally). But if the use of sanctions can increase the supply of a global public good, then the overall effect may be welfare-enhancing. More remarkably, this paper shows that, for a range of parameter values, the

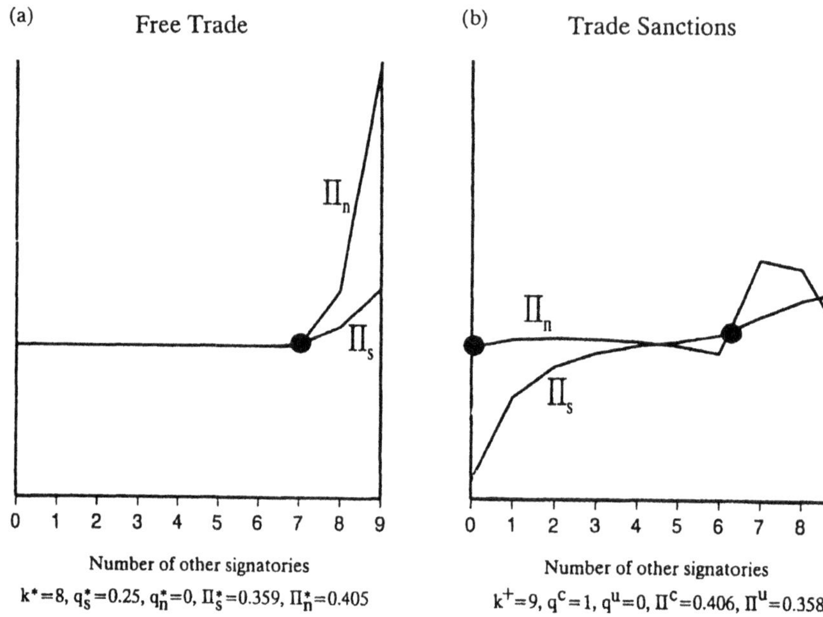

Fig. 3. Self-enforcing IEAs — $\omega = 0.0152$, $\sigma = 0.095$.

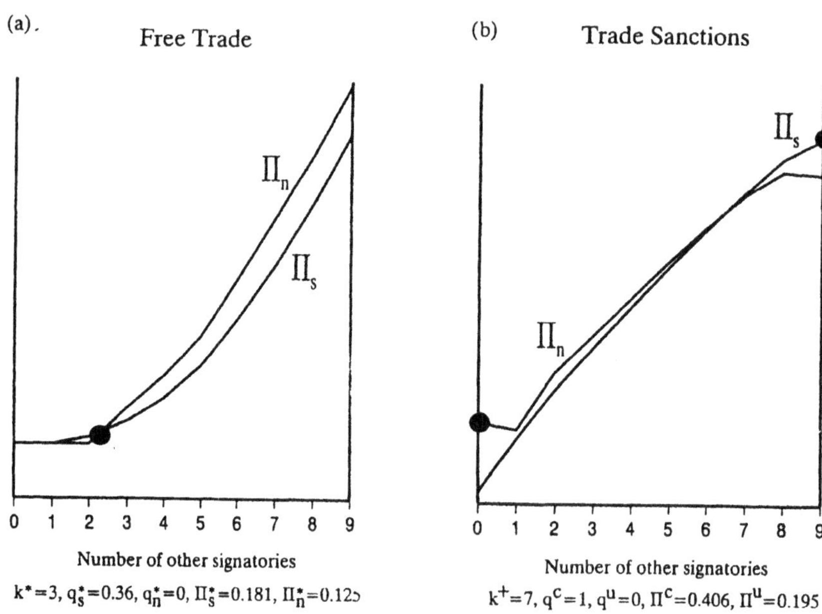

Fig. 4. Self-enforcing IEAs — $\omega = 0.076$, $\sigma = 0.095$.

credible threat to impose sanctions is enough to sustain full cooperation in environmental policy; in equilibrium, trade is not restricted. However, this result may not hold generally. For this and other reasons, the multilateral trading system should not allow signatories to impose sanctions simply because it serves their own interests in a particular instance. Sanctions should be permitted, but only if they satisfy certain general principles.

The success of the Montreal Protocol might also suggest that, if sanctions were used more frequently in IEAs, the environment would be better protected. However, for a number of reasons the Montreal Protocol is most likely an unusual case. Where trade sanctions are not sufficient to deter free-riding, countries will inevitably search for other punishments. But virtually every punishment will harm signatories as well as non-signatories, and it is this fact which is the principal obstacle to sustaining international cooperation.

Acknowledgements

I am grateful to the Centre for Social and Economic Research on the Global Environment for funding this research, to Richard Cooper and Martin Weitzman for comments at a seminar presentation, and to John Vickers and three anonymous referees for suggesting improvements to previous drafts.

Appendix

Proof of Proposition 1. In the symmetric equilibrium, we know from Eq. 3a that $x = N(1 - \sigma q)/(N+1)$, where x and q are, respectively, the output level of each firm and the abatement standard imposed by each government. Upon substituting into Eq. 6 we obtain

$$\frac{\partial \Pi_j}{\partial q_j} = \frac{N}{(N+1)^2}\{\omega(N+1) - \sigma(2N+1) + \sigma\omega(N+1) - \sigma q^{u}[2\omega(N+1) - \sigma(2N+1)]\} \qquad (A.1)$$

The Kuhn Tucker conditions (Eq. 5a,5b) are necessary and sufficient for $\omega/\sigma > (2N^3+1)/2N^2(N+1)$. Provided this condition is satisfied, the interior solution is found by setting Eq. A.1 equal to zero; the solution for $q^u = 0$ is found by setting $q^u = 0$ in Eq. A.1 and solving for $\partial \Pi_j/\partial q_j \leq 0$; and the solution for $q^u = 1$ is found by setting $q^u = 1$ in Eq. A.1 and solving for $\partial \Pi_j/\partial q_j \geq 0$.

If $\omega/\sigma \leq (2N^3+1)/2N^2(N+1)$, then $2\omega(N+1) - \sigma(2N+1) \leq 0$. So $\partial \Pi_j/\partial q_j$ is non-decreasing in q_j. This means that, for $q_j \in [0,1]$, $\partial \Pi_j/\partial q_j$ is maximal at $q_j = 1$. Setting $q^u = 1$ in Eq. A.1 we find that, in equilibrium, $\partial \Pi_j/\partial q_j = N\{(1-\sigma)\,[\omega(N+1) - \sigma(2N+1)]\}/(N+1)^2$. By assumption, $\sigma < 1$ (to ensure output is positive). Also, $2\omega(N+1) - \sigma(2N+1) \leq 0 \Rightarrow \omega(N+1) - \sigma(2N+1) < 0$. So we have $\partial \Pi_j/\partial q_j < 0$ in equilibrium. From Eq.

5a, $\partial \Pi_j / \partial q_j < 0 \Rightarrow q^{u} = 0$.||

Proof of Proposition 2. The proof is analogous to the proof for Proposition 1. Expression 8 can be rewritten

$$\frac{\partial \Pi^{c}}{\partial q} = \frac{N^2}{(N+1)^2}\{\omega N(N+1) - \sigma(N+2) + \sigma\omega N(N+1)$$
$$- \sigma q[2\omega N(N+1) - \sigma(N+2)]\} \qquad (A.2)$$

The second order conditions are $\partial^2 \Pi^{c}/\partial q^2 < 0 \Rightarrow N\omega/\sigma > (N+2)/2(N+1)$. When this inequality holds, $\partial \Pi^{c}/\partial q$ is decreasing in q. Hence $\partial \Pi^{c}/\partial q > 0$ for $q = 1$ implies $\partial \Pi^{c}/\partial q > 0 \forall q \in [0,1]$. Setting $q = 1$ in Eq. A.2, we find $q^{c} = 1$ provided $\omega N/\sigma \geq (N+2)/(N+1)$. Similarly, $\partial \Pi^{c}/\partial q < 0$ for $q = 0$ implies $\partial \Pi^{c}/\partial q < 0 \forall q \in [0,1]$. Setting $q = 0$ in Eq. A.2, we find that $q^{c} = 0$ provided $\omega N/\sigma \leq (N+2)/(1+\sigma)(N+1)$. Obviously, for intermediate values of $\omega N/\sigma$ we have an interior solution and q^{c} is found by setting $\partial \Pi^{c}/\partial q = 0$.

If $N\omega/\sigma \leq (N+2)/2(N+1)$, $\partial \Pi^{c}/\partial q$ is non-decreasing in q. Hence, $\partial \Pi^{c}/\partial q < 0$ for $q = 1$ implies $\partial \Pi^{c}/\partial q < 0 \forall q \in [0,1]$. Setting $q = 1$ in Eq. A.2, I find $\partial \Pi^{c}/\partial q < 0$ provided $\omega N/\sigma < (N+2)/(N+1)$, assuming $\sigma < 1$ (i.e., output by firms is positive). But $\omega N/\sigma < (N+2)/2(N+1) \Rightarrow \omega N/\sigma < (N+2)/(N+1)$, so that where the second order conditions fail to hold, $q^{c} = 0$ is (second-best) optimal.||

Proof of Lemma;. In equilibrium, the net marginal benefit of abatement for a representative non-signatory is

$$\frac{\partial \Pi_n}{\partial q_n} = \frac{1}{(N+1)^2}\{N[\omega(N+1) - \sigma(2N+1) + \sigma\omega(N+1)]$$
$$- q_n\sigma[2\omega N(N+1)(k+1) - \sigma[2N^2(k+1) + N - k]]$$
$$+ q_s\sigma k[2\omega N(N+1) - \sigma(2N^2 - 1)]\} \qquad (A.3)$$

If Eq. A.3 is non-positive $\forall$ feasible values of q_n, q_s and k, then non-signatories will play $q_n = 0$, irrespective of the number of signatories and their chosen abatement levels. We thus want to show that the maximal value of Eq. A.3 is non-positive.

If Eq. 11 holds, then $\partial \Pi_j/\partial q_j$ is maximal for $q_s = 0$. Inequality Eq. 11 also implies that $\partial \Pi_j/\partial q_j$ is increasing in q_n. To see this, note that $\partial \Pi_j/\partial q_j$ will be increasing in q_n if $\omega/\sigma < [2N^2(k+1) + N - k]/2N(N+1)(k+1) \; \forall \; k$. The RHS of this inequality is decreasing in k. Hence, if the inequality holds for $k = N-1$ then it must hold for all k, $N - 1 \geq k \geq 0$. If $k = N-1$, then the inequality becomes $\omega/\sigma < (2N^3+1)/2N^2(N+1)$. But $(2N^3+1)/2N^2(N+1) > (2N^2-1)/2N(N+1)$. Hence if Eq. 11 holds then $\partial \Pi_j/\partial q_j$

is increasing in q_n and $\partial \Pi_j / \partial q_j$ is maximal for $q_n = 1$ and $k = N - 1$.

Setting $q_s = 0$, $q_n = 1$, $k = N - 1$, Eq. A.3 can be rewritten

$$\frac{\partial \Pi_j}{\partial q_j} = \frac{[\omega N(2N^2 + N - 1) - \sigma(2N^3 + 1)]}{(N+1)^2} \times \left(\frac{[\omega N(N+1) - \sigma N(2N+1)]}{[\omega N(2N^2 + N - 1) - \sigma(2N^3 + 1)]} - \sigma \right) \qquad (A.4)$$

Inequality Eq. 11 implies $\omega N(2N^2 + N - 1) - \sigma(2N^3 + 1) < 0$. By assumption, $\sigma < 1$ (output by each firm is positive). Hence, to prove the lemma we need only show that $[\omega N(N+1) - \sigma N(2N+1)] \geq [\omega N(2N^2 + N - 1) - \sigma(2N^3 + 1)]$. But this inequality merely restates Eq. 11.||

References

Barrett, S., 1992. International Environmental Agreements as Games. In: R. Pethig (Ed.), Conflict and Cooperation in Managing Environmental Resources, Berlin: Springer–Verlag.

Barrett, S., 1994a. Self-enforcing international environmental agreements. Oxford Economic Papers 46, 878–894.

Barrett, S., 1994b. Strategic Environmental Policy and International Trade. J. Public Economics 54, 325–338.

Benedick, R.E., 1991. Ozone Diplomacy, Cambridge, MA, Harvard University Press.

Black, J., Levi, M.D., deMeza, D., 1992. Creating a good atmosphere: minimum participation for tackling the greenhouse effect. Economica 60, 281–293.

Brander, J., 1981. Intra-industry trade in identical commodities. J. Int. Economics 11, 1–14.

Brander, J.A., Krugman, P.R., 1983. A reciprocal dumping model of international trade. J. Int. Economics 15, 313–323.

Carraro, C., Siniscalco, D., 1993. Strategies for the international protection of the environment. J. Public Economics 52, 309–328.

Carraro, C., Siniscalco, D., 1994. R and D Cooperation and the Stability of International Environmental Agreements, Nota di Lavoro 65.94, Fondazione Eni Enrico Mattei, Milano.

Cesar, H., de Zeeuw, A., 1994. Issue Linkage in Global Environmental Problems, Nota ke Lavoro 56.94, Fondazione Eni Enrico Mattei, Milano.

Helpman, E., Krugman, P.R., 1985. Market Structure and Foreign Trade, Cambridge, MA: MIT Press.

Hoel, M., 1992. International Environment Conventions: The Case of Uniform Reductions of Emissions. Environ. Res. Economics 2, 141–159.

Hoel, M., 1996. Should a carbon tax be differentiated across sectors?. J. Public Economics 59, 17–32.

Kennedy, P.W., 1994. Equilbrium Pollutin Taxes in Open Economies with Imperfect Competition. J. Environ. Economics Management 27, 49–63.

Markusen, J.R., 1975. International externalities and optimal tax structures. J. International Economics 5, 15–29.

Ulph, A., 1994. Environmental Policy and International Trade: A Survey of Recent Economic Analysis, Discussion Paper 53.94, Fondazione ENI Enrico Mattei.

Xing, Y. and C.D. Kolstad, 1996. Environment and Trade: A Review of Theory and Issues, Working Paper 2-96, Department of Economics, University of California, Santa Barbara.

Transborder Pollution Controls, Trade and Welfare

[26]

JOURNAL OF ENVIRONMENTAL ECONOMICS AND MANAGEMENT 15, 259–284 (1988)

The Impact of Selected Abatement Strategies on Transnational Pollution, the Terms of Trade, and Factor Rewards: A General Equilibrium Approach

JOHN D. MERRIFIELD*

Department of Economics and Finance, University of Texas, San Antonio, Texas 78285-0633

Received November 5, 1985; revised January 4, 1987

Widespread publicity of international conflict over transfrontier pollutants, such as acid deposition and the November 1986 chemical spill in the Rhine River, has increased the public's awareness of the need to devise abatement strategies appropriate for transnational pollution. This article develops a general equilibrium approach for analyzing the economic impacts of selected abatement strategies. The model includes internationally mobile goods, capital and pollution flows, and flexible output and factor prices. The general equilibrium approach provides policymakers with important information which is usually not revealed by a partial equilibrium approach. That is demonstrated by applying the model to the North American acid deposition issue. © 1988 Academic Press, Inc.

I. INTRODUCTION

Governments throughout the world have grappled with the issue of transnational pollution for some time. A long-time problem has been Europe's Rhine River; a recipient of wastes from several countries, including a major chemical spill in November 1986 (*Time*, 11/24/86). In 1909, the United States (U.S.) and Canada negotiated the Boundary Waters Treaty to control pollution in the lower Great Lakes and the St. Lawrence Seaway [26]. The *Trail Smelter* case [27] put transfrontier air pollution in the headlines in the 1920s. Pollution of the Great Lakes is still a subject of U.S.–Canadian negotiation and cooperation, resulting in 1983 in an agreement to limit phosphorous pollution (*USA Today*, 10/1/83).

Acid deposition, more often referred to as acid rain (wet acid deposition), has received widespread publicity in North America.[1] Pictures of decaying structures (such as the Statue of Liberty), reports of fish kills, possible soil productivity losses, and the high cost of abatement have aroused[2] the general public. The high cost of action and inaction,[3] and the income and geographic distributional effects of proposed abatement strategies, has made acid deposition into a hot political issue. Controversy within the Reagan Administration and the Congress, demands for

*Assistant Professor of Economics. This article is based on Dr. Merrifield's dissertation research, conducted at the University of Wyoming in Laramie.

[1]Acid deposition is also a major issue in Europe [20]. Other current North American transnational pollution problems include air pollution in Cuidad Juarez–El Paso (U.S.–Mexico), Gulf of Mexico oil spills (mostly U.S.–Mexico), Lower Colorado River basin salinity (U.S.–Mexico), and water pollution in the Great Lakes (U.S.–Canada).

[2]According to a Louis Harris poll, 90% of the American people think acid rain is a serious problem. Awareness of the problem has doubled since 1980 [5].

[3]The only published estimate of abatement benefits for the U.S. is a 1978 figure of $5 billion annually [8].

0095-0696/88 $3.00

action by affected domestic groups,[4] and by the Canadian government have, until recently, only prompted numerous studies of the problem. In March 1987, President Reagan endorsed a $2.5 billion, 5-year effort to find cleaner methods of burning coal.

The primary purpose of this paper is to develop and illustrate the properties of a model that shows how transnational pollution flows, production, the terms of trade, and factor prices are affected by two abatement strategies. A welfare index summarizes the impact of both strategies on national welfare. After discussing the general properties of the model, it is applied to the North American acid deposition issue. The acid deposition issue is employed primarily to put the discussion of the model on a more concrete basis. A secondary objective of the paper is to demonstrate how a general equilibrium (GE) model can reveal some important aspects of a transnational pollution issue, which a partial equilibrium analysis often fails to discover. No attempt is made to provide a thorough economic analysis of acid deposition or all the proposed abatement strategies.

Production taxes and regulations requiring a certain amount of pollution abatement equipment at each source (Best Available Control Technology standards) are analyzed because, in the U.S., existing practices suggest that such strategies will be considered for any pollution problem and are likely to be implemented again in the future [25].

The model is an advance over previous work in this area. Pollutants, goods, and capital are internationally mobile, and prices of factors and goods are determined endogenously. Both countries are explicitly included in the model, and each has some price-setting power. In contrast, previous work in this area generally has assumed that some prices are constant, with frequently only one country explicitly included in the model, and usually only one model component (goods, factors, or pollutants) is internationally mobile. Section II provides a brief review of previous, related work, including trade models with externalities and public goods, and GE models with pollution.

Following the literature review, a GE trade model with transnational pollution is introduced (Section III) and discussed in some detail. The supply and demand sides of the economy are included, but the supply side is emphasized. An increase in the economic activity of either country raises the pollution flow of both countries (pollution is a pure public bad). The scarcity of capital services and the pollution flow are directly related. Capital (defined to include natural resources) is damaged by the pollutant. The model's endogenous variables are the factor rewards, the terms of trade, each country's total output, each country's share of the available stock of capital, and the pollution flow.

In Section IV, general properties of the model are discussed. Then the model is used to analyze the abatement strategies in the context of the acid deposition issue. For a more realistic analysis, pollution flows are allowed to vary between the two countries; pollution is no longer a pure public bad. Comparative static results of changes in production taxes and abatement equipment standards are presented. The welfare implications of each strategy for each country are discussed in section V.

[4]Six northeastern states (Maine, New York, Rhode Island, Vermont, Massachusetts, and Connecticut) and four environmental groups (no specifics given) have sued the Environmental Protection Agency to use existing authority to curtail sulfur emissions [4]. In addition, the National Governors Association voted 24–10 to back immediate action to control acid rain [3].

Together, the results indicate that Canada has more unilateral policy options likely to increase its welfare. That result was unexpected, because Canada is a much smaller country and receives a much larger share of its acid deposition from the U.S. than the U.S. receives from Canada. It occurs because Canadian emissions account for a larger share of either country's acid deposition than its share of the total internationally mobile capital stock. Also, the imposition of a production tax or a tightening of the abatement equipment standard by either country or jointly by both countries is more likely to increase Canadian than the U.S. welfare. Each country's net creditor–debtor status is the major determinant of that result. A summary and conclusions are presented in Section VI.

II. LITERATURE REVIEW

The effort to advance economic theory and improve policy-making is continuing on at least two fronts. The purpose of this section is to show how existing work with GE models with pollution but no international trade[5] ([6, 9, 10, 28]), trade models with pollution ([1, 21]), and the work of McGuire [16] and Siebert *et al.* [23] including trade and pollution in a GE setting have increased our understanding of transnational pollution.

The following pages will be devoted to a somewhat detailed discussion of the articles mentioned above. This section concludes with a discussion of how those articles have contributed to and facilitated further advances by this research effort.

A. General Equilibrium Models with Pollution

GE models are now being applied to the problems of pollution damage and pollution control because of growing interest in the incidence (who bears the burden) and distributional effects of pollution abatement policies. The comparative advantage of GE models is their ability to reflect the distributional effects of policy changes. Furthermore, it is often possible to summarize the comparative static results with a welfare index (Section V of this paper).

Of the four papers to be discussed here, only the Yohe [28] and Forster [10] articles address the income distribution–incidence question directly. Distributional–incidence implications are extracted from the models of Comolli [6] and Forster [9] by Forster [10].

Comolli developed a static model and a dynamic model to consider the comparative statics of more stringent abatement requirements and the adjustment process set in motion by requiring increased abatement effort. The distinctive features of the Comolli model arise from the assumptions about pollution damages and the mechanism for pollution control. Pollution is a by-product of producing the first good (X_1), it can accumulate over time, and the stock (not flow) of pollution enters the production function of the second good as an input with a negative marginal product. The pollutant either does not directly enter the utility functions of individuals, or if it does, it is assumed that goods consumption and the pollution stock are additively separable arguments within the utility function. In other words, the pollution level is taken as given by each consumer, and so does not affect the

[5] Trade does occur between sectors within the single country.

consumption mix decision. Abatement occurs when a larger share (β) of X_1 output goes to pollution control. The value of β is set by the government.

The mechanism that reduces pollution is the key to the distributional–incidence implications of the Comolli model. As the amount of X_1 available to consumers is reduced its relative price is bid up, which then increases the return of the factor used intensively in its production. That result is obtained from both the static and the dynamic versions of Comolli's model. If, instead, X_2 is diverted for the pollution abatement effort, the return of X_1's intensive factor falls, while the return of X_2's intensive factor rises.

In Forster [9], pollution is a result of producing and consuming both goods. The stock of pollutants is an argument in the social welfare function, but it is not in the production function of either good. As in Comolli's model, individual consumers take the stock of pollution as given. Without government regulation, the aggregate purchases of consumers will not be the socially optimal amount.

For the "more polluting commodity," the producer's price is too high and the consumer's price is too low. The authorities correct the market failure with a tax on the more polluting commodity. The reduction in the producer's price reduces the price of the input used intensively to produce the more polluting commodity. With a different policy tool for increasing pollution abatement, a result opposite of Comolli's is derived. The reversal occurs because Forster's per unit tax reduces the producer's price, while Comolli's hike in β raises the producer's price.

Yohe [28] adapts the model of Batra and Casas [2] to look at how selected abatement strategies affect factor rewards. Pollution occurs because X_1 producers require the environment as a waste disposal sink. The ability to pollute is a specific, productive factor of X_1 producers, which makes pollution their intensive factor. In contrast to the Comolli and Forster models, the Yohe model is static and why abatement is desirable is not indicated. Pollution does not explicitly damage producers or consumers in the model, but the authorities specify the maximum rate of pollution.

Early in this paper, Yohe assumes that output prices are fixed. That assumption, along with incomplete specialization, would normally[6] break the link between factor endowments (including the permissible rate of pollution in Yohe's model) and factor prices. However, with more factors than goods,[7] factor prices are affected by a tightening of the pollution standard. The shadow price of waste emissions rises, the non-intensive factor (of both goods) reward falls, and the return to X_2's intensive factor rises. Tightening the pollution standard reduces the supply of an important X_1 input, and thereby reduces the supply of X_1. That releases capital and labor to X_2 producers. If labor (capital) is X_2's intensive factor, the shift of some capital and labor from X_1 to X_2 will raise (lower) K_2/L_2 and increase (decrease) the return to labor while reducing (raising) the price of capital.

Yohe's result is similar to Forster's [9] but occurs for different reasons. In Forster's model, price changes alter factor rewards. In Yohe's model, with prices fixed, a change in the availability of the environmental factor, plus the difference in the number of goods and factors, alters factor prices. When output prices are flexible, the effect of a tighter pollution standard on factor rewards is qualitatively

[6] See Jones [13] for an explanation of that result.

[7] Jones [14] has demonstrated some of the ramifications for factor rewards of having more factors than goods.

identical to the result with fixed output prices, but the size of the effect will vary with the price elasticity of demand for each good.

Forster [10] also introduces extensions of a model similar to Yohe's. Forster [10] first considers a situation in which waste emissions are not homogeneous. Labor, initially the only other productive input, is mobile between industries. With a mobile factor and two specific factors, the model is similar to Jones' [14] three factor, two good model. The two factors employed in each industry are continuously substitutable. With flexible factor prices and the other restrictions, labor is fully employed. The authorities regulate the flow of pollution (static model, no stock accumulation) by selling transferable pollution permits to each industry.

With fixed output prices, fewer pollution permits for either industry means a rise in the market price of permits in both industries. It also reduces the price of labor, by increasing the labor–pollution ratio in each sector. The sector facing the permit cutback reduces its output and its demand for labor. The full employment assumption requires that the wage rate fall so that the sector not directly affected by the permit reduction can expand its labor force.

Additional results are obtained from the model by varying the pollution control mechanism. When the authorities levy an emissions' tax, factor rewards respond to an increase in one of the taxes like they did to a reduction in the number of one sector's pollution permits. Again, the price of labor falls, but since the government now controls the price of pollution in each sector, the return to emissions does not change. With an emissions' tax, the government no longer directly controls the rate of pollution. An attempt to reduce the waste emissions of one sector can increase the emissions of the other sector. For instance, if the government raises the tax on the X_1 industry's emissions, X_1 falls, some workers move to X_2 industry jobs, and the marginal product of X_2 emissions rises. With no change in X_2's emissions' tax or the price of X_2, the X_2 industry releases more pollutants so as to reestablish equality between the cost of polluting and the value of its marginal product.

Intersectoral trade has an important role in the papers just discussed, but the effect of introducing international trade was not considered. Selected models combining international trade and pollution are discussed next.

B. International Trade Models with Pollution

Papers such as Pethig [21] and Asako [1] are of greatest interest. The Pethig model was set up to show that the expected welfare gains from trade may not materialize or they may be accentuated when the pollution intensiveness of the two goods varies. A fixed consumption ratio assures that the international ratio of X_1 to X_2 production cannot change. Only the location of production can change. Pollution is not physically mobile between countries, but it can be indirectly imported or exported. For instance, if the pollution-intensive commodity (X_1) is exported by country A, increased trade could lower A's welfare. Additional pollution damages could offset the usual material gains from trade. If A exports X_2, an expansion of trade would add the benefits of reduced pollution to the material gains from trade. The country that exports the pollution-intensive good may not gain from trade, while the other country always gains. Pollution concerns provide an incentive for one country to expand trade, and for the other country to restrict trade. However, if the same good is pollution intensive in both countries, the fixed worldwide output ratio prevents both countries from simultaneously tightening their environmental policies.

With binding pollution control constraints, the country with the least restrictive controls will export the pollution-intensive good. In effect, the Ricardian basis for trade is reinforced or replaced by a factor endowments basis for trade. The country with the lowest shadow (with a standard) or real (with an emissions' tax) price for pollution becomes the one relatively well-endowed with the pollution factor. It follows that the two countries' welfare is interdependent, because a change in one country's environmental policy will affect the location of production, and thereby affect the pollution level and welfare of both countries.

Asako's results are similar to Pethig's, despite some differences in their models. In both models, only commodity trade links the two countries. However, in Asako's model, the foreign country's existence is implicit rather than explicit. Other significant differences are Asako's policy tools and his treatment of pollution. Pollution is a joint product, rather than an input. Labor is the only explicit productive factor in the model. In Asako's model, the authorities pursue their environmental quality objectives by altering the pattern of trade with a tax-subsidy approach. By directly linking trade policy and environmental quality concerns, the Pethig result that it may be unwise to expand trade if the export good is the more polluting commodity is also obtained by Asako.

C. *Static General Equilibrium Trade Models*

Most relevant to this research is the work of McGuire [16]. The setup is similar to Yohe's [28]. Permission to pollute is an input only for the X_1 industry of both countries. Unlike Yohe, damages are included in the model. The marginal social cost of pollution is assumed to be a known constant. With no regulation, pollution is "employed" such that its marginal product is zero. Trade occurs because of differences in factor endowments. Prior to the introduction of environmental regulation,[8] the model is identical to the Hecksher–Ohlin (H-O) model. Consequently, with no regulation, prices are the same in both countries. Demand factors are discussed occasionally but are not explicitly included in the model.

To analyze the effects of a reduction in the permissible rate of pollution, McGuire further assumes that capital and emissions and labor and emissions are equally substitutable. In other words, the elasticities of substitution, σ_{LT} and σ_{KT}, are equal (in McGuire's notation T denotes the pollution input). Thus, when regulation of T occurs, the production function's shape is not altered. The only change is a renumbering of the isoquants. Before introducing international trade into the analysis, the impact of regulation on a closed economy is considered. The results are identical to Yohe's analysis and contrary to Forster's [10] homogeneous pollution model. Because only one sector "employs" pollution in Yohe and McGuire, regulation prompts the factor rewards of K and L to move in opposite directions, with the factor used intensively in the non-polluting, and hence unregulated, industry gaining absolutely in terms of both goods.

When international trade is added to the analysis, it is important to distinguish between coordinated and uncoordinated regulation. Coordinated regulation means

[8]McGuire [16] mentions that for some issues it may matter whether pollution is internationally mobile, but the model does not formally incorporate that feature.

that the shadow price of permission to pollute is uniform in the two countries. The factor price equalization result will not be disturbed by coordinated regulation. The autarchy result that the intensive factor of the unregulated industry benefits and the other factor suffers is also retained. With uncoordinated regulation, factor price equalization is lost. For a small country facing fixed world commodity prices, pollution restrictions depress the price of the factor used intensively to produce the polluting good, so that when output is reduced, the released factors can be absorbed by the unregulated industry. The other factor reward rises. If the country is large enough to influence world prices, the change in factor rewards is definitely reversed from the small country case for all but the country enacting the regulations. Since McGuire's pollution control mechanism does not separate producer and consumer prices, producer prices will be bid up when regulation curtails production of the polluting good. This latter result is identical to the factor incidence outcome derived from Comolli's model by Forster [10]. The importance of the choice of pollution control mechanism to the factor incidence result was illustrated earlier by the differences in the Comolli and Forster [9] results.

For the bulk of the paper, McGuire assumes that productive factors are internationally immobile. Just prior to the concluding remarks, McGuire provides a discussion of the intuitive results of uncoordinated regulation when factors move freely between the two countries. With H-O assumptions, in particular the identical technology assumption, the international equality of factor prices cannot be restored until all of the polluting industry has departed the country imposing the strictest environmental regulations. With uncoordinated regulation of pollution, factor prices cannot be equalized so long as both countries are incompletely specialized. Thus, if even one factor is internationally mobile, uncoordinated regulation leads to complete specialization in at least one country, and perhaps both. If the pollutant is an international public bad, uncoordinated regulation is futile, because their only effect is to relocate the source of emissions.

An extension of Pethig's work [23] incorporates mobile capital and international trade in a general equilibrium model. Pollution is not internationally mobile, and as in Pethig, the expenditure ratio for the two goods is fixed. Permission to pollute is an input and is thus desired by producers. However, pollution-caused damages are not explicitly incorporated. The authorities pursue the implicit public good, environmental quality, with either an emissions tax or an emissions standard. H-O type conclusions are drawn from the model. The country with the least restrictive environmental laws exports the pollution-intensive good. The impact of tighter pollution control laws on capital flows and income distribution depends on relative factor intensities of the goods and the abatement technology.

D. Another Step Forward

The model presented in detail in Section III contains elements of many of the models discussed in this section. Because of its static[9] nature, and its treatment of pollution as an input, the model most closely resembles the work of Yohe [28] and McGuire [16].

[9]Contrary to models such as Forster [9] and Comolli's [6] dynamic model, damages are related to the rate of pollution, rather than to the size of an accumulated stock of pollution. The model provides a steady state, zero discount rate perspective.

The model allows commodity and input prices to be determined endogenously, and goods, pollution, and capital are internationally mobile, yet the assumptions are generally less restrictive (except for its static nature). In the models just discussed, only McGuire considers the impact of factor mobility. Another significant improvement over previous models is the ability to consider the economic impact of tighter abatement equipment standards. Because of perceived low monitoring costs, equipment standards appear to be much more popular abatement strategies than emissions' taxes or salable pollution permits, the strategies most often considered by economists. This section has shown that the economic consequences of an abatement effort are very sensitive to changes in the abatement strategy.

III. THE MODEL[10]

The essence of an analysis of transnational pollution is the impact of abatement strategies on prices, and hence on the movement of goods and productive resources between the countries. Price changes effect the profit functions of producers and the welfare of households. Pollution damages are also likely to alter prices. Therefore, the model's features include endogenous input (capital[11] and labor) and goods' prices and capital mobility between countries. As Siebert *et al.* [23] point out: "Pollutants ambient to the environment may affect the quality of inputs in production processes, the production procedures, produced commodities, capital goods (wealth damages) etc." Because damages to capital (broadly defined) by transnational pollutants are well known, the model incorporates a damage function in which the scarcity of capital services varies directly with the pollution flow.[12] The model is static, so there is no mechanism which permits pollutants to accumulate with time. The total final demand output of each country is treated as a single composite good in the model. Country A produces X_1, consumes some of it, and exports the balance to country B. X_1 serves as a numeraire good with a constant price of one. B produces X_2 consumes some of it, and exports the remainder of its output to A. The price of X_2 is P, where P is a relative price ($P_2/P_1 = P_2/1 = P$) determined endogenously. The two economy-wide production functions are

$$X_i = X_i(g(R)K_i, L_i, E_i, Z_i) \tag{1}$$

where:

K_i = capital used to produce X_i; $i = 1, 2$.

L_i = labor used to produce X_i.

E_i = emissions released to the environment in the course of producing X_i.

Z_i = pollution abatement equipment employed by producers of X_i. Z is a pure intermediate good.

[10] For notational simplicity and to emphasize the general applicability of the model, the countries are referred to as A and B rather than U.S. and Canada. Many equations and complete mathematical derivations of the model are relegated to the Appendix.

[11] In a two factor model, capital must include natural resources, which can certainly be thought of as part of a country's "capital" stock (i.e., non-labor resource base).

[12] A damage function for labor could be included without sacrificing mathematical certainty in the general case as long as the elasticity of productivity with respect to pollution flows is smaller for labor than for capital.

R = transnational pollutant flow.

$g(R)K$ = capital scarcity varies directly with the transnational pollutant flows ($g' < 0$).

For individual firms (1) is homogeneous degree one. Total output is exhausted by factor payments at the firm level (zero economic profits),

$$C_{L1}W_A + C_{K1}r + C_{Z1}P_{Z1} = 1 \quad (2)$$

$$C_{L2}W_B + C_{K2}r + C_{Z2}P_{Z2} = P \quad (3)$$

$$C_{LZ1}W_A + C_{KZ1}r = P_{Z1} \quad (4)$$

$$C_{LZ}2W_B + C_{KZ2}r = P_{Z2}, \quad (5)$$

where

C_{ij} = input i per output j; $i = L, K, Z$; $j = X_1, X_2, Z_1, Z_2$.

W_A = price of labor in country A.

r = price of capital.

P_{Z_i} = price of Z_i employed as an intermediate good by X_i producers; $i = 1, 2$.

The linear homogeneity assumption eliminates any complications which could result from variability in firm size or numbers in the initial equilibrium. With an equilibrium as a starting point, it also follows that each firm is using the best available technology.

Several restrictions apply to (1). Capital can be substituted for labor, and Z can be substituted for emissions, but capital cannot be substituted for Z. It follows that the input substitution elasticities σ_{KE}, σ_{KZ}, σ_{LE}, and σ_{LZ} are equal to zero. For the acid deposition issue, recent research[13] suggests that opportunities to marginally reduce emissions through production process modifications are very limited. The alternative processes in use or available represented major capital investments which would have only permitted the firms to install less expensive new abatement equipment. For the small changes in policy variables the model is able to consider, it is not overly heroic to assume that individual firms cannot substitute productive capital or labor for emissions' or abatement equipment. With $\sigma_{KE} = \sigma_{LE} = \sigma_{KZ} = \sigma_{LZ} = 0$, output cannot be increased by employing additional E or Z without also acquiring additional K or L.

Economy wide, a doubling of inputs will not result in a doubling of output. That conclusion follows from the feedback effect of the externality on the scarcity of capital. When many firms seek to increase output, emissions increase significantly and some of the service flow they expect from their capital stock fails to materialize. Because private marginal products can be shown to equal social average products (Markusen [15], 1983), the externality will not block the exhaustion of total output at the firm level. Consequently, the simplifying features of linear homogeneity indicated by the preceding paragraphs are not ruled out by the externality's impact on capital scarcity.

In this model, both governments enforce a minimum ratio of Z to output for each firm. Thus, although additional Z is by itself a non-productive factor, government

[13]Summarized in the final report of Work Group 3B formed under the U.S.–Canada Memorandum of Intent on Transboundary Air Pollution [17].

regulation ensures that an increase in X_i $(i = 1, 2)$ will require an equal percentage increase in Z_i. With homogeneous degree one production functions, the expansion path is linear. With constant input prices, an effort to increase output by N percent means an $N\%$ increase in the use of all inputs, including Z. It will be assumed that an unregulated firm would use the environment for waste disposal to the point where the marginal product of emissions is zero.

While individual firms are unable to substitute capital or labor for Z, for the economy as a whole, they are indirect substitutes for Z.[14] Indirect substitution occurs because increasing the demand for Z will divert capital and labor away from the production of final demand goods X_1 and X_2. A change in the government-controlled ratio of Z_i to X_i is analogous to Comolli's shift in β. Both divert resources from final demand to pollution abatement:

$$Z_i = Z_i(g(R)K_{Zi}, L_{Zi}), \qquad i = 1, 2. \tag{6}$$

With flexible factor prices and the ability to substitute capital for labor, productive inputs will be fully employed in both countries:

$$C_{L1}X_1 + C_{LZ1}Z_1 = L_A \tag{7}$$

$$C_{L2}X_2 + C_{LZ2}Z_2 = L_B \tag{8}$$

$$C_{K1}X_1 + C_{KZ1}Z_1 = K_A \tag{9}$$

$$C_{K2}X_2 + C_{KZ2}Z_2 = K_B \tag{10}$$

$$\bar{C}_{Z1}X_1 = Z_1 \tag{11}$$

$$\bar{C}_{Z2}X_2 = Z_2 \tag{12}$$

$$K_A + K_B = \bar{K} \tag{13}$$

$$\kappa_A + \kappa_B = \bar{K}, \tag{14}$$

where κ_i = capital owned in country i; i = A, B,

$$C_{L1} = C_{L1}(W_A, r) \tag{15}$$

$$C_{LZ1} = C_{LZ1}(W_A, r) \tag{16}$$

$$C_{K1} = C_{K1}(W_A, r, R). \tag{17}$$

For C_{L2}, C_{KZ2}, and C_{K2} replace W_A with W_B in (15)–(17). Labor is assumed to be immobile between countries and fixed in quantity.[15] Input–output ratios are a function of input prices. The capital–output ratios also vary inversely with pollution

[14] Z is assumed to be a nontraded good. While it is certainly conceivable that Z could be exported by one of the countries, that feature was omitted from the model. Adding trade in Z to the model would have added much more in the way of analytic complexity to the model than increased realness would warrant. That conclusion is based on the fact that most industrialized nations devote but 1 to 2% of their resources to pollution abatement [24].

[15] That assumption is consistent with the immigration restrictions existing between most nations. Where intranational labor mobility is restricted by cultural ties, incomplete information, or high transport costs, that assumption may still be reasonable for analyses of regions within a nation.

flows.[16] The total capital endowment available to the economic system which A and B comprise is assumed fixed, but at the margin, capital is assumed to be freely mobile between A and B. Capital ownership is immobile internationally.

The demand for X_1 and X_2 is assumed to depend on their relative price (P) and total income ($Y = Y_A + Y_B$). Only one demand equation is included explicitly in the model, because, according to Walras' law, when all but one market clears the remaining market must also clear. The X_2 market was arbitrarily selected as the one to explicitly include in the model:

$$X_2 = X_2(P, Y) \tag{18}$$

$$Y = Y_A + Y_B \tag{19}$$

$$Y_A = X_1 + r(\kappa_A - K_A) \tag{20}$$

$$Y_B = PX_2 + r(\kappa_B - K_B). \tag{21}$$

Tastes are assumed to be identical. The identical tastes assumption allows demand to be expressed as a function of the combined income of A and B. With no net saving, identical tastes (equal income elasticities) ensure a balance of payments between the two countries. Homotheticity is also assumed, but is not a critical assumption. Homotheticity simplifies the mathematics and rules out cases where income elasticities are negative (inferior goods) or large (luxury goods).

The model is completed with the addition of the transnational pollution relationships. The pollution flow depends on emissions emanating from both countries. As suggested by (1) and (6), the emissions released by each country depend on output and on the pollution abatement equipment standard:

$$R = R(E_A, E_B) \tag{22}$$

$$E_A = E_A(X_1, Z_1) \tag{23}$$

$$E_B = E_B(X_2, Z_2). \tag{24}$$

Many of the preceding assumptions are necessary only for mathematical certainty (unambiguously signed matrix determinant) in the general case. For simulation purposes, the static model could be constructed without all but the competitive markets, constant returns to scale, and factor supply assumptions in most cases. In addition, each country's single composite good could be disaggregated into at least two composite goods; the ones responsible for the pollution of interest and all other goods. Merrifield [18] showed that the model could be extended to consider abatement strategies other than production taxes and abatement equipment standards (e.g., emissions taxes, fuel switching, and tariffs), and that more than two countries could be explicitly included.

Total differentiation of each equation (except (1) and (6)), and some substitutions, produces an eight-equation, operational model.[17] The mathematical oper-

[16]For many transnational pollutants, including acid deposition, no direct health effects have been identified. Indirect effects, so far, are only speculative and seem limited to certain subpopulations. In addition, the health impacts would probably not be observed until long after the initial exposure to the pollutant.

[17]The determinant of the equation system is unambiguously positive. No additional assumptions are required to obtain that result.

ations which transform the equations above into the eight equations below are explained in the Appendix:

$$X_1^* - \gamma_{L1}W_A^* + \gamma_{L1}r^* = L_A^* - \lambda_{LZ1}C_{Z1}^* \quad (25)$$

$$X_2^* - \gamma_{L2}W_B^* + \gamma_{L2}r^* = L_B^* - \lambda_{LZ2}C_{Z2}^* \quad (26)$$

$$X_1^* + \gamma_{K1}W_A^* - \gamma_{K1}r^* + \varepsilon R^* - K_A^* = -\lambda_{KZ1}C_{Z1}^* \quad (27)$$

$$X_2^* + \gamma_{K2}W_B^* + \gamma_{K2}r^* + \varepsilon R^* + \psi K_A^* = -\lambda_{KZ2}C_{Z2}^* \quad (28)$$

$$\theta_{L1}W_A^* + \theta_{K1}r^* = -\theta_{V1}V_A^* \quad (29)$$

$$\theta_{L2}W_B^* + \theta_{K2}r^* - P^* = -\theta_{V2}V_B^* \quad (30)$$

$$\pi_1 X_2^* + \pi_1 X_1^* - \alpha'_P P^* = 0 \quad (31)$$

$$\delta_{X1}X_1^* + \delta_{X2}X_2^* - R^* = -\delta_{Z1}C_{Z1}^* + \delta_{Z2}C_{Z2}^*, \quad (32)$$

where

$i^* = di/i$ – the percentage change in i.

$\psi = K_A/K_B$.

V_i = production tax on output of country i; i = A, B.

$\gamma_{L1} = \lambda_{L1}\rho_{K1}\sigma_{LK}^1 + \lambda_{LZ1}\rho_{KZ1}\sigma_{LK}^1$.

$\gamma_{L2} = \lambda_{L2}\rho_{K2}\sigma_{LK}^2 + \lambda_{LZ2}\rho_{KZ2}\sigma_{LK}^2$.

$\gamma_{K1} = \lambda_{K1}\rho_{L1}\sigma_{LK}^1 + \lambda_{KZ1}\rho_{LZ1}\sigma_{LK}^1 + \lambda_{K2}\rho_{L2}\sigma_{LK}^2 + \lambda_{KZ2}\rho_{LZ2}\sigma_{LK}^2$.

σ_{LK}^i = elasticity of substitution of K for L in the production of i.

$i = X_1, X_2, Z_1, Z_2$.

ρ_{ij} = *net* or direct share of input i of the revenues generated from the production of j; $i = L, K$; $j = X_1, X_2, Z_1, Z_2$.

λ_{ij} = *net* or direct share of a country's endowment of i employed in the production of j; $i = L, K$; $j = X_1, X_2, Z_1, Z_2$.

θ_{ij} = *gross* or direct plus indirect share of input i of the revenues generated from the production of j.

π_i = share of total income accounted for by X_i production.

α = price elasticity of demand for X_2; $\alpha < 0$.

α'_P = income compensated price elasticity of demand for X_2; $\alpha'_P < 0$.

δ_{Xi} = partial elasticity of the pollution flow with respect to X_i production; $i = 1, 2$.

ϕ_{Xi} = partial elasticity of country B's pollution flow with respect to X_i production; $i = 1, 2$.

δ_{Zi} = partial elasticity of the pollution flow (country A's flow for acid deposition example) with respect to C_{Zi}; the abatement equipment standard for X_i; $i = 1, 2$.

ϕ_{Zi} = like δ_{Zi} but for country B's pollution flow.

ε = elasticity of capital productivity with respect to the pollution flow.

The eight unknowns or endogenous variables are capital stock of country A (K_A), X_1, X_2, wages (W_A, W_B), price of capital (r), P, R. The policy variables to be examined with the model are changes in abatement equipment standards and production taxes. In the next section, comparative static results will be presented. Welfare implications are discussed after the comparative statics section.

IV. COMPARATIVE STATIC RESULTS

The two control strategies will be discussed first from a general perspective, and then in the context of the acid deposition issue.

A. The General Case

A general property of the model is that with internationally mobile goods, capital, and pollutants, only the equipment standard strategy has an unambiguous impact on pollution flows. That conclusion alone is remarkable. An attempt to reduce pollution by way of a new tax on the output of polluting industries could actually increase pollution! The ambiguity exists because the change in pollution flows due to a reduction in one country's emissions may be more than offset if capital movements increase the other country's output and emissions. In fact, a number of the comparative static results are ambiguously signed. The sign depends on international differences in the pollution and capital intensiveness of production functions, international differences in input substitution elasticities, and the sensitivity of the capital stock to pollution damage.

The change in pollution flows which results from a new production tax imposed by either country depends on which country produces the more pollution-intensive good. Assume country A employs $n\%$ of the total, internationally mobile, capital stock and its emissions account for $m\%$ of pollution flows. If m is greater (less) than n, A's (B's) output is pollution intensive. A new tax on X_2 (B's output) will result in a net increase in pollution flows. A new tax on X_2 (A's output) reduces pollution flows.

The changes in the price of capital, the price of labor, the terms of trade, and the outputs of each country that normally follow imposition of a new production tax are reinforced when pollution flows and the scarcity of capital are directly related. For example, if a tax on X_2 is introduced, the price consumers face rises and the price received by producers falls. Factor rewards fall in country B, prompting some capital to migrate to A. X_1 producers demand additional capital because its price has fallen relative to W_A, and because the higher consumer price for X_2 increases the demand for X_1. If the tax has a net negative (positive) effect on pollution flows, the bulk of additional (diminished) capital services are employed in (taken from) A (B).

The comparative statics of a change in the abatement equipment standard are slightly more complicated. A tightening of the standard in either country reduces the pollution flow[18] and is likely to increase the relative scarcity of the good produced in the country tightening its standard. A country could reduce the relative scarcity of its output by tightening its standard if they are best able to absorb the additional capital services released when pollution is reduced. Unless the production

[18] The unambiguity of this result is lost if pollution flows are not identical (not a public bad) in the two countries, clearly the case for acid deposition in the U.S. and Canada which is considered in Subsection IVB.

of abatement equipment is tremendously capital intensive, the availability of additional capital services depresses the price of capital and raises the price of labor in both countries. Labor prices may fall if the passive country's share of total income is large and the acting country can more easily substitute capital for labor. Then the drop in the price of the acting country's output necessitates a reduction in its payments to labor. Changes in the output of either country are uncertain because the diversion of capital and labor into pollution abatement contradicts the reduced scarcity of capital services.

The discussion of comparative static results becomes more concrete and is thus easier to follow if the model is applied to a particular transnational pollution issue. Information relevant to the North American acid deposition controversy is used to help interpret the comparative static results discussed in Subsection IVB.

B. The North American Acid Deposition Issue

Preliminary research suggests that long range transport of oxides of sulfur and nitrogen generated in both countries is responsible for acid deposition in each country. The sulfur oxides are more important than the oxides of nitrogen. Canada receives at least 3 units of airborne sulfur from the U.S. for each unit the U.S. receives from Canada [12]. U.S. sulfur emissions are responsible for about 50% of Canada's sulfur deposition [12], while Canadian emissions are to blame for only 10 to 20% ([22] and Forster, personal communication, 1984) of U.S. sulfur deposition.

Distributive shares data ([7, 19]) were also useful in reducing the ambiguity of comparative static results. For the period 1976–1979, labor's share of total output was 78% in the U.S. and 76% in Canada, with the remainder going to capital. The U.S.'s capital stock is 10 times larger than Canada's [11]. Because it is unreasonable to assume that acid deposition flows are identical in the two countries, an additional equation and endogenous variable are added to the model. R is replaced by R_A and R_B, where R_A and R_B are still functions of the emissions of both countries. The determinant of the nine-equation system remains unambiguously positive. The mathematical expression for each comparative static result is in the Appendix.

If Canada levies a production tax on its output, X_2, the relative selling price increases, which lowers X_2 and raises X_1. As in Forster [9], the pollution abatement effort reduces factor rewards. The price of capital falls, so that the capital leaving Canada can be absorbed in the U.S. The loss (addition) of capital in Canada (the U.S.) reduces (raises) the productivity of labor, and thereby lowers (increases) the wage rate. Because of the difference in the size of the U.S. and Canada, the effect on Canadian acid deposition of the reduction in X_2 is much more significant than the much smaller increase in X_1. Canadian acid deposition is reduced by the tax on X_2. The Canadian tax has a small, but negative, effect on acid deposition in the U.S. The effect of the reduction in Canadian emissions is not quite offset by the increase in U.S. emissions.

If the U.S. imposes a tax on X_1, most of the comparative static results are the reverse of those which follow a tax on X_2. However, there are some similarities. The price of capital falls so that capital leaving one country can be absorbed by the other. The price of capital will fall by much more as a result of a tax on X_1, than a tax on X_2. The smaller Canadian economy will be required to absorb a relatively large amount of capital. Again, there is little or no change in U.S. acid deposition.

The effect of a reduction in one country's emissions is offset by an increase in the other country's emissions. In percentage terms, X_2, rises much more than X_1 falls. As a result, the tax on X_1 increases acid deposition in Canada, while leaving it virtually unchanged in the U.S.

If the two countries act jointly and simultaneously levy a production tax, X_1 and X_2 production will not be altered.[19] Consequently, the terms of trade will not change. However, the price received by producers is reduced by the taxes, which means that the price of capital and wages in both countries fall. With no change in X_1 or X_2, acid deposition is unchanged in both countries.

In Canada, a stricter abatement equipment standard means an increase in C_{Z2}, the ratio of Z_2 to X_2. The initial direct effect acts to reduce acid deposition in two ways. The additional Z_2 directly reduces the release of Canadian emissions, and the production of additional Z_2 means the diversion of some capital and labor from producers of X_2, thereby further reducing emissions. Furthermore, the initial tightening of Canada's capital market causes some capital to leave the U.S. thereby curtailing U.S. emissions. That impact is more significant the easier the U.S. firms can substitute labor for capital, and the greater the difficulty in making input substitutions in Canada. The reduction in acid deposition in both countries reduces the scarcity of capital. If the reduction in K scarcity is significant, X_1 and X_2 go up, instead of down.

The key to understanding the impact of an increase in C_{Z2} is the realization that comparative static results are a combination of first- and second-round effects. In the first round, production and use of additional Z_2 reduces emissions and acid deposition in both countries. X_1 and X_2 are reduced, and the price of capital increases to shift some capital from the U.S. to Canada. That, in turn, reduces U.S. wages. The change in the terms of trade, and the fate of Canadian wages, depends on whether the relative scarcity of X_2 increases or decreases. Since X_2 producers lose workers and capital to Z_2 producers, while X_1 producers lost only capital, it seems likely that the relative scarcity of X_2 will increase. However, that cannot be stated with certainty. If labor is much more readily substituted for capital in the U.S. than in Canada, the relative scarcity of X_1 increases.

The first-round may be offset, overwhelmed, or complemented by the second-round effects. The curtailment of acid deposition reduces the scarcity of capital services, thereby lowering the price of capital, increasing the production of both goods, and increasing emissions in both countries.

Therefore, there is some degree of uncertainty about each of the comparative static results of an increase in C_{Z2}. In general, the sign of the results depends on differences in σ_{LK} between the two nations, the capital intensiveness of Z_2, and the sensitivity of capital productivity to changes in acid deposition (ε_A and ε_B). As suggested earlier, when A and B are the U.S. and Canada, respectively, the composite goods X_1 and X_2 include many of the same goods and services. With similar technologies available in both countries, σ_{LK} is not likely to differ significantly between them. Furthermore, since most industrialized nations only devote 1 to 2% of their resources to pollution control [24] the degree of capital intensiveness of Z_2 is likely to be a trivial factor in determining the sign of a comparative static

[19] Households receive the tax proceeds in lump-sum payments. With unchanged relative prices, consumers purchase the same amount of X_1 and X_2 because the income effect of the tax proceeds offsets the effect of the increase in the absolute price of both goods.

result. From that additional information it follows that an increase in C_{Z2} will shift the terms of trade in Canada's favor (the price effect of Comolli's [6] increase in β was the same), lower the price of capital, and raise the wages of workers in both countries. Acid deposition falls in both countries.

The remaining comparative static results (X_1 and X_2) depend on values of ε_A and ε_B, in the initial equilibrium. For small values of ε_A and ε_B output decreases, and for larger values production of X_1 and X_2 increases. To gain some insight on what constitutes a small or large value of the ε's, some numerical illustration is useful. If the price elasticity of demand and input substitution elasticities are unity, the critical value of the ε's is 0.17. If ε_A and ε_B are less than 0.17, a 1% increase in C_{Z2} reduces X_2 production. If a 1% reduction in acid deposition in each country reduces the scarcity of each country's capital stock by 0.17%, the 1% increase in C_{Z2} leaves X_2 production unchanged. Since only a small part of the capital services of either nation is affected by acid deposition, it would seem, *a priori*, that the true value[20] of the ε's is well below one, close to the critical value of 0.17 suggested by this illustration.

Recall that for the U.S., a production tax does not reduce acid deposition. fortunately, an increase in C_{Z1} cannot fail to reduce U.S. acid deposition. The first-round effects of the increase in C_{Z1} are analogous to the Canadian case, with second-round effects again either complementing, offsetting, or overwhelming the first-round effects. Using the same information with regard to the capital intensiveness of pollution abatement equipment and similarity of σ_{LK} in the U.S. and Canada to analyze the comparative static results of the increase in C_{Z1}, the following results emerge. The terms of trade shift in favor of the U.S., the price of capital falls, wages of U.S. workers rise, and there is little or no change in Canadian wages. The relative scarcity of X_1 increases, because its producers lose L and K to Z_1 producers, while X_2 producers lose only K. Pollution cleanup reduces damage to capital, thereby increasing the effective supply of capital. In the U.S., additional capital and an improvement in the terms of trade raises wages. For Canadian wages, the terms of trade effect and additional capital work in opposite directions.

The R_B, X_1, and X_2 comparative statics depend on the ε's. Unless ε_A is greater than seven, an increase in C_{Z1} reduces R_B. It seems unlikely that a 1% decrease in U.S. acid deposition would reduce capital scarcity by over 7%. The critical value of the ε's for the X_1 and X_2 comparative static results is less than 0.1, a number probably closer to the true values of the ε's.

If both countries agree to raise their abatement equipment standards, there will be no change in the terms of trade if the σ_{LK} are similar in the two countries. The reduced scarcity of capital services lowers the price of capital, raises wages in both countries, and reduces acid deposition in both countries.

V. WELFARE ANALYSIS

A government's decision to adopt a particular abatement strategy depends less on the expected reduction in pollution than on the expected increase in welfare. The strategy which reduces pollution the most may not be the welfare maximizing

[20] There is no reason why ε_A and ε_B should be equal. This discussion is only intended to suggest what general range ε_A and ε_B should be in for X_1 and X_2 to be uncertain.

strategy. Pollution affects only production directly, so welfare is defined as

$$U_i = U_i(D_{1i}, D_{2i}), \qquad i = \text{A, B}, \tag{33}$$

where

U_i = welfare of country i.

D_{1i} = quantity of X_1 consumed in country i; i = A, B.

D_{2i} = quantity of X_2 consumed in country i; i = A, B.

Changes in A's welfare ($d\omega_A$) and B's welfare ($d\omega_B$) can be written:

$$d\omega_A = r^*(\kappa_A - K_A)(r/Y_A) - P^*(PD_{2A}/Y_A) \tag{34}$$

$$d\omega_B = r^*(\kappa_B - K_B)(r/Y_B) + P^*(X_2 - D_{2B})(P/Y_B). \tag{35}$$

For the complete derivation of (34) and (35) see the Appendix. Country A will seek a strategy which reduces P and increases r if it is a net creditor, or reduces r otherwise. The opposite is true for country B. The data ([7, 19]) suggest that Canada was a net debtor and that the U.S. was a net creditor.[21]

A tax on X_2 will raise Canadian welfare. The resulting increase in P and reduction in r raise the Canadian welfare index. Furthermore, acid deposition in Canada is reduced. A reduction in the wages of Canadian workers is also an outgrowth of the tax. A potentially undesirable distributional consequence of the tax could be eliminated by redistributing the tax receipts to workers, rather than in the lump-sum manner assumed so far.

In the U.S., the welfare implications of a production tax are less clear-cut, because for the U.S., the drop in r has a detrimental effect on welfare. The wages of American workers are also reduced. The welfare implications are further complicated, because acid deposition in the U.S. is not greatly affected by the tax.

If the two countries jointly impose a production tax, that is, a new, small production tax is introduced simultaneously for X_1 and X_2, U.S. welfare is reduced and Canadian welfare increases. The terms of trade are not affected, so the welfare implications are the result of the reduction in the price of capital. The production taxes drive a wedge between the producer and consumer price of the goods, thereby reducing the return to labor and capital in both countries. Those results could be altered by changing the formula for redistributing the tax revenues.

A Canadian decision to increase C_{Z2} is also likely to raise the Canadian welfare index, but with less certainty than the new tax on X_2. Recall that the increase in P, the reduction in r, and the raise for Canadian workers are certain to follow the hike in C_{Z2} only if U.S. and Canadian σ_{LK}'s are similar, and if Z_2 production is not a nationally significant capital-intensive process. The changes in P and r which follow an increase in C_{Z1}, again, appear to have contradictory welfare implications for the U.S., although with the same reasons for uncertainty as in Canada. Joint

[21] While a precise measure of the importance of capital payments in the total welfare equation depends on the year of the data and whether stock or flow data are used, it seems safe to say that net income from foreign investment is at least 10% of the U.S. capital owner's total income. Likewise, at least 10% of Canada's net capital income goes to foreigners. Consequently, changes in the price of capital are important in each country's welfare outlook. As a side note, it appears as if ballooning government budget deficits caused the U.S. to join the ranks of net debtor nations in 1984. The older data suffice for the illustrative purposes to which they are being applied.

action again favors Canada. With similar σ_{LK}'s, the simultaneous increase in C_{Z1} and C_{Z2} has little or no impact on the terms of trade, but it reduces the price of capital.

Which of the two strategies discussed so far will be favored in each country, either acting independently or in preparing a negotiating position for joint action? In Canada, the production tax might be favored. The new tax on X_2 unambiguously increases welfare. While the welfare implications of an increase in C_{Z2} are less certain (welfare could actually be reduced), the potential for Canada to significantly improve its welfare is greater. Recall expression (35). Introducing a production tax will reduce X_2 and D_{2B} proportionately, resulting in a smaller absolute difference between them. The larger the price elasticity of demand for X_2, the larger the drop in X_2 and D_{2B} following the introduction of the tax. If the marginal damage to capital (the ε's) is large in the neighborhood of the initial equilibrium, the increase in C_{Z2} could increase P and X_2 simultaneously and reduce r while some foreign-owned capital leaves, the best possible outcome. However, if production technologies in the two countries are such that σ^2_{LK} is significantly greater than σ^1_{LK}, the terms of trade will not be shifted in Canada's favor by the increase in C_{Z2}. Whether Canada will favor the production tax or the tighter abatement equipment standard depends on risk aversion and prior knowledge of the value of the ε's, the price elasticity of demand for X_2, and input substitution elasticities. If the price elasticity of demand for X_2 were known to be large, and if σ^2_{LK} were significantly greater than σ^1_{LK}, the best course of action for Canada might be to refrain from taking any unilateral abatement efforts and instead pressure the U.S., through diplomatic channels, to reduce its emissions. As the net importer of acid deposition precursers, Canada does have the advantage of the so-called diplomatic high ground in demanding action from the U.S.

The U.S. decision is more difficult, and in another sense easier to make. It is more difficult, because both the tax and the hike in C_{Z1} will lower the price of capital. Although the terms of trade are definitely improved by the production tax, and very probably improved by the increase in C_{Z1}, the drop in r prevents either strategy from producing an unambiguous welfare improvement. The decision is made easier, because with an increase in C_{Z1} acid deposition is reduced, and there is at least some chance that P and r will both move in the desired direction. If the marginal damage to capital is high, X_1 could increase even while its relative price increases. If the U.S.'s apparent recent switch to net debtor status is permanent, the decision becomes even less difficult.

VI. SUMMARY AND CONCLUSIONS

The model discussed has shown the importance of capital flows and trade in determining the best strategy to reduce transfrontier pollution. An open economy does not make it impossible for either country to take effective unilateral action against a transnational pollutant, but each country must recognize that some policies could increase, rather than decrease, pollution flows. Foreign emissions could be increased by the policy enough to offset the effect of reduced domestic emissions. The model has also shown that the distributional and terms of trade effects vary with the abatement strategy. Along with the effect on pollution flows, those factors will weigh heavily in the decision on which abatement strategy is best.

Assuming the σ_{LK} do not differ greatly between the U.S. and Canada, and that ε_A and ε_B are much less than one, the following general conclusions emerge. Canada is more likely to benefit (or less likely to suffer) from the implementation of unilateral or joint pollution abatement efforts. Even though Canada is the smaller country and it receives a larger share of acid deposition from the U.S. than the U.S. receives from Canada, both abatement options will reduce Canada's acid deposition, while only the hike in C_{Z1} reduces U.S. acid deposition. While the first result appears to be consistent with the observed behavior of the Canadian and U.S. federal governments, the conclusion stated in the preceding sentence is not. The conclusion drawn from this model that Canada appears to have more unilateral abatement options is due primarily to two factors: the international mobility of capital, and the fact that Canada's capital stock is only a tenth as large as the U.S. capital stock, even though Canadian emissions account for more than a tenth of the acid deposition occurring in both countries.

The welfare index adopted in Section V suggests that changes in the terms of trade and the price of capital by themselves capture welfare changes. However, politicians will certainly continue to weigh the distributional effects of policy. In addition, if factors such as the existence value of historic structures, visibility, and biodiversity (which are not explicitly included in the model) are significant in the decision-making process, the impact of an abatement strategy on pollution flows is important independent of the welfare changes measured by $d\omega_A$ and $d\omega_B$.

Certainly, this research is not the final word on transnational pollution abatement strategies, either generally, or on the more specific North American acid deposition issue. Rather it offers a beginning by expanding the use of GE trade models to new analytical territory, and for policymakers it suggests several questions which should be given additional, more in-depth attention.

MATHEMATICAL APPENDIX

1. Transformation of a Zero Profit Equation into Percentage Change Form

a. Begin with (3) and (5).

b. Totally differentiate each:

$$dC_{L2}\,W_B + C_{L2}\,dW_B + dC_{K2}\,r + C_{K2}\,dr + C_{Z2}\,dP_{Z2} = dP \tag{A1}$$

$$dC_{LZ2}\,W_B + C_{LZ2}\,dW_B + dC_{KZ2}\,r + C_{KZ2}\,dr = dP_{Z2}. \tag{A2}$$

c. Divide through by P in (A1) and P_{Z2} in (A2) and multiply each term by i/i = one, where i = the change variable of that term:

$$C^*_{L2}\rho_{L2} + \rho_{L2}W^*_B + C_{K2}\rho^*_{K2} + \rho_{K2}r^* + \rho_{Z2}P^*_{Z2} = P^* \tag{A3}$$

$$C^*_{LZ2}\rho_{LZ2} + \rho_{LZ2}W^*_B + C^*_{KZ2}\rho_{KZ2} + \rho_{KZ2}r^* = P_{Z2}. \tag{A4}$$

d. Note that for homogeneous production functions

$$C_{L2}\rho^*_{L2} + C^*_{K2}\rho_{K2} = C^*_{LZ2}\rho_{LZ2} + C^*_{KZ2}\rho_{KZ2} = 0$$

then substitute (A4) for P_{Z2} in (A3),

$$\theta_{L2}W_B^* + \theta_{K2}r^* - P^* = 0, \tag{A5}$$

where $\theta_{K2} = \rho_{L2} + \rho_{Z2}\rho_{LZ2}$ and $\theta_{K2} = \rho_{K2} + \rho_{Z2}\rho_{KZ2}$.

2. Transformation of a Full Employment Equation into Percentage Change Form

a. Begin with (10): $C_{K2}X_2 + C_{KZ2}Z_2 = K_B$.

b. Substitute (12) into (10) and obtain

$$C_{K2}X_2 + C_{KZ2}C_{Z2}X_2 = K_B. \tag{A6}$$

c. Totally differentiate:

$$dC_{K2}\,X_2 + C_{KZ2}X_2 + dC_{KZ}\,2C_{Z2}X_2 + C_{KZ2}\,dC_{Z2}\,X_2 + C_{KZ2}C_{Z2}\,dX_2 = dK_B. \tag{A7}$$

d. Divide every term by K_B and multiply each term by one i/i, where i for each term is the change variable:

$$\lambda_{L2}C_{K2}^* + X_2^* + \lambda_{KZ2}C_{Z2}^* + \lambda_{KZ2}C_{KZ2}^* = K_B^*. \tag{A8}$$

e. Input–output ratios are a function of input prices, and in the case of capital, they are also a function of the pollution flow:

$$C_{K2}^* = \rho_{L2}\sigma_{lk}W_B^* + \rho_{K2}\sigma_K r^* + \beta_2 R^* \tag{A9}$$

$$C_{KZ2} = \rho_{LZ2}\sigma_{LK}W_B^* + \rho_{KZ2}\sigma_{KK}r^* + \beta_{Z2}R^*. \tag{A10}$$

If all factor prices change in the same proportion, and the pollution flow does not change ($R^* = 0$), $C_{K2} = C_{KZ2} = 0$. That implies the following:

$$\rho_{K2}\sigma_{KK} = -\rho_{L2}\sigma_{LK} \tag{A11}$$

$$\rho_{KZ2}\sigma_{KK} = -\rho_{LZ2}\sigma_{LK}. \tag{A12}$$

f. After substituting (A11) and (A12) into (A9) and (A10), (A9) and (A10) replace C_{K2} and C_{KZ2} in (A8). Also ψK_A replaces K_B,

$$\psi K_A^* + X_2^* + \gamma_{K2}r^* + \varepsilon R^* = -\lambda_{KZ2}C_{Z2}^*, \tag{A13}$$

where $\varepsilon = \lambda_{K2}\beta_2 + \lambda_{KZ2}\beta_{Z2}$.

3. Transformation of the Demand Equations into a Single Percentage Change Equation

a. Begin with (18)–(21).

b. Totally differentiate and rewrite in percentage change form.

c. Transformed (20) and (21) are then substituted for Y_A^* and Y_B^* in transformed (19), which is then substituted for Y^* in transformed (18):

$$\pi_1 X_2^* - \pi_1 X_1^* - \alpha_p P^* = 0. \tag{A14}$$

4. Transformation of the Pollution Flow Equations into a Single Percentage Change Equation

a. Begin with (22), (23), and (24).

b. Totally differentiate each, divide through by R, E_A, and E_B, respectively, and divide each term by i/i, where i is each term's change variable.

c. Substitute E_A and E_B from the transformed versions of (23) and (24), respectively, into transformed (22):

$$\delta_{X1} X_1^* + \delta_{X2} X_2^* - R^* = -\delta_{Z1} C_{Z1}^* - \delta_{Z2} C_{Z2}^* \tag{A15}$$

5. Derivation of the Welfare Index for Country A

a. Begin with (A16) and (A17)

$$U_A = U_A(D_{1A}, D_{2A}) \tag{A16}$$

$$Y_A = D_{1A} + PD_{2A} = r\kappa_A + W_A L_A. \tag{A17}$$

b. Totally differentiate (A16) and divide through by

$$dU_A/dD_{1A} = U_{1A}$$

$$dU_A/U_{1A} = d\omega_A = dD_{1A} + U_{2A}/U_{1A} dD_{2A} \tag{A18}$$

In equilibrium, the ratio of marginal utilities (U_{2A}/U_{1A}) is equal to P (P_2/P_1), the price ratio.

c. Totally differentiate (A17):

$$dY_A = dD_{1A} + P\,dD_{2A} + D_{2A}\,dP = dr\,\kappa_A + dW_A\,L_A \tag{A19}$$

d. Note the $d\omega_A$ in (A18) equals the left two terms in the middle of (A19). Substitute $d\omega_A$ into (A19) and divide through by Y_A:

$$Y_A = d\omega_A/Y_A + dP\,D_{2A}/Y_A = dr\,\kappa_A/Y_A + dW_A\,L_A/Y_A \tag{A20}$$

e. Redefine $d\omega_A = d\omega_A/Y_A$, reduce (A20) to the two sides of the right equal sign, and convert to percentage change form:

$$d\omega_A = r^*(r\kappa_A/Y_A) + W_A^*(W_A L_A/Y_A) - P^*(PD_{2A}/Y_A). \tag{A21}$$

f. Use (29) to define W_A^* in terms of r^*:

$$W_A^* = -\theta_{K1}/\theta_{L1} r^*. \tag{A22}$$

g. Substitute (A22) for W_A in (A21) and then simplify:

$$d\omega_A = r^*(r\kappa_A/Y_A) - (rK_A/W_AL_A)(W_AL_A/Y_A)r^* - P^*(PD_{2A}/Y_A) \tag{A23}$$

$$d\omega_A = (r/Y_A)(\kappa_A - K_A)r^* - P^*(PD_{2A}/Y_A). \tag{A24}$$

Comparative Static Results

6. A New Production Tax Is Levied on X_2. Assume $\theta_{V2} = 0.01$

a. $R_B^* = \alpha_P \cdot 0.01 \cdot [\psi\gamma_{L2}\phi_{XB}(\gamma_{K1} + \gamma_{L1}) - \phi_{XA}\gamma_{L1}(\gamma_{K2} + \gamma_{L2})]V_B^*$
inverse relationship

b. $R_A^* = (-0.01) \cdot \alpha_P[-\varepsilon_B\gamma_{L1}\gamma_{L2}(\phi_{XA}\delta_{XB} - \phi_{XB}\delta_{XA}) + \delta_{XA}\gamma_{L1}(\gamma_{L2} + \gamma_{K2}) - \psi\gamma_{L2}\delta_{XB}(\gamma_{K1} + \gamma_{L1})]V_B^*$

c. $X_2^* = \alpha_P\gamma_{L2} \cdot 0.01 \cdot [\phi_{XA}\varepsilon_B\gamma_{L1} + \psi(\delta_{XA}\varepsilon_A\gamma_{L1} + \gamma_{K1} + \gamma_{L1})]V_B^*$
inverse relationship

d. $P^* = 0.01 \cdot \pi_1[\gamma_{L1}(\gamma_{K2} + \gamma_{L2} + \phi_{XB}\gamma_{L2}\varepsilon_B + \psi\gamma_{L2}\delta_{XB}\varepsilon_A + \gamma_{L2}\phi_{XA}\varepsilon_B) + \psi\gamma_{L2}(\delta_{XA}\varepsilon_A\gamma_{L1} + \gamma_{K1} - \gamma_{K1})]V_B^*$ positive relationship

e. $W_B^* = \alpha_P \cdot 0.01 \cdot [\theta_{L1}(\phi_{XB}\gamma_{L2}\varepsilon_B + \gamma_{L2} + \gamma_{K2}) + \phi_{XA}\varepsilon_B\gamma_{L1} + \psi(\delta_{XA}\varepsilon_A\gamma_{L1} + \gamma_{L1} + \gamma_{K1} + \delta_{XB}\gamma_{L2}\varepsilon_A\gamma_{L1})]V_B^*$ inverse relationship

f. $X_1^* = \alpha_P\theta_{L1} \cdot (-0.01) \cdot [\gamma_{L2} + \gamma_{K2} + \phi_{XB}\gamma_{L2}\varepsilon_B + \psi\gamma_{L2}\varepsilon_A\delta_{XB}]V_B^*$
positive relationship

g. $W_A^* = \alpha_P\theta_{K1} \cdot (-0.01) \cdot [\gamma_{L2} + \gamma_{K2} + \phi_{XB}\gamma_{L2}\varepsilon_B + \psi\gamma_{L2}\varepsilon_A\delta_{XB}]V_B^*$
positive relationship

h. $r^* = \alpha_P\theta_{L1} \cdot (-0.01) \cdot [\gamma_{L2} + \gamma_{K2} + \phi_{XB}\gamma_{L2}\varepsilon_B + \psi\gamma_{L2}\varepsilon_A\delta_{XB}$
inverse relationship

i. $K_A^* = \alpha_P \cdot 0.01 \cdot [\gamma_{L2}\{\varepsilon_B(-\delta_{XB}\varepsilon_A\gamma_{L1} + \phi_{XB}(\delta_{XA}\varepsilon_A\gamma_{L1} + \gamma_{K1} + \gamma_{L1})) - \delta_{XA}\varepsilon_A\gamma_{L1} - \gamma_{K1} - \gamma_{L1}\} - \gamma_{K1}(\varepsilon_A\delta_{XA}\gamma_{L1} + \gamma_{K1} + \gamma_{L1})]V_B^*$
positive relationship.

7. An Increase in C_{Z2}^*

a. $R_B^* = C_{Z2}^*\lambda_{LZ2}[\alpha_P\{\phi_{XB}\theta_{L1}\gamma_{K2} + \theta_{L2}\gamma_{L1}(\psi\phi_{XB} - \phi_{XA}) + \psi\theta_{L2}(\varepsilon_A\gamma_{L1}(\phi_{XB}\delta_{XA} - \phi_{XA}\delta_{XB}) + \phi_{XB}\gamma_{K1})\} - \gamma_{L1}\gamma_{K2}\pi_1(\phi_{XB} + \phi_{XA})] - C_{Z2}^*(\lambda_{KZ2} + \delta_{Z2}\varepsilon_A\psi)[-\alpha_P(\phi_{XB}\theta_{L1}\gamma_{L2} + \phi_{XA}\theta_{L2}\gamma_{L1}) + \gamma_{L2}\gamma_{L1}\pi_1(\phi_{XB} + \phi_{XA})] - \phi_{Z2}C_{Z2}^*[\alpha_P\{\theta_{L1}(\gamma_{K2} + \gamma_{L2}) + \psi(\theta_{L2}(\gamma_{K1} + \gamma_{L1}) + \varepsilon_A(\delta_{XA}\theta_{L2}\gamma_{L1} + \delta_{XB}\theta_{L1}\gamma_{L2}))\} - \pi_1\{\gamma_{L1}(\varepsilon_A\psi\gamma_{L2}\delta_{XB} + \gamma_{K2} + \gamma_{L2}) + \gamma_{L2}\psi(\delta_{XA}\varepsilon_A\gamma_{L1} + \gamma_{L1} + \gamma_{K1})\}]$

b. $X_2^* = \lambda_{LZ2}C_{Z2}^*[\alpha_P\{\theta_{L1}\gamma_{K2} + \phi_{XA}\varepsilon_B\theta_{L2}\gamma_{L1}$
$+\psi\theta_{L2}(\gamma_{L1} + \gamma_{K1} + \delta_{XA}\varepsilon_A\gamma_{L1})\} - \pi_1\gamma_{K2}\gamma_{L1}]$
$-C_{Z2}^*\gamma_{L2}(\pi_1\gamma_{L1} - \alpha_P\theta_{L1})(\lambda_{K2} + \delta_{Z2}\varepsilon_A\psi + \phi_{Z2}\varepsilon_B)$

c. $X_1^* = -C_{Z2}^*\lambda_{LZ2}[\alpha_P\{\gamma_{L1}\theta_{L2}(1 + \varepsilon_B\phi_{XB} + \psi\delta_{XB}\varepsilon_A\gamma_{L1})\} + \gamma_{K2}\pi_1\gamma_{L1}]$
$-\gamma_{L1}C_{Z2}^*(\lambda_{KZ2} + \delta_{Z2}\varepsilon_A\psi + \phi_{Z2}\varepsilon_B)(\pi_1\gamma_{L2} - \alpha_P\theta_{L2})$

d. $W_A^* = -\lambda_{LZ2}\theta_{K1}C_{Z2}^*[\alpha_P\theta_{L2}\{1 + \varepsilon_B\phi_{XB} + \psi\varepsilon_A\delta_{XB}\} + \pi_1\gamma_{K2}]$
$-\theta_{K1}C_{Z2}^*(\lambda_{KZ2} + \delta_{Z2}\varepsilon_A\psi + \phi_{Z2}\varepsilon_B)(\pi_1\gamma_{L2} - \alpha_P\theta_{L2})$

e. $r^* = -W_A^*\theta_{L1}/\theta_{K1}$

f. $W_B^* = \lambda_{LZ2}C_{Z2}^*[-\alpha_P\theta_{L1}\theta_{K2}(1 + \varepsilon_B\phi_{XB} + \psi\delta_{XB}\varepsilon_A) + \pi_1\{\gamma_{L1}(1 + \varepsilon_B\phi_{XB}$
$+\psi\delta_{XB}\varepsilon_A + \phi_{XA}\varepsilon_B + \psi\delta_{XA} + \psi) + \theta_{L1}\gamma_{K2} + \psi\gamma_{K1}\}]$
$-C_{Z2}^*(\lambda_{KZ2} + \delta_{Z2}\varepsilon_A\psi + \phi_{Z2}\varepsilon_B)(-\alpha_P\theta_{L1}\theta_{K2} + \pi_1(\gamma_{L1} - \gamma_{L2}\theta_{L1}))$

g. $P^* = \lambda_{LZ2}\pi_1C_{Z2}^*[\gamma_{L1}\theta_{L2}(1 + \varepsilon_B) + \theta_{L1}\gamma_{K2} + \psi\theta_{L2}\gamma_{L1}(1 + \varepsilon_A) + \psi\theta_{L2}\gamma_{K1}]$
$-\pi_1C_{Z2}^*(\lambda_{KZ2} + \delta_{Z2}\varepsilon_A\psi + \phi_{Z2}\varepsilon_B)(\theta_{L2}\gamma_{L1} - \theta_{L1}\gamma_{L2})$

h. $K_A^* = -\lambda_{LZ2}C_{Z2}^*[\alpha_P\{\varepsilon_B\theta_{L2}\gamma_{L1}(\phi_{XA}\delta_{XB}\varepsilon_A + \phi_{XB} + \phi_{XB}\delta_{XA}\varepsilon_A)$
$+\gamma_{K1}\theta_{L2}(1 + \phi_{XB}\varepsilon_B) + \gamma_{L1}\theta_{L2}(1 + \delta_{XA}\varepsilon_A) - \delta_{XB}\varepsilon_A\theta_{L1}\gamma_{K2}\}$
$+\gamma_{L1}\pi_1\gamma_{K2}(\varepsilon_A + 1) + \gamma_{K2}\pi_1\gamma_{K1}] - C_{Z2}^*(\lambda_{KZ2} + \phi_{Z2}\varepsilon_B)[-\alpha_P\{\theta_{L2}\gamma_{L1}(1$
$+\delta_{XA}\varepsilon_A) + \theta_{L2}\gamma_{K1} + \delta_{XB}\gamma_{L2}\theta_{L1}\varepsilon\} + \gamma_{L2}\gamma_{L1}\pi(1 + \varepsilon_A) + \gamma_{L2}\gamma_{K1}\pi_1]$
$+\delta_{Z2}\varepsilon_AC_{Z2}^*[-\alpha_P\{\theta_{L2}(\delta_{XA}\varepsilon_A\gamma_{L1}\gamma_{L1} + \gamma_{K1}) + \delta_{XB}\varepsilon_A\theta_{L1}\gamma_{L2}\}$
$+\pi_1\gamma_{L1}\gamma_{L2}(1 + \varepsilon_B) + \pi_1\gamma_{L2}\gamma_{K2}]$

i. $R_A^* = \lambda_{LZ2}C_{Z2}^*[\alpha_P\{-\delta_{XA}\gamma_{L1}\theta_{L2}(1 + \phi_{XB}\varepsilon_B)$
$+\delta_{XB}(\theta_{L1}\gamma_{K2} + \phi_{XA}\varepsilon_B\theta_{L2}\gamma_{L1} + \psi\theta_{L2}(\gamma_{K1} + \gamma_{L1}))\} - \gamma_{K2}\pi_1\gamma_{L1}]$
$+C_{Z2}^*(\lambda_{KZ2} + \phi_{Z2}\varepsilon_B)[\alpha_P(\delta_{XB}\theta_{L1}\gamma_{L2} + \delta_{XA}\theta_{L2}\gamma_{L1}) - \gamma_{L2}\gamma_{L1}\pi_1]$
$-\delta_{Z2}C_{Z2}^*[\alpha_P\{\theta_{L1}\gamma_{L2}(1 + \phi_{XB}\varepsilon_B) + \theta_{L1}\gamma_{K2}$
$+\psi\theta_{L2}\gamma_{K1} + \theta_{L2}\gamma_{L1}(\phi_{XA}\varepsilon_B + \psi)\}$
$-\pi_1\{\gamma_{L1}\gamma_{L2}(1 + \varepsilon_B + \psi) + \gamma_{L1}\gamma_{K2} + \gamma_{L2}\psi\gamma_{K1}\}]$.

8. A Production Tax is Levied on X_1. Assume $\theta_{V1} = 0.01$

a. $R_A^* = \alpha_P \cdot 0.01 \cdot [\delta_{XA}(\phi_{XB}\varepsilon_B\gamma_{L2} + \gamma_{L2} + \gamma_{K2}) - \delta_{XB}\phi_{XA}\varepsilon_B\gamma_{L2}$
$-\psi\delta_{XB}\gamma_{L2}(\gamma_{K1} + \gamma_{L1})]V_A^*$

b. $R_B^* = \alpha_P \cdot 0.01 \cdot [\gamma_{L1}\phi_{XA}(\gamma_{K2} + \gamma_{L2}) - \psi\phi_{XB}\gamma_{L2}(\gamma_{K1} + \gamma_{L1})$
$-\psi\gamma_{L1}\varepsilon_A\gamma_{L2}(\phi_{XA}\delta_{XB} - \phi_{XB}\delta_{XA})]V_A^*$

c. $K_A^* = \alpha_P \cdot 0.01 \cdot [\gamma_{L1}\gamma_{L2}\{\varepsilon_A\varepsilon_B(\phi_{XB}\delta_{XA} - \phi_{XA}\delta_{XB}) + \varepsilon_B\phi_{XB} + \gamma_{K2} + \gamma_{L2}$
$+\varepsilon_A\delta_{XA}(\gamma_{K2} + \gamma_{L2})\} + \gamma_{K1}(\gamma_{L2} + \gamma_{K2} + \phi_{XB}\varepsilon_B\gamma_{L2})]V_A^*$
inverse relationship

d. $X_1^* = \alpha_P\gamma_{L1} \cdot 0.01 \cdot [\gamma_{L2}(\phi_{XB}\varepsilon_B + 1 + \psi\delta_{XB}\varepsilon_A) + \gamma_{K2}]V_A^*$
inverse relationship

e. $X_2^* = \alpha_P\gamma_{L2} \cdot (-0.01) \cdot [\gamma_{L1}(\varepsilon_B\phi_{XA} + \psi + \psi\varepsilon_A\delta_{XA}) + \psi\gamma_{K1}]V_A^*$
positive relationship

f. $W_{\mathrm{A}}^{*} = \alpha_{P} \cdot 0.01 \cdot [\gamma_{L2}(\phi_{X\mathrm{B}}\varepsilon_{\mathrm{B}} + 1) + \phi_{X\mathrm{A}}\gamma_{L1}\varepsilon_{\mathrm{B}}\theta_{L2} + \gamma_{K2}$
$+\psi\{\theta_{L2}(\delta_{X\mathrm{A}}\gamma_{L1}\varepsilon_{Z} + \gamma_{L1} + \gamma_{K1}) + \delta_{X\mathrm{B}}\varepsilon_{\mathrm{A}}\gamma_{L2}\}]V_{\mathrm{A}}^{*}$
$-\pi_{1}[\gamma_{L1}\gamma_{L2}(1 + \varepsilon_{\mathrm{B}} + \psi\varepsilon_{\mathrm{A}} + \psi) + \gamma_{L1}\gamma_{K2} + \gamma_{L2}\gamma_{K1}]V_{\mathrm{A}}^{*}$

g. $W_{\mathrm{B}}^{*} = \alpha_{P}\theta_{K2} \cdot (-0.01) \cdot [\gamma_{L1}(\varepsilon_{\mathrm{B}}\phi_{X\mathrm{A}} + \psi\phi_{X\mathrm{A}}\varepsilon_{\mathrm{A}} + \psi) + \psi\gamma_{K1}]V_{\mathrm{A}}^{*}$
$-\pi_{1}[\gamma_{L1}\gamma_{L2}(1 + \varepsilon_{\mathrm{B}} + \psi + \psi\varepsilon_{\mathrm{A}}) + \gamma_{L1}\gamma_{K1}\psi]V_{\mathrm{A}}^{*}$

h. $r^{*} = \alpha_{P}\theta_{L2} \cdot 0.01 \cdot [(\varepsilon_{\mathrm{B}}\phi_{X\mathrm{A}} + \psi\delta_{X\mathrm{A}}\varepsilon_{\mathrm{A}} + \psi)\gamma_{L1} + \psi\gamma_{K1}]V_{\mathrm{A}}^{*}$
$-\pi_{1} \cdot 0.01 \cdot [\gamma_{L1}\gamma_{L2}(1 + \varepsilon_{\mathrm{B}} + \psi + \psi\varepsilon_{\mathrm{A}}) + \gamma_{L1}\gamma_{K2} + \gamma_{L2}\gamma_{K1}\psi]V_{\mathrm{A}}^{*}$
inverse relationship

i. $P^{*} = -\pi_{1} \cdot 0.01 \cdot [\gamma_{L1}\gamma_{L2}(\varepsilon_{\mathrm{B}} + 1 + \psi + \psi\varepsilon_{\mathrm{A}}) + \gamma_{L1}\gamma_{K2} + \gamma_{L2}\gamma_{K1}\psi]V_{\mathrm{A}}^{*}$
inverse relationship.

9. An Increase in C_{Z1}

a. $R_{\mathrm{A}}^{*} = -\lambda_{LZ1}C_{Z1}^{*}[-\alpha_{P}\{\theta_{L1}\varepsilon_{\mathrm{B}}\gamma_{L2}(\delta_{X\mathrm{A}}\phi_{X\mathrm{B}} - \delta_{X\mathrm{B}}\phi_{X\mathrm{A}}) + \theta_{L1}\delta_{X\mathrm{A}}(\gamma_{K2}$
$+\gamma_{L2}) + \psi(\delta_{X\mathrm{A}}\theta_{L2}\gamma_{K1} - \delta_{X\mathrm{B}}\theta_{L1}\gamma_{L2})\} + \psi\gamma_{L2}\gamma_{K1}\pi_{1}]$
$-\lambda_{KZ1}\psi C_{Z1}^{*}[-\alpha_{P}(\delta_{X\mathrm{A}}\theta_{L2}\gamma_{L1} + \delta_{X\mathrm{B}}\theta_{L1}\gamma_{L2}) + \gamma_{L2}\gamma_{L1}\pi_{1}]$
$+\delta_{Z1}C_{Z1}^{*}[-\alpha_{P}\{\varepsilon_{\mathrm{B}}(\phi_{X\mathrm{A}}\theta_{L2}\gamma_{L1} + \phi_{X\mathrm{B}}\theta_{L1}\gamma_{L2}) + \theta_{L1}(\gamma_{K2} + \gamma_{L2}) + \psi\theta_{L2}(\gamma_{K1}$
$+\gamma_{L1})\} + \pi_{1}\{\gamma_{L1}(\gamma_{K2} + \phi_{X\mathrm{B}}\gamma_{L2}\varepsilon_{\mathrm{B}} + \gamma_{L2}\phi_{X\mathrm{A}}\varepsilon_{\mathrm{B}}) + \psi\gamma_{L2}(\gamma_{K1} + \gamma_{L1})\}]$
$-(\phi_{Z1}\varepsilon_{\mathrm{B}}C_{Z1}^{*}[\gamma_{L1}\gamma_{L2}\pi_{1} - \alpha_{P}(\delta_{X\mathrm{A}}\theta_{L2}\gamma_{L1} + \delta_{X\mathrm{B}}\theta_{L1}\gamma_{L2})]$
inverse relationship

b. $R_{\mathrm{B}}^{*} = -\lambda_{LZ1}C_{Z1}^{*}[\alpha_{P}\{-\phi_{X\mathrm{A}}\theta_{L1}(\gamma_{L2} + \gamma_{K2}) + \psi(-\phi_{X\mathrm{A}}\theta_{L2}\gamma_{K1}$
$+\delta_{X\mathrm{B}}\varepsilon_{\mathrm{A}}\theta_{L1}\gamma_{L2} + \phi_{X\mathrm{B}}\gamma_{L1}\theta_{L2}(1 + \delta_{X\mathrm{A}}\varepsilon_{\mathrm{A}})))\} + \psi\pi_{1}\gamma_{L2}\gamma_{K1}] - \psi C_{Z1}^{*}(\lambda_{KZ1}$
$+\delta_{Z1}\varepsilon_{\mathrm{A}})[-\alpha_{P}(\phi_{X\mathrm{B}}\theta_{L1}\gamma_{L2} + \phi_{X\mathrm{A}}\theta_{L2}\gamma_{L1}) + \gamma_{L2}\pi_{1}\gamma_{L1}]$
$-\phi_{Z1}[\alpha_{P}\{\theta_{L1}(\gamma_{K2} + \gamma_{L2}) + \psi(\theta_{L2}\delta_{X\mathrm{A}}\varepsilon_{A}\gamma_{L1} + \gamma_{L1} + \gamma_{K1}) + \delta_{X\mathrm{B}}\varepsilon_{\mathrm{A}}\theta_{L1}\gamma_{L2})\}$
$-\pi_{1}\{\gamma_{L1}(\gamma_{K2} + \gamma_{L2} + \psi\gamma_{L2}\delta_{X}X_{\mathrm{B}}\varepsilon_{\mathrm{A}}) + \gamma_{L2}\psi(\delta_{X\mathrm{A}}\varepsilon_{\mathrm{A}}\gamma_{L1} + \gamma_{K1} + \gamma_{L1})\}]$

c. $K_{\mathrm{A}}^{*} = \lambda_{LZ1}C_{Z1}^{*}[\alpha_{P}\{\varepsilon_{\mathrm{A}}\theta_{L1}(\delta_{X\mathrm{A}}(\phi_{X\mathrm{B}}\varepsilon_{\mathrm{B}}\gamma_{L2} + \gamma_{L2} + \gamma_{K2})$
$-\delta_{X\mathrm{B}}\phi_{X\mathrm{A}}\varepsilon_{\mathrm{B}}\gamma_{L2}) + \theta_{L1}(\phi_{X\mathrm{B}}\varepsilon_{\mathrm{B}}\gamma_{L2} + \gamma_{L2} + \gamma_{K2}) - \phi_{X\mathrm{A}}\varepsilon_{\mathrm{B}}\theta_{L2}\gamma_{K1}\}$
$+\pi_{1}\{\gamma_{K1}\theta_{K1}(\gamma_{K2} + \gamma_{L2} + \phi_{X\mathrm{B}}\gamma_{L2}\varepsilon_{\mathrm{B}}) + \theta_{L1}(\phi_{X\mathrm{B}}\varepsilon_{\mathrm{B}}\gamma_{L2}\gamma_{K1} + \gamma_{K1}(\gamma_{K2} + \gamma_{L2}))$
$+\gamma_{L2}\gamma_{K1}\phi_{X\mathrm{A}}\varepsilon_{\mathrm{B}}\}] - C_{Z1}^{*}(\lambda_{KZ1} + \delta_{Z1}\varepsilon_{\mathrm{A}})[\alpha_{P}\{\theta_{L1}(\theta_{X\mathrm{B}}\varepsilon_{\mathrm{B}}\gamma_{L2} + \gamma_{L2} + \gamma_{K2})$
$+\phi_{X\mathrm{A}}\gamma_{L1}\theta_{L2}\varepsilon_{\mathrm{B}}\} - \pi_{1}\gamma_{L1}((\phi_{X\mathrm{B}}\gamma_{L2}\varepsilon_{\mathrm{B}} + \gamma_{L2} + \gamma_{K2}) - \gamma_{L2}\phi_{X\mathrm{A}}\varepsilon_{\mathrm{B}})]$
$-C_{Z1}^{*}\phi_{Z1}\varepsilon_{\mathrm{B}}[-\alpha_{P}\{\theta_{L2}(\gamma_{K1} + \gamma_{L1} + \delta_{X\mathrm{A}}\varepsilon_{\mathrm{A}}\gamma_{L1}) + \delta_{X\mathrm{B}}\varepsilon_{\mathrm{A}}\theta_{L1}\gamma_{L2}\}$
$+\gamma_{L2}\gamma_{L1}\pi_{1}(\varepsilon_{\mathrm{A}} + 1) + \gamma_{L2}\pi_{1}\gamma_{K1}]$

d. $X_{1}^{*} = -\lambda_{LZ1}C_{Z1}^{*}[-\alpha_{P}\{\theta_{L1}(\gamma_{K2} + \gamma_{L2} + \phi_{X\mathrm{B}}\varepsilon_{\mathrm{B}}\gamma_{L2})$
$+\psi(\phi_{L2}\gamma_{K1} + \delta_{X\mathrm{B}}\varepsilon_{\mathrm{A}}\theta_{L1}\gamma_{L2})\} + \pi_{1}\gamma_{L2}\psi\gamma_{K1}]$
$-\gamma_{L1}C_{Z1}^{*}(\lambda_{KZ1}\psi + \delta_{Z1}\varepsilon_{\mathrm{A}}\psi + \phi_{Z1}\varepsilon_{\mathrm{B}}\gamma_{L1})(\pi_{1}\gamma_{L2} - \alpha_{P}\theta_{L2})$

e. $X_{2}^{*} = -\lambda_{LZ1}C_{Z1}[\alpha_{P}\gamma_{L2}\theta_{L1}(\varepsilon_{\mathrm{A}}\phi_{X\mathrm{A}} + \psi + \psi\varepsilon_{\mathrm{A}}\delta_{X\mathrm{A}}) + \pi_{1}\gamma_{L2}\psi\gamma_{K1}]$
$-C_{Z1}^{*}\gamma_{L2}(\lambda_{KZ1}\psi + \delta_{Z1}\varepsilon_{\mathrm{A}}\psi + \phi_{Z1}\varepsilon_{\mathrm{B}})(\pi_{1}\gamma_{L1} - \alpha_{P}\theta_{L1})$

f. $P^{*} = -\lambda_{LZ1}\pi_{1}C_{Z1}^{*}[\theta_{L1}(\phi_{X\mathrm{B}}\varepsilon_{\mathrm{B}}\gamma_{L2} + \gamma_{L2} + \gamma_{K2}) + \psi(\theta_{L2}\gamma_{K1} + \delta_{X\mathrm{B}}\varepsilon_{\mathrm{A}}\theta_{L1}\gamma_{L2})$
$-\gamma_{L2}\theta_{L1}(\varepsilon_{\mathrm{B}}\phi_{X\mathrm{A}} + \psi + \psi\varepsilon_{\mathrm{A}}\delta_{X\mathrm{A}})] + \pi_{1}C_{Z1}^{*}(\lambda_{KZ1}\psi + \delta_{Z1}\psi\varepsilon_{\mathrm{A}}$
$+\phi_{Z1}\varepsilon_{\mathrm{B}})(\theta_{L1}\gamma_{L2} - \theta_{L2}\gamma_{L1})$

g. $r^* = -\lambda_{LZ1}\theta_{L1}C^*_{Z1}[-\alpha_P\theta_{L2}(\varepsilon_B\phi_{XA} + \psi(1 + \delta_{XA}\varepsilon_A)) + \pi_1\gamma_{L2}(1 + \phi_{XB}\varepsilon_B$
$+\psi\delta_{XB}\varepsilon_A + \varepsilon_B\phi_{XA} + \psi + \psi\varepsilon_A\delta_{XA}) + \pi_1\gamma_{K2}] + \theta_{L1}C^*_{Z1}(\lambda_{KZ1}\psi$
$+\delta_{Z1}\psi\varepsilon_A + \phi_{Z1}\varepsilon_B)(\pi_1\gamma_{L2} - \alpha_P\theta_{L2})$

h. $W^*_A = -\theta_{K1}/\theta_{L1}r^*$

i. $W^*_B = -\lambda_{LZ1}C^*_{Z1}[\alpha_P\theta_{K2}\theta_{L1}(\varepsilon_B\phi_{XA} + \psi(1 + \delta_{XA}\varepsilon_A)) + \pi_1\gamma_{L2}\{\theta_{L1}(1$
$+\phi_{XB}\varepsilon_B) + \psi\delta_{XB}\varepsilon_A\gamma_{L2}\theta_{L1} + \varepsilon_B\theta_{L1}\phi_{XA} + \psi\theta_{L1}(1 + \varepsilon_A\delta_{XA})\} + \pi_1(\theta_{L1}\gamma_{K2}$
$+\psi\gamma_{K1})] - C^*_{Z1}(\lambda_{KZ1}\psi + \delta_{Z1}\varepsilon_A\psi + \phi_{Z1}\varepsilon_B)[-\alpha_P\theta_{L1}\theta_{K2} + \pi_1(\gamma_{L1} - \gamma_{L2}\theta_{L1})].$

ACKNOWLEDGMENTS

This paper would not have been possible without the generous assistance of several individuals. Special thanks are due Shelby Gerking, Jack Mutti, and Bruce Forster for their numerous helpful suggestions and moral support. David Brookshire, Ralph d'Arge, and Larry Ostresh also provided helpful comments and encouragement. Susan Kalima, Lori Tobias, Joe Krismer, and Frank Goodale typed and printed the manuscript, a formidable task with the numerous equations and symbols. Remaining shortcomings and errors are the sole responsibility of the author.

REFERENCES

1. K. Asako, Environmental pollution in an open economy, *Econom. Rec.* **55**, 359–367 (1979).
2. R. Batra and F. Casas, A synthesis of the Heckscher-Ohlin and the neoclassical models of international trade, *J. Internat. Econom.* **6**, 21–38 (1976).
3. NGA backs acid rain controls, "Coal Outlook," Vol. 8, No. 9, p. 3 (March 5, 1984).
4. Northeast states blast EPA SO2 stance, "Coal Outlook," Vol. 8, No. 12, p. 1 (March 26, 1984).
5. Panel probes Reagan's acid rain view, "Coal Outlook," Vol. 8, No. 13, p. 4 (April 2, 1984).
6. P. Comolli, Pollution control in a simplified general equilibrium model with production externalities, *J. Environ. Econom. Management* **4**, 289–304 (1977).
7. Council Of Economic Advisors, "Economic Report of the President," U.S. Govt. Printing Office, Washington, DC (1983).
8. T. D. Crocker, What economics can currently say about the benefits of acid deposition control, *in* "Proceedings Michigan State University Institute of Public Utilities Fourteenth Annual Conference," p. 724–744 (1983).
9. B. Forster, Pollution control in a two-sector dynamic general equilibrium model, *J. Environ. Econom. Management* **4**, 305–312 (1977).
10. B. Forster, Environmental regulation and the distribution of income in simple general equilibrium models, *in* "Economic Perspectives" (M. B. Ballabon, Ed.), Harwood Academic Pub., New York (1981).
11. B. Forster, "Acid Rain in North America: An International Externality," Research Report or Occasional Paper No. 84, Department of Economics, University of Newcastle (1983).
12. J. Galloway and D. Whelpdale, An atmospheric sulfur budget for eastern North America, *Atmos. Environ.* **14**, 409–417 (1980).
13. R. Jones, The structure of simple general equilibrium models, *J. Polit. Econom.* **73**, 557–572 (1965).
14. R. Jones, A three-factor model in theory, trade, and history, *in* "Trade, the Balance of Payments and Growth" (J. Bhagwati, Ed.), North Holland, Amsterdam (1971).
15. J. Markusen, Factor movements and commodity trade as complements. *J. Internat. Econom.* **14**, 341–356 (1983).
16. M. McGuire, Regulation, factor rewards, and international trade, *J. Public Econom.* **17**, 335–354 (1982).
17. "Memorandum of Intent on Transboundary Air Pollutants," Interim Report of Work Groups (1981).
18. J. D. Merrifield, "The Impact of Selected Abatement Strategies on Transnational Pollution, the Terms of Trade, and Factor Rewards: A General Equilibrium Approach," Mimeographed Ph.D. dissertation, University of Wyoming, Laramie (1984).

19. Ministry of Supply and Services, "Canada Yearbook, 1980–1981," Bryant Press Limited, Ottawa (1981).
20. P. Ohlendorf, Unexplained deaths in the forest, *MacLeans* **97**, No. 13:50 (1984).
21. R. Pethig, Pollution, welfare, and environmental policy in the theory of comparative advantage, *J. Environ. Econom. Management* **2**, 160–169 (1976).
22. R. Robinson, Recognizing the true cost of acid rain, *in* "Acid Rain," Canadian-American Centre SUNY Buffalo (1982).
23. H. Siebert, J. Eichberger, R. Gronych, and R. Pethig, "Trade and Environment: A Theoretical Enquiry," Elsevier, Amsterdam (1980).
24. U.S. Department of Commerce, "The Effects of Pollution Abatement on International Trade—III," U.S. Govt. Printing Office, Washington, DC (1975).
25. U.S. General Accounting Office, "A Market Approach to Air Pollution Control Could Reduce Compliance Costs without Jeopardizing Clean Air Goals," U.S. Govt. Printing Office, Washington, DC (1982).
26. I. Walter (Ed.), "International Economics of Pollution," Macmillan, London (1975).
27. I. Walter (Ed.), "Studies in International Environmental Economics," Wiley, New York (1976).
28. G. W. Yohe, The backward incidence of pollution control—Some comparative statics in general equilibrium. *J. Environ. Econom. Management* **6**, 187–198 (1979).

[27]

Cutting CO_2 Emissions:

The Effects of Alternative Policy Approaches*

*John Whalley*** *and Randall Wigle****

This paper starts from the premise that attempts to curtail global emissions of greenhouse gases are likely to be made in the next few decades. We discuss some of the possible international effects which could result from attempts to achieve such a cutback, and illustrate a methodology which we hope to extend, in subsequent work, to further evaluating the consequences of responding to the problem of global warming. We identify possible magnitudes of effects of cutting global CO_2 emissions, and illustrate ways in which inter-country terms-of-trade effects and changes in trade patterns may occur.

INTRODUCTION

Rather than debate the wisdom of curtailing greenhouse gas emissions, this paper starts from the premise that attempts to curtail emissions of greenhouse gases are likely to be made in the next few decades.[1] Given this, we discuss some of the possible international effects which could result from attempts to achieve such a cutback, and illustrate a methodology which we hope to extend, in subsequent work, to further evaluating the consequences of responding to the problem of global warming. In the paper, we concentrate

The Energy Journal, Volume 12, Number 1.

*The authors would like to thank, without implicating, T. Hertel, M. Rothschild, G. Harrison and C. Waddell, as well as two anonymous referees, for helpful comments. Earlier drafts of this paper were presented to the Annaul Meetings of the Canadian Economics Association, Quebec City, June 5, 1989, and to a conference on Applied General Equilibrium Modelling, San Diego, September 8-9, 1989. A further version of this paper is to be subsequently published in the conference proceedings. Wigle acknowledges support from the Social Sciences and Humanities Research Council of Canada.

**Department of Economics, University of Western Ontario
***Department of Economics, Wilfrid Laurier University

1. See the final statement from the Environment Canada Conference in Toronto in June 1988, entitled *The Changing Atmosphere: Implications for Global Security*, which we discuss below.

on identifying possible magnitudes of effects of cutting CO_2 emissions, and illustrate the ways in which terms-of-trade effects and changes in trade patterns may occur.

One point which emerges is that a given reduction target can be achieved via a number of alternative policy instruments. Not surprisingly, the burden of the resulting adjustments by country is sensitive to the allocations of cutbacks among the countries. Somewhat less obvious is that the choice between production and consumption taxes affects the allocation of the burden of adjustment.

ALTERNATIVE APPROACHES TO CUTTING EMISSIONS

A number of issues will arise with the implementation of any future cut of global CO_2 emissions. The first is the depth of cut to be adopted. Once the target proportionate cut is chosen, a given cut could be achieved in one of several ways, but two 'polar cases' may be illustrative. The most direct way to achieve a 20% reduction would be to have all countries agree to reduce their own emissions by 20%. An alternative would be to have countries agree to reduce their emissions to an equal per capita amount, with the level set so as to reduce total emissions by 20%.

These proposals are, however, deceptively different from one another. The equi-proportionate reduction approach effectively confers squatters' rights on the heaviest-emitting countries, while forcing reductions by the least-offending countries. By contrast, the equal per capita standard would require significant cutbacks by high-emissions countries, with no cutbacks at all (even in projected growth to 2005) by the lowest-income countries. The first scheme is the more regressive in impact, since the low-emissions countries also tend to be the lowest-income countries.

Targets for cutbacks could be set in terms of global or national consumption, although proposed cutbacks could be achieved in a number of different ways. Taxes could be applied to either fossil fuel use, or production. Quotas could be placed on either the use, or production, of fossil fuels. Further, the revenues from any taxes or quota sales could be collected either by national governments, or by an international body such as the proposed World Atmospheric Fund.

If taxes are used, or if quota rights are sold, the disposition of these revenues also becomes a significant issue. If consumption taxes are used and national governments receive the revenues, high-emission countries would receive the bulk of the revenues. In contrast, if quotas were sold and revenues collected by an international agency, the issue of the distribution of the revenues would become a significant one. (Below, we estimate that revenues could amount to several hundred billions of dollars annually.) Once again the most obvious scheme would be to have national governments collect and redistribute the revenues as they wish, while a less obvious and dramatically different alternative would be either to allocate revenues from quotas on an equal per capita basis between all countries around the world, or to allocate them more than proportionately to lower-income countries.

Restrictions on the use of "greenhouse" energy would cause the producers' price of fossil fuels to fall, with the users' price rising. Energy-intensive products would increase in price relative to those which are not. Associated with these would be changes in the terms of trade against fossil-fuel exporters, higher prices for consumers of energy-intensive products, and lower returns for producers of energy-intensive products. One would also expect the price of energy from non-greenhouse sources to rise.

Since the size of each of these effects is hard to estimate in isolation, we use a simple numerical general equilibrium model of global trade and production to provide an indication of the possible incidence, terms of trade, and transfer effects associated with a number of emission reduction proposals, all loosely modelled after the Toronto proposal outlined above.

A NUMERICAL GENERAL EQUILIBRIUM MODEL FOR ASSESSING THE EFFECTS OF CO_2 EMISSION REDUCTIONS

We have used a single-period computable general equilibrium model to evaluate the possible effects of alternative CO_2 emission cuts. In it, the world is divided into three regions, as indicated in Table 1. The Developed Region includes all countries with per capita income, in 1986, greater than $2,000 US, and with less than 25% of their exports made up of fuels. The Developing Region includes all countries with per capita incomes below $2,000 US, and with fuel exports accounting for less than 25% of total exports. The Oil Exporting Region includes all countries where fuel exports account for more than 25% of exports.

The nested functional structures used in the model to represent production and demand in each region are set out in Table 2. Each region is endowed with three non-traded primary factors: (i) primary factors, exclusive of energy resources, (ii) greenhouse energy resources (deposits of oil, gas and coal), and (iii) other energy resources (hydroelectric capacity and nuclear). Both energy resources are converted into the relevant energy products through a refining/extraction process, which uses other resources (primary factors). There are three internationally traded commodities in the equilibrium system: greenhouse energy products, energy-intensive manufactures, and other goods (all other GNP). Energy-intensive manufactures, other goods, and the composite energy product (greenhouse and non-greenhouse energy) are the commodities which enter final demands.

For each of five produced goods in each region (listed in Table 2), production is represented by a constant elasticity of substitution (CES) function. Greenhouse and non-greenhouse energy products use the respective energy resources and primary factors. Non-greenhouse energy products are non-traded, since hydroelectric, solar and nuclear power are not traded in

Table 1. Regions in the Equilibrium Model Used to Evaluate Options for Reductions in CO_2 Emissions

Developed World:

All countries with per capita income (1986) above $2,000 US, with less than 25% of exports in fossil fuels.

Developing World:

All countries with per capita income (1986) below $2,000 US, with less than 25% of exports in fossil fuels.

Oil Exporters:

All countries with fuel more than 25% of their exports.

significant quantities between the regions as defined here[2]. A domestic energy composite is produced by a third (energy conversion) industry, using inputs of the two energy products. The two final-goods (energy-intensive manufactures, and other goods) use primary factors and the composite domestic energy product as inputs. Perfect competition is assumed throughout for all sectors and in all regions.

Equilibrium, in this model, involves full global market clearing in all three traded goods (greenhouse energy products, energy-intensive manufactures, and other goods). For the two non-traded goods (non-greenhouse energy products, and composite energy) there is domestic market clearing within each economy. Since prices in this system are treated as completely flexible, they will adjust to the levels required to clear the relevant international and domestic markets.

The introduction of carbon taxes into this system will raise prices of greenhouse energy products, and hence the price of composite energy to users, and reduce prices to producers. This will have the effect of cutting both consumption and production of greenhouse energy products, with prices adjusting until the global market in greenhouse energy products clears. If prices to consumers increase fully by the amount of the tax, the tax will have been fully passed on to users of carbon. If prices to consumers change little, then the tax will have been passed backwards to producers of greenhouse energy products. Substitution will also occur between greenhouse and non-greenhouse energy products, and between the energy composite product, and other inputs. The strength of all of these effects depends on the elasticity values used at the respective nodes in the nesting of substitution possibilities set out in Table 2.

2. While there is trade in radionuclides, this is ignored.

Table 2. Structure of Equilibrium Model Used to Evaluate Options for Reductions in CO_2 Emissions

Factors and Goods:

Endowments

"Greenhouse" Energy Resources (GR), Other Energy Resources (ER), Primary Factors (PF)

Produced Goods

Greenhouse Energy Products (GP), Other Energy Products (EP), Composite Energy (E), Energy-Intensive Goods (EI), Non-Energy Intensive Goods (NEI)

Structure of Production:

Stage 1 Production of energy products

```
PF    GR        PF    ER
 \    /          \    /
   GP              EP
```

Stage 2 Production of composite energy

```
GP    EP
 \    /
   E
```

Stage 3 Production of energy-intensive and non-energy intensive products

```
E     PF        E     PF
 \    /          \    /
   EI              NEI
```

Arguments in Final Demands

EI, NEI, E

To evaluate effects of alternative carbon tax schemes on the three regions, we use the model in what we term counterfactual mode[3]. This involves constructing a base (or reference) case solution to which the equilibrium model is calibrated[4] (i.e., parameters are chosen such that the model will reproduce the base case data as a full equilibrium solution prior to any policy change being introduced). The base case data thus fully describes a no-policy change model solution. Different carbon tax schemes can then be introduced, with a new equilibrium (counterfactual equilibrium) solution computed for each. Using a pair-wise comparison (base case versus

3. This is a technical term used in the applied general equilibrium modelling literature; see Shoven and Whalley (1984, and forthcoming) for more details.

4. See Mansur and Whalley, 1984.

counterfactual), international incidence effects are evaluated following each such calculation.

An important characteristic of the model is the ease, specified through substitution elasticities, with which outputs can be shifted between the two energy products, relative to the ease of substitution between the two energy products in consumption. The former is assumed to be relatively low, while the latter is relatively high. This configuration reflects energy resources being non-tradeable and in fixed supply. As a result, the elasticity of input substitution in the energy products sectors is set to 0.2. The "energy" sector in each region uses inputs of the two energy products, and substitution between them is relatively easy (the elasticity of substitution is set to 4). This reflects the fact that inputs of coal or hydroelectricity in the proper ratio are close substitutes for the purpose of heating a house, or running an industrial plant. Final demand is for the energy-intensive and non-intensive goods plus the (region-specific) energy aggregate. All of the traded goods produced in each of the three regions are perfect substitutes (i.e., we do not adopt the Armington structure for traded goods).

This structure allows us to readily identify the ease of shifting outputs between the greenhouse and other energy products sector as well as the ease of substitution in consumption between the final demand products.

Data

The model is calibrated to a 1986 global benchmark equilibrium data set built using available sources (see Table 3). Data on GNP, population and exchange rates are obtained from the World Tables. Energy consumption production and trade data are obtained from a secondary source (Filion, 1988). Finally, trade data assembled for another purpose from the UN trade tapes are used to complete the trade data for the non-energy products.

One of the most striking differences between the developed and developing countries is that the developing countries have dramatically higher per capita emissions than developed countries. As we split the countries, the GNP of developed countries is about three times that of the developing countries, while emissions are (roughly) equal. Developing countries account for a higher share of emissions than GNP because they tend to use less energy-efficient technologies, and a higher share of coal in total energy products. The production of one BTU of energy with coal generates significantly more CO_2 than with either oil or natural gas.

Developed countries are net exporters of both energy-intensive goods and non energy-intensive goods, and are significant importers of fossil fuels. The developing countries import both fossil fuels (greenhouse energy products) and energy-intensive goods, and export non-energy-intensive goods. Finally, the "oil" region is a significant net exporter of fossil fuels and has correspondingly large imports of the two other traded goods. The goods

Table 3. Global Benchmark data for 1986 Used in the General Equilibrium Model

Production and Consumption of Energy by Region:

Bloc	Greenhouse Energy (Billions of US$) Production	Consumption	Share of Other Energy To Total Energy Use
Developed	189.8	339.8	15.4%
Developing	247.4	287.0	7.1%
Oil Exporters	232.6	48.4	11.2%

Trade Pattern by Region (New Exports in Billions of US$):

	Developed	Low-Income	Oil
G Energy	-150.0	-39.6	189.7
E Intensive	38.0	-26.8	-11.2
Other (non-intensive)	+112.0	66.5	-178.5

Population and GNP by Region:

	Product	Share of World's Population	Emissions
Developed	74.8%	15.6%	50.7%
Developing	22.2%	80.6%	42.8%
Oil Exporters	3.0%	3.7%	6.4%

Sources: GNP, production, population and non-energy trade data were based on The World Bank's World Tables. Data for the USSR and People's Republic of China were generated from estimates in Holzman (1976) and Rosefielde (1973). Energy use and trade flows are based on Filion, ed., *The Canadian World Almanac*, 1989. See pages 419 and 461. Trade data for energy-intensive goods are based on UN trade tapes.

which we call energy-intensive are mostly what might be called primary manufactures (for example, metals, basic products, glass, ceramics, fabricated goods). The net trade between these large blocs is a relatively small fraction of world trade, since much of recorded trade takes place within our regions.

As emphasized earlier, the developed bloc accounts for much higher shares of the world's emissions and production, than population. Trade was forced to balance without capital flows. The energy-intensive goods sector includes what is often referred to as primary manufacturing. Notably, it includes primary metal manufacturing, as well as the glass, pottery, and plastics industries. These are identified as having the highest energy input requirements in Ross (1989), and the input ratios used in that paper were used to infer energy input requirements for the respective industries.

SOME COUNTERFACTUAL POLICY EXPERIMENTS USING THE MODEL

As mentioned earlier, two proposals made at the Toronto conference on the changing atmosphere called for a 20% cut and a 50% cut in CO_2 emissions, respectively, by 2005. In what follows we model the effects of a 50% cut in emissions, abstracting from the impact this would have on atmospheric CO_2 concentrations. The limitations inherent in using a static general equilibrium model for this purpose are discussed in the conclusion.

The main experiments we consider are the following:

1. Production taxes collected by national governments to achieve a 50% reduction in their respective production of greenhouse energy, and hence CO_2 emissions.

2. Consumption taxes collected by national governments to achieve a 50% reduction in their own consumption of greenhouse energy, and hence CO_2 emissions.

3. A global consumption (or production) tax collected by an international body such as the "UN," with revenues distributed to countries according to population, and achieving the same 50% reduction.

4. A reduction of global emissions by 50% achieved by establishing a ceiling on per capita emissions.

Implementation[5]

As a first approximation, we assume that the rate of CO_2 emissions is proportional to the use of greenhouse energy products. In particular, if reductions are achieved by scaling back proportionally on the use of all fossil fuels, this assumption is reasonable. Switching between coal and natural gas, for a given level of energy consumption, would reduce CO_2 emissions.

The evaluation of national production and consumption taxes is achieved by imposing (respectively, production or consumption) quotas in each country to correspond to the required cut. Since industries are all modelled as perfectly competitive, the quota values determined in this way correspond to the taxes required to bring about the specified reduction in emissions. For the case of "global" taxes, revenue is distributed on an equal per capita basis. Production and consumption taxes are formally equivalent in this case because all consumers pay the same price and all producers receive the same price.

5. The model was implemented using MPS/GE. See Rutherford, 1988.

Given that the revenue distribution is exactly the same for the two taxes, the size of tax required to reduce global consumption (and thus production) by 50% is equivalent.

National Taxes

The effects shown by the model, from imposing national production taxes on greenhouse energy products such as oil, gas and coal, to achieve a target of 50% cut in emissions, are shown in Table 4. The proportionate effects on consumption are similar in all the regions, but welfare effects are dissimilar. Also, while the reductions in greenhouse energy trade are easy to understand, there is a dramatic increase in trade of energy-intensive for non-intensive products. The other energy sectors in each economy expand by over 58%.

These welfare effects by region may at first seem surprising, since the oil region experiences a welfare gain, even though they are the largest producers (and are thus subject to the most tax). The welfare effects reflect two considerations. First, the national production taxes raise revenue which goes to countries proportional to their own production. This means that revenues accrue disproportionately to the net exporters, so that the national production taxes operate much like an export tax. This explains why the loss of the developed region is so large, while the oil region experiences a small welfare (and terms of trade) gain. We further note that the revenue collected by such a tax is significant, amounting to almost $200 billion in the developed region alone. Implied tax rates from these restrictions are about 80%.

The effects of achieving 50% reductions in CO_2 emissions through national consumption taxes are shown in Table 5. Results for national consumption taxes are different from those for national production taxes in a number of ways. The most striking are the welfare effects. The revenues generated by these consumption taxes accrue to countries proportional to their consumption. This means that the bulk of the revenue is received by the developed region (in effect acting somewhat like an import tariff from the point of view of that region). As a result, the oil region experiences a large welfare loss in this case, and collects little of the revenue. Most of the burden of the emission reduction effort is borne by the oil-exporting region.

In both experiments, dramatic changes in the pattern of trade occur. This occurs partly because of the simple production structure used, but also because trade in the energy intensive and non-energy intensive goods are such a small share of total production and consumption (see Table 3).

A Global Tax

Table 6 shows the effects of a global tax on either consumption or production of greenhouse energy products. The tax is computed by imposing

Table 4. Reduction of CO_2 Emissions by 50% Through National Production Taxes

Energy Quantities and Prices (% Changes):[a]

Region	Greenhouse Energy Production	Other Energy Consumption	Other Energy Production	Price
Developed	-50.0	-72.6	7.0	58.9
Developing	-50.0	-28.0	9.5	101.2
Oil Exporters	-50.0	-17.7	9.8	108.0
Price of Greenhouse Energy			-56.3	

Trade Pattern (% Changes in Trade Volume):[b]

	Developed	Developing	Oil
Greenhouse energy	+ + +	109.15	-57.31
Energy-Intensive	---	+ + +	+ + +
Non-Energy-Intensive	1419.87	---	99.36

Welfare and Revenue Effects (Billions of US$):

	Welfare[c] (%)	Revenue Generated	Tax Rate
Developed	-179.70 (-1.68)	170.54	80.42
Developing	-151.23 (-4.76)	223.26	80.78
Oil Exporting	46.99 (10.80)	209.92	80.78
World Total	-283.94 (-1.98)		

a. Price effects are % changes in producers' prices.

b. % changes in trade volumes (net exports) expressed as a percentage of original net exports. + + + denotes that the region has changed from an importer to an exporter, while --- indicates the converse.

c. Welfare effects are in billions of US$ (% of changes in brackets).

a global quota on production and calculating the value of one unit's worth of quota. The quota is sold by a UN agency which, in turn, redistributes the revenues proportionally to each region's population.

The implementation of this scheme leads to a reduction in the producer's price of greenhouse energy products and, at the same time, a terms of trade loss to the oil-exporting region. Further, the majority of the revenues associated with the plan accrue to the developing region, which is,

Table 5. Reduction of CO_2 Emissions by 50% Through National Consumption Taxes

Energy Quantitites and Prices (% Changes):[a]

Region	Greenhouse Energy Production	Consumption	Other Energy Production	Price
Developed	-55.7	-50.0	7.9	73.4
Developing	-48.0	-50.0	9.7	106.9
Oil Exporters	-47.4	-50.0	10.0	113.1
Price of Greenhouse Energy				-56.9

Trade Pattern (% Changes in Trade Volumes):[b]

	Developed	Developing	Oil
Greenhouse Energy	-42.76	-62.34	-46.86
Energy-Intensive	---	265.68	+ + +
Non-Energy-Intensive	-45.69	67.07	-3.70

Welfare and Revenue Effects (Billions of US$):

	Welfare[c] (%)	Revenue Generated	Tax Rate
Developed	-67.39 (-0.63)	283.99	79.51
Developing	-120.60 (-3.80)	299.55	82.89
Oil Exporting	-108.13 (-24.85)	46.44	83.41
World Total	-269.12 (-2.07)		

a. Price effects are % changes in producers' prices.

b. % changes in trade volumes (net exports) expressed as a percentage of original net exports. + + + denotes that the region has changed from an importer to an exporter, while --- indicates the converse.

b. Welfare effects are in billions of US$ (% of changes in brackets).

in effect, rewarded for its low emissions by a significant transfer. The oil region's terms of trade losses exceed their share of the revenues, resulting in a welfare loss. In the case of the developing region, the terms of trade work against them, but a significant transfer in their favour leads to a sizable gain. This contrasts with similar sized welfare losses under either of the alternative "national" tax schemes. This reinforces the significant implications of the redistributive scheme suggested here. Note that total tax revenue amounts to $601 billion, of which $484 billion would be received by the developing region.

Table 6. Reduction of CO_2 Emissions by 50% Through Global Production Taxes

Energy Quantities and Prices (% Changes):[a]

Region	Greenhouse Energy Production	Consumption	Other Energy Production	Price
Developed	-54.3	-72.8	6.9	58.2
Developing	-48.1	-24.5	9.6	102.8
Oil Exporters	-48.5	-39.9	9.1	91.8
Price of Greenhouse Energy				-56.8

Trade Pattern (% Changes in Trade Volumes):[b]

	Developed	Developing	Oil
Greenhouse Energy	-96.11	122.3	-50.45
Energy-Intensive	---	+ + +	+ + +
Non-Energy-Intensive	479.24	---	29.05

Welfare and Revenue Effects (Billions of US$):

	Welfare[c] (%)	Revenue Generated	Tax Rate
Developed	-252.92 (-2.36)	93.85	80.59
Developing	+93.98 (+2.96)	484.49	
Oil Exporting	-122.84 (-28.23)	22.61	
World Total	-281.78 (-1.97)		

a. Price effects are % changes in producers' prices.

b. % changes in trade volumes (net exports) expressed as a percentage of original net exports. + + + denotes that the region has changed from an importer to an exporter, while --- indicates the converse.

c. Welfare is measured in billions of US$ (% changes in brackets).

Emissions Ceilings

We finally consider reductions in emissions through per capita ceilings on levels of emissions. As we mentioned earlier, this differs from previous cases where all regions experience similar (or the same) reductions in consumption or production of greenhouse energy-intensive products. In this case, we assume that a per capita standard is established in such a way as to reduce total emissions by 50%. As a practical matter, this would mean that the developed region reduces consumption by more than 50%, with smaller cuts in both the developing and oil region. This follows, since the per capita emissions in the developed region are approximately six times those of the rest of the world combined.

We consider two cases: first, emissions of the developing and oil region are restricted to 75% of their original value (a 25% cut), with the developed region required to cut by 74% to achieve the required overall reduction. This case is shown in Table 7. We also evaluate a case where the required reductions correspond exactly to both a 50% reduction in emissions, and equal per capita emissions. This case is presented in Table 8. This involves an 84% cut for the developed region, a 6% cut by the developing region and a 69% cut by the oil-exporting region.

The pattern of gainers and losers under both ceilings cases is the same as that under the global tax case. This highlights the importance of revenues, since under the latter proposal revenues generated by the taxes used to fulfil the "national" ceilings will be distributed exactly the same way as the revenue from a global tax. Correspondingly, the welfare effects in these two cases (Tables 6 and 8) are similar. The developing region has a small welfare gain in the case of the first ceiling because, although it loses from having to cut greenhouse-energy consumption by 25%, it has a revenue gain. In the second "ceiling" experiment it has a much smaller cut in consumption and almost the same revenue gain.

A further aspect of the policy approaches used here deserves further comment. In all the experiments involving taxes or limits on consumption of greenhouse energy, we have taken consumption to include both intermediate and final consumption of energy. One reason for choosing this approach is that such a tax would be much easier to collect than one which distinguished between these uses. In the case where limits are stricter in the developed than in the developing region, the pattern of production of energy-intensive products changes dramatically. The developed region becomes a significant net importer of these goods in both "ceilings" experiments. An unanticipated effect of treating intermediate use the same as final demand is thus to move the location of intermediate consumption of fossil fuels (as well as the intended effect of reducing total consumption).

SUMMARY AND CONCLUSIONS

While the model used in this paper has some obvious weaknesses (some of which we discuss below), a few general observations about the implications of policies aimed at responding to the global warming problem do suggest themselves from the model results.

First, the rule for distributing tax or quota revenues between regions, and particularly between the developing and developed regions, is important. In the two extreme cases (national collection and distribution of taxes versus

Table 7. Reduction of CO_2 Emissions by 50% Through Per Capita Emissions Ceilings

Energy Quantities and Prices (% Changes):[a]

Region	Greenhouse Energy Production	Consumption	Other Energy Production	Price
Developed	-51.6	-74.0	7.4	65.6
Developing	-46.5	-25.0	9.4	99.4
Oil Exporters	-52.0	-25.0	7.7	69.7
Price of Greenhouse Energy				-56.5

Trade Pattern (% Changes in Trade Volumes):[b]

	Developed	Developing	Oil
Greenhouse Energy	+ + +	108.96	-58.14
Energy-Intensive	—	+ + +	+ + +
Non-Energy-Intensive	1420.68	—	40.50

Welfare and Revenue Effects (BIllions of US$):

	Welfare[c] (%)	Revenue Generated	Tax Rate
Developed	-188.28 (-1.76)	170.14	81.56
Developing	0.41 (0.01)	377.95	80.14
Oil Exporting	-91.73 (-21.08)	45.75	76.55
World Total	-279.60 (-1.95)		

a. Price effects are % changes in producers' prices.

b. % changes in trade volumes (net exports) expressed as a percentage of original net exports. + + + denotes that the region has changed from an importer to an exporter, while — indicates the converse.

c. Welfare is measured in billions of US$ (% changes in brackets).

collection and distribution by an international agency), the developing region receives transfers from the revenues equal to $223 billion or $484 billion, respectively. This leads to a welfare loss of about 5% of GNP in the case where consumption tax revenues are collected and distributed by national governments, and a welfare gain as high as 3% in the case of revenue distribution proportional to population.

Table 8. Reduction of CO_2 Emissions by 50% Through Alternative Per Capita Ceilings

	Welfare[a] (%)	Revenue Generated	Tax Rate
Developed	-247.28 (-2.31)	190.12	88.97
Developing	54.61 (1.72)	357.25	75.34
Oil Exporting	-122.81 (-28.22)	36.68	86.42

a. Welfare is measured in billions of US$ (% changes in brackets).

Second, the choice between national production and consumption taxes is of some significance -- and to the oil region in particular -- as production taxes act to some extent like export taxes, benefiting the oil bloc through positive terms of trade effects. National consumption taxes act to some degree like an import tariff, hurting the oil region and benefiting the developing region.

A third observation is that the oil-exporters bear a significant burden from responding to CO_2 reductions under all plans, except under the production tax scheme. This should not be surprising as in these calculations the target for reduction is greenhouse energy products (fossil fuels), of which this group is a dominant exporter. In the case of the national production taxes they generate significant revenue, leading to a small welfare gain, but in all other cases the welfare loss they suffer exceeds 20% of GNP.

Finally, while the alternative of per capita limits on emissions may have appeal from an equity point of view, such a policy could cause a severe distortion of trade patterns, with the production of energy-intensive products shifting from the developed to the developing countries. The trade restructuring we show is partly due to the simple production structure used, but the incentives generated by differential cutbacks are quite clear. The asymmetric restrictions on the use of fossil fuels in the developed world generate significant incentives for this type of restructuring. In terms of the sum of the region welfare changes criteria, the most equitable of the "per capita ceilings" approaches (Table 8) fares the worst in terms of efficiency, perhaps partly due to the implied distortion.

REFERENCES

Filion, John, ed., (1988). *The Canadian World Almanac, 1989*. Toronto: Global Press.

Mansur, A. and J. Whalley (1984). "Numerical Specification of Applied General Equilibrium Models: Estimation, Calibration and Data." In J.B. Shoven and H. Scarf, eds., *Applied General Equilibrium Analysis*. Cambridge, MA: Cambridge University Press.

Ross, Marc (1989). "Improving the Efficiency of Electricity Use in Manufacturing." *Science* 244(4902): 311-317.

Rutherford Thomas F. (1988). "General Equilibrium Modelling with MPS/GE." London, Ontario: Department of Economics, University of Western Ontario.

Shoven, J. and J. Whalley (1984). "Applied General Equilibrium Models of Taxation and International Trade: An Introduction and Survey." *Journal of Economic Literature* (September): 1007-1051.

Shoven, J. and J. Whalley (forthcoming). *Applying General Equilibrium*. Cambridge, MA: Cambridge University Press.

The Climate Institute (1988). "Toronto Conference Calls for Sharp Cuts in Carbon Dioxide Emissions." *Climate Alert* 1(3).

The World Bank (1987). *World Tables 1960-1986*. Washington: International Bank for Reconstruction and Development.

[28]

International trade and environmental quality: how important are the linkages?

CARLO PERRONI University of Western Ontario
RANDALL M. WIGLE Wilfrid Laurier University

Abstract. This paper develops a numerical general equilibrium model of the world economy with local and global environmental externalities. The model is then used to investigate the relationship between trade and the environment. Our results suggest that international trade has little impact on environmental quality. Furthermore, the magnitude of the welfare effects of environmental policies is not significantly affected by changes in trade policies. At the same time, the size and distribution of the gains from trade liberalization appear to be little affected by changes in environmental policies.

Commerce international et qualité de l'environnement: quelle est l'importance des liens? Ce mémoire développe un modèle numérique d'équilibre général de l'économie mondiale qui tient compte des effets externes locaux et globaux sur l'environnement. Le modèle est utilisé pour explorer le rapport entre commerce international et environnement. Les résultats obtenus suggèrent que le commerce international a peu d'effet sur la qualité de l'environnement. De plus, la taille des effets de bien-être des politiques environnementales n'est pas affectée de manière significative par les changements dans les politiques commerciales. D'autre part, la taille et la répartition des gains provenant de la libéralisation du commerce semblent peu affectées par les changements dans les politiques environnementales.

I. INTRODUCTION

The last few years have seen a remarkable increase in environmental concerns, both in the public at large and among policy makers. One particular focus of these concerns is the interrelationship between international trade and the environment. A widely held view is that international trade is a primary contributor to environmental

This paper was presented at the CEA annual meetings in June 1992, and at the EEA annual meetings in March 1993. The authors wish to thank participants in workshops at Brock University, the University of Western Ontario, and the University of Guelph. We also wish to thank Nick Hanley, Glenn Harrison, and a number of anonymous referees for their comments on earlier drafts. Financial support from the Social Sciences and Humanities Research Council of Canada is gratefully acknowledged. Perroni acknowledges support from the Ford Foundation.

Canadian Journal of Economics Revue canadienne d'Economique, XXVII, No. 3
August août 1994. Printed in Canada Imprimé au Canada

0008-4085 / 94 / 551–67 $1.50

degradation (Shrybman 1990). Trade liberalization has also come under criticism on the grounds that domestic environmental policies can be significantly undercut through trade diversion and relocation of dirty industries to 'pollution havens,' particularly when governments are restricted by trade treaties.[1]

The implications of the environmental externalities for the theory of comparative advantage have been extensively explored in the literature. Environmental emissions affect the pattern of comparative advantage: countries with comparatively higher levels of environmental assimilative capacity, or with comparatively lower valuations of environmental quality have a comparative advantage in the production of pollution-intensive goods (Siebert 1977; Blackhurst 1977). Less than full internalization of environmental externalities may have implications both for equity (if the victims of the externalities are not compensated) and for efficiency (emission levels will be above optimal). With respect to international trade, the lack of internalization distorts the pattern of comparative advantage, resulting in non-optimal levels of trade. In addition to these efficiency effects, the lack of internalization affects the distribution of the gains from trade. In this situation, a country might find autarky to be preferable to free trade (Pethig 1976).

The thrust of the literature on trade and the environment is mainly theoretical and few of the results are even qualitatively robust. Nevertheless, there appears to be some consensus among economists that trade barriers are a very poor substitute for domestic environmental policies (Bhagwati 1981a), and that trade liberalization and environmental protection may be treated as separable objectives, but to our knowledge no previous study has attempted to provide quantitative support for this conjecture.

This paper represents an attempt to assess the relative contribution of international trade to environmental degradation, and the extent to which environmental policies affect the size and distribution of the gains from trade liberalization. To this end we formulate an operational general equilibrium model encompassing international trade and environmental externalities, which is calibrated to a consistent world data set for 1986. We employ the model to explore the quantitative significance of the links between international trade and the environment.

The main obstacle to performing such an exercise is simply our limited information on how economic activities affect the natural environment, and on how individuals value environmental quality. Although there is a large literature on the valuation of environmental damages, there are many parameters we use for our model for which there are no estimates. In this respect our results are of necessity speculative. Nevertheless, we feel that the urgency of the debate on trade and environment warrants a first attempt to assess the importance of these linkages.

Given our parameterization, numerical simulations indicate that although trade liberalization appears to have a discernible impact on the environment, its relative contribution to environmental degradation is very limited, and that this impact is likely to be virtually zero when appropriate environmental policies are in place.

1 Specific GATT rules have come under attack, especially those concerning subsidies and 'National Treatment' (see Whalley 1991).

Furthermore, we find that environmental policies and trade policies are not as interdependent as some appear to believe. Specifically, environmental policy seems to have little effect on the size and distribution of the gains from trade liberalization. Similarly, we find that trade policy has a very limited impact on the welfare effects of environmental policies.

The plan of the paper is as follows. Section II outlines the general methodology employed to model environmental externalities, while section III details the structure of our model. Section IV describes the data set and the calibration procedure. Our experiments and numerical results are presented in section V.

II. ENVIRONMENTAL EXTERNALITIES IN THE GLOBAL ECONOMY

The processes that link environmental externalities to both the damage caused by them and the costs of reducing them can be grouped into four categories.

- *Institutional processes*. While there is normally a market mechanism to mediate transactions in private goods, there may be no private market for environmental quality. In the absence of a market or some other corrective policy, polluters do not pay for their 'use' of environmental resources.
- *Technological processes*. Production activities generate emissions that reduce environmental quality. These emissions can be reduced by switching to cleaner technologies or through the cleaning up of existing technologies ('end-of-pipe treatment'). Just as there are different technical processes for production, there are alternative processes of abatement.
- *Natural and geographical processes*. The impact of emissions on environmental quality varies across regions, depending on the nature of the emissions (local/transnational/global) and on the assimilative capacity of the environment. The latter will depend on the geographical pattern of emissions and on the local characteristics of the natural environment.
- *Subjective processes*. The value placed by consumers on environmental quality depends on consumers' preferences and there is a strong presumption among economists that the willingness to pay for environmental quality is positively correlated with lifetime wealth.[2]

The connections between these processes, the economy's agents and the environment are summarized in figure 1.

These categories may become quite blurred in practice. For instance, we may observe that the valuation of environmental externalities appears to be higher in rich countries than it is in poor ones, but it is hard to tell whether this effect is mainly due to differences in assimilative capacity or differences in income levels. Also, the distinction between technological and physical processes is largely conventional and depends on how we define the pollutant being emitted. Thus, unless

2 There is limited evidence on the matter. Braden and Kolstad (1991) give a good discussion of the associated problems. The general conclusion of Radetzki (1992) is consistent with the view that valuation rises with income.

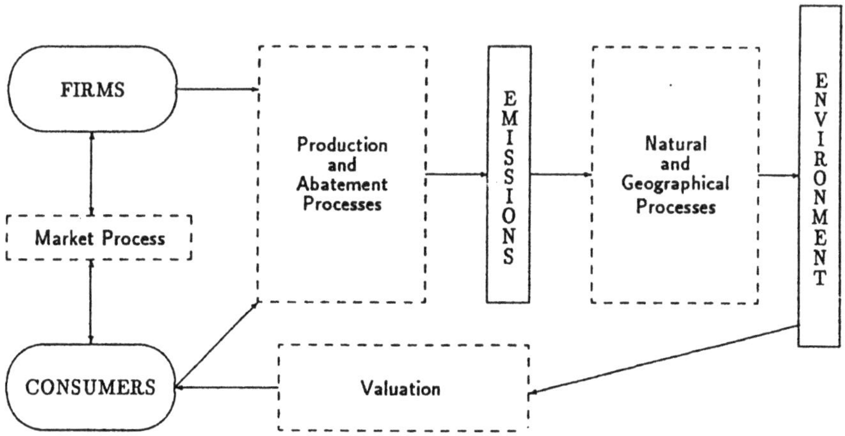

FIGURE 1 Economy–environment linkages

detailed information on the various aspects of environmental externalities is available, one may be tempted to abandon some of the above distinctions. In our view, however, maintaining these distinctions is important *precisely because of* the lack of detailed information: a careful categorization provides structure to the analysis and order to the policy debate. Also, maintaining such distinctions is essential for an interdisciplinary approach to the problem of environmental externalities.

The fact that these distinctions are often subtle means that they are often ignored in quantitative models; the need for preserving these distinctions in a model with fully integrated international trade spurred our modelling efforts. In order to explore the relationship between trade and the environment, in the next section we develop a model of the global economy that attempts explicitly to include all of the above aspects of environmental externalities.

III. MODEL STRUCTURE

This section describes the structure of our model, with a special emphasis on the modelling of environmental externalities. A complete description of the model is available from the authors by request.

1. Emissions and abatement

As mentioned above, we distinguish between externalities arising from production and from consumption activities, as well as between local and global externalities.[3] Gross environmental emissions, in the absence of any regulation, represent a fixed

3 There is nothing in the model structure to prevent us from having 'regional' externalities that affect only geographically close countries. Since our country aggregation is not based on geography, such a categorization becomes meaningless.

proportion of activity levels. To illustratc, let us denote by m^L and m^G, respectively, the local and global emission coefficients of a given production or consumption sector.[4] Then the sector's gross emissions are simply equal to m^LX and m^GX, where X represents the level of output or consumption. Net emissions depend on gross emissions and on the degree of emission abatement. Denoting by A^L and A^G, respectively, the proportional abatement of local and global emissions by this sector, its net emissions can be expressed as $m^LX\ (1 - A^L)$ and $m^GX\ (1 - A^G)$.

Abatement activities are sector specific. We assume that there exists some degree of output complementarity in the 'production' of abatement of local and global emissions. This is achieved by postulating a constant-elasticity transformation (CET) function linking 'aggregate abatement,' A, with the proportional abatement levels for local and global emissions with elasticity of transformation τ between the two types of abatement. Unit abatement costs are assumed to be independent of production levels; as sectors increase the level of abatement as a proportion of their emissions (i.e., as they decrease their per-unit emissions), however, unit emission abatement costs rise (Ballard and Medema 1988). We represent this cost structure by means of a constant-elasticity unit cost function of the form

$$\frac{F(\vec{p}, A)}{A} = \frac{f(\vec{p})}{1+\eta}A^{\eta}, \tag{1}$$

where $F(\vec{p}, A)$ is the cost of abating a given proportion, A, of emissions for each unit of output or consumption, $\vec{p}$ is a vector of input prices, and η (which is positive) is the elasticity of unit abatement costs with respect to A. Marginal abatement costs as a function of A are then

$$f(\vec{p})A^{\eta}. \tag{2}$$

The government levies unit local and global emission fees. The resulting emission charges, z^jL and z^jG, paid on each physical unit of the 'unabated' portion of output or consumption, are equal to the emission fee times the amount of emissions per unit of output or consumption (i.e., the emission coefficient). For given emission fees, producers and consumers select cost-minimizing abatement levels for which marginal abatement costs equal private marginal abatement benefits. The latter are equal to a CET aggregation of unit emission charges. Notice that we assume abatement technologies to be identical in all regions, which implies that differences in abatement choices across regions arise exclusively from differences in emission charges or in factor prices.[5]

2. Damage and valuation

Total local emissions experienced by a certain region, E^L, are the sum of net local emissions by all sectors in that region. Total global emissions experienced

4 By consumption sector, we mean merely the domestic consumption of the good in question.

5 We assume that no region is inherently 'dirtier' than others.

by a region, E^G, are the sum of net global emissions by all sectors in all regions. The relationship between emissions experienced and environmental damage D is modelled by means of convex, constant-elasticity damage functions:

$$D^L(E^L) = k^L(E^L)^{\rho^L} \tag{3}$$

$$D^G(E^G) = k^G(E^G)^{\rho^G}, \tag{4}$$

where k^L and k^G are constants, and ρ^L and ρ^G represent elasticities of damage with respect to emissions (assumed to be greater than unity) (Dewees 1992). These elasticities are likely to be different for different types of emissions and to vary across regions to reflect differences in assimilative capacity. Further discussion of the parameters of the damage functions follows below.

We also distinguish between a local dimension and a global dimension of environmental quality on the consumption side of the economy. Environmental quality is equal to the difference between endowments of environmental quality and damage:

$$Q^L = \bar{Q}^L - D^L(E^L) \tag{5}$$

$$Q^G = \bar{Q}^G - D^G(E^G). \tag{6}$$

It follows that the marginal valuation of emissions experienced by a region is simply equal to

$$p_E^L = Np_Q^L \frac{dD^L}{dE^L} \tag{7}$$

$$p_E^G = Np_Q^G \frac{dD^G}{dE^G}, \tag{8}$$

where N is population, and p_Q^L and p_Q^G are individual marginal valuations for local and global environmental quality, respectively.

The individual valuations of environmental quality in turn depend on the level of environmental quality and on per capita consumption of goods. We model this relationship via a utility function defined over consumption goods and environmental quality. First we aggregate the two types of environmental quality by means of a constant-elasticity of substitution (CES) function with an elasticity of substitution of σ. Combined environmental quality then enters a CES utility function together with per capita consumption, with an elasticity of substitution equal to γ.[6] It can be easily shown that the reciprocal of γ equals the income elasticity of environmental quality valuation, ω.[7] Also notice that the degree of responsiveness of the marginal

6 We assume strong separability between consumption and environmental quality, which enables us to treat environmental quality as a single consumption aggregate (Forster 1981).

7 Notice that since individuals are rationed in their consumption of environmental quality, and since observable income does not include the value of environmental quality consumed, it is possible to obtain a positive income elasticity of the marginal valuation of environmental quality from a homothetic formulation of preferences (Lucas et al., 1992).

valuation of environmental quality to an increase in damage depends on the size of environmental quality endowments. Thus, we can choose these endowments so as to reflect an exogenously selected value for the elasticity of marginal valuation with respect to damage, ζ.

Because of the static nature of the model, we implicitly assume that environmental quality is a renewable resource. If all pollutants were 'fund' pollutants (i.e., if the environment has some assimilative capacity for them) this inaccuracy may not be too serious. For 'stock' pollutants (those for which the assimilative capacity is very small or zero), this assumption leads to an underestimation of the social cost of environmental emissions.[8]

3. Environmental policies

Environmental controls are modelled as emission fees that force the emitting party to internalize part or all of the external cost. For local emissions generated by a sector in region j, emission charges per unit of unabated output or consumption are

$$z^j L = \pi_D^j p_E^{jL} m^L, \tag{9}$$

where π_D^j represents the rate at which the emitter is forced to internalize the externality. For global emissions, charges are

$$z^j G = \pi j_D p_E^{jG} m^G + \pi_X^j \sum_{r \neq j} p_E^{rG} m^G, \tag{10}$$

where π_D^j is an internalization rate for the domestic component of the externality, and π_X^j is the rate of internalization for international spillovers. Even when π_X^j is greater than zero, we assume that the revenue of emission charges is transferred not to the affected parties but to the residents of the country where the emissions originate. In our model structure this approach – unlike real-world environmental regulatory schemes – is inherently efficient, though not necessarily equitable.

4. Key parameters

The respective shapes of the marginal cost and benefit functions for emission abatement are crucial determinants of optimal abatement choices and their responsiveness to policy changes. This subsection summarizes how the key parameters and variables in our environmental submodel affect the shape of these functions.

The level of marginal abatement costs depends on factor prices and is increasing in the proportion of emissions abated. The marginal cost schedule is steeper the larger is the elasticity of unit abatement costs with respect to proportional abatement, η. This relation merely reflects the fact that a given incremental reduction in emissions is easier to achieve when emissions are high than when almost all emissions have been eliminated.

8 The terms 'stock' and 'fund' pollutants are suggested in Tietenberg (1991).

The marginal benefits of abatement depend on internalization rates, population size, and the marginal valuation of environmental quality, which in turn depends directly on per capita income and inversely on the level of environmental quality. The marginal benefit schedule is decreasing in the level of abatement, since an increase in environmental quality results in a reduced marginal valuation of environmental quality and thus in lower emission charges for a given rate of internalization. The marginal benefit schedule is steeper the larger are the elasticity of environmental damage with respect to emissions, ρ, and the elasticity of damage valuation with respect to damage, ζ.

5. Production and trade

The environmental submodel described above is embedded in a multisectoral-multiregional trade model with non-homogeneous traded goods. Primary factors, labour and capital, are domestically mobile but internationally immobile, and factor endowments differ across regions. Because of capital immobility, and the static nature of the model, dirty industries are prevented from relocating to regions with low emission charges, a possibility that some authors indicate as a primary source of environmental 'leakage' (Lucas et al., 1992). As we shall mention below, we view this as a main limitation to our analysis. Production technologies are identical across regions and are modelled by means of constant returns to scale CES production functions. Preferences are modelled through homothetic nested CES functions, as discussed above. Substitution elasticities are identical across regions, but demand share parameters are region specific. In order to accommodate cross-hauling in trade flows, we adopt an 'Armington' structure: goods of the same type produced in different regions are less than perfect substitutes.[9]

IV. DATA AND PARAMETER CALIBRATION

In this section we describe the basic data used to calibrate the model. The commodities were chosen with the idea of identifying goods by their factor intensities in labour, skills, capital, and 'environmental inputs.' As a result, there are six goods (and sectors) chosen to separate industries with more emissions from those with less and also to separate higher-technology industries from lower-technology industries.

Countries were grouped according to their per capita incomes (since it is an important determinant of the valuation of environmental quality) and the relative levels of environmental quality they enjoy. The following abbreviations are used:

NA United States and Canada (assumed to have relatively low unit emissions and limited assimilative capacity)

9 From a theoretical point of view an Armington structure is inconsistent with the assumption that technologies are identical across regions. Nevertheless, in a model with aggregated flows, the assumption of imperfect substitutability between imports and domestically produced goods may be justified by the existence of discrepancies in the commodity compositions of trade and production flows.

OD Other Developed Countries (assumed to have relatively low unit emissions and limited assimilative capacity).

LI Low- and Middle-Income Countries (assumed to have relatively high unit emissions and abundant assimilative capacity).

For standard CGE models the calibration procedure is straightforward, but for the environmental portion of our model, calibration is complicated by the inadequacy of data, and specifically by the absence of markets for environmental quality.

Population, trade, demand and value added data were used to calibrate the model to 1986.[10]

Sectoral abatement costs as a percentage of total costs in NA were obtained from Lucas et al. (1992) and Low (1992b). Since data on abatement costs for consumption emissions were not available to us, we simply assumed that these costs are one-half of the abatement costs in the corresponding production sectors. For this specification, total abatement costs represent less than 1 per cent of GNP, which is in line with typical estimates (Low 1992a).

Although the choice of a reference abatement level is somewhat arbitrary, if we assume a 50 per cent abatement level in conjunction with a value of 1/3 for η (the elasticity of unit abatement costs with respect to proportional abatement), the resulting abatement cost schedules behave consistently with empirical findings.[11]

The parameters of damage functions are specified as follows. For global emissions we assume identical parameters for all regions. With respect to local emissions, we specify different scale coefficients in the various regions. These coefficients, k^{jL}, reflect the degree of dispersion of local emissions in the local environment and are likely to be different for different pollutants and to depend on the size and physical characteristics of the local environment. Since we were not able to find aggregate estimates for these coefficients, as a first approximation they were specified according to the formula $k^{jL} = \kappa^L (N^j)^{-\rho^{jL}}$, where N^j is the population of region j, and κ^L is a scaling parameter that is endogenously determined by our calibration procedure. Given this specification, if two regions of different size (and with an identical ρ^L) experienced local emissions that are in proportion to their respective population sizes, then they would experience the same level of local environmental damage. For the elasticities of damage with respect to emissions, we employ educated guesses based on a comparison of emission data with concentration levels for selected air and water pollutants in different regions (World Resources Institute 1990).

To calculate emission coefficients, we first compute marginal abatement costs, given our choice of η (see above) and for given unit abatement costs. Notice that our choice of functional form implies that marginal abatement cost is simply equal to average cost times $(1 + \eta)$. These marginal abatement costs provide an

10 Further details are available from the authors by request.

11 Maloney and Yandle (1984) focus on the price elasticity of demand for emission permits, which, given our specification of abatement costs, can be expressed as $\Omega = A/[\eta(1 - A)]$. For $A = 0.5$ and $\eta = 1/3$ one obtains $\Omega = 3$, which is consistent with their findings (they report values of 3 and above).

estimate of the implied emission charges (which equal the marginal benefit of abatement). We then employ an exogenous imputation scheme to obtain separate local and global emission charges.[12] For given domestic internalization rates, and assuming zero internalization rates for international spillovers, we can compute net emissions values per unit of output. Given reference abatement levels, we obtain gross emission values. We then arbitrarily choose units for physical emission so that, in the benchmark equilibrium, the marginal valuation in NA is equal to unity. We thus obtain physical sectoral unit coefficients of gross emissions, which we adopt for all regions.

Clearly, the absolute size of environmental externalities that we obtain through this process is crucially dependent on the choice of benchmark internalization rates: the higher the benchmark rate of internalization rate, the smaller the implied external effects in the benchmark equilibrium. Since no reliable estimate is available for the value of environmental damages generated by economic activities, any choice of internalization rates must by necessity be purely speculative. In order to reflect this indeterminacy, we choose a base case value of 0.33 for the domestic internalization rate in all regions and subsequently perform sensitivity analysis around this central value. Notice that assuming identical internalization rates for all regions does *not* contradict the idea that environmental controls are tighter in high-income countries, since, for a given internalization rate, emission charges and abatement levels will be higher in high-income regions, where the marginal valuation for environmental quality is higher.[13]

For the income elasticity of the marginal valuation of environmental quality, ω, the elasticity of marginal valuation of environmental quality with respect to environmental damage, ζ, and the elasticity of substitution between local and global environmental quality, σ, we select, respectively, central-case values of 1.0, 0.5, and 1. Although the available evidence on the parameters characterizing preferences for environmental quality is rather scant,[14] there seems to be an agreement that, given a certain level of environmental quality, its marginal valuation would be substantially higher in rich countries than in low- and middle-income countries. Given our choice of parameters, we obtain equilibrium values for the social marginal valuation of environmental quality in different regions that do not conflict with our prior beliefs: 1.0 for NA, 0.63 for OD, and 0.12 for LI.

For all production and abatement functions, as well as for the aggregation of domestic demand, we employ a Cobb-Douglas specification, which implies a unitary

12 For production emissions, we assume that local emissions charges account for 80 per cent of total emission charges. For consumption emissions, 100 per cent of emission charges are assumed to account for local emission charges in all sectors except EH, where this share is reduced to 80 per cent (to reflect the presence of taxes on consumption of fossil fuels).

13 This assumption, however, contradicts the observation that internalization rates appear to differ across countries by type of emission. For example, taxes on fossil fuels in the EEC are substantially higher than they are in North America, suggesting that the internalization rate for global emissions is higher in the EEC than in North America.

14 'Economists are as far now from placing a single dollar value on fishable water, unimpaired scenery, or other environmental phenomena as they were two decades ago, perhaps farther' (Braden and Kolstad 1991, 324).

elasticity of substitution. Finally, for the elasticity of substitution between domestically produced goods and imports we use a value of 2.5, while the elasticity of substitution between imports of different origin is made equal to 5 (see discussion in Jomini et al. 1991).

When the model is calibrated, a direct computation of benchmark emissions and abatement levels in all regions would require a previous knowledge of the values of the marginal valuations of environmental quality in all regions, which in turn depend on net emissions. This requirement forces us to resort to a simultaneous calibration procedure: all parameters are endogenized, and the model is augmented by a set of calibration restrictions. This augmented model, together with our assumed data and parameters, is sufficient to identify all the parameters of the model. The final step of our calibration procedure consists of solving the augmented model numerically to obtain a set of parameters that is consistent with our data set.[15] The calibration procedure is detailed in model documentation available from the authors.

V. SIMULATIONS AND RESULTS

We performed simulations with our model to assess the relative contribution of international trade (including trade policy changes) to environmental degradation and to explore the implications of environmental externalities for the size and distribution of the gains from trade liberalization. Specifically, we explore the effects on environmental quality and welfare of all combinations of the following trade-policy configurations:

1. Business as usual (current levels of environmental protection)
2. A move to full, global internalization (i.e., $\pi_D^j = 1$ and $\pi_X^j = 1$ in all regions)
3. Unilateral domestic environmental action by NA (i.e., $\pi_D^j = 1$ in NA);

and of the following three trade-policy scenarios:

a. Benchmark trade barriers (benchmark)
b. A removal of all trade barriers (free trade)
c. A three-fold increase in trade barriers (trade wars).

The results of our simulations for all cases are summarized in tables 1 and 2.[16] The rest of this section is devoted to a discussion of our findings. Some limited sensitivity analysis is presented in subsection 1.

At the benchmark levels of internalization, international trade does appear to have some negative impact on environmental quality. A move to free trade slightly

15 The model is conceived and solved using MPS/GE (Rutherford 1988).

16 The numbers in these tables should all be interpreted as percentage changes compared with the initial situation (benchmark trade barriers and benchmark internalization in all countries). Given our parameterization, in the benchmark equilibrium a 1 per cent increase in net emissions produces approximately a 1 per cent decrease in the level of environmental quality in the NA bloc. Admittedly, the figures representing changes in environmental quality cannot be given any cardinal interpretation, since in our model environmental quality is defined only in a conventional fashion; these figures, however, may provide information on the *relative* effects of different policies. Percentage welfare changes are computed as equivalent variations as a proportion of benchmark full income (income plus the value of environmental quality enjoyed by consumers).

TABLE 1
Per cent changes in combined environmental quality – central case

Region	NA	OD	LI
	Benchmark internalization		
Benchmark	0.0	0.0	0.0
Free trade	−1.3	−0.9	−0.7
Trade wars	+0.8	+0.5	+0.4
	Global internalization		
Benchmark	+95.9	+68.1	+39.4
Free trade	+95.5	+67.5	+39.5
Trade wars	+96.1	+68.6	+39.5
	Unilateral action by NA		
Benchmark	+45.7	+2.0	+2.3
Free trade	+44.5	+1.2	+1.7
Trade wars	+46.5	+2.5	+2.7

TABLE 2
Per cent welfare changes – central case

Region	NA	OD	LI
	Benchmark internalization		
Benchmark	0.0	0.0	0.0
Free trade	+0.4	+1.3	0.0
Trade wars	−1.1	−2.6	−1.6
	Global internalization		
Benchmark	+1.3	+0.8	+0.8
Free trade	+1.7	+2.2	+0.8
Trade wars	+0.2	−1.8	−0.8
	Unilateral action by NA		
Benchmark	+0.4	+0.1	+0.2
Free trade	+0.8	+1.4	+0.1
Trade wars	−0.7	−2.5	−1.4

worsens the environment, while an increase in trade barriers has a small but positive impact on the environment. Trade liberalization produces sizable welfare gains only for NA and OD. On the other hand, an increase in trade barriers has a substantial negative welfare impact on all regions.

Full internalization of all externalities causes marked improvements in environmental quality in all regions. All countries that fully internalize externalities experience an improvement in environmental quality of more than 39 per cent, regardless of the trade policy regime. By contrast, the improvement in environmental quality brought about by a move from free trade to a trade war is never more than 2 per cent. Full internalization also yields substantial welfare gains for all regions.

The most striking message of the results is that compared with environmental policies, trade policies have very little impact on environmental quality. This finding suggests that the relative contribution of international trade to environmental degradation is quite modest. Notice also that the size and the distribution of the gains from trade liberalization are not substantially affected by the change in environmental policies.

Unilateral domestic internalization by NA causes a marked improvement in NA environmental quality, but the addition of trade restrictions has virtually no added effect on environmental quality. However, trade restrictions still cause a large welfare loss. The idea that appropriate environmental policies, when implemented unilaterally, must be buttressed by trade restrictions is not supported by our results. Even though NA internalizes only the 'domestic' impact of the emissions, such a policy still produces a reduction in global emissions. As a result, the welfare of non-participants rises and their environmental quality improves.

The *qualitative* effect of trade policy on environmental quality is unrelated to the environmental policy regime. Liberalization causes small quality losses, and trade restriction causes small gains in environmental quality. In most cases, environmental quality is highest for all environmental policies when trade is restricted. In the LI region, virtually the same environmental quality is achieved when global internalization is combined with free trade as it is when it is combined with trade wars. In the other cases, the reduction in environmental quality caused by free trade is smallest (sometimes almost zero), however, when appropriate environmental policies are in place. Stated differently, the indirect negative impact of trade liberalization on environmental quality is likely to be smaller the higher the level of internalization of environmental externalities.

1. Sensitivity analysis

Given the acknowledged uncertainty about many of our parameters, we performed some limited sensitivity runs on two experiments (Global internalization and Trade Wars). The central case elasticities and alternate values used are reported in table 3. The choice of values was based on a number of considerations. First, where we had some evidence (as in the case of the elasticity of marginal abatement cost with respect to the degree of abatement), we used this evidence to choose the midpoint. Where there was no directly applicable evidence, we adopted values that seemed plausible. We also did a run corresponding to the case where the internalization rates in the developed regions are higher (0.5) than the low-middle income region (0.33). This run is reported in the last column of our sensitivity results. (See tables 4 and 5.)

The main message from the sensitivity runs is that the main conclusion of our analysis is robust to the range of parameters we tried. In all configurations, trade restrictions have relatively minor effects on environmental quality and cause significant welfare losses to all regions, whereas following appropriate environ-

TABLE 3
Parameter values used in sensitivity analysis

Parameter	LOW	CC	HIGH
Domestic internalization rate (π_D^j)	0.10	0.33	0.50
MAC w.r.t. degree of abatement (η)	0.25	0.33	0.50
Valuation w.r.t. income (ω)	0.95	1.00	1.05
Valuation w.r.t. damage (ζ)	0.25	0.50	0.75
Local-global substitution (σ)	0.85	1.00	1.15

TABLE 4
Sensitivity: global internalization

Environmental quality (per cent changes)

		π_D^j		η		ω		ζ		σ		$\pi_D^{NA,OD} = 0.5$
Region	CC	*L*	*H*	*L*	*H*	*L*	*H*	*L*	*H*	*L*	*H*	$\pi_D^{LL} = 0.33$
NA	95.9	100.0	77.2	98.5	91.7	97.4	94.2	49.9	132.3	95.9	95.8	81.7
OD	68.1	106.2	54.0	72.5	60.9	64.9	69.8	37.3	95.1	68.4	67.9	63.1
LL	39.4	42.8	38.1	43.0	34.1	32.3	43.9	21.7	54.5	39.9	39.1	50.5

Welfare (per cent changes)

		π_D^j		η		ω		ζ		σ		$\pi_D^{NA,OD} = 0.5$
Region	CC	*L*	*H*	*L*	*H*	*L*	*H*	*L*	*H*	*L*	*H*	$\pi_D^{LL} = 0.33$
NA	1.3	5.6	0.6	1.4	1.2	1.0	1.5	1.6	1.1	1.3	1.3	1.0
OD	0.8	5.4	0.3	0.9	0.7	0.6	1.0	1.0	0.7	0.8	0.8	0.7
LL	0.8	2.8	0.5	0.8	0.8	0.8	0.8	0.9	0.7	0.8	0.8	0.6

mental policies significantly improves environmental quality and raises economic welfare.

The analysis also identifies two parameters that are crucial to the analysis. The first is the domestic internalization rate (π_D^j). The lower the benchmark internalization rate, the higher the (welfare and environmental quality) returns to internalization. The other important parameter is the elasticity of marginal valuation with respect to damages. The higher this value is, the higher are the returns to liberalization as well.

2. *Summary of results*

Our numerical findings must be viewed as exploratory for a number of reasons, not least of which is our limited knowledge of precisely how environmental emissions affect the environment. The main qualifications to our results fall into the following categories.

TABLE 5
Sensitivity: trade wars

Environmental quality (per cent changes)

		π_D^j		η		ω		ζ		σ		$\pi_D^{NA,OD} = 0.5$
Region	CC	*L*	*H*	*L*	*H*	*L*	*H*	*L*	*H*	*L*	*H*	$\pi_D^{LI} = 0.33$
NA	0.8	0.8	0.8	0.8	0.8	0.8	0.8	0.6	0.9	0.8	0.8	0.6
OD	0.5	0.9	0.4	0.5	0.5	0.5	0.5	0.4	0.6	0.5	0.5	0.4
LI	0.4	0.4	0.4	0.4	0.4	0.3	0.4	0.3	0.5	0.4	0.4	0.3

Welfare (per cent changes)

		π_D^j		η		ω		ζ		σ		$\pi_D^{NA,OD} = 0.5$
Region	CC	*L*	*H*	*L*	*H*	*L*	*H*	*L*	*H*	*L*	*H*	$\pi_D^{LI} = 0.33$
NA	−1.1	−1.0	−1.1	−1.1	−1.1	−1.1	−1.1	−1.0	−1.1	−1.1	−1.1	−1.1
OD	−2.6	−2.4	−2.6	−2.6	−2.6	−2.6	−2.6	−2.5	−2.6	−2.6	−2.6	−2.6
LI	−1.6	−1.5	−1.6	−1.6	−1.6	−1.6	−1.6	−1.5	−1.6	−1.6	−1.6	−1.6

- *Parameters.* Our reading did not yield consensus values for a number of key parameters in the model, particularly those describing individual and social valuation of environmental quality, which crucially determine the size of the benefits of internalization.
- *Data.* Data on policy regimes, emissions and environmental quality are inadequate, particularly for the LI bloc.
- *Model structure.* Because of the static nature of our model, our results do not capture the potential effects of trade and environmental policies on industrial location and on technological change. The model is very highly aggregated.
- *Policy regime.* Both benchmark and counterfactual environmental policies are implemented as emission fees, which are at least cost effective and can be efficient. This regime contrasts with the actual policy regimes in many countries that employ inefficient regulatory schemes.

VI. SUMMARY AND CONCLUSION

The model developed in this paper represents an attempt to achieve a comprehensive treatment of local and global environmental externalities in a static framework and of their linkages with international trade. In spite of our efforts carefully to separate the various aspects of environmental externalities, our numerical findings must be viewed as exploratory, owing to our limited knowledge of precisely how environmental emissions impact on the environment. We also realize that two features of the model, perfect competition and capital immobility, are likely to dampen the impact of both trade and environmental policies. Even with these limitations, we believe that the results of our simulations shed some light on some fundamental questions concerning the linkages between environmental and trade policies.

Our results suggest that, although free trade may have a negative impact on environmental quality, its relative contribution to environmental degradation appears to be limited. Further, achieving significant environmental quality improvements via trade policy is likely to be extremely costly. This finding can be attributed to the following circumstances.

1. Trade accounts for a relatively small share of world production.
2. A large share of trade involves trade in environmentally 'clean' goods.
3. Estimates suggest that, even for 'dirty' traded goods, abatement costs account for a relatively modest share of total costs.

These facts contribute to our conclusion that trade restrictions are a very poor substitute for direct environmental protection.

Our experiments also indicate that the welfare gains from environmental protection are not significantly affected by changes in trade policies; at the same time, the size and distribution of the gains from trade liberalization are little affected by the presence of environmental externalities. These findings suggest that trade restrictions are not necessary companions to effective environmental policy, and that well-conceived environmental policies are unlikely to be disastrous in an open economy, as some appear to believe.

Protection of the environment is becoming a dominant concern in the design of economic policies, and our numerical results indeed suggest that the gains from increased environmental action may be very substantial. Nevertheless, the importance of coordinating trade and environmental policies should not be overstated. Even in the absence of international cooperation on environmental policies, the process of trade liberalization may promote a more efficient use of world resources.

REFERENCES

Ballard, Charles L., and Steven G. Medema 1988 (March) 'The efficiency effects of pigouvian taxes and subsidies: a computational general equilibrium approach. Paper presented at the NBER Applied General Equilibrium Workshop

Bhagwat, Jagdish (1981a) 'The generalized theory of distortions and welfare.' In Bhagwati (1981b)

— ed. (1981b) *International Trade: Selected Readings*, Second ed. (Cambridge, MA: MIT Press)

Blackhurst, Richard (1977) 'International trade and domestic environmental policies in a growing economy.' In *International Relations in a Changing World*, ed. R. Blackhurst et al. (Leiden: Sijthoff)

Braden, John B., and Charles D. Kolstad eds (1991) *Measuring the Demand for Environmental Quality* (New York: Elsevier Science Publishers)

Dewees, Donald N (1992) 'The efficiency of pursuing environmental quality objectives: the shape of damage functions.' Mimeo, Department of Economics, University of Toronto, June

Forster, B.A. (1981) Separability, functional structure and aggregation for a class of

models in environmental economics.' *Journal of Environmental Economics and Management* 8, 118–33
Jomini, Patrick, et al. (1991) *SALTER: A General Equilibrium Model of the World Economy – Volume 1: Model Structure, Database and Parameters.* Study undertaken by the Industry Commission for the Department of Foreign Affairs and Trade
Low, Patrick, ed. (1992a) *International Trade and the Environment* (Washington DC: International Bank for Reconstruction and Development)
— (1992b) 'Trade measures and environmental quality: the implications for Mexico's exports.' In Low (1992a)
Lucas, Robert E.B., David Wheeler, and Hemamala Hettig (1992) 'Economic development, environmental regulation and the international migration of toxic industrial pollution: 1960–88.' In Low (1992a)
Maloney, M.T., and B. Yandle (1984) 'Estimation of the cost of air pollution control regulation. *Journal of Environmental Economics and Management* 11, 244–63
Pethig, R. (1976) 'Pollution, welfare, and environmental policy in the theory of comparative advantage.' *Journal of Environmental Economics and Management 3*, 160–69
Radetzki, Marian (1992) 'Economic growth and the environment.' In Low (1992a)
Rutherford, Thomas Fox (1988) 'General equilibrium modelling with *MPS/GE*.' Paper, Department of Economics, University of Western Ontario
Shrybman, Steven (1990) 'International trade and the environment: an environmental assessment of the General Agreement on Tariffs and Trade.' *Ecologist* 20, 30–4
Siebert, Horst (1977) 'Environmental quality and the gains from trade.' *KYKLOS* 30, 657–73
Tietenberg, Tom (1991) *Environmental and Natural Resource Economics*, third ed. (Harper Collins)
Whalley, John (1991) 'The interface between environmental and trade policies.' *Economic Journal* 101, 180–9
World Resources Institute (1990) *World Resources, 1990–1991* (London: Oxford University Press)

[29]

Environment and Development Economics 5 (2000): 457–481

Reducing coal subsidies and trade barriers: their contribution to greenhouse gas abatement

KYM ANDERSON
CEPR, and School of Economics and Centre for International Economic Studies, University of Adelaide, Adelaide, SA 5005.
Email: kym.anderson@adelaide.edu.au

WARWICK J. McKIBBIN
Research School of Pacific and Asian Studies, Australian National University, ACT 0200 and the Brookings Institution, Washington, DC.
Email: Warwick.McKibbin@anu.edu.au

ABSTRACT. International negotiations for an agreement to reduce the emission of greenhouse gases have not produced cost-effective policies for reducing emissions, not least because they are unlikely to prevent 'leakage' through a re-location of carbon-intensive activities to poorer countries. An alternative or supplementary approach that is more likely to achieve at least some emission reductions, and at the same time generate national and global economic benefits rather than costs, involves lowering coal subsidies and trade barriers. Past coal policies have encouraged excessive production of coal in a number of industrial countries and excessive coal consumption in numerous developing and transition economies. This paper documents those distortions and outlines the circumstances under which their reform (currently under way in some countries) could both improve the economy and lower greenhouse gas emissions globally. It then quantifies the effects on economic activity as well as global carbon emissions, using the G-Cubed multi-country general equilibrium model of the world economy. Both the gains in economic efficiency and the reductions in carbon dioxide emissions that could result from such reforms are found to be substantial—a 'no regrets' outcome or win–win Pareto improvement for the economy and the environment.

Keywords: Coal subsidies, trade and environment, carbon emissions, global warming, greenhouse gases, IPCC

This paper draws on two earlier ones: an Invited Paper for the 41st Australian Agricultural and Resource Economics Society Conference, held at Broadbeach, January 20–25, 1997, and a paper prepared for the Global Environment and Trade Study based at the London Business School, Yale University, and the University of London's Foundation for International Environmental Law and Development. The authors are grateful for very helpful comments from conference participants plus Scott Barrett and two anonymous referees. Financial support from the Australian Research Council and the MacArthur Foundation is gratefully acknowledged. Since this paper used the G-Cubed model developed jointly with Peter Wilcoxen, it has also benefited from funding of a project at the Brookings Institution and has received financial support from the US Environmental Protection Agency through Cooperative Agreement CR818579–01–0 and from the National Science Foundation through grant SBR–9321010. The views expressed are those of the authors and should not be interpreted as reflecting the views of others including the trustees, officers or other staff of the University of Adelaide, the Australian National University, the Brookings Institution, the Environmental Protection Agency, or the National Science Foundation.

1. Introduction

With respect to the environment, governments are often blamed for not doing enough, such as taxing polluters. Their reticence is understandable from a political viewpoint: the interventions advocated by environmental groups are typically harmful to the economic interests of powerful industry groups. Yet there are many situations where it would be more appropriate for environmentalists to ask governments not so much to 'do something' as to 'undo something'. Among the innovative suggestions being made by economists for addressing environmental problems, following the Rio Earth Summit in 1992, is the removal of excessive government subsidies to pollutive activities (World Bank, 1997a). This action is attractive both because it benefits rather than retards the national economy involved and because it can be done unilaterally rather than requiring collective international action with attendant free-rider problems.

A classic example has to do with 'greenhouse' gases. The scientific community continues to debate the question as to whether the build-up of carbon dioxide, ethane, and other greenhouse gases is contributing to a significant warming of the earth's surface; what the economic consequences of global warming might be; and even whether the world as a whole will be better or worse off. Yet, despite these gaps in our knowledge, there seems to be a widespread presumption that governments must intervene to ensure greenhouse gas emissions are reduced. For example, 150 countries gathered in Geneva in July 1996 to reach a United Nations consensus on setting binding targets for reducing carbon emissions in stages over the next 25 years. Given the uncertainty surrounding the likelihood and possible consequences of global warming, it would seem prudent to first search for ways to reduce greenhouse gas emissions with policy changes that can be justified on standard economic and local environmental grounds. That is, to what extent are there unambiguous win–win possibilities for reducing those emissions that would benefit the global economy *and* the global environment? This paper explores one such set of reforms that have recently begun to be implemented, namely reductions in government distortions to the world's coal markets, bearing in mind that coal accounts for around 30 per cent of the world's primary energy supply and 40 per cent of carbon emissions from energy use (ignoring firewood).

Since both coal mining and coal burning are pollutive, it would be optimal to tax the pollutive contributions of both production and consumption of coal. Yet we observe several industrial countries subsidizing coal mining, and many developing and former socialist countries subsidizing coal burning, either explicitly and/or implicitly with the help of coal trade barriers. To what extent is it possible that replacing those effective production and consumption subsidies with optimal taxes—or even just removing the subsidies and trade barriers—could simultaneously improve the efficiency of resource use, reduce damage to local environments, and lower greenhouse gas emissions? Earlier studies suggest there may well be such possibilities (Burniaux, Martin and Oliveira-Martins, 1992; Hoeller and Coppel, 1992; Larson and Shah, 1995), but they focus on all fossil fuels rather than just on coal. It is of interest to examine the contribution of coal policies alone, since policies affecting the export supply of the other fossil fuels are controlled largely by OPEC and, unlike coal policies, are not under political pressure to change.

This paper addresses the issue in a series of steps. It first provides some details of the environmental externalities on the demand and supply sides of the coal market, from which it is then clear what the optimal policy interventions would be for national governments if they ignore international pollution spillovers. These are then compared with the actual policy interventions we observe in key national coal markets around the world. The evidence on the extent of divergences between domestic and international coal prices in various groups of countries shows that, as with agriculture, coal producer and consumer prices have tended to be well below border prices in developing and former socialist countries, and to be well above border prices in several large industrial countries that are net importers of coal. The possible consequences for economic activity and greenhouse gas emissions of removing those subsidies—as has begun to happen in the 1990s—are then explored. This is done first using a simple theoretical partial equilibrium approach. Then some empirical results are summarized from a recent study that uses a global computable general equilibrium model known as G-Cubed. That model is able not only to capture the effects exposed through partial equilibrium thinking but also to take into account the possibilities for substitution in production and consumption between products (including within the energy group) both within and across countries when domestic relative prices are changed in some or all regions. Notwithstanding the reforms of recent years, those results suggest that significantly lower greenhouse gas emissions could result from further reducing the remaining coal mining subsidies in the OECD. Even larger benefits would result if poorer countries also raised their artificially low domestic prices for coal. Some qualifications and the environmental, trade, and policy implications of the analysis are discussed in the final section of the paper.

2. Environmental externalities and optimal policy intervention in the coal market

Traditionally, the externality most commonly thought of with respect to coal was local air pollution in the form of smog generated from the burning of coal by households and industry. That pollution is substantially greater per unit of energy provided than that generated from other fuel sources (except perhaps from firewood).[1] More recently we have come to appreciate the contribution also of sulphur dioxide emissions from coal burning, especially in the form of acid rain. Those sulphur emissions—which can vary considerably among coal sources—have down-wind trans-border as well as intra-national effects that are undesirable. And even more recently the additional worry has been coal's contribution to global greenhouse gases, most notably through carbon dioxide emissions:

[1] Apart from emitting far less visual pollution than coal, oil emits into the atmosphere only about two-thirds as much carbon per unit of energy as does coal, and gas only about half as much (World Bank, 1997b, table 4.1).

40 per cent of the CO_2 emitted globally from energy use came from coal in the early 1990s (World Resources Institute, 1996). The distinguishing feature of those emissions is that their contribution to global warming occurs regardless of the location on the globe of the coal-burning activity.

Much less appreciated are the adverse environmental effects on the production side, from coal mining. They include not just the visual eyesore of holes in the ground in the case of open-cut mines or of mine overburden, but also run-off and leaching from tailings and coal washeries can pollute rivers and lakes. And of significance internationally are the contributions to global warming from methane (CH_4) from the mine, which increase with mine depth. Coal mining contributed 13 per cent of global methane emissions in the early 1990s (World Resources Institute, 1996). As it happens, many of the mines in Europe are now extremely deep, and are providing coal with relatively high sulphur content. Moreover, once pit mines are exhausted, problems continue. During normal working of a mine, water is pumped out virtually as soon as it enters, which prevents it being contaminated by soluble minerals; but if that pumping is not continued after the mine closes, unpumped water gradually builds up and eventually contaminates groundwater (Steenblik and Coroyannakis, 1995). Government subsidies and protection from imports for such mines thus add present and future production externalities to the more-commonly understood local, regional, and global externalities on the consumption side from coal burning.

These facts suggest the social marginal benefit curve in a national coal market is below the private demand curve, and the social marginal cost curve is above the private supply curve, and more so if the welfare of other countries is also taken into account. Even ignoring the latter, the optimal intervention in the presence of these externalities (assuming optimal interventions are in place in all other markets) involves taxing the undesired pollution both from coal mining and from coal burning.[2] Thus the removal of any subsidies to coal mining or coal consumption, including indirect subsidies via trade policies, are likely to be at least a partial step towards the optimal measures and levels of government intervention in coal markets.

3. Coal markets and current coal policies in various parts of the world[3]

The world's coal production is remarkably concentrated. As of 1993 there were just 13 countries whose production accounted for more than 1 per cent of the world's coal. They accounted for 91 per cent of global coal production. They also accounted for 83 per cent of global coal consumption, which suggests that countries which have coal use it but do not export it much. In fact international trade accounts for only about one tenth of global coal sales. (North America, Australia, and South Africa supply three-quarters of that trade, with another 15 per cent coming from the

[2] In the past a case might have been made for some restriction of coal imports on energy supply security grounds, but that is no longer valid now that coal is a much smaller contributor to energy in coal-importing countries.

[3] This and the next section draw on and extend analysis in Anderson (1992, 1995b).

former Soviet Union, China and Poland.) The trade propensity is low partly because of the bulkiness of the product (high transport costs per unit of energy), so that only the highest quality hard coal is worth trading. But also to blame for the small share of production traded are the distortionary subsidy and trade policies in both importing and exporting countries, which happen to have a strong anti-trade bias.

Coal producer subsidies in Western Europe and Japan have been enormous since the 1960s. On the other hand, the opposite policy bias has prevailed in Eastern Europe and the former Soviet Union where policies have kept coal prices below international levels, with perhaps even worse economic and environmental consequences. Coal prices have been kept artificially low in other developing countries too, most notably in the two big coal-burning countries of China and India. In examining these distortions, it is therefore helpful to separate the high-priced OECD countries from the low-priced non-OECD countries.

OECD countries

Within the OECD, North American and Australasian coal markets are reasonably free of coal market distortions. In Western Europe, by contrast, costs of coal production per ton are as much as two to three times import prices. These differences are maintained partly by restricting imports to raise the domestic coal price, partly by the treasury subsidizing producers directly, and partly by imposing minimum purchase obligations on electricity generating utilities, requiring them to buy certain volumes of coal from local mines at above international prices. In Germany, for example, the electricity utilities agreed to buy during 1992–1995 at least 87 per cent of their coal needs from local mines, with only a quarter of that coal priced at import parity and the rest at more than twice the import price—in return for which the utilities have been allowed to pass on the high input cost to electricity consumers, who also contribute an 8 per cent tax to help finance the coal producer subsidy (Newbery, 1995).

The producer subsidy equivalent (PSE) of assistance to production of hard coal, shown in table 1 as a percentage of the import price, reveals that assistance to European Union and Japanese coal production has been very large and grew rapidly during the 1980s. By the early 1990s it was equivalent to providing a domestic producer price that was more than three times the import price in Belgium and Germany, two times in Spain, and 40 per cent higher in France and the UK. There has in addition been considerable assistance to coal producers that is not price related. In fact, over the 1986–1992 period the assistance to production shown in table 1, as a fraction of total assistance, was just two thirds for the UK, about half for Germany and Spain, only a third for Belgium, and less than one tenth for France (IEA, 1993, and earlier editions, and, for France, EC, 1992).

These estimated rates of assistance exceed those for agriculture in Western Europe and Japan. As shown in the middle rows of table 1, in the 1990s the PSE is estimated to have averaged near 90 per cent of the border price for EU agriculture, compared with more than 150 per cent for EU coal. When expressed on a per worker basis, the difference in support has been even larger. During 1987–1993, for example, the support in the EU for

Table 1. *Production subsidies in Western Europe's and Japan's hard coal and farm sectors, 1979–1997 (per unit producer price subsidy equivalent as a percentage of the border price)*

Hard coal[a]

	1979–1981	*1982–1984*	*1985–1987*	*1988–1990*	*1991–1992*	*1993–1996*
Belgium	na	47	124	215	267	na
France[c]	67	54	68	40	39	na
Germany, West	56	45	113	205	228	223
Spain[c]	na	na	58[b]	74	98	107
United Kingdom	na	65	55	107	40	17[f]
EU-12[d]	**na**	**52**	**91**	**165**	**163**	**na**
Japan	na	62	205	267	226	263

Agriculture

	1979–1986	*1985–1987*	*1988–1990*	*1991–1993*	*1994–1997*
EU-12	**57**	**85**	**78**	**90**	**84**
Japan	147	250	184	187	267

Hard coal support per miner employed (1990 US dollars)

	1982	*1986*	*1990*	*(1990)*[e]
Belgium	14,800	23,800	33,600	(84,400)
Germany	14,200	26,900	45,100	(90,200)
United Kingdom	6,500	18,700	26,600	(38,000)

Notes: [a] The United States thermal coal export price fob plus $7 per tonne for freight was used as a proxy for the cif import price for Western Europe, while for Japan Australia's export price fob plus $7 was used. Only subsidies affecting current production are included.

[b] 1986–1987 only.

[c] The numbers for Spain and France are lower-bound estimates. In the case of France (and Germany in 1979–1981) they are based only on the extent to which domestic prices exceed import prices, from EC (1992).

[d] Weighted average with weights based on coal production in 1985–1989, and with Spain's PSE in 1982–1985 assumed to be 50 per cent. The 7 EU member countries not listed have weights under 0.5 per cent so their exclusion has almost no affect on the EU average.

[e] Values in parentheses include 1990 assistance that does not directly affect current production.

[f] Fiscal years ending 31 March.

Sources: Based on PSE estimates from Steenblik and Wigley (1990), IEA (1993, 1997), and EC (1992) for coal, and OECD (1994, 1998) for agriculture.

current production per full-time worker equivalent was $11,400 for farmers (OECD, 1994),[4] compared with two to four times that for coal miners. Indeed total assistance per coal miner employed was close to $90,000 for Belgium and Germany (nearly half of which was supporting current production) and $38,000 for the UK in 1990 (see final three rows of table 1). And, based on EC (1992) data, it was well over $100,000 for France. According to these estimates—which were three times as large in real terms as a decade earlier—it would have been far cheaper to close all coal production in these countries (and Spain) and pay miners their current wage to do nothing.

Estimates of the extent of consumer price distortion are more difficult to determine, but the IEA (1994b) does provide user prices and import prices for coal. Based on those data, it would appear that for Western Europe as a whole both coking and steaming coal prices for users as compared with the prices of imports from outside Western Europe have become steadily greater. On average during 1984–1991, coking coal was priced to industry about 15 per cent above the price of the most expensive imported US coal, and steaming coal was about 40 per cent above for electricity utilities and 55 per cent above for industry users. Again this rivals the extent to which food prices for consumers exceed border prices, which for the EU averaged 55 per cent during 1979–1993 (OECD, 1994). In addition, because coal mined in the EU is 'dirtier' than its imported coal (Steenblik and Coroyannakis, 1995, table 7), the utilities' minimum local purchase obligations require more to be spent on filters to burn the higher-priced domestic coal.

An indication of the extent to which user prices in the most protective European countries exceed those in the United States is given in table 2. Steaming coal in the early 1990s was four times higher than the US price in Germany, twice as high in the United Kingdom, and between 1.3 and 2.3 times as high in Belgium and France. Not surprisingly, electricity prices were roughly double those of the US as well. Some of those differ-

Table 2. *Steaming coal and electricity prices in Europe relative to the United States, 1990–1992 (US = 100)*

	Coal price for industry	*Coal price for electricity*	*Electricity price for households*
Belgium	133	143	212
France	234	130	191
Germany	459	377	205
United Kingdom	212	227	144
Hungary	250	197	55
Poland	81	55	33
Slovakia	72	58	32
India[a]	90	39	na

Note: [a] 1990 only.
Source: IEA (1994b).

[4] It had risen to $21,000 by 1995–1997 (OECD, 1998: 40).

ences may reflect costs of transporting coal (and other energy raw materials) to power plants, some is the result of different preferences for preserving the environment, and some may reflect the greater need to tax emissions in densely populated Europe; but much of it is the result of protective producer coal subsidies and associated barriers to coal import competition.

During the 1990s, these subsidies have come under domestic political pressure to be reduced. Belgium and the United Kingdom began the process with actual cuts, and now France and Germany have made commitments to gradually reduce government support to coal mining over the next decade. For the United Kingdom at least, that has shown up as a fall in the estimated coal PSE to 1996 (last column of table 1). The potential to reform these policies is thus very real, making an examination of the effects of such reform timely.

Non-OECD countries

Obtaining estimates of price distortions in Eastern Europe, the former Soviet Union, and other transition and developing countries is more problematic. What is clear, though, is that in the past coal has been grossly underpriced there, which helps explain the relatively high consumption levels in some of those countries. Except in Hungary, the price of steaming coal paid by electricity utilities in Eastern Europe has been only a fraction (half or less) of the border price. Industry users paid somewhat more, but they still received it at well below its opportunity cost on the world market. The extent of underpricing is currently being reduced though, with Hungary's coal prices now matching the user prices in Western Europe. Even so, it appears from the lower part of table 2 that electricity users in the early 1990s were still hugely subsidised in Eastern Europe, as in India, with prices between one third and one half those of the United States. Thus the OECD's GREEN model, calibrated to 1985, assumes that coal prices average close to half border prices for each of Eastern Europe, the former Soviet Union, China and India, which together account for all but a sixth of the non-OECD coal market (Lee, Oliveira-Martins, and Mensbrugghe, 1994). Table 3 shows that even up to the mid 1990s coal prices in China were less than three-quarters of border prices, although the higher 'market' as distinct from 'plan' prices there are applying to an

Table 3. *Domestic and border prices for coal, China, 1990–1995 (yuan per tonne)*

	Plan price	*Market price*	*Border[a] price*	*Market-to-border price*
1990	56[b]	150	225	0.67
1991	na	160	237	0.68
1992	na	147	248	0.59
1993	na	173	307	0.56
1994	na	189	285	0.66
1995	na	214	284	0.75

Notes: [a] Converted to yuan at market exchange rates.
[b] Unweighted average of 'basic' and 'high' plan prices.
Source: Anderson and Peng (1998).

increasing proportion (now more than half) of sales as non-state owned mines develop (Wang, 1996).[5]

What would be the implications of completely dismantling these coal subsidies and trade barriers? We begin using a simple theoretical partial equilibrium approach and then turn to some empirical results that draw on a global computable general equilibrium model known as G-Cubed.

4. Effects of dismantling coal subsidies: partial equilibrium analysis

Consider the coal market of a small open economy under the following assumptions: coal is a homogeneous product; the domestic coal-mining industry competes with imports that are freely available at a landed price of P_w; there are negative production and consumption externalities associated with coal mining that are both intra- and inter-national/global such that the private marginal cost curve for mining, S_p, is below the national social marginal cost curve S_s, which in turn would be below the global social marginal cost curve (not shown) if international pollution spillovers were to be taken into account, and the private marginal benefit curve D_p is above the national social marginal benefit curve D_s, which in turn would be above the global social benefit curve (not shown) if international pollution spillovers were to be taken into account; and the demand and supply curves incorporate changes in productivity and any international factor movements that would accompany domestic price changes. Under these conditions, and assuming also that in related markets in the economy there are no other distortions nor any externalities that are not offset with optimal intervention measures, then this coal market can be depicted as in figure 1.

Laissez faire versus optimal intervention

Equilibrium in figure 1 in the absence of any government intervention in this coal market would involve a domestic price equal to P_w that would induce OQ being produced and OC being consumed each year, with QC imports satisfying the excess domestic demand at that price. These levels differ from the optimal levels, however, given the presence of externalities in this market. To simplify the analysis, assume transactions costs of taxing environmental damage at the source (e.g., water contamination from mining or sulphur emissions from burning coal) are sufficiently expensive as to make coal production and consumption taxes the optimal intervention instruments, and that this small nation ignores its contribution to neighbouring countries' and global pollution. Then on the production side, OQ* is the optimal output level since it is where the national social marginal cost curve S_s intersects the import price line that represents the

[5] A rough preliminary set of estimates by the World Bank (1997b) suggests the rate of underpricing of coal has halved in EEFSU and fallen by one-sixth in China and India during the 1990s. Why coal, like food, should have been underpriced in poorer countries and overpriced in coal-importing richer countries, and why those policies are now beginning to be reformed, are important questions. Space limitations preclude discussing them here, but see Anderson (1995a, b).

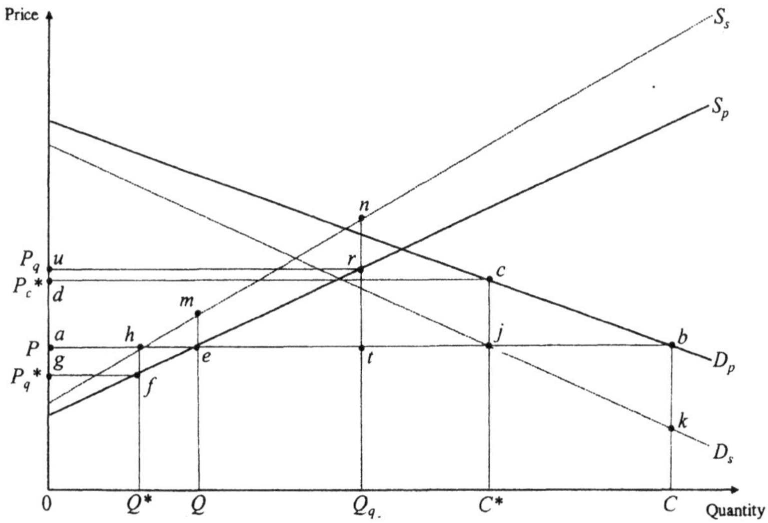

Figure 1. *The effects of removing a subsidy to coal mining in a small open economy*

opportunity cost of producing domestically. That output level would be attained if a tax on coal production were imposed which lowered the domestic price received by miners from P_w to P_q*. And, on the demand side, OC* is the optimal consumption level. At that level the curve representing the national social marginal benefit from coal burning, D_s, intersects the import price line; it would be attained if a tax on coal consumption were imposed which raised the domestic price paid for coal from P_w to P_c*.

The welfare effects of imposing the tax on production can be shown in areas in figure 1. That tax reduces coal producer welfare by *aefg*, raises government tax revenue by *ahfg*, boosts the welfare of those outside this market who are harmed by coal mining activities by *hmef*, and thus increases net economic welfare in this country by (−*aefg* + *ahfg* + *hmef* =) *hme*. Welfare also is increased by imposing the optimal tax on coal consumption. In that case coal consumer welfare is lowered by *abcd*, government tax revenue is raised by *ajcd*, the welfare of those outside this market but within the country who are harmed by local pollution from coal burning activities is raised by *bkjc*, and thus net economic welfare in this country is increased by (−*abcd* + *ajcd* + *bkjc* =) *bkj*.

Effects of removing coal production subsidies

Now suppose this economy has in fact put in place a tax on coal consumption that has raised the domestic price to P_c* and reduced coal use to the optimal level of OC*; but instead of also putting in place a tax on domestic production it has subsidised coal mining by offering a producer price of P_q which has induced production to the level OQ_q and thus lowered imports to Q_qC^*.[6] Removing that inappropriate production subsidy would lower production by QQ_q and producer welfare by *aeru*, but it would also lower government outlays by *atru* and boost the welfare of those outside this market who are harmed by coal mining activities by *emnr*, hence net economic welfare would be greater by *emnt*.[7] (If the government not only abolished the producer subsidy but also imposed the optimal producer tax of $P_wP_q^*$, there would be the additional net social welfare gain of *hme*, or a total gain of *hnt*.) Thus both the economy and the environment in this reforming economy would improve by removing that coal production subsidy.

Should enough small open economies simultaneously remove their subsidies to coal mining (and replace any associated coal import tariff with an optimal consumption tax—see footnotes 2 and 3), import demand for and hence the price of coal in the international market would rise. That would reduce coal consumption globally and induce substitution towards using other fuels, virtually all of which are less environmentally damaging and in particular contribute less greenhouse gases than coal. Thus there would be an environmental improvement not only in the reforming economies (less local damage from coal mining and burning) but also in the world at large (less greenhouse gas emissions of methane and carbon). Should domestically mined coal in the reforming countries also be more sulphuric than imported coal, the substitution by consumers away from domestic to imported coal in these countries also would reduce acid rain at home and in neighbouring down-wind countries.

Other countries that are net exporters of coal would benefit from the rise in the international coal price, as would net exporters of substitute fuels to a lesser extent, and conversely for net importers of energy. (This would have second-round effects on aggregate demand including the demand for coal, not shown in the diagram). But the world economy as a whole would be better off, in addition there would be less local pollution in both the reforming countries and other economies[8] as well as less greenhouse gas emissions (and even more so if those coal producer subsidies were replaced by optimal producer taxes).

It is true that, if enough coal-importing economies removed their coal production subsidies simultaneously, their loss from the adverse change in their terms of trade may more than offset their gain from reducing their

[6] The equivalent result would be achieved with an import tariff of $P_c^*P_w$ and an additional production subsidy of $P_qP_c^*$. In that case government direct outlays to producers would have been smaller but there would have been no consumer tax revenue, so the net impact on government revenue is the same.

[7] If $P_q = P_c^*$, then only an import tariff would have been necessary and the equivalent reform would be a replacement of that tariff with an optimal consumption tax of $P_c^*P_w$.

[8] The only possible exception is in those non-reforming countries where the extra pollution from coal production expansion may more than offset the reduced pollution from cuts in coal use. Globally the increase in pollution from such production expansion is likely to be less than the reduction in pollution from coal mining in reforming countries, however, since the latter tend to be among the deepest in the world.

coal market distortion. Even so, that does not alter the fact that each small reforming nation is better off economically and environmentally from so reforming, for to abstain while others reformed would make them even worse off because they would not have the domestic efficiency and environmental gains to offset their deteriorating terms of trade.

Effects of removing coal consumer subsidies

Consider now another type of small open economy that is a net exporter of coal, as depicted in figure 2. The notation and assumptions are otherwise as for figure 1 and in particular both production and consumption externalities are still present. In this case, however, the country is pricing coal below rather than above the price at its border, P_w. Specifically, suppose the country has taxed production so as to set the producer price optimally at P_q* so that 0Q* is being mined per year; but instead of also taxing coal use it has provided a consumption subsidy equal to P_wP_c so that $0C_c$ rather than the optimal quantity of just 0C* is being consumed each year. Thus instead of exports being C*Q* as under optimal national policies, they are just C_cQ*. Removing that inappropriate consumer subsidy would lower consumption by CC_c and consumer welfare by *abvw*, but it would also lower government outlays by *ayvw* and boost the welfare of those domestic residents outside this market who are harmed by the local pollution from coal burning by *bvzk*, hence net economic welfare would be greater by *byzk*.[9] (If the govern-

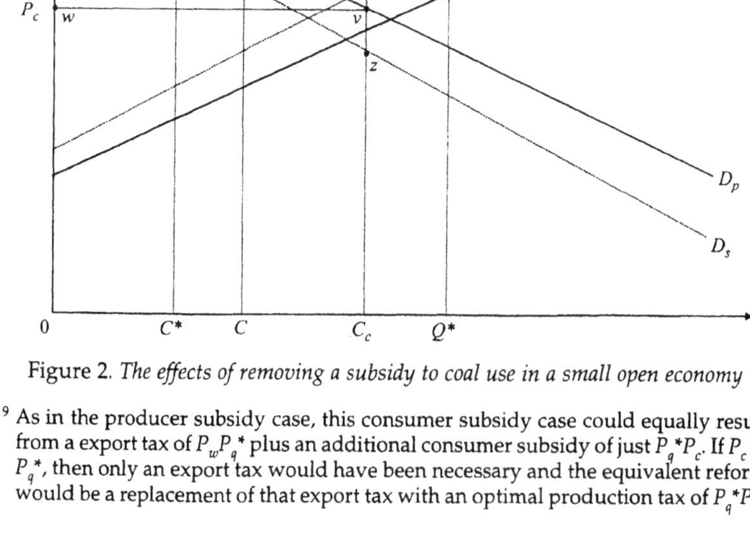

Figure 2. *The effects of removing a subsidy to coal use in a small open economy*

[9] As in the producer subsidy case, this consumer subsidy case could equally result from a export tax of P_wP_q* plus an additional consumer subsidy of just P_q*P_c. If P_c = P_q*, then only an export tax would have been necessary and the equivalent reform would be a replacement of that export tax with an optimal production tax of P_q*P_w.

ment not only abolished the consumer subsidy but also imposed the optimal consumer tax of $P_c{*}P_w$, there would be the additional net social welfare gain of *jbk*, or a total gain of *jyz*.) Thus both the economy and the environment in this reforming economy would improve. Should coal burning in these countries also contribute to acid rain at home and in neighbouring down-wind countries, the reduction in coal use would reduce that environmental damage too.

Should enough small open economies simultaneously reduce their subsidies to coal users (and replace any associated coal export tax with an optimal production tax—see footnote 5), two offsetting effects on the global environment would result. One is that coal consumption in these reforming economies would fall, lowering global carbon emissions. The other is that coal export supplies in the international market would rise, causing the price of coal in that market to fall. That would encourage coal consumption in the rest of the world. Thus it is an empirical question as to whether there would be a net improvement or worsening of the global environment from carbon emissions, even though there is an unequivocal improvement in the local environment of these reforming countries.

Given their current low incomes, it is possible that some of these countries may place little or no negative value on their pollution from coal mining. In that case their optimal producer price would be P_w and so reform would also involve lifting the currently low prices received by miners in those countries. That would add to production and to the increase in net exports from these reforming economies, and hence to their downward pressure on the international price of coal.

Other countries that are net importers of coal would benefit from the fall in the international coal price, as would net importers of substitute fuels to a lesser extent, and conversely for net energy exporters. (Again this would have second-round effects on aggregate demand, including the demand for coal, that are not shown in the diagram.) But the world economy as a whole would be better off by the removal of coal consumer subsidies, so long as the welfare gains in the reforming economies are not more than offset by the welfare loss from any increase in greenhouse gas emissions, should the latter occur.

If enough coal-exporting economies simultaneously removed their coal consumer subsidies (and possible also their coal producer taxes), it is true that their loss from the adverse change in their terms of trade may more than offset their gain from removing their coal market distortions. Even so, as with the case of producer subsidy reform in the coal-importing countries, that does not alter the fact that each small reforming nation is better off economically and environmentally from so reforming, for if it abstained while others reformed it would be even worse off because it would not have the domestic efficiency and environmental gains to offset its deteriorating terms of trade.

Reforming producer and consumer subsidies simultaneously

If both sets of countries were to remove their coal subsidies simultaneously, the coal trade expansion would be greater but the change in the price of coal in the international market from producer subsidy cuts in rich countries would be more or less than offset by the change as a result of removing the coal price distortions in poorer countries. Hence the sign of the net price change, and of the changes in economic welfare in most countries, are empirical questions. The answers to those questions also depend on the degrees of substitution in production and consumption as between coal, other fuels, and other products, the net effects of which can only be captured using a global multi-commodity model. In the next section we describe an intertemporal multi-country global general equilibrium model useful for that purpose, known as G-Cubed, discuss the simulation design to be used, and then present some empirical results.

5. Effects of dismantling coal subsidies: empirical general equilibrium analysis

The G-Cubed multi-country model of the world economy

The G-Cubed multi-country model has been constructed specifically to contribute to the current policy debate on global warming, but it has many features that make it useful for answering a range of issues in environmental regulation and other economic policy questions. It is a global model with substantial regional disaggregation and sectoral detail. In the present version the world economy is divided into eight regions and the model distinguishes five energy sectors (electric utilities, natural gas utilities, petroleum processing, coal extraction, and crude oil and gas extraction) and seven non-energy sectors (mining, agriculture, forestry and wood products, durable manufacturing, non-durable manufacturing, transportation, and services). A key feature of the model is that substitution possibilities in production and consumption are based on econometrically estimated cost functions. Intertemporal budget constraints of households, governments, and nations (the latter through accumulations of foreign debt) are imposed. To accommodate these constraints, forward-looking behaviour is incorporated in consumption and investment decisions. Countries are linked not only by the flow of goods and factors of production but also flows of financial assets with rates of return based on returns in the real economy. The model has an internally consistent macroeconomic framework in which saving and investment decisions are determined endogenously. Overall, the model is designed to provide a bridge between computable general equilibrium models and macroeconomic models by integrating the more desirable features of both approaches. In addition, it includes an environmental module which provides information on changes in carbon emissions as economic activities change. Full details of the model are documented in McKibbin and Wilcoxen (1995).

Simulation design

Using this model we assume the divergences between domestic and international coal prices in 1990 were as shown in table 4. That table also shows the shares of each region in global coal production, consumption, and greenhouse gas emissions, as well as the importance of coal in primary energy use in each region at that time. The model is then used to project the world economy from 1990 to 2050 under the assumption of no change

Table 4. *Shares of global hard coal production and consumption, of coal's contribution to global CO_2 and methane emissions, and coal producer subsidy and consumer tax equivalents (PSEs and CTEs), various countries/regions, circa 1990 (per cent)*

	Share of world coal production	*Share of world coal consumption*	*Share of primary energy consumption from coal*	*Coal mining's contribn. to global methane emissions*	*Coal burning's contribn. to global CO_2 emissions*	**PSE**[a] *coal mining*	**CTE**[a] *coal used by industry*	**PSE**[a] *coal used for electricity*
United States and Canada	26	24	23	3.8	8.7	0	0	0
Australia and New Zealand	6	2	43	0.5	0.7	0	0	0
Japan	0	3	17	0.0	1.5	250	100	180
Western Europe	7	11	21	0.7	6.6	140	130	170
C. and E. Europe and former USSR	19	18	30	1.8	6.3	−50	−50	−50
China	26	25	76	5.6	9.3	−40	−40	−40
India	6	6	66	0.8	2.3	−40	−40	−40
Other developing countries	12	13	18	0.1	4.6	−40	−40	−40
WORLD	**100**	**100**	**30**	**13.3**	**40.0**			

Notes: [a] 'Guesstimated' percentage by which the domestic price exceeds the border price.
Source: IEA (1994a, b, c, d), BP (1994), World Resources Institute (1996) and the references on distortions cited in the text and the above tables.

in coal or any other policies. Given this baseline scenario we then present two scenarios as alternatives to a continuation of the policies of the early 1990s, both phased in over the period to 2005. One scenario involves coal policy reforms just in OECD countries; the second scenario explores coal policy reforms in non-OECD regions as well. In so far as some reform has already taken place during the 1990s our results exaggerate the benefits that *remain* to be reaped from continuing the process, but do not exaggerate the benefits of the overall reform.

Specifically, we analyse in the first case the effects of completely removing the coal producer subsidies and import restrictions in Japan and Western Europe, on the assumption that current consumer taxes there are optimal from the viewpoint of society's concerns with pollution from coal in those densely populated countries.[10] Removing coal producer subsidies and import restrictions in the protective OECD economies would be expected to lower their coal production and raise their coal imports, causing coal prices in international markets to rise and stimulating substitution away from coal use in all economies with open coal markets. In the second scenario, we also raise domestic coal prices in non-OECD countries up to international levels. This should have the effect of reducing coal consumption in these countries, thereby lowering their carbon emissions in so far as they use less fossil fuels in aggregate and they substitute towards less carbon-intensive fuels than coal. But that reform also raises prices received by coal producers in those non-OECD countries. This encourages coal production and hence net exports of coal from these countries, which would depress international coal prices and so encourage coal use and hence greenhouse gas emissions elsewhere.[11] The interesting empirical question is whether the removal also of policies that depress domestic coal prices in non-OECD countries adds to or offsets the positive environmental effects of removing coal production subsidies and import restrictions in Western Europe and Japan.

Empirical results: removing OECD production subsidies and import restrictions
The assumed policy decision to phase out production subsidies for coal in Western Europe (denoted ROECD in the figures below) and Japan has the effects expected within those regions, but some non-intuitive results emerge for other regions. Figure 3 shows that global carbon dioxide emissions fall over time as those production subsidies are gradually eliminated.

[10] In fact, according to Hoeller and Coppel (1992, chart 2), the coal consumption tax per ton of carbon is far smaller in all OECD countries than the user taxes on oil and gas, whereas if coal is more pollutive its use should be taxed more rather than less than those other fuels. This suggests there is further scope for beneficial reform beyond that considered in this paper.

[11] We assume that by the beginning of the simulated reform the coal-mining enterprises in transition economies are operating as normal profit centres. In so far as some state-owned mining enterprises are in fact still being propped up by government subsidies to cover operating losses and these are removed over the simulated reform period to 2005, then we will have overstated the coal supply response in these economies and thereby understated the contribution of reform to reducing global carbon emission.

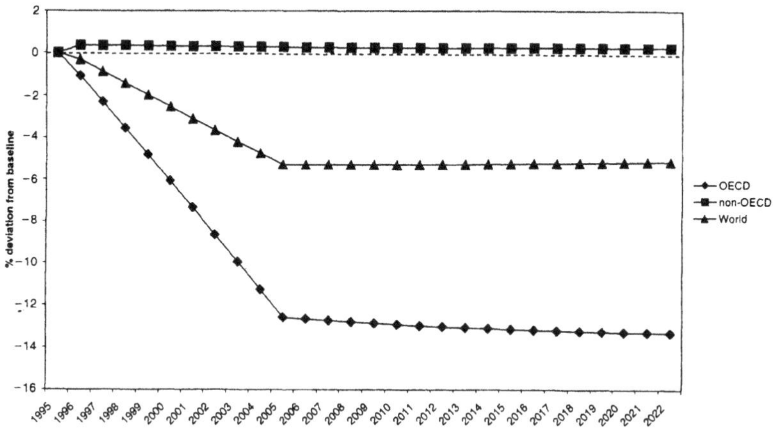

Figure 3. CO_2 *emissions*

(This and subsequent figures present results as percentage deviations from the baseline. Thus a value of zero indicates that the variable is equal to its baseline value.) By 2005, global emissions are permanently reduced by over 5 per cent per year forever. This fall in global emissions (relative to what otherwise would happen) is almost entirely the result of a fall, of one-eighth, in emissions from the OECD countries. Most of this decline occurs in Western Europe, but emissions also decline in Japan and the United States.

These changes can be understood by first recognizing that the removal of OECD coal production subsidies leads to a rise in the price of coal in international markets and hence in all regions where domestic prices respond to change in international prices. That stimulates coal output in and net exports from all other regions. The rise in the user price of coal also leads to a substitution away from coal as an energy source and away from producing carbon-intensive goods whose prices in international markets also rise. Thus emissions fall in most OECD countries. The exception is Australia where, as in the non-OECD regions, carbon emissions rise very slightly. This is because those regions, as net exporters of coal, enjoy a terms of trade gain and hence an income boost: although their coal prices rise and the share of carbon-intensive energy falls relative to other energy sources used (as occurs elsewhere in the world), the absolute amount of carbon-based energy use nonetheless increases as a result of the effects of higher incomes and foreign direct investment inflows in aggregate demand in these economies.

In addition to these effects, a number of other factors are at work. In particular, the phasing out of coal production subsidies has a direct impact on the fiscal positions of governments that have been paying the subsidies. The saving in fiscal outlays is assumed to be used to reduce fiscal deficits in those countries. In Western Europe especially this is a substantial saving which, through macroeconomic adjustments, helps to offset the effect on

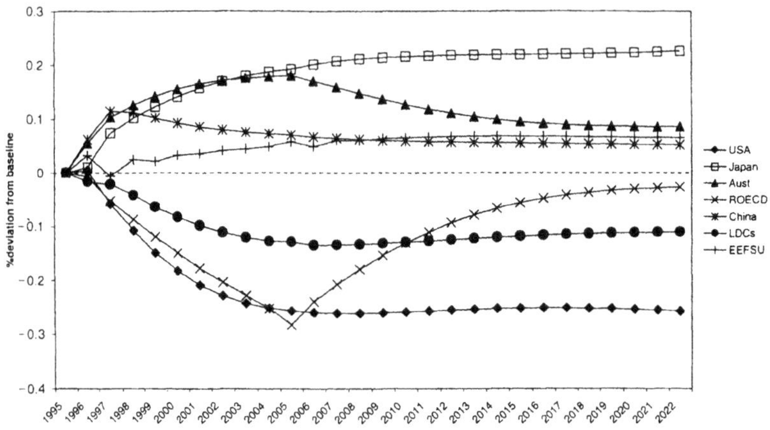

Figure 4. *Gross domestic product (GDP)*

the economy of the adverse terms of trade change resulting from the rise in the international price of coal. This beneficial fiscal effect is absent in North America, Australasia, and the non-OECD regions where there are assumed to be no policy changes; hence firms in these regions face higher input costs for energy without any compensatory offset from greater domestic saving lowering the cost of capital.

It should be stressed that the decline in carbon dioxide emissions from fossil fuel use that is depicted in figure 3 is a decline relative to a baseline in which global emissions are projected to rise from around 22 billion tonnes in 1990 to around 32 billion tonnes by 2010 (IEA, 1994c), and hence to almost 30 billion tonnes by 2005. Under this scenario they would still rise, but only to about 28 billion tonnes by 2005.

The effects on national outputs and incomes are more diverse. Figure 4 contains results for real GDP, again as a deviation from baseline. GDP is the value added by domestically located factors of production in each economy. This is a measure of aggregate domestic production change; but it does not take into account the international movements of capital allowed for in the G-Cubed model. GNP, on the other hand, is a measure of income to domestically owned factors of production no matter whether they are located at home or abroad. Thus it is a better measure of economic well-being of domestic residents than GDP since it measures their income from all their owned factors of production.[12] It does not include the negative valuation society places on greenhouse gas emissions though, and so will understate the gains in well-being from policy changes that reduce those emissions.

[12] Both GDP and GNP are measured in constant (1990) US dollars at the prices prevailing in each scenario. Thus the difference between scenarios in estimated GDP or GNP includes the effect of both quantity and price differences. Even GNP is not an ideal measure of utility, however, but it is the best indicator of welfare that is available in the model.

In Western Europe (ROECD in the figures), the rise in energy import prices and hence the prices to users leads to a fall in GDP during the adjustment period as industries respond to higher input cost and the economy adjusts to the deterioration in its terms of trade. By 2005, when the coal production subsidies are completely removed, the gains from reallocating resources within Western Europe begin to offset the negative shock of higher energy import prices.[13] By about 2020 those economies have adjusted to the change in relative prices and GDP returns to close to baseline. The recovery in its GDP is also the result of the permanently higher level of saving by Western European governments as a result of the fiscal savings from the reduction in subsidies. As in Japan, gains from an improvement in economic efficiency and the government budget in Europe outweigh the impact of slightly higher coal import prices and hence user prices of coal within the domestic economy. Countries with a relative abundance of coal experience a terms of trade improvement, by contrast, and hence enjoy a rise in GDP (most notably Australia, China, and the EEFSU region).

Bear in mind, though, that these GDP changes are not the same as changes in GNP in particular regions. This is because the G-Cubed model used here allows for foreign capital flows which adjust to changes in market conditions, as is evident by comparing figures 4 and 5. Western Europe, for example, exports financial capital to other regions under this scenario so as to take advantage of the now higher earnings abroad than at home. These higher earnings are reflected in GNP. Thus the reforms, although leading to a lower level of GDP relative to baseline for Western Europe, raise incomes there by 2014 because some of the capital released

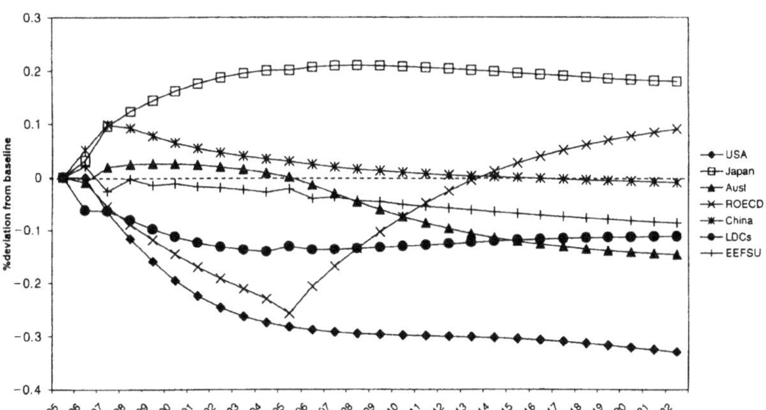

Figure 5. *Gross national product (GNP)*

[13] That negative shock is exaggerated in our modelling because we have not incorporated the fact that some electricity utilities in Western Europe are currently forced to use more high-cost local coal than they would prefer at prevailing prices (see section 3 above and Newbery, 1995).

from the coal- and fossil-fuel intensive industries (or what would otherwise have been invested in those industries) eventually earns a higher return overseas than it would have if it had stayed in those industries as in the baseline.

Overall, the effect of cutting coal production subsidies in the OECD is to reduce significantly the emission of carbon dioxide, particularly in the OECD. Even though this leads to some minor increase in carbon dioxide emissions in relatively carbon-intensive developing countries as a result of substitution away from the production of carbon-intensive goods in the OECD, this 'leakage' effect is a negligible offset to the OECD's carbon emission reduction—in contrast to the leakage that would occur under an international agreement in which only OECD countries voluntarily agreed to curtail their carbon dioxide emissions while imposing no discipline on non-OECD countries' emissions. The reason to expect substantial leakage in the latter case is because a voluntary cut-back in carbon emissions in the OECD would cause a major reduction in OECD coal use and hence in the international price of coal, thereby encouraging expanded use of coal in non-OECD regions.[14]

Empirical results: effects of removing also coal consumer subsidies and export taxes in non-OECD regions

Now consider the effect of adding to the phase-out of OECD production subsidies (which began earlier this decade) a phase-out of coal market distortions in non-OECD economies (which are just beginning, most notably in China and Central Europe). In this scenario we also completely remove the subsidy to consumption of coal and the tax on coal production (together with any associated export restriction) to bring coal prices to international market levels in the non-OECD economies. The results for the combined simulation are shown in figures 6 through 8.

As expected, the consequent rise in coal prices in the non-OECD economies leads to an expansion of coal production and a contraction of coal use within those economies. The expansion of production relative to consumption implies an increase in net exports from non-OECD to OECD economies, which on its own reduces the price of coal in international markets and hence in these economies, offsetting slightly the rise resulting from the OECD's production subsidy cuts. The effects on total carbon emissions, shown in figure 6, are the net effect of the removal of both OECD and non-OECD coal market distortions compared with no reform. In this case emissions from non-OECD countries also fall as their consumption subsides are removed. By 2005 carbon dioxide emissions from non-OECD economies are 4 per cent lower, when both OECD and non-OECD policies are reformed together, than otherwise would have been the case.

[14] How large that leakage would be depends on the nature of any international agreement of course. Numerous attempts have been made to simulate various possibilities. An early example is Piggott, Whalley, and Wigle (1992). See also ABARE and DFAT (1995), McKibbin and Wilcoxen (1996), and the surveys in Winters (1992) and IPCC (1996, ch. 11).

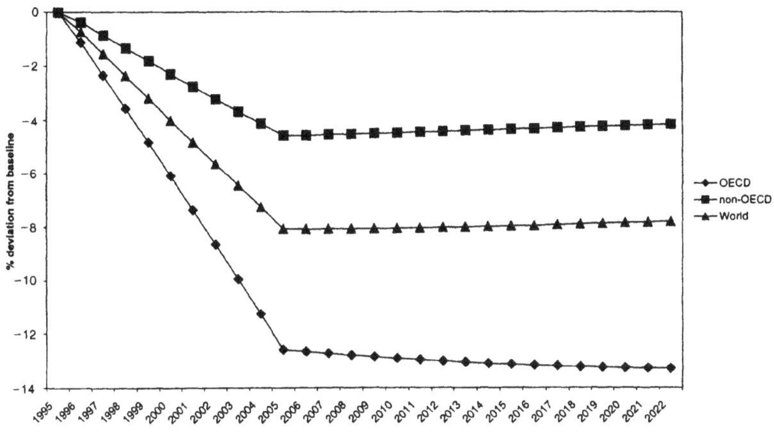

Figure 6. *CO_2 emissions*

To understand the effect of the non-OECD policy reform alone, the first set of simulation results should be subtracted from the combined results. We showed in the simulation results for the OECD policy reform that emissions from non-OECD economies rise slightly. Thus the effect of non-OECD policies on reducing non-OECD emissions are slightly larger than shown in figure 6. There is only a very slight rise in OECD emissions as a result of the lower price of coal in international markets in this as compared with the previous scenario, an effect that is dwarfed by the reduction resulting from the OECD's policy reform. Overall, global carbon dioxide emissions fall by 8 per cent relative to what otherwise would have been experienced by 2005, compared with just 5 per cent in the first scenario involving only OECD reform. That is, despite the fact that reforms in the non-OECD regions raise their net exports and hence lower the international price of coal, global carbon emissions are estimated to fall more, evidently because the effect of eliminating coal consumption subsidies turns out to dominate the effect of encouraging more coal mining in those regions.

Not only do the transition and developing economies gain in terms of emission reduction, but as well the changes in production contained in figure 7 show that GDP rises in each of these regions. This is the result of the efficiency gains from reducing their production and consumption distortions. Resources are freed up from the distorted sectors and reallocated through the global economy, yielding higher rates of return. EEFSU output expands substantially, while developing country output hardly alters in this combined scenario as compared with the reduction in output shown in figure 4, in which just the OECD countries reform.

Again the GNP effects are somewhat different from the GDP ones. While the GNPs of the transition and developing economies are raised by this combined reform, as compared with either no policy changes or just OECD reform, Australia's GNP is eventually lowered slightly when the

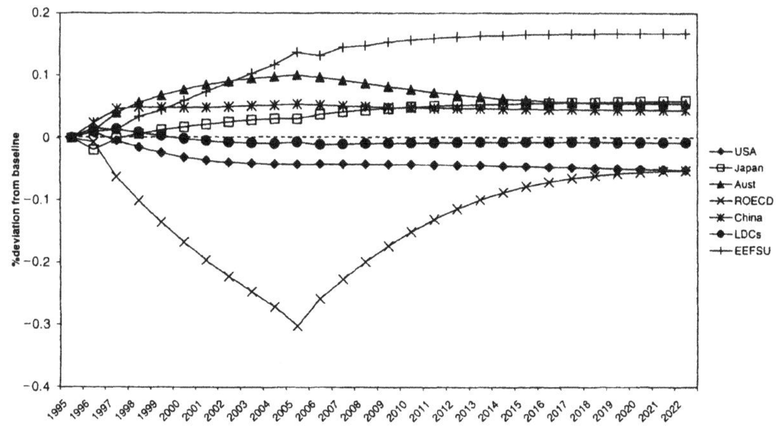

Figure 7. *Gross domestic product (GDP)*

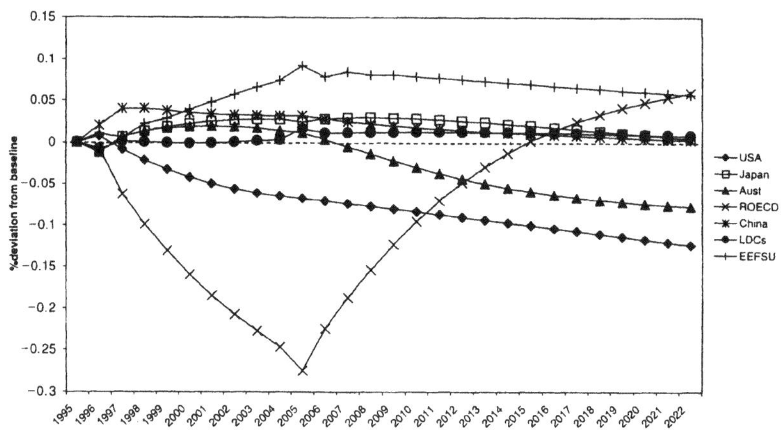

Figure 8. *Gross national product (GNP)*

non-OECD countries also reform. The latter is mainly because the terms of trade of coal-exporting and capital-importing Australia gradually deteriorate as the non-OECD countries' net exports of coal expand.

6. Conclusion

This paper has examined distortions in global coal markets that point to a significant subsidization of coal production in OECD economies and significant coal consumption subsidies in developing and transition economies—when the opposite policies are what are needed to overcome the environmental policies associated with coal mining and burning. Model-based empirical evidence summarized here suggests that the gradual removal of production subsidies in the OECD and the removal of distortions to coal markets in developing and transition economies can potentially reduce global emissions of carbon dioxide by up to 8 per cent relative to emissions that otherwise would have been experienced early next century. This environmental gain is achieved with gains in economic efficiency rather than economic costs—a win–win outcome for the environment and the economy. Both gains would be even greater if Western European countries also raised their low coal consumer tax rates as they phase out their coal producer subsidies, since those consumer taxes are currently relatively low (see footnotes 10 and 13 above), presumably to lower the cost to electricity utilities of requiring them to use lower-quality locally mined coal. And both gains would also be enhanced if countries taxed domestic coal production optimally so as to ensure coal mining enterprises compensate society for the pollution they cause.

Thankfully the process of lowering coal subsidies and trade barriers has already begun, with some EU economies (most notably Belgium and the UK) already advanced in dismantling their coal production subsidies and others (France and Germany) committing themselves to do so. And in some transition economies the low prices of coal (and also oil and gas) are gradually being raised. For example, in China many state-owned coal mines are being transferred out of the hands of the state and gradually subjected to domestic market forces. The results in this paper suggest these reforms should be applauded as a positive contribution to the reduction of greenhouse gas emissions, and countries should be encouraged to complete the process.[15]

References

ABARE and DFAT (1995), *Global Climate Change: Economic Dimensions of a Cooperative International Policy Response Beyond 2000*, Canberra: ABARE.

Anderson, K. (1992), 'Effects on the environment and welfare of liberalizing world trade: the cases of coal and food', in K. Anderson and R. Blackhurst (eds.), *The Greening of World Trade Issues*, Ann Arbor: University of Michigan Press and London: Harvester Wheatsheaf, chapter 8.

Anderson, K. (1995a), 'Lobbying incentives and the pattern of protection in rich and poor countries', *Economic Development and Cultural Change*, **43**(2): 401–423.

[15] Three caveats need to be kept in mind though. One is that the above results are for reforms from the 1990 level of price distortions, so the gains that *remain* to be reaped from completing the reform are less than those presented above. The second caveat is that in so far as electricity utilities in Western Europe were forced to use coal more than they would have preferred at prevailing prices, they may opt to use other fuel sources after the reform—in which case there would be less upward pressure on international coal prices (but more on the price of other energy raw materials). Also, under electricity de-regulation in the European Union the prospects for freer international trade in electricity may further alter the location of its production and hence the demand for the different fuels used to produce it (Hoster, 1997). These factors are not accounted for in our analysis. And, thirdly, no account is taken of the possible technological changes that might occur with or without these reforms.

Anderson K. (1995b), 'The political economy of coal subsidies in Europe', *Energy Policy* **23**(6): 485–496.

Anderson, K. and C.Y. Peng (1998), 'Feeding and fueling China in the 21st century', *World Development*, **26**(8): 1413–1429.

BP (1994), *Statistical Review of World Energy*, London: British Petroleum (annual).

Burniaux, J.-M., J.P. Martin, and J. Oliveira-Martins (1992), 'The effect of existing distortions in energy markets on the cost of policies to reduce CO_2 emissions: evidence from GREEN', *OECD Economic Studies*, **19**: 141–165.

EC (1992), *Commission Report on the Application of the Community Rules for State Aid to the Coal Industry*, Brussels: EC Commission (annual).

Hoeller, P. and J. Coppel (1992), 'Carbon taxes and current energy policies in OECD countries', *OECD Economic Studies*, **19**: 167–193.

Hoster, F. (1997), 'Effects of national energy policies on carbon dioxide emissions in a European internal electricity market: results from a simulation model of the European power system', Working Paper 79.97, Fondazione Eni Enrico Mattei, Milan, November.

IEA (1993), *Energy Policies of IEA Countries*, Paris: OECD's International Energy Agency (annual).

IEA (1994a), 'Coal information' (diskette), Paris: OECD's International Energy Agency.

IEA (1994b), *Energy Prices and Taxes*, Paris: OECD's International Energy Agency (quarterly).

IEA (1994c), *World Energy Outlook*, Paris: OECD's International Energy Agency (annual).

IEA (1994d), *Energy Statistics and Balances of Non-OECD Countries*, Paris: OECD's International Energy Agency (annual).

IEA (1997), *Energy Policies of IEA Countries*, Paris: OECD's International Energy Agency (annual).

IPCC (Intergovernmental Panel on Climate Change) (1996), *Climate Change 1995* (IPCC Second Assessment Report), Cambridge and New York: Cambridge University Press.

Larsen, B. and A. Shah (1995), 'Global climate change, energy subsidies, and national carbon taxes', in L. Bovenberg and S. Cnossen (eds.), *Public Economics and the Environment in an Imperfect World*, Dordrecht: Kluwer.

Lee, H., J. Oliveira-Martins, and D. van der Mensbrugghe (1994), 'The OECD GREEN model: an updated overview', Technical Paper No. 97, OECD Development Centre, Paris.

McKibbin, W. and P. Wilcoxen (1995), 'The theoretical and empirical structure of the G-Cubed model', Brookings Discussion Paper in International Economics No. 118, The Brookings Institution, Washington DC.

McKibbin, W. and P. Wilcoxen (1996), 'The economic implications of greenhouse gas policy', in H. English and D. Runnals (eds.), *Environment and Development in the Pacific: Problems and Policy Options*, Melbourne: Addison Wesley Longman, pp. 8–34.

Newbery, D. (1995), 'Removing coal subsidies: implications for European electricity markets', *Energy Policy*, **23**(6): 523–534.

OECD (1994), *Agricultural Policies, Markets and Trade: Monitoring and Outlook 1994*, Paris: OECD (annual).

OECD (1998), *Agricultural Policies of OECD Countries: Measurement of Support and Background Information 1998*, Paris: OECD.

Piggott, J., J. Whalley, and R. Wigle (1992), 'International linkages and carbon reduction initiatives', in K. Anderson and R. Blackhurst (eds.), *The Greening of World Trade Issues*, Ann Arbor: University of Michigan Press and London: Harvester Wheatsheaf, chapter 6.

Steenblik, R.P. and P. Coroyannakis (1995), 'Reform of coal policies in Western and Central Europe: implication for the environment', *Energy Policy*, **23**(6): 537–554.

Steenblik, R.P. and K.J. Wigley (1990), 'Coal policies and trade barriers', *Energy Policy*, **18**(5): 351–369.

Wang, X. (1996), 'China's coal sector: moving to a market economy', mimeo, China Country Department, The World Bank, Washington DC.

Winters, L.A. (1992), 'The trade and welfare effects of greenhouse gas abatement: a survey of empirical estimates', in K. Anderson and R. Blackhurst (eds.), *The Greening of World Trade Issues*, Ann Arbor: University of Michigan Press and London: Harvester Wheatsheaf, chapter 5.

World Bank (1997a), *Five Years After Rio: Innovations in Environmental Policy*, Washington, DC: The World Bank, Environment Department.

World Bank (1997b), 'Subsidy Policies and the Environment', in *Expanding the Measure of Wealth: Indicators of Environmentally Sustainable Development*, Washington, DC: The World Bank, Environment Bank.

World Resources Institute (1996), *World Resources 1996–97*, New York: Oxford University Press.

Name Index

For Product Safety Concerns and Information please contact our EU representative GPSR@taylorandfrancis.com Taylor & Francis Verlag GmbH, Kaufingerstraße 24, 80331 München, Germany

Batch number: 10726302

Printed by Printforce, the Netherlands